Week by Week

Documenting the Development of Young Children

Third Edition

Week by Week

Documenting the Development of Young Children

Third Edition

Barbara Ann Nilsen, Ed.D.
Broome Community College

THOMSON

DELMAR LEARNING

Australia   Canada   Mexico   Singapore   Spain   United Kingdom   United States

THOMSON
™
DELMAR LEARNING

Vice President,
Career Education SBU:
Dawn Gerrain

Director of Editorial:
Sherry Gomoll

Acquisitions Editor:
Erin O'Connor

Developmental Editor:
Alexis Breen Ferraro

Editorial Assistant:
Ivy Ip

Director of Production:
Wendy A. Troeger

Production Editor:
Eileen M. Clawson

Composition:
Stratford Publishing Services, Inc.

Director of Marketing:
Wendy E. Mapstone

Channel Manager:
Donna J. Lewis

Cover Design:
Andrew Wright

Printed in United States of America
1 2 3 4 5 6 7 8 9 10   XXX   08 07 06 05 04

For more information, contact Delmar Learning, 5 Maxwell Drive, Clifton Park, NY 12065-2919

Or you can visit our Internet site at http://www.delmarlearning.com

For permission to use material from this text or product contact us by
Tel (800) 730-2214
Fax (900) 730-2215

Library of Congress Cataloging-in-Publication Data

Nilsen, Barbara.
    Week by week : documenting the development of young children /
Barbara Ann Nilsen.—3rd ed.
      p. cm.
Includes bibliographical references and index.
ISBN 1-4018-7092-9
    1. Behavioral assessment of children. 2. Observation (Psychology)
3. Observation (Educational method) 4. Child development. I. Title.

BF722.N53 2004
370.15--dc22

                              2004010251

NOTICE TO THE READER

Contents

Preface

Week by Week is a documentation guidebook for students and practitioners in early childhood education who work with toddlers through second grade children. Each chapter has three main parts: the documentation method, the child development overview, and the plans that integrate the method to document children's development. The purpose is to organize and plan deliberately, week by week, to build each child's portfolio. *Week by Week* presents a manageable plan that will help you gather documentation on *all* the children in the class or group in *all* the developmental areas.

The first two editions of *Week by Week* have been used in a number of ways. Freshman students in associate degree programs use the text for a course in techniques of documentation. Students in subsequent semesters in both associate-degree and bachelor-degree programs use the text for child development study and in field experiences. The text has been used in baccalaureate and master's teaching preparation programs. Classroom teachers have used the text as a tool to help them organize their observations into meaningful portfolios that document their children's development. It has also been used in Head Start, Even Start, child care, and nursery-school settings. In this third edition I recognize the differences in how the book is used and have added specific instructions in each chapter for students and for practitioners.

How this Book Came to Be Written

My original idea for the book was to share my system of child observations with practitioners like myself. The title, *Week by Week*, describes a year-long systematic plan for teachers to document each child's development by forming an extensive portfolio that shows each child's progress in all areas of development. As my teaching venue changed from the preschool classroom to the college classroom, the book became a textbook. As a college textbook, it introduces students to these methods—in the context of child development—that can be used and practiced in periodic visits into a classroom. It may be used for the sole purpose of observing, or as students participate in a field experience. It has been well-received by students and it is my hope that they will keep the book and renew their acquaintance with it when they get a classroom of their own. Then the full week-by-week plan will take on new meaning. I've found books from my college days and it is like meeting an old friend—we take up where we left off.

Organization of *Week by Week*

If you are new to *Week by Week*, you will find a wide variety of information in it. Everyone comments on the "It Happened to Me" feature—short vignettes, funny stories, and experiences that anyone who works with children, and even those who don't, will find interesting. Each chapter introduces a recording method, its best uses and disadvantages. There are examples in the chapter and forms in the Appendix and in the Online Resource. Each chapter also reviews an area of child development because you have to know what you are looking for and must be able to recognize it when you see it. There are interactive exercises to focus thinking. Topics in Observation bring out an issue or expand an idea, and curriculum actions based on observations are included along with children's book suggestions. Plans for the week (or assignments for students to practice the method) are included, along with tips on sharing observations with families, and what to actually do with the documentation products.

New to this Edition

Since the second edition was written, I have changed in my own involvement in early childhood education. I continue to teach college courses but have expanded my interest and responsibility both up and down.

In my expanded role I now chair the department that prepares students to transfer into teacher certification programs, as well as move into the early childhood workforce. My new experiences have led me to make some changes in *Week by Week* for those teachers who are preparing for Head Start positions, prekindergarten programs requiring teacher certification (which many states have inaugurated), and kindergarten and first grade classrooms, where there is now national pressure on performance. We who believe that portfolio assessment is the best way to document the competencies of children under age eight need to demonstrate the authenticity of portfolios and advocate for their acceptance over standardized tests for this population.

My other role is overseeing a project with infant and toddler teachers who facilitate the development of our littlest ones. This is the result of our expanding knowledge of the critical role of those teachers. Those two ends of the spectrum of early childhood education will be apparent in this edition.

Another change in the educational and personal world, and so too in *Week by Week,* is the increasing opportunity to use electronic media. Technology has been slower in coming into the classroom and even slower in record-keeping duties, but I have added some suggestions for how it can be used with each of the methods explored in the book.

The main idea of *Week by Week* is to organize a gargantuan task into manageable, weekly assignments. However, students and teachers still moan, "But I don't have time!" Therefore, I have included a section to give suggestions for how to either make time for recording or how to record more efficiently.

Previous readers of this book will notice the greatest change in the chapter on cognitive development. Because the reality of testing has permeated our educational venues, that chapter discusses testing as an observation tool. This does not imply a recommendation of testing for young children. However, for those who will be compelled to use standardized tests, the information provided will help them become more aware and better prepared.

Key terms have been added at the end of each chapter, along with a comprehensive Glossary at the end of the volume.

Ancillaries

The following ancillary materials are available to accompany *Week by Week: Documenting the Development of Young Children, Third Edition.*

Online Instructor's Manual

The instructor's manual to accompany this text contains classroom learning suggestions and assignment grading rubrics. It is password protected and can be accessed by visiting the instructor's lounge located at *http://www.earlychilded.delmar.com.* In order to gain access, you must first be validated as an instructor. Please complete the instuctor validation form found in the instructor's lounge. When you are approved, a username and password will be e-mailed to you within 48 hours.

Computerized Test Bank

The computerized test bank is comprised of true/false, multiple choice, short answer, and completion questions for each chapter. Instructors can use the computerized test bank software to create sample quizzes for students. Refer to the CTB User's Guide for more information on how to create and post quizzes to your school's Internet or Intranet.

Online Resources™

Online Resources™ to accompany the third edition of *Week by Week: Documenting the Development of Young Children* is your link to early childhood resources on the Internet. It contains useful features to help students and practitioners implement documentation plans. It includes downloadable forms from the chapters, a case study related to chapter content, learning activities to help you understand the chapter concepts, and Web links related to chapter content.

The Online Resources™ icon appears at the end of each chapter to prompt you to go on-line and take advantage of the many feratures provided. You can find the Online Resources™ Web site at *http://www.earlychilded.delmar.com.*

Web Tutor

The Web Tutor to accompany *Week by Week: Documenting the Development of Young Children, Third Edition,* allows you to take learning beyond the classroom. This Online Courseware is designed to complement the text and benefits students in that it enables them to better manage their time, prepare for exams, organize their notes, and more. Special features include Chapter Learning Objectives, Online Course Preparation, Study Sheets, Glossary, Discussion Topics, Frequently Asked Questions, Online Class Notes, Online Chapter Quizzes, and Web Links related to chapter content. Printing features allow students to print their own customized study guides.

A benefit for instructors as well as students, the Web Tutor allows for on-line discussion with the instructor and other class members, real-time chats to enable virtual office hours and encourage collaborative learning environments, a calendar of syllabus information for easy reference, e-mail connections to facilitate communication among classmates and between students and instructors, and customization tools that help educators tailor their course to fit their needs by adding or changing content.

Web Tutor allows you to extend your reach beyond the classroom and is available on either the WebCT or Blackboard platform.

Acknowledgments

My thanks and love to family who are my biggest supporters, my friend Carol who loves me like a sister, my colleagues near and far who dedicate themselves to the care and education of America's children, and to my students who teach me something every day.

Sincere appreciation to Erin O'Connor who believes in my work, Alexis Breen Ferraro and the staff at Delmar for their assistance, patience, and creativity in putting my ideas into reality. A special "thank you" to the reviewers who provided valuable feedback and helped to shape the final work:

Nancy Baptiste, Ed.D.
New Mexico State University
Las Cruces, NM

Jennifer Berke, Ph.D.
Mercyhurst College North East
North East, PA

Alice Beyrent
Hesser College
Manchester, NH

Irene Cook
Taft College
Taft, CA

Brenda Schin
Private Child Care Provider
Selkirk, NY

Joan Wyde, Ph.D.
Houston Community College System
Houston, TX

About the Author

Barbara Nilsen is professor and chair of the Teacher Education and Early Childhood Department at Broome Community College, Binghamton, New York, where she teaches in the classroom and on-line. She is also the grant director of NYSECEONLINE and the Early Learning Opportunities collaborative project for Building Brighter Futures for Broome. The author received her Ed.D. in Early and Middle Childhood from Nova University. She has been active in local, state, and national early childhood professional development initiatives such as Career Pathways, Chil-

dren's Program Administrator Credential, Infant/Toddler Credential, and Early Childhood Associate Degree Program Accreditation project. She is coauthor, with Virginia Albertalli, of *An Introduction to Learning and Teaching: Infants through Sixth Grade*.

This text is dedicated to the busy hands, open minds, and caring hearts of all who work with young children. You bear the worthy name: Teacher. I welcome your communication by e-mail at NILSEN_B@sunybroome.edu.

Introduction: Getting Started

THE WHYS OF OBSERVING

EXERCISE: Observe (or imagine):

- a clock
- the inside of a refrigerator
- a traffic light

Exactly what do you see? What are your observations telling you? What will you do as a result of what you see? Write down what decisions you might make based on those observations.

The word *observe* brings to mind the action of looking, seeing, not participating but viewing the action as an outsider. In any context, **observing** is just the first step in determining action. The first stage, taking in information, occurs simultaneously with evaluation and selection of a course of action. The clock is observed, usually not to admire the design, but to determine the time. Looking inside a refrigerator may indicate a trip to the store is needed or that the source of a foul odor should be investigated. The traffic light is a lovely shade of green, but its meaning is more important. That observation produces action: Go!

Everything we see is not just observed but immediately interpreted for meaning. A decision is made either to do nothing or to act. The observation may be so insignificant that it is sensed but not acted upon. Later it might prove to be important, like that traffic light that was green but the car in the cross street came through the intersection anyway. When filling out the accident report, those details are important.

Why Observe?

When a teacher observes a child, information is collected and could be measured against a whole body

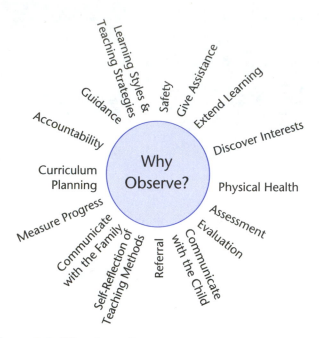

Figure I–1 Why observe?

of knowledge about child development in general and that child in particular (Figure I–1). Information is then used to make decisions about the next actions. Someone has estimated that a teacher makes thousands of decisions in a day. They are all based on observations evaluated for meaning and most appropriate responses. This *observe, decide, act* sequence is repeated over and over again throughout the day.

Let's observe a child painting at the easel and see what we can see in Figure I–2.

Safety. The most important reason for watching children is to keep them safe. Seeing a potentially

Figure I–2 Common activities yield knowledge of the child.

dangerous situation and rushing to prevent an injury is the most basic example of observe, decide, act. A child waiting to paint may be observed trying to wrestle the brush away from the painter. With angry looks and harsh words, she is trying to gain control of the painting area. The teacher rushes over and intervenes before the painter is knocked aside or a brush is poked into someone's eye.

Physical Health. Recognizing the signs of sickness or disease is another reason to observe, decide, and act. This also can protect the physical health of others. The teacher may notice a few small red spots behind the painter's ear. She casually pats the child's arm and feels bumps beneath the skin. These observations, along with the knowledge that the child's brother had chicken pox two weeks ago, prompts the teacher's decision to isolate the child and call the child's family to take the child home. For chicken pox, of course, it's already too late. Everyone's been exposed! A child painted this upon her return to school after having chicken pox (Figure I–3).

Assistance. Observation may indicate that help is needed. A child is observed preparing to paint at the easel. The teacher sees that the paper supply is gone. He gets more from the cupboard and shows the child

Figure I–3 Observing a child's work, as well as the child as she works, gives valuable information.

how to attach the sheets with the big clips and where to hang the painting to dry.

Guidance. Prevention is always better than remedy. Redirection is better than discipline or punishment. From observations, potential problems can be averted. The painter's brush is approaching the wall. The teacher says, "We paint on paper," guiding the brush back to the paper on the easel.

Discover Interests. The adult watches the child choose a play area and talks with the child about the play. This watching, remembering, and affirming is a friendly thing to do. It also is another way of building bridges from interests to planning, from home to school, and making the curriculum relevant. The theme of animals (in the beginning stages of drawing recognizable objects!) emerges in the painting. The observer remembers the home visit where this child showed a menagerie of pets, who might be potential classroom visitors!

Learning Styles and Teaching Strategies. Watching a child reveals personality, learning styles, and could give clues to teaching strategies. By observing the painter, learning styles are indicated that will work better for her, maybe verbal directions, or being shown, or trial and error. Reflective observation of the student's learning process leads the teacher to adapt teaching strategies to the child's styles and needs.

Extend Children's Learning. Through observations, teachers can see that teachable moment, that budding interest, that blossoming skill. Providing materials, activities, and opportunities to build on that observed development will capitalize on it. From observing the painting filled with alphabet letters, the teacher decides this is a good time to bring out the alphabet magnets and invite the painter to play with them.

Curriculum Planning. Teaching is building bridges, making connections between new information and old. The teacher plans related experiences and activities. The group has enjoyed and mastered easel painting so the teacher plans that next week he will introduce watercolors, demonstrating the technique of washing the brush between colors.

Communication with the Child. Teachers should talk with every child, and what better subject to discuss with them than the child's activities. Every child deserves the individual attention of the teacher. By discussing what the teacher sees with the child, the child can give the reason or explanation in a way that makes sense if only the teacher asks the child. That is

the basis for Piaget's cognitive questioning method (Piaget & Inhelder, 1969), to delve more deeply into children's "wrong" answers. In that way, thinking processes are explored. Results or answers are not simply evaluated. Woodward (1993) calls this "negotiated evaluation." This process involves discussing observations with the child, and also the family.

The teacher says to the painter, "You worked hard on that painting. You used red, blue, and yellow, and you made straight lines and curved lines. Would you like to tell me how you did it? What did you do first?"

Communication with the Family. Talking with the family about the child's daily activities communicates to them:

- Your child is under a watchful eye.
- This teacher sees and relates important development in your child's actions, rather than giving you a test score you do not understand.
- You are included in the world that the teacher and your child share.

Unfortunately, many children and families have come to expect to receive bad reports, phone calls, and notes from school, bringing a sense of dread. Too often, they relate misbehaviors, failure to perform to expectations, or commands to the child or family to take remedial action. Discussing the observations from the day's observed activities or documentation from the portfolio with the child's family will give positive, substantive information about the child's progress, compared only to her previous work, not anyone else's. Observation gives descriptive accounts of the child's behavior and skills from the point of view of achievement rather than deficit, what she can or has done, rather than cannot or will not. Observations are shared with families in formal and informal ways.

The paintings in the child's portfolio previously were scribbles, then become pages filled with lines and deliberate designs. The teacher and child show her family the collection in the portfolio. The family realizes the teacher *knows* their child and sees their child's work from a different point of view.

Measure Progress. Children change so quickly. Based on knowledge of child development, certain changes are expected and anticipated. Comparisons over time can measure that development. The teacher sees that the painter moved from experimentation with line and color to painting recognizable objects. She proclaims the smiling face with dots is a picture of her brother who is just getting over the chicken pox. The teacher can see her control of small muscles and frustration when the paint does not flow in the way the painter thinks it should. The child's social world is portrayed in the pictures she paints. Many areas of development can be observed in this one activity and in changes from paintings done a few weeks ago.

Assessment. Teachers watch children to gather information. That is assessment, the process of documenting a child's skills and development. Assessment may take many forms but the premise here is that observation is the best method. Information is gathered to measure the child's development against accepted stages or set of norms of development. Assessment measures where the child is at this point and indicates what stage comes next. It alerts the observer to unusually delayed or accelerated development. The painter paints first with the right hand then switches to the left and back again. The observer assesses the lack of "handedness" at this point in the child's development. Alphabet letters emerge from the painter's strokes as the observer watches. Ah ha!

Evaluation. Evaluation is the decision-making step of assessment. Woodward (1993) uses the following definition: "Evaluation is the collection and analysis of data, from a variety of sources and perspectives, which will contribute to:

- making judgments of merit and worth
- making decisions about future planning
- informing learning." (p. 2)

The observer of the painter has collected paintings over several weeks and judges that this child is in the Preschematic Stage, beginning to represent thought. A sticky note as to the importance of this example may be placed on the back of the painting, noting, "She has moved from making circles and controlled straight lines to painting faces, and has a positive mood at the time of the painting." The teacher may decide to read a story about sick children, or bring out the skeleton for the Science Area to give the painter ideas about anatomy. A copy of this drawing is filed in the child's portfolio to make later comparisons.

Referral. Sometimes questions or even red flags arise when a teacher watches a child. Certain behaviors, actions, skills, or lack of them, will send an alert calling for a closer look at a developmental area.

From the child's paintings, the teacher sees some alarming messages. The teacher may ask a probing question, such as, "Would you like to tell me about your painting?" and the child's answers may lead only to more questions.

Thought and closer observation of behavior over time may warrant the discussion of the concern first with the family or other professionals within the agency, and then perhaps a suggested referral to the family. The referral may be for further evaluation in a specific area, such as hearing, speech, physical, or cognitive development. Family involvement and decision-making in the referral process are the pivotal factors. Families are recognized and deferred to as the authority on the child.

There may be situations where it is necessary to report suspicions of neglect or abuse. Knowledge, careful judgment, empathy, and consideration are important skills for the teacher in all of these circumstances, both referrals and reporting.

Self-Reflection of Teaching Methods. Observing is not just looking at a child but thinking about our influence on the child and the child's effect on us. The teacher notices that no one is painting anymore and wonders what the cause could be. By observing and recording, questions can be answered and the teacher's own effectiveness can be measured. The interest a child has in the planned activities will indicate to the teacher if the activities are appropriate. Activities that are not challenging or are too difficult will be avoided or abandoned by the child. By closely observing what keeps a child involved, the observer can learn what skills the child is working on and then modify activities to meet those needs.

This type of observation is active research, constantly accumulating data to analyze for its meaning. Yetta Goodman (1989) says "kid watching" is "teachers who interact with students and who monitor class activities in order to understand more about teaching and learning, mostly learning."

Accountability. Is the teacher, curriculum, or school doing what it says it will do? Proof is needed to show that children are learning and meeting the standards and expected outcomes. "This child's painting shows increases in small muscle control, attention span, interest in alphabet, and is increasingly detailed." The teacher's notes on the back of the painting relate the significance of this work in the light of developmental progress. It shows the child is learning. Documentation of all types can

- provide evidence of children's learning in all domains.
- provide insight into learning experiences.
- provide a framework for recording each child's interests and developmental progress.
- emphasize learning as an interactive process.

- show advantages of concrete activities and materials as opposed to group testing situations.
- enable teachers to assess knowledge and abilities in order to increase the challenge to match the child's level (Helm, Beneke, & Steinheimer, 1997).

Why Write It Down?

EXERCISE: Using a separate sheet of paper, list the kinds of writing you do in a day. Jot down the reason for each.

"I'll remember this and write it down later." Everyone has said that and then did not write it down. It is lost with all the other details of life that intercede and blur the image, blotting out specifics and erasing the exact words. **Recording** is used here to refer to a written account or notation of what has been observed. What are the reasons for writing down what has been seen? See Figure I–4.

To Remember. The grocery list (Figure I–5), even if it is left home on the refrigerator door, sticks in the memory longer because it was written down. Many students copy their notes over or condense them as a study technique. There is a connection between writing and memory. The words that are written form a visual and kinetic connection in the brain, assisting memory and recall even when the visual cues are not present.

To Compare. A child's height is measured with a line on the wall, and it is surprising a few months later how much she has grown without anyone realizing it. If that mark had not been made, the change would not have been noticed. Children are expected

Grocery List

eggs	vegetable soup
milk	toothpicks
chocolate chips	paper towels
banking	
dry cleaning	
birthday card for Louise	

Figure I–5 Write to remember.

to change, so a mark of comparison is needed. Relying on the memory of the child one, three, or six months ago is inaccurate and unreliable. By writing observations down, teachers have tangible comparison points. Portfolios, collections of the child's work and written observations, are becoming an accepted method of documenting a child's progress. Written observations that are thorough, objective, regular, and done in the natural classroom environment are accurate measures of the child's progress.

To Amplify Later. Sometimes there is no time to write the whole incident, so a few strategic notes written and dated at the time can be just enough to jog the memory for a longer, more complete narrative written later.

The teacher shows a new song chart and has just said, "I need all your eyes up here." Andrew asks, "What's sixteen plus sixteen?" A puzzled look comes over the teacher's face, followed immediately by one of irritation for the interruption. He repeats his question louder. "Thirty-two, now let's look at this new song chart." Andrew replies, "Oh, you want all thirty-two eyes looking at the chart." This tells us about Andrew's thinking, his beginning understanding of math concepts, and causes the teacher to vow to listen more closely to children's questions. This is a wonderful incident to relay to Andrew's family to

Figure I–4 Why write?

demonstrate his thinking and his humor. The teacher just had time to write "eyes, 16, 32" with the ever-present pad and pen. That was enough to enable the teacher to fully write about the incident later.

To Catch and Preserve Details. Details are quickly forgotten. Insurance companies want auto accident reports written at the scene because of the frailty of human memory. Fine details that seem so clear or seem so unimportant now, can best be preserved by writing them down. These details can give clues to trends or correlations that are not seen at the time. Upon closer examination and comparisons later, they gain significance. For example, keeping some data on where and how long each child spends in certain areas of free time gives much information about the child. Without some method of tracking, there is no way to recall details like this that can yield important information.

To Serve as a Literacy Role Model. Children need to see adults writing. Literacy is an important concept to teach young children. The importance of the written word is emphasized when children see the usefulness and practical applications by their role models, the adults in their lives. When an adult writes something down, a child often asks, "What are you doing?" A reply such as, "I'm writing this down so I won't forget" is laying literacy foundations for the child (Figure I–6). It shows that writing is a way to help memory, that what is written is constant and stirs the child's desire to want to write himself. Accessible materials encourage him to do that (Figure I–7).

To Document. Reliable research demands hard data. It is necessary to preserve in writing—to **document**—what has been observed to substantiate it.

Figure I–6 Busy teachers jot short notes to amplify later.

Dramatic Play Area—paper and pencil next to the play phone, sheets cut for grocery lists attached to a pad on the play refrigerator, calendars on which children can write important events to remember

Block Area—paper, markers, tape for signs on buildings

Large Motor—paper, markers, tape for signs signifying what the climber is today (a rocket ship, a house on fire, Jenny's house)

Sand/Water—paper and pencil nearby to write down a mark at what sinks or floats, draw pictures of what has been found hidden in the sand; paper to list who is waiting for a turn

Cubbies—paper and pencil to list what children say they want to do outside today to decide which toys to load in the wagon

Group Area—chart paper, markers to take surveys of favorite things, lists of things to remember contributed by the group, safety rules

Figure I–7 A Literacy-Rich Environment

Recording methods that include facts rather than inferences along with date and time of the recording are essential to meaningful documentation. The details must be preserved to see progress, trends, and correlations.

It is especially critical if a child discloses an incident of abuse. The reports must be accurate and show the child was not led or influenced in order for the disclosure to be supportable evidence. One would like never to deal with this. For the protection of the child, it is important not to jeopardize the testimony by negligence or inaccuracy.

Why Use Different Methods?

EXERCISE: How many ways can you cook a chicken? Make a list. Here's a start:

- fry
- broil
- stew
- microwave

Why are there so many ways to cook a chicken? Because there are different end results from each method. The cook may be looking for a certain consistency, lowering calories, tenderizing, or working within a short period of time. There are many different methods of recording observations because the end result from each method is different. Yes, they are all based on observing the child and measuring the observation against standards in order to make decisions about immediate and future actions, but they differ in technique, content, and approach. *Week by Week* presents many different methods, along with a review of a developmental area, but the method is not limited to recording only that particular area. In the cooking example above, once the technique of frying or stewing or microwaving is mastered, it can be applied to other foods and modified for a variety of desired results. Just like cooking, once the recording technique is mastered, it can be applied to other developmental areas and modified to fit the recorder's style and selected outcome. The recording methods can be classified using the web design (Figure I–8).

Each method is a technique to focus on a behavior, skill, or action of an individual child or the whole group. The **narrative** recordings, such as anecdotal, running records, and interviews, tell a story. They bring the reader along by providing the actual details of actions, words, and results. The **criterion-referenced** recordings, such as class list logs, checklists, and rating scales, provide a predetermined standard or guideline to look for and measure against. The **quantitative** recordings, such as time samples and frequency counts, provide a numerical count of individual or group actions that then can be interpreted in various ways. These methods lose most of the raw data, the actual details that narratives preserve, but are useful for certain purposes. The **work samples**, such as drawings, writings, constructions, sculptures, and media-preserved work (audio or video recordings or photographs), give a visual account of the child's activities from which assessments are made. Each category and method within the category is distinctive and useful with its own specific technique, advantages and disadvantages, and best applications. These methods will be presented, practiced, and recommended for specific purposes throughout this book.

PORTFOLIOS

The systematic gathering of information about the child is **portfolio** assessment. Portfolios are more than a scrapbook or folder full of unrelated pieces of paper. Gronlund (2003) states, "Simply collecting samples of students' work and putting it in a file does not constitute a portfolio. Much greater care is required in the development of a portfolio that will be useful in instruction and assessment" (p. 159). Portfolios provide information on each child as an individual, on child development in general, and on the diversity of children. Portfolios give the opportunity for family involvement through communication centered on the child's work and they help the family become involved in the curriculum. From building portfolios, teachers learn to assess and plan curriculum for each child individually, see progress over time, and reflect on teaching practices (Shores & Grace, 1998).

Danielson and Abrutyn (1997) describe three types of portfolios. *Display* portfolios are scrapbooks of photographs of children's activities and learning experiences in the classroom without teacher comment or showing progress over time. *Showcase* portfolios are the best pieces of the child's work either self- or teacher-selected without evaluation or information about progress or affecting the curriculum. *Working* portfolios include selected but typical work samples along with teacher documentation to show the child's progress, the teacher's observations, and on which curriculum is based and future actions are planned for the child, with the child, the family, and other professionals if needed.

Portfolios draw from multiple information sources and are gathered in the child's natural surroundings by persons familiar with the child and the environment. They are collected over time so they clearly show the child's progress.

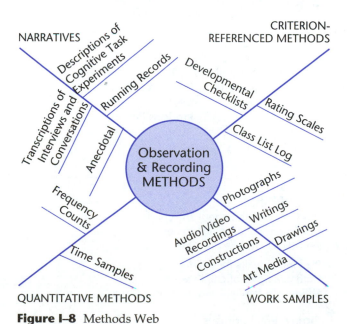

Figure I–8 Methods Web

What Is in the Portfolio?

A portfolio is an individual folder for each child in the class. Eventually it may hold many pieces of the child's work, teachers' observations, photos, video or audio tapes, so it should be expandable. All portfolios should be stored in a locked file cabinet or file box. This assures they are accessible only to authorized people, including the staff working with the children and the director. The portfolio is available to the family upon request and to the child.

McAfee and Leong (2002) suggest that the following types of items are appropriate for portfolios.

- Work products done on paper—samples of cutting, drawing, and any art medium; printing; practice papers; pasting; writings (initial drafts, editing, final drafts). Dictations by nonwriters.
- "Journals" for math, science, writing—children's drawings, scribbles, collages reflecting their experiences and growth.
- Records of data collection and presentation in math, science, social studies, health.
- Sketches of a child's work, made by the child or an adult (block structure, pattern blocks, sand, any 3-D work). Sketches of the plan for that work.
- Photographs of a child engaged in significant work or play.
- Photographs of exhibits and displays prepared by child or group.
- Audio tapes and video tapes.
- Printouts of work done on computer—draw/paint, math, writing programs, games.
- Participation chart—what a child did on a given day or during a given period. Include qualitative information.
- Logs of activities and results (books read to or by child; family can help).
- Time sample or count of what a child did on a given day or period.
- Interviews—audio/video/written. Elicit reports or descriptions of a process, such as how to make a favorite food, get to school, make friends, or play a game; or "favorite" activities, books, or things to do. The child can draw it and then dictate the explanation to an adult.
- Structured observation, performance assessment, or dynamic assessment results. Do one or two children a day.
- Anecdotal records or jottings grouped according to the portfolio categories and/or affixed in chronological order. Use Post-its, gummed labels, or quarter sheets of recycled office paper (tape them on).
- Awards, certificates, citations.

- Families' comments and goals, notes from family–teacher and child–teacher conferences; drawings and dictated or written messages to families from children (p. 99).

(From McAfee, *Assessing and Guiding Young Children's Development and Learning, 3e.* Published by Allyn and Bacon, Boston, MA. Copyright © 2002 by Pearson Education. Reprinted by permission of the publisher.)

The systematic plan to build the portfolio will gather information from multiple sources (Figure I–9):

Child. The child contributes work samples, such as drawings, art work, samples of writing and language. Media, such as audio and video tapes and

Figure I–9 Portfolios

photographs, also can be included. The portfolio is a book about the child so from a very early age, the child has a voice in the included works.

Families. Families, the true authority on the child—since they know the child better than anyone—submit information to the portfolio on forms and written comments.

Teachers. Teachers and caregivers, who see the child regularly, submit formal observations using a variety of methods to best record different kinds of data in the most objective styles. Informal observations are included as important events worthy of remembering for a variety of reasons.

Staff. Staff in the program who have contact with the child may write a submission for the portfolio. The cook, the bus driver, the nurse, all see the child from a different perspective in different settings and have information to contribute.

Previous Teachers. Previous teachers' records may be passed on in the portfolio.

Referral agents. Referral agencies may include reports or suggestions for working with the child in the portfolio.

What Is Not in the Portfolio?

If there are any suspected, but as yet unsubstantiated, concerns about possible child abuse, those records should be kept in a confidential file, separate from the child's records. Any anecdotal recordings that document a possible disclosure of child abuse should be placed in this confidential file. A copy of the filed Child Abuse Reporting form and notations tracking the action should also be retained there. The teacher's Reflective Journal is the writer's private property, not to be kept with children's records, preferably kept at home.

Who Can Read the Portfolio?

The portfolio includes documentation of all developmental areas for helping, measuring, and reporting the child's progress. Documentation is arranged chronologically and in developmental areas, logged in on an Overview Sheet so that contents are noted. Because of the completeness and intimacy of a portfolio, its contents must be protected from unauthorized viewers. The National Association for the Education of Young Children's *Code of Ethical Conduct* (Feeney & Kipnis, 1998) under the section on Ethical Responsibilities to Families reads:

P–2.8—We shall develop written policies for the protection of confidentiality and the disclosure of children's records. These policy documents shall be made available to all program personnel and families. Disclosure of children's records beyond family members, program personnel, and consultants having an obligation of confidentiality shall require familial consent (except in cases of abuse or neglect).

P–2.9—We shall maintain confidentiality and shall respect the family's right to privacy, refraining from disclosure of confidential information and intrusion into family life. However, when we have reason to believe that a child's welfare is at risk, it is permissible to reveal confidential information with agencies and individuals who may be able to intervene in the child's interest (p. 7).

Custodial parents or legal guardians have a right to see and control school records under the Family Educational Rights and Privacy Act (Buckley Amendment) passed by Congress in 1974. In the basic belief that early childhood programs are in partnership with families, the records are subject to their inspection. The systematic plan of gathering information has nothing to hide, for it seeks to provide objective, descriptive documentation.

Occasionally people who have a need or a right to know may see the contents of the portfolio. Those people may include: health professionals who are doing updates on a child's immunizations; a program evaluator who is gathering developmental level data, not on individual children but on an aggregate of all the children; or an accreditor looking at how the program records developmental information or seeking proof of a systematic authentic assessment plan. An ethical way to inform the families and the program of who has seen the contents of the file is to include a **file access log** (Figure I–10) in each file. Each person who views the file, other than the teacher(s), signs the log, providing the date, identity, agency represented, and reason for looking at the file.

Program handbooks should inform families that their child's portfolio is open to them any time. They usually have final determination of it at the end of the year, whether it will go to the next teacher, next center, on to the public school, or taken home. The school will obtain written permission before releasing any portfolio document to others. The exceptions are school officials with a legitimate educational interest and officials for use in audit or accreditation associations (with names deleted). In emergencies, the information is used to protect the health of the individual (Berger, 1994).

The record of _____ was reviewed by the following:
(child's name)

DATE	NAME/TITLE	AGENCY	REASON	SIGNATURE

Figure I–10 File Access Log

Why Use Portfolio Assessment Rather than Testing?

Chapter 8 will discuss standardized testing and its use and misuse; this book will guide you in using portfolios as an authentic, reliable way to assess children's development. Much has been written to promote portfolio assessments (Anderson, 1998; Bredekamp & Rosegrant, 1992; Kamii, 1990; Meisels, 1987, 1989; NAEYC, 1997; Shepard, 1989). A review of the benefits of portfolio assessment include its ongoing purposeful assessment done during authentic activities in a naturalistic setting without diverting children from natural learning processes.

Portfolios can be a valid, reliable replacement for standardized testing. Organizations like the NAEYC and National Association of Early Childhood Specialists in State Departments of Education (NAECS/ SDE) take the position that "Information gained from assessments of young children's progress with respect to standards must be used to benefit children. Assessment and accountability systems should be used to improve practices and services and should not be used to rank, sort, or penalize young children" (NAEYC, 2002). They call for more authentic assessment methods that provide documentation gathered from multiple sources over a period of time in the child's natural environment (Figure I–11).

The *Week by Week* systematic plan for portfolio building will enable the user to gather data to meet the need of authentic assessment in a manageable way. It meets the guidelines for appropriate assessment for planning instruction and communicating with families, identifying children with special needs, and for program evaluation and accountability. For a full discussion of these guidelines see *Reaching Potentials: Appropriate Curriculum and Assessment for Young Children* (Bredekamp & Rosegrant, 1992, p. 22–26).

Boehm and Weinberg (1997) remind readers of the valuable work of many social scientists, sociologists, and anthropologists who have gathered observational field data. An ecological view is studying in naturalistic settings, not in the traditional control experimental atmosphere. An early childhood set-

Figure I–11 Close observation of routine events helps the teacher evaluate and make decisions.

ting is not a controlled laboratory but an environment that is just a part of the child's larger realm.

EXERCISE: How long do these big projects take? What steps lead to completion of the project?

- Conception to birth:
- Earn a college degree:
- Lose twenty-five pounds:
- Crochet a bedspread:

Some of those projects take months, some take years, some take a lifetime. Each one begins with a plan with small steps along the way, leading to the completion of the project. None can happen overnight. Some may even seem impossible but when broken down into manageable steps, planned and worked on over a period of time, they can be accomplished. Eventually the desired goal will be reached.

Teachers of young children *know* they should be keeping written records on each child's behavior for many good reasons, but there is one seemingly insurmountable obstacle: *time*. This book begins with the premise that writing down observations of children's activities is the preferred method of assessing and documenting children's development.

"But I don't have time!" Every busy adult working with children has said it. The teacher's priority is to applaud the climb to the top of the ladder, redirect that arm ready to throw a block, or give a thoughtful response to a family member as she hurriedly says on her way out, "He's running a little fever and had a touch of diarrhea this morning, but he says he feels fine." The role of the teacher is to provide physical and psychological safety and intellectual challenge to each child. The teacher also strives to maximize the teachable moment and expand on the child's interests and conversations.

Those two assumptions, accurate record keeping and responsiveness to the needs of each child, seem incompatible. Time and attention for record keeping is minimal. Teachers who know they should be making written records are caught in a bind. They recognize the importance of keeping accurate records on which to base evaluations or plan individualized curriculum. The difficulty, and for some the impossibility, is doing that while interacting with the children.

Major accomplishments require time and planning. A meaningful portfolio of a child's develop-

ment and work is not gathered in a few days. Authentic assessment is achieved when each child's development is observed and documented objectively and periodically (Figure I–11). The results are strategies to facilitate the child's progress to the next developmental level by individualizing the curriculum. When the teacher knows that one or more children in the class have reached a certain level of development, plans can be specified for them to advance. There is a pattern of observe, assess, plan, and record. This is repeated in each developmental area for each child but only when an authentic performance-based assessment system is in place that allows this to happen efficiently.

In order to accomplish this desirable goal, the task must be broken down into manageable segments, planned and executed in a systematic manner. Doris Bergen (1993/94) says "Developing a systematic way of evaluating every child's performance and carefully recording assessment results is a crucial component of authentic assessment" (p. 102). Newman and Roskos (1993) point out "Programs need to *build in* the means and opportunities for all caregivers to watch and record what young children do in some systematic way over time" (p. 22). Benjamin (1994) suggests scattering observation chairs in strategic places around the room in preplanning and organizing for successful recording of observations. Skills, tools, materials, help, and dedication to the plan are needed to systematically build a portfolio demonstrating a child's development.

I was teaching a college course in observation techniques but struggling to apply the methods in my own classroom. There were mounds of checklists, one for each child, index cards, and notepads all over the room. When I tried to write a daily journal or mark a checklist, I could not remember children like Johnny who floated all over the room, never doing anything "noteworthy." This plagued me until I realized *I had to have a plan*. I went looking for one but had no success. After calculating the weeks in the school year, what I wanted to know, and the appropriate method to record it, I had a systematic plan. That plan, refined through many years of teaching and research, is presented in this book.

In *Week by Week*, when the word *teacher* is used, it refers to the recorder who is documenting the child's behavior. It may be the early childhood student in a practicum experience, caregiver in a child care setting, or teacher in a classroom setting. The recorder may have the minimum required hours of in-service training, a CDA (Child Development Associate), associate degree to advanced degrees, or teacher certification. Whatever the qualifications on paper, the children call this person "teacher" because she is in the teacher role and will be called by that worthy name in this text.

Users of *Week by Week*

This book is written for two audiences. It is a textbook for students in preparation programs (as well as being a resource for those same students when they have a classroom of their own) and for practitioners in the field.

***Week by Week* for the Student.** As a college textbook this book will be used for 13, 15, or 16 weeks. Each week you will be introduced to a different method and will be given one assignment to practice the method. If you are in a field placement for the whole semester you can incorporate the *Week by Week* plan as you participate in the classroom activities. If you are taking a course in observation methods, you can make weekly visits just for observation, or you may be able to plan three or four longer visits and do several of the practice assignments in each visit. In either of these two plans you will miss the day-to-day interactions. This is just for practice, a simulation of what you will be doing when you have a classroom of your own. CAUTION: Seeing children intermittently makes it impossible to draw decisive conclusions about their development. Also, it is important *not to talk specifically* about a child, teacher, or program by name when you are in your college classroom, dorm, or out with friends. **Confidentiality** is a part of the ethical responsibility of professionals.

***Week by Week* for the Practitioner.** Maybe you used this book in your college class and now have your own classroom. Or perhaps you found this book and are making a commitment to better organize your contributions to each child's portfolio. Appendix A provides information on how to schedule a manageable number of observations each week over the school year, returning to each developmental area several times. You will find a calendar in Appendix C that will help you. Some additional forms are included in Appendix E for your use in organizing the portfolio and using it to individualize the curriculum. After all, that's what observing is all about. You observe, you assess, you plan, you implement, you observe, you assess, you plan. Well, you get the idea by now. Remember that when you are totally responsible for the classroom that you will have to steal moments to write things down. That is the biggest hurdle to observing and recording. For help with this, note especially the "How to Find the Time" sections in each chapter.

The teacher using the *Week by Week* system will gain skill in using various methods of recording observations and will be reviewing child development and good teaching practices. Knowledge of child development, observation methods, and curriculum are not separate from each other but are interdependent. One must know what to look for in order to be a good observer, and mindful teachers make decisions based on what they see. The *Week by Week* system will enable the teacher to document important information about each child, usable for measurement and reporting, and information that is accurate and objective.

Chapter Features

Each chapter has three major sections. First, we introduce a recording method and acquaint you with its uses. A child development section follows for which that specific recording method is appropriate. This is an important part of each chapter, for without the child development framework, you would not know what to look for. Finally, each chapter has assignments for the student and the practitioner, with some accompanying helpful information. Here is an expansion of the features of each section.

Exercises. Scattered throughout the book are interactive sections inviting the reader to answer a question or formulate a list. Readers should write their "answers" in pencil to be erased for privacy or on a separate sheet of paper. These exercises are designed to introduce a concept which is applied in the following portion of the text. These are designed to be fun with a purpose so the reader is encouraged to complete them as they appear. Here's an example:

EXERCISE: Select one of the long-term projects in the exercise and list the steps needed to get to the end result.

The purpose of this book is to enable the reader to break down the huge task of portfolio building for assessment and curriculum planning into manageable steps, organized by weeks, methods, and developmental areas. Dividing the group of children into smaller, manageable numbers to observe in any one week also provides a realistic goal.

Using the . . .

EXERCISE: A house builder uses many tools. Next to each of the following, write its purpose:

- Hammer
- Screwdriver

- Saw
- Tape measurer
- Sand paper

Just as a builder has many tools, each with a distinctive purpose, so should the teacher have many recording tools and observation methods to use for specific purposes. There are several different kinds for different occasions or situations. Some are better than others at capturing certain kinds of behaviors, skills, and activities. If it were physical development we were observing and recording then a developmental checklist would be more efficient than a narrative describing every action of the child's movements. Speech and language are best captured on an audio tape but can also be recorded efficiently on a checklist, but then we lose the exact words, inflections, and context of the situation. Each chapter will present a method or technique along with a description and examples of that method linked to one of the developmental areas in which it can be used. That is not the *only* method for that development area, nor is that method only to be used in that developmental area.

Advantages and Disadvantages. A hammer is not adequate to turn a screw; likewise, a screwdriver does not efficiently drive in a nail (although some of us have attempted to do so). We present an observation in each chapter, described and illustrated with examples. Some are methods that will be familiar, some will be new. Some will be simple to grasp and use while others will take more practice. Some are used often while others are used periodically or only in special circumstances.

Pitfalls to Avoid. With every one of the builder's tools, incorrect use may result in a dangerous situation or an outcome that is less than desirable. Using a stiff paintbrush leaves unwanted streaks in the paint or varnish, for example. The description of the observation method will also include some cautions about the method or its use. These are not necessarily disadvantages, but are included to maximize the usefulness of the method.

Using Technology. New products and electronic devices can be used to more efficiently manage documenting children's development. This section in each chapter will suggest some products or applications that could be used to collect, organize, store, and report the documentation. Some are inexpensive and handy while others may require financial investment and a change in practice. Teachers are change agents, seeking to facilitate change in others so we, of all people, should be open to change ourselves.

How to Find the Time. In this section there will be some suggestions for how to find the few minutes that it takes to accomplish the documenting of children's behavior while managing the classroom at the same time. I repeat, it can be done!

Time? When is there time to write? A developmentally appropriate classroom for young children dedicates blocks of time to children's choice of activities. These are self-initiated, with materials and equipment available on shelves the children can reach themselves. Whole group activities are limited to very short periods, if at all. That leaves the caregiver with time, once the environment is prepared, to observe, make notes, and even closely follow and document a child's play. If there is no time for this, the teacher should look at the environment, the schedule, the ratio of children to adults, the curriculum, and the teaching practices. Perhaps there is work to be done in those areas before observation techniques can be implemented.

If you are a student using the recording method to complete an assignment, you have a luxury. Time. You can concentrate on children's movements and listen and write down their exact words without interruption. Now imagine yourself as the teacher trying to capture the same information using the same method while supervising the whole room for safety, reading a book, wiping a nose, washing your hands, and keeping track of the time to transition to the next part of the daily routine. It is tough but it can be done. However, it takes time-management skills, flexibility, concentration, classroom organization, and cooperation from the other adults in the classroom.

Review Box. At the end of each recording method section is a short definition of the method and other areas of development or behavior on which it can be used now that you have a working knowledge of the method's procedure, advantages, and disadvantages. At the end of each child development section, other recording methods are suggested to use to document the progress in that area. This demonstrates that the methods and areas of development are linked in *Week by Week* and are not exclusive to each other. Using some kind of reliable, regular documentation system is the goal.

Looking at . . .

The other half of each chapter is a discussion of one area of child development. That is what you are recording, each child's development, so you need to know what to look for. When the radiologist shows the X ray of a broken bone to the parents of the crying child, they look at it but may not *see it as she does*. Without her specialized knowledge, they look at the same visual image but understand it at a different level. The teacher needs the knowledge base of child development (Figure I–12).

Without it, behavior is observed, seen, but not recognized for its importance. For that reason, each chapter includes an overview of a developmental area discussing influences, milestones, terminology, and key theories. There is an emphasis on the child's observable skills and behaviors that demonstrate progress. Developmentally appropriate activities and practices are suggested to help foster that development.

Topics in Observation. These are discussions on issues related to observing and recording children's development. They are intended to help the reader gain a broader understanding of a specific topic in teaching, learning, or authentic assessment. These essays offer a deeper consideration of a certain aspect of the field of observing and recording. An example is shown on page 15.

It Happened to Me. Vignettes of my classroom experiences are scattered throughout the book. These anecdotes illustrate points about child development from children I have known and mistakes I have made that taught me what not to do. Some are observations my college students have written. Others are humorous stories related to me. All are stories, incredible, yet true. There are millions that *got away* because I never wrote them down! Many of these are remembered because after reflection on the real

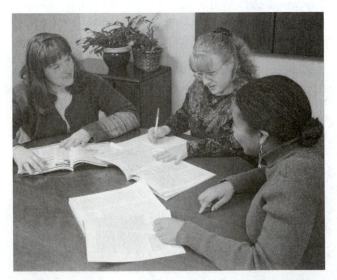

Figure I–12 Observation is based on a knowledge of child development.

IT HAPPENED TO ME

Why Doesn't Johnny Paint?

Early in my preschool teaching career, a mother asked me after class, "Why doesn't my Johnny ever paint? He never has any paintings to bring home." I thought, "Of course he paints! Everyone paints at the easel. There are always children on both sides for more than an hour every day. We use gallons of paint and reams of paper every year. Of course, he paints!" I started watching Johnny closely. Sure enough, he never chose easel painting. Even more revealing from my closer observation was how little I knew about what Johnny ever did. He was one of those children who did not draw attention to himself by negative behavior. He played and followed the rules of the classroom. At the end of the day, I had no idea what Johnny, and many others like him, had done. This is why we need to plan observations to include all children, not just those who demand our attention.

meaning of the incident, they taught me a lesson. Why is it that we often learn best from our mistakes? Many events became more important than I thought they were at the time. I hope you will begin to collect your own stories that have taught you lessons about teaching and life.

Helping All Children. Every child is unique, as different from one another as observers are. There are sometimes special considerations when observing the widely diverse populations in today's early childhood programs. Inclusion of children with special abilities in schools and programs call for attention to staff training, adaptability of facilities and environments, and inclusive practices. These are supported in this book by the emphasis on individual assessment, documentation, and individualizing the curriculum based on that assessment. At the risk of reinforcing stereotypes, this section is included to suggest insight relevant to the developmental area or the observation and recording process. It is a reminder that all children are children first, with circumstances that cannot be ignored. Recognizing their individuality influences the responses of thoughtful practitioners.

TOPICS IN OBSERVATION

The Ecological View of the Child

Urie Bronfenbrenner (1979) reminds us that each human exists in the context of society, illustrated by concentric circles of influence that make that person's life unique from all others. We use this same principle in looking at one aspect of a child's behavior such as when a teacher observes a small segment of a child's behavior—how the child holds the scissors to cut (Figure I–13). This is reflected against what the teacher knows about stages of normal small muscle development. The teacher recognizes the family influences on the child, both biologically and socially. How are her other small muscle skills and large muscle skills? Has she been allowed to use scissors at home? The family's situation in the community is appraised, along with the political and economic influences. Does this family value independence in a child or is it so stressed over not having enough food that providing opportunities to write and draw are not a priority? Did this family just emigrate to this country after months of nomadic life? National and world conditions have influenced the life of this family and ultimately the development of the child. Historical events in far distant lands and another time have brought the child to this point in time.

The **ecological view** of the child takes steps backward to visualize a broader view than just cutting with scissors. This ecological view of development gives the observer multiple perspectives on the child, looking at the big picture.

Scientists do not jump to conclusions based on one view through the microscope. The same is true when observing a child's behavior or skill, frozen in time on a particular day. Other developmental areas overlap to influence that observation. What is observed must be considered in context of the whole child, this child in particular, and added to the body of knowledge about children, families, and the society around them.

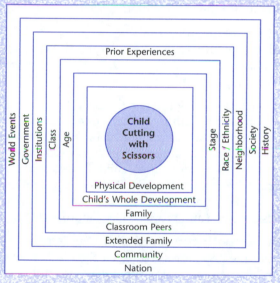

Figure I–13 The Ecological View of the Child from the Teacher's Viewpoint.

Helping Professionals. When working with children and families, teachers are often the resource or intermediary between people who need specialized advice and services and the professionals and agencies. This section is included in each chapter to acquaint the reader with the terminology of specialists to whom the teacher may refer the family. Each program should have a list of specific referral agencies and professionals from which the family can select, with guidance from the people they trust.

Other Methods. The recording method and developmental areas are linked in this book to familiarize you with both. However, once you have learned about the methods, you will see that development may be recorded and assessed using several different methods. At the conclusion of each chapter there is a feature that suggests which other methods would be suitable for documenting the developmental area featured in the chapter.

Key Terms. Throughout the chapter important words appear in bold type to draw your attention. They are listed at the end of each chapter; you can use this list as a self-check to be sure you understand their meaning. Each term is listed and defined in the Glossary at the end of the book.

Week by Week Plans. In the preface, and earlier in this chapter, I explained the dual purpose for this book. It is primarily a textbook to introduce early childhood students to the importance of documenting children's development and building individual child portfolios for authentic assessment and curriculum planning, all within the context of child development milestones. At the end of each chapter is a student assignment to complete during that week of field experience. Alternatively, several chapter assignments could be combined and completed in three or four lengthy visits over a semester.

For the Student. You will practice this recording method by following the assignment at the end of the chapter. You or your instructor may need to modify this depending on your field placement situation.

For the Practitioner. To achieve the goal of gathering a fairly equal amount of documentation on each child, use various methods, and revisit developmental areas three times over a school year. An organizational system can be used to ensure that you are gathering an approximately equal distribution of portfolio documentation on all children.

The monumental task of documenting every child in the class will become a series of small weekly plans, using the methods learned in that chapter to observe the developmental area that has been reviewed. *Week by Week* is a systematic plan to gather documentation on each child, in every developmental area, over a period of time, using a variety of recording methods. Some methods record small specific bits of information on all the children in the class. Other methods focus on one child, gathering detailed information. The Week by Week Plan usually gathers both kinds of information each week, rotating developmental areas and individual children. The children are arbitrarily divided evenly into four observation groups (A, B, C, D) so that selection of children for individual focus is by predesigned plan (Figure I–14). This gives every child a fair representation rather than depending on attention-getting behavior as the documentation cue, resulting in large folders on some children and thin ones on others.

You will notice that new methods are introduced each week and preceding ones are used again, perhaps in a different developmental area and on a different group of children. This shows the versatility of various methods while assuring that all children are recorded equally and in all developmental areas. Appendix A includes an extended chart so that the teacher can continue to plan past the first fourteen weeks, following them to build a meaningful progressive portfolio on which to base curriculum decisions and to chart achievement.

What to Do with It. This phrase will become familiar to the reader. At the end of each chapter presenting a recording method, a filing place is suggested along with a Portfolio Overview Sheet on which to note its presence, similar to a table of contents. These recordings are the teacher's contributions to the portfolio being built on each child. The child, the family, and other program personnel also may contribute meaningful data to the portfolio. Again, the purpose is not just a collection of papers but a working, growing body of knowledge about the child for the purposes of:

- documenting progress
- documenting typical and atypical behavior for intervention
- planning curriculum

Much has been written in the last ten years concerning portfolio building. The lack of a systematic plan for gathering that information, using a variety of methods, has led to this book. The purpose of the methods, rationale, instruction, and child development is to come to *know the whole child*. By knowing, then reflecting on this knowing, the teacher can truly plan and assess learning and progress (see Figure I–15).

Sharing with the Child and the Family. At the end of the day or session, what the teacher sees can be related to the child. What a wonderful send-off when the teacher says, "You painted a long time at the easel today," or "Today was a good day of sharing toys for you." The teacher shows by specific *positive* reference to the child's action that what they did today was noticed and important. This is not the time for reminders of misdeeds or warnings about tomorrow. This is also an opportune time to share that same kind of positive information with the family member picking the child up. If the routine does not provide that face-to-face contact, a note or a phone call, even to an answering machine, an e-mail account, or a digital photo through e-mail, communicates to the family that the teacher has been carefully watching their child and saw something important. It builds relationships between child, family, and school, and the self-esteem of all. Examples of this type of communication are included in each of the weekly observation plans.

WEEK	METHOD	AREA	ON WHOM
1	Class List Log Work Samples Reflective Journal	Separation and Adjustment Art	All All Self
2	Anecdotal Record Class List Log Reflective Journal	Self-Care Self-Care	Group A All Self
3	Checklist Anecdotal Record Reflective Journal	Physical Development Physical Development	All Group B Self
4	Running Record Class List Log Reflective Journal	Social Development Social Play Stage	Group C All Self
5	Frequency Count Anecdotal Record Reflective Journal	Emotional Development Emotional Development	All Group D Self
6	Interview and Checklist Class List Log Reflective Journal	Speech and Language Speech and Language	Group A All Self
7	Time Sample Interview and Checklist Reflective Journal	Attention Span Speech and Language	All Group B Self
8	Developmental Checklist Checklist Interview and Checklist Reflective Journal	Cognitive Math and Science Speech Language	Choice All Group C Self

(continued)

Figure I–14 Week by Week Plan

As a student, most likely it will not be your role to communicate with the family although it depends on your field experience situation. Examples are included for those who do have this responsibility and as a model for those who will someday have direct communication with families. Communication with the child and family members about what we see as teachers is an important part of our job yet one for which little preparation exists. Reading this section will help you begin to formulate your own family communication attitudes and practices.

In an effort to reflect the lives of many children today, the term *family* has been used throughout the book rather than *parent*. This is not meant to negate the importance of parents in the lives of children but to broaden the importance of those significant people in the child's life that vary for each child. At times it seems awkward and contrived but its concept is so important that I invite you to join me in this retraining of ourselves. Chapter 14 contains a further discussion of this rationale when it addresses sharing the portfolio in family conferences (formerly Parent Conferences).

WEEK	METHOD	AREA	ON WHOM
9	Rating Scale Interview and Checklist Reflective Journal	Literacy Speech and Language	All Group D Self
10	Work Samples Anecdotal Record Progress Reports* Reflective Journal	Creative Creative Process	All Group A Group A Self
11	Media Running Record Progress Reports* Reflective Journal	Dramatic Play and Blocks Dramatic Play	All Group B Group B Self
12	Class List Log Anecdotal Record Progress Reports* Reflective Journal	Self-Esteem Self-Identity	All Group C Group C Self
13	Setting Observation Class List Log Anecdotal Record Progress Reports* Reflective Journal	Environment Group Interactions Group Interactions	Visit All Group D Group D Self
14	Class List Log Checklist Progress Reports Reflective Journal *See Week 14, Assignment C	Interactions with Adults Physical Development	All All Group D Self

Figure I–14 (continued)

Actions. Because observations are meant to stimulate a decision, a section called *Actions* is included with *Read a Book* suggestions of a few books to read with children about the area of development. *In the Environment* suggests small changes or additions to the environment to help stimulate this area of development. *In the Curriculum* gives a few ideas about curriculum projects based on children's interests. Read Katz and Chard, *Engaging Children's Minds: The Project Approach* (2000) for a full description of this topic. This section also includes ways to individualize the curriculum. *In the Newsletter* suggests topics for newsletter articles or ways of sharing anecdotes or children's work.

The Reflective Journal. Each week a group of open-ended questions are provided to guide the teacher in looking inward. These are for the writer's own consideration of the events of the week, personal attitudes, self-analysis, and promises for the future. These are private journal entries, not a part of the child's records. These will be discussed again in

PORTFOLIO OVERVIEW SHEET

NAME _____ BIRTH DATE _____

SEPARATIONS AND ADJUSTMENT

Documentation	Location	Recorder	Date
_____	_____	_____	_____
_____	_____	_____	_____
_____	_____	_____	_____

SELF-CARE

Documentation	Location	Recorder	Date
_____	_____	_____	_____
_____	_____	_____	_____
_____	_____	_____	_____

PHYSICAL DEVELOPMENT

Documentation	Location	Recorder	Date
_____	_____	_____	_____
_____	_____	_____	_____
_____	_____	_____	_____

SOCIAL DEVELOPMENT

Documentation	Location	Recorder	Date
_____	_____	_____	_____
_____	_____	_____	_____
_____	_____	_____	_____

EMOTIONAL DEVELOPMENT

Documentation	Location	Recorder	Date
_____	_____	_____	_____
_____	_____	_____	_____
_____	_____	_____	_____

SPEECH AND LANGUAGE

Documentation	Location	Recorder	Date
_____	_____	_____	_____
_____	_____	_____	_____
_____	_____	_____	_____

MEMORY AND ATTENTION SPAN

Documentation	Location	Recorder	Date
_____	_____	_____	_____
_____	_____	_____	_____
_____	_____	_____	_____

COGNITIVE DEVELOPMENT

Documentation	Location	Recorder	Date
_____	_____	_____	_____
_____	_____	_____	_____
_____	_____	_____	_____

LITERACY DEVELOPMENT

Documentation	Location	Recorder	Date
_____	_____	_____	_____
_____	_____	_____	_____
_____	_____	_____	_____

CREATIVITY— ART AND BLOCKS

Documentation	Location	Recorder	Date
_____	_____	_____	_____
_____	_____	_____	_____
_____	_____	_____	_____

CREATIVE—DRAMATIC PLAY

Documentation	Location	Recorder	Date
_____	_____	_____	_____
_____	_____	_____	_____
_____	_____	_____	_____

SELF-IDENTITY

Documentation	Location	Recorder	Date
_____	_____	_____	_____
_____	_____	_____	_____
_____	_____	_____	_____

GROUP INTERACTIONS

Documentation	Location	Recorder	Date
_____	_____	_____	_____
_____	_____	_____	_____
_____	_____	_____	_____

INTERACTIONS WITH ADULTS

Documentation	Location	Recorder	Date
_____	_____	_____	_____
_____	_____	_____	_____
_____	_____	_____	_____

OTHER DOCUMENTATION

_____
_____
_____

REPRODUCED WITH THE PERMISSION OF AUTHOR: Nilsen, B. (2005). *Week by Week: Plans for Documenting the Development of Young Children, 3E.* Clifton Park, NY: Thomson Delmar Learning.

Figure I-15 Portfolio Overview Sheet

Chapter 1. These are found grouped together in Appendix E and are perforated so you can tear them out, keep them in a safe place, and work through them week by week.

Resources. Resources listing helpful books and articles on selected topics are included at the end of the chapters following the references.

NOW YOU CAN GET STARTED

In fourteen weeks, many recording methods are presented and practiced. An overview of child development principles gives a knowledge base or review from which to observe. The Plan systemizes recordings so that all developmental areas are observed at least once. In real life, the areas must be revisited repeatedly to accomplish the objective of seeing change over time so the plans are extended to forty weeks in Appendix A. Care has been taken to observe each child equally in all developmental areas using a variety of methods. (See Appendix B for an overview of that plan.) The weekly plans for the rest of the year are included in Appendix C so this book can be a manual for use in an early childhood program throughout the year. Adaptations for class size and situation are explained.

That is how this book is arranged. It is meant to be a weekly plan for recording observations of each child's development and used as a basis for planning curriculum. The outcome of the plan is a meaningful, comprehensive portfolio.

You will need a new file folder for each child in your class, plus a few extras for new children through the year. Write names on tabs, last name first, and place the folders in alphabetical order. Place in the file any information supplied by the parents.

A Portfolio Overview Sheet is a summary of all the recordings in the portfolio so the reader can see at a glance what is contained there, a type of table of contents. You will duplicate the one supplied at the end of Chapter 1 to place in each portfolio.

This introduction sets the stage, gives you the background, and acquaints you with the format of the book. The next steps are yours. Complete the exercises and adapt the plans for your particular group of children. At the end of fourteen weeks, you will have accumulated sizable portfolios on each child, with documentation in each developmental area. If you continue the plans throughout the year (Appendix B), you will see the progress they make and become a better observer, recorder, and teacher.

A WORD ABOUT ETHICS AND CONFIDENTIALITY

Ethics of Documentation

As professionals (or developing professionals) we are bound by ethical principles. **Ethics** should guide documentation in the following ways.

Accuracy. With every method of observation there is a responsibility to record the raw data (facts) as accurately as possible. This is done by making notes as completely and promptly after observing as possible. As time passes our memory dims and details slip away. The best recording is done *as the behavior is observed*. Some methods you will learn about are strictly factual while others do have elements of judgment inherent in them. Carefully choose those methods and use them wisely.

Objectivity. Methods that preserve the raw data (just record the facts) are more **objective** (without bias or opinion) than others. That does not mean that one method is better than another or that biases and opinions can't enter into any recording. It is the responsibility of the recorder to capture what is seen and heard without interpretation. Again, the methods will contribute to the recording of data or interpretation. Be aware of that possibility.

Another aspect of objectivity is selecting children to document. By leaving it to the observer it is possible to have thick files on a child who has challenging behavior, resists classroom routines, or has social difficulties with other children or teachers. This child is interesting to write about for we are drawn to negative examples. However, there are children who follow the rules, flow with the routines, and get along with other children and adults. These children seldom are chosen for specimen recordings but all children deserve an equal representation in observing practices. The Week by Week Plan seeks to make that selection of subjects more arbitrary, thus equalizing the number and topic of the documentation added to each child's portfolio.

Labeling. We all sort and categorize the information we take in. That is how we attempt to make sense of the world. It is important not to draw premature conclusions or diagnoses about a child based on limited information, or to label a child or behavior. Our observation methods are designed to document the facts and try to avoid categorizing a child as "bold," "hyperactive," or "shy." As observers our role is to describe, document, and measure progress.

Intended Purposes. Students are writing about children for the purpose of observing and interpreting milestones in child development, to see theories in action, and to practice recording methods. The actual files should be destroyed once the course is completed since their purpose has been served.

Practitioners' purpose in recording is to document a child's behavior, assess, and plan for that child accordingly. Documenting should not be used to build a case against a child for any reason or to threaten or humiliate a child or family.

Sharing with the Family. For students, sharing with the family is only done under the direction of and with the approval of the teacher. For practitioners, observations should be related to parents using tact and much deliberation about how they will be received. Occasionally what the teacher thinks is a triumph the parent may see otherwise because of a different perspective or value.

Talking to the child in front of the family should also be done with consideration. Sometimes children want privacy and a sense of being a person apart from the family. The teacher could ask the child, "May I tell your family about how long you painted today as we show them the painting?" Sometimes the child needs to hear their accomplishments related to their family. Misdeeds or concerns however must be done in private, away from the child and other families, of course.

Confidentiality

Students will mask the identity of the children they observe by using only initials or some other neutral identifier. No last names should ever appear on any student's recording. Permission from a family member may be required by the school or program. It is the student's responsibility to inquire about the policy and abide by it. The file must keep the documentation private from anyone other than the instructor, the child, the child's family, and those who have a legal "right to know."

Writing enhances memory. That point has been strongly emphasized as the reason for writing observations. It is also true that what is remembered is discussed. As one becomes a better observer and recorder, it will also be only natural that conversations will be full of anecdotes. Cute stories, interesting quotes, and even concerns and *inside* information are on the observer's mind and sometimes lips.

Discussions outside the classroom with friends, or one's own family, require discretion. Sometimes stories are related for illustration, but should never include children's names. Complaining, satirizing, or criticizing children or families is unprofessional. Professional behavior is guided by judgment, kindness, and most of all, respect for an individual's privacy. Let's make a commitment to uphold NAEYC'S *Code of Ethical Conduct* (Feeney & Kipnis, 1998).

KEY TERMS

assessment	narrative
confidentiality	objective
criterion-referenced	observing
document	portfolio
ecological view	quantitative
ethics	recording
evaluation	referral
family	work samples
file access log	

REFERENCES

Each chapter will include references used in the chapter.

Anderson, S. R. (1998). The trouble with testing. *Young Children, 53* (4), 25–29.

Benjamin, A. (1994). Observations in early childhood classrooms: Advice from the field. *Young Children, 49* (6), 14–21.

Bergen, D. (1993/94). Authentic performance assessments. *Childhood Education, 70* (2), 102.

Berger, E. (1994). *Parents as partners in education: The school and home working together.* New York: Prentice Hall.

Boehm, A. E., & Weinberg, R. A. (1997). *The classroom observer: Developing observation skills in early childhood settings,* 3rd ed. New York: Teachers College Press.

Bredekamp, S., & Rosegrant, T. (1992). Reaching potentials: Appropriate curriculum and assessment for young children (Vol. 1). Washington, DC: National Association for the Education of Young Children.

Bronfenbrenner, U. (1979). *The ecology of human development.* Cambridge, MA: Harvard University Press.

Danielson, C., & Abrutyn, L. (1997). *An introduction to using portfolios in the classroom.* Alexandria, VA: Association for Supervision and Curriculum Development.

Feeney. S., & Kipnis, K. (1998). *Code of ethical conduct.* Washington, DC: National Association for the Education of Young Children.

Goodman, Y. M. (1989). Evaluation of students. In K. S. Goodman, Y. M. Goodman, & W. J. Hood (Eds.). *The whole language evaluation book.* Portsmouth, NH: Heinemann.

Gronlund, N. E. (2003). *Assessment of student achievement,* 7th ed. Boston: Allyn and Bacon.

Helm, J. H., Beneke, S., & Steinheimer, K. (1997). Documenting children's learning. *Childhood Education, 73* (4), 200–205.

Kamii, C. (1990). *Achievement testing in the early grades: The games people play.* Washington, DC: National Association for the Education of Young Children.

Katz, L., & Chard, S. (2000). *Engaging children's minds: The project approach.* Norwood, NJ: Ablex Publishing Corporation.

McAfee, O., & Leong, D. J. (2002). *Assessing and guiding young children's development and learning,* 3rd ed. Boston: Allyn and Bacon.

Meisels, S. J. (1987). Uses and abuses of developmental screening and school readiness testing. *Young Children, 42 (2),* 4–6.

Meisels, S. J. (1989). High stakes testing in kindergarten. *Educational Leadership, 46 (7),* 16–22.

NAEYC. (1997). Position statement. Developmentally appropriate practice in early childhood programs serving children from birth through age 8. In *Developmentally appropriate practice in early childhood programs,* Revised edition. Eds. S. Bredekamp & C. Copple, 3–30. Washington, DC: Author.

NAEYC. (2002). *Early learning standards: Creating the conditions for success. Executive Summary.* Washington, DC: National Association for the Education of Young Children.

Neuman, S. B., & Roskos, K. A. (1993). *Language and literacy learning in the early years: An integrated approach.* New York: Harcourt Brace Janovich.

Piaget, J., & Inhelder, B. (1969). *The psychology of the child.* New York: Basic Books.

Shephard, L. A. (1989). Why we need better assessments. *Educational Leadership, 46 (7),* 4–9.

Shores, E. F., & Grace, C. (1998). *The portfolio book: A step-by-step guide for teachers.* Beltsville, MD: Gryphon House.

Woodward, H. (1993). *Negotiated evaluation: Involving children and parents in the process.* Portsmouth, NH: Heinemann.

RESOURCES

For more on portfolios and documentation, see:

Bredekamp, S., & Rosegrant, T. (1992). *Reaching potentials: Appropriate curriculum and assessment for young children, Vol I.* Washington, DC: National Association for the Education of Young Children.

Helm, J. H., Beneke, S., Steinheimer, K. (1998). *Windows on learning: Documenting young children's work.* New York: Teachers College Press.

Shores, E. F., & Grace, C. (1998). *The portfolio book: A step-by-step guide for teachers.* Beltsville, MD: Gryphon House.

Using the Class List Log to Look at Separation and School Adjustment

IN THIS CHAPTER

- **Using the Class List Log**

- **Topics in Observation: Why Not Use a Diary or Daily Journal?**

- **Using the Reflective Journal**

- **Looking at Separation and School Adjustment**

- **Helping All Children with Separation and School Adjustment**

- **Helping Professionals for Separation and School Adjustment Concerns**

USING THE CLASS LIST LOG

EXERCISE: Make a list of all the people you have had contact with today. Note what color shirt each person was wearing.

Some assumptions can be made about the list in the preceding exercise. It may be difficult to list every person one is with but easy to remember more significant people. It also may be difficult to remember the color of the shirt each person wore, especially casual contacts. It would have been easier if one knew at the beginning of the day what the assignment was and noted it as it occurred. At the end of the day, or after the fact, recall is more accurate concerning some people and some facts than others. Memory might fail regarding people who demanded no attention and received none.

The teacher's clearest recollection at the end of the day is usually of those children who did memorable things. The memory might be a child splashing paint across the room or one singing every song from the latest Disney movie. Children who cause no trouble or draw no attention to themselves might not be remembered at the end of the day.

A method is needed to guide the teacher to record information about every child in the class. The same category of information should be recorded on every child in the group on the same day: It is more equitable to standardize the criteria and collect data on all the children in the group. Memory cannot be trusted for accuracy or remembering each child.

The **Class List Log** is a method or format to record one or more short, specific pieces of information about each child present on that day. It is designed to be quick and easy (something every teacher is looking for). However, it provides information on every child in the group. It records facts that may be interpreted later or incorporated into another type of developmental comparison over time. The Class List Log criterion is determined in advance and is the same for each child (Figure 1–1).

Blank forms are made by alphabetically arranging the first names of the children. This arrangement allows for the quickest way to find the space to jot a note. There is a line at the top for the date. Using a date stamp is a good routine to follow. This assures the date is on every recording, including the year. Leave as much space between names as possible.

Two forms may be made vertically on one page and kept on hand for various purposes. Bits of information then can be copied over or cut apart and stapled into each child's file. (Blank Class List Logs are provided in Appendix D.) The availability of the Class List Log form is essential to its usefulness.

While actively engaged in play or work, the recorder uses the Class List Log to record information on one skill or behavior on each child in the group. This provides a natural information-gathering process. For example, cutting could be observed by placing children's scissors on a table with interesting papers to cut, such as gift wrap, wallpaper samples, or comics. The observer sits nearby with a Class List Log and makes notes as each child works in that area. Large motor skills can be observed easily as children go through a maze that includes climbing, balancing,

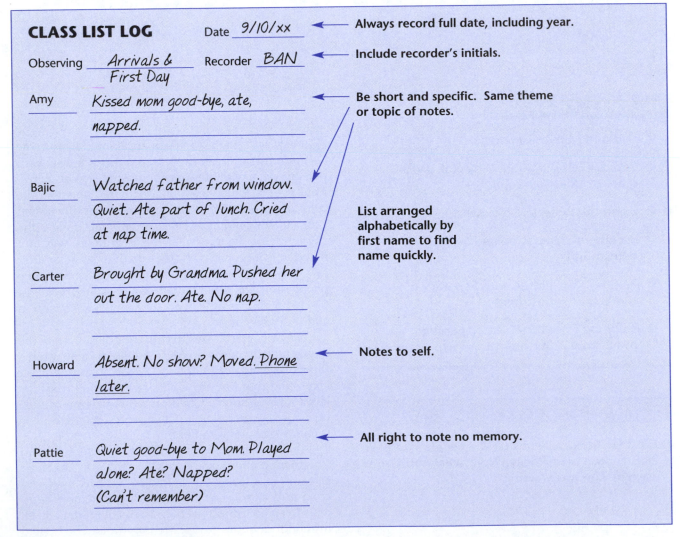

Figure 1–1 Class List Log Example

throwing, jumping, and crawling skills. It is important to date every observation, including the year.

EXERCISE: Mark the following *Yes* or *No* for suitability of Class List Log criteria.

_____ has toileting accidents
_____ is able to cut
_____ listens to story
_____ pours own juice, usually without spilling
_____ sleeps at rest time
_____ considerate of others' feelings
_____ can pedal a tricycle
_____ understands concepts of front/back, up/down, loud/soft
_____ uses words to resolve conflicts
_____ follows classroom rules

Now go back to the list and record in which setting or activity this most easily could be observed for every child in the group in one class session. If that is difficult, then that skill or behavior probably is not suitable for a Class List Log.

Remember that the Class List Log is best for recording on-the-spot observations or memorable frequent events so "toileting accidents" would be useful in the toddler class but hopefully not in older groups. "Can pedal a tricycle" could be recorded on a Class List Log if that day most of the children have the opportunity to ride while the teacher observes and records. "Understands concepts of front/back, up/down, loud/soft" probably is not best recorded by a Class List Log. It would take several observations or a specific planned activity to observe and record each of these concepts on all the children. "Follows classroom rules" could be recorded on a Class List Log from memory but it would be untrustworthy (as memories are) and possibly biased so other recording methods would be better for this behavior.

Uses

The Class List Log might be used to take attendance or to make notes on one behavior for a specific purpose. For example:

- separation from family
- large motor: specific skills such as climbing, standing on one leg for five seconds, walking the length of the balance beam, alternating feet coming down stairs, or hopping
- small motor: cutting with scissors, printing first name, rolling a ball, folding a napkin or paper in half, or putting together an eight-piece puzzle

- language: reciting nursery rhymes; responding to vocabulary of over, under, small, bigger, biggest
- literacy: looking at a book from front to back, "reading" pictures
- math: rote counting, using one-to-one correspondence
- science: placing items in sequence, sorting items by color or size
- art: painting lines, circles, human figures, alphabet letters (use Class List Log at the easel to tally each time a child chooses to paint in a week)
- blocks and dramatic play: note level of play, role in dramatic play, or type of constructions made

Advantages

The Class List Log is an efficient recording method because it

- is quick and easy.
- records specific information on every child in the group.
- gives specific, dated, brief, factual information.
- can be transferred to other forms of recording as base information.
- can be used later for comparison.

Disadvantages

The Class List Log may not be desirable because

- the form becomes outdated as children enter or leave group.
- rewriting is time-consuming.
- limited information or data is recorded.
- it must be repeated to be valuable for comparison.

Pitfalls to Avoid

The recorder should remember to

- always date each entry (a stamp dater is great).
- include the time of day, if pertinent.
- select an observable criterion.
- write short, factual notes.

Technology

Technology refers to tools that make a task easier. While we may think it means only electronic equipment, the term also includes any object or supply that helps make a job easier or more efficient. Here are some tools that will help you manage information you gather with a Class List Log.

Mailing Labels. These can be used to efficiently transfer information gathered in a Class List Log format. By preparing sheets of labels with children's first names in alphabetical order, either by hand or on the computer, the important developmental information gathered from observations can then be transferred to a sheet of paper in each child's portfolio.

Date Stamp. Small stamp-pad tools with moveable dates are invaluable to help with one of the most important and basic pieces of information we gather. How many of us have photos from past years without dates on the back, making it difficult to remember when they were taken? The date stamp can be used on each of the mailing labels, on portfolio entries, and on children's work as it is added to the portfolio. They are inexpensive and can be placed in many areas of the classroom. Children can be taught to date their own paintings and artwork.

Hand-held Computer. A personal digital assistant can be very useful for the Class List Log. Using the program Documents to Go® the Class List Log can be produced on the computer, then transferred to the hand-held computer where notes can be entered. Later the information is transferred back to the main computer and sorted into individual children's files in a matter of minutes. You won't have to copy notes over, cut up lists and tape them into file folders, or even use address labels. The Portfolio Overview Sheet can then be used as the outline for storing each piece of documentation according to developmental area. This week's recording on separations or adjustments (discussed later in the chapter) would be electronically pasted under that heading with the date; others later in the year will be added there for a cumulative record.

How to Find the Time

Having the forms already made and available around the room make Class List Logs easy to use. Because they are designed to record one small piece of data—the same one on each child—they are not time consuming. By carefully selecting the observable, important developmental task or behavior that you are recording, information can be gathered on every child in the group in a relatively short period of time.

What to Do with This Information

On the Portfolio Overview Sheet, note the type of documentation that provides information for this developmental area (e.g., Class List Log by entering "CLL"). If it is a recording on the individual child it is filed in the child's folder. If it is a recording method that includes the whole class or a group of children it is

SEPARATIONS AND ADJUSTMENT			
Documentation	Location	Recorder	Date
CL		BAN	9/7
CL		BAN	2/14
CL		MS	4/5
RR		BAN	5/9

Figure 1–2 Portfolio Overview Sheet Example

filed in the Class File. The individual information may either be copied in the child's file, appear as a summary in the child's file, or referred to directly from the Class File. The recorder's name and date are noted (Figure 1–2). If bits of data are on mailing labels, these are attached to a page in each child's portfolio with the date. Class List Log sheets can be cut apart and each child's portion stapled, taped, or pasted on a sheet in the portfolio. Later, observations in this category will be added to this page. Remember, this is your index of all pieces of data you have on the child.

If the program uses a developmental checklist, the bits of information can be transferred to the checklist category in the child's portfolio, with the date and specifics. For example, Class List Log information gathered on cutting may be transferred to a developmental checklist on small muscle development.

Information gathered with the Class List Log could be shared with the family verbally at the end of the day. "Today, Aillio used the scissors to cut up the funny papers. He worked hard at cutting along the lines." A written happy note (Figure 1–3) could be sent home informing families, "Today, Aillio worked hard at cutting."

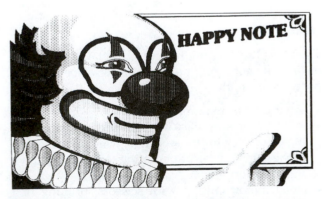

Figure 1–3 Happy notes are a method of communicating with families.

If a skill below the expected level of development at this age or stage is observed, a curriculum plan is implemented to address this area. This gives the child the opportunity to practice and advance the skill.

The Class List Log is an effective method to use in the first week of school to record observations. This method recognizes the teacher's first priority is making relationships with the child and family. The observations of separations and first impressions are important ones to record, however, providing an understanding of the foundations and outward manifestations of attachment and separation. The Class List Log provides a quick, easy format on which to record first observations without consuming much of the recorder's time.

Why Not Use a Diary or Daily Journal?

EXERCISE: Write a diary entry for yesterday on a separate piece of paper (for your eyes only).

Many people working with children know they should write about the children. Many even have written diligently in a notebook or in each child's file every day. The difficulty comes when this type of record keeping is considered in light of objectivity and comprehensiveness across the developmental areas.

An entry in a **diary** written at the end of the day is likely to omit details in sequence (Figure 1–4). Exact conversations and movements, which give so much important information to the assessment of children's development, are forgotten. At the end of the day, the strongest memories are those frustrations and difficulties. When it comes to remembering what each child did, the few who were the most difficult are most vividly recalled. Some are remembered at the end of the day because of an unexpectedly advanced skill or a novel, cute incident. The problem occurs when trying to remember the children in the middle. Those are the children who cause no trouble, who quietly abide by the rules, float through the day, doing nothing out of the ordinary to attract attention. Informal diary writing leaves those children out day after day after day.

This same difficulty occurs when writing in each child's page in a notebook. At the end of the day, try as one might, some children are not memorable. How can a teacher say to a parent, "I don't know what your child did today. I can't remember a thing." So instead, general comments are made, not based on hard data. The child is cheated out of being the focus of the observer's attention. It is not out of malice but because of the unsystematic way this type of recording is done. There is no hard data. Observations are written from memory, after the event.

The other shortcoming of the diary as an observational method is its subjectivity. People have used diaries traditionally for writing their innermost thoughts and feelings. **Subjective** recordings are those that are influenced by state of mind, point of view, or inferences into the meaning of events. The opposite is objective recordings, which are detached, impersonal, unprejudiced, recording facts rather than feelings and generalities. For the purpose of fair assessment and documentation of each child's development in all areas, objective methods should be used. The goal is an objective measurement system for each child. Diary entries do not help the teacher meet that goal.

Analyze your diary entry written in the preceding exercise. Can you separate the objective and subjective parts?

9/10   The First Day! It's a large class with many more boys than girls. They're going to give me a run for my money! They seem to have adjusted well for the first day 😊 and are eager to learn the routines, especially to explore the classroom. Carter was already in the Teacher's Cupboard. Said "What else ya got in here? Can I have that?" He's so cute. I'm especially interested in who makes friends. Today Jeff, Pia, Maurice, Jan & Chanique played together. I think this clearly will help me be a better observer. I'm so tired!

9/20   Day 2: I found out today that I need to find ways to separate Scott & Jeff -- together they're dynamite! They had me so busy doing damage control I can't remember what the other children did. Oh yes, Casper left to visit another class for 45 min. before I realized he was gone!

12/3   Wow has it been that long since I last wrote. I have parent conferences in two weeks. I better start better record keeping!

Figure 1–4 This diary example was written at the end of the day. It was difficult to remember details about every child.

EXERCISE: Mark these phrases *S* for subjective or *O* for objective.

_____ jumped from 18 inches
_____ very smart
_____ nice boy
_____ grabbed toy and said, "Mine!"
_____ doing fine
_____ she's a challenge
_____ polite
_____ counted to 8
_____ recognized nametag
_____ called someone a bad name
_____ clapped to "Bingo" song
_____ enjoyed music time

Check yourself: OSSOSSSOOSOS

USING THE REFLECTIVE JOURNAL

EXERCISE: Which of the following things would you rather discover yourself than have someone else tell you?

_____ You have bad breath.
_____ You are unzipped or unbuttoned.
_____ You have food stuck between your teeth.
_____ You are prejudiced against something.
_____ You are acting unprofessionally.

The **Reflective Journal** is a teacher's diary for personal thoughts. The word _reflective_ brings the image of deliberating, wondering, pondering, thinking, and rethinking. Teachers need to also be learners and that learning begins within, inquiring about one's own motivations, influences, molding experiences, culture and cultural biases, values, and beliefs (Balaban, 1995). Observing children in their natural setting includes the observer as a participant and a partner in the research (Swick, DaRose, & Pavia, 1998/99). Thinking and wondering about the child, the teacher's role, the classroom environment, the policies, all help the teacher to evaluate and transform what needs to be changed or modified. Teachers need opportunities to inquire into their own experiences and tell their own stories as a method of action research, collecting and analyzing data, and coming to conclusions. These reflections may be very private or may be shared with a mentor and discussed for further reflections. Some fascinating examples of those inquiries are:

Aaronsohn, E. (1996). _Going Against the Grain: Supporting the Student-Centered Teacher_ is a dialogue between a mentor and a beginning teacher who is bearing up under pressure to abandon developmental teaching philosophies.

Hendrick, J. (1997). _First Steps Toward Teaching the Reggio Way_ features stories of how teachers implemented the philosophies of the Reggio Emilia schools in the United States.

Terte, Klein, and Jewett (1998). _When Teachers Reflect_ includes several teacher's journeys with self-doubts and evolving practices into inclusion and individualizing curriculum. These reflections are valuable as written documentation of the teacher's private thoughts.

The Reflective Journal is like looking into a mirror (Figure 1–5):

- External view—When looking into a mirror, the viewpoint is from the outside, as others see the person. The Reflective Journal is an opportunity to explore the view that others see and com-

Figure 1–5 The Reflective Journal is like a mirror.

pare it to the inner, deeper meaning. It helps the observer see as others see.

- Quick check—Often the mirror is used for a quick, overall glance to see that clothes, hair, and makeup are satisfactory. A Reflective Journal can be a place for a cursory overview of performance, feelings, or events of the day without getting into deep analysis.

- See changes—Changes in appearance are identified by looking in the mirror. Grey hairs (or disappearing ones) or extra pounds are noticed visually when reflected in the mirror. The Reflective Journal can help the writer notice changes about thinking and attitudes.

- Close examination—The mirror can be used for a concentrated examination of a certain area. It may be a changing spot on the skin, clothing alignment, or a new wrinkle that has appeared overnight. The Reflective Journal can be a private place to self-examine a troublesome area. It may be premature or too private to discuss with someone else. An attitude toward a child or coworker, a creeping doubt about one's ability, or a prejudice that has come into one's consciousness can be closely examined in a journal.

- Make changes—When a look in the mirror shows something is askew, missing, or undone, the resultant action is an adjustment to correct the problem. Reaction to visions in the mirror is one of the purposes of looking. Writing in a Reflective Journal raises issues that call for change and presents the opportunity to resolve to take action. The Reflective Journal becomes an agent of change.

- Done repeatedly—Glances in the mirror are done many times a day, sometimes using substitutes such as windows in storefronts to re-examine certain areas. The Reflective Journal brings the teacher to inward examination again and again, whether in writing or in thinking.
- Reflection becomes a memory—The vision in the mirror is remembered. Looking internally through a Reflective Journal to examine values, beliefs, and feelings also forms memories. Those become as real as physical experiences. Reflection is more than daydreaming. It can be a life-changing experience.

EXERCISE: **Try some Reflective Journal writing:**

When I enter a new place for the first time I feel . . .
Writing about myself is . . .
An area I would like to explore about myself is my . . .
I chose to work with children because . . .

What Is Its Purpose?

Just like a personal diary, the teacher's Reflective Journal is a place to express emotions, make judgments, and form hypotheses (Figure 1–6). It is not a part of the child's file but the personal property of the writer, providing a healthy outlet for emotions. This type of recording must be kept separate from the assessments

9/10	I'm so excited about the first day of school. I wonder if having so many boys in the class will affect behavior & class management? Hey -- do I expect a difference? I guess I do! How can I keep my "active boy" bias from influencing what I see? Maybe these new methods of recording will help. I think I'll look for some things to read about sex differences and behavior.
9/13	I heard Mary & Ted next door talking about my new room arrangement breaking down the barrier between blocks and dramatic play. Do I let blocks go in the "oven"? Or in purses & briefcases? What about high heels and cowboy boots in the block area? We'll see!
9/20	Boy, this nit-picking is getting to me. Today Mary made me so angry when she said to the director, "my orderly classroom."

Figure 1–6 Reflective Journal Example

of the development of the child. For privacy, it must be kept at home, away from the work site.

Uses

The Reflective Journal is useful

- to express emotions or questions; to let off "steam," anger, frustration, elation; to express worry concerning a child, a coworker, a parent, a supervisor, or self.
- for self-examination of attitudes, biases, or prejudices.
- to pose theories about a child's behavior that are from intuition.
- to explore remedies, strategies, advantages, and disadvantages of possible solutions.

Advantages

- an outlet for emotions
- process writing to work through theories and to clarify and expand thinking
- becomes a record of professional development

Disadvantages

It is not useful for assessing children's development because it is

- written after the event when facts are lost.
- highly inferential and emotionally based.
- not comprehensive in recording information remembered on each and every child, only those who stand out.

What to Do with the Reflective Journal

Because of the confidential, subjective nature, it must be

- kept secure and private, away from the workplace.
- used as an emotional release that may not be possible in any other form.
- used to take a measurement of your personal and professional development in working with children and their families and with coworkers.
- used to explore questions, develop theories, and examine biases.
- reviewed at intervals to examine changes in thinking and attitudes, and measure professional development.

Pitfalls to Avoid

The Reflective Journal is very personal. It is important to maintain trust that what is written there will

---

R E V I E W

Class List Log: Alphabetical first name list to record small, specific pieces of information on each child in the class.

Types of Information to Record:

single elements of adjustment to routines

single elements of self-care

single elements of physical development

social development stage

clear articulation of speech

single elements of understanding math, science concepts

single elements of literacy development

frequency of choices of learning centers (one Class List Log in each center for logging choice), such as painting easel, dramatic play area, computer blocks

Reflective Journal: Personal diary kept separate and private from children's recording.

thoughts

expressions of emotion

questions

self-evaluation

reminders

---

not be read by anyone. Keep it at home. Get in the habit of writing in it every week. Go beyond the guided questions and use it to vent your feelings, questions, ideas, and theories. Keep it safe.

Using Technology

Many people now are in the habit of reading their e-mail once a day. Getting in the habit of entering a reflective journal entry is a convenient way to record thoughts, preserving them in a computer document, and printing them out periodically to review them.

How to Find the Time

The Reflective Journal, because it is personal and not used for direct assessment, takes personal time. This is done after the work day has ended, or at home. For many people, writing is a chore; for those people this task may be difficult. For others, writing is therapeutic and this task may be enjoyable. In either case, setting aside the time is well spent.

LOOKING AT SEPARATION AND SCHOOL ADJUSTMENT

A smooth transition from home to school at the beginning of the year or as a child enters a program provides for the child's immediate comfort and contributes to later success.

Attachment's Relationship to Separation

EXERCISE: Using a separate sheet of paper, make a list of objects that are important to you. How did they become so valued? How would you feel if they were destroyed in a fire, lost, or stolen?

People form an **attachment** to objects and other people for a variety of reasons. An object might be something attained after hard work and much preparation. It may be a gift received as an expression of love. Sometimes the longer an item is possessed, the more valuable it becomes. Strong attachment or value makes it hard to part with that object or person. Familiarity provides comfort. Separation brings a feeling of loss.

The infant's relationship with adults begins at birth when needs are met (Figure 1–7). This attachment to the family emerges from built-in survival techniques and responses. In the early weeks, the provider of those needs is irrelevant to the infant, as long as the needs are met. The infant begins to focus on the face, voice, and smells of those close to him, and begins to form mental images of those who hold him. Bowlby (1969), Yarrow (1964), Shaffer and Emerson (1964), and Ainsworth, Blehar, Waters, and Wall (1978) have all done important studies of this process of attachment. These studies are the basis for guiding expectations and practices. The professional caregiver's role is to build the child's bond to the parent as the primary adult and to the caregiver as a trustworthy substitute.

In the first few weeks of life, the infant responds to and attends to any nearby person, parent, or caregiver. This is the survival instinct: Without adult provision of needs, the infant could not live.

Between eight weeks and six months, the infant begins to discriminate between familiar people, such as parents, and unfamiliar people. The child is more responsive, and smiles and vocalizes more to familiar people than to unfamiliar people. There are implications for infants entering child care prior to six months old. As the infant is beginning to differentiate between self and significant others, the primary caregivers should be consistent people who are

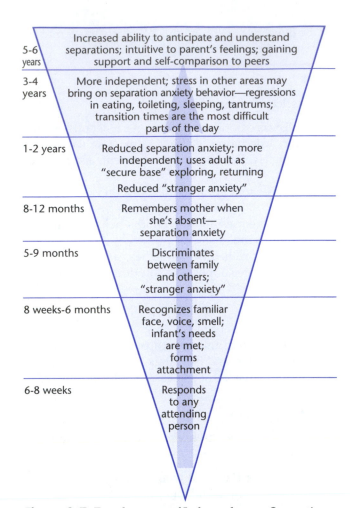

5-6 years	Increased ability to anticipate and understand separations; intuitive to parent's feelings; gaining support and self-comparison to peers
3-4 years	More independent; stress in other areas may bring on separation anxiety behavior—regressions in eating, toileting, sleeping, tantrums; transition times are the most difficult parts of the day
1-2 years	Reduced separation anxiety; more independent; uses adult as "secure base" exploring, returning. Reduced "stranger anxiety"
8-12 months	Remembers mother when she's absent— separation anxiety
5-9 months	Discriminates between family and others; "stranger anxiety"
8 weeks-6 months	Recognizes familiar face, voice, smell; infant's needs are met; forms attachment
6-8 weeks	Responds to any attending person

Figure 1–7 Development of Independence—Separation and Adjustment to Out-of-Home Experiences

responsive to the infant's needs. Infants may exhibit **stranger anxiety** as they are increasingly aware of the difference between close family and other people. However, Shaffer and Emerson (1964) found that most infants are capable of forming a number of attachments at the same time. The role of the caregiver is to keep the infant primarily attached to the parents. This can be done by providing reminders of the parents. Images (photographs), voices (tapes), and smells (belongings) surrounding the child during the day at the center will help to maintain that attachment during the family's absence. This gives assurance to parent and child that their bond is the primary one. The caregiver maintains that bond during their hours away from each other.

The infant and toddler maintain contact or stay near the attached person by creeping, walking, and following those important people. The child uses vocal signals, cooing, crying, and eventually words to maintain contact. Older infants and toddlers begin to anticipate the coming separation. This may happen when they see their coat and diaper bag being readied by the caregiver at the end of the day, or when they see the family member. This is what is called **separation anxiety.** This is a normal part of development but is distressing to all involved. The intensity of this stage is dependent on many factors: attachment to the parents, temperament of the child, and experiences with consistent responsive caregivers. It can be minimized by establishing those **good-bye rituals** that Balaban (1995) speaks about in a very helpful book on this subject, *Learning to Say Good-bye.* She advises families to establish a good-bye routine that is consistent every time they part (Figure 1–8). It serves as a dependable signal that leads the child to trust that the family member will return, even though parting may be full of tears and anger.

The toddler or preschooler engages in forming relationships with the attachment figures, learning how to get families and caregivers to change their behavior to conform to child's wishes. Preschoolers still experience separation anxiety because they now realize their power to manipulate others to meet their desires. They may not want the parent to have a life outside of their realm. Life in group care is different from life at home. Adjusting to discontinuity between home and the center may be stressful. The child learns to use separation anxiety as a tool to receive special attention and special promises. It often results in a

Figure 1–8 Good-bye rituals help the child and the parent with the transition and separation.

relaxation of standards of behavior. The family member may feel guilt or ambivalence for leaving. The caregiver's responsibility is to help the child cope and empower the family member to leave without guilt or losing a battle. Good-bye routines, once established, work very well at helping to ease tension.

Why all the attention to this area? Research has indicated some serious long-term consequences from separations of families and children. Bjorklund and Bjorklund (1992) summarized the attachment research of Bowlby (1969) and Ainsworth, et al. (1978), and others to suggest that securely attached children

- are more independent (than unattached children).
- have a more positive self-image.
- engage in positive social interactions with peers.
- have fewer behavioral problems.
- are able to negotiate in conflicts.
- score higher in IQ and standardized tests.
- are more socially competent, self-directed, and attentive at age 35.
- are more curious, flexible, and persistent.
- have better impulse control. (pp. 321–323)

With important outcomes associated with attachment, giving attention and developing strategies to assist in this important developmental area are critical.

Preparation for Entering Programs and Schools

EXERCISE: Using a separate sheet of paper, list important "first" events in a lifetime (such as birth, first step, first tooth, first date).

Beginnings are memorable events. They are celebrated with much thought, preparation, and anticipation. Photographs, videos, and certificates are concrete remembrances of the occasion. Memories are recited in detailed stories of the process. Lengthy discussions relate what went well and reflect on what did not and how it could have been done differently.

Beginning a new school year, entrance to a new child care center, and even the beginning of every day, is an important event. These beginnings are worthy of careful preparations, thoughtful processes, and detailed recording. Making smooth transitions into the program, whether for the first time ever or the first time that day, begins long before the parent and child come through the door.

Important Information Gathering Prior to the First Day. Every program has its own information-gathering form for facts about the child from the parents. The type of program, the objectives, and state regulations prescribe the type of information gathered on this form. A copy is placed in the child's portfolio for the teacher's reference. The original is kept in the program office.

EXERCISE: On a separate sheet of paper, make a list of information you think should be included on a family information form.

Refer to the family information form (Figure 1–9), and see how many pieces of information you thought of and which ones you feel are the highest priority.

The family is the most important source of information for assessing the child's development. By requesting developmental information, the program is recognizing the family unit as the child's first teachers, the ones who know the child best. In special education programs where children have been formally evaluated, Bloch (1987) stresses the importance of collaboration with families as information gatherers. She makes the point that "a radical rethinking of the way professionals work with parents and families is required" (p. 4). Bloch's parent assessment component in the Five P's (Parent Professional PreSchool Performance Profile) program, teaches them to

- learn to observe their child's behavior.
- systematically collect data about their child's performance at home.
- understand early childhood development.
- acquire rating skills.
- recognize behaviors that interfere with learning.
- share and compare assessments with the school.
- develop more realistic expectations for their child (p. 5).

Many questionnaires have been developed for parents to assess their own child's development, used as a screening device to identify those children who may have developmental delays. The *Ages and Stages Questionnaires System* (Bricker, 1999) is an especially easy tool to use, along with home visits (Figure 1–10). It has a few selected questions in developmental areas at eleven intervals between four months and four years of age.

Families should be consulted concerning their goals for the child and expectations of the program. This can be done in an informal conversation, a more formal interview, or in a questionnaire. McAfee and Leong (2002) recommend these procedures for eliciting information from families:

- Be respectful of family and community culture, customs, and language.

- Advise families about what information will be helpful.
- Use existing communication opportunities.
- Be able to get needed information related to a problem or concern.
- Have parents do some assessment and documentation. (pp. 62–63)

Personal Meetings. Building a relationship with the child and the families begins before the first day at school. This can be done in a variety of ways, depending on the program, the timing, and the age of the child.

EXERCISE: Check the ways you get acquainted with someone:

_____ phone conversations
_____ reading a questionnaire they have answered
_____ visiting one another's home
_____ introductions
_____ work on a task together
_____ have a common interest

Home Visits. One of the best ways to get to know the child in the family context is to make a home visit. This can be used to fill out the necessary paperwork and begin to establish a bond with the child in the child's surroundings. A home visit is not to inspect or to judge but to better understand the family situation. It is usually done in pairs, by the people who will be directly interacting with the child. It often helps to bring an activity or some piece of the school's equipment along, such as a toy or a book. Families and children would be interested in an album of photographs of school activities and people. It is important to provide time for the family and child to ask questions and tell stories of their family. The visitors will not only talk but listen.

This is a friendly, short visit to get acquainted. It can determine the families' needs of assistance from the program. Families can ask questions or express concerns they may have. They could both explore ways in which they can be involved in the life of the program. A home visit can be an excellent opportunity to explain the typical arrival and departure procedures. It informs the family and the child of the daily schedule, and what they should provide (Figure 1–11).

The visitor talks and begins to make friends with the child by smiling and making gestures of friendship without overpowering or demanding their participation. The family watches the developing relationship. Reactions may vary depending on their knowledge and trust of the program and feelings

THE B.C. CENTER
FAMILY, HEALTH, AND DEVELOPMENT FORM

Child's Name: _____ Date of Birth: _____

HEALTH HISTORY

Type of Birth: _____ Was the child preterm? _____

Does your child have a history of the following:

Frequent Colds: _____ Frequent Diarrhea: _____ Asthma: _____ Nosebleeds: _____

Ear Infections: _____ Stomach Aches: _____ Seizures: _____ Headaches: _____

Urinary Infections: _____ Please indicate what brings on the above conditions if you know: _____

_____

_____

What illness(es) has your child had? At what age?

Chicken Pox: _____ Scarlet Fever: _____ Hepatitis: _____ Diabetes: _____ Mumps: _____

Measles: _____ Other: _____

Does your child vomit easily? _____ Does your child run high fevers often? _____

Has your child had any serious accidents? If so, please explain: _____

_____

Does your child have allergies? _____ If so, how are they manifested?

Asthma: _____ Hay Fever: _____ Hives: _____ Other: _____

What causes the allergy? _____

Does your child have any food allergies? _____

Does your child receive any medication regularly? _____

Do you have any concerns in these areas: Speech: _____ Physical: _____ Hearing: _____

DEVELOPMENTAL HISTORY

Please answer to the best of your memory!

At what age child: crept _____ sat alone _____ walked alone _____

named simple objects _____ spoke in sentences _____ slept through the night _____

dressed self _____ began toilet training _____

Words child uses for urination/bowel movement: _____

Are there any eating problems? _____

Any dietary restrictions (vegetarian, etc.)? _____

How would you describe your child's personality? _____

Are there other child care arrangements during hours when the child does not attend this center?

_____

How does your child respond to other children? _____

Has your child had any other group play experiences? _____

How does your child cope with separation? _____

Have there been any recent family changes that we should be aware of? _____

What do you find best comforts your child? _____

Does your child have any fears that you are aware of? _____

How does your child show stress and what do you do to relieve it? _____

Do you have any concerns about your child's development? _____

Is there any other information you wish to share with us regarding your child? _____

_____

_____

_____

Figure 1–9 Family Information Form (Reproduced with permission, BC Center, Broome Community College, Binghamton, NY.)

GROSS MOTOR *Be sure to try each activity with your child.*

	YES	SOMETIMES	NOT YET	

1. Does your child catch a large ball with both hands? You should stand about 5 feet away and give your child two or three tries. ☐ ☐ ☐ ____

2. Does your child climb the rungs of a ladder of a playground slide and slide down without help? ☐ ☐ ☐ ____

3. While standing, does your child throw a ball overhand in the direction of a person standing at least 6 feet away? To throw overhand, your child must raise her arm to shoulder height and throw the ball forward. (Dropping the ball, letting the ball go, or throwing the ball underhand should be scored as "not yet.") ☐ ☐ ☐ ____

4. Does your child hop up and down on either the right or left foot at least one time without losing his balance or falling?

5. Does your child jump forward a distance of 20 inches from a standing position, starting with her feet together? ☐ ☐ ☐ ____

6. Without holding onto anything, does your child stand on one foot for at least 5 seconds without losing his balance and putting his foot down? You may give your child two or three tries before you mark the question. ☐ ☐ ☐ ____

GROSS MOTOR TOTAL ____

FINE MOTOR *Be sure to try each activity with your child.*

1. Does your child put together a six-piece interlocking puzzle? (If one is not available, take a full-page picture from a magazine or catalog and cut it into six pieces. Does your child put it back together correctly?) ☐ ☐ ☐ ____

2. Using child-safe scissors, does your child cut a paper in half on a more or less straight line, making the blades go up and down? (Carefully watch your child's use of scissors for safety reasons.) ☐ ☐ ☐ ____

3. Using the shapes below to look at, does your child copy at least three shapes onto a large piece of paper using a pencil or crayon, without tracing? Your child's drawings should look similar to the design of the shapes below, but they may be different in size. ☐ ☐ ☐ ____

L + I O

4. Does your child unbutton one or more buttons? Your child may use his own clothing or a doll's clothing. ☐ ☐ ☐ ____

5. Does your child draw pictures of people that have at least three of the following features: head, eyes, nose, mouth, neck, hair, trunk, arms, hands, legs, or feet? ☐ ☐ ☐ ____

6. Does your child color mostly within the lines in a coloring book? Your child should not go more than ¼ inch outside the lines on most of the picture. ☐ ☐ ☐ ____

FINE MOTOR TOTAL ____

Figure 1–10 Gross and Fine Motor Checklist (Reprinted with permission. Bricker, D. et al. (1999). Ages & Stages Questionnaire, 2nd ed. Baltimore, MD: Brookes.)

Figure 1–11 A home visit is a way to establish a relationship between the teacher, the child, and the family.

about the impending separation. Some visitors take a photograph of the family that will greet them on the first day. Giving the child a photograph of the teachers will begin the acquaintance on a visual level also. Of course, notes about the visit are written and placed in the class or program's file and are confidential, open only to those directly responsible for the child, including the parents. There are many well-known home visitation programs that deliver parent education and seek to reduce child abuse. The most successful are those that do less modeling and more family support and take advising roles during the visit (Peterson, 1999). Early Head Start attributes its success to effectively engaging families with their child in home visits, with families reporting a feeling of partnership with the home visitor and an improved relationship with their child (Roggman, Boyce, Cook, & Jump, 2001). (See the resources list at the end of this chapter for more information about home visits.)

Home visits for public school teachers have been found to be effective in school adjustment, family involvement in the child's learning, and changes in teacher attitudes. "After home visits we found ourselves relating more often, verbally and emotionally, with the children. . . . After talking to parents in such a personal way, we began to view all of the children in our classes more compassionately and with greater understanding" (Gorter-Reu & Anderson, 1998, p. 73). Unfortunately, teacher–family contact, direct and informal and with less negative content, declines once children enter kindergarten (Rimm-Kaufman & Pianta, 1999).

Visit to the School or Center. Another effective way to become acquainted is for the family to bring

the child to visit the center by appointment, so they receive individual attention. After-hours seems to work best. A typical day's routine is reviewed, from arrival through departure. They can take a tour of the center to see the rooms and areas the child will be using. The child can play and become familiar with the room and equipment. This is easier without the distraction of other children and the impending separation from the parent. A nutritional snack time with the visitors sets a social atmosphere. An unhurried visit can help the child adjust to the environment. The child forms a visual image of the center and begins to build positive images of herself at play there. This also builds the relationship of trust with the family. They see this is a good place for the child, and families experience the center's willingness to be a part of the support system to their family.

Formal Family Orientation. Many centers have a "family only" orientation where staff is introduced, policies are reviewed, and relationships between the family and the center are established. Food, adult chairs, and friendly greetings set the tone of partnership and cooperation. Providing child care will not only assist more families to attend but will be one of the first signs that this is a family-friendly place.

A tour of the center and a short video or slide presentation showing the "action" of the program help establish a positive atmosphere. Families' questions and concerns are anticipated in a short, reassuring presentation. The staff communicates the recognition of the needs of families and the dedication of the program to cooperate and accommodate as much as possible. Humor, understanding, and active listening are characteristics that will make this step in the transition smoother. Individual relationship-building between family and staff at this orientation helps alleviate the anxiety for the family, the child, and the staff. This is useful not only on the first day, but throughout the year, as situations develop that no one can foresee right now. An opportunity for individual questions or even anonymous questions will help to provide an open forum.

Working with Families for Arrivals and Departures

EXERCISE: Think about the necessary foundations or building blocks of family–teacher relationships. Write the characteristics in the blocks in Figure 1–12.

Building blocks help the child adjust to a new environment; they are necessities in growth and

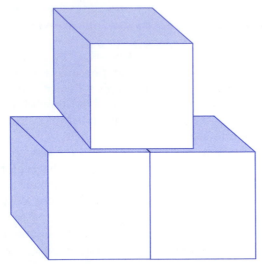

Figure 1–12 Building Blocks of Family–Teacher Relationships. Fill in the skills, qualities, and activities that will build strong relationships.

development. Qualities such as trust, open communication, respect, a friendly face, approachability, kindness, and understanding might appear in the blocks. The partnership of families and teachers gives the child the confidence that needs will be met by trustworthy adults. When there are barriers such as jealousy, fear, or differences in value systems that are not addressed, it is more difficult for the child to adjust to and develop in that environment. Open communication between parents and program personnel is an important process.

If it is the beginning of the school year and all children are entering for the first time, a staggered first day, or first week, may be possible: Half, or a portion, of the children attend one day or one morning with the other portion coming on a second day or in the afternoon. The rationale is that children are learning the routine and adjusting to the setting in small groups. This allows the staff to closely observe and interact with fewer children, forming friendships with them. Staff also can anticipate if there may be a separation stage to work through and begin to consult with families about strategies.

Every child should be greeted as they arrive. The greeter or door person sets the mood for the day, letting the child know he is important. The smile communicates acceptance and friendship. Greeting the child by name, and commenting on an event in the day that he particularly will enjoy, helps to prepare him for a good day ahead. This cannot be stated emphatically enough. Every child should be greeted and made to feel welcome!

EXERCISE: A family member brings his child to your program for the first time. He gets the child interested in the water table, then walks over to you and says, "I'm just going to slip out so he won't cause a scene." What would you say?

"Separation is a natural part of life. When you build strategies with parents and children to alleviate anxieties, you're giving everyone the chance to start each day off right" says Susan Miller, author of many books on infant and toddler care and education (2002). Families should be encouraged to establish a good-bye routine, stay for a while, and leave firmly. This allows the child to slowly adjust and not feel rushed or rejected. The child can anticipate the family member's departure by dependable cues. Caution should be taken that the child not manipulate the family member into "one more kiss, one more hug, one more. . . . " Sneaking out is discouraged no matter how much the family member sees it as an easier way. For the child, this builds mistrust and a fear that every time he gets involved in play or turns his back, the loved one will leave. Families witness the staff's concern for the child and are assured that the needed comfort is given. The staff assists the family in involving the child in the routines and activities of the classroom. A phone call to the family later to say the child is no longer crying will alleviate the anxiety.

Alice Honig (2002) reminds families and caregivers to arrange for comfort spaces and to make the transition into the day gradual and relaxed. She says to look for the sparkle in the child's eyes as a sign that the child is ready to be engaged in play and exploration. Szamreta (2003) relates her experiences using and expanding peekaboo games and materials to help toddlers practice going-away/coming-back behavior, as a motivation for engagement with materials, and to transition from home to school (p. 88).

Planning for the end of the day is an important part of curriculum as well. It helps to have the child's belongings all in one place, like the cubby or a mailbox system, so there is no last-minute hunt for paintings or library books. When dismissal time is the same for everyone, some programs have closing circles, hand squeeze, or recall and review of the day.

If children leave at different but predictable times, it is up to the teacher to give the child a cue that the departure time is approaching so the child can bring closure to the activity and mentally prepare for the change. When the family picks up unpredictably, the teacher can help the child cope with the change by assisting in the closing of the activity and engaging the family member in conversation so the child can work independently to prepare to leave.

Separation Anxiety and Difficulties

EXERCISE: Describe an incident of separation difficulty you have witnessed.

As families consider leaving their child in someone else's care, there are psychological issues for all concerned: the family, the child, and the caregiver. It is important to know about how a child develops attachments, and the possible effects of separation on those attachments. There are strategies for helping the child and the family cope with the trauma of separation that reinforce the primary family–child relationship.

EXERCISE: Describe what feelings each of these people might have upon the first day of school or care in a new program: the family, the child, and the teacher or caregiver.

Separation Anxiety Behavior. A child in the midst of a "separation anxiety attack" may display out-of-control behavior. It is embarrassing for the family, who is fearful that the teacher will judge the child or the family in a negative way. It is difficult for the caregiver to address the emotional needs of an unfamiliar child. The family and many other children and families as well may be looking on. It is equally difficult for the child who is distressed and out of control, needing someone to help. These extreme moments call for calm reassurance that the family will return at the end of the day. An established good-bye routine, such as "kiss, kiss, hug, nose rub, bye-bye" and a prompt departure helps the child anticipate the family member's departure and come to rely on the family member's return.

The distressed child, of course, should receive holding and comforting as long as necessary to help overcome the feeling of abandonment. Often the child rejects any physical contact or comforting from this new adult. The teacher respects that but shows reliability of care and interest in the child's difficult moment. The teacher offers choices of activities that may be of interest to the child. The child may be kicking and screaming. This should be ignored if it is hurting no one, or gently restrained if it is aimed at the caregiver, other children, or furniture. Removal of the child from the curious stares of other children prevents embarrassment and copycat behavior from others.

Verbal and body language convey understanding for the feelings of loneliness and anger. Reassurances are given that the family member will return. The teacher communicates the desire to help the child

gain control and have a safe, happy time while she is here. Reading a book, singing a song, rocking, or stroking the back sometimes help soothe those feelings. Continued violent reactions call for patience, tolerance, and endurance. They will eventually subside. Sometimes the most effective caregiver action is just quiet acceptance of the strong emotions without overtures to distract the child. Each child has individual behavior patterns to be learned. The caregiver seeks the most effective relaxation techniques for each child. The child builds trust in the family member's **return** and learns **coping mechanisms.**

EXERCISE: What would you say to this child? See Figure 1–13.

Separation Anxiety Warning Signs

Difficulties with separation may not always appear at the beginning of the year, the beginning of the day, or in a violent emotional outburst. Sometimes partway through the day or the year, a child who appeared adjusted to school, begins to display some difficulties: Crying at the family member's leaving, inability to eat, sleep, play, all can happen at any time. What is going on? It may be the aging process. As the child develops, thinking changes. She may be passing into a new stage. That happy baby who held out her arms wide to the caregiver is now burying her head in her dad's coat. She may be the toddler who takes one look at the caregiver, looks at mom, and kicks and shrieks as her coat is removed. The child grabs it back, latches onto her mom's pocketbook strap like it is a life preserver, and will not let go. It may be that child who came happily each day with a smile and a picture she drew for the teacher who now says, "I don't like it here. I wanna go home." It is just as important for the teacher to

Figure 1–13 What would you say to this child?

respond promptly to more subtle separation behavior. They can take many forms: difficulties in eating, sleeping, toileting, learning, or social difficulties.

Eating. For the infant, refusal to take nourishment is an immediate danger signal. Teachers can try various positions of holding during feeding, and even blocking the infant's view of the caregiver. Communication with the family member about feeding routines ahead of time, and even a phone call to verify and seek advice, may be helpful. A joint effort of family member and caregiver should make this difficulty short-lived. Continued difficulty may need the involvement of the pediatrician and other support personnel.

For toddlers and preschoolers, eating away from home may be distressing, perceived as a betrayal of that very personal time with close family members.

A relaxed environment without pressure from caregivers, along with familiar foods and utensils, will help ease this time. It usually is just a matter of days until children adjust and join in the sociability of mealtime and look forward to it with enthusiasm. If a child is crying at mealtime, refusing food day after day, or indicating by behaviors that this is a stressful time, it demands attention. Family member–caregiver communication, sometimes with a referral agent, such as the director, and the pediatrician, can usually work this through.

Sleeping. Environmental changes can affect sleep, so children in new places may have difficulty resting. Other children's schedules and sleep patterns may keep the child from sleeping. The new environment, governed by licensing regulations, may add to the child's difficulty in adjustment to sleeping away from home. The caregiver gathers information from the family on the child's sleep patterns. Upon each day's arrival, family members give information about last night's sleep. Everything possible is done to make the environment conducive to the child's relaxation. Music, favorite toys, books, or a blanket help with sleep routines and should be individual choices for children. Children having adjustment problems to center care may have continued sleep disturbances. Again, the close observation and responsiveness of the caregiver to the individual child's needs will help. Communication with the family for understanding and accommodating the child's needs to the center's practices also helps (Figure 1–14). Sleep deprivation might result in the child's irritable behavior and increased anxiety for the adults.

Making notes on the child's sleepy times of day, indicators of sleep needs, techniques that relax the child, positions of sleep, and toys or physical items

IT HAPPENED TO ME

Wrapped in Love

I was visiting in an infant room and saw a baby about six months old wrapped in a large red shawl while the caregiver fed him. She later explained he was having difficulty adjusting and would not eat at the center. Through trial and error she and his mother came up with the idea of bringing in something of the mother's from home. Wrapped in his mother's shawl, he was wrapped in the essence of her love and security. Now he could eat.

normally taken to bed are important pieces of information for the child's file. Sharing and exchanging information such as this with the family will help the child's adjustment to sleeping away from home. It assists substitute caregivers in meeting the child's needs when the regular teacher is absent.

Toileting. For two-year-olds, managing toilet needs on their own is a big accomplishment but is not without its relapses for a variety of reasons. Adjustment to a new place may upset that delicate balance. The child is curious and may frequently use the child-sized toilet as a novelty. The new stimulating environment full of active play areas and new playmates may result in forgetfulness or inattention to toileting cues, leading to accidents. A matter-of-fact attitude

Figure 1–14 Family members and teachers need to communicate about children's routines.

USING THE CLASS LIST LOG TO LOOK AT SEPARATION AND SCHOOL ADJUSTMENT   41

by caregivers, along with a change into familiar clothing after a toileting accident, usually is all that is necessary to help the child cope with these events.

Some children, however, have a delicate emotional response to new places, making it difficult to eliminate in this new surrounding. A child may hold the genitals, lay over a chair until the urge passes, or even cry from a severe stomachache. It is up to the teacher to be a detective, interpreting these subtle clues. Once the cause is determined, appropriate action can be taken. Again, communication with the family about the child's patterns, times, and physical cues is an important part of making the child comfortable. Family members taking the child into the bathroom and talking about using it should be part of the first visit or first day at the center. Continued disruption in toileting may cause bladder infections or constipation and other disorders. A daily, unobtrusive observation of the child's toileting behavior is also a part of the record-keeping procedure. Any extraordinary behavior should be noted factually and shared at the end of the day with the family member, away from the presence of the child.

Participation. The child who is experiencing separation difficulties may not be able to attend to the learning activities that are planned. He may have difficulty making choices or staying with a task. Transitions from one area to another or interacting positively with other children may precipitate crying or tantrums. After a normal adjustment period, if this behavior is observed, it should be recorded. Reference to it later will indicate the stages the child has gone through in the separation process.

Social Interactions. When a child is in emotional turmoil, it may affect the child's outward behavior to others. The child may cling to one caregiver, transferring parental attachment to another adult. That is a healthy coping mechanism in an infant and toddler and, temporarily, for the preschooler. A branching out of friendships and social contacts is expected after a time. Some interventions may be necessary if that is not observed.

Children who are experiencing separation difficulties may be socially withdrawn. The group situation may be overwhelming. The child just needs some time to watch and see how other children are handling it. A sensitive caregiver will allow the child this luxury of watching, along with an occasional commentary on what the other children are doing. The child is invited to join the play. The caregiver will also be familiar with the stages of play and have realistic expectations for the child's positive social interactions. Communication with the family to know the child's social his-

tory will also help to better understand the child's reactions. It would be helpful to know the positive or negative experiences the child has had with siblings and other children who are the same age.

Acting Out as a Symptom of Separation Anxiety. For some children, the new environment is so stimulating that their self-control is not strong enough to govern their behavior. The child may be unaccustomed to so many playmates and play areas. Inappropriate and unsafe actions may erupt, which might result in rejection by other children. The teacher redirects or restricts behavior. The staggered first day can help to ease this transition. For the child entering the program once it has already begun, it may be overwhelming. Other children are already established in routines and have formed friendships. The teacher coaches the new child through routines and introduces expectations in various areas to help the child adjust.

The child comes into a new situation, not knowing the rules and the people; she feels rejected and abandoned by the family. When the teacher places herself in those little sneakers, it will help to ease the child through these first days.

The child is sending a signal of distress or going through a new phase and the best defense is that close communication and understanding between family member and caregiver. It is helpful to have a talk, outside of the child's hearing, about the change. This may reveal some unusual events at home that are manifested in behaviors of insecurity and separation anxiety. Together, some ideas can be generated about how to help everyone cope with changes or troubled times.

Permanent Departures and Good-byes

Just as beginnings are important, so are endings.

EXERCISE: Using a separate sheet of paper, make a list of ending celebrations, rituals, or customs.

Bringing closure to a letter, a day, or a life has emotional importance. It closes the circle.

A good-bye party for a child who is moving or leaving the program helps recognize the child for the contribution she made to the class. Classmates can present physical reminders of her friends there. Though it is a sad occasion, it can be a part of learning to say good-bye. By attempting to remain in contact, a sense of the larger community is felt with her as a link to the next city, state, or country. This helps both the child leaving and those remaining.

At the end of the year, a child-centered farewell celebration (as opposed to cap-and-gown commencement for preschoolers) can be planned. This is also a

IT HAPPENED TO ME

Mid-September Reflection

We had gotten through those first days and weeks. All those plans for smooth transitions seemed to have paid off. Each child came ready to play and said good-bye to parents willingly. They had fallen into the routine of the day. Today during free play, I could move from area to area, observe their play, comment on their actions, add a prop here and there, and enjoy their absorption with activities of their choosing.

Then I heard a noise, a long sucking in of air with a quiet sort of high-pitched wail. Where did it come from? I looked around the room. Children were climbing and sliding and going in and out the door on the climber, which was their spaceship today. A boy was sitting at the table in the dramatic play area with a police hat on. He was packing a lunch pail with dishes and silverware, talking to another boy who was stirring "soup." Several children were in the block area piling blocks, laying out carpet squares, and standing up farm animals. Sand box players were pouring, shoveling, and digging for shells they found hidden there. Two children at the easel, a boy on one side and a girl on the other, were busily making lines and circles. There it was again! I looked around again. Same scene as before but now I could locate the source of the sound. It seemed to be coming from the boy at the easel. As I looked closer, he stared at his paper as his hands moved methodically up and down. He watched the paint as it dripped from the brush, then I heard the sound again and saw his face muscles tense into a frozen stare.

I walked over and placed my hand on his shoulder. The dam broke. He let out all those sobs he had been trying to hold in! He was missing his mom and had tried to hide it for an hour but just could not hold it in any longer. Were there signs I could have seen before it got to this point? Are there others who were feeling this internal sadness, holding it in check but inwardly hurting? Was I being smug and self-congratulating without really addressing the issue of separation with those who were least capable of coping with it—the children? I vowed to be a more empathetic observer and to use more touch as a message to each child that I am here to support and comfort if they need me. Tomorrow I'll read *Are You My Mother?* by Eastman to stimulate some discussion about separation and the ever-returning parent.

time for remembering (part of the cognitive process); expressing positive feelings for one another (social and emotional development); and drawing, dictating, or writing the remembrances (literacy and art activities).

Planning for departures as well as arrivals is an important part of the teacher's responsibilities and also can be opportunities to observe. How does the child organize for the end of the day? What is the child's response to the cue of the approaching end to an activity? How does the child greet the family member at the end of the day? These are possible Class List Log criterion.

HELPING ALL CHILDREN WITH SEPARATION AND SCHOOL ADJUSTMENT

Children with special needs and children from nonmainstream cultures or who may not speak English are entering programs nationwide. The practitioner has the responsibility to be prepared to help these children make the transition into the program as stress-free as possible. Prior knowledge of the child, no matter what the situation, helps this process. Specific knowledge of these special populations is imperative. Research, family, and professionals providing information, and extra observation and patience will be required.

Children with Special Needs

The Americans with Disabilities Act of 1990 (P.L. 101–336) protects against discrimination based on a person's disability. Children with disabilities must be admitted into settings that have been adapted to accommodate them. When children with special needs are integrated into a group, it is important to have knowledge and information concerning the handicapping condition and this child's situation in particular before the first day they come to school.

This can be obtained from the family information form, a home visit, or the child's report from helping professionals if the parents have given permission for its release. The family of a child with a disability may be more anxious about leaving the child in a school setting. That anxiety may be transferred to the child—making separation more difficult for all. Child and family alike need the reassurance that the child will be well cared for and accepted. In fact, inclusive settings often help to foster children's ideas about helping others, the understanding of emotions, and acceptance of individuals with disabilities (Diamond, 2001).

For children with visual impairments, tape recordings about the routines and what to expect from a typical day would be helpful. If the child is hearing-impaired, this could be done through a picture album. The caregivers should become familiar with the language the child will be using to communicate. Knowledge of a child's physical impairments will help modify the setting to be more accessible. Of course, the building already meets the guidelines for accessibility under the Americans with Disabilities Act (P.L. 101–336). Modifications may need to be made within the classroom arrangement and in the thinking and approach of the staff. Any modifications for the child preferably are made before the child enters the program. Emotional or behavioral disabilities should be understood thoroughly by conferences with the family and helping professionals so that the teachers are prepared and react in a consistent way.

Diverse Cultures

The attachment between family and child varies for different cultures. For some, the infant never is physically apart from an adult, being held, carried, or touched almost constantly. For these children, the physical and emotional separation needs special attention. In other cultures, children are expected to become independent very quickly so any expectation of separation anxiety is not understood or tolerated. An awareness of cultural parenting styles and the attachment and separation practices will help the teacher adjust expectations and actions.

For the child who is non-English speaking, it is most helpful if the teacher learns a few of the most important words such as greetings, routines like "Eat," "Toilet," "Mother returning soon," and "I can help you." This can be accomplished by asking the family, working through an interpreter, or researching translations at the library. The child will need time and an environment that is child-centered.

When the environment is restricted by teacher's directions and highly emphasizes following directions, the non-English speaking child will have difficulty adjusting. Play is a universal language, and once the child feels comfortable, the lure of play will help her feel more comfortable.

Meeting the needs of each child as an individual necessitate preparation, understanding, and careful observation skills.

HELPING PROFESSIONALS FOR SEPARATION AND SCHOOL ADJUSTMENT CONCERNS

If a child is having separation or classroom adjustment problems beyond his ability to cope, it may be necessary to consult helping professionals. After consultations with families and the director or program personnel, outside professionals who may help are the:

pediatrician—physician specifically trained to care for the health and well-being of children

child psychologist—conducts screenings for diagnosis and treatment of children with emotional, behavioral, or developmental problems

child psychiatrist—provides counseling or consultative services to individuals or families who may be experiencing problems

play therapist—child psychologist who uses play to diagnose and treat children who may be withdrawn, nonverbal, or traumatized

OTHER METHODS

Other Methods to Record Separation and Adjustment:

Anecdotal and Running Records
Checklists/Rating Scales
Conversations and Interviews
Work Samples
Media

KEY TERMS

attachment
Class List Log
coping mechanisms
diary
good-bye rituals

Reflective Journal
separation anxiety
stranger anxiety
subjective

WEEK 1: PLAN A

CLASS LIST LOG—SEPARATION AND SCHOOL ADJUSTMENT

Materials: 8–10 file folders, Class List Log forms.

Label one file folder "Class File." Select eight children from the class and set up eight file folders with a Portfolio Overview Sheet in each. Remember to use the children's initials only, and before you observe, get permission from the teacher or the family if that is the school's policy. Get each child's birth date from the teacher and enter on the Portfolio Overview Sheet.

Practitioners

Materials: File folders for each of the children in your group. Class List Log forms.

Same as above, but use children's real names.

Photocopy the Class List Log found in Appendix D. Alphabetize the class by first names down the left side. Make a supply of these partially completed Class List Log forms.

Fill out the heading of one Class List Log form. Observe the group this week. Make short, descriptive notes about each one's arrival or departure, noting how each child is greeted while separating from family members.

What to Do with It

Filing. Note presence of a Class List Log in each child's portfolio overview under this section (Figure 1–15). A blank portfolio overview appears in Appendix D.

If further action is needed, write a note, place it in the Class File, and follow it up.

Completed Class List Logs contain information on all the children in the class, so it is not appropriate to file them in a child's portfolio. Establish a Class File that will hold those recordings that contain information on all the children. (Other methods of this type are explained later in this book.) This is the teacher's and the program's property and should be stored separately from the portfolios to protect confidentiality.

File Week 1, Plan A, in the class file.

SEPARATIONS AND ADJUSTMENT			
Documentation	Location	Recorder	Date
CL	Class file	BAN	9/7
CL	"	BAN	2/14
CL	"	MS	4/5
RR	Portfolio	BAN	5/9

Figure 1–15 Portfolio Overview Example

Sharing with Child and Family. This type of observation can be shared by the teacher with the family and the child, if appropriate. For example: "Mrs. Jones, the way you are helping Joshua become accustomed to being here has given me ideas to share with other parents. I was observing yesterday and saw some of the things you did to make him feel comfortable here and confident of your return before you left. He had a wonderful day and I believe it was because of that."

If difficulties persist, based on observations and recordings, the teacher may meet with the family and discuss what has been observed and work together on a plan to help the child adjust.

Actions.

Read a Book. There are many appropriate books to prepare for adjustments to school or to ease separations. Read the book to the individual child, the whole class, or suggest it to family members.

Boelts, M. (1996). *Little Bunny's Preschool Countdown.* Morton Grove, IL: A. Whitman.
Eastman, P. D. (1988). *Are You My Mother?* New York: Random House.
Fowler, S. G. (1994). *I'll See You When the Moon is Full.* New York: Greenwillow Books.
Hutchins, P. (1994). *Three Star Billy.* New York: Greenwillow Books.

In the Environment.

- photographs, tape recordings of child's family members
- soft spaces for comfort and safe withdrawal
- place to store and retrieve comforting objects

In the Curriculum.

- play "Hide and Seek" and have follow-up conversations about the permanency of relationships and temporary or permanent separations
- projects regarding parents' activities while children are at school

In the Newsletter.

- article regarding separation: program policies, advice for smooth transitions at the beginning and end of the day or session
- reminders later in the year of the importance of smooth, sensitive transitions

WEEK 1: PLAN B

WORK SAMPLES FOR ALL

This week encourage each child to draw or decorate the cover (one panel) of his or her own portfolio. This is a good one-on-one activity to help you get acquainted with each child. Write the date in the corner. Explain to the child, if the child is old enough to understand, that this is a place where you, the teacher, will be collecting writing about the child at school and some artwork throughout the year. Invite the child to add samples of her work to the portfolio. You will show her the file at times throughout the year.

If the child wants to fill the folder with work, you might want to establish separate work sample folders that are accessible to each child. The children can store their own work.

WEEK 1: PLAN C

REFLECTIVE JOURNAL

Respond to the following in your Reflective Journal, kept in a private file at home.

As I approach this year, my life seems . . .

This year I hope that . . .

When I walk into a place I have never been before I feel . . .

Maybe a child feels . . .

The one different approach I will try this year will be . . .

I wonder . . .

REFERENCES

Ainsworth, M., Blehar, M., Waters, E., & Wall, S. (1978). *Patterns of attachment.* Hillsdale, NJ: Lawrence Erlbaum Associates.

Balaban, N. (1995). *Learning to say good-bye: Starting school and other early childhood separations.* New York: New American Library.

Bjorklund, D. F., & Bjorklund, B. R. (1992). *Looking at children: An introduction to child development.* Pacific Grove, CA: Brooks/Cole Publishing Co.

Bloch, J. S. (1987). *The five P's manual.* Syosset, NY: Variety Pre-Schooler's Workshop.

Bowlby, J. (1969). *Attachment.* New York: Basic Books.

Bricker, (1999). *ASQ Questionnaire System,* 2nd ed. Baltimore, MD: Brookes.

Diamond, K. E. (2001). Relationships among young children's ideas, emotional understanding and social contact with classmates with disabilities. *Topics in Early Childhood Special Education, 21* (2), 104–114.

Eastman, P. D. (1988). *Are you my mother?* New York: Random House.

Gorter-Reu, M. S., & Anderson, J. M. (1998). Home kits, home visits, and more! *Young Children,* 53 (3), 73.

Honig, A. S. (2002). Soothing separations. *Scholastic Early Childhood Today,* 17 (1), 20–22.

McAfee, O., & Leong, D. (2002). *Assessing and guiding young children's development and learning,* 3rd ed. Boston: Allyn and Bacon.

Miller, S. A. (2002). Easing the transition from home to school. *Scholastic Early Childhood Today,* 17 (1), 33–34.

Peterson, E. (1999, Fall) Home-grown advice: Tips on making your program's home visits rewarding for parents and children. *Children and Families,* 18 (4), 30–33.

Rimm-Kaufman, S. E., & Pianta, R. C. (1999). Patterns of family–school contact in preschool and kindergarten. *School Psychology Review, 28* (3), 426.

Roggman, L. A., Boyce, L. K., Cook, G. A., & Jump, V. K. (2001). Inside home visits: A collaborative look at process and quality. *Early Childhood Research Quarterly, 16* (1), 53–71.

Shaffer, H., & Emerson, P. E. (1964). The development of social attachments in infancy. *Monographs of the Society for Child Development, 29* (3), serial No. 94.

Swick, K. J., DaRose, D., & Pavia, L. (1998/99). Inquiry as key to early childhood teacher education. *Childhood Education 75* (2), 66–70.

Szamreta, J. M. (2003). Peekaboo power: To ease separation and build secure relationships. *Young Children, 58* (1), 88.

Yarrow, L. J. (1964). Separation from parents during early childhood. In M. L. Hoffman & L. W. Hoffman (Eds.) *Review of child development research, Vol. I.* New York: Russell Sage Foundation.

RESOURCES

Aaronsohn, E. (1996). *Going Against the Grain: Supporting the Student-Centered Teacher.* Thousand Oaks, CA: Corwin Press.

Balaban, N. (1987). *Learning to say good-bye: Starting school and other early childhood separations.* New York: New American Library.

Blecher-Sass, H. (1997). Good-byes can build trust. *Young Children, 52* (7), 12–14.

Brodkin, A. (1994). "She cries when I leave." *Early Childhood Today, 9* (1), 38–39.

Church, E. B. (1992). Separation: Helping kids and families through the transition. *Pre-K Today, 7* (1), 62–78.

Hendrick, J. (1997). *First Steps toward Teaching the Reggio Way.* Upper Saddle River, NJ: Merrill, an imprint of Prentice Hall.

Johnson, L., & Mermen, J. (1994). Easing children's entry to school: Home visits help. *Young Children, 49* (4), 62–68.

Terte, E. A., Klein, S. M., & Jewett, J. L. Eds. (1998). *When Teachers Reflect: Journeys Toward Effective, Inclusive Practice.* Washington, DC: NAEYC.

Using Anecdotal Recordings to Look at Self-Care

USING THE ANECDOTAL RECORDING

Maralyce went into the bathroom in the three-year-old classroom. After considerable time, she could be heard screaming and crying. The teacher rushed to the door to find Maralyce standing by the toilet, pants around ankles, trying to adjust streams of toilet paper to cover the seat. Every time she put one strip on, another would slide off. The teacher asked "What's wrong, Maralyce? Why are you crying?" Maralyce sobbed, "Mommy said I can't go potty 'til I cover the seat, and it won't stay on." The teacher went and quickly got tape and gave it to Maralyce. She taped the paper on the seat, sat down quickly,

and let out a "Wooo!" (The teacher saw the still-developing coordination of a three-year-old in conflict with a parental expectation. She was inclined to say, "You don't need that paper. The seat is clean." However, she wanted Maralyce to have a way to do it herself, and did not want to contradict the family's authority and instructions.)

There are incidents that need to be remembered exactly as they happened. They tell a story that lets the reader see, hear, and feel as if he were there. The story contains a factual account of an incident that may be typical or out of the ordinary. The incident, however, is best remembered in its entirety. The most factual recording method is **Anecdotal Recording.** It can be used to

- portray an incident that indicates a child's development in a specific area.
- record a humorous incident to share with families.
- preserve the details of a curious incident for later reflection.
- record the exact details of a child's disclosure of an incidence of abuse.
- exemplify a child's typical behavior.
- record the details of an incident that is totally foreign to the child's typical behavior.

The Anecdotal Recording is a **narrative** account of an incident that may be a few seconds or several minutes in length. The Anecdotal Recording recounts the event, telling the reader when, where, who, and what. It does not answer the question *why* in the body of the recording. That conclusion or **inference** is separated from the recording. An inference is an informed judgment or conclusion based on observation. When we see a child crying our inference is that the child is sad or hurt. We may or may not be correct.

Every newspaper reporter, police officer, and insurance claims adjuster knows that facts written on the scene or very shortly thereafter are the most accurate. When an event occurs that is important to remember, a few notes are jotted down to refer to later. If an interesting conversation is happening, it is recorded word for word. It is written, as much as possible, as it is happening (Figure 2–1). By the end of the day, the notes are amplified and rewritten into a full account while the details are still fresh. It can be

Figure 2–1 Anecdotal Recording Example

written on regular lined paper. It helps to fold the paper in half vertically and write on the left side so explanatory comments can be written in the right-hand column. In this way, comments of the recorder are placed separately from the recording. The reader then knows the difference between the actual recounting of the incident and the writer's inferences. It also is possible to fold the paper so the comments are not visible. Another reader can then draw independent conclusions about the incident.

Bentzen (2001) calls this an **open method,** a narrative that preserves the details so that different interpretations can be made, determined by the reader's focus. The reader receives a mental picture of that event by reading the words.

An Anecdotal Recording is a written replay of an incident. In Figure 2–1, note these characteristics of an Anecdotal Recording: (1) it sets the stage for the reader, "In cubbies dressing for outdoor play," (2) it identifies the characters, target child by name: Sherita, other child by initial for anonymity: D (this may even need to be blotted out later) "Sherita and D and Teacher." Abbreviations are used in the writing for speed, (3) the account describes the action in detail: "Sherita bends over with eyes close to D's zipper," (4) it describes the interaction between the characters "T bends down and says," (5) it records exact quotes, including pronunciation as it is heard, "I tan't dit it!" (6) it concludes with result or reaction between characters, "You're my buddy, right?" Sherita: "Right, Davi."

Separate from that account in the right-hand column, the teacher writes comments, inferences, judgments, questions, and reminders: (1) comments on development: "Helper attitude" (2) actions: "Talk to speech therapist for an update" (3) reminders: "Place Sherita and Davi together at lunch (4) curriculum plans: "Bring in dress-up clothing with separating zippers (5) on a separate note the teacher reminds herself to copy the anecdote for Davi's file and then she will make appropriate notes in the right-hand column relating to Davi's part in the incident, perhaps blocking out Sherita's name for anonymity.

With the inferences in the right-hand column separate from the actual recording of the incident, it is easily folded back for a fresh viewpoint. Other readers may interpret the incident differently. Inferences or evaluations may differ, depending on the role of the observer. Davi's family might infer she is not getting proper attention from the teacher. Another child's family might wonder why this helpless child is in such an advanced class, demanding time from the teacher. Another teacher might deduce that this child needs some instruction in self-care skills. The speech pathologist might be overjoyed to hear Sherita express herself in nearly recognizable words. The teacher might write a comment to the side, "Sherita is the youngest in her family so seldom has a chance to be the helper. Davi has often excluded Sherita from play so this may be the beginning of a friendship." All people read the same account, but their inferences are different because of their perspectives.

Frank (1999) calls this "using ethnographic eyes." It is the difference between *note taking* and *note making*. Note taking is the descriptive field notes that give the reader a re-creation of the sensory information (seeing, hearing, feeling, smelling). Note making is the interpretation of what is being observed. In Figure 2–1 the description of zipping the coat and the

Figure 2–2 Diary Example

exact quotes are examples of note taking. "Helper attitude!" is the interpretation—it is note making.

Many people use the term *Anecdotal Recording* when what actually has been written is a diary account (Figure 2–2). This type of recording is true, but it is not factual. It summarizes actions, draws conclusions, and leaves out information that could be useful. Compare Figure 2–2 to Figure 2–1. See that the Anecdotal Recording in Figure 2–1 gives enough detail so that the reader has the feeling of being there. The anecdotal recording relates:

body positions—"bent over, eyes closed"
actions—"puts two parts together," "slips out"
reactions—"grits teeth," "stomps foot," "looks up"
exact words—"Davi, you hold this," "Thanks Sherita"
inflection and pronunciation—"I tan't dit it"

The reader "sees" the incident. She "hears" the conversation along with emphasis as it was spoken. Then more accurate and individual judgments based on the reader's perspective are made.

Uses

Anecdotal Recordings can be

- used for preserving details about any developmental skill, behavior, or incident for later judgments and reflection.
- given to other people for their independent evaluation.
- used as an accurate, detailed recording method in suspicion or disclosure of child abuse.

EXERCISE: What advantages and disadvantages do you see in using an Anecdotal Recording?

Read those that follow and see if you agree.

Advantages

Anecdotal Recordings

- need no special forms.
- are preserved facts and details for any reader to draw conclusions.
- give a short, contextual account of an incident.
- give the reader a "sense of being there."
- separate judgments or inferences from details of incident.
- are useful for recording all areas of development.
- are necessary for capturing exact details for specific purposes, such as speech/language development and child abuse disclosure.

Disadvantages

Shortcomings of Anecdotal Recordings are

- choosing which incidents to record gives the writer selectivity that may influence positive or negative collections.
- intense writing to capture all details, quotes, body movements.
- diverts attention from interactions with children.
- can only focus on a few minutes of action.
- can only focus on one or two children at a time.

Pitfalls to Avoid

Random selection of children to write about in an anecdotal format presents the same problem as diary entries. There is usually some child who is performing attention-getting behavior. Others would never have a focused anecdotal record in their file. They are placid, follow the rules, and rarely draw attention to themselves.

This is overcome by the *Week by Week* portfolio plan. It specifies a few children a week as the focus of in-depth recordings. These children are not selected randomly but from a planned numbering system from the alphabetical Class List Log. In addition, the developmental area to be observed is suggested so that the selection of what and when to write about is more objective and documentation is collected in all developmental areas. With the *Week by Week* plan, information is gathered on all the children every week in a different developmental area. In addition to that, a more focused observation and recording is done on a specified group of children. Over the course of a year, using the *Week by Week* plan, each developmental area is revisited at least three times for each child. Also, each child is the focus of at least three Anecdotal Recordings. Appendix A contains the full *Week by Week* plan. Appendix C illustrates how the *Week by Week* plan documents the developmental areas for each child in the class.

The most difficult part of Anecdotal Recording is just writing factually. Those little inferences, explanations, reasons, feelings, and biases just slip in. The recorder constantly needs to test if the reader will "see it in the mind." If it is not describing an event exactly as it occurred then the writer is summarizing and it ceases to be an accurate recording. It requires the recorder to stretch vocabulary to describe actions in noninferential, nonjudgmental terms

"zipped Davi's jacket," not "helped"
"jumped and fell," not "clumsy"

"gave a piece of Play Doh" not "shared"
"eyes widened, mouth open," not "looked surprised"

EXERCISE 1: Mark the following sentences *Yes* if they fit the criteria for Anecdotal Recording or *No* if they are inferences, explanations, or not exact quotes.

_____ a. Tara ran over to the cubby area.
_____ b. She had on a short shirt and wanted to get her jacket.
_____ c. Stacey asked her, "Why do you want your jacket on?"
_____ d. She said her stomach was cold.
_____ e. Tara shrugged her shoulders.
_____ f. Stacey went over and zipped the jacket for Tara.
_____ g. Tara thanked her.

Answers:

a. Yes. It tells where she went and how she went there.
b. No. How does the reader know what she wanted? Just describe what is visible: "She had on a short shirt. She got her jacket from the hook."
c. Yes. These were the exact words.
d. No. This is not a direct quote. Instead, write, "Tara said, 'My belly is cold.'"
e. Yes. Body motion is described.
f. Yes. Action is described.
g. No. This is not a direct quote. Instead, Tara said, "Thank you, my dear."

EXERCISE 2: Make a list of descriptive, but noninferential, nonjudgmental words to use in place of these to give the reader more information about the nature of how the action was carried out:

stood
walked
said
cried
laughed

EXERCISE 3: Look at Figure 2–3. Write an imaginary Anecdotal Recording as if you were there. Remember the technique: description and quotes. Have someone else read it and ask if they can picture exactly what happened from your writing.

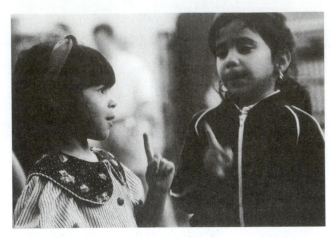

Figure 2–3 Examine this photograph and write an imaginary Anecdotal Record.

EXERCISE 4: Watch a person performing a routine task, such as walking to and turning on a light, getting something from a purse, or coming into a room and finding a seat. Write an Anecdotal Recording so the reader can mentally visualize exactly the motions of that person. Have someone else read it to determine if it is descriptive and not inferential.

Using Technology

There are various electronic recording devices that may be used to capture events as they are happening that may be faster and more accurate than writing about the incident while it is happening (or shortly thereafter).

Audio Recording. Dictating into small tape recorders can be useful for capturing the details that will later help you write an anecdotal recording. Transcribing tape-recorded notes can be done quickly by a fast typist into a computer file. The transcription can be placed in the corresponding developmental area of the electronic Portfolio Overview Sheet. Printing out the Anecdotal Record stored in this way also makes it easier for the family or other staff to read.

Video Recording. This is the best way to capture all the detail of an incident. Unfortunately, the very advantage—capturing everything—is a disadvantage in that it takes too much time to sift through what is mundane and what is important developmental information. It is also difficult to focus the camera on one specific child without the child becoming self-conscious and then changing behavior from natural to unnatural. Filtering out background noise and action is also difficult for all but the most experienced videographers. Video recordings can be useful for practicing Anecdotal Recording skills.

Voice Programs. There are computer programs that are inexpensive, or even free, that allow your speech to be transferred into electronic text. This makes Anecdotal Recording easier to do and easier to read than handwriting.

How to Find the Time

Using the small tape recorder (as discussed above) can save time. Using the voice program (mentioned above) can also speed the transfer of notes into a detailed account. When you are writing about self-help skills, keep a pad and pen nearby at mealtime, in the cubby area, and in the bathroom; this will enable you to capture those details where they happen.

What to Do with This Information

An Anecdotal Recording preserves specific information that can be used in many ways. It contributes to the overall assessment and evaluation of the child when combined with other information-gathering resources. It is stored in the child's portfolio (Figure 2–4).

Child's Portfolio. If the incident captured in an Anecdotal Recording involves more than one child, it can be copied and the names of other children blocked out to place in more than one file. Block out names other than the child of this portfolio. The previous incident could be placed in Sherita's file with Davi's name blocked out. It could be copied for Davi's file with Sherita's name blocked out. In this particular incident, blocking the name may not be necessary but it does establish a practice of confidentiality. Sometimes it is unpredictable what judgments the reader will make about the other children involved. The teacher's copy in the class file preserves all names for reference.

In the portfolio, this Anecdotal Recording will serve as documentation for judgments made about the child: "Sherita is using words in conversations now (language development) and even helping other children (social development)."

This recording can be compared to earlier incidents: "Compare anecdotal record of 2/13 to those of 9/27, 10/14, and 12/20 to see the progress Sherita has made."

Curriculum Planning. Class activity ideas come from close observations: "I think I'll bring in some clothes with separating zippers for the dramatic play area to give all the children some practice. That sequined vest I got at a garage sale will be a hit."

It can be the basis for making an individual plan: "Sherita is beginning to play near other children. Strategies: Model play and sharing behaviors, connect Sherita with Davi in a cooperative activity, read a book to small group including Sherita, and initiate playmate discussion."

The recorder may decide to further investigate or question a concern: "Listen more closely to Sherita's language and ask the speech pathologist if this is age-appropriate."

Other Teachers on the Team. The recording may be read by others on the team to gather their opinions on the meaning of the incident: "Does this incident seem like unusual behavior for Davi from what you've been seeing?" Seeking the advice of colleagues not responsible for the child is also a way to gain the perspective of an uninvolved professional. Of course, the names would all be blocked out. Without parental written permission, records are not shown to anyone outside the team.

Sharing with Families. If you are a student using this textbook, you should not be sharing information directly with the family. That is the teacher's job. However, students may share their written observations with families if they have been cleared by the teacher in charge of the classroom and perhaps the instructor of the course.

When sharing information with the family the teacher should always be aware of the program or school's protocol, especially when suggesting there may be a developmental problem and suggesting a referral. Remember, "the child is an extension of the family" and this is a very sensitive area. Suggesting that there might be a problem should not be undertaken without first conferring with a supervisor, or thinking through exactly how it should be worded.

Giving the family a copy of the incident provides them with a glimpse into the child's day: "Here's a

SELF-CARE			
Documentation	Location	Recorder	Date
CL		BAN	9/14
AR		MS	3/15

Figure 2–4 Portfolio Overview Sheet Example

REVIEW

Anecdotal Recordings: Detailed incident on one child (others may interact in the incident), including the setting, action/reaction, exact quotes, and result. It should be detailed enough for the reader to "be there."

Types of Information to Record Using Anecdotal Recording: This method is useful for recording any incident, usual or unusual. It can give information on:

- separation and adjustment
- self-care skills
- physical development
- social development
- emotional development
- language and speech
- attention span and interests
- cognitive development
- literacy
- creativity
- sociodramatic play
- child abuse disclosure
- self-esteem

little incident I wrote down today about Davi getting some help getting ready for outside play. I know you've been working on her manners. She spontaneously said, 'Thank you' and invited the other child to be her friend."

Actions or behavior are recorded descriptively as a way to explain development to the family: "Sherita initiated helping another child today for the first time. I thought you'd like to read about it. We'll be working on helping her develop more ways to play cooperatively."

Factual examples illustrate the teacher's assessment or concern to the family: "Sherita's language seems to be at a younger stage. Here are some examples I tape recorded. Maybe you'd like to take these to talk with the speech pathologist and see if a full evaluation is recommended."

Conferring with Helping Professionals. Upon permission from the family, Anecdotal Recordings can be read by helping professionals. This allows people such as the speech and language pathologist, child psychologist, art teacher, and social worker to draw their own conclusions. They evaluate the incident based on their specialized knowledge and area of expertise: "The strategies you've been working on

with Sherita in therapy seem to be working. Here's an incident in which she helped another child. What do you think we should do next?"

Talking with the Child. The child can give insight into an incident and also should be aware of the recorder's interest and writing about her actions: "Davi, I wrote down about how Sherita helped you with your jacket today. Then you invited her to be your buddy." The child may respond with an explanation or further conversation.

Evidence to Child Protective Services. An Anecdotal Recording is acceptable evidence to document a child abuse disclosure. When a child reveals information that may indicate abuse, it is important to accurately write down how the disclosure came about. The record must contain exact questions and comments of the adult and the child. Behavior or visual indicators may raise suspicions of abuse. The Anecdotal Recording preserves details and factual descriptions without conclusions or judgments.

LOOKING AT SELF-CARE SKILLS

EXERCISE: On a separate sheet of paper, list the things you do for yourself that give you pride, for example, changing a tire, programming the videocassette recorder, cruising the Internet.

"I can do it myself!" Those words spoken, sometimes defiantly, stand as a declaration of independence or a statement proclaiming a milestone accomplishment. Why are a child's **self-care** (sometimes called self-help) skills important, other than to free the adult from tasks previously done for the child? The accomplishment of taking care of one's own needs is a progression throughout childhood. It can be viewed as **development,** moving from simple to complex tasks, in an orderly predictable sequence yet at an individual rate for each person. The sequences of self-care skills incorporate many other components of developmental areas and contribute to self-worth and competency. The observer can assess, facilitate, and celebrate those accomplishments (Figure 2–5).

The self-care skills are closely allied to the areas that are affected by separation anxiety. This is probably because they are the tasks a parent does for a child. These are the most tenuous when the parent is no longer present. For the youngest child, they are the basis of survival and comfort. They become common elements in different environments for the older

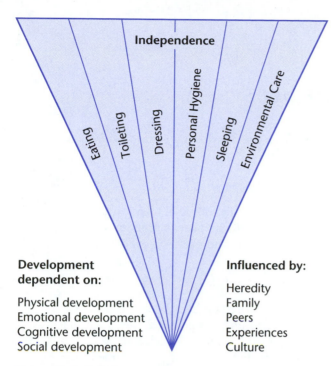

Figure 2–5 Self-Care Development

Each self-care skill meets that definition of development. Babies suck before they chew, eat with their fingers before they use a spoon, spoon before fork, fork before knife, knife before melon baller. This series always follows this progression because it depends on physical growth and development and builds on the skills and experience with the preceding attainment. The skills do not appear then disappear. They last a lifetime unless some trauma or drastic event interrupts or prevents the accomplishment of the task.

The reason for knowing the progression of self-care skills is the same as it is for every other area of development. Watching for the first time is a reassurance that development is taking place. It is a milestone, a marker. The first time the baby reaches out to hold her own bottle or takes the spoon and feeds herself is a momentous occasion. It demonstrates an increasing self-responsibility that is an indicator of maturity. Besides recognizing the mastery of a new skill, the adult then provides practice and more opportunities for the child to perform that task independently. The caregiver will also be looking to the next task in the progression and providing experiences for the child to attempt that task.

Once the child has mastered the spoon, the family introduces a little fork and demonstrates the stabbing motion that differentiates a fork from a spoon. This is planning curriculum based on developmental level. The caregiver sees that one child is ready for this at 10 months. Another is still working on the spoon at 12 months. This is individualizing the curriculum, developmental education. Families and teachers do it all the time without realizing it.

Self-Care and Autonomy

EXERCISE: At what point did you feel independent of your family? List the milestones toward that accomplishment.

Autonomy, the process of governing oneself and providing for one's own needs, is the goal of childhood. For twenty-first-century children, that seems to be a very long process. The human infant is born totally helpless but by one-and-a-half years, he is mobile and wanting to do more things for himself. Caregivers still need to be protective and restrictive while allowing the child opportunities to begin to be more independent. Erikson (1963) describes this conflict as Autonomy vs. Shame and Doubt. To develop autonomy children need both ability and opportunity. Ability is readiness. A child who has not yet developed small-muscle skills cannot be expected to

child. They are actions that are expected responsibilities of the caregiver, routines that can be sources of observation and assessment of development, and the basis for curricula planning.

Development of Self-Care Skills

The word *development* is an important one to understand. It is more than just change. The changes are

- interdependent on other developmental areas.
- sequential and build on prior learning.
- at varying rates from child to child and within different areas in the same child.
- affected by early experiences.
- from simple to complex.
- influenced by social and emotional contexts.
- actively and culturally transmitted.
- influenced by biological and environmental factors.
- facilitated through play.
- practiced and challenged.
- represented in different modalities. (adapted from Bredekamp, 1997)

The inverted triangle, illustrating the expanding nature of development, is used throughout the book to represent the expansion of skills and knowledge that begins in a limited, crude way but broadens and builds upon prior experiences.

TOPICS IN OBSERVATION

Using All Our Senses

EXERCISE: Using a separate piece of paper, make a list of what you can observe about a child from senses other than seeing:

hearing　　　　smelling　　　　touching　　　　tasting

The word *observe* is understood to use sight as the primary source of taking in information; however, all senses are receptors of information on which to base decisions. As observers of young children, all senses can be used to assess and evaluate the child.

Visual Cues	Inferences
Height, weight, body proportions, coordination, glasses, brace on leg, hearing aid	Physical growth and development, health, developmental delays, physical limitations
Skin color, hair color, eye shape	Racial or ethnic group, health, cosmetic use
Clothing, hairstyle, hygiene	Socioeconomic level, family style and care
Activity level	Emotional state, health factors
Facial expressions and body language	Emotional states, attention, interest
Playmates, interactions	Social stage, personality, sexual preference of playmates, aggressiveness
Approach to play, work, other people	Self-esteem, learning style, cognitive level and style
Mannerisms	Role models—family, TV characters, other children
Evidence of injury	Accident, surgery, abuse

Figure 2–6 Visual cues may lead one to make inferences about a child.

Seeing

Visually, information is gathered on the child's physical appearance; size; attributes, such as hair, coloring, features, facial expressions; coordination; actions; location in the room; and choices of activities. From all those visual cues, inferences are made regarding the child (Figure 2–6).

Hearing

The adult attunes to the message being communicated, from the first "coos" to intricate stories recounted with sound effects and voice. Many areas of development can be assessed from listening.

Emotional state—laughter, crying, whining, teasing, anger, silence

Cognitive development—vocabulary, content, grammar, problem-solving strategies, humor, storybook characters

Physical development—formation of teeth, tongue, and jaw

Health—nasal or bronchial congestion, wheezing, possible hearing difficulties affecting speech, digestive sounds

Family—home language, activities, siblings, other family members, other significant people in the child's life, television and video usage

Sociability—play stage, themes, playmates, leadership

Touching

Some information may not be apparent to sight or sound. The reaction to an adult's soft touch might seem unusual, giving rise to conjecture about the origin of that response.

(continued)

TOPICS IN OBSERVATION

Using All Our Senses (continued)

Muscle tone—firm muscle tissue, eating disorders, and some diseases
Illness—fever, rashes, cold, clammy skin
Stress—tension in the body, trembling, goosebumps
Injury—swelling, reaction to touch indicating a tenderness
Response to touch—cuddly, withdrawal, rigid

Smelling

The most obvious information gathered by smelling is that a diaper change is needed. In a one-year-old, that observation is common and demands a standard response. In a six-year-old that observation, of course, also calls for the action of cleaning up, but it is noteworthy and a red flag for other assessments. Smelling gives the keen observer clues about:

Hygiene—cleanliness, tooth decay, bed wetting
Illness—respiratory infections, diseases such as diabetes that may give off a sweet odor
Home odors—smoking, seasonings, animals, perfume
Safety—ingestion of a poisonous substance

Tasting

Taste probably would not be used to gather information on the child.

The "Sixth Sense"

The observer's instinct, or "gut" feeling should receive attention. Sometimes there is something about a child sensed not by eyes, ears, nose, or touch but by a feeling. Professionals must rely on substantive information but often have a heightened awareness. This is not to be used as a measurement but as an indicator that further hard evidence needs to be gathered. The observer makes a closer investigation with detailed documentation for later analysis. This may involve other professionals, with the permission of the parents, such as a social worker, health coordinator, psychologist, or speech therapist.

The keen observer uses all senses to gather information. The knowledge of child development is applied, using multiple methods of documentation of the observations. All of this information-gathering is used to benefit the child and the program.

manage buttons and zippers on clothing. While they want to dress themselves, or more likely, undress themselves, their ability may prevent them from doing so. The other aspect of autonomy is opportunity. When a child never is allowed to feed herself because she makes a mess, or to wash his own hands because he doesn't do it thoroughly, the child will be dependent longer and will feel incompetent. Autonomy is also culturally related. Some cultures

want children to be dependent for much longer than we do in the United States.

Children who have had no experience of success in becoming independent have a fundamental lack of confidence in their own self-worth. In *Miseducation: Preschoolers at Risk*, David Elkind (1987) gives the practical advice "children are just learning these skills, so it is important not to force them. . . . The important thing, as I have tried to suggest, is to find a healthy middle ground between doing everything for children and doing nothing for them and expecting them to cope with the adult-sized world" (p. 111).

Self-Care Skills in the Curriculum

By observing with the developmental progression in mind, observations become assessments and tools for planning curriculum. The area of self-care is not always recognized as a curriculum. It is taken for granted, probably because it develops so naturally. Self-care skills are recognized as a very important part of the curriculum for children with special needs (Bowe, 2004). Upon consideration, taking care of one's own body functions involves many areas of development and contributes not only to physical but emotional well-being. Both large and small muscle strength and coordination are necessary for these tasks. A great many thinking processes are involved in each skill, beginning with body awareness of the cues of hunger, tiredness, need to eliminate, and feeling cold or hot. The connections between past experiences build and form new thinking patterns.

Certainly self-care skills are necessary for social acceptance. It is part of that whole realm of manners and out-in-public actions. These are learned by observing and imitating role models and from direct instruction. The learning depends on the child's desire to be accepted and liked. There is a feeling of accomplishment and increased self-esteem when one can do something independently, without assistance. Following surgery or an illness, people report how good it feels just to be able to brush their own teeth or go up a few steps. Those actions become so natural, done without thinking or appreciating their complexity. In childhood, they are skills to learn, moving from basic to complex levels.

Individual differences are significant in self-care skills. Predictability of body rhythmicity is seen dramatically in the Thomas and Chess (1977, 1980) longitudinal studies. The studies indicated that feeding, elimination, and sleeping patterns at two months were consistent or at least similar at 10 years old. In addition to physical differences, social, racial, and cultural influences as well as birth order may affect self-care development. Marci Hanson (1998) warns, "Expectations for children concerning feeding, sleeping and speaking, as well as the use of discipline, to mention only a few may vary widely across cultural groups" (p. 13). The book reviews many different cultural beliefs important for teachers to know. Information on the child's self-care skills can be gathered from families as well as observed in the natural routines of the day in the group setting. Figure 2–7, Ire-

ton (1995), is a checklist that could be used to assess self-help skills with the ages at which these normally occur. These are part of the developmental process so the observer realizes that each child attains these milestones in an individual timetable.

Self-Care Skills

Self-care skills are points of observing and recording used to recognize milestones, plot and share progress, and plan curriculum (Figure 2–8).

Eating. In infancy, the adult is the source of nourishment to the child, whether by breast or by bottle. The infant depends on the adult to provide the acceptable food at regular times and as the infant gives signals of hunger. Reflex actions of rooting (turning toward the cheek that is touched) and sucking once the nipple is felt on the lips are built-in muscle responses. They enable the infant to receive nourishment. By three or four months, the baby will begin to recognize the breast or bottle, reach for it, and hold it firmly. In another month, the baby begins to push it away when full. By six months, the pincer grasp of thumb and forefinger enables the baby to indiscriminately pick up small food items (and fuzz balls) and get them into the mouth. This means the caregiver must give extra caution to the cleanliness of the environment. The caregiver must be vigilant regarding small ingestible and undigestible items. Soon the caregiver will begin to give the baby the opportunity to eat small bits of appropriate food items while the child is securely strapped in a high chair or infant seat.

In the second year, the child begins to assert independence by grabbing the spoon, the bottle, or the cracker. He now has the small motor skills to get them to his mouth fairly accurately and teeth to chew. Three- and four-year-olds gain skill at using utensils: spoon first, then the fork, then the knife. They should be given the opportunity to practice under supervision (Figure 2–9). Gentle reminders and pointers for using the silverware effectively are given. They can efficiently pour, if the pitcher is lightweight and clear, so they can see the liquid approaching the spout. It helps if the glass or paper cup has a fill line for a visual cue to stop pouring. It helps to place the glass on a tray to catch "over pours" until control is gained.

By late four and early five years, children have the physical mobility and manual dexterity to help themselves to food as it is passed. They love to assist in preparation of peeling foods with proper utensils and supervision. They can set the table, fold napkins,

SELF-HELP

Includes eating, dressing, bathing, toileting, independence, and responsibility

Age 1-2

- Removes socks. — 12m
- Lifts a cup to mouth and drinks. — 12m
- Feeds self with a spoon. — 15m
- Hands empty dish to adult. — 15m
- Ⓟ Remembers where things are kept in the house. — 15m
- Uses a small pail or other container for carrying things. Or used to. — 15m
- Tries to put on shoes. Or puts them on. — 15m
- Climbs on chair, stool, or box to reach things. — 15m
- Eats with a fork. — 18m
- Eats with a spoon with little spilling. — 21m
- Takes off shoes and socks. — 21m
- Unzips zippers. — 21m

Age 2-3

- Ⓟ Wipes up spills, using cloth or sponge. — 2-0
- Ⓟ Takes off unbuttoned shirt/blouse without help. — 2-0
- Ⓟ Opens door by turning knob and pulling. — 2-0
- Ⓟ Washes and dries hands. — 2-6
- Ⓟ Goes around the house independently; requires little supervision. — 2-6
- Ⓟ Washes self in bathtub—may need a little help. — 2-6

Ages 3-4

- Puts on a shirt/blouse or jacket without help. — 3-0
- Toilet trained for urine control and bowel movements. — 3-0, 2-6
- Ⓟ Brushes teeth without help. — 3-0
- Ⓟ Takes responsibility for self in eating, dressing, and washing—but may need a little help. — 3-3
- Ⓟ Undresses completely without help. — 3-6, 3-0
- Ⓟ Washes face without help. — 3-9, 3-3
- Ⓟ Notices when shirt/blouse or pants are inside-out and turns them right-side-out. — 3-9
- Ⓟ Dresses and undresses without help, except for tying shoelaces. — 3-9, 3-6
- Ⓟ Stays dry all night. — 4-3, 3-3

Age 4-5

- Uses table knife for spreading. — 4-3
- Buttons one or more buttons. — 4-3
- Ⓟ Usually looks both ways when crossing streets. — 4-6
- Buttons a shirt, blouse, or coat, having all the buttons in the correct holes. — 5-0, 4-3
- Goes to the toilet without help; wipes self, flushes toilet, and washes hands. — 5-0, 4-3
- Takes care of personal belongings. — 5-3, 4-6

Age 5-6

- Puts shoes on the correct feet. — 5-0
- Ⓟ Pours self a drink. — 5-0
- Ⓟ Pours dry cereal and milk into a bowl without spilling. — 5-3

OTHER SKILLS

- _____
- _____
- _____

PROBLEMS

- Immature; acts much younger than age
- Disorganized; messy, careless, irresponsible
- Can't sit still; may be hyperactive
- Passive; seldom shows initiative
- Lacks self-confidence; says "I'm dumb," etc.

Figure 2–7 Self-Help Milestones (Ireton, H. *Child Development Inventory Teacher's Observation Guide,* ©1995. Reprinted by permission of Behavior Science Systems, Inc., Box 580274, Minneapolis, MN 55458. [612] 929-6220).

clear the table, and be quite helpful in the whole mealtime routine.

Learning and language connected with eating begins with the recognition of food sources, such as

Passes food as served

Cuts soft foods with knife

Uses knife for spreading

Pours, serves self from bowl

Eats with fork

Drinks from cup alone

Discriminates edible substances

Uses spoon, some spilling

Drinks from cup if held

Holds food, bites, chews

Feeds self—whole hand

Grabs for spoon

Holds bottle with both hands

Reaches for breast or bottle

Figure 2–8 Eating Skills

Figure 2–9 Pouring takes physical skills, concentration, and patience.

the breast or bottle. Accompanying vocabulary is built as the caregiver says, "Here comes the baba, baby hungry?" The creeper finds tidbits on the floor but her ability to discriminate between food and non-food items is not developed, possibly placing her in danger.

By one year she begins to display likes and dislikes of foods by their appearance or a single taste. As language explodes in the second year, she can recognize and name many foods. The sorting skills of the three- and four-year-old transfer into food groups. It begins with likes and dislikes. Eventually, she can classify meat, vegetables, fruits, drinks, and breads. She is learning the names for the individual items based on visual and aromatic cues.

EXERCISE: What table rules did you learn as a child? How did you learn them?

The social-emotional aspects of eating are lessons that are learned early. The aura of mealtime lasts a lifetime. It may be a relaxed, social gathering, or a tense, emotion-laden time of restrictions and prohibitions. Adults are responsible for the physical environment of cleanliness, safety, appropriateness of menu, cognitive connections, and language and vocabulary expansion. They are modeling social graces and providing an emotional atmosphere where psychological safety and individualism are recognized (Figure 2–10).

When children sit at a table that fits them and participate to their ability with the preparation, serving, and feeding of the meal, it builds the feeling of competency. The interaction with peers and adults in pleasant conversation teaches many social lessons. Verna Hildebrand (1999) reminds teachers:

Figure 2–10 Eating is a social event in which many lessons may be learned.

IT HAPPENED TO ME

Bad Example

I was observing in a child care center at morning snack time. Some of the children had been doing puzzles and playing with Play Doh at the table while others had been painting, stacking with blocks, shoveling sand, and looking at books. The teacher rattled a box of Coco Puffs and the children came running to sit at the table. She stood behind each child, scooped up a handful of cereal from the box and placed it on the bare table in front of each one. She poured juice from a can into paper cups and set them in front of each child. She said, "OK, eat, and no spilling." She stepped away from the table and ate a candy bar from her pocket.

Mealtime can also foster children's feelings of connectedness to each other and to their cultural heritages. Just think of how many of your interactions with other people seem to involve sharing food, whether to mark a happy or sad occasion, or simply to enjoy each others' company. Social development is nurtured through the conversations that naturally accompany pleasant meals. (p. 192)

Children learn they are trusted when they are given autonomy over choices among healthy foods. By participating in the food preparation, serving, and self-feeding they feel competent. When they interact with others during mealtime, they learn skills that they will be using around the table the rest of their life. Because eating disorders are beginning as early as three and four, close attention should be given to mealtimes and the emotions involved.

EXERCISE: "It Happened to Me: Bad Example" is a true Anecdotal Recording, unfortunately! What was wrong with the teacher's practices?

Toileting. Control of body eliminations is truly an illustration of development: from no control with only reflex actions, through the steps dependent on physical growth, to a complex set of controls and releases dependent on many other factors (Figure 2–11).

Of course, the infant has no control over body eliminations so the adult performs all necessary tasks of absorbing, catching, cleaning, and rediapering.

This routine function, like any other done with an infant, is not without its effect on the infant's cognitive, language, and social-emotional realm.

Adults give many messages to the infant during diapering, such as messages about safety, gentleness, hygiene, acceptance of body elimination, and sexual attitudes. When a caregiver expresses unpleasantness at the task, the infant confuses the message. He does not know it is the task, and not him, that is the cause of the unpleasant facial expressions and expressive language.

EXERCISE: Ask a parent to recount a toilet-training story (everyone has at least one), and write it down as it is told. Use the criteria for an Anecdotal Recording.

Usually children are well into the second year before they begin to recognize the body signals of an impending bowel movement and, even later, the need to urinate. The physical growth of muscles is occurring, along with the mental attention to body signals. Unfortunately, it is at a time when there is a strong desire to gain more control of the world. In this battle to control the body, the child and the adult are often at opposite poles, making toilet training a chore many adults dread. The struggle can be eased by recognizing the turmoil going on inside the child. She is given control, since the adult cannot control it anyway. Psaltis and Stonehouse (1990) give the strong warning, "As in other areas of care, *there is no place in learning self toileting for shaming, embarrassing, or making a toddler feel guilty*" (p. 83, italics in original work). Curriculum for this area is in environment preparation, positive role models, and sometimes direct instruction.

Environment. The adult's role is to provide an environment that encourages the desired action: potty chair, steps to the toilet, child-sized toilet seat, books, pictures, pleasant room decor. The bathroom often is overlooked as a place where learning occurs. Interesting pictures at the side and back of the toilet give "goers" thought-provoking visual aids. Of course, visual reminders of hand washing will link toileting with personal hygiene.

EXERCISE: Toileting is an emotionally charged subject for child and adult. Finish these reflective questions:

The most uncomfortable part for me about working with children surrounding toileting is . . .
I think it is because . . .
Maybe it would be better if I . . .

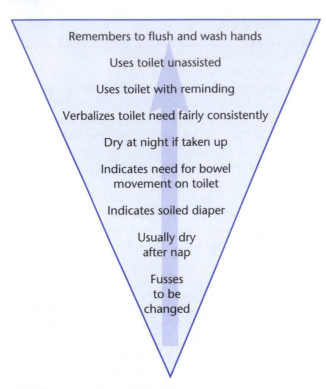

Remembers to flush and wash hands

Uses toilet unassisted

Uses toilet with reminding

Verbalizes toilet need fairly consistently

Dry at night if taken up

Indicates need for bowel movement on toilet

Indicates soiled diaper

Usually dry after nap

Fusses to be changed

Figure 2–11 Toileting Development

Role Models. Toileting is sometimes aided by the social aspect in group care because of the child's natural imitative nature. When one child uses the toilet, others will want to do it also. When a child is praised for potty use, it is likely to occur again and again and eventually become a routine.

EXERCISE: What does "It Happened to Me: Am I Clean?" tell you about the child's stage of development? Home influence? The teacher?

Direct Instruction. Some children may need to be taught proper use of the toilet and toilet paper. This is best accomplished on an anatomically correct doll. Teachers should avoid performing this task on a child in an enclosed bathroom stall. For children still needing assistance, stalls are without doors or the task is done with the door propped open. This is a precaution to possible child abuse allegations.

As the child is expanding her vocabulary, a consideration of which words to use for body elimination functions should be explored so that families and teachers attain consistency. This also gives a positive rather than negative connotation to the function. The struggle over toilet training is an emotionally

IT HAPPENED TO ME

Am I Clean?

This happened to a friend of mine. In a four-year-old class, a child had gone to the bathroom while they were having snack. She waddled back from the bathroom with her pants around her ankles, bent over, looking through her legs yelled, "Am I clean?" "Yes, you're clean. Good job wiping," said the teacher matter-of-factly. The girl returned to the bathroom, dressed, washed hands, and returned to snack.

and culturally sensitive topic that is enhanced by the caregiver's partnership with the family and the child. Hanson (1998) gives the reminder that "in the United States, toilet training between the child's second and third birthday is a common practice and is highly valued by many families. However, this practice may be viewed by many other cultural groups as unnecessary and too early" (p. 13).

Dressing. It is always easier to knock down a building than to build it, delete a page of type than to write it, criticize than to praise. So it is with dressing—the first step in self-care is taking clothing off. Parents have all experienced, at least once, the shock of a stark-naked child appearing when they were just fully clothed a few minutes ago. Dressing is a developmental progression of skills (Figure 2–12).

Children can be given the power to take off the articles of clothing they can manage. By the time they are two or three years old, they can take off their shoes at nap time, their hat after coming in from outside play, and all their clothes at bath time. They should do what they can do. By selecting clothing that children can manage themselves, such as boxer pants, the child finds the task much easier. It is easier than a one-piece jumpsuit or buttons up the back of a dress.

EXERCISE: Make a list of clothing fasteners that are difficult even for adults. How could it have been designed differently?

Teachers can add play items with buttons, snaps, zippers, and ties to the curriculum to encourage practice of those skills. It is always amazing how a child can squeeze into a leotard and tutu over a pair of jeans and a sweatshirt and sneakers. If they want it

Ties hood
Ties shoes
Pulls on boots
Zips separating zippers
Puts on shoes, usually right feet
Puts on coat unassisted
Buttons, zips, snaps
Dresses with some help
Pulls down pants to toilet
Pulls up pants
Removes coat
Unzips
Pulls off socks
Takes off hat and shoes
Holds out arms and legs

Figure 2–12 Dressing Development

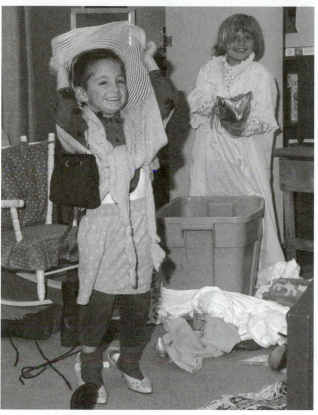

Figure 2–13 Dress-up clothes give practice in buttoning, zipping, and tying.

on, they will find a way. Inviting dress-up props stimulate interest and practice skills (Figure 2–13).

When helping a child after toileting or getting ready to go outside, the child should be assisted with what they cannot do and encouraged to do what they can. The adult can pull up the pants and let the child pull up the suspenders. The teacher can start the separating zipper and let her finish it, or finish tying the bow after she has crossed the ties.

"Never do for a children what they can do for themselves."

Personal Hygiene. Body cleanliness and care of the infant is, of course, the sole responsibility of the adult (Figure 2–14). It is a physical function performed which is building associations in the infant between certain events. "They change my diaper and wash my body and hands." "They set me in the high chair, wash my hands, then give me food." "They take me away from the table and wash my face and hands." In the first year, these associations are being made. In the second year when the child gains mobility and small muscle control, she can go to the sink, which is adapted so she can reach it, and wash her hands. She is taught to do this after going to the toilet or wiping her nose, or before eating. She can manage to turn on the water, wash, dry, and go on with play. In the fourth and fifth years, small muscle control is more

developed. The child can now efficiently handle combing hair, brushing teeth, and bathing in the tub with supervision.

Recognition of the need for washing is a difficult lesson for young children to learn because of the "invisible" germs. They are concrete thinkers. When they look at their hands and see no dirt, they find it incomprehensible that they should wash, especially if they did it once today already. It is the social acceptance and cognitive bridging that reinforce the personal hygiene habits until the child is into the elementary school years when microscopic particles are understood.

Sleeping. Sleep needs and patterns are individual but follow a developmental pattern. Individual differences are seen in the amount of sleep children need, how they get to sleep, how soundly they sleep, and their usual waking-up routines.

Children in group care tend to be overstimulated because of many available playmates and play things. It is lessened by stress reduction throughout the day and by planning for smooth transitions, and alternating active and quiet activity choices. Prior to nap time, consistent routines, such as mealtime, teeth

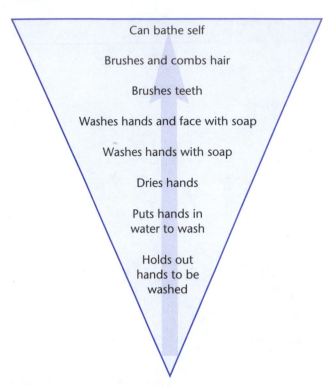

Can bathe self

Brushes and combs hair

Brushes teeth

Washes hands and face with soap

Washes hands with soap

Dries hands

Puts hands in water to wash

Holds out hands to be washed

Figure 2–14 Personal Hygiene Skill Development

brushing, and music listening or a story, help to prepare the children for sleep. Attention is given to the program schedule and environment to allow for resting and sleeping time on self-demand. Sleeping arrangements often are strictly mandated by state regulations for safety and supervision. The National Association for the Education of Young Children's (NAEYC) *Developmentally Appropriate Practice* (Bredekamp, 1997) mandates children have their own cribs, bedding, feeding utensils, clothing, diapers, pacifiers, and other special comforting objects. Infant's names are used to label every personal item. Individual programs develop routines of backrubs, soft music, and quiet play preceding rest times to help children relax and sleep if they need to (Figure 2–15). Allowances are made for those children who are no longer taking naps to look quietly at books in the napping area or to play in a quiet learning center.

Individual children have sleep patterns such as sleeping position or what soothes them into sleep. They may require possessions nearby to fall asleep. By noting a reduction in sleep times, modifications are made for the child who no longer requires a nap. Communication of daily sleep patterns between home and school assists both family and center in meeting the needs of the child.

Family and staff daily reports are used in most centers to convey this type of information at arrival

Figure 2–15 Allowances should be made for children's individual sleeping patterns.

and departure times. Sharing "what works" benefits the child at home and at the center.

Self-Care in the Classroom

Caring for the classroom environment is another area of development.

EXERCISE: Observe the room you are in. What are the items in the room or the arrangement that encourages self-care? (Example: Wastebasket is available.)

Some observable signs of a child's participation in classroom self-care are

- selects toys for play
- puts a toy back in its place
- plays actively without adult leadership
- follows classroom routines
- cleans up spills
- helps prepare for activity
- can carry breakable objects
- performs "job chart" tasks
- demonstrates safety awareness
- assists another child to do a task

With the movie *Home Alone* and its sequels in mind, many have visions of the immense capacities of a child's competency. On the other hand, there have been newspaper horror stories of children left alone at a very young age. Some of these children are caring for even younger siblings and often there are tragedies. This self-care concept is not to hurry the child along to independence before he is ready. It allows him the freedom and responsibility for self-care. This is done in small, manageable steps that build confidence and competency. They eventually form the ability to make safe self-care decisions. The age at which a child can be allowed to play unattended in a room at home, go down the street alone, and eventually stay at home alone for a short time varies with the individual child. It also is affected by the home setting, the neighborhood, and prior experiences. There should be a history of smaller, success-

ful instances of self-care. Parents are in the business of working themselves out of a job and building into the child the competencies for self-care. It is done one day at a time.

Many classrooms and home environments use job charts for daily responsibilities. This is an organized way to ensure care of the environment. It also teaches that each one must do a part for the good of the group (Figure 2–16).

In the classroom as well, children become competent in self-care as they learn the routines. They can meet realistic expectations for cleaning up after themselves and should be given responsibilities for themselves and others. There are children who are so

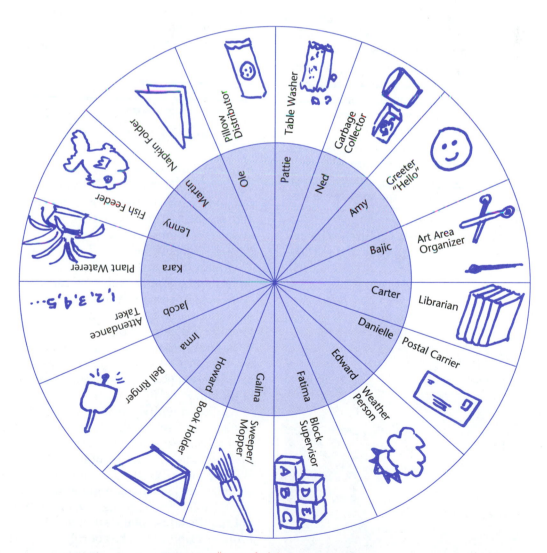

Names (inner circle) move each day.

Figure 2–16 Job Chart. (Reprinted with permission from Carol Fuller, Conklin Presbyterian Preschool, Conklin, NY.)

averse to cleaning up that they are reluctant to play with anything so they do not have to put anything away. Clean-up time is easier with the aid of effective transitions. These begin with a warning time that playtime is almost over, which helps to prepare children to end play and begin to pick up. Little ritual songs or signals, such as music or a bell, work better than an adult yelling "Pick-up time!" See Figure 2–17.

Adults can make pick-up time fun by using child-sized brooms, small vacuum cleaners, and toy trucks to transport toys back to their places that clearly are labeled. This reinforces the group participation in taking care of the classroom and initiates the concept of environmental responsibility.

If the Child Is Having Difficulty. The teacher begins with a closer examination of the environment. Modifications are made to help the child, such as low clothes hooks, reduced lighting in the nap area, or steps up to the changing table or toilet. If the environment is appropriate, the expectations for the child may not be reasonable. Other areas of the child's development are considered (language, cognitive, small muscle). Are these self-care expectations realistic? After this, a talk with the family is the next step to find out if they can give advice, insight, or assistance.

The teacher should be aware of the families' expectations for the child at home, how the child does these things at home, and what may be the reason for this inability here. More time may be all that is needed.

The Importance of Self-Care. Children who can care for their own bodies are physically and psycho-logically strong. It is a progression. It may have relapses, need reminders, and result in frustration. Families sometimes wonder if their child will be graduating from high school in diapers, sucking on a bottle, with zippers unzipped. That rarely happens; they do learn it along the way. The adult's role is consideration of the environment, realistic expectations, positive role models, and direct, specific instructions. Clean-up involves classification, seriation, and organizational skills. It builds a respect for the environment and a sense of responsibility. A model teacher was observed using a variety of creative clean-up strategies. He acted like a human crane, made dot picker uppers with masking tape, sticky side up on blocks, created a sympathetic response to a story about "home for lost toys" to find places for displaced items, and used chairs as bulldozers to push toys to their rightful place (Bauer & Sheerer, 1997). Children then develop these self-care skills that allow them to be independent and socially accepted.

HELPING ALL CHILDREN WITH SELF-CARE SKILLS

It has already been mentioned that cultural differences are seen most in the area of self-care skills. The caregiver needs to be sensitive to different attitudes and practices. The family role of providing cultural socialization must be accommodated in the program through the cultural competence (Hanson, Lynch & Wayman, 1990) of the teachers, clarifying their own values and assumptions. This can be done through home visits, research, family questionnaires, and gaining information from watching the child and family together. Adjustment of routines for these differences is the appropriate action, rather than forcing the child to conform. Communication and coordination between school and home must occur for the benefit of the child.

Children with special needs, as previously mentioned, need to be allowed to do all they can for themselves. Self-care routines provide opportunities for assessment, intervention, and development of skills (Benner, 2003). They are frequent, common to all children, and involve identified sequences. They do not interfere with regular programming and do not require additional staff or special training. These routines also need to be coordinated with family life so collaboration between program and family is necessary for continuity of practice. A survey of the routines of the day and setting specific goals for the child

Pick up, pick up.

Everybody do your share.

Pick up, pick up.

Pick up everywhere.

To the traditional "Today Is Monday" tune:

It's time to pick up.

It's time to pick up.

Mary's picking up blocks.

Jack's sweeping sand.

Tania's finishing her painting.

Soon it will be snack.

Figure 2–17 Pick-up songs help make an orderly environment everyone's responsibility.

in each routine can be implemented and serve as communication between all team members, family, and the child (Cripe & Lee, 1997). It may mean that some modifications are made to the environment and expectations. All children have the need to feel competent and responsible.

HELPING PROFESSIONALS FOR SELF-CARE SKILLS

Other professionals may be consulted depending on the area of difficulty, such as a

pediatrician—for a thorough physical checkup to rule out any possible physical reasons for difficulties

social worker—for advice on family and center practices and expectations

occupational therapist—to examine more closely fine muscle skills involved in self-care

child psychologist—to explore the child's attitudes and reasons for refusing to care for herself

OTHER METHODS

Other Methods to Record Self-Care

Class List Log
Checklists/Rating Scales
Running Records
Frequency Counts
Conversations and Interviews
Work Samples
Media

KEY TERMS

Anecdotal Recording
autonomy
development
inference
narrative
open method
self-care

WEEK 2

NOTE FOR ADJUSTING WEEK BY WEEK PLAN TO YOUR CLASS

Practitioners

Each week's plans will include recordings on the whole class and on individual children. In our effort to record fairly and equally, divide the class into four groups by taking one of the Class List Log forms and dividing it as equally as you can into four groups: Groups A, B, C, and D. These children will be in these recording groups for the rest of the year, so keep this as your master group plan.

When the weekly plan is to observe each child in Group A (or B, C, or D) use the Class List Log of the children in that group to determine how many children you must observe each day. (In this way you can factor in short weeks and so on.) Write those names on the calendar. For example, if you had 16 children in your class, Group A will have child 1, 2, 3, and 4. On Monday, child 1 will be the focus of the recording; on Tuesday, child 2, and so on. If you had 23 in your class, Group A will have child 1, 2, 3, 4, 5, and 6. You may decide that on Tuesday and Wednesday you will focus on child 2 in the morning and child 3 in the afternoon for the plan. The following week, the plan for individual recordings probably will be Group B, so you would focus on each of the children in the next group, one or two per day.

WEEK 2: PLAN A

ANECDOTAL RECORDING— SELF-CARE FOR GROUP A

Student

Select the four oldest children in the group of eight that you will be observing this semester. Look for opportunities to write an anecdotal record on each of them in the area of self-help skills. This can be a description of a child's arrival and how the child stores belongings. It can be at snack or mealtime or when the child is using the bathroom. (Note that this does not mean you should accompany and observe the child using the toilet, but observe how the child indicates the need to go, handles undressing and dressing, and handwashing.) In the case of infants or toddlers, write about the skills the child has—reaching for the bottle or spoon, pulling off socks, or attempting to dress.

Practitioners

Select each of the children in Group A. On Monday, while working with the children through the day, focus attention skills displayed by child 1 during eating, dressing, toileting, taking care of themselves, or taking care of the room. Jot notes. Later in the day, on the left-hand column of a sheet of paper, write an Anecdotal Recording as an illustration of child 1's self-care skills. Remember to just be a detail writer, including actions and exact quotes to give the reader the feeling of being there. On Tuesday, repeat the assignment for child 2, Wednesday for child 3, and so on. In the right-hand column, make notes about what this self-care incident shows about the child's physical, cognitive, language, and social-emotional development. In the right column, you make comments such as, "This is the first time she's done this by herself. She was so proud," or "This is unusual for him," or "I wonder if she would have done this if she hadn't felt me watching her."

What to Do with It

Filing. On each child's Portfolio Overview Sheet, note that the Anecdotal Record is being included that documents an aspect of self-care, along with your name and date (Figure 2–18). File the recording in the child's portfolio.

SELF–CARE			
Documentation	Location	Recorder	Date
CL	Class file	BAN	9/14
AR	Portfolio	MS	3/15

Figure 2–18 Portfolio Overview Example

Sharing with Family and Child. Share the incident with family and the child, if it is appropriate. For example: "I was observing Boneva today and noticed how well she's handling the butter knife for spreading and even cutting up her potato into small pieces. That's quite an advanced skill."

Actions:

Read a Book.

DeFelice, C. J. (1996). *Casey in the Bath.* New York: Farrar Strauss Giroux

Linnea, R. (1997). *Mouse Mess.* New York: Scholastic

Shihab, N. (1997) *Lullaby Raft.* New York: Simon and Schuster

Takabataki. (1993). *Rub-a-dub-dub: Who's in the Tub?* San Francisco: Chronicle Books

Cole, J. (1989). *Your New Potty.* New York: William Morrow & Co. Books

VanVeeuwen, J. (1998). *Amanda Pig and Her Best Friend Lollipop.* New York: Deal Books

Vivas, J. (1997). *Let's Eat.* New York: Scholastic

In the Environment.

- Provide equipment that fosters self-care success: child-sized eating utensils and small pitchers, child-sized toilet, low sink, soap and towel dispenser, time and space for dressing and undressing for outdoors.
- Provide a place for everything for a sense of orderliness.
- Provide time to clean up without pressure.
- Make clean-up fun, not a time of punishment for playing and making messes.

In the Newsletter.

- Investigate the consequences of *not* caring for hygiene with concrete experiences, growing mold, dissolving enamel in cola, wearing the wrong kinds of clothing.

- Develop a project of how a toilet or drain works.
- Explore the sleeping habits of various animals.

Communication with Families in Newsletters.

mold, dissolving enamel in cola, wearing the wrong kinds of clothing.
- Develop a project of how a toilet or drain works.
- Explore the sleeping habits of various animals.

Communication with Families in Newsletters.
- This is a great topic for a series of articles with helpful advice on eating, toileting, sleeping, and home chores.
- Article on family self-care practices in various cultures.

WEEK 2: PLAN B

CLASS LIST LOG—SELF-CARE FOR ALL

Use a Class List Log form to record selected skills from eating, toileting, dressing, personal hygiene, sleeping, or classroom self-care. Review the developmental milestones for the age of the children in your class and observe this week, noting the degree of self-care each child exhibits in these areas. Be sure you are allowing each child to do for themselves what they can do.

What to Do with It

Filing. In each child's Portfolio Overview Sheet, note the date of the Class List Log, the self-care level observed, and the recorder's name (yours). File the completed Class List Log in your class file. You will refer to it again later in the year.

Make a note if further action is indicated and follow through on further observation. Discuss with the teaching team, your supervisor, or the child's family.

WEEK 2: PLAN C

REFLECTIVE JOURNAL

Respond to the following in your Reflective Journal, kept in a private file at home.

I need to be giving children more opportunities for self-care. I think I'll . . .

I find myself doing more for _____ than the other children.
The reasons for this may be . . .

When I'm trying to do something and someone tries to help me, it makes me . . .

These are the things I can do for myself that make me feel competent:

3

Using Checklists to Look at Physical Development

USING THE CHECKLIST

EXERCISE: Complete this Checklist.

_____ I read Chapters 1 and 2.
_____ I completed each exercise in Chapters 1 and 2.
_____ I enjoyed writing in my Reflective Journal.
_____ I underlined key passages.
_____ I know the definition of *development*.

A **Checklist** is a predetermined list of criteria against which the recorder answers *yes* or *no*. In Checklist ratings, the recorder reads the criterion, decides on an answer, and makes a checkmark as an indication of an affirmative answer. Some of the preceding criterion are observable while others are judgmental or inferential. Mark those with a *J*. The third and fifth items are not observable.

Bentzen (2005) describes Checklists as a **closed method** because no raw data or evidence is recorded, just the decision (inference) of the recorder about the criterion. Checklists are highly selective, only giving the recorder the opportunity to record a decision concerning the criterion. That does not mean it is not useful or accurate, but the reader has no raw data or details to check the recorder's decision. This is a characteristic of Checklist recording.

A valid child development Checklist records the attainment of accepted developmental milestones of knowledge, behavior, and skills. All Checklists depend on the familiarity of the observer with the criteria and ability to assess the criteria accurately. Therefore, the criteria should be clearly observable, leaving little room for subjective judgments. If not, two raters may see the same child performing a skill, yet rate the skill differently. Checklists' criteria should

REFERENCES

Bauer, K. L., & Sheerer, M. A. with Dettore, Jr., E. (1997). Creative strategies in Ernie's childhood classroom. *Young Children.* 52 (6)

Benner, S. M. (2003). *Assessment of young children with special needs: A context-based approach.* Clifton Park, NY: Thomson Delmar Learning.

Bentzen, W. (2001). *Seeing young children: A guide to deserving and rewarding behavior* (4th ed.) Clifton Park, NY: Thomson Delmar Learning.

Bowe, F. G. (2004). *Birth to five: Early childhood special education* (3rd ed.) Clifton Park, NY: Thomson Delmar Learning.

Bredekamp, S. (1997). *Developmentally appropriate practice in early childhood programs.* Revised edition. Washington, DC: National Association for the Education of Young Children.

Cripe, J. W., & Lee, J. M. (1997). Activity-based intervention strategies for serving young children with developmental delays in early childhood programs. In W. H. Brown & M. A. Conroy, *Including and supporting preschool children with developmental delays in early childhood programs.* Little Rock, AR: Southern Early Childhood Association, 49–63.

Elkind. D. (1987). *Miseducation: Preschoolers at risk.* New York: Alfred A. Knopf.

Erikson, E. (1963). *Childhood and society* (2nd ed.). New York: Norton.

Frank, C. (1999). *Ethographic eyes.* Portsmouth, NH: Heinemann.

Hanson, M. J. (1998). Ethnic, cultural, and language diversity in intervention settings. In E. W. Lynch, & M. J. Hanson. *Developing cross-cultural competence: A guide for working with young children and their families.* (2nd ed.) Baltimore, MD: Brookes.

Hanson, M. J., Lynch, E. W. & Wayman, K. I. (1990). Honoring the cultural diversity of families when gathering data. *Topics in Early Childhood Special Education 10,* 112–131.

Hildebrand, V. (1999). *Guiding young children.* New York: Macmillan Publishing Co.

Ireton, H. R. (1995). *Teacher's observation guide.* Minneapolis, MN: Behavioral Science Systems.

Psaltis, M., & Stonehouse, A. (1990). Toddler-centered routines. In A. Stonehouse, *Trusting toddlers: Planning for one- to three-year-olds in child care centers.* St. Paul, MN: Toys 'n Things Press.

Thomas, A., & Chess, S. (1977). *Temperament and development.* New York: Brunner/Mazel.

Thomas, A., & Chess, S. (1980). *The dynamics of psychological development.* New York: Brunner/Mazel.

RESOURCES

Feldman, J. (1995). *Transition time: Let's do something different!* Beltsville, MD: Gryphon House.

Lynch, E. W., & Hanson, M. J. *Developing cross-cultural competence: A guide for working with young children and their families* (2nd ed.) Baltimore: Brookes.

Psaltis, M., & Stonehouse, A. (1990). Toddler-centered routines. In A. Stonehouse. *Trusting Toddlers: Planning for one- to three-year-olds in child care centers.* St. Paul, MN: Toys 'n Things Press.

Using Checklists to Look at Physical Development

USING THE CHECKLIST

EXERCISE: Complete this Checklist.

_____ I read Chapters 1 and 2.

_____ I completed each exercise in Chapters 1 and 2.

_____ I enjoyed writing in my Reflective Journal.

_____ I underlined key passages.

_____ I know the definition of *development*.

A **Checklist** is a predetermined list of criteria against which the recorder answers *yes* or *no*. In Checklist ratings, the recorder reads the criterion, decides on an answer, and makes a checkmark as an indication of an affirmative answer. Some of the preceding criterion are observable while others are judgmental or inferential. Mark those with a *J*. The third and fifth items are not observable.

Bentzen (2005) describes Checklists as a **closed method** because no raw data or evidence is recorded, just the decision (inference) of the recorder about the criterion. Checklists are highly selective, only giving the recorder the opportunity to record a decision concerning the criterion. That does not mean it is not useful or accurate, but the reader has no raw data or details to check the recorder's decision. This is a characteristic of Checklist recording.

A valid child development Checklist records the attainment of accepted developmental milestones of knowledge, behavior, and skills. All Checklists depend on the familiarity of the observer with the criteria and ability to assess the criteria accurately. Therefore, the criteria should be clearly observable, leaving little room for subjective judgments. If not, two raters may see the same child performing a skill, yet rate the skill differently. Checklists' criteria should

REFERENCES

Bauer, K. L., & Sheerer, M. A. with Dettore, Jr., E. (1997). Creative strategies in Ernie's childhood classroom. *Young Children. 52* (6)

Benner, S. M. (2003). *Assessment of young children with special needs: A context-based approach.* Clifton Park, NY: Thomson Delmar Learning.

Bentzen, W. (2001). *Seeing young children: A guide to deserving and rewarding behavior* (4th ed.) Clifton Park, NY: Thomson Delmar Learning.

Bowe, F. G. (2004). *Birth to five: Early childhood special education* (3rd ed.) Clifton Park, NY: Thomson Delmar Learning.

Bredekamp, S. (1997). *Developmentally appropriate practice in early childhood programs.* Revised edition. Washington, DC: National Association for the Education of Young Children.

Cripe, J. W., & Lee, J. M. (1997). Activity-based intervention strategies for serving young children with developmental delays in early childhood programs. In W. H. Brown & M. A. Conroy, *Including and supporting preschool children with developmental delays in early childhood programs.* Little Rock, AR: Southern Early Childhood Association, 49–63.

Elkind. D. (1987). *Miseducation: Preschoolers at risk.* New York: Alfred A. Knopf.

Erikson, E. (1963). *Childhood and society* (2nd ed.). New York: Norton.

Frank, C. (1999). *Ethographic eyes.* Portsmouth, NH: Heinemann.

Hanson, M. J. (1998). Ethnic, cultural, and language diversity in intervention settings. In E. W. Lynch, & M. J. Hanson. *Developing cross-cultural competence: A guide for working with young children and their families.* (2nd ed.) Baltimore, MD: Brookes.

Hanson, M. J., Lynch, E. W. & Wayman, K. I. (1990). Honoring the cultural diversity of families when gathering data. *Topics in Early Childhood Special Education 10,* 112–131.

Hildebrand, V. (1999). *Guiding young children.* New York: Macmillan Publishing Co.

Ireton, H. R. (1995). *Teacher's observation guide.* Minneapolis, MN: Behavioral Science Systems.

Psaltis, M., & Stonehouse, A. (1990). Toddler-centered routines. In A. Stonehouse, *Trusting toddlers: Planning for one- to three-year-olds in child care centers.* St. Paul, MN: Toys 'n Things Press.

Thomas, A., & Chess, S. (1977). *Temperament and development.* New York: Brunner/Mazel.

Thomas, A., & Chess, S. (1980). *The dynamics of psychological development.* New York: Brunner/Mazel.

RESOURCES

Feldman, J. (1995). *Transition time: Let's do something different!* Beltsville, MD: Gryphon House.

Lynch, E. W., & Hanson, M. J. *Developing cross-cultural competence: A guide for working with young children and their families* (2nd ed.) Baltimore: Brookes.

Psaltis, M., & Stonehouse, A. (1990). Toddler-centered routines. In A. Stonehouse. *Trusting Toddlers: Planning for one- to three-year-olds in child care centers.* St. Paul, MN: Toys 'n Things Press.

For additional information on early education curriculum, visit our Web site at http://www.earlychilded.delmar.com

be closely examined for appropriateness to the population it is assessing and the developmental sequence of the criterion. Many programs and teachers design their own Checklists to fit the goals and objectives of the program and the population the program serves.

The developmental sequence of a Checklist makes it a forecaster or predictor of the skills or behaviors that will appear next. In this way, they help the teacher to individualize the curriculum by suggesting what experiences to provide in the next stage. For example:

    __X__ Child sits unassisted.
    __X__ Child creeps.
    _____ Child pulls to a standing position.
    _____ Child walks holding onto furniture.
    _____ Child walks alone.

By seeing that the next stage is pulling to a standing position, the teacher will provide an environment that stimulates pulling up to a standing position, such as stable furniture and interesting things to look at above the creeping level. The teacher may plan activities in which the child is lifted to a standing position and supported for short periods of time.

Each criterion should measure the presence or absence of the knowledge, behavior, or skill. Checklists sometimes contain criterion that ask the recorder to judge or summarize groups of actions. For example, a Checklist item on small muscle skills may list:

    _____ Coordinated eye/hand movements.

The teacher observed the child putting puzzle pieces into the correct holes. The meaning or summary of that skill could be inferred as "coordinated eye/hand movements." This type of criterion leaves much room for interpretation and the greater chance that it is subjective rather than factual, objective recording. Valid Checklists list specific knowledge, behaviors, and skills, in developmental sequence, that describe exactly a movement, skill, or behavior. This leaves the recorder only to answer the basic question, "Is the child doing that or not?"

EXERCISE: Mark the following Checklist items O for observed, or I for interpreted.

    _____ 1. Can sit unassisted for two minutes
    _____ 2. Uses pincer grasp to pick up small objects
    _____ 3. Enjoys pulling self up on furniture
    _____ 4. Able to do most small muscle skills
    _____ 5. Can walk six feet on a four-inch balance beam
    _____ 6. Can cut
    _____ 7. Moves gracefully
    _____ 8. Increasing strength and dexterity
    _____ 9. Gives little attention to small muscle activities
    _____ 10. Balances on one foot for five seconds

Check yourself:

1. O—The position is observable, and time is measured.
2. O—How the child picks up the object is observed.
3. I—If the child enjoys it or not is interpreted by observing behavior and forming a conclusion. If the criteria were "Pulls self up on furniture," it would be O.
4. I—What are *most small muscle tasks*? It is not clear what they are, and if they are observed or not.
5. O—The length and width of board is a precise measurement, and action is observable.
6. I—The criteria is too broad. More accurate criteria is "Can cut a straight line" or "Can cut a curved line."
7. I—The observer has much latitude in deciding if the movement is "graceful." An observable criteria is "Moves without bumping into objects in the room" or "Moves to rhythm of music."
8. I—Increasing from what? This is not measurable. An observable criteria is "Can suspend body weight on bars for 10 seconds" or "Can catch an 8-inch ball from 10 feet."
9. I—Judgment of the observer is recorded rather than observed behavior. An observable criteria is "Spends ____ minutes on small muscle activity."
10. O—Position and time measurement is specific. This is an objective criteria.

If Checklists were used for every increment, in every skill or behavior, in every developmental area, the Checklist would be unwieldy. Well-constructed Checklists are specific and limited to observable milestones. They are used with other methods of recording to document the specifics of observations.

The Checklist is reused periodically to measure the progress along the developmental continuum. If progress is not indicated by observing criterion farther along the scale, the teacher takes a closer look to be sure the data is correct. The Checklist may indicate significant lags that need to be addressed. A discussion is held with the family, possibly referring them to helping professionals for a full evaluation. The decision may be made just to wait and watch for another period to see if the skills develop.

A Checklist is an effective tool to share with the family. It shows expected developmental progression and the level attained within those expectations. It indicates the dates of the observations and how much progress has taken place over that time. It may reveal accelerated or delayed development in specific areas, showing the child's strengths or areas yet to be developed. The Checklist becomes a permanent part of the child's portfolio or file.

Checklists, their content or format, can be varied to meet the needs of the recorder or program (Figures 3–1 and 3–2). Some recorders recommend that different colored pens be used for each rating period. Many observers and Checklists are entering the technological age with computer scanning and analysis.

Limitations to Checklists

1. It does not preserve the details of a conversation where vocabulary, tone of voice, and exact words give the essence of the exchange.
2. The observer sees behaviors and skills and makes a decision as to the presence or absence of the criteria. Once the checkmark or indication is made, there is no further notation about the event. You will notice that most of the items in the Checklists in Figure 3-1 and Figure 3-2 (Gober, 2002) are directly observable. These Checklists could be modified by entering the date the behavior was observed instead of just including a checkmark in the box. Beaty, in *Observing Development of the Young Child* (2002), inserts a column next to each criterion to use for note-taking in order to make the Checklist more of an open method. Beaty refers to these notes as "evidence" because they retain details of why the observer made that judgment. Of course, it will be necessary to return to the lists periodically to record the child's progress.
3. Some Checklists are sequential (see 0–12 months in Figure 3–1) but some are not (see 6–8-year-olds in Figure 3–2). Nonsequential Checklists are not as useful for anticipating emerging development or in planning curriculum to help the child reach the next milestone.
4. The observer's decision may be influenced by personal biases. The Checklist provides no way for the reader to form an independent opinion. The reader has to trust the recorder's judgment. This shortcoming of Checklists can be overcome by having various individuals recording with the Checklist. This gives more than one person's opinion on the decision of the criteria.
5. Because of its lack of detail, the Checklist is not a method that is reliable for documentation of suspected child abuse.

EXERCISE: Look through the Checklists of Physical Development in Figure 3–1 and mark each criterion that is based directly on observations with an O, with a J if it is a judgment based on the observation, and a P if it is a perception of the child's inner feelings. Talk about your findings with a classmate.

Uses

The Checklist method of recording

- records the presence or absence of predetermined criterion.
- shows the sequence of developmental progress.
- measures progress.
- can be used as a screening for developmental lags.
- can be used as a curriculum planning tool for individualizing the curriculum.

Advantages

The Checklist is

- time- and labor-efficient.
- comprehensive. (It may cover many developmental areas in one Checklist.)
- documentation of development.
- individual documentation on each child.
- a clear illustration of the developmental continuum.

Disadvantages

The Checklist

- loses the details of events.
- may be biased by the recorder.
- depends on the criteria to be clearly observable.
- may have many items to check, making it time-consuming.

Pitfalls to Avoid

Checklists seem like they can be done from memory but memories are inaccurate and can be biased. The recordings should be from direct observation.

Checklists can be unwieldy if the recorder is trying to do too much at one time. To actually observe and record on a Checklist, it helps to either select one child to observe over a period of a day in all developmental areas, or one developmental area and observe all children in that area.

Be sure that the Checklist is broad enough to include skills and behavioral milestones at prior levels as well as future ones. Children's development is uneven and a child may be functioning at a young level in one area and an advanced level in another. The unchecked criteria give guidance about curriculum planning.

Many Checklists are covered by copyright. Either purchase the rating sheets or receive permission to copy them. It's the honest thing to do.

0–12 Months

	Observed	Not Observed
Physical Growth/Motor Development		
Looks around (2 months)	☐	☐
Laughs aloud (3–5 months)	☐	☐
Controls head movements (about 4 months)	☐	☐
Notices hands/feet and plays with them (3–5 months)	☐	☐
Rolls over (4–6 months)	☐	☐
Sits up without support (6–8 months)	☐	☐
Holds bottle (6–8 months)	☐	☐
Crawls (6–8 months)	☐	☐
Walks with support	☐	☐
Imitates adults' facial gestures	☐	☐
Reaches, grasps	☐	☐
Puts objects in mouth	☐	☐
Picks things up with thumb and finger	☐	☐
Picks up toys that are dropped	☐	☐
Teeth appear (6–12 months)	☐	☐

12–24 Months

	Observed	Not Observed
Physical Growth/Motor Development		
Teething continues	☐	☐
Crawls well, stands alone well	☐	☐
Walks without help	☐	☐
Pushes, pulls toys	☐	☐
Sits in chair	☐	☐
Moves to music	☐	☐
Throws, kicks a ball	☐	☐
Crawls down stairs backward	☐	☐
Stacks blocks	☐	☐
Uses a spoon, chews food	☐	☐
Turns book pages	☐	☐
Jumps up and down	☐	☐
Holds glass	☐	☐
Opens doors and cabinets	☐	☐
Scribbles, paints with whole arm	☐	☐
Starts elimination control	☐	☐

24–36 Months

	Observed	Not Observed
Physical Growth/Motor Development		
Uses a spoon without spilling	☐	☐
Opens doors	☐	☐
Washes and dries hands	☐	☐
Begins to cut with scissors	☐	☐
Uses one hand consistently	☐	☐
Runs forward, jumps in place, climbs	☐	☐
Stands on one foot	☐	☐
Walks on tiptoes	☐	☐
Kicks ball forward	☐	☐
Rides a tricycle	☐	☐
Marches to music	☐	☐

Figure 3–1 Developmental Checklist, 0–36 Months. (Courtesy of Gober, S. Y. 2002. *Six Simple Ways to Assess Young Children*. Clifton Park, NY: Thomson Delmar Learning.)

3-Year Olds		
	Observed	**Not Observed**
Physical Growth/Motor Development		
Copies circles	☐	☐
Manipulates clay, puzzles, scissors	☐	☐
Builds	☐	☐
Runs around obstacles	☐	☐
Walks on a line	☐	☐
Hops/balances on one foot	☐	☐
Steers and pedals tricycle	☐	☐
Throws ball overhand	☐	☐
Jumps with two feet	☐	☐
Begins to use zippers, buttons to dress	☐	☐
4-Year-Olds		
Physical Growth/Motor Development		
Draws, paints, uses scissors	☐	☐
Dresses and undresses without assistance	☐	☐
Walks stairs alone, alternating feet	☐	☐
Self-reliant in bathroom	☐	☐
Kicks, throws, bounces, catches a ball	☐	☐
Runs, hops, skips, jumps, gallops	☐	☐
Developing eye–hand coordination	☐	☐
5-Year-Olds		
Physical Growth/Motor Development		
Takes care of personal needs (ties shoes, buttons, zips, etc.)	☐	☐
Coordinates body parts (biking, swimming, etc.)	☐	☐
Cuts accurately	☐	☐
Uses pencil and scissors correctly	☐	☐
Basic grasp of right and left, but confuses them	☐	☐
Movements appear smooth	☐	☐
Walks backward	☐	☐
Skips	☐	☐
Right or left handedness is established	☐	☐
Uses glue correctly and easily	☐	☐
6–8-Year-Olds		
Physical Growth/Motor Development		
Rate of growth slows, but growth spurts occur	☐	☐
Enjoys team sports	☐	☐
Repeats skill for mastery (bike riding, skating, swimming, etc.)	☐	☐
Forms letters and numbers well	☐	☐
Loss of teeth	☐	☐
Body develops more proportionately	☐	☐
Visual difficulties may surface	☐	☐
Shows coordination of large and small motor skills	☐	☐
Draws a person with clothes and body parts	☐	☐

Figure 3–2 Developmental Checklist, 3- to 8-Year-Olds. (Courtesy of Gober, S. Y. 2002. *Six Simple Ways to Assess Young Children.* Clifton Park, NY: Thomson Delmar Learning.)

Using Technology

A Checklist can easily be loaded on a personal digital assistant or a small laptop using Documents to Go®. In the classroom, all you have to do is open the document, check what the child has attained, and save the document with the child's name. It can later be downloaded into the child's electronic portfolio.

How to Find the Time

Checklists are not time-consuming if you select only a portion of the Checklist and observe all the children for the chosen developmental area. On another day, select a different developmental area. This procedure will help you to focus your attention on one type of behavior and you can observe each of the children in that particular way.

What to Do with It

Programs usually purchase or develop a Checklist to match program goals and the age range of the children in the program or class. An individual Checklist is kept in each child's portfolio or file. Periodically, the recorder reexamines each developmental area. It is objective only as long as the Checklist closely describes exact observable behavior rather than vague generalizations that may be interpreted many ways.

Families have access to this portfolio and the Checklist. It is a good tool to show families the developmental sequence and the documentation of the accomplishments of their child. Focusing on the accomplishments, rather than the areas yet to be attained, is a positive way of evaluating a child's development.

Some Examples of Checklists

Ages and Stages Questionnaires (ASQ)™, 2nd edition, is by D. Bricker and J. Squires (1999). It is an age-related series of developmental screening questions answered by parents or primary caregivers and is designed to identify the few infants and young children who require more extensive evaluation.

The *Brigance Diagnostic Inventory of Early Development,* 2nd edition, is by A. H. Brigance (Curriculum Associates, Inc., 1999). It is a comprehensive Checklist to assess development and diagnose developmental delay.

The *Child Development Inventory (CDI)* is by H. Ireton (Behavior Science Systems, 1992). It is a Parent Checklist for ages six months to six years to measure development and identify potential problems for further assessment.

The *Child Observation Record (COR)* is by High/Scope Press (1992). It is an ascending Checklist for cognitive, movement, and social-emotional development.

The *Denver Developmental Screening Test II (DDST-II)* is by W. Frankenburg, et al. (Denver Developmental Materials, Inc., 1990). It is a range of criterion over four domains: social-emotional, fine motor, gross motor, and language. Can be used for screening at-risk children.

Developmental Profiles: Pre-birth Through Twelve, 4th edition, is by K. E. Allen and L. Marotz (Delmar, 2003). One-page-for-one-year developmental Checklists give the milestones for that year. The text provides more specific information, learning activities, and developmental alerts.

Observing Development of the Young Child, 5th edition, is by J. Beaty (Macmillan Publishing Company, 2002). It is a Checklist with an evidence column for three- to six-year-olds with ascending criteria in all developmental areas. Child development and curriculum planning resources.

The *Peabody Developmental Motor Scales, 2nd edition,* is by M. R. Folio and R. R. Fewell (2000). It is an assessment of gross and fine motor skills birth through five years.

The *Work Sampling System* is by S. Meisels, et al. (Rebus Planning Associates, 1994). It has Checklist components in personal and social development, language and literacy, mathematical and scientific thinking, social studies, the arts, and physical development. It assesses children's skills, knowledge, behavior, and accomplishments.

R E V I E W

Checklist: Listing of related criteria against which skills, knowledge, or behavior is measured indicating yes or no, present or not present. Can indicate milestones attained and areas yet to be developed.

Types of Information to Record Using Checklists:

self-care skills

physical development—large muscle/small muscle skills

stages of social development

stages of emotional development

stages of language development

stages of cognitive development

specific criteria such as "knows colors, shapes, recognizes numbers"

stages of literacy development

stages of creative development

stages of sociodramatic play

aspects of self-concept

Your Frame of Reference

Everyone looks at the world through a unique **frame of reference.** That frame of reference can be compared to a picture frame to help understand the concept (Figure 3–3).

A frame is the boundary or outer limits around a picture. The frame around the perimeter of a piece of glass sets the boundaries all around and limits vision beyond. Each person's understanding or "vision" is limited by boundaries different from every other person. The frame of reference is formed from past experiences but is very influential in viewing the present and the future. For the teacher, the frame of reference must be considered when observing children because it determines how the child is viewed. Some experiences that form the frame of reference follow.

Childhood. Each person's childhood is unique, even for children born in the same family, even for twins. Birth order, health, dynamics of personality in interactions with family members, inborn characteristics, and family environment all have an effect on childhood. When observing a child, adults subconsciously reflect on their own childhoods. These are factors in limiting how the adult sees the child. They unconsciously ask themselves, "How is this child like me or different from me as a child? What advantages or disadvantages does this child have that might influence the child in a different way from my own childhood? Can I even relate to the situation of this child because of the kind of childhood I have had?"

Education and Training. The educational level and philosophies learned affect the teacher's perceptions and judgments of the child being viewed. From a psychological background, the viewer may look for the meaning behind the behavior. From a psychosocial background, the viewer may look for conflict between biological and social demands at each maturational stage. From a behaviorist background, the viewer might look for the stimulus and responses reinforced in the behavior.

Past Experiences with Children. Many people working with children have a long history. They may be parents and grandparents or started out their career caring for younger siblings, babysitting as a teenager, and now caring for extended family members. The past is the keyhole through which the present is viewed. This observed behavior may trigger memories and situations from the past and send up a warning signal, while other observers ignore the same action or regard it as insignificant. What is seen is always reflected back to what has been experienced in the past. Those new to the profession with little experience are going to see behaviors and incidents differently from those with much experience.

Own Learning Styles. With the advent of more knowledge of individual learning styles, it becomes clearer that a teacher's learning style is as important as the student's. Depending on the acute sensory reception, the observer will absorb information in different ways:

Auditory learner—from language and sounds the child makes

Figure 3–3 Frame of Reference

Own Learning Styles

Education and Training

Past Experiences with Children

Childhood

Smudges:
Biases
Personal factors

(continued)

Your Frame of Reference (continued)

Visual learner—from actions, scenes, pictures of the child's behavior
Tactile learner—from touching the child

Values. Society has influenced each person differently in the formation of values and viewpoints. The societal influences of socioeconomic level, race, ethnicity, and gender enter into the observation framework. There is little control over the formation until an awareness is raised.

Smudges on the Glass

The frame of reference is the perimeter but the viewing is done through the glass. There may be smudges on the glass. Those smudges are biases that keep the observer from seeing the child objectively.

Biases For or Against the Child. Individual bias and prejudice are human factors that may interfere with a clear view of the child. Those biases may be positive, causing a child's needs to be overlooked because of personal feelings that get in the way. Strengths of the child may be overlooked because of a prejudice or bias that will negatively affect objective observation. Some might be:

Sex—may prefer boys or girls better
Hair color—may love or hate redheads
Racial or ethnic—stereotypic beliefs
Economic or social status—rich or poor may interfere with how the child is perceived
Personality clashes—may love or hate children who are whiny, mischievous, active, sassy, bold, shy
Prior contact with the family—older child was in the class
Physical attributes—beauty, handicaps, weight
Hearsay—prior teachers influence opinion

Personal Factors that Affect Observation. Adults may have their own situations that have nothing to do with the child but may affect the observer enough to interfere with objective recording:

Health—headache, awaiting test results, impending surgery, pregnancy, or premenstrual syndrome
Stress—financial, personal, or workplace tension
Outside pressure—gathering evidence to document a decision or a referral

The observer's consciousness is raised on these issues through reflection. By selecting objective observation methods, communicating and sharing observations and inferences with coworkers and parents, these biases can be minimized.

All of these—the framework, the biases, and the daily situation—influence observation. Because observation is subjective, many criticize it as untrustworthy for evaluation. Many prefer standardized tests as more objective measuring tools. Testing will be discussed in a later section. These warnings of influences on observations are discussed here as a prelude to offer evidence for the necessity of carefully choosing recording methods. When limitations are recognized, efforts can be made to overcome the possible negative influences. "Forewarned is forearmed" as the saying goes. "We do, because we know." Some recording methods can be biased. Some days might not be good ones to gather information and make decisions. The professional acts ethically.

LOOKING AT GROWTH AND DEVELOPMENT

EXERCISE: Using a separate sheet of paper, list five phrases to describe your body.

Read the chapter, then return to your descriptions and mark them *G* for growth areas and *D* for development areas.

Bodies change. They grow and develop. What is the difference? **Growth** refers to changes in size, *quantitative* change, those changes that can be measured in increasing numbers such as height, weight, head circumference, and teeth.

- Most infants range in length from 18 to 21 inches at birth and are expected to grow longer and taller.
- By 36 months, the toddler has molars and a total of 20 "baby" teeth and is expected to grow more.
- The average five-year-old weighs 38 to 45 pounds and is expected to increase in weight as she grows older.

There are norms, or averages, established by statistical analysis of large groups of people. These are the established ranges for average growth at specific ages (Figure 3–4). Tables like these can alert observers to significant variations that warrant further investigation for the cause.

Other changes can be measured in numbers that are not physical. Vocabulary also "grows" because it can be measured in numbers. The toddler has a vocabulary of 50 to 300 words. The attention span is growing. It can be measured in minutes (sometimes seconds) and is expected to increase as the child matures.

Development is also change, but *qualitative change*, increasingly better, more complex, and more coordinated. Development, like growth, occurs in sequential, predictable stages, yet is different for every individual based on several factors. Physical development, both large and small muscle coordination begins with reflex actions to rudimentary then fundamental movement quality during the preschool years. It forms the basis for refinements that are used in all active sports.

EXERCISE: List all the factors you can think of that affect physical development.

Now read on and see how many factors correlate to your list.

Many factors affect growth and development.

- Genetics determines thousands of characteristics of growth and development, such as body size, sex, and coloring.

- Prenatal care, including the mother's nutrition and physical condition, and even age, contribute to prebirth growth and development.
- Health factors, such as preventive care, diseases, illnesses, and accidents in childhood, can affect both the growth and development of the body.
- Environmental factors, such as nutrition, quality of air, and geographic location, affect physical growth and development.
- Age or maturation is a determining factor in the changing body's size and development.
- Social factors, such as opportunities, experiences, and role models, affect development.
- Economic level has an effect on both physical growth and development through nutrition, experiences, and opportunities.

Other areas of development have a two-way influence.

- Cognitive development affects physical development. As the child's thinking changes to higher levels, her movements change. She can do a more complex puzzle, not just because of physical dexterity but ability to visualize pieces of the whole. It is also through physically manipulating materials that the child's cognitive structures build, experiencing soft and hard, hot and cold.
- Language and physical development are interdependent. As the child physically develops, he also learns new vocabulary words for the movements (jump, skip, pirouette). By following verbal directions, processing language, he learns how to perform physical tasks. "Hold the bat up straighter, away from your body."
- Social interactions with other people encourage physical development. By imitating the actions of others, children learn to perform tasks, such as painting, swinging, and riding a bike. As they perform these actions, they interact with other people and their physical development is used to play and work cooperatively.
- Emotional deprivation has been known to stunt physical growth. Emotional development is affected by body growth. Abnormal growth and physical disabilities can affect self-esteem. It influences development because lack of confidence can make someone awkward.

When physical growth or development is adversely affected, whatever the cause, modifications can be made to the environment. This minimizes the social-emotional effects and helps compensate for or improve the skill. This can be accomplished through observation, evaluation, and individualized curriculum planning.

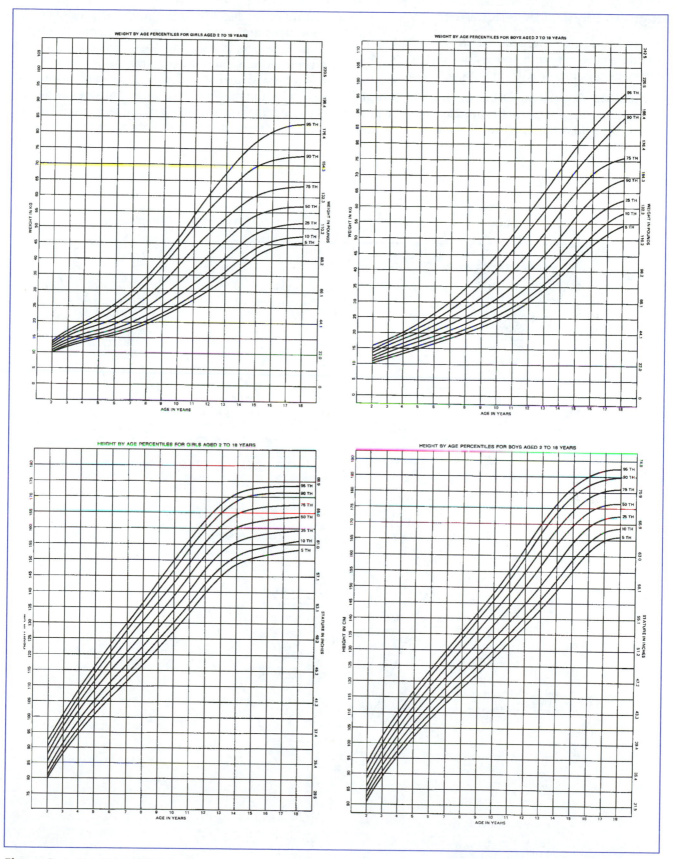

Figure 3–4 Height and Weight Charts

Stages of Physical Development

The common characteristics of development: predictable sequences with individual differences are very evident in physical development (Figure 3–5).

Predictable Sequence. Development and coordination (voluntary control of the muscles) occur in predictable directions (Figure 3–6). The infant first gains control of the head by using neck muscles, then the shoulders and torso. When development reaches the thighs and calves and toes, real crawling and creeping are accomplished. This head-to-toe direction of development is described as **cephalocaudal**. Control of the shoulders and arms comes before hands, then fingers, from the center of the body outward described as **proximodistal,** or near to far (Figure 3–7).

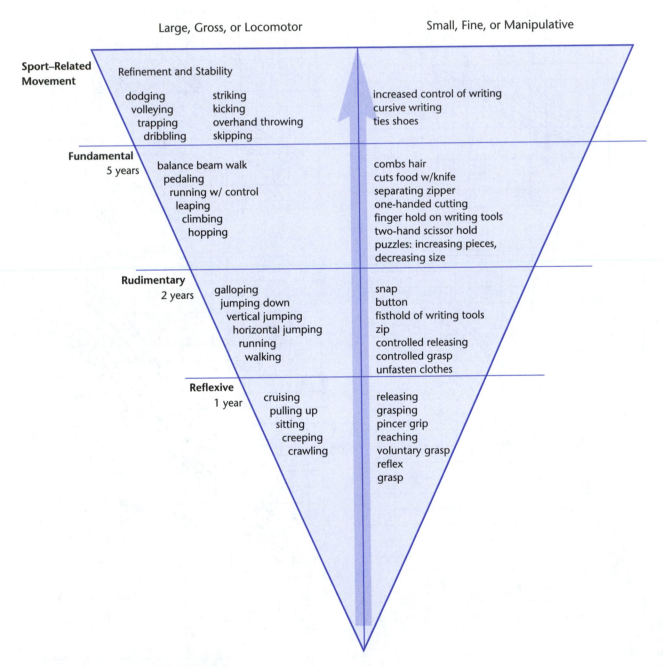

Figure 3–5 Muscle Control and Skill Development

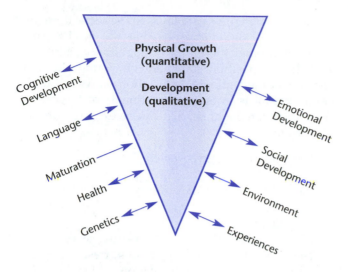

Figure 3–6 Interrelated Factors in Physical Growth and Development

Gaining Control of Muscles in a
Downward and Outward Sequence

Figure 3–7 Cephalocaudal and Proximodistal Muscle Control Development

Individual Timetable. Some infants purposefully pick up their head and look for the source of a voice or sound by one month. Some do this earlier than others. Some children are walking by 10 months and others not until 16 months. A baby will not walk until she *can*. An adult cannot make a baby walk before the muscles are strong and coordinated enough to accomplish the task.

Readiness. Physical development vividly illustrates the predictable, sequential, individual aspects of development. In other areas of development, such as emotional and cognitive development, the stages are not as easily observed. This visual reminder is an important concept to apply to curriculum planning in all areas. The child's body and mind must be ready before she can accomplish the skill. All the other steps have come before it to lead the way, serving as a benchmark of readiness for the next step.

By the age of one and a half, a child has accomplished the basic physical skills of mobility (**large muscle** or gross motor) and manipulation (**small muscle** or fine motor). The next 48 months will see vast increases in coordination and integration of all body structures. By the time children are five, they have acquired body control. The skills of walking, running, climbing, balancing, pushing, pulling, lifting, carrying, throwing, catching, and striking prepare them for life functions and all the sports and recreation skills.

Why Physical Development Is Important

The principle that developmental areas are interrelated is very plainly seen in physical development.

Early physical development and fitness affects lifelong health in areas such as posture, balance, muscular strength, cardiovascular endurance, and body leanness. Declining fitness and increasing obesity are national concerns.

Physical Development and Health. Studies have shown that even among children aged three to four years, those who were less active tended to remain less active than most of their peers after age three years so it seems that early experiences have lifelong effects (Pate, Baranowski, Dowda, & Trost, 1996). The alarming increase in rates of heart disease, diabetes, and high blood pressure are connected to physical activity. In 2000, the United States Department of Health and Human Services launched Healthy People 2010, a campaign to advocate and plan for a more active population. It is based on studies of obesity and has concrete plans for changing behavior and measuring success [http://www.surgeongeneral.gov/]. It is important for families and educators to become positive role models and to be actively involved in physical activity on a regular basis.

There are many theories about the factors leading to this physical decline. One study found that one-quarter of U.S. children spend four hours or more watching television each day (Anderson, 1998). Television, video watching and game playing, and computers have been attributed as a major contribution to obesity. Because of children's inactivity and advertisements for high-calorie, fat-laden foods, television is blamed (Bar-Or, 2000). Changes in family structures with both parents working outside the home turning child-rearing over to others, or to the children themselves, have been blamed for children not playing actively. Violence in the neighborhood has kept some children from playgrounds or playing outside in the street or yard. Schools have been reducing the emphasis on physical education as mandates for academic areas and budgetary woes increase.

Family physicians urge adults to

- moderate the amount of time children spend in front of television, computers, and video terminals.
- encourage spontaneous physical activity during recess and physical education classes.
- provide safe opportunities for play. (Stephens, 2002)

Physical Development and Cognition. While the importance of early physical activity to life-long fitness is obvious, researchers are finding its importance to cognitive and emotional development. Neuroscientists studying the brain with Positron Emission Tomography or PET scans observe and measure brain activity levels. Physical movement that involves both hemispheres of the brain like creeping and crawling heighten cognitive functioning (Hannaford, 1995). As the infant's brain is developing, sensory systems such as vision, hearing, taste, smell, touch, balance, and body awareness are functioning at their most primary stage. The body's central nervous system is beginning to integrate these systems. As the infant continues to grow and develop this integration comes under the control of the infant and responses to senses become automatic and unconscious. This sensory integration allows the brain to then process more complex information. When this integration is interrupted for some reason, it may result in the child acting disorganized, confused, and frustrated, and may ultimately interfere with learning (Bakley, 2001). Early perceptual sensory motor experiences can increase brain functioning and lead to cognitive gains. There is no doubt that exercise as well as good nutrition are necessary for learning and growing.

Even though physical play is in the social domain, Bjorklund (1998) reminds us that the mechanisms involved expand the realm of cognitive benefits as well. In the position statement on young children and recess, the National Association on Early Childhood Specialists in State Departments of Education (1997) lists content areas that can be explored on the playground.

Natural elements: experiencing wind, dirt, water, seasons

Physics: using a see-saw, merry-go-round, swings

Architecture and design: building with natural materials

Math and numbers: counting, keeping score

Language development: explaining, describing, articulating, seeking information, and making use of oral language/vocabulary/word power

Therefore, they recommend all early childhood and elementary schools include periods within the instructional day for free and active outdoor play.

Hannaford, in *Smart Moves: Why Learning Is Not All in Your Head* (1995), suggests children create their own toys, be encouraged to make up imaginative stories, participate in rational dialogue by the age of four years, honor care of people, pets, and objects, be encouraged to delay gratification, be discouraged to watch TV and play video games, and above all, take part in lots of body movement opportunities for full limbic system development. It is vital to brain development. The interplay of mind and body is not surprising but is a reemphasis of the importance of physical activity to overall success in learning and living.

Physical Development and Social-Emotional Development. Researchers also point out the social and emotional effects of large muscle skills are children's views of themselves and their perceptions of how others feel about them (Gallahue, 2003; Purkey, 1996; Coakley, 2001). Success-oriented physical education not only meets the child's need for motor skill development but the social-emotional development qualities of competence, belonging, and self-worth (Weiller & Richardson, 1993).

Obesity can cause children (especially girls) to be ridiculed and rejected, which may cause low self-esteem, and lead to dieting and food-related problems like bulimia and anorexia (Lowey, 1998).

Cortisol, the hormone released during stress into saliva, undermines neurological development and can affect cognitive, motor, and social development. Pica (2000) makes the case for the importance of physical development beyond fitness, emphasizing the relationship to social-emotional, creative, and cognitive development. She relates movement to all curriculum areas.

Physical Development and Play. As infants become more social, they interact with objects and other people in play. At first play is a sensory manipulation. The infant reaches out and takes hold of a rattle or a toy, or grabs his father's nose. As the child's muscles eventually become coordinated through experience, he will discover that he can cause the toy to make a sound, or can make someone smile. In an ever-increasing spiral of complex actions and reactions, the child's play repertoire expands. The child learns that play is pleasurable, self-motivating, not expected to produce a specific outcome, and requires the integration of several different skills to continue. This play is inborn in animals and humans. Playing appears to be linked to social adjustment and improved physical condition (Power, 2000).

As children mature, their physical ability to run, throw, catch, climb, and kick are often channeled into more formal kinds of play, such as sports games with rules. Success in sports depends not only on physical ability but emotional stability, self-control, and social competence. Games for young children should be those in which all children can find success, so there should be no competition. Cooperative games, *not* those with one winner and the rest losers, can help young children develop team spirit, and seek out game-playing for its intrinsic rewards. In addition, losing produces negative feelings which can affect emotional development (low self-esteem) and social development (promoting self over others.)

Young children should be given every possible opportunity to build their physical skills. The opposite actually happens in competitive games—those who need the most practice, get the least amount of time to play. Children cannot develop their physical skills if they are on the sidelines.

Free play in a well-equipped area is important. Programs should also provide an appropriate movement curriculum to develop physical fitness and perceptual motor activities (Poest, Williams, Witt, & Atwood, 1990). Even for children with severe disabilities, formal psychomotor programs were not as effective as training specific to diagnosis of individual needs. These were most effective when planned individually for children, conducted by the child's teacher and in close communication with families (Frost, 1992). That is exactly a description of observation, assessment, and individualized curriculum planning with family involvement. That is appropri-

ate and effective for all children. Scofield (1987) in *School Age NOTES* points out the uses and abuses of free play (Figure 3–8).

The Role of Observation in Physical Development

EXERCISE: Watch two people walk across the room. Write a description of how each one walks. What contributed to the differences?

Observation and Recording for Assessment. Watching children move gives the observer information, leading knowledge, and theories about the contributing factors:

> *height*—parents' height
> *weight*—nutrition, metabolism, television habits, family's physical fitness
> *movement*—age, experiences, inherited capabilities, self-esteem, physical energy level, possible disabilities

Written observations provide documentation for comparisons over time to show progress. From observations, assessments may be made as to the child's growth and development. Further evaluations may

---

USES OF FREE PLAY

- Free play increases creativity.
- Children learn to set own limits, accept responsibility for operating within those limits, and develop a sense of independence and competency.
- It provides time for one-to-one relationship building of staff to children.
- It provides time for observation of particular children or groups of children and their interests and interactions.

ABUSES OF FREE PLAY

- Not enough activities or raw materials are provided.
- Caregivers begin to see it as a "break" for themselves, then become resentful when children want their attention while they are gossiping or reading the paper.

Figure 3–8 Uses of Free Play. (Courtesy of Scofield, R. T. *School Age NOTES*, 1987. Nashville, TN. Reprinted with permission.)

be recommended if assessments indicate results fall below the normal range.

Observation for Safety Maintenance. It is the adult's responsibility to prepare a safe environment for children.

EXERCISE: Using a separate sheet of paper, list five safety features you would plan if you were designing a room for young children.

Accidents occur frequently in the early years because of increased mobility, lack of coordination, inability to anticipate and avoid dangerous actions, or lack of supervision. The newly mobile infant requires crawling surfaces that are sanitary and safe from ingestible objects. Beds and changing tables must have high sides, safety straps, and adult supervision. For the infant and toddler, surrounding equipment must be a stable base as the standing infant pulls himself up. He uses furniture for handles and stabilizers as he begins to walk around. Children are built to climb, motivated by curiosity and newfound physical skills. Readdick (1998) has outlined the developmental stages of climbing, beginning with anticipatory, clambering, initial, transitional, elementary, and mature, each with increasing coordination of arms, body, and legs to ascend and descend. When climbing is seen as a form of active learning, physical coordination, and source of self-esteem, then modifications to the environment are made to provide for safe climbing. Climbing on objects not meant to be climbed can be dangerous, so the furniture must be secured. Other climbing experiences should be provided, within a manageable range of the child's climbing ability. A soft mat is placed underneath to cushion inevitable falls. All stairways and doorways must be blocked from the little cruiser.

Frost (1992) has devised a Playground Maintenance Checklist for Ages 3 to 8 that features criteria on surfaces, equipment, natural aspects, security, storage, safety, and educational usefulness (Figure 3–9).

EXERCISE: Use the Playground Maintenance Checklist to practice Checklist recording and review the criteria for safe environments.

Preschoolers have greater mobility and coordination, increasing the risk of accidents. The independent two-, three-, and four-year-olds have the urge to get things for themselves. Leaving an area, climbing into a cupboard or onto shelves, or attempting tasks beyond their capability and judgment present dangers. Preschoolers need an environment with

Date Detected	Date Repaired	
		• Hard surfaces under and around equipment in fall zones
		• Resilient surface material pitted or scattered
		• Insufficient space between equipment
		• Equipment not sized for age of children
		• Entrapment areas
		• Excessive or unprotected heights
		• Shearing and crushing mechanisms
		• Cracking, bending, warping, rusting, breaking, or missing components
		• Pinching actions, open S hooks, deformed rings, links, etc.
		• Loose or uncapped bolts, nuts, etc.
		• Worn bearings or axles
		• Worn swing hangers (swivels) or chains
		• Metal slides in direct path of sun
		• Slide beds loose, metal edges accessible to fingers
		• Heavy swing seats or seats with protruding elements
		• Exposed or damaged concrete footings
		• Equipment improperly anchored
		• Sharp edges and points
		• Exposed or projecting elements, caps missing
		• Railings of insufficient height
		• Railings invite climbing (horizontal instead of vertical)
		• Exposed metal in tires or swing seats
		• Suspended elements (e.g., ropes, cables) in movement areas
		• Deteriorated (splintered, cracked, rotting) wood
		• Broken or missing railings, steps, swing seats, rungs, deck components, etc.
		• Slippery footing areas on decks, steps, walkways
		• Trash (broken glass, foreign objects, etc.) in area
		• Vandalism (fire damage, broken or missing parts)
		• Obstacles (rocks, roots, trash, badly placed equipment) in movement area
		• Poor drainage (standing water)
		• Accessible electrical apparatus (air conditioners, switch boxes) climbable poles, guy wires, ladders accessing electrical lines
		• Fence not installed or in need of repair, gates not securable (younger children), extra protection for pools
		• Signs illegible and in poor repair
		• Moving parts not lubricated
		• Toxic materials
		• Foreign materials or equipment parts in fall zone

Figure 3–9 Maintenance Checklist. (Courtesy of Frost, J. L., 1992, pp. 348, 349. *Play and Playscapes*. Clifton Park, NY: Thomson Delmar Learning. Reprinted with permission.)

interesting things to do, opportunities to help themselves in learning centers, and adequate supervision for safety and facilitating play. Then the potential for accidents can be reduced.

Assessing Muscle Development through the Environment. It is the teacher's role and responsibility to provide a safe environment to meet the developmental needs of the children. Usually the classroom space is predetermined so the teacher makes decisions of furnishings and room arrangement based on teaching philosophies and priorities for space.

Indoor Play. Lack of space is the reason given by many teachers for not including classroom space for a large muscle area. A climber, space to jump, tumble, and run require open, nonfurnished areas. A clear floor space of 35 square feet per child is the minimum needed for toddlers and preschoolers. Less than 25 square feet of usable space reduces gross motor activity and group play and may increase aggression.

Designer of innovative developmental environmental facilities for children, Ania Rui Olds (1994), bases designs on three essentials:

1. extensive experiences in the natural world and the inclusion of natural elements indoors
2. identifiable places for gross motor play inside
3. use of lofts and varied types of equipment to encourage children's use of their bodies continuously (p. 34)

In the physical environment, the adult assures safety, provides opportunities, and gives support. The developing skill determines the environment (Figure 3–10) that includes all the skill opportunities that have already been attained so they can be refined and practiced. New experiences are added to the old.

Traffic, school, and work schedules, less play space, even neighborhood dangers contribute to what Rivkin (1995) calls "vanishing habitats for play." The benefits of outdoor play to physical development as well as sensory learning, appreciation for nature, and space for expending energy are obvious but families and teachers seem to give it less and less attention.

Outdoor Play. The outdoor environment should also be considered to maximize development in all areas.

EXERCISE: If you were designing a playground for infants, what kinds of equipment and surfaces would it have?

Crawlers and walkers need materials that are safe and soft for first crawling and walking efforts indoors and out. Carriage and stroller paths past

SKILL	ENVIRONMENT
Infants	
Rhythmic movement	Rocking chair, music
Crawling	Clean, cushioned surfaces to crawl on, under, through
Pulling up/standing	Stable furniture to hold
Walking, holding on (cruising)	Furnishings placed close together
Walking alone	Smooth, nonslip carpeted surface
Climbing	Low, padded platforms with padded surface beneath
Pushing, pulling, and lifting	Movable materials, tubs, wheeled toys
Toddlers: Above, plus	
Climbing	More challenging apparatus, three or four stairs with railing
Scooting	Wheeled toys
Running	Clear, carpeted area for running
Jumping	Sturdy, low platforms
Pushing, pulling, and lifting	Heavier, movable equipment
Throwing	Large, lightweight balls
Preschoolers: Above, plus	
Balancing	Climbing and balance apparatus
Pedalling	Tricycles, scooters
Hopping	Floor games and patterns
Throwing and catching	Balls and beanbags, targets
Striking	Bats, rackets, foam balls, wiffle balls suspended from ceiling
Schoolagers: Above, plus	
Dribbling and shooting	Basketballs, baskets, and court
Running races	Team games
Gymnastics	Padded surface, horse, and parallel bars
Dancing	Rhythmic group dancing

Figure 3–10 Developing skills determine the environment.

interesting things to look at begin the infant's outdoor experience. Paths later can be used for toddling, walking, and wheeled toys. Gentle inclines provide climbing and rolling down fun. A variety of natural materials such as grass, sand, wood, and smooth rocks provide sensory experiences in texture. Wind chimes, birdfeeders, and portable tape players provide hearing experiences. The area is enriched with a variety of toys for manipulation, pretend play, and construction (Figure 3–11).

Preschoolers need the same type of equipment and surfaces as the younger children but more challenging and separate. They need climbing apparatus and balancing equipment. They need steep hills to climb and roll down and movable construction materials. Riding toys, swings, and sports equipment such as balls, bats, nets, and ropes also facilitate physical development.

Outdoor play can be enhanced by nonpermanent, moveable equipment. Griffin and Rinn (1998) give many examples using such materials as used tires, large boxes, plastic trash barrels, and carpet remnants. The goals of an obstacle course are to

- develop a means for children to understand spatial awareness in connection with their own bodies.
- offer adventure.
- enhance gross motor skills and cooperative skills.
- provide opportunities for experimentation and exploration.
- offer creative and dramatic-play outlets.
- enhance positive self-esteem.
- provide challenge. (p. 18)

Sutterby and Frost (2002), playground researchers, recommend

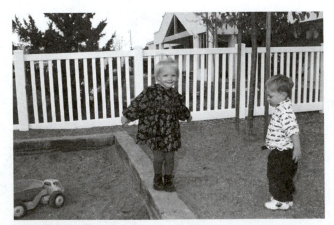

Figure 3–11 Even the littlest ones need an enriched outdoor environment full of sights, sounds, and a variety of textures.

- playgrounds that include gardening and nature areas.
- Fitness homework assignments that involve the family.
- outdoor cooking activities linked to culture.
- dress code for teachers that allows for active participation with children.
- walking to and from school where possible.

In elementary school, recess is usually the one free-play time of the day when children can make choices. As children's opportunities for outdoor play are reduced by busy lives, neighborhood risks, and the culture of inactivity, the need for recess is greater. However, in the climate of pressure for academic performance, recess is sometimes sacrificed for remedial work or disciplinary measures. It is often the time when children are supervised by aides rather than their teachers. If teachers were on the playground, a great deal could be learned about children's physical and social behavior (O'Brien, 2003).

Physically challenged children can use the paths for wheelchairs and raised water and sand play areas for accessibility. Children with visual impairments are provided tactile and auditory stimulation materials. A real garden provides gross motor exercise as it is dug, raked, and weeded; it also encourages science, language, and sensory pleasure.

"Making playgrounds fit for children and children fit on playgrounds is essential for increasing the fitness and improving the health of today's children and tomorrow's adults" (Sutterby & Frost, 2002).

Cognitive and emotional development can have an effect on physical development. Through physical development and achievement, children's self-esteem and confidence are enhanced. Encouraging a healthy and fit lifestyle should begin early in life. The National Association for Sport and Physical Education (NASPE, 1995) has defined standards with benchmarks and assessment examples for young children's physical education. They include motor skills, physical fitness, social behavior in physical activity settings, understanding and respect for differences among people, and physical activity for enjoyment, challenge, self-expression, and social interaction. In order for young children to achieve these standards, the teacher must incorporate a regular, purposeful, physical activity into the curriculum.

Observation for Curriculum Planning. For infants, body awareness, learning names for the parts of the body, and naming parts as they are washed and moved are the beginnings of large muscle curriculum. Using the Developmental Assessment Checklist, the adult can see what the child has accomplished and continue to give her practice to refine that skill. If she can roll over, then she is frequently placed on the floor and coaxed, called, lured by a toy, or gently rocked to practice the rolling. She will be sitting up soon, so she can be propped in a sitting position several times a day for short periods to give her a new view. Moving to a beat is an important curriculum goal, so music, rhythm instruments, singing, and dancing are planned daily.

Older infants and toddlers begin the quest to explore beyond their body. Toys and activities to manipulate and move are a necessary part of the curriculum. Activities are planned for interaction with adults and materials chosen to keep interest. The adult models and introduces new ways of playing.

Locomotor movement, such as creeping and crawling, transfers weight from one side of the body to the other. This is a necessary skill for walking because all the more complex skills build on that one. To stimulate creeping and crawling, interesting objects and pictures are placed at floor level, not too far away to be frustrating, but alluring enough to produce forward motion. Crawlers want interesting things to crawl on, such as unbreakable mirrors or pictures under sheets of plexiglass on the floor. A texture maze on the floor and up the first two feet of the wall are stimulating environments planned for infant and toddler motor development. Feeling the steady beat, Weikart (2000) believes, is a primary ability to basic motor skill development so those games of "Patty Cake" and baby rumbas are planned curriculum activities. Reading poetry, repeating fingerplays, and reading stories with repetitive lines provide verbal experiences with rhythm.

For preschoolers, an old but useful book of activities for four- to eight-year-olds, *Until the Whistle Blows* (Hall & Sweeny, 1976), suggests large muscle curriculum consists of activities that address the following components of fitness:

- *strength*—working together to lift and move heavy objects
- *coordination*—obstacle courses that involve multiple movements such as climbing, crawling, and balance
- *flexibility*—bending, stretching, and dramatic movement
- *stamina*—increasing number of repetitive movements
- *speed*—moving quickly, stopping accurately
- *equilibrium*—balance beam, walking backward
- *power*—kicking balls, batting balloons
- *cardiovascular recovery*—cool down to normal heartbeat through relaxation techniques (p. 10)

Planned activities can be documented using different methods to indicate the child's reaction to the experiences and development of skills. Over time, this record becomes valuable evidence of the efforts and celebrations of accomplishments. The developmental Checklists show skills for practicing to improve and the next skill that is to be introduced and encouraged. Vygotsky (1978) calls this the zone of proximal development, the "distance between the actual developmental level . . . and the level of potential development . . . under adult guidance or in collaboration with more capable peers" (p. 86). With the help of an adult or another child, the developing child can approximate the skill before he really can accomplish it on his own. This brings the promise, the feeling of success, and builds rapport with those who support the attempt.

The curriculum is individualized by referring to assessments to determine the level of motor development each child has attained. Daily plans for the whole group would include a variety of large muscle activities. They address the key experiences previously discussed. Individual children benefit from specifically focused activities to help them achieve the next level of development. They must, however, have many opportunities for success at their present level without feeling pressured or required to try something they are not sure they will attain. The skillful teacher uses a blend of addressing needs by combining it with interests like the song line "a little bit of sugar makes the medicine go down."

Planning for exceptional children will build on the abilities they do have. The curriculum is adapted so they have the closest match to what the rest of the class is doing. This is what is known as the **least restrictive environment.** If the class is marching, the child in the wheelchair can push along in the parade or beat the drum. The child with a hearing impairment can watch the beat being tapped out and feel the vibration of the drum. The child who does not speak can lead the band. The child who is visually impaired can play an instrument in one location. The child who speaks no English can move and play with everyone else.

Share Observations with Children and Families. Relating observations to families not only informs them of the child's activity that day but is an opportunity to teach child development principles and raise the child's self-esteem.

EXERCISE: How do you think a child would feel about the following comments?

"Now you can stand up all by yourself!"
"Look at how you are sitting up! You're so strong."

"You worked so hard at that balance beam today."
"You climbed to the top of the climber today. How did it feel up there?"

Accomplishments, as well as attempts, should be relayed to the child and the family. Telling the family good news in front of the child is a self-esteem booster for all of them. When the formal observation documentation such as Checklists or Anecdotal Records are shown or given to families, they see the progress and become involved in setting goals and strategies for the next skill or level. If the assessment indicates a significant developmental lag or regression, the family is consulted in private. This is to determine if this coincides with what they have observed. Then a follow-up action can be decided. It may be just to wait a while for the skill to develop or to seek further advice depending on the situation and the family's decision.

Differences between Girls and Boys

EXERCISE: How are boys and girls different other than anatomically?

Physiologically, men are stronger than women but women have greater endurance. There are other differences seen very early in life. Male one-year-olds already spend more time in gross motor activities while girls of that age spend more time in fine motor activities.

The social treatment of girls and boys, regarding toys and movement, begins very early. It is virtually impossible to control for that factor. This makes it difficult to determine what indeed is genetic and what is learned. Many studies have shown gender differences in toy selection, adult interactions with girls and boys, fantasy play themes, and types of play. Boys were found to be more aggressive (Figure 3–12) and girls more domestic, boys more physical and girls more verbal. The exact cause of those differences is still under debate.

EXERCISE: How does Figure 3–12 make you feel? What would you do if you were the adult in charge?

Because early childhood care and education is a field with predominately female personnel, their own genetic and social predispositions guide play expectations for girls and boys. That subtle bias can be seen in the low priority for large muscle equipment and curriculum in early childhood programs. Often female personnel give quick responses and attempt to dis-

Figure 3–12 Boys engage in more rough-and-tumble play.

courage rough-and-tumble play in the classroom. The biases are not so subtle in comments such as "Boys don't cry," or "Young ladies don't do that."

Pellegrini and Smith (1998) have done longitudinal studies of rough-and-tumble play, defined as active physical running and wrestling accompanied by laughter rather than frowning and hitting. Rough-and-tumble play is not about territories or possessions. Participants take turns as victim and victimizer. Their studies found that rough-and-tumble play was engaged in typically by boys who had high social skills. They contend observation of rough-and-tumble play can be a social competence indicator. It leads to games with rules, role taking, and problem solving. Its use with established guidelines is promoted by Porter (1994). He claims it is a safe, fun activity to be encouraged as "a natural expression of children's exuberance, joy, and affection for each other" (p. 45). The implications give early childhood educators issues to consider:

- Does the environment meet the large muscle needs of all the children in the class?
- What is the response of adults when children are spontaneously using large muscles to run, wrestle, or pretend to box in the classroom?
- Is the dramatic play area designed to attract domestic players and not active players, thereby reinforcing the sex stereotypic play?
- Do children wear casual clothing for physical, indoor, and outdoor activities?
- Do adults wear casual clothing for physical, indoor, and outdoor activities?

Small Muscle Development

The coordinated functions of arm, hand, and fingers are taken for granted.

EXERCISE: Pick up each of the following items: chair, book, dime, hair. Perform each of the following tasks: zip a zipper; tie a shoe; write your name. Now perform the above tasks with your nondominant hand. Notice the different movements and functions of your small muscles.

For the first few months of life, the small muscles of hands and feet are moved by **reflexes,** rather than purposeful movements controlled by thought. Apply pressure to the palms of the infant and her mouth opens and her head flexes forward (Babkin reflex). Stroke her palm and her hand closes into a grip around the object so strong it can hold her weight. Stroke the sole of her foot and her toes extend. Over the course of the first year, the infant develops control over these small muscles, first by reaching, corralling, and grasping with the entire hand. By age one, the infant can use the thumb and forefinger in a pincer grasp. Letting go, or releasing, comes later than grasping. This explains why an infant holding onto an earring or a lock of hair has a hard time letting go of it.

These small muscle skills are connected to eye and hand coordination, the cephalocaudal and proximodistal development of the whole body, and thought processes. They will continue to develop in the more specific motions needed to twist, squeeze, pinch, button, snap, zip, pour, pick up small objects, insert, and cut. All of these skills are leading to the achievement of readiness to write. Other developmental skills also signal that the child is ready for writing:

> balance without using the hands
> grasp and release objects voluntarily
> handedness predominates with one hand leading and the other following
> eye–hand coordination
> construction experiences—putting things together, parts and whole concept
> increased attention span

The developmental sequence is:

> scribbling, holding tool in a hammer hold
> scribbling, with finger hold
> control of tool to close a circle shape
> making straight lines
> drawing with the characteristics of writing
> beginning of alphabet letters
> ability to make a square
> printing name—in uppercase letters
> printing name—in upper- and lowercase
> left-to-right progression of letters and words

IT HAPPENED TO ME

He Sure Can Cut!

We had been working with Andy's small muscle skills, finding ways to interest him in trying some cutting instead of always playing with blocks and on the climber. We found some construction machinery catalogs and invited him to cut and paste to make a book to take home. He worked for several days at it and we saw those cutting skills improve so dramatically we sent home a "Happy Note" about the news. Mom came in a few days later and said, "You know those cutting skills you've been working on with Andy? He's been working on them at home too. He got the scissors and cut up all the chains in my jewelry box into little pieces!" Gulp! Teaching should come with disclaimers, "We cannot be responsible for the application of newly learned skills in a nonsupervised environment."

Observing Small Muscle Development. The physical environment includes materials and opportunities for the child to practice small muscle skills. The baby touches and grasps any objects within its reach, appropriate or not, grandpa's glasses, a hot coffee cup, or a dust mote floating through the air. The toddler grabs, carries, dumps, fills, manipulates whatever is movable: toilet paper, stones in the driveway, knickknacks on the coffee table, or items on the supermarket shelf. The preschooler practices writing with whatever tools are available, a stick in the dust, Mommy's lipstick, or a paintbrush in tar. The important observer role is to watch what the child is touching, then evaluate its potential for harm. If necessary, the adult intervenes before damage is done to the child, the object, or the environment.

The observer in an educational setting sees the movements as indicators of development and documents what the child can do on this date so that periodically the record is updated to check if progress is being made. Knowledge of the child's abilities at this stage influences the kinds of equipment, materials, and activities the teacher provides. An infant is given items that are easy to grasp and gives some immediate signal such as a rattle, toy with a bell or squeak. The toddler is given items to stack, fill and dump, pound, squeeze, and manipulate such as Play Doh and puzzles with simple, large pieces. The preschooler is provided with smaller manipulatives, such as building bricks, smaller piece puzzles, lacing cards, scissors, and a wide array of writing tools and papers.

Documentation of small muscle development can be made with Checklists, Anecdotal Records, and samples of the child's work on paper. The first scribbles, the first alphabet letters, the first name writing, the first "I love you" note are precious and graphic illustrations of the small muscle development as it leads to literacy. These are important evidence to be added to the portfolio and shared with families to illustrate the child's small muscle development. Stages of small muscle development also are integrally involved in both art and literacy and are discussed again in later chapters.

HELPING ALL CHILDREN WITH PHYSICAL DEVELOPMENT

Adapting the environment for children with special needs already has been addressed. Just as with any other child, the basis for planning curriculum begins with the assessment of where the child is in that developmental area. More information is usually present about the area of disability, from family information and the child's file with reports from helping professionals. It is in the areas other than the one affected that the observer needs to attune. It sometimes is the bias or unconscious attitude that other developmental areas are similarly affected. That is not true. Other areas could be right at the age or stage level with other children. They could just as easily be advanced. Objective observation and recording, without bias concerning the disability, is important.

Non-English-speaking children, and children of diverse cultures are not different physically than others in the group. It may be in the communication of expectations with both groups that any difficulties may arise. Modeling and acceptance will help all children feel the freedom to try physical activities.

HELPING PROFESSIONALS FOR PHYSICAL DEVELOPMENT CONCERNS

If observation reveals a developmental lag, the family is consulted, following confirmation by others on the team. They can be referred to their medical helper, such as the pediatrician, for evaluation. Others who may become involved in evaluations of physical developmental lags follow:

occupational therapist—a specialist who evaluates activities of daily living (feeding or dressing themselves) and provides therapy for assisting in the mastery of these activities

neurologist—a physician who specializes in the diagnosis and treatment of disorders of the nervous system, treating symptoms of pain and motor impairments

physical therapist—a specialist who evaluates capabilities for standing, sitting, and ambulation and provides therapy for people who have problems with these functions

OTHER METHODS

Other Methods to Record Physical Development:

Class Log List
Anecdotal/Running Record
Media such as photographs or video recording

KEY TERMS

bias	large muscle
cephalocaudal	least restrictive environment
Checklist	proximodistal
closed method	reflexes
frame of reference	small muscle
growth	

WEEK 3: PLAN A

CHECKLIST ON PHYSICAL DEVELOPMENT FOR ALL

Copy the Gober Checklist (Figures 3–1 and 3–2) for eight children and this week observe them in the physical development portion of the Checklist. If the program where you are doing your field experience has a Checklist, you may want to use it to help the teacher, gathering information on a portion of the group.

Practitioners

Use your program-approved Checklist and gather information on physical development on all the children in the group this week as the children work and play.

What to Do with It

Filing. Enter on the Portfolio Overview Sheet that the Checklist on physical development has been used, the recorder's name (you), and the date. Place the Checklist in each child's portfolio (Figure 3–13).

Sharing with Child and Family. Share the child's accomplishments with the family and the child, if appropriate. For example: "This week we are closely observing the child's muscle development and coordination. I noticed Madeline can skip, walk downstairs using alternating feet, and balance on one leg for several seconds. Those are unusual skills for one not yet four years old," or "Frank, I noticed that you can cut with scissors with either your left hand or your right hand. Do you write better with one hand or the other? Can you show me?"

Actions.

Read a Book.
Here are a few great stories about physical development to share with the group or individual children:

PHYSICAL DEVELOPMENT			
Documentation	Location	Recorder	Date
CK	Portfolio	BAN	9/19
CK	"		12/12
CK	"		5/16

Figure 3–13 Portfolio Overview Example

Buller, J. (1996). *Ready, Set, Hop!* New York: Harper Collins.

Nye, P. (1997). *I Love to Dance.* Dallas, TX: Penny Laine Papers.

Wilkes, A. (1994). *See How I Grow.* New York: D. K. Publishing.

In the Environment.
- Provide equipment within the classroom for large muscle development, available by choice throughout the day.
- Provide a variety of tools and materials to stimulate a small muscle development.
- Outside play area—provide:
  - enough space and equipment that encourages active participation
  - large and small group play spaces
  - areas of sun and shade

In the Curriculum.
- Match a child's interest with the area that needs more development to stimulate interest and practice.
- Use height and weight changes as a curriculum theme incorporating measurement, charting, change. This could develop into a project about influences on growth, infant growth and development and monthly baby visits, or a class-initiated and designed exercise program.
- Outside materials extend indoor curricular areas including art, literacy, and science.

In the Newsletter.
- List what physical development milestones are occurring in a wide age range. (Be sure to add an explanation that all children develop at different rates in the various developmental areas and that serious developmental lags will be noted by teachers and discussed with families.)
- Article on common household objects and activities that promote small muscle development such as pinching clothespins; playing with kitchen tools such as tongs, pizza wheels; sorting pasta shapes, etc.
- Article on home play yard safety—cushioning under climbers and slides, rope swing cautions, clothing without neck strings.
- Article on the importance of outdoor play.
- Location of some interesting neighborhood play places.

Look at the next level or skill to be developed for each child. Plan activities to encourage that skill, especially inviting this child to participate. Make a note of the child's response. For example, "Monday—put out new building blocks, invite Ben and X, and Y, and Z. Ben worked with blocks for three minutes but had difficulty. I took out the larger blocks, which he worked with for seven minutes."

Date these notes and place them in the child's portfolio.

If a significant lag appears, discuss it with your supervisor to confirm it, then with the family. Together you can decide on a course of action.

WEEK 3: PLAN B

ANECDOTAL RECORDING PHYSICAL DEVELOPMENT FOR GROUP B

Students

Select two children and complete an Anecdotal Recording.

Practitioners

Select children in Group B. On Monday observe the first child in Group B, looking for an episode demonstrating physical development. On Tuesday observe the next child, planning so that by the end of the week, each child in Group B has an Anecdotal Recording on muscle development in the portfolio.

Write an Anecdotal Recording with as many details about how the child moves and uses the body. If the child makes any comments about physical ability, be sure to note it word for word. Comment in the right column on the significance of this event. Was it usual or unusual, above or below expected level for this age? Give some possible contributing factors if

you know them. The reader should have the feeling of seeing the episode through your eyes.

What to Do with It

Filing. On the child's portfolio overview, note the Anecdotal Record is being included, your name as recorder, and the date. (See the preceding portfolio overview entry.)

If a significant lag is indicated, speak with your supervisor. Discuss with the family to decide on a course of action.

Plan specific curriculum activities to practice the accomplished skill and next-level skills to give experiences to develop with help.

Sharing with the Child and Family. Share the recording with the child's family and the child, if appropriate. For example, "Megan traced her hand and cut it out today. That's quite a difficult task for a three-year-old, but she did it." File the Anecdotal Recordings in each child's portfolio.

WEEK 3: PLAN C

REFLECTIVE JOURNAL

Respond to the following in your Reflective Journal, kept in a private file at home.

Physical activities in my daily routine include...

In thinking about physical development, my own large muscle skills are...

My small muscle skills are...

I think I'm this way because...

It's affected other areas of my life by...

REFERENCES

Allen, K. E., & Marotz, L. (2003). *Developmental profiles: Pre-birth through twelve* (4th ed.). Albany, NY: Delmar.

Anderson, R. E., Crespo, C. J., Bartlett, S. J., Cheskin, L. J., & Pratt. M. (1998). Relationship of physical activity and television watching with body weight and level of fatness among children: Results from the Third National Health and Nutrition Examination Survey. *Journal of the American Medical Association, 279*, 938–942.

Bakley, S. (2001). Through the lens of sensory integration: A different way of analyzing challenging behavior. *Young Children, 56* (6), 70–76.

Bar-Or, O. (2000). Juvenile obesity, physical activity, and lifestyle changes. *The Physician and Sports Medicine, 28* (11), 51–58.

Beaty, J. (2002). *Observing development of the young child* (5th ed.). New York: Macmillan Publishing Co.

Bentzen, W. R. (2005). *Seeing young children: A guide to*

observing and recording behavior (5th ed.). Clifton Park, NY: Thomson Delmar Learning.

Bjorklund, D. F., & Brown, R. K. (1998). Physical play and cognitive development: Integrating activity, cognition and education. *Child Development, 69* (3), 604–606.

Bricker, D., & Squires, J. (1999). *Ages and Stages Questionnaires (ASQ)™* (2nd ed.). Baltimore, MD: Brookes.

Brigance, A. H. (1999). *Brigance diagnostic inventory of early development* (2nd ed.). Woburn, MA: Curriculum Associates, Inc.

Coakley, J. J. (2001). *Sport in society: Issues and controversies* (7th ed.). St. Louis: Mosby.

Folio, M. R., & Fewell, R. R. (2000). *Peabody Developmental Motor Scales* (2nd ed.). Allen, TX: Developmental Learning Materials Teaching Resources.

Frankenburg, W. K., Dodds, J. B., & Fandal, A. W. (1990). Denver Developmental Screening II (DDST-II). Denver: Denver Developmental Materials, Inc.

Frost, J. (1992). *Play and playscapes.* Clifton Park, NY: Thomson Delmar Learning.

Gallahue, D. L. (2003). *Developmental physical education for children.* Champaign, IL: Human Kinetics.

Gober, S. Y. (2002). *Six simple ways to assess young children.* Clifton Park, NY: Thomson Delmar Learning.

Griffin, C., & Rinn, B. (1998). Enhancing outdoor play with an obstacle course. *Young Children, 53* (3), 18–23.

Hall, J. T., & Sweeny, N. H. (1976). *Until the whistle blows: A collection of games, dances, and activities for four-to-eight year olds.* Santa Monica, CA: Goodyear Publishing Co.

Hannaford, C. (1995). *Smart moves: Why learning is not all in your head.* Arlington, VA: Great Ocean Publishers.

High/Scope Educational Research Foundation. (1992). *Child Observation Record (COR) and Child Assessment Record (CAR).* Ypsilanti, MI: High/Scope Educational Research Foundation.

Ireton, H. (1992). *Child Development Inventory (CDI).* Minneapolis, MN: Behavioral Science Systems.

Lowey, M. (1998). Suggestions for working with fat children in schools. *Professional School Counseling, 1* (4), 18–23.

Meisels, S., Jablon, J., Marsden, D., Dichtmiller, D., & Dorfman, A. (1994). *The work sampling system.* Ann Arbor, MI: Rebus Planning Associates, Inc.

National Association for Sport and Physical Education. (1995). *Moving into the future: National standards for physical education.* Reston, VA: Author.

National Association of Early Childhood Specialists in State Departments of Education. (1997). *Recess and the importance of play: A position statement on young children and recess.* http://ericps.crc.uiuc.edu/naecs/position/recessplay.html. Accessed April 8, 2003.

Novak, D. E. (2000). *Help! It's an indoor recess day.* Thousand Oaks, CA: Corwin Press.

Olds, A. R. (1994). From cartwheels to caterpillars: Children's need to move indoors and out. *Child Care Information Exchange, 96,* May/June 1994.

O'Brien, L. M. (2003). The rewards and restrictions of recess: Reflections on being a playground volunteer. *Childhood Education, 79* (3), 161.

Pate, R. R., Baranowski, T., Dowda, M., & Trost, S. G. (1996). *Tracking of physical activity in young children. Medicine and Science in Sports and Exercise 28* (1), 92–96.

Pellegrini, A. D., & Smith, P. K. (1998). Physical activity play: The nature and function of a neglected aspect of play. *Child Development, 69* (3), 577–598.

Pica, R. (2000). *Moving and learning series. Preschoolers & kindergartners.* Clifton Park, NY: Thomson Delmar Learning.

Poest, C. A., Williams, J. F, Witt, D. D., & Atwood, M. E. (1990). Challenge me to move: Large muscle development in young children. *Young Children 45* (5).

Porter, R. (1994). Roughhousing as a style of play. *Child Care Information Exchange 96,* May/June 1994.

Power, T. (2000). *Play and exploration in children and animals.* Mahwah, NJ: Lawrence Erlbaum Associates.

Purkey, W. W., & Novak, J. M. (1996). *Inviting school success: a self-concept approach to teaching, learning and democracy.* Belmont, CA: Wadsworth.

Readdick, C. A., & Park, J. J. (1998). Achieving great heights: The climbing child. *Young Children, 53* (6), 14–19.

Rivkin, M. S. (1995). *The great outdoors: Restoring children's right to play outside.* Washington, DC: National Association for the Education of Young Children.

Stephens, M. (2002). Children, physical activity, and public health: Another call to action. *American Family Physician, 65* (6), 1033.

Sutterby, J. A., & Frost, J. L. (2002). Making playgrounds fit for children and children fit on playgrounds. *Young Children, 57* (3), 36–41.

Vygotsky, L. S. (1978). *Mind in society: The development of higher psychological processes.* Cambridge, MA: Harvard University Press.

Weikart, Phyllis S. (2000). *Round the circle* (2nd ed.). Ypsilanti, MI: High/Scope Press.

Weiller, K. H., & Richardson, P. A. (1993). A program for kids: Success-oriented physical education. *Childhood Education, 69* (3).

RESOURCES

Hall, J. T., & Sweeny, N. H. (1976). *Until the whistle blows: A collection of games, dances, and activities for four-to-eight year olds.* Santa Monica, CA: Goodyear Publishing Co.

Novak, D. E. (2000). *Help! It's an indoor recess day.* Thousand Oaks, CA: Corwin Press.

Rivkin, M. S. (1995). *The great outdoors: Restoring children's right to play outside.* Washington, DC: National Association for the Education of Young Children.

Sanders, S. W. (2002). *Active for life: Developmentally appropriate movement programs for young children.* Washington, DC: National Association for the Education of Young Children. http://www.surgeongeneral.gov

Weikart, P. S. (2000). *Round the circle* (2nd ed.). Ypsilanti, MI: High/ Scope Press.

Weiller, K. H. & Richardson, P. A. (1993). A program for kids: Success-oriented physical education. *Childhood Education, 69* (3), Spring, 1993.

For additional information on early education curriculum, visit our Web site at http://www.earlychilded.delmar.com

Using Running Records to Look at Social Development

USING RUNNING RECORDS

EXERCISE: Read the Running Record that focuses on Larry (Figure 4–1). Cover the right-hand column with a sheet of paper, make comments or inferences about Larry as indicated from this incident.

From the exercise you see that a **Running Record** uses the same technique as the Anecdotal Recording. It is a factual, detailed, written account over a span of time. Actions are described and quotes are recorded as precisely as possible. Commentary or interpretation about the recording is written separately from the actual account. The recorder decides to observe and write for a period of time, focusing on one child or one play area. A nonselective narrative documents a specimen of that child or that area's action.

The Running Record is written as the events are happening, while the Anecdotal Recording usually is written shortly after a significant event. The Anecdotal Recording is a little story with a beginning, the action, and an ending. Running Records are indiscriminate, giving a more objective glimpse into a normal (or what may turn out to be abnormal) segment of time. That is not known, however, before the recorder begins to write. Everything that happens in that time segment is recorded: the mundane, the boring, the unexplained. At the end of a time period, the recording stops. This may not necessarily be at the end of the event. A Running Record is like turning on a video and just letting it run for a certain amount of time, recording whatever occurs. A Running Record

Time Recording   Recorder
Began

Nov. 14   10:15 a.m.   BAN recorder
    LARRY   4 Yrs., 2 mo.

Larry is in the play kitchen with Susan, Allison, and Marie. M: put the eggs in the refrigerator. L. took 2 dishes and 2 forks and set the dishes on the table. Hands forks to Andrea, sitting at the table. L. gets another plate and fork and sets it at another chair. Andrea goes by on a big truck and L. gets on the back. A: yells, Get off! L. gets off then stands watching her as she goes on. L. stands watching. Still watching, L. walks into other room where A. went with truck. To Mike: These robbers stole our truck, pointing to A. M. has the gas tank. He just looks up. L: She needs some gas, points to A. A: No, they didn't tell ya. M. holds gas tank to chest. A. rolls towards them. L. puts two hands out to stop the truck. She drives by and he just watches. L. walks back into other room and gets into rocker boat. A. and S. come by on two trucks. A to L: Can you show us the cemetery? L. doesn't answer. H. rocks fast with Lucy and S. gets on. L. rocks fast. They hand him dolls. He holds them. Kevin gets in and rocks. S: You need to get off this boat. Lucy to L: You're our neighbor. L: I can stay on here. Sets dolls down. Picks them up. Lucy purposely falls out of boat. She laughs, gets back in and rocks fast. Lucy: You're making me fall off. L. stops rocking. Steven comes over to get in. L: You're too heavy. K. comes with blocks. L. drops them into trucks parked nearby. L: We need some money. Jumps out. Climbs up climber, runs down slide, back to boat. Chews on fingernail. Other boys dropping blocks into boat. L. laughs loudly. Stands up in boat, smiling. No more money he says loudly. He takes the doll and throws it out, throws out some blocks. L. gets out and throws some blocks back in. 1: More money, more money. Gets back in the boat. Girls in boat tip over backwards on purpose, laughing. He pulls blocks out and takes 2 over to the shelf and drops them nearby. Screws up face, arms out. Too much money. Why are you doing this? Gets into boat and starts stacking the blocks in it. Kevin gets in. They rock and sing, Do, do, do, ya need some gas?
10:26

Time ended   Teacher's   Should blocks be
                questions   allowed in this
                        area? Ask Betty.

Use initials after first mention of name for time saving.

Action

Exact Quotes

Follow target child

Comments: Play entry tactic

Comments: Where did this come from?

Asserts himself

Uncertain?

Accepted into the game

Beginning cleanup!

A new friend!

Note:
Bare record could be copied for other children's files if no negative events took place or block other names

Figure 4–1 Running Record Example

is the most useful in giving a naturalistic view of a short time in the life of the child.

When a learning center or area of the classroom is the focus of a Running Record, it can evaluate the usefulness of the area and if the area needs any modifications. Particular learning centers or classroom areas are more suitable for viewing specific skills. A Running Record in the large muscle area obviously gives information on children's climbing, running, or jumping skills but also can yield valuable information on social, emotional, and verbal development. Imaginative play, social interactions, and self-concept are illustrated vividly in the dramatic play area as well as the block area. Small muscle skills, literacy development, and social and verbal skills are observed easily in the art area or during play at the sand or water table. Running Records of ten minutes at any one of these areas can be extremely informative.

The Running Record requires intense concentration and focused attention. Other staff are needed in the room to be sure all children are supervised adequately. Of course, any recording in progress is secondary to a child in need. Any time recording must be interrupted, a line is drawn and the ending and return time is noted. It may be resumed if the situation is now under control.

EXERCISE: **On a separate sheet of paper, describe how you might feel if someone were watching you for ten minutes and writing notes.**

One caution in using the Running Record, or any other recording technique, is the possible effect it may have on the child's behavior (Figure 4–2). It may make them uncomfortable or act in an artificial way. The

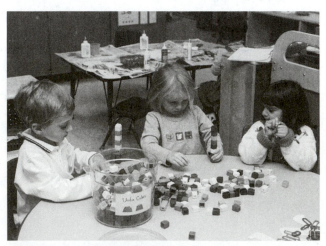

Figure 4–2 Observation may change behavior, so the observer attempts to be unobtrusive.

Using Running Records to Look at Social Development

USING RUNNING RECORDS

EXERCISE: Read the Running Record that focuses on Larry (Figure 4–1). Cover the right-hand column with a sheet of paper, make comments or inferences about Larry as indicated from this incident.

From the exercise you see that a **Running Record** uses the same technique as the Anecdotal Recording. It is a factual, detailed, written account over a span of time. Actions are described and quotes are recorded as precisely as possible. Commentary or interpretation about the recording is written separately from the actual account. The recorder decides to observe and write for a period of time, focusing on one child or one play area. A nonselective narrative documents a specimen of that child or that area's action.

The Running Record is written as the events are happening, while the Anecdotal Recording usually is written shortly after a significant event. The Anecdotal Recording is a little story with a beginning, the action, and an ending. Running Records are indiscriminate, giving a more objective glimpse into a normal (or what may turn out to be abnormal) segment of time. That is not known, however, before the recorder begins to write. Everything that happens in that time segment is recorded: the mundane, the boring, the unexplained. At the end of a time period, the recording stops. This may not necessarily be at the end of the event. A Running Record is like turning on a video and just letting it run for a certain amount of time, recording whatever occurs. A Running Record

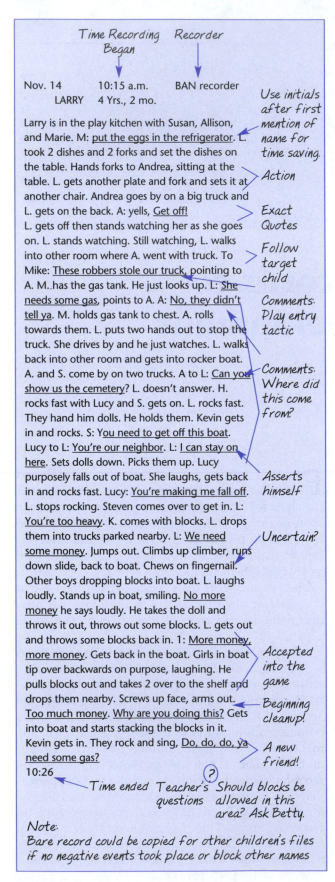

Figure 4–1 Running Record Example

The annotations shown in the running record figure:

Time Recording Began
Recorder

Nov. 14   10:15 a.m.   BAN recorder
    LARRY   4 Yrs., 2 mo.

Larry is in the play kitchen with Susan, Allison, and Marie. M: put the eggs in the refrigerator. L. took 2 dishes and 2 forks and set the dishes on the table. Hands forks to Andrea, sitting at the table. L. gets another plate and fork and sets it at another chair. Andrea goes by on a big truck and L. gets on the back. A: yells, Get off! L. gets off then stands watching her as she goes on. L. stands watching. Still watching, L. walks into other room where A. went with truck. To Mike: These robbers stole our truck, pointing to A. M..has the gas tank. He just looks up. L: She needs some gas, points to A. A: No, they didn't tell ya. M. holds gas tank to chest. A. rolls towards them. L. puts two hands out to stop the truck. She drives by and he just watches. L. walks back into other room and gets into rocker boat. A. and S. come by on two trucks. A to L: Can you show us the cemetery? L. doesn't answer. H. rocks fast with Lucy and S. gets on. L. rocks fast. They hand him dolls. He holds them. Kevin gets in and rocks. S: You need to get off this boat. Lucy to L: You're our neighbor. L: I can stay on here. Sets dolls down. Picks them up. Lucy purposely falls out of boat. She laughs, gets back in and rocks fast. Lucy: You're making me fall off. L. stops rocking. Steven comes over to get in. L: You're too heavy. K. comes with blocks. L. drops them into trucks parked nearby. L: We need some money. Jumps out. Climbs up climber, runs down slide, back to boat. Chews on fingernail. Other boys dropping blocks into boat. L. laughs loudly. Stands up in boat, smiling. No more money he says loudly. He takes the doll and throws it out, throws out some blocks. L. gets out and throws some blocks back in. 1: More money, more money. Gets back in the boat. Girls in boat tip over backwards on purpose, laughing. He pulls blocks out and takes 2 over to the shelf and drops them nearby. Screws up face, arms out. Too much money. Why are you doing this? Gets into boat and starts stacking the blocks in it. Kevin gets in. They rock and sing, Do, do, do, ya need some gas?

10:26

Time ended   Teacher's Should blocks be
    questions   allowed in this
              area? Ask Betty.

Note:
Bare record could be copied for other children's files if no negative events took place or block other names

Margin annotations:
- Use initials after first mention of name for time saving.
- Action
- Exact Quotes
- Follow target child
- Comments: Play entry tactic
- Comments: Where did this come from?
- Asserts himself
- Uncertain?
- Accepted into the game
- Beginning cleanup!
- A new friend!
- ?

is the most useful in giving a naturalistic view of a short time in the life of the child.

When a learning center or area of the classroom is the focus of a Running Record, it can evaluate the usefulness of the area and if the area needs any modifications. Particular learning centers or classroom areas are more suitable for viewing specific skills. A Running Record in the large muscle area obviously gives information on children's climbing, running, or jumping skills but also can yield valuable information on social, emotional, and verbal development. Imaginative play, social interactions, and self-concept are illustrated vividly in the dramatic play area as well as the block area. Small muscle skills, literacy development, and social and verbal skills are observed easily in the art area or during play at the sand or water table. Running Records of ten minutes at any one of these areas can be extremely informative.

The Running Record requires intense concentration and focused attention. Other staff are needed in the room to be sure all children are supervised adequately. Of course, any recording in progress is secondary to a child in need. Any time recording must be interrupted, a line is drawn and the ending and return time is noted. It may be resumed if the situation is now under control.

EXERCISE: On a separate sheet of paper, describe how you might feel if someone were watching you for ten minutes and writing notes.

One caution in using the Running Record, or any other recording technique, is the possible effect it may have on the child's behavior (Figure 4–2). It may make them uncomfortable or act in an artificial way. The

Figure 4–2 Observation may change behavior, so the observer attempts to be unobtrusive.

IT HAPPENED TO ME

Artist's Model?

I was sightseeing on a bus in a foreign country, feeling very special, looking all around at the scenery, when I felt someone watching me. A young man toward the rear of the bus was sketching on a pad. "Oh," I thought, "He's an artist. This country's full of artists. He must be sketching me." So I turned my best side toward him, sat up straighter in the seat, and sat still with a facial expression I wanted captured on his pad. As he was leaving the bus I craned my neck to see the pad. It was a forest scene, apparently from memory, he was working on. Because I thought he was watching me, I changed my behavior.

recorder must be sensitive to that self-consciousness. The writing would then stop and efforts made to be less obvious in the future. In a classroom where observation and recording go on all the time as a natural part of everyday life, children often cease to notice. By showing them the notes, even if they are not able to read, they feel more comfortable about the writing. Talking with them about what was observed helps them understand the purpose behind the writing. When they hear the teacher talk with their family about the episodes from the notes, they realize that their actions are important and meaningful. **Warning:** Any negative occurrences or difficulties observed should not be discussed with the family in the presence of the child.

Uses

The Running Record

- records detailed segments of behavior occurring in a certain time block.
- focuses on an individual child to show a naturalistic view of a part of the day.
- can be analyzed for evaluation of many developmental areas: physical, social, emotional, language, self-concept, attention span, problem solving, memory, learning style.
- documents evaluation of developmental areas for child study.
- can focus on a particular learning center or classroom area to see what typically occurs there.

Advantages

The Running Record is helpful because it

- details a normal segment of time in the day, giving a more natural view.
- reveals many areas of development in one recording.
- can evaluate the effectiveness of a learning center or area.

Disadvantages

The Running Record may

- make the subject feel watched, become uncomfortable, and change behavior, destroying the nature of the recording.
- not show in the time segment what normally occurs.
- make the adult unavailable to facilitate or observe what is happening in the rest of the room because attention is focused on the recording.
- tire and drain the recorder because of its intensity.

EXERCISE: Practice writing a Running Record. Take a separate sheet of paper right now, fold it in half, select a person to watch, and write down everything that person does and says for ten minutes.

Rate your Running Record.

- Did you mention the setting so the reader knows where it took place?
- Did you write the date and time you started?
- Did you write your name on it as the recorder?

Look over the words you used to make sure they described actions, not summarized them, or gave reasons. The words should form mental pictures.

- If you used any of the following words, perhaps you fell in the trap of summarizing: *because, wanted to, tried, saw, played, looked (emotion), noticed, pretended.*
- If more than one person was involved, did you write down the conversation word for word?
- Now go back and on the right column write what judgments you would make about this person's physical, cognitive, social, and emotional development. What did this segment of action show about that person? What questions did it raise about why the person acted that way?

EXERCISE: The following pages contain Running Records on which to practice. Find the recorder's mistakes, then return to this point and check yourself.

ABCCenter   AnnWade
4 yr. old class   BANrecorder

Sep. 28

9:30	Ann plays with other children at the sand table. She talks with Q
●	most of the time.
	She picks up a shovel and scoops sand into a sifter, watching it
	sprinkle and calling it snow.
	When Q. picks up the shovel, Ann thinks she should have it back so she
	grabs it away. Q. gets another one. As children come over, Ann gives
	them attention and asks them questions.
	After a while, Ann skips over to another group of children she
	wants to play with. She says, "Hey, watcha doin?"

Figure 4–3 Find the recorder's errors: Running Record #1.

In Figure 4–3 the term *plays* is too generic. The recorder should be specific and mention who else is there. "Talks" is not exact quotes. This was an example of good action description. How does the observer know what Ann thinks? Exact quotes were not written down. This is fifteen minutes of action? The recorder exactly documented pronunciation giving the reader more information about the child.

Read Figure 4–4. "Play a lot" is a summary, there is no documentation. It is a good description of placing blocks, but there are no quotes. "As usual" is an unsubstantiated comment. It could be written in the right-hand column. "Convenient" is a judgment. Perhaps the writer set up the room? Movement on the trucks and blocks was well described. How does the writer know J. does not like it? "Vicious" is a subjective term with some bias showing. "Because" is a red flag. The open record only describes action. The reasons for the action or reaction can be written in the right-hand column. What exactly did the teacher say? "Go over and apologize and build that back up!" "Look at T.'s face. He is sad. You knocked over his building. Helping him build it back up is a friendly thing to do."

In Figure 4–5, "started playing" is a summary of their actions with no descriptions. Were they just piling them or making the Eiffel Tower? Twenty minutes of playing should contain more details. How did the recorder know what N. wanted? The teacher's words are lost, and it doesn't matter if she loved it. It should be satisfying to the builder unless she commissioned it to be built. "Got bored," what does that *look* like? "Decided" is another red-flag word. A recorder only writes what actually happens, not what is decided. That is determined by the actions.

Running and Anecdotal Records are like written movie scripts, exactly describing actions, facial expressions, and exact words of the players.

Pitfalls to Avoid

Running Records are time and energy intensive so the recorder must be sure that the children are safely involved, under the supervision of at least one other adult for interaction, and only then should a running record be started. Because of the objective technique, it probably is not a method that a volunteer could be asked to do but the supervision could be assigned.

ABC Center   JimmyFresno
4 yr old class   BAN recorder

Sep. 29

8:20am.

Jimmy and T. are in the block area where they play alot together. J. places four longer blocks in a square on the rug and tells T. to go get some more. T. obeys as usual and gets on the big truck, making motor noises. Scoots over to the convenient block shelf. He picks up blocks with each hand, loads the truck, then drives it slowly to where J. has started building. J takes 4 blocks & sets them on end. He decides he doesn't like it so he gives a vicious kick & knocks them down. T. jumps up screaming at J. because he is so angry. The teacher tells J. to help build the building up and he does.

Figure 4–4 Find the recorder's errors: Running Record #2.

Attention to safety and the interactive needs of children always takes precedence over recording.

Another pitfall is that close observation tends to make the target child feel observed and perhaps change behavior. The recorder must be very careful to observe from far enough away as to not interfere with the child's actions but close enough to hear conversations. Sometimes the location of a chair on the other side of a piece of equipment, behind the child's line of vision but within hearing distance, can be effective.

Often other children enter into the Running Record in interactions with the target child. Because this will be filed in one child's portfolio, other children's names should be blotted from this particular recording for anonymity.

A Running Record can yield a great deal of insight into a child's usual activities, but it can be so mundane as to seem unimportant. It is not. As a true measure of a child's development and behavior, naturalistic observation like a Running Record is invaluable.

Using Technology

A video camera is a wonderful tool for capturing live action. There is no way a written Anecdotal or Running Record can compare, but using a video camera does take time, patience, and the knack for being in the right place at the right time. Using a video camera can also be intrusive. Whenever anyone but the most experienced model sees a camera aimed their way, they change their behavior. It is very difficult to capture spontaneous, meaningful video footage.

Hand-held computers can accommodate a portable keyboard that unfolds, which can be helpful because many people can type faster than they can write. Using a keyboard also makes it easier to add the Running Record to an electronic file on each child. Electronic files, mentioned in Chapter 3, are easy to manipulate, do not take up classroom storage space, are easier to keep confidential, and can also store artwork and photographs.

How to Find the Time

Running Records are one of the most time-intensive recording methods. To concentrate fully on one child and write accurately and descriptively about the child's every action and conversation takes undivided attention. That means that this recording method, in its purest sense, done as the action is

ABC Center   Nora Camp
4 yr. old class   BAN recorder

Sep. 30

10:35   After circle time the children had free play. N. and her friend T.

went over to the block area and dumped the blocks on the floor

and started playing. They play for about 20 minutes. One girl

stayed by the blocks while N. wanted the teacher to see their

building. The teacher said she loved it and the two girls smiled.

After the teacher walked away, the two girls stared at it, then

they knocked it down and started to build something new. N. got

bored then and decided to go over to the dramatic play area.

11:00

Figure 4–5 Find the recorder's errors: Running Record #3.

taking place, is not practical for the person who is also responsible for the classroom. A modification can be to jot notes and amplify them later; however, time dulls the accuracy of the memory so it is never as rich as what really happened. So we are faced with the dilemma of how to make time to complete Running Records.

The student teacher or student visitor may have the luxury of doing Running Records and having no other classroom responsibility. This is a wonderful learning experience and one that should be practiced. Not only can it be a great help to the teacher but it can be a learning experience for the student by sharing the Running Record with the teacher and then discussing the interpretation. Another option is for the teacher to arrange for classroom coverage for a brief period each day to sit and watch children's play. Or, a classroom volunteer could be trained in this method under the direction of the teacher. However it is arranged, Running Records are valuable pieces of documentation and a 10-minute observation in every developmental area usually provides

enough detail or depth to enable the observer and the reader to draw some conclusions about the child's level.

What to Do with It

Following the actual recording, the teacher can make notes in the right-hand column in the same categories as the Anecdotal Record.

- explanations
- comments about development
- questions for further investigation
- plans for the child based on the observation

The Running Record is filed in the target child's portfolio after noting its presence on the Portfolio Overview Sheet. It may be read to the child at a later date for the basis of a conversation about the child's activities. The teacher can ask questions like, "When you were piling the blocks up and ran out of blocks, you stopped building. Is there something else you could have used to continue playing there?" or

"When you were at the Writing Center, I heard you say something about writing a letter and an elephant but I couldn't hear what you said. Do you remember?"

The Running Record that includes other children who interacted with the target child can be copied with the teacher then making notations in the right-hand column about the second child. When the record is filed in a child's portfolio, it should only contain the name of that child with other names blotted out.

LOOKING AT SOCIAL DEVELOPMENT

Two children are pulling on the same toy. "It's mine!" "No I want it!" An adult comes over, takes it away from one and gives it to the other. "You've got to share! Don't be so selfish."

That is not sharing. That is robbery. That is reinforcing the concept that bigger people can take things away from small people. True sharing is the willing relinquishing of one's rightful possession to another person. But how do children learn not to be so selfish?

The Need for a Selfless Society

Moving from selfish to selfless takes more than changing a few alphabet letters. It is a total transformation from self-centered, immediate gratification to other-centered, altruistic, generosity. The goal of maturity in a moral society is to become less concerned with one's own needs and desires by giving priority to others'. A

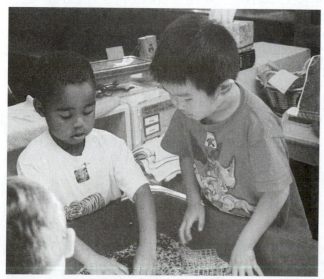

Figure 4–6 Attaining social development is not without its struggles.

> ### R E V I E W
>
> ***Running Record:*** Detailed account of a segment of the child's day, written as it is observed. Includes settings, descriptions of actions and interactions, and exact quotes.
>
> ***Types of Information to Record Using Running Records:*** Any segment of the child's day, usual or unusual. It can yield information on:
>
> separation and adjustment
>
> self-care skills
>
> physical development
>
> social development
>
> emotional development
>
> language and speech
>
> attention span and interests
>
> cognitive development
>
> literacy
>
> creativity
>
> socio-dramatic play
>
> self-esteem

person, group, or society, which only lives for itself, is constantly in conflict. Often more than one person wants the object or their own opinion to prevail and both cannot be satisfied. From that conflict came the rules of the tribe, then laws. Now laws are so numerous and complex that buildings are needed to hold the books that list and interpret them all. People devote their lives to interpreting, enforcing, changing, and even breaking them. There are also some people in a society who cannot fill their own needs so others are needed to generously help if they are to survive. The task of raising the young to be selfless is for the survival of the society. What a responsibility! This is a long struggle that begins with small steps.

EXERCISE: Think about how the following laws or rules restrict your freedom for the good of society.

- Only licensed physicians can practice medicine.
- Drive on the right side of the road.
- Items in a store must be exchanged for payment.
- Use utensils, not hands, for serving items from the salad bar.
- Buckle up your seat belt in the car.

TOPICS IN OBSERVATION

"The Stew"

Once upon a time a chef set out to make a stew by preparing the ingredients and placing them on the stove to cook. After a period of time, the chef took a deep ladle and sampled a bit of each of the ingredients to judge the progress of the stew. Some needed more time to cook so the chef extended the cooking time. The broth was lacking in flavor so the chef added some spices. It was too salty so the chef added a potato to take away some saltiness. The chef still was unsatisfied with the taste, so a chef, a stew expert, was called in to give an opinion. More modifications were made to the stew.

The stew was then served to the first diner, the chef's mother who declared the stew, "Marvelous!" The Board of Health inspector closely examined each part of the stew, looking for irregularities, without actually caring about the whole stew. The vegetarian, repulsed by the meat in the stew, stopped eating, vowing to make comments to the cook. One diner thought it needed more salt, while another thought it was too salty. The unserved portions of the stew were refrigerated and reheated the next day with flavors mellowed and texture softer. The smart chef wrote down the recipe so that future stews could be as flavorful but the chef knew it all depended on the ingredients available. But alas, some of the diners had moved on to other restaurants so they never got the full, aged taste of the stew. Ah, if they could only taste the stew now.

Meaning:

The stew is the child made up of many areas of development. The family brings the child to the teacher with knowledge, skills, and abilities. The teacher works with those to bring them to a certain expected level. A sample of the child's development is made to determine progress in development and further actions. In some areas, nothing is needed but time. In other areas, additions are made in the curriculum to assist in development. Sometimes behaviors that are getting in the way of learning are modified. Expert advice is sometimes needed so the family and teachers seek the referral and advice of helping professionals.

Hopefully, the family is pleased with the progress of the child, overlooking some areas still developing. Some observers look at specific areas while not seeing the whole child, such as a speech pathologist, dentist, or physical therapist. The child's progress may not be acceptable to some who have special interests or biases. Over time, the child grows, develops, and changes but past teachers and resource people do not have the opportunity to observe the progress. The family and teachers who have a record of the changes know what worked for that child. Each child is unique though and the teacher realizes the necessity for adapting environment and curriculum for each child and group. It is sad that not everyone gets the opportunity to appreciate the transformation.

In caring, teaching, or working with young children, the development of the social domain has a high priority. It does not develop separately from physical, cognitive, emotional areas but simultaneously moves forward, influenced by many of the same factors of genetics, environment, culture, and society. Helping a child to learn the rules of the tribe will help him to function in that group. It is a necessary skill for both physical and psychological well-being.

EXERCISE: List some social rules, not developed naturally, that children must be taught.

The infant is born being concerned only with its own needs, totally dependent on reflexes and signals calling for responses to those signals. The hungry baby never considers the mother's dinner getting cold. The baby crying in the middle of the night pays no heed to parents' early work schedules. The crawler pulls the cat's tail, or the toddler takes a truck from another. The needs and wants of the other person are not deliberated, or weighed, or even considered at all. Years and much growing and developing must take place before the child sees the point of view of the other person. It takes even longer before she can place the other person's needs ahead of her own with generosity and empathy. She has much growing up to do before living up to society's expectations and taking on the responsibility for others. Along that path there are stages, developmental milestones, that can be observed, aided in their arrival by interactions with adults.

Theories of Social Development and Their Implications on Early Childhood Professional Practice

Many in the past have pondered the origins of how people relate to one another. Freud (1953) attributes social behavior to the sexual nature of humans hidden in the subconscious. He saw the strong parental role in developing the superego or conscience to balance the id, demanding satisfaction of desires. The parental influences on the child's knowledge and feelings of right and wrong are deeply ingrained and different from one family to another. It is important for the teacher to know and work cooperatively with parents, reducing the dissonance of differing messages and how to cope with them. Freudian theory also reminds teachers that the child also has a sexual nature. Although they are very young, basic sex roles and attitudes are forming through experiences in early childhood.

Erikson's psychosocial developmental theory (1950) looks at not just biology but the changing mind and emotions and the effects of society in forming behavior patterns. His Eight Stages of Man illustrates the observable, predictable stages through which humans move. They include the positive task of the social role in each stage. Unlike Freud, who looked into the past to find reasons for pathological behavior, Erikson looked to the future, not giving up hope that the past can be overcome. Erikson's theory also stresses the importance of the adults in understanding and meeting children's needs in each stage. This affects how the child feels about himself and interacts with others.

Piaget's work in cognitive theory (Flavell, 1977) has meaning for children's social development. Children's thinking governs their actions. As the child takes in new information, the child interprets it differently at different stages. Before the infant reaches **object permanence,** the knowledge that objects exist outside their sight, the infant will not "miss" his mother. Once he has cognitively reached that stage, other people's faces are compared to his mental image of hers and that mismatch results in separation anxiety. The young child is described in Piaget's theory as **egocentric,** only able to see things from his own point of view. "I want this ball so I should have it," and takes the ball from another child. When the adult says, "How would you like it if he did that to you?" it has no meaning. He cannot mentally place himself with the ball in his hands with another child taking the ball away. This is just too much abstract cognitive processing for his ability at this stage. This is the underlying factor of social actions in the preschool years: the conflict between what one child wants (and thinks he should have) and that of another. Recognizing this, the adults take many actions, such as having enough duplicate toys that the need for possession is met. Once the child becomes verbal, the adult repeats phrases children can use. These help function socially, such as "You could say, 'I want to play with that ball when you're done,'" or "Tell her 'I don't like it when you take that away from me.'"

Behaviorists' social learning theory (Skinner, 1953; Watson, 1950) describe how learning takes place when it is reinforced either negatively or positively. This behaviorism is the reason that spanking or punishment works (for a while) and praise causes that behavior to occur again. This is external reinforcement of behavior. Parents and teachers want the child to be *intrinsically motivated,* to do the right thing even when no one is there to say, "Good job," or "No, No." When appropriate recognition for *right* and *wrong* deeds is given, the child sees the results from those actions and forms a thinking process for making choices about right and wrong for next time. Hopefully, the adult does not have to be present for reinforcement for the child to make the *right choice.*

Maslow's work (1970) investigating the causes of behavior also was based on met or unmet needs. His "Hierarchy of Needs" chart is familiar to students of psychology. It has the most basic survival needs at the bottom of the triangle, moving up to social needs, and eventually to self-actualization. This is where satisfaction comes, from serving others rather than self. Physical and psychological safety are necessary for children to develop. Schools have learned that a hungry child cannot learn, so national programs provide nutritious breakfasts and lunches. The physical environment influences behavior so homes, schools, restaurants, arcades, and businesses spend millions of dollars on color, furnishings, lighting, and aesthetics to influence human behavior. The classroom environment is an important factor in learning by attending to the physical and psychological needs of the children and adults. The affective needs of acceptance, recognition, affection, belonging, and love are the work of the curriculum of the social development area. From names on the cubbies, to hugs at the end of the day, children thrive socially in the environment that meets their emotional needs.

Hartup (1992) and many others have studied the importance of peer relationships. The critical social purposes of early childhood education are reinforced by his statement:

> Indeed, the single best childhood predictor of adult adaptation is not IQ, not school grades, and not classroom behavior, but rather, the adequacy with which the child gets along with other children. Children who are generally disliked, who are aggressive and disruptive, who are unable to sustain close relationships with other children, and who cannot establish a place for themselves in the peer culture are seriously at risk.

Implications of Social Learning Theory on Early Childhood Practices. In recent years, there has been an increased interest in identifying social factors such as the ability to have friends, maintain interactions, and cultivate social competence (Fabes et al., 1999). Children who are able to control their own physiological, emotional, and behavioral responses are socially competent, which enables them to function in a social atmosphere as well as in a learning environment. It is during the preschool years that this regulatory control system is formed (Rothbart & Bates, 1998). Five major clusters of social skill behaviors, with the acronym CARES, have been identified (Elliott, McKevitt, & DiPerna, 2002).

1. *Cooperation*—Behaviors such as helping others, sharing materials with a peer, and complying with rules.
2. *Assertion*—Initiating behaviors such as asking others for information and behaviors that are responses to others' actions, such as responding to peer pressure.
3. *Responsibility*—Behaviors that demonstrate the ability to communicate with adults and show concern about one's property.
4. *Empathy*—Behaviors that reflect concern for peers' or significant adults' feelings.
5. *Self-control*—Behaviors that often emerge in conflict situations such as responding appropriately to teasing or to corrective feedback from an adult. (p. 1042)

Positive social interactions, including friendships between children and adults, are beneficial not only for emotional health but physical health as well. Lacking close relationships can negatively affect every area of life (Lawhon, 1997). For this reason teachers need to

- work cooperatively and closely with the family.
- be aware of the sex role formation in young children.
- meet children's needs.
- consider child's cognitive level for realistic social expectations.
- give appropriate recognition for right and wrong deeds, along with resulting consequences.
- assist each child toward social competence.

Stages of Social Development

The word *development* indicates the change that takes place in the way the child interacts with other people is qualitative. It is not a change that can be measured in numbers but in refinement. It moves from simple to more complex, in a predictable sequence, but at different rates for individual people (Figure 4–7).

Self. The newborn infant (neonate) has no social competence. Interactions with other people are governed by reflexes:

Rooting reflex—When stroked on the cheek, the neonate turns toward that side. (It is not to see his mother better.)

Babkin reflex—When the palms are stimulated, the neonate's fingers curl around it and grasp it. (It is not to play with daddy's finger.)

Walking and stepping reflex—When held so that feet or toes touch the floor, the neonate makes a walking, stepping motion. (It is not to dance with her sister.)

Moro reflex—When a loud noise, bright light, loss of support is experienced, the neonate startles and flings out his arms. (It is not reaching out to be held because he was scared.)

What is the neonate doing socially? The infant can see very well close up, looking at close faces and registering information about what it sees and hears. The baby's kinesthetic sense (body movement and position) is present so the baby senses she is held, rocked, or touched. Babies usually cry less and are soothed by motion. The baby imitates and matches facial expressions. There is a wonderful example of this in the video *Exploring First Feelings* (1986). An adult is holding a newborn and opens her mouth. The baby gazes intently and matches the movement.

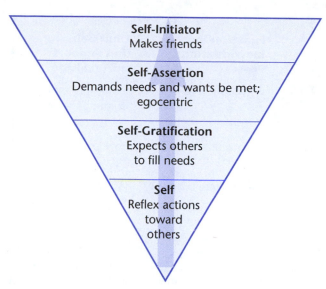

Figure 4–7 Stages of Social Development

Some babies right from the start are more gregarious, responsive to others, open to friendly overtures (Figure 4–8). Others are much more serious, reserved, limiting social contacts to just a few people. This personality type affects social interactions, and may be evident throughout the child's life. All areas of development—physical, cognitive, and emotional—are being affected and are affecting social development.

The implications for social development seem clear. The adult role is to meet the baby's needs, first of all in physical care. The infant who has attention and is prompted to respond to coos and words is being prepared for verbal conversations. The environment stimulates cognitive development. Psychological needs are met by being close, and handling the baby gently and responsively. Interactions are initiated and provide an interesting environment that responds to what the baby indicates she likes. These met needs give the infant a secure base from which to emerge into the social realm with the abilities to function in it.

Self-Gratification. During the first year, the infant is focused on receiving what he needs to survive and be happy, whatever that takes. This is the stage of attachment to his parents and is the beginning of his independence from them. During the first months of life, the baby increases the imitative behavior with smiles and laughs as the adult feeds, dresses, and cares for him. In the second half of the first year, the baby shows separation anxiety, trying to recapture the presence of the ones who meet his needs. He also begins some social exchanges by reaching out his hands and arms to be held, kicking, and making noises to gain attention. He is becoming mobile so he now can crawl to mother and pull on her leg. He is beginning to learn that he is no longer allowed to cry, sleep, play, eat, or act by his own desires. He may be put down for a nap when he is not "ready" or be told "No" when he reaches for grandpa's glasses. He cries and uses whatever social skills he has learned to get what he wants. He also is beginning to exert social control by withdrawing, by turning away from the spoon, a play thing, or a smiling auntie, pulling back her social self.

The play that infants engage in during the first year is mainly manipulation. They experience the object in every way possible: touching, squeezing, biting, smelling, shaking to listen, and throwing to see the reaction. A favorite game is peekaboo, which builds the cognitive structure of what goes away is not gone forever but returns. This game prepares the infant for separation. Another favorite game is to throw the toy away and have someone return it. It is a social give and take, action and response. It also reinforces the object permanence, but also that power over other people to do what he wants them to do. It is the precursor for taking turns, sharing, and playing baseball.

This process over the first two years is moving from self to the consideration of others. It is dependent on the infant's capabilities and the supportive adult behaviors. Figure 4–9 graphically portrays the stages, the roles of child and adult, with the desired outcomes (Kostelnik, et al., 2002).

Figure 4–8 Social development begins with the infant's needs being met.

Phase	Age of Onset in Months	Infant Capabilities	Social Outcome	Function in Individuations Process	Adult Behaviors That Support Individuation
I	0	Sucking, visual tracking; grasping; cuddling; vocalizes	Reflexes	Proximity to mother	Observation of states; prompt basic care
II	1–2	More time quietly alert; sensory learning about people and objects; molding to caregiver's body; continues interesting activities; coos and goos	Mother–infant pair perceived as a unit; beginning social responsiveness; mutual cueing, gazing	Begins differentiation between self and objects; more ways of maintaining proximity	Provide objects; engage in turn-taking play; give prompt basic care; respond sensitively to different states
III	4–8	Sits, grasps; creeps; increased interest in objects; sensory learning: mouthing, manipulating, examining, banging; laughs, yells, and squeals; babbling	Recognizes familiar people; shows clear preferences among people; intentionality limited to previously learned actions; playful; social smile, laughter	No self-awareness; beginnings of social expectations; stranger fear; maintains proximity by following, checking back on caregiver after short excursions	Provide a safe environment for floor exploration; establish limit for child; respond predictably
IV	9–12	Walking, climbing, running; joyful exploration; curious, excited; beginning use of language and gesture; person and object permanence becoming clearer; trial-and-error problem solving; intentions conveyed by language, gesture, and action; makes requests; comprehends words; complex babbling	Strong desire for approval, inclined to comply; self-willed; increased self-control; variety of emotions; social play with adults; interest in events	Beginning to recognize that mother is not part of self; maintains proximity by following and calling mother; strong preferences for particular people; protests separation; uses mother as a "base of operations" and moves outward	Protect from hazards (child has mobility without judgment); respond promptly to communicative acts; set and maintain routines and limits; provide opportunity for independence; use language to comfort, explain; leave child with familiar adults; have patience
V	15–24	Increase of all motor tasks; skillful exploration; rapid increase in language and nonverbal communication skills; offers objects to preferred adults; self-recognition person permanence achieved at end of phase V; pointing, says words then word combinations	Is likely to cling, then run away; plays "mother chase me!"; self willed: "No" before compliance; considerable amount of self-control; self-comforting; may show sudden fear after departure from mother; may cry from relief at her return	Realizes mother's goals are not own goals; may be ambivalent about dependence/independence; can play happily in absence of preferred person; uses "gifts" of toys in seeking proximity, more language	Verbalize about departures, reassure; tolerate rapid changes in approach and withdrawal; use language to discuss events, relationships, objects, etc.; allow child to control some holding on, letting go; make social expectations clear over and over; have patience
VI	24–30	Good understanding of ordinary language; intentionally well developed; mental problem solving; ability to ask for help based on need; goal-directed behavior; self-definition of gender and age	Increasing interest in other children; peer play and communication stronger; mutually regulated social interactions; pretend play	Realistic sense of self and others; uses a wide array of techniques to maintain proximity (helping, conversation, play, stories); can cope well with separations	Continue to reassure, support, and provide affection; praise efforts at self-control and independent behavior; provide experience with another toddler

Figure 4–9 The Individuation Process and Appropriate Adult Responses. (Courtesy of Kostelnik, M. J., Whiren, A. P., Soderman, A. K., Stein, L. C., & Gregory, K., 2002, p. 36. *Guiding Children's Social Development 4th Edition.* Clifton Park, NY: Thomson Delmar Learning. Reprinted with permission.)

Self-Assertion.   In the second year, the child generalizes all other social relationships. She expects that everyone, especially other children, will treat her in the same way as her parents: accepting, acquiescent, providing what she needs and wants. When this does not happen, she cannot understand it.

Language is developing at this time also, so vocabulary and verbal expression come into the social realm. Words and phrases like "No!" "Mine!" and "Gimme" are repeatedly used in social gatherings. "Please" is expected to yield miraculous results with objects or toys being the lure of toddler friendships.

Stages of Play.   Parten's Stages of Social Play (cited in Rogers & Sawyers, 1988) have long been referred to when classifying the development of social play (Figure 4–10). In **unoccupied play,** the child is not focused on any toy or activity: he follows the adult but does not engage in any sustained way. In **onlooker play,** the child watches other children play but does not get involved. This is used frequently by children in new situations. They can scope out the territory. It is also the style of children who are shy, emotionally depressed, or just not feeling like getting involved. The caregiver attends to both behaviors, assesses possible causes, and decides if action is indicated. The adult may decide to issue an invitation to play. In this way, she can role model how to join in the play. The decision may be to allow the child to have control over joining or not.

Solitary play, playing alone or totally focused on one's own play, is used for manipulation and practice, stress release, or by choice. It is the way of gaining familiarity with a new toy, game, or sports equipment. It is the repetitive motion to make a skill become natural. Many find this relaxing and rewarding.

In **parallel play,** there is minimal social contact. It is not solitary play, but it is not involved either. It involves companionship but not cooperation, affiliation but not association. The young child at this stage is not developmentally able to sustain a higher level of play.

This stage is mainly manipulative, seeing how things work. The developing small muscles are used to twist, insert, pound, shovel, grasp, release, and pinch. The large muscles are used for climbing, pedaling, running, and jumping. The child, at the beginning of this stage, cannot sustain interactive play because of limited language, cognitive, social, and emotional skills. That does not keep the child from seeking out those social contacts. In the second year, walking widens the social world considerably. Now the child can walk over to other children and initiate interactions. Because of social immaturity, however,

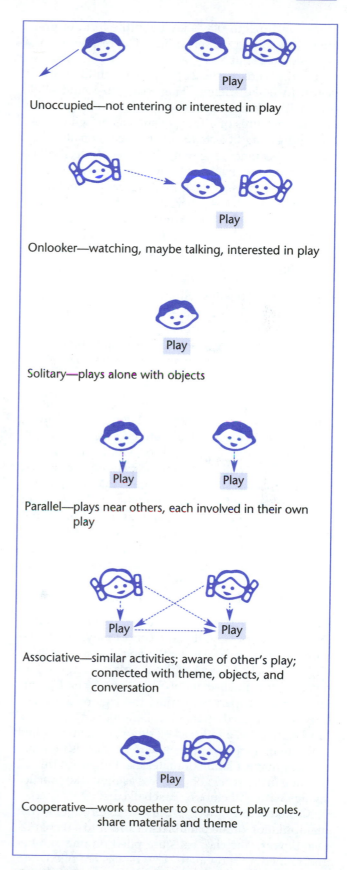

Unoccupied—not entering or interested in play

Onlooker—watching, maybe talking, interested in play

Solitary—plays alone with objects

Parallel—plays near others, each involved in their own play

Associative—similar activities; aware of other's play; connected with theme, objects, and conversation

Cooperative—work together to construct, play roles, share materials and theme

Figure 4–10   The Stages of Social Play

those overtures to play may be in the form of grab-bing a toy, biting, or screaming. The responses may be less than friendly.

By the end of the second year, children have begun to make friends. They recognize other chil-dren with whom they have frequent contact. They imitate overtures of affection, such as hugging, kiss-ing, and giving objects to others. Occasionally, they make eye contact, engaging in little conversations. Mostly they are involved in their own play and play objects. Still possessing immature cognitive, social, emotional structures, sharing and turn taking are limited, if present at all. Some very young children have been observed in friendships. Rubin (1980) listed some factors that contributed to these early friendships.

- secure relationships with their mothers
- relationships with older siblings or children
- their mothers were friends
- the children were at similar developmental levels, had similar temperaments, and behavioral styles (pp. 26, 27)

Children's play can be observed and coded using Rubin's play matrix (Rubin, Maioni, & Hornung, 1976) of Functional (explorative, repetitive play), Constructive (creating a product), Dramatic (pretend-ing), and Play with Rules (game playing), combined with the social stages of solitary (alone), parallel (alongside), and interactive (with others). The stages of play are developmental stages that are attained and built upon for the next stage but are revisited again and again throughout life for various reasons. Regres-sion to an earlier stage is not viewed as peculiar or cause for alarm. The setting, the person's style, and the situation determine how the person will interact.

Types of Play. Besides the stages of play, another dynamic enters play. It is the *how* of play. Four cate-gories of play are seen in the social stages of play (Figure 4–11). In **functional play,** actions are repeated for practice and exploration. A child paints all over the paper, his hands, the legs of the easel. Clay is squeezed, patted, rolled, poked, and cut. Blocks are piled and knocked down, containers filled with them, then dumped. No end product is in mind; it is just manipulation of materials. People do this all the time in sporting goods stores as they take practice swings with golf clubs or baseball bats.

Constructive play produces a product. That manipulation of the paintbrush turns into a recogniz-able flower. The clay balls are piled on one another and named a "snowman." The blocks are piled, and the builder calls it "The Umpire (sic) State Building."

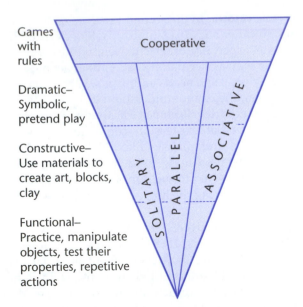

Figure 4–11 Types and stages of play

Dramatic play takes the player into the world of pretend. The paintbrush becomes a bee buzzing toward the flower, gathering nectar. The snowman is moved along the table, talking to other clay creations and wondering what will happen when the sun comes out. The builder takes a monkey from the jun-gle set and has King Kong climbing up the building. Participation, with or without props, in the world of fantasy is classified as this type of play.

As children move toward the fifth and sixth years, **games with rules** become part of their play repertoire. This coincides with mathematical reason-ing and the social-emotional stage of industry, putting things in order. By this age, children are bringing themselves into control, passing the egocen-tric stage, so now they can see from another's point of view. This stage also appears at a time when chil-dren's language skills are more developed and they are able to play in a more cooperative way.

Self-Initiator. Three-, four-, and five-year-olds are blossoming social beings. They now have the verbal, physical, and cognitive skills to begin to interact more with each other. They engage in **associative play,** doing a similar type of activity, involved in the same play theme or with similar types of toys, but in this stage they still are "doing their own thing." They are not working together toward a common goal, they just happen to be near each other, talking about what each of them is doing.

Cooperative play produces a common product, such as a block building, a road in the sand connecting areas, or dinner in the dramatic area. All players are working out a common plan. Preschoolers are still in the Preoperational Stage, still egocentric, but they are making advances. The teacher prepares an environment that will enhance social development by providing enough materials so that solitary and parallel play is not thwarted by having to "steal" from others. Cooperation and sharing are planned into the routines and curriculum by such things as helper charts, joint projects, songs, stories, and puppet plays. Competition during this period is not understood, so it is not an appropriate method of group interactions. Games with winners and losers, who can be the best, the fastest, or the neatest reinforce selfish attitudes. Cooperation and concern for others are the major social tasks of this age. Children who have had experiences in rule-making for the classroom and in their enforcement in an acceptable way get along better. They know and understand the reasons for why rules exist. They are careful observers of others who are breaking the rules. This is the beginning of moral development, recognizing right from wrong.

Difficulties between children are best handled not by the teacher as the judge. The teacher's role is facilitator for negotiation, helping those involved to tell each other their point of view. The children decide in a democratic manner.

Excluded children, those who have difficulty being accepted by peers, have some common characteristics. Disliked children often ignore other children's overtures to play, misunderstand peers' emotions, and are aggressive (Kemple, 1992). A strategy to help excluded or disliked children is to pair them with a younger child with whom they can feel more socially confident. Likewise, they may be paired with those who are socially competent as a model. Alternatives to aggressiveness through role plays, books, and puppet plays may give problem-solving ideas to be remembered when conflicts arise.

The Importance of Play to Social Development

EXERCISE: How do you play?

Play is a part of life, not just for children but for adults as well. Some early childhood programs are criticized for allowing play. "They're not learning anything there. All they ever do is just play." The word *play* is used repeatedly in discussing social development and many other areas as well. An understanding of play and its importance is necessary to child observers because it is a vehicle for learning.

The phrase "Play is the child's work," or variations of it, have been the theme or motto for defending play. The Concept Map in Figure 4–12 illustrates the developmental areas involved in play, kinds of play, its connection with language arts, and the necessary provisions for play. The opposite word from *play* is *work*. The constructivist theory (DeVries & Kohlberg 1987) contends it is through play and interaction with the environment that children construct mental images and processes. This is *work* in the sense that it has purpose and a definite goal. When an attempt is made to differentiate play from work, the dividing line becomes blurred. Play has been described and researched by many people. Rubin, Fein, and Vandenberg (1983) formed this description of play.

1. Play is intrinsically motivated.
2. Play is relatively free of externally imposed rules.
3. Play is carried out as if the activity were real.
4. Play focuses on the process rather than any product.
5. Play is dominated by the players.
6. Play requires the active involvement of the players.

The International Association for the Child's Right to Play (IPA) has in its declaration that play, along with the basic needs of nutrition, health, shelter, and education, is vital to develop the potential of all children. Play is instinctive, voluntary, and spontaneous. Play helps children develop physically, mentally, emotionally, and socially. Play is a means of learning to live, not merely a way to pass time (Brett, Moore, & Provenzo, 1993).

It is obvious that play can take place without other people, so solitary play is not just a stage but a type of play. Play with other people involved is democratic, without rules. Each player has some authority over the play. By observing, it is evident that not every player has equal power or as much power as they may want. Conflict in play erupts when the social development of the players is uneven. All the other developmental areas such as cognitive, language, physical, and emotional contribute to play's success.

Observing Play and Social Development

"Kidwatching" (Goodman, Goodman, & Hood, 1989) as children interact with each other can be extremely amusing. They reveal so much of themselves and all areas of development as they play. Information on physical, cognitive, language, emotional, and social development can be gathered as children interact with the environment and other people.

Figure 4–12 Concept Map

Anecdotal and Running Record. Social play observations are caught vividly with Anecdotal and Running Recordings that capture the actions and the words. A narrative gives a lasting memory of an event that can be wrought with meaning to every reader. One of the foremost kidwatchers is Vivian Paley. Her books of Anecdotal Recordings, many about boys and girls in dramatic play, are not only entertaining but full of meaning. In *Boys & Girls:* *Superheroes in the Doll Corner* (1984), she relates a discussion with the children about where the real work of school is happening in the classroom.

Paley is so skillful in asking open-ended questions such as, "How can you tell if you're working or playing?" She accurately records children's conversations and her questions that explore their thinking. Reeny in *The Girl with the Brown Crayon* (Paley, 1997) joins her classmates through a study of the books of

Leo Lionni as well as leads them to learn about self-identity. These books are wonderful examples of anecdotal recording and thoughtful teaching.

Classifications of Play. Observers of social development should be able to recognize and label social play using Parten's stages (unoccupied, onlooker, solitary, parallel, associative, cooperative) and Smilansky's and Piaget's play categories (functional, constructive, dramatic, games with rules).

EXERCISE: Using Parten's, Smilansky's and Piaget's terms, classify the following players.

1. Jake and Donald are sitting across from each other, building with separate erector sets. Jake and Donald are in the _____ stage, demonstrating the _____ type of play.
2. Heather, Greg, and Lisa are putting on a puppet play in a cardboard stage. Louise has been watching for several minutes. Louise is in the _____ stage, while Heather, Greg, and Lisa are in the _____ stage, demonstrating _____ type of play.
3. Piku is at the art table making balls of clay and poking them with a pencil. He is in the _____ stage of play, demonstrating _____ type of play.
4. Barry is laying parallel rows of blocks and Birdie is riding a truck back and forth between them. Barry and Birdie are in the _____ stage of play, Barry demonstrating _____ type of play. Birdie is demonstrating _____. She says, "I'm delivering bread to the store." Now her play is _____.

In checking your understanding of the play stages and types, you should have recognized: (1) parallel, constructive, (2) onlooker, cooperative, dramatic; (3) solitary, functional; (4) associative, constructive, functional, dramatic.

Checklists. Most developmental checklists have a section for social play, usually using the stages and types previously mentioned. One that has been developed to help teachers and parents monitor a child's social behavior is shown in Figure 4–13. It comes with the admonition from the authors, McClellan and Katz (1993), that the intent is not to prescribe "correct social behavior." It is to uncover children who may be doing poorly on many items on the list. Those children may have personality and temperament differences that are completely normal for them. Children from diverse cultural and family backgrounds may not *usually* do many of these things. When this checklist

I. Individual Attributes

The child:
1. Is **usually** in a positive mood
2. Is not **excessively** dependent on the teacher, assistant, or other adults
3. **Usually** comes to the program or setting willingly
4. **Usually** copes with rebuffs and reverses adequately
5. Shows the capacity to empathize
6. Has a positive relationship with one or two peers; shows capacity to really care about them, miss them if absent, etc.
7. Displays the capacity for humor
8. Does not seem to be acutely or chronically lonely

II. Social Skill Attributes

The child **usually**
1. Approaches others positively
2. Expresses wishes and preferences clearly; gives reasons for actions and positions
3. Asserts own rights and needs appropriately
4. Is not easily intimidated by bullies
5. Expresses frustrations and anger effectively and without harming others or property
6. Gains access to ongoing groups at play and work
7. Enters ongoing discussion on the subject; makes relevant contributions to ongoing activities
8. Takes turns fairly easily
9. Shows interest in others; exchanges information with and requests information from others appropriately
10. Negotiates and compromises with others appropriately
11. Does not draw inappropriate attention to self
12. Accepts and enjoys peers and adults of ethnic groups other than his or her own
13. Gains access to ongoing groups at play and work
14. Interacts nonverbally with other children with smiles, waves, nods, etc.

III. Peer Relationship Attributes

The child is
1. **Usually** accepted, versus neglected or rejected, by other children
2. **Sometimes** invited by other children to join them in play, friendship, and work.

Figure 4–13 The Social Attributes Checklist. (Reprinted from McClellan, D. E., & Katz, L. *Young Children's Social Development: A Checklist.* Urbana, IL: ERIC Clearinghouse on Elementary and Early Childhood Education, 1993. EDO-PS-93-6.)

shows children are having social difficulties, the teacher assesses the cause and plans for a classroom that is supportive and accepting.

There are two published rating scales with preschool norms: the Social Skills Rating Scale (SSRS) (Gresham & Elliott, 1990) and the Preschool and

Kindergarten Behavior Scales (PKBS) (Merrell, 1994). These tools can be used for social skills assessment and intervention planning.

HELPING ALL CHILDREN WITH SOCIAL DEVELOPMENT

Free play in smaller spaces for close proximity play, with teachers providing low structure with minimal rules but a wide variety of toys, provides the best environment for social interactions for children with or without disabilities. While meeting the learning needs of children with disabilities, inclusive settings have been shown to contribute to emotional understanding and acceptance in typically developing children (Diamond, 2001). There seems to be little difference between the number of friendships for children with disabilities and typically developing children in inclusive settings (Buysse, Goldman, & Skinner, 2002). This environment promotes imitation of peers by younger children and those with developmental delays. Some modifications to the environment are made specific to the child's need.

Social interactions depend heavily on communication. For the child with a hearing loss, this is a barrier. Early involvement with hearing children as social role models and alternative communication techniques are helpful in promoting social development. For the teacher, this also means learning some way to communicate with the child to facilitate social interactions with the child's peers and interpret the classroom environment.

Vision impairment does not necessarily cause social problems but more likely it is society's reaction to the impairment. The more severe the impairment the less negative the reaction, possibly because of the sympathy effect. Children with thick corrective lenses may be rejected as a playmate by other children just from appearances. The teacher can inform children of the nature of the child's vision and how it may affect the child in the classroom, inviting other children's assistance and acceptance. The teacher as a role model provides an environment that is safe but allows all the freedom and challenge other children receive.

Children with physical limitations are now included in regular classrooms, advertisements, and television shows. Familiarity with prostheses, walkers, and wheelchairs are helping to bring more social peer acceptance in group settings. Children have a desire to be helpful yet the danger exists for them to do too much, reinforcing learned helplessness. It is important for every child to be included in every classroom activity to the fullest of her ability. That will go a long way in facilitating peer acceptance as well.

Children from other cultures may have different social styles, depending on cultural values and practices. The teacher familiarizes himself with the cultures of the children in the group and transfers that awareness to assist the child to feel comfortable socially in the classroom. If a child does not speak English, the teacher, even though he may not speak the child's language, can act as a body language translator and an advocate for the child with the other children. The family, through an interpreter, can supply the teacher with a list of common words and their meanings.

The social climate of acceptance for all children will be extended to any child with differences. Having a friend is one of the most important motivators in learning and feeling successful and happy. The teacher must do all in his power to make that happen.

HELPING PROFESSIONALS FOR SOCIAL DEVELOPMENT CONCERNS

If all the efforts of the staff and observations documented by Anecdotal and Running Records or social checklists indicate a child is having a problem in this area, some action must be taken. In a talk with the family, the teacher can discuss his concerns. This is a sensitive area since no family wants to hear that their child is rejected and friendless. Family dynamics and values are closely woven with social development, so the utmost care should be taken in this approach. The family probably already has clues the child is having difficulty. The child may be reluctant to come to school, with crying and tantrums every morning. The child may be getting into fights, hurting and being hurt. Together some of the possible causes are explored and some plans agreed upon.

If the problem is prolonged or so severe it seems inadvisable to wait, then helping professionals may be consulted. After the medial personnel have ruled out any possible physical cause, then the psychological causes could be examined. Some of those professionals might include a

social worker—counsels individuals and families, serves as advocate or consultant to agencies or schools

family therapist—psychologist specializing in working with families in the treatment of an individual or family group *play therapist*—psychologist or psychiatrist using play for diagnosis, dialogue, and treatment of childhood social-emotional disorders

child psychologist—evaluates, diagnoses, and treats children for emotional, social, cognitive, and behavioral disorders

interviews or discussions about friends

time samples—Who the child is with during free choice time

work samples—child's friends depicted in art work, collaborative work such as murals, joint buildings

photographs, audio or video tape capturing child's interactions with others

OTHER METHODS

Other Methods to Record Social Development:

Class List Log—who plays with whom

Notation of level of social play stage:

anecdotal recording

checklists and rating scales

frequency counts—How many play encounters occur with another child during one day? How frequently a child leads/follows another child during one day?

KEY TERMS

associative play	object permanence
constructive play	onlooker play
cooperative play	parallel play
dramatic play	Running Record
egocentric	social competence
functional play	solitary play
games with rules	unoccupied play

WEEK 4: PLAN A

RUNNING RECORD OF SOCIAL DEVELOPMENT FOR GROUP C

Students

Select two children, and follow the directions below. From Group C, assign each of the children to a day this week.

Decide on a 10-minute time block to observe each child. Fold lined paper down the middle and write in the left-hand column. When that time comes, whatever that child is doing, begin your recording. Start with the child's name, date, time, and in which area or activity the child is engaged. From that point, write down each action and movement, and any conversation. Be as descriptive as you can without summarizing or giving reasons for the behavior. Record conversations word for word. Later in the day, take the recording and make comments, write questions, or pose theories in the right-hand column. Review the stages of social play. Identify which stage or stages the child demonstrated, and write that in the right column as well.

What to Do with It

Filing. Write a few summary words, the date, and your name on the Portfolio Overview Sheet (Figure

4–14). Make a note if further action is indicated and follow through. File the Running Record in each child's portfolio.

Sharing with Child and Family. Share with the family and the child, if appropriate. For example: "Mrs. Stento, today when I was watching Tony play he was deeply engrossed in pouring sand from one container to another. Another child came to the table and began to play next to Tony. Without missing a beat in pouring, Tony slid one of his containers toward the other child, who took it and also began filling it. Not a word was exchanged but that was a big step for Tony, sharing one of his toys," or "Maxine, I was making some notes as you played

SOCIAL DEVELOPMENT

Documentation	Location	Recorder	Date
CL	Class file	MS	9/26
CL	"	BAN	1/10
CK	Portfolio	BAN	4/30
CK	"		5/20

Figure 4–14 Portfolio Overview Example

today and I wrote down about how you played the big sister going to the doctor with her baby brother. You were very gentle with Robert. That must be the way your sister Irene is gentle with you."

Actions.

Read a Book.

Bridwell, N. (1998). *Clifford Makes a Friend*. New York: Scholastic.

Carle, E. (1971). *Do You Want to be My Friend?* New York: HarperCollins.

Lyon, G. (1989). *Together*. New York: Orchard Books.

MacDonald, A. (1997). *Little Beaver and the Echo*. New York: Talman Co.

McPhail, D. M. (1998). *A Bug, a Bear, and a Boy*. New York: Scholastic.

Oram, H. (1998). *Badger's Bad Mood*. New York: Scholastic.

In the Environment.
- Provide dramatic play props such as male and female dress-up clothes, dolls and home-type furniture and accessories, large muscle play equipment such as climbers, jumping and swinging apparatus, and boxes, balls, and tunnels.
- Attach photographs of each child in the classroom to individual blocks in the block area to be used as props.

In the Curriculum.
- Include children's names in songs and chants.
- Pair children together for simple cooperative play activities.

In the Newsletter.
- Article about children's friendships at this age. Many families expect friendships to form at a very early age while the child is still centered on self (not in a negative but developmental way). Help families see how this is a part of development.
- Article to encourage "play dates" but discourage "exclusive parties."

WEEK 4: PLAN B

CLASS LIST LOG OF SOCIAL DEVELOPMENT FOR ALL

Copy a Class List Log from Appendix D and write the names of the children in your class alphabetically. Draw vertical lines to indicate the social play stages: onlooker, solitary, parallel, associative, and cooperative. This week during free play time, observe the children as they interact with each other. Place a check mark in the stage next to their name. If you can, you could also indicate what type of play it is: functional (F), constructive (C), dramatic (D), or games with rules (G).

What to Do with It

Filing. At the end of the week, take the Class List Log and transfer the stage you observed onto the Portfolio Overview Sheet with your name and date of the observation. (See the example in Plan A, Figure 4–14.)

File the Class List Log in the class file. Make note if any further action is indicated.

Sharing with Child and Family. Share with the family and the child, if it is appropriate. For example: "Mr. Nugent, I noticed Max playing for a long time by himself today with the Legos," or "Kathy, I noticed you building together with Laura today in the block area."

WEEK 4: PLAN C

REFLECTIVE JOURNAL

Respond to the following in your Refective Journal, kept in a private file at home.

One difference in the way boys and girls played this week was ...

I noticed this week that there was no difference in the way boys and girls ...

When children have difficulty sharing, I ...

When I think about my own social development, I prefer (Onlooker, Solitary, Parallel, Associative, or Cooperative) play. I think it's because ...

I wish I could ...

REFERENCES

Brett, A., Moore, R. C., & Provenzo, Jr., E. F. (1993). *The complete playground book.* Syracuse, NY: Syracuse University Press.

Buysse, V. Goldman, B. D., & Skinner, M. L. (2002). Setting effects on friendship formation among young children with and without disabilities. *Exceptional Children, 68* (4) 503–517.

DeVries, R., & Kohlberg, L. (1987). *Constructivist early childhood education: Overview and comparison with other programs.* Washington, DC: National Association for the Education of Young Children.

Diamond, K. E. (2001). Relationships among young children's ideas, emotional understanding and social contact with classmates with disabilities. *Topics in Early Childhood Special Education, 21* (2), 104.

Elliott, S. N., McKevitt, B. C., & DiPerna, J. C. (2002). Best practices in preschool social skills training. In A. Thomas & J. Grimes, *Best practices in school psychology IV.* Bethesda, MD: National Association of School Psychologists.

Erikson. E. H. (1950). *Childhood and society.* New York: Norton.

Exploring first feelings: Milestones in the emotional development of babies. (1985). [Videorecording]. Washington, DC: Institute for Mental Health Initiatives.

Fabes, R. A., Eisenberg, N., Jones, S., Smigh, M., Guthrie, I., Poulin, R., Shepard, S., & Friedman, J. (1999). Regulation, emotionality and preschoolers' socially competent peer interactions. *Child Development, 70* (2), 432–442.

Flavell, J. (1977). *Cognitive development.* Englewood Cliffs, NJ: Prentice Hall.

Freud, S. (1953). *The standard edition of the complete psychological works of Sigmund Freud.* (J. Strachey, Ed. and Trans.). London: Hogarth and the Institute of Psychoanalysis.

Goodman, K. S., Goodman, Y. M., & Hood, W. J. (1989). *The whole language evaluation book.* Portsmouth, NH: Heinemann.

Gresham, F. M., & Elliott, S. N. (1990). *Social skills rating system.* Circle Pines, MN: American Guidance System.

Hartup, W. W. (1992). *Having friends, making friends, and keeping friends: Relationships as educational contexts.* Urbana, IL: ERIC Clearinghouse on Elementary and Early Childhood Education, ED 354 854.

Kemple, K. (1992). *Understanding and facilitating preschool children's peer acceptance.* Urbana, IL: ERIC Clearinghouse on Elementary and Early Childhood Education, EDO-PS-92-5.

Kostelnik, M. J., Whiren, A. P., Soderman, A. K., Stein, L. C., & Gregory, K. (2002). *Guiding children's social development: Theory to practice,* 4th ed. Clifton Park, NY: Thomson Delmar Learning.

Lawhon, T. (1997). Encouraging friendships among children. *Childhood Education, 73* (4), 228–231.

Maslow, A. H. (1970). *Motivation and personality.* New York: Harper & Row.

McClellan, D., & Katz, L. (1993). *Young children's social development: A checklist.* Urbana, IL: ERIC Clearinghouse on Elementary and Early Childhood Education. EDO-PS-93-6.

Merrell, K. W. (1994). *Preschool and kindergarten behavior scales.* Austin, TX: PRO-ED.

Paley, V. G. (1984). *Boys & girls: Superheroes in the doll corner.* Chicago: The University of Chicago Press.

Paley, V. G. (1997). *The girl with the brown crayon.* Cambridge, MA: Harvard University Press.

Rogers, C. S., & Sawyers, J. K. (1988). *Play in the lives of children.* Washington, DC: National Association for the Education of Young Children.

Rothbart, M. K., & Bates, J. E. (1998). In N. Eisenberg (Ed.), W. Damon (Series Ed.), *Handbook of child psychology: Vol. 3, Social, emotional and personality development* (pp. 105–176). New York: Wiley.

Rubin, K. H., Maioni, T., & Hornung, M. (1976). Free play behaviors in lower-class and middle-class preschoolers: Parten and Piaget revisited. *Child Development, 47,* 414–419.

Rubin, K., Fein, G. G., & Vandenberg, B. (1983). Play. In E. M. Hetherington (Ed.), P. H. Mussen (Series Ed.), *Handbook of child psychology: Vol. 4. Socialization, personality, and social development* (pp. 693–774). New York: Wiley.

Rubin, Z. (1980). *Children's friendships.* Cambridge, MA: Harvard University Press.

Skinner, B. F. (1953). *Science and human behavior.* New York: Macmillan.

Watson, J. B. (1950). *Behaviorism.* New York: Norton.

RESOURCES

Katz, L. G., & McClellan, D. C. (1997). *Fostering children's social competence: The teacher's role.* Washington, DC: NAEYC.

Kostelnik, M. J., Whiren, A. P., Soderman, A. K., Stein, L. C., & Gregory, K. (2002). *Guiding children's social development* (4th ed.). Clifton Park, NY: Thomson Delmar Learning.

Rogers, C. S., & Sawyers, J. K. (1988). *Play in the lives of children.* Washington, DC: National Association for the Education of Young Children.

For additional information on early education curriculum, visit our Web site at http://www.earlychilded.delmar.com

5

Using Frequency Counts to Look at Emotional Development

IN THIS CHAPTER

- **Using Frequency Counts**

- **Looking at Emotional Development**

- **Helping All Children with Emotional Development**

- **Helping Professionals for Emotional Concerns**

- **Topics in Observation: The Assessment and Curriculum Braid**

USING FREQUENCY COUNTS

EXERCISE: How often did you do each of the following today?

eat
go to the bathroom
talk on the phone
say your pet phrase ("Oh well," "Basically,"
    or "Whatever")

Much behavior is habitual, done without thinking. Occasionally, those habitual actions become really important. More attention is given to how often and what food is eaten when someone is on a diet. Measuring or counting is a part of decision making. If a person is experiencing an illness, the number of times one goes to the bathroom may be an important symptom. Legislators tally the number of pro and con calls received on an issue. Weight before beginning a diet, the number of phone calls, or an unusual change in body functions is an indicator that provides information for comparison. In behavior modification, a measurement is made, action taken, and then measured again to see the significance of the change.

In the classroom, a **Frequency Count** can measure repeated actions of a child, the whole group, or the teacher. It is sometimes necessary to count behaviors that occur often in one day or session, such as hitting, children running, or the teacher saying, "Don't." Strategies are implemented then to reduce negative actions or behavior, or increase desirable ones.

EXERCISE: Frequently occurring actions that may occur in a group of preschool children follow. What is your estimate of how many times a day

each happens? In the following list, place a +
next to the ones you would like to increase and a
– next to ones you would like to decrease.

1. spills
2. biting
3. punching
4. "Thank you."
5. vomiting
6. using the book area
7. sharing
8. "Don't . . ."
9. "OK, guys."
10. "Teacher, Teacher . . ."

Candidates for a reduction are numbers 1, 2, 3, 8,
9, and 10. Numbers 4, 6, and 7 could be increased.
Number 5 is an infrequent event and would not be
a measurable criterion for a Frequency Count or a
reduction plan. It is necessary to note that incident,
however, on a health form or a short anecdotal. In an
infant room, this may be a more frequent event.
Number 2 is more likely to occur in a toddler room,
because it is an expected behavior. If it were a frequent behavior in a kindergarten room, with an individual child, or many children, the teacher would
begin to search for answers, after she applied first
aid, of course. Biting is not expected behavior for
kindergarten students.

Frequency Counts are a way of seeing just how
often an event happens. The purpose is to try to
change undesirable behavior. If the action is negative
and excessive for the age or stage expectations, then a
plan is implemented to try to reduce it. If an expected
behavior is not present or not happening often
enough, then a plan is made to try to increase it. After
a period of time, another Frequency Count is taken to
measure the success. The process is documented by a
Frequency Count to "prove" if the remedy or theory
works.

This is not recommending a program of behavior
modification where positive behavior is rewarded
so it will increase, and negative behavior is punished
so it will decrease. It is more a measurement of the
teacher or learning process, like a pretest and a post-
test. It assumes a change will take place. The agents
of that change may be time, direct instruction, modeling, planned experiences, and self-regulation. Bandura's social learning theory (1977) recognized that
the change, called learning, results from an interaction
between thinking, acting, and the environment.

Figure 5–1 is an example of a Frequency Count.
Spills seem to be happening many times a day in this
classroom and the staff is concerned, besides irri-

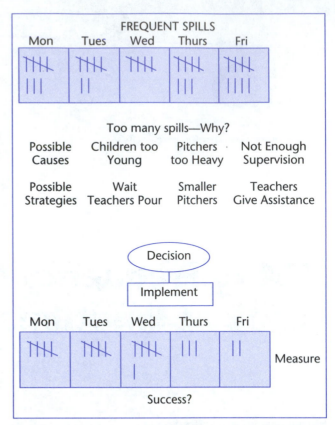

Figure 5–1 Frequency Counts to Measure Reduction of
Undesirable Behavior

tated, at the messes. They complain then talk about
some possible reasons. The children may be too
young to initiate pouring, or the pitchers available
are too heavy with no lids and opaque so the liquid
comes out unexpectedly for novice pourers. Perhaps
the adults are not sitting at the table with the children
but using that time to prepare for the next activity.
Each of the possible reasons suggests possible strate-

IT HAPPENED TO ME

The Spilling Song

In a center I visited recently, a spill occurred. Immediately, a teacher jumped up and turned on a
record player with a little song about spilling. She
later remarked, "That same child deliberately spills
every day." I asked about the song. "Oh, they love
it." Do you think the teacher's response to spilling
increased or decreased spilling at snack time?

gies. A decision is reached and the strategy is implemented. A later Frequency Count measures whether the strategy is successful or not.

Using the Frequency Count to Document Frequently Occurring Behaviors

Other classroom situations and possible strategies for Frequency Count measurement follow:

- decrease aggressive acts—prosocial or emotional curriculum
- decrease the need for teacher intervention—more self-help shelves for materials and supplies
- decrease inappropriate use of materials—helper chart to encourage responsibility
- document individual child with transition difficulties—individual Frequency Count and implementation of special warning before it is time to change activities
- decrease use of punitive guidance techniques—training in positive guidance
- decrease teacher chatting on the playground—coffee break for chatting before playground duty
- decrease domination of adult voices in the classroom—tape recorder to monitor and make teachers aware of voice level
- increase cooperative play—buddy time when each child and a friend choose an activity to do together
- increase interactions with families—weekly happy notes
- increase eye-level talking with children—small chairs in each learning center for teacher to sit on while observing play and talking to children
- increase scanning supervision of whole room—reminder posters for teachers on every wall that display "SCAN"
- increase use of learning area—place an adult there to interact with the children
- increase self-care—equip room with cleaning equipment, low shelves, paint smocks with Velcro, dress-up clothes with elastic and Velcro

Using Frequency Counts to Measure Prosocial and Antisocial Behavior

Groups of young children are emotionally and socially immature, resulting in disagreements and a lack of empathy for one another. The goals of adults who work with children are to decrease antisocial behavior and increase prosocial behavior. Frequency Counts can measure the effectiveness of a chosen strategy or intervention, or the progress that children make just from maturation and experience in a group setting.

A Frequency Count tallies each time a specified behavior occurs. The Frequency Count example in Figure 5–2 shows a group of eleven children on a certain day. Huy made no social contacts. What does that mean? We cannot tell from this recording. That means that it is a closed method. All the details except for the name of the child involved and the fact that it occurred are lost. The reader does not know the nature of the action, what precipitated it, any conversation from the incident, or the result. The purpose is solely to count.

EXERCISE: Interpret what the information in Figure 5–2 could mean.

> What kind of a player is Carol? Solitary, parallel, cooperative (not the traditional meaning, but play stage meaning)?
> What do you think Edward did?
> What about Huy? Why do you think he has no tallies?

Probably Carol is in the cooperative stage of play but immature socially. She had a lot of social contacts, but she may not have her emotions under control. After reading the rest of the chapter, particularly the difference between girls and boys, come back and think about Edward here. Huy probably is not making many social contacts because of his language barrier. Isolated children are neither prosocial or antisocial. The common definition of an introverted, withdrawn, quiet person is, "He's antisocial." In this case, it probably is not deliberate or willful, just lack of confidence: "When in doubt, do nothing" syndrome.

Prosocial and antisocial Frequency Counts give indicators of the emotional tone of the classroom. Prosocial behavior is the outward manifestation of empathy, caring for another person through an action. In encouraging caring communities, Frequency Counts help the teacher clearly see patterns of individuals who are displaying these behaviors.

Frequency Counts can be used in selected circumstances, not a usual part of the classroom information gathering. Effectively measuring before and after a strategy or a period of time gives important documentation to the significance of the interval.

Using Technology

If you are counting the frequency of one child's target behavior or actions, you can attach a counter to your belt. If counting a specific behavior of a group of children, the tallies on each child should be separate so a pencil-and-paper tally sheet would be the most efficient tool.

FREQUENCY COUNT

Date _March 01 Year_ Recorder _BAN_

Make a tally mark in the column next to the child's name each time you observe a behavior that you would classify as prosocial or antisocial.

CHILD'S NAME	PROSOCIAL Helping, sharing, hugging, calling another child by a kind name	ANTISOCIAL Hurting, hoarding, bad name calling, rejecting another child
Amy	✓ ✓	
Bajic	✓ ✓ ✓	✓ ✓ ✓ ✓
Carol	✓ ✓ ✓ ✓ ✓	✓ ✓ ✓ ✓ ✓
Danielle	✓	✓ ✓
Edward		✓ ✓ ✓ ✓ ✓ ✓
Fatima	✓	
Galina	✓ ✓ ✓	
Huy		
Irma	✓ ✓	✓
Jacob	✓ ✓	✓ ✓
Kara	✓ ✓ ✓ ✓	
Totals	24	22

Figure 5–2 Frequency Count Example

How to Find the Time

This method takes very little time. It may be one of the least time-consuming methods. Details, quotes, and situations are not recorded; only record the occurrence of the target behavior.

What to Do with the Information

The information gathered from a Frequency Count is more than food for an inquiring mind, although it may indicate that no change is needed. It is a tool to measure a baseline, the commonplace, not out of the ordinary. It is the basis for judgments about the need for change. A strategy is implemented to attempt the change then more Frequency Counts are taken to measure progress and success. The process is a mini-research and experiment in a behavior modification format. Depending on the topic and subject of the research, it can be shared as a victory in progress with families, other teachers, and the administration. It can be used as a needs assessment for equipment, materials, or teacher training. The postintervention Frequency Count can be used in reporting to funders or the administration the difference the new equipment or the training made. Periodic return to the Frequency Count method will measure how long-lasting the effects of the project have been.

Advantages

Frequency Counts are

- a quantitative measurement on which to base strategies for change.
- quick to record, with no details, just tallies to write.

- useful for quantitatively and objectively measuring frequently occurring behaviors.

Disadvantages

Frequency Counts can

- lose the raw data, with no details recorded.
- only measure one kind of behavior, making the results highly selective.
- allow the recorder's bias to enter the recording.

Pitfalls to Avoid

Frequency Counts

- can select behaviors to measure that do not occur often (we hope), such as: accidents requiring stitches, incidents of child abuse, guinea pig escapes.
- infer from one sample that this is normal behavior. (It may have been an unusual day so results are not indicative of a normal day.)
- allow much interpretation from one recorder to another. (For example, "Was that sharing when Aiko handed Katerina the Play Doh because Katerina demanded it?")
- are an intense recording method that requires the adult to be free from child-interaction responsibilities, which is not always possible.

LOOKING AT EMOTIONAL DEVELOPMENT

Stages of Emotional Development

EXERCISE: **What emotions would these events stir in you? How would you express it?**

You won the $3 million lottery.
You are asked by your best friend to co-sign a $20,000 loan.
You are told the plane has lost power, prepare for a crash landing.
You have lost an heirloom ring that has been in your family for five generations.
You just got a phone call from the lottery office that they made a mistake. You did not win the money after all.

Emotions are not grown. They change over time from simple to complex. Their development occurs in predictable stages but in very individual ways. Development of emotions is in the expression and control. As the human matures, the capacity for distinguishing between various emotions intensifies, and along with it the ability to recognize those same emotions in others. Finding acceptable expressions and control of those emotions is a lifelong struggle for the ability to control the intensity at both ends of the emotional balance.

Studies of emotions have found that there are emotions common to all humans (Figure 5–3). These **core emotions**—fear, rage, and love—were researched in the work of J. B. Watson (1914). These form the basis for all emotions that are just more finite distinctions of fear, rage, and love. Core emotions are, at first, purely responses to stimuli. Within the first year, however, their appearance becomes more deliberate and recognizable (Figure 5–4).

In the infant, these emotions are expressed first by reflexes, varying in intensity. They are usually governed not as much by the situation but by temperament. One baby expressing joy or contentment may lie passively, while others may move actively about. Babies differ in the intensity of their crying dependent more on their particular style than the range of their discontent. These temperaments are genetic but over time other influences will affect change in responses. Parental influence on temperament has been studied by many researchers. Thomas and Chess (1977) have done research on long-term effects of mother–child interactions on personality and emotional development. They identified nine temperamental qualities that can be observed not only in the infant but continued throughout life.

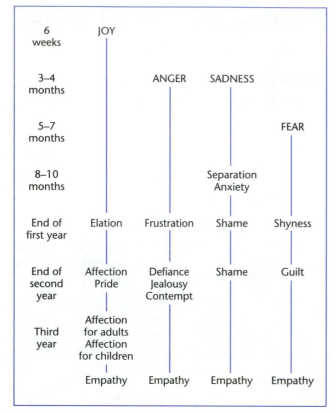

Figure 5–3 Emergence of children's emotions during the first three years of life.

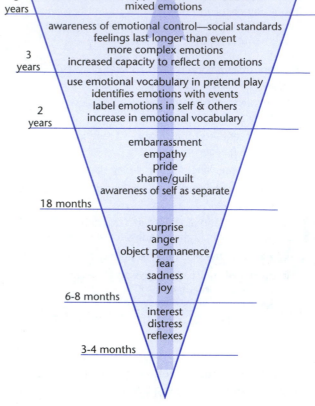

Figure 5–4 Emotional Development

1. *Activity level*—physical motion
2. *Rhythmicity*—regularity of biological functions
3. *Approach or withdrawal*—initial reaction to new stimulation
4. *Adaptability*—flexibility after initial reaction
5. *Intensity of reaction*—energy level of responses
6. *Threshold of responsiveness*—intensity of stimulation needed to produce a response
7. *Quality of mood*—general behavior
8. *Distractibility*—outside stimulation changing ongoing behavior
9. *Attention span and persistence*—length of time activities are maintained

EXERCISE: Think of yourself and one other person you know well and jot down, on a separate sheet of paper, descriptors in the nine categories of temperament.

	Self	Friend
1.		
2.		
3.		
4.		

5.
6.
7.
8.
9.

Examine the differences. Why are you different from your friend? Genetics? Family influences? Experiences with peers?

Socialization of Emotions

Emotional development has several aspects. The first is recognizing and interpreting the emotions in others. This is accomplished very early in life when an infant can distinguish between a smile and a serious face or frown. Infants whose mothers suffer from depression and therefore may lack certain facial expressions, especially friendly, approving ones, may internalize the expresssions as displeasure or rejection. This could affect attachment, one of the most basic necessities in future emotional development.

IT HAPPENED TO ME

When Are You Going to Control Your Temper?

My two sons and I were sitting at the dining room table doing homework when they started arguing over a pencil, the way seven- and nine-year-olds will. The argument got more and more heated until the furious nine-year-old flung the pencil at his brother. The pencil seemed to spin in slow motion as it narrowly missed his brother's eye. I was relieved that it missed but outraged that he would do such a dangerous thing. I got right in his face, and yelled, "When are you going to learn to control your temper!?" At that moment I realized I was out of control and he was wise not to say, "When you do, Mother."

As the child develops a more complex thinking process, he can differentiate the range of feelings from pleasant to elated and select expressive behaviors appropriate to the range. Emotional development then is the recognition of the feelings and range of emotions. Most of all, emotional development is learning to control and express emotions in a socially acceptable way. Humans spend the rest of their lives trying to interpret the feelings of others, which in turn has implications for the development of self. Goldman describes this ability as **emotional intelligence** (1995), recognizing emotions of others and self-awareness and impulse control. School readiness, early school success, and later accomplishments in the workplace are dependent on this emotional intelligence or competence (Peth-Pierce, 2000). Intervention programs have been successful in teaching children how to do this, making them better able to function in relationships in school, home, and ultimately the workplace.

Infants are born with the basic emotional responses that will become more defined in how they are expressed as other areas of development become more mature. As thinking levels develop, the causes of the feelings and more choices of expression are understood.

Emotional regulation is the ability to display spontaneous reactions and the ability to delay or control reactions as needed. Control and appropriate expression of emotions are learned, just as other skills are, through

Modeling—seeing how others react and express emotions

Direct instruction—"When you feel like that, this is what you can do or shouldn't do"

Positive or negative reinforcement—Smiles, nods, verbal praise or scowls, stern looks, no-no head shake, or harsh physical touching.

Inhibited children repress their emotions resulting not only in added stress but inability to learn how to practice social competencies, not learning how to appropriately express anger, fear, and frustration. Children without social skills and language to express emotions resort to socially unacceptable words and actions that cause them to be rejected by peers and labeled by adults as acting out.

Emotions are socialized or influenced in their recognition and expression by adults in the child's world. Americans display more intense expression of emotions than Chinese and Japanese people. This may cause children from Eastern cultures to be ill at ease in a setting where discussion and free expression of emotions are encouraged.

It is difficult to interpret the inner cause for the outward display of emotions. The observer infers the cause based on prior knowledge of development and behavioral cues. Each individual is different, and before language appears, it is impossible to be certain of the emotions of the observed. Between two and three years old, children use the words *mad, scared,* and *happy* to describe their own and other's emotions. Notice the correlation to the core emotions. By five years old they could match and label a broader range of emotions from pictures (Kuebli, 1994).

Help With Emotional Expression

EXERCISE: How do you feel when someone says, "I know just how you feel"?

Do you want to say, "No, you don't. How can you? Your experience was different from mine. You had different supports to lean on. You are different from me. You can't know how I really feel. I'm only letting you see a bit of what I really feel"?

How do you feel when someone says, "Don't feel that way"?

Will you stop feeling because they said that? Does it make the hurt or anger go away because they commanded it? You *do* feel that way. What you are trying to do is deal with it.

Emotions and their expression are very personal. As much as someone would like to alleviate another's pain, it is one of those times when a person only knows what they feel. The role of the family and teacher is to respect the child's emotions, not deny that they exist. "I can see that you are really sad over that." The adult models an acceptable way to express the emotion, "When I get sad or hurt, I sometimes cry and want to be alone." And everyone needs a friend who offers, "When you are ready to talk about it, or need a hug, I'm here."

In the case of angry and aggressive emotions, the same technique can be used. "I can see that you are really angry over that, but I can't let you hurt other people. When you are ready to tell your friend what made you so angry and try to work out the problem, I'll be here to help you. Until then you can paint at the easel or cut Play Doh with scissors to get yourself under control."

Figure 5–5 Joy is easy to recognize!

Joy, Love, and Happiness

EXERCISE: **What does happiness look like? What might be some causes of happiness?**

The most recognizable characteristic that suggests joy or happiness is smiling. Those first smiles are reputed to be reflex responses to digestion rather than an emotional state. Smiles in response to human voices are seen at three weeks and to familiar faces by three-and-one-half months. Laughter, in response to physical stimulation like tickling, then to more social situations, begins at four months. The reciprocal sharing of smiles, coos, and laughter is part of the attachment process needed for the coming separation, cognitively and physically. Emotional development is closely aligned with social interactions and cognitive development. When the infant can differentiate between self and others and realizes the primary caregiver is not with her, anger and fear combine to form separation anxiety. The emotional task of infancy is the formation of trust (Erikson, 1950), the confidence that needs will be met, mother will return, and all is well. That is the foundation for mental health (Figure 5–5).

Joy is manifested after the age of one from situations that have favorable results. To young children, that means it satisfies their own desires. As they work on autonomy, the accomplishment of tasks brings joy in the form of pride. As they near four and five years old, happiness is meeting adults' expectations. They are working toward empathy. They can now find joy for what is happening to others rather than self. That is a goal of social development for the benefit of the whole community.

The Absence of Joy. Factors that influence this emotion begin, as always, with what is inborn. Some infants just have a generally happy behavior. Others are more irritable and harder to find in a state of satisfaction and calm. That inborn temperament may be the beginning point. Interactions with mother, the primary caregivers, and others are extremely important. In cases studied in which infants were deprived of social interactions, physical, mental, and emotional disorders were seen contributing to the **failure to thrive.** In situations of neglect, conditions of poverty, or physical illness, emotional damage can be seen as well.

EXERCISE: **Think of someone you know who has had a life of really difficult experiences yet appears to have overcome the obstacles and is emotionally whole. What made the difference for that person?**

EXERCISE: **How do you deal with difficult situations?**

Some children display behaviors that will allow them to deal with the absence of joy in their life. First, children may be in denial. They may use fantasy or refuse to recognize the difficult situation by acting as if it were not so. Children use this technique to come through abuse, removing themselves emotionally from the situation until it becomes unreal, a sealed-off part of their life. Children may regress to an earlier stage of behavior to escape the reality of the difficulty. By recording a child's progress, an observation of regression can be a warning that something may be bothering the child. Withdrawal might be used as protection from facing the absence of joy. By not interacting socially, the pain or risk of pain is thought to make it hurt less. By evaluating children's social behaviors against the typical stages, clues may be noticed that suggest a possible emotional trauma. When children act out, there may be many causes. It may be a realistic behavior for this age or stage, a bid for attention, or a disregard for others because of the emotional pain the child is experiencing. Observing the indicators of defense mechanisms should be noted and studied further.

An interesting phenomenon that puzzles researchers, as well as anyone who wonders about cause and effect, is the coping mechanisms that some children develop. Some children can remain emotionally healthy after experiencing traumatic events. Anthony and Cohler (1987) looked at the common factors in the **invulnerable child,** the one who survives and can rise above expected dire outcomes from difficult, seemingly impossible circumstances. They exhibit empathy, detachment from the dysfunctional behaviors of others, a sense of humor, and personal power. Teachers or caregivers have incredible belief in the capacity for the spirit to overcome difficult situations. This leads them to assist every child learning **coping skills.** The child's competency and empowerment will help bring joy and happiness out of deprivation.

When a child displays a lack of joy, the teacher has some steps to take (Figure 5–6). The first one is to recognize the emotion and not show disapproval or denial even if the emotion is not justified. So often adults say "Smile for me," or "You shouldn't feel that way." The emotion is real to the person feeling it and should not be denied by an outsider. Second, trying

to get the child to forget about the feeling is a short-term solution. Pretending happiness does not help when the child is experiencing loneliness from missing the family member who left him at day care. Acting silly to get the child to smile or involving him in an activity only temporarily relieves the difficulty.

When children learn coping skills, they can generalize to any situation that is unpleasant. In this way, they can address the difficulty in an emotionally healthy way.

Coping skills are learned in the same ways other skills are learned. The first step is the recognition of the cause of the problem. This will help the child, at her developmental level, understand why she has this feeling. The emotion is named and the normalcy of these feelings will help the child move toward a solution. For example: "You're not happy today because you didn't want to say good-bye to your dad and see him leave you. Everyone feels sad sometimes when they want to be with someone and they can't. What are some things you could do until he comes back?"

Adults can role model coping mechanisms for children. "I think I'll put on this happy record. It always makes me feel like smiling when I hear this song." Some direct instruction can take place by using discussions following books or puppet scenarios in which characters have similar feelings of sadness or loneliness. Helping children to learn ways to deal with their feelings is a part of the social-emotional curriculum.

Anger and Aggression

EXERCISE: Using a separate sheet of paper, list 10 things that make you angry. What do you do when you are angry?

Developmental Stages of Anger. Anger grows from the unmet needs of the self. When a baby rolls over and gets stuck next to the bars of the crib, that cry is an angry one. She wants to move, but something is preventing her from carrying out that urge to move. That same feeling will overcome her twenty years later when she is late for work but stuck in traffic. The response is usually different (sometimes not). Anger is energizing. It motivates the child to chase down the one who took his tricycle while he was off picking dandelions. It enables the adult to clean the whole house after an argument with a friend. Some of those actions may address the cause of the anger while others act as a valve to let off steam. This **displacement** of anger's energy has been the subject of much research with varying results. The major

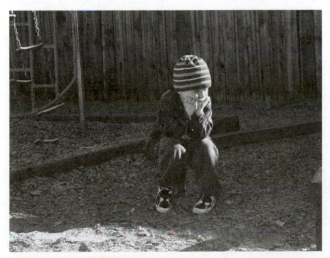

Figure 5–6 A child with an absence of joy is a concern.

Figure 5–7 Tantrums are common in toddlers, displaying newly developed emotions without the inner controls to manage them.

objection to it is that it does not solve the problem, just vents the energy.

In the child's second year, she is seeking to be autonomous, to rule herself. She is angry when those attempts are resisted, even if it is for her own safety. Her lack of full language development makes it difficult for her to express her desires or her feelings about being thwarted or denied, so anger and frustration are increased (Figure 5–7). The egocentricism contributes to angry feelings. The child can only see her own point of view. She cannot understand why she cannot have the tricycle back after leaving it for 10 minutes, just because she wants it. She wants it so she believes she should have it. With the struggle for autonomy it is not surprising that defiance, an angry stance against authority, would begin in the second year. The battle of wills is beginning here, and depending on the child's temperament and the parenting style, it may be a long, difficult one or less severe.

Toward the end of the second year a more complicated form of anger—jealousy—appears. It could be caused by adult attention diverted away from the child or a desirable object seen in the hands of someone else. A common reaction to this jealousy is a temper tantrum. These are often seen in the grocery store, or the mall, where there is so much visual stimulation. Attractive, desirable objects are all around but so are restrictions the child cannot understand. They are told not to touch when their mother is

touching. They are told they cannot have it when it is placed at eye level and within their reach.

The temper tantrum can be seen in the classroom for just the same reasons. With the teacher's time divided among several children, demands for time and attention are many and are divided. Equipment and materials in the toddler room are well thought out to provide many duplicates so that competition for toys is kept to a minimum. Tantrums will still occur, so the caregiver should be prepared to understand their causes and deal with them in an understanding way. He gives attention to the causes and the safety of the child, not the behavior. That prevents it from becoming a battle of wills.

Aggression. Aggression is the display of anger that results in physical or emotional damage to people or property. Aggression has been the subject of much research. Jacquelyn Gentry of the American Psychological Association states, "Violence is primarily a learned behavior, and kids who see constructive ways to deal with anger, frustration, and disappointment are learning violence prevention" (Chamberlin, 2000). Genetic or biological causes are being researched to learn if medications or genetic manipulation could reduce aggressiveness. Family influence on aggressive behavior is being studied to find the cycle over the generations and try to intervene in its recurrence. Society's influence, especially violent television programming, has been a large segment of the aggression research with much of it pointing to high correlations. The predictability and treatment of childhood aggression and the sex differences are other aspects of the studies. All of these underscore the problematic nature of childhood aggression and the complexity of its effects on behavior. These cannot be minimized or trivialized but there are some basic understandings about children and aggression that every teacher should recognize.

EXERCISE: What does aggression in the classroom look like?

Aggression is developmental. Children are aggressive at various predictable stages (Kostelnik, Stein, Whiren, Soderman, & Gregory, 2002) (Figure 5–8).

Two- and three-year-olds display aggressiveness mainly to attain or maintain possession of items or territories. They will use physical violence, hitting, kicking, and biting to keep or get what they want. "It is important not to assume that such behaviors represent a personality trait," writes Jewett (1992). It is a developmental phase, not a prediction of a lifestyle.

Two-year-old aggressiveness is described as instrumental aggression. It works! Hit the person

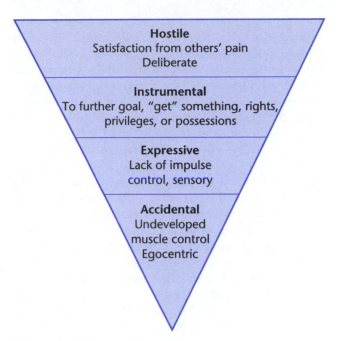

Figure 5–8 Types of Aggression

Figure 5–9 Accidental Aggression

who has the toy and he lets go. Knock the person off the bicycle so now she can get on. As language skills increase, the child can speak rather than act, and eventually negotiate. Preschoolers are beginning to use words to express their desires but may still be resorting to grabbing, stealing, or hiding items to keep them.

Early school-age children use negotiation more often but shift from physical aggression to verbal aggression. Name calling, mean talk, and threatening to withdraw friendships are the ways school-age children are aggressive.

Aggression Can Be Accidental. Young children are physically uncoordinated. Much of the hurtful actions take place because they are inaccurate walkers and touchers (Figure 5–9). Stepping on each others' fingers, exploratory touches that end up hurting, and manipulation of materials and equipment in ways that hurt someone else are common. While digging vigorously in the sand, it flies into someone's eyes. While walking through the block area, she knocks down a pile of blocks. A child slides down the slide and knocks down the person standing at the bottom. All are incidents that can be classified as aggression but were unintentional. However, young children cannot understand intentionality. If they are hurt, they interpret it as aggression, and feel vindicated in hitting back. When the adult says, "She didn't mean it," those words have little meaning for the young child. The observant adult can only reduce

this type of aggression by creating a safe environment and constant supervision. Positive guidance techniques such as, "Shovel the sand into the bucket," "Build inside these dividing lines," or "Wait to slide down until that person is out of the way" can help preschool children have a little more control over their behavior.

Aggression Can Be Changed to Assertion. The adult will not always be present to prevent scuffles over toys or disagreements over turns or rights. Helping children become more assertive is another of those lessons that has many rewards (Figure 5–10). The child who can express what he wants or needs is more likely to receive it than the child who grabs. The child who can defend himself verbally from aggressors gains self-esteem and prevents himself from becoming a victim. The assertion skills will give the individual the autonomy to make their own needs known. When others must guess, they may do so incorrectly. Assertion too is developmental. It progresses from the two-year-old saying, "Mine," the three-year-old saying, "I had that first," and the four-year-old saying, "Maybe we could take turns."

Aggressiveness Is Not an Outcome of Child Care But of Strict Discipline. Studies have reported that children in child care are more aggressive than those children reared exclusively at home (Belsky, 2002; Haskins, 1985; Thornburg, Pearl, Crompton, & Ispa,

Figure 5–10 Aggression—No! Assertion—Yes!

Figure 5–11 Child care is not the cause of aggression. Punitive discipline is.

1990) (Figure 5–11). Caldwell, a researcher with the National Institute of Child Health and Human Development, refutes Belsky's conclusions by pointing out that the high incidence of aggression was correlated with multiple factors, such as maternal sensitivity (2001). When children see the aggressor getting what she wants, getting attention, or other children copying the aggressive behavior, increased aggressive acts result (Goldstein, Arnold, Rosenberg, Stowe, & Ortiz, 2001). Teacher presence and prevention of aggression were cited as important to prevent the chain reaction of aggression.

Another study of preschoolers and aggression (Clarke-Stewart, Graber, & Fitzgerald, 1994) found the correlating factor was not the setting or the quantity of aggressive acts but physical control and punishment. The punitive discipline techniques used by either child care workers or families was the common factor. This is another in the growing body of research that punitive adult behavior increases child aggression. It calls for families and teachers to develop more appropriate discipline strategies.

Aggression Must Be Reduced. The first reason to reduce aggression is safety, in the classroom or at home (Figure 5–12). This is not just for the present, but for the future. Bullying has come into national focus following tragic school violence events. More than 30% of school youth reported participating in bullying behavior or being bullied themselves

(Nansel et al., 2001) and a majority of former bullies had at least one violent crime conviction. Garbarino (1999), who has studied boys who have been involved in violence, says that they suffer from "emotional illiteracy," a restricted range of emotional expression and a restricted language to express emotions. Many studies have shown that aggressiveness in the early elementary grades predicts aggressiveness in early adulthood (Huesmann, Eron, & Lefkowitz, 1984). This continuity is disturbing yet holds the promise for early childhood education. The goal of emotional control is a critical one. By lowering aggression before the early elementary age, it can have long-lasting effects. Farrington's study (1991) found high percentages of other causes for aggression. Economic deprivation, family criminality, poor child-rearing behavior, and school failure were all measurable at eight to ten years of age. Physically abused and neglected children are at risk of antisocial behavior (Finzi, Ram, Har-Even, Shnit, & Weizman, 2001) and a meta-analysis of the use of violent video games found a correlation to aggressive behavior in children and young adults (Anderson & Bushman, 2001).

Aggression Is Different in Boys and Girls. For many years, research has looked at hostile aggression as a greater problem for boys than girls (Figure 5–13). More boys are reported by teachers and families as aggressive. It has been thought that hormonal differences accounted for this aggressiveness but recent studies are causing scientists to rethink that belief (Seligman, 1995). Kellam, Ling, Merisca, Brown, and Ialongo (1998), at Johns Hopkins University, have found that first grade is a critical point in boys' pathway to or away from aggression. Tremblay (1991) suggests that girls may be less aggressive in the school years. However, the more aggressive girls tended to show later effects.

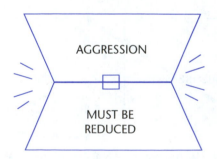

Figure 5–12 Aggression must be reduced!

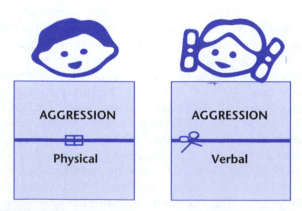

Figure 5–13 Differences in Aggression of Boys and Girls

- More became adolescent mothers
- More were single parents
- They experienced higher levels of psychiatric disorders
- They had children who were more aggressive

No matter what the cause, aggression is a problem in group settings of children, in the home, and in society as a whole. A task of the early childhood field then is to attempt to reduce the aggression.

Aggression Can Be Reduced. Children can learn to exhibit prosocial behavior through a variety of strategies (Figure 5–14) (Kostelnik, et al., 2002):

> modeling
> reinforcement
> reducing the frustration in children's lives
> helping children feel more competent
> fostering empathy among children
> teaching children prosocial behaviors
> helping children recognize instances of accidental aggression
> re-channeling children's expressive aggression
> helping children de-escalate potentially aggressive play
> making it clear aggression is unacceptable
> teaching children alternatives to gunplay
> teaching children to generate potential responses to the aggression of others
> teaching alternatives to aggression through planned activities
> teaching alternatives to aggression through conflict mediation (Kostelnik, et al., 2002, pp. 367–371)

Other social prevention programs have been found to reduce antisocial behaviors (Burchard & Burchard, 1987). *Early Violence Prevention: Tools for Teachers of Young Children* (Slaby, Roedell, Arezzo, & Hendrix, 1995) offers many suggestions for the physical environment, materials, cooperative activities, guidance techniques, responding, and teaching problem solving and assertiveness skills.

Novick (2002), a language and literacy expert, suggests that expanding children's (especially boys') emotional vocabulary helps in social interactions and brings an awareness of the power of words to hurt or heal. Teaching children the skill of negotiation has been used successfully in one Head Start's Fussbusters initiative (Gillespie & Chick, 2001). Classroom disputes were discussed at a Peace Table. A classmate not in the dispute but chosen by participants mediated the conversation. Children developed their own set of classroom rules and conflicts were reduced when children took control of their own solutions. In another initiative, a whole-school bullying intervention was found to be more effective than a focus on individual students (Bullying Prevention, 2002). Educators are becoming more aware of the social effects of aggression on learning and are infusing curriculum with social development objectives.

Fear and Shyness

EXERCISE: What are you afraid of?

Fear and Development. The first fear is of strangers. That only happens after the child has developed an awareness of separateness from others and has formed mental images of those familiar faces that are seen frequently. Sometimes even these may cause terrified screams. This change, at around six months, signals a changing cognitive development. The infant is constantly matching new pictures with the old. Any discrepancy, glasses/no glasses, hair up/hair worn down, that does not match the mental image, triggers the fear response (Figure 5–15).

AGGRESSION

Prosocial Teaching

AGGRESSION

Figure 5–14 Prosocial teaching reduces antisocial behavior, including aggression.

Figure 5–15 Children have many fears.

Other fears develop around two-and-a-half once a child's thinking is more advanced. Fears develop from the child's inability to make sense of the world. With limited understanding, everything is magic and anything is possible. There could be a grizzly bear under the bed. The house might blow away. The closet might be full of scary things that come out at night. These fears can be planted by tales the child hears from other people, adults included. Television or a fantasy book, read for fun and imagination, can produce fears. Fears of monsters, and being hurt, and nightmares, persist into the sixth and seventh year, when a firmer understanding of reality and fantasy is formed.

EXERCISE: What does fear look like?

Fear is exhibited by wide, open eyes; screaming; crying; rigid body; sometimes uncontrollable trembling; retreat or withdrawal; or seeking adult help. Some of the same strategies to help the child deal with anger can be used with fear. Talking about the fear by naming the emotion, not denying the feeling, and working together to help the child cope with the feeling are approaches that have been successful. The child can be encouraged to draw or act out the fear, write or dictate a story about it, or eventually face up to it little by little.

Shame, a Form of Fear. During the second year, when the child is struggling with autonomy, a stronger sense of guilt or shame is developed. This shows the thinking processes have been categorizing actions as acceptable and not acceptable. This is a necessary step in moral development. When the child does something perceived as unacceptable, feelings of shame develop. These are extremely strong in children who have strong family authority without the opportunity to make decisions for themselves.

Four- and five-year-olds are in what Lickona (1983) calls Stage 1 of Moral Development, "You Should Do What You're Told." Children at this age, he says, believe that "what's right is doing what grown-ups tell you and the reason to do what you're told is you could get in trouble if you don't" (p. 114). Children who develop shame are those who are constantly reminded that they are not doing as they were told. It sometimes leads them to believe there is something inherently wrong with them. It may be the adult's expectations were unrealistic for the child's ability to comply. The feelings of inadequacy and shame are all the child knows in this situation.

Shyness, a Form of Fear. Shyness may be a type of fear that appears at the end of the first year because so many situations and people are new. The child at this age realizes the separateness from parents. The

---

IT HAPPENED TO ME

The Beginning of Conscience

I was talking with the mother of a two-year-old when the mother looked down. Her little girl had a fistful of little pieces of paper. She admonished her, "Don't throw those pieces on the floor." The little girl looked up at her mom, closed her eyes, and opened her hand. This was a great example of a beginning conscience. She only believed something was wrong if someone is watching. She displayed her egocentric thinking: if she did not see it, neither did her mother.

---

new freedom in mobility and competency is accompanied by feelings of inadequacy. Extra attention causes them discomfort (Figure 5–16). They are often most comfortable observing or withdrawing from the action until they are sure they can function. This should be accepted as a feeling, not to be denied, changed, or negated. The adult helps the child find ways to understand and cope with the feeling. Empty praise is not helpful nor is labeling like, "the shy one." Care should be taken to give opportunities without pushing.

Shyness in our culture carries many messages: feminine/masculine, powerful/weak, smart/slow, low/high self-esteem, bold/timid. Swallow (2000)

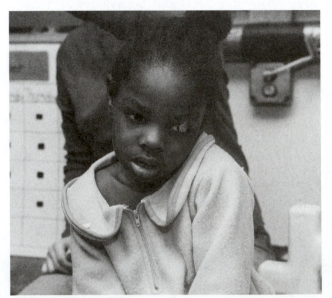

Figure 5–16 Children who are labeled "shy" often continue that behavior.

says that 20% of children are born shy and another 20% develop shyness before adulthood. Possible causes for developing shyness may be a stage the child is going through, a trauma, teasing, moving, poor parenting, or school pressures. He says, "Shyness is a personality style shared by millions," (p. 9) but it can interfere with development, school performance, and social experiences. The teacher should

- get to know each child as an individual.
- provide quiet and observation spaces in the classroom.
- make all children aware of the routine and changes.
- use transition techniques that allow for children to conclude previous activity before moving on.
- give choices in participation, allowing observing without embarrassment.
- work with family to determine the best approach for each child.

Children under Stress. There are three major sources of **stress** for children. The first is within the child, from a temperament that is slow to adjust to change and fearful of new people and experiences. As the child matures and builds confidence, the feeling of stress due to change may dissipate or the child may develop coping mechanisms to alleviate the negative feelings. Stress may cause the child to become more withdrawn, less socially outgoing, and less prone to engage in risky behavior.

The family can be a source of stress for the child. An abusive or neglectful family is stressful and damaging to developing social and emotional well-being. Family situations such as poverty, ill health, death, divorce, remarriage, new siblings, and moving are stressful as well. Even families with no pathology and who only want the best for their child may involve the child in so many scheduled activities that the child has no downtime, no time to relax, to unwind naturally, which can be stressful.

The world itself is a stressful place. Instant and graphic images of dramatic, scary events such as war, accidents, disease, and famine play out in every living room, giving the child (and adults too) a feeling of vulnerability, leaving all to question, "Am I safe anywhere? Will it happen to me? Can anybody take care of me and protect me?" It is not surprising that children display signs of stress.

The Emotionally Secure Environment

The role of the family and early childhood environment is to reduce the effects of negative emotions. They can help the child develop healthy attitudes,

---

IT HAPPENED TO ME

A Scary Dream

A four-year-old girl came into day care one morning, carrying her blanket and looking very serious. (No one spoke to her father as he dropped her off. No one greeted the little girl or noticed her facial or body expressions.) I was there observing a student teacher involved in an activity who also did not notice the girl. She walked over to me, a perfect stranger, and laid her head on my shoulder.

"You look like you're still sleepy," I said.

"No, I had a bad dream last night," she said quietly.

"Do you remember what the dream was about?" I asked.

"It was scary. Dreams are what you think about when you're sleeping."

That was profound, I thought.

"But dreams aren't real," I replied, thinking that might help.

"I know, but you still wake up scared." How true. I needed a four-year-old to remind me that even unreal things can make us feel real feelings. We trust that someone will notice, care, give voice to our fears, and help us face them not feeling alone. *Listen to the children.*

---

inner controls, and acceptable expressions. It begins with an atmosphere of mutual trust between the home and the program. The program with predictable room arrangements and routines is reassuring and stress-reducing. The rooms are physically comfortable without too much sensory stimulation. The curriculum is appropriate for the age and stage of the child, reflecting an attitude of acceptance of mistakes and responsiveness to the individual. Learning activities promote internal satisfaction, rather than emphasis on strict obedience or pleasing the adult. The schedule gives freedom to move, make choices, and use creative play outlets. These all contribute to a stress-free environment, control of negative emotions, encouragement of the positive ones of interest, curiosity, and enjoyment. This is accomplished by assessing the children's developmental levels and planning curriculum from topics or themes or projects that come from the children's world.

EXERCISE: Using a separate sheet of paper, make a list of prosocial (caring and empathetic) actions you would like to see in your classroom. Now make a list of antisocial actions you probably witnessed but wished you did not. (These are typical behaviors of young children without emotional self-control.)

This is the connection between emotional development and Frequency Counts on prosocial and antisocial actions. They are done occasionally to take the social-emotional temperature of the room. It gives an objective, quantitative measurement of the environment. It may be the temperature is "normal" so nothing else needs to be done. It may reveal there are "hot zones," certain children who are having difficulty controlling aggressive tendencies. They could benefit from some intervention, since aggressive behavior affects social relationships, self-esteem, and ultimately success in school.

The physical environment is the first area to assess in providing for the emotional and prosocial development of children. An environment that is not safe or comfortable may contribute to stress and misbehavior. Kostelnik et al. (2002, p. 258) identify possible environmental factors that can affect behavior, such as: temperature; cleanliness; equipment; and interior design, including color, displays and textures, sound, and lighting.

The Socialization of Emotional Competence

Denham (1998) stresses three components of the socialization of emotional competence: modeling, coaching, and contingency. This is how children learn to comprehend others' emotions, interpret their own feelings, and express their feelings in appropriate ways:

Modeling. Whenever an adult shows emotion, intentionally or not, the child observes the behavior and adds it to his own storehouse of reactions to replay in later situations. He learns the emotional significance of events and common behaviors associated with expression of emotions such as yelling, swearing, crying, silence, increased activity, talking it out, and coping. *Example:* The car is stalled in traffic and the driver leans on the horn and utters some profanity.

Coaching. Talking about emotions is an important function of language. Discussing feelings and their causes and subsequent actions is a way to teach emotional competence. *Example:* "You were angry when

IT HAPPENED TO ME

The Red Telephone Struggle

Two four-year-old girls wanted the red telephone in the dramatic play area. They each had a tight hold on an end of the receiver. This meant they were very close together, struggling in a pulling match. Gritting their teeth, looking eye to eye, they each grunted, "I want it," "I want it." I observed this but waited a few seconds to see what would happen. I could have gotten the other phone and talked to them about it, but I waited. It went on longer and longer. Their faces turned red and neither showed signs of increasing violence nor of giving up. Minutes went by. I had to restrain myself from entering in but I knew they could learn from the experience and I was curious as to how it would end. Finally, after many minutes of stalemate, one dropped her end, turned, and flounced away. The one left holding the phone (you guessed it) dropped it and flounced off herself.

you thought Aaron was taking your toy but then you saw that he had one just like yours and got them mixed up. When you said, 'That's mine,' it made him look closely and see the one in his hand wasn't his. Next time you might say, 'I have one like that. Is that one mine or yours?'"

Contingency. Adult reactions to a child's emotions reflects to the child the seriousness of the event, the adult's concern over it, and a comforting knowledge that the adult understands and will help. *Example:* The child stumbles and hits her head. The adult looks over, assesses the situation, and continues talking or rushes over and says, "Ouch, that must have hurt. Let me see if you need a bandage." Contingency reactions by the adult are moderated by the age of the child. Younger children with limited emotional experience need constant reassurance that the adult is watching, and cares about emotional situations. As a child gets older, the adult uses more judgment in when to assist or intervene, or when to allow the child to take control of the situation and work it out on her own.

Through observation, children's emotional and social situations are examined closely. From that examination, the teacher takes actions to assist the child to move on in the developmental stage. The adult helps the child recognize emotional and social states, gain control of behavior, feel more competent, and move on to the next level of social development. Observation and recording are closely entwined with curriculum to assist this process. This is similar to making a braid (Figure 5–17).

HELPING ALL CHILDREN WITH EMOTIONAL DEVELOPMENT

The factors influencing emotional development are observed in all children. For children with developmental delays or disabilities, emotions are affected as well. A growing awareness of differences increases with maturity and experiences outside the home. When children with physical disabilities are included in programs with other children, self-comparisons are made. The other children are also learners with still-developing social skills, understanding, and empathy. Fear, rejection, and curiosity may be the emotions displayed by the classmates causing loneliness, doubt, and low self-esteem in the child with the disability. The teacher prepares the other children in the group, just as the environment is prepared, to receive the child with handicaps. Providing adaptive apparatus, such as wheelchairs, walkers, hearing aid cases, and eyeglass frames, the children can experiment with how it feels to use these things. Many more books now include children with differing abilities, both in regular storylines and in nonfictional, child-level explanations of disabilities.

Children with emotional disorders in the classroom will affect the emotions of both the staff and other children. Difficult behaviors, aggressiveness, withdrawal, and acting out always are challenges for staff. For the child with chronic emotional disorders, it is an even greater challenge. Acceptance and a knowledge of the disorder and approaches to use will be part of the preparation for this child. Information from families, records from other professionals working with the child and the family, and individual research will provide the teacher with a background and strategies to deal with the child. The other children can be informed and helped to under-stand the nature of this child's needs so that a caring atmosphere is created for all.

HELPING PROFESSIONALS FOR EMOTIONAL CONCERNS

Helping professionals, such as social workers, psychologists, or psychiatrists may be involved in consultations, assisting in emotional development difficulties. The staff will use each other for resources to seek answers to emotional behavior problems. Discussions with parents in the initial interview and intake process, in open communication opportunities such as open house, parent meetings, and social events give the teacher insight about the child. When all other attempts are not working, a more formalized discussion with the parents may be necessary. The emotional realm is subjective and also personally connected with the families' and teacher's emotions. This conference should be approached sensitively, seeking a partnership of ways to help the child. Caution is taken not to lay blame, make diagnoses, or criticize. The teacher is prepared to suggest referrals for further evaluation. They may include

medical personnel—pediatrician, neurologist (treatment of brain and central nervous system disorders)

mental health professionals—psychiatrists, psychologists, social workers, therapists

support groups—mentor families; family resource centers; cooperative extension agents; school, religious, or community agencies

OTHER METHODS

Other Methods to Record Emotional Development:

Anecdotal/Running Records
Developmental Checklist or Rating Scale with emotional development component
Dialogs/Discussions with child about emotions
Media recordings depicting emotions

KEY TERMS

aggression	displacement	Frequency Count	stress
coping skills	emotional intelligence	invulnerable child	zone of proximal
core emotions	failure to thrive	shyness	development

The Assessment and Curriculum Braid

EXERCISE: Try making a French braid in a volunteer's hair. Here are the directions: Section the top and separate into three parts. Place the left strand across the center. Bring the center strand to the left, switching their positions. Place the right strand across the center, bring the center strand to the right, switching their positions. Gather additional hair from behind the left ear, and add it to the strand that is now on the left. Place the strand with the added hair across the center strand. Use the right thumb to gather additional hair from the back of the right ear and add it to the strand that is now on the right. Place the strand with the added hair across the center strand. Keep taking additional hair and combining it with the main strands.

Think of development, assessment, and curriculum as the three main strands (Figure 5–17). It all begins with the knowledge of child development; the normal expectations of how the child will change over time physically, socially, emotionally, and cognitively. Every group of children brings its own range of development, interests, and today's reality. Assessing their knowledge and interest will determine the curriculum vehicle. Reggio Emilia's projects (Edwards, Gandini, & Foreman, 1993) are based on children's interests and happenings in their town. The projects about the race or the fountains in town demonstrate how the curriculum was real to the children before the activities began. They could then relate it to prior knowledge. Left on their own, children will play the Olympics *after* rather than *before* they happen. The children have then seen it on television and have heard their parents talk about it. It is a part of their real world. When teachers introduce the Olympic theme weeks before it happens, it is a part of the teachers' world but not the child's.

Knowledge of what two-year-olds, or threes or fours are like is one of the main strands in the braid. The specific group is observed and assessed through knowledgeable eyes. They are measured against a range of expectations. They also are observed to poll their interests. This makes assessment another strand of the braid. Documentation is the process of writing down what is seen. It will be remembered and used for a variety of purposes. That also will be a strand that runs through the braid, making a formalized record of what is known, done, and questioned.

Figure 5–17 Development, assessment, and curriculum are three strands of the braid of appropriate programs for young children.

Curriculum is the strand that carries the experiences and opportunities for exploration and discovery through the senses. By planning activities that children touch, taste, hear, see, and smell, all the developmental areas are being stimulated. If the experiences are familiar to

The Assessment and Curriculum Braid *(continued)*

their world, they make associations or matches. "Oh, I tasted this before. It's a sweet pickle." If the experiences are new ones, they seek to find equilibrium. "This is *called* a pickle but it's *made* out of a cucumber?" The association with the cucumber is unbalanced. What makes a pickle a pickle? A worthy curriculum theme? Science is seeing cause-and-effect changes. Math is following the recipe. Language is learning vocabulary and new, fun songs and rhymes about pickles. Visual perception is the comparison of shades of green in varieties of pickles. They appear in drawings and easel paintings. Social interactions take place in exploring who likes dill and who likes sweet pickles. People like different kinds of pickles, and people are different like pickles. Playing "Who's in the Pickle Jar" promotes social and physical development as children run to catch each other. The unstressful, nonacademic theme will produce emotional relaxation through enjoyment and self-esteem. "These are the pickles I made in school today. Bet you can't guess they're made out of cucumbers." Weaving all these activities together is the web, that very fragile but definite unending thread.

Implementation of curriculum is another strand of the braid. The teacher may have the background training in the "plan, do, review" model of High/Scope (Hohmann & Weikart, 2002). The teacher may follow the Creative Curriculum (Trister-Dodge, 2002), which carries the curriculum through the physical environment. The Montessori training may lead the teacher to set up formal lessons with defined procedures for children to follow. If the teacher is like most, the teaching philosophy or professional practice is eclectic. It is a combination of many philosophies that fit into their own learning style, personality, educational background, and also the program goals.

While the curriculum is being carried out, the teacher is the observer. She notes such things as how each child is running in the game, who can count the pickles in the jar, and who has never seen a cucumber before. The teacher writes down the wonderful stories they tell about how the seeds got in there and what will happen if they are swallowed. Every developmental area can be evaluated as children interact with the environment without intrusion or pressure. There will be children on both ends of the range of normal who will need some adaptation of the environment. The child who has not yet reached the levels of most of the other children will need to have some teacher assistance and facilitation to bridge the gap. This is what Vygotsky calls the **zone of proximal development** (Hills, 1992). It allows the child to approximate a level of competency, held up by the teacher's scaffold or mediation. The observer will document (to remember) what the child knows, what he can do, how he behaves, and how he feels about himself. This is all while observing the pickle game.

The teacher evaluates each child against what is expected for this age or developmental stage. Added to that is what the teacher knows about this particular child's circumstances. Because of that knowledge, a decision is made to modify the curriculum for a particular child. A child may need to have a pickle sign placed in his hand as the signal that it is his turn to chase because he cannot hear his name called. Another may need to hear the word in Spanish. The observer may notice that a particular child is easily frustrated when matching the lids to the pickle jars. She notes to take a closer look at possible vision or small muscle problems. The observer may notice that a child was reading all the ingredients to the recipe chart. That child needs a simple reader about pickles to keep him interested and a way to tape record so that others can listen to it. By writing this down (documenting) the teacher will remember to follow through on the plan, or follow up on questions to be answered.

(continued)

The Assessment and Curriculum Braid (continued)

The evaluations are communicated first to the family. The best way is that face-to-face exchange about specific incidents and their relation to the child's developing knowledge and skill. This is a form of family education about child development and shows the family that the teacher is closely watching and recognizing the accomplishments of their child. The child should also hear of their accomplishments. Empty valuative words like "Wonderful" or "Good" are meaningless, compared to specific statements, such as, "When you counted those pickles it was higher than I've ever heard you count before." The communication of evaluations of child development can be used effectively to initiate early intervention. Through careful observation and documentation, developmental concerns are raised that need to be investigated further. After additional observations and consultations with other team members, the validity of the concern is confirmed. The family and teacher can pursue a course of action to address the concern.

The teacher activates the curriculum and evaluates development. Another strand in the braid reflects on the professional and personal efforts of the process. Attitudes are monitored and decisions reconsidered. Receptiveness to change is measured. The reflective practitioner returns to the strands of child development and assessment. The process begins again.

As this braid weaves in all these components, it becomes stronger. When any of the strands is weak, broken, or absent, the result is not as effective. In many programs, the documentation of assessment is the weakest strand, leaving individualization and communication to rely on memory and chance. Those are too important to not be supported by data, collected in a natural way through multiple sources. That is how assessment/documentation/evaluation drives curriculum.

What does observing and recording have to do with curriculum? Everything or nothing—it depends on the program and the teacher. All the methods and assignments in this book could be used to compile a vast and impressive portfolio on each child. It would be useless if it only showed where the child was at any given point. It becomes dynamic information when it is used to help guide curriculum. "How is that done?" becomes the question.

How is curriculum formed? Schweinhart (1995) is studying the use of various curriculum models that are being used by early childhood leaders and how extensively they are used. High/Scope, the Creative Curriculum, and the Bank Street model were the three predominant curriculums being used. Preliminary findings suggest that less than one-third espouse any one model while more than two-thirds use parts of some models, though not extensively. This indicates that curriculum is individualized for program needs and to fit teaching styles of individual teachers.

Schweinhart's study was undertaken to try to measure and compare the outcomes of various models. With this much variation in how they are used, it is impossible to assess the outcomes of any one model using standardized testing. By observing and assessing individual children, however, the curriculum and the teaching methods can be evaluated, not just measured to a standard but to become the basis for change. That is what Rosegrant and Bredekamp (1991) call transformational curriculum—curriculum that helps bring about change. One strand of the braid is assessment of prosocial and emotional control with a Frequency Count. Another is implementation of curriculum. The third is evaluation of individual children's social interactions and emotional nature and controls. These are woven together in the braid to make a strong, efficient, and neat model.

WEEK 5: PLAN A

FREQUENCY COUNT–SOCIAL/EMOTIONAL

Students

Using the Frequency Count form in Appendix D, follow the directions below.

Practitioners

Make at least two copies of the Frequency Count form in Appendix D. List the children in Groups A and B on one form and Groups C and D on another. Use the alphabetical name list from the Class List Log.

On one day during free choice time, observe for thirty minutes, looking for evidence of prosocial or antisocial behaviors on one sheet. On another day, observe the children on the second sheet. Each time one of these behaviors occurs, make a tally mark next to the name of the child in the appropriate column.

What to Do with It

Filing. The Frequency Count is filed in the class file because it contains information on all the children observed. Notes may be made on each child's Portfolio Overview Sheet under Emotional Development or the topic of the Frequency Count.

Analyze and plan. Look at the results. Do you see a few children with very high numbers in the antisocial column? Write a short theory as to why these children have scored in this way. (Do not put this in the child's portfolio. This is for your use.) Use some of the Resources to make a plan for the class or for individual children to foster prosocial/emotional development. You may want to try another Frequency Count at intervals during and following your plan to measure if it has been effective.

Sharing with Child and Family. The Frequency Count is a method on which the teacher can base decisions or measure results. It probably would not be shared with the family unless on a very general basis and then only after the intervention has been made and results tabulated. It may be a statement such as: "We have been working very hard to be kinder and gentler with one another. We experimented by measuring the number of unkind and aggressive actions in a day—a number that was too high. Then we have been doing the following: Reading books about friendship, using the word *friend* more often as we speak to the children, playing games that promote cooperation rather than competition, encouraging and giving recognition for all kind and gentle acts that we see. And low and

behold, it is working! We measured again and the numbers were lower. We'll keep at it!"

Actions.

Read a Book.

> Aliki. (1998). *Painted Words, Spoken Memories.* New York: Greenwillow.
>
> Altman, L. J. (1993). *Amelia's Road.* New York: Lee & Low.
>
> Bunting, E. (1991). *Fly Away Home.* New York: Clarion.
>
> Bunting, E. (1996). *Going Home.* New York: HarperCollins.
>
> Coles, R. (1995). *The Story of Ruby Bridges.* New York: Scholastic.
>
> Falwell, C. (1992). *Nicky Loves Daddy.* New York: Houghton Mifflin.
>
> Fox, M. (1994). *Tough Boris.* New York: Harcourt Brace & Co.
>
> Frasier, D. (1991). *On the Day You Were Born.* San Diego, CA: Harcourt Brace Jovanovich.
>
> Rosenberg, L. (1993). *Monster Mama.* New York: Putnam.
>
> Williams, V. (1984). *A Chair for My Mother.* New York: Greenwillow.

In the Environment.

- Reflect on the positive emotional climate provided in the classroom by the adults. Be sure that each child is valued and respected.

In the Curriculum.

- Incorporate the affective dimension in curriculum planning—how people feel under certain circumstances, what feelings the projects invoke in the participants, what differences and problems arise from working together and how they can be solved with empathy.
- Use puppets and class meetings to work out problems based on hypothetical common situations before they arise. Then when those situations do arise, such as difficulties over turn taking, or sharing, or inadvertently hurting someone physically or emotionally, some strategies or resolutions have already been worked out. A script, so to speak, has already been written.

In the Newsletter.

- Article on development of emotional controls
- Article on handling pet deaths and hard emotional issues

- Article on aggression, its causes and appropriate responses
- Article on children's fears
- Article on shyness—causes and appropriate
- Article on Action Research through Frequency Counts and implementation. Action research, such as frequency counts to measure the success of a classroom strategy, is a way to inform families of the seriousness and professional-

ism with which the teacher is addressing change in the classroom. When it is described in general terms, without naming specific children, of course, it lets families know that the teacher is attending to behavioral aspects of learning in a positive way, working to promote each child's social competence and mental well-being. It can also suggest strategies that may be replicated at home.

WEEK 5: PLAN B

ANECDOTAL RECORDING OF EMOTIONAL DEVELOPMENT FOR GROUP D

Students

Select an incident that illustrates a principle in emotional development. Record the incident using an Anecdotal Record. In the right-hand column write about the principle that this incident illustrates.

Practitioners

Select the children in Group D. Divide them among the days of this week

Write an Anecdotal Recording on each child about an incident that gives information about emotional development, such as the child displaying joy, happiness, anger, aggression, or fear. Make notes as the incident is happening, or shortly thereafter. By the end of the day, write an Anecdotal Recording about the incident. Include as many details as possible about the incident in the left column of a sheet of paper. In the right-hand column, comment on the significance of the incident, if it was usual or unusual, and possible contributing factors. You may want to comment on:

Knowledge—recognition of emotions, vocabulary of emotions
Skills—what the child can do to control emotions
Dispositions—behaviors related to emotions

Feelings—how the child's self-concept is involved with emotions

What to Do with It

Filing. In the child's portfolio, jot a few summary words on the overview sheet that the Anecdotal Recording is present, the date, and your name (Figure 5–18).

If a strategy to help the child cope with emotions is indicated, discuss it with the family or your supervisor to decide on a course of action. Follow through.

Sharing with Child and Family. Share the observation with family and the child, if appropriate, such as "I was observing Carlos today and saw him go to the bathroom all by himself. He had been afraid to go down the hall alone, but today he did it." File in each child's portfolio.

EMOTIONAL DEVELOPMENT			
Documentation	Location	Recorder	Date
FC	Class file	MS	10/6
RR	Portfolio	MS	12/27
FC	Class file		3/30
FC	Class file		5/25

Figure 5–18 Portfolio Overview Example

WEEK 5: PLAN C

REFLECTIVE JOURNAL

Would you describe yourself as shy? If so, think about these suggestions from Zimbardo and Radl (1981), *The Shy Child:*

Decide to get over it.
Learn *why.*

Build self-esteem: What are your best qualities?
Pay attention to your personal appearance.
Be your own best friend.
Practice social skills. (pp. 214–227)

Respond to the following in your Reflective Journal, kept in a private file at home.

I feel shy when . . .

I think it's because . . .

From the above list, maybe I could try . . .

When I see a child angry, it makes me . . .

When I looked at the Frequency Count and compared boys to girls, I was surprised to see . . .

It might make me . . .

I really would like to help _____ control emotions. I'll try . . .

REFERENCES

Anderson, C. A., & Bushman, B. J. (2001). Effects of violent videogames on aggressive behavior, aggressive cognition, aggressive affect, physiological arousal, and prosocial behavior: A meta-analytic review of the scientific literature. *Psychological Science, 12* (5), 353.

Anthony, J. E., & Cohler, B. J. (Eds.). (1987). *The invulnerable child.* New York: The Guilford Press.

Bandura, A. (1977). *Social learning theory.* Englewood Cliffs, NJ: Prentice Hall.

Belsky, J. (2002). Quantity counts: Amount of child care and children's socioemotional development. *Journal of Developmental & Behavioral Pediatrics, 23* (3), 167–170.

Bullying prevention program may reduce aggression. (2002). *The Brown University Child and Adolescent Behavior Letter, 18* (12) 5(1).

Burchard, J. D., & Burchard, S. N. (Eds.) (1987). *Prevention of delinquent behavior.* Beverly Hills, CA: Sage.

Caldwell, B. M. (2001). Déjà vu all over again: A researcher explains the NICHD Study. *Young Children, 56* (4) 58–59.

Chamberlin, J. (2000). Working to create a violence free future for young children. *Monitor on Psychology, 31* (8), 54–55.

Clarke-Stewart, K. A., Gruber, C. P., & Fitzgerald, L. M. (1994). *Children at home and in day care.* Hillsdale, NJ: Lawrence Erlbaum Associates, Publishers.

Denham, S. A. (1998). *Emotional development in young children.* New York: The Guilford Press.

Edwards, C., Gandini, L., & Forman, G. (Eds.) (1993). *The hundred languages of children: The Reggio Emilia approach to early childhood education.* Norwood, NJ: Ablex.

Erikson, E. H. (1950). *Childhood and society.* New York: Norton.

Farrington, D. P. (1991). Childhood aggression and adult violence: Early precursors and later-life outcomes. In D. J. Furman, (1995, January). Helping children cope with stress and deal with feelings. *Young Children, 50* (2).

Finzi, R., Ram, A., Har-Even, D., Shnit, D., &Weizman, A. (2001). Attachment styles and aggression in physically abused and neglected children. *Journal of Youth and Adolescence, 30* (6), 769.

Garbarino, J. (1999, July/August). *Boys to Men: Questions of Violence.* Harvard Education Letter Research online, http://www.edletter.org/past/issues/1999-ja/forum.shtml Accessed February 15, 2003.

Gillespie, C. W., & Chick, A. (2001). Fussbusters: Using peers to mediate conflict resolution in a Head Start classroom. *Childhood Education, 77* (4), 192–195.

Goldman, D. (1995). *Emotional intelligence: Why it can matter more than IQ.* New York: Bantam Books.

Goldstein, N. E., Arnold, D. H., Rosenberg, J. L., Stowe, R. M., & Ortiz, C. (2001). Contagion of aggression in day care classrooms as a function of peer and teacher responses. *Journal of Educational Psychology, 93* (4), 708.

Haskins, R. (1985). Public school aggression among children with varying day-care experience. *Child Development, 56,* 689–703.

Hills, T. W. (1992). Reach potentials through appropriate assessment. In Bredekamp, S., & Rosegrant, T. (Eds.), *Reaching Potentials: Appropriate Curriculum and Assessment for Young Children, Volume 1.* Washington, DC: National Association for the Education of Young Children.

Hohmann, M., & Weikart, D. P. (2002). *Educating young children: Active learning practices for preschool and child care programs.* Ypsilanti, MI: High/Scope Press.

Huesmann, L. R., Eron, L. D., Lefkowitz, M. M., & Walder, L. O. (1984). Stability of aggression over time and generations. *Developmental Psychology, 20,* 1120–1134.

Jewett, J. (1992). *Aggression and cooperation: Helping young children develop constructive strategies.* Urbana, IL: ERIC Clearinghouse on Elementary and Early Childhood Education, EDO-PS-92-10.

Kellam, S. G., Ling, X., Merisca, R., Brown, C. H., & Ialongo, N. (1998). The effect of the level of aggression in the first grade classroom on the course and malleability of aggressive behavior in middle school. *Development and Psychopathology, 10,* 165–185.

Kostelnik, M. J., Stein, L. C., Whiren, A. P., Soderman, A. K., & Gregory, K. (2002). *Guiding Young Children's Social Development* (4th ed.). Clifton Park, NY: Thomson Delmar Learning.

Kuebli, J. (1994, March). Young children's understanding of everyday emotions. *Young Children, 49* (3), 44.

Lickona, T. (1983). *Raising good children.* New York: Bantam Books.

Nansel, T. R., Overpeck, M., Pilla, R. S., Ruan, W. J., Simons-Morton, B., & Scheidt, P. (2001). Bullying behaviors among US youth: Prevalence and association with psychosocial adjustment. *Journal of American Medical Association, 285,* 2094–2100.

Novick, R. (2002). Learning to read the heart: Nurturing emotional literacy. *Young Children, 57* (3), 84–89.

Peth-Pierce, R. (2000). A good beginning: Sending America's children to school with the social and emotional competence they need to succeed. *Monograph from the Children's Mental Health Foundations and Agencies Network, 9.* Bethesda, MD: National Institute of Mental Health. Available on-line at http://www.nimh.nih.gov/childhp/fdnconsb.htm.

Rosegrant, T., & Bredekamp, S. (1991). Reaching individual potentials through transformational curriculum. In S. Bredekamp and T. Rosegrant (Eds.). *Reaching Potentials: Appropriate Curriculum and Assessment for Young Children, Volume 1.* Washington, DC: National Association for the Education of Young Children.

Schweinhart, L. (1995, June). *Early childhood curriculum models: Who needs them?* Research presented at the meeting of the National Institute for Early Childhood Professional Development, San Francisco, CA.

Seligman, J. (July 3, 1995). Testosterone wimping out? *Newsweek,* p. 61.

Slaby, R. G., Roedell, W. C., Arezzo, D., & Hendrix, K. (1995). *Early violence prevention: Tools for teachers of young children.* Washington, DC: National Association for the Education of Young Children.

Swallow, W. K. (2000). *The shy child: Helping children triumph over shyness.* New York: Warner Books.

Thomas, A., & Chess, S. (1977). *Temperament and development.* New York: Brunner/Mazel.

Thornburg, K. R., Pearl, P., Crompton, D., & Ispa, J. M. (1990). Development of kindergarten children based on child care arrangements. *Early Childhood Research Quarterly, 5,* 27–42.

Tremblay, R. E. (1991). Aggression, prosocial behavior, and gender: Three magic words but no magic wand. In D. J. Pepler & K. H. Rubin (Eds.), *The development and treatment of childhood aggression.* Hillsdale, NJ: Lawrence Erlbaum Associates.

Trister-Dodge, D. (2002). *The creative curriculum for early childhood,* 4th ed. Washington, DC: Creative Associates International, Inc.

Watson, J. B. (1914). *Behavior: An introduction to comparative psychology.* New York: Holt, Rinehart, & Winston.

Zimbardo, P., & Radl, S. (1981). *The shy child: A parent's guide to preventing and overcoming shyness from infancy to adulthood.* New York: McGraw-Hill.

RESOURCES

Bos, B. (1990). *Together we're better.* Roseville, CA: Turn the Page Press.

Segal, M., & Adcock, D. (1993). *Play together, grow together: A cooperative curriculum for young children.* Ft. Lauderdale, FL: Nova University Publications.

Slaby, R. G., Roedell, W. C., Arezzo, D., & Hendrix, K. (1995). *Early violence prevention: Tools for teachers of young children.* Washington, DC: National Association for the Education of Young Children.

Smith, C. A. (1993). *The peaceful classroom: 162 easy activities to teach preschoolers compassion and cooperation.* Mt. Rainer, MD: Gryphon House.

Online Resources

For additional information on early education curriculum, visit our Web site at http://www.earlychilded.delmar.com

Using Conversations to Listen to Language and Speech

USING CONVERSATIONS AS AN OBSERVATION METHOD

EXERCISE: What might the following sentences tell you about the person speaking?

"Howdy, ya'll."

"I've just had a dialogue with my stock broker . . ."

"When I was in France . . ."

"I'm so stupid . . ."

"Thith ith fun!"

"I ain't got no job."

"Dey gonna come get you bein' bad."

"Wa wa."

"You raise sheep? How do e-w-e do it?" (spells out *ewe*)

"Na na, na na, na."

"You sister him?"

Observing by listening is done naturally all the time. The message received by the listener is not just the words and their meaning. Inferences are made about where the speaker is from, their self-esteem, educational background, social situation, ethnic group, and even mental age. Subtle, and sometimes not so subtle, clues are given about their interests, economics, and experiences. The listener notices teeth formation, facial expression, body language, eye contact, sense of humor, and vocabulary choice. All of these may give more information about the speaker than the actual words spoken.

EXERCISE: When you want to know something about the following subjects, whom do you ask?

What postage is due on this package I'm mailing?

How many automobiles were shipped into the United States last year?

How long do I cook a five-pound roast?
What medicine can I take for this cold?
Do I need a haircut?
Where does it hurt?

To receive a reliable answer to a question, it must be addressed to the person who most likely knows the answer. Scramble the answers to the questions in the preceding exercise to see how foolish it is to ask the wrong person, or even guess the answer. It only makes sense, then, to gather information *about* the child *from* the child. Harste, Woodward, and Burke (1984) use the phrase, "the child as the informant." By listening to the child, both what is said and how it is said, information is transferred upon which evaluations are made.

EXERCISE: Using a tape recorder, talk to five children of different ages. Try to find a child of one, two, three, four, and five. This tape will be used repeatedly in this chapter to illustrate speech and language development.

Carry on a little conversation beginning with a greeting, "My name is _____. What's your name? How old are you? What are you doing? Where did you get that? What are you going to do with it?"

What differences did you hear in the way children of various ages answered the questions?

Interviewing, or asking children questions to find out what they know or what they are thinking about, is an age-old technique. The early childhood field has a prestigious role model for interviewing children in Piaget (Evans, 1973), who used the "clinical" interview, writing meticulous notes on the questions and answers. He began with his own children but extended his interviews to others to delve deeper into their thinking and understand their wrong answers to questions.

Talking with young children can be interesting and rewarding (Figure 6–1). It also can be frustrating because of their short attention span and egocentricism (only understanding from their point of view). Sometimes they do not speak clearly enough to be understood. Questioning children brings surprising results: Ask a child, "What color is a banana?" The child may say white or may say yellow. The part we eat is white. Ask a child, "What color is an apple?" The answer may be white. Is that a wrong answer? It probably would be considered wrong on a standardized test, although it is correct technically.

There are many formal tests of speech and language that use picture recognition, imitating letter

Figure 6–1 Talking with a child can be interesting and a source of developmental assessment.

sounds, comprehension, and sentence completion. These are used primarily by speech and language pathologists in determining a child's level of speech and language ability. The family, teacher, or caregiver is most concerned, however, in communicating with the child. Formal evaluation measures are used only when that communication seems to be hampered by speech or language delays or difficulties.

Social discourse or discussions and questioning methods were first called **action research** by Kurt Lewin in 1948. It is a way for teachers to find out what they want to know and to seek answers about their own classroom. Talking with children and their self-reporting are accepted fact-finding methods (Moxley, Kenny, & Hunt, 1990). Conversations take several forms, depending on the age of the child, situation, and information to be gathered. **Informal conversations** happen all the time in the normal functioning of the child in the environment. As the adult talks with the child about her actions, he asks, "Wow! How did you get that to stand up on that little end like that?" or "Can you think of another way to use these old pieces of plastic someone gave us?" Snack, mealtimes, and discussions after stories are excellent times for informal discussions or interviews. This style allows the conversation to flow in a natural way and to gather spontaneous samples of what the child is doing and thinking. Besides listening to the message, the hearer can also examine how the child is using language and the quality of the speech production. It then becomes an informal **diagnostic interview** as well. Interviewing can be a process to confirm a problem that may need remediation. Both casual conversations and structured interviews can be diagnostic.

A more **structured interview** gathers specific information about the child's understanding of certain concepts. The adult sets up items for the child to choose—big/little; short/long; over/under; red/blue; things that go together or things that do not belong. Selected pictures or books often are used to elicit conversation. During the interview, speech and language skills are assessed (Wortham, 2001). An Interest Questionnaire (Almy & Genishi, 1979) can give older children an opportunity to express their likes and dislikes and give insight into a child's happiness or self-esteem, with questions like: "What would you like to know more about?" or "The most interesting thing I have done at our school during the past week is?" or "What is your favorite thing to do at school?"

Responses may be written in a log by older children or dictated to the teacher (Figure 6–2). Dictation gives the child a role model for literacy, seeing spo-

ken words translated into permanent print. It also gives the child an opportunity to think and reflect on the past. Through dictation, the child expresses feelings by elaborating on thoughts and feelings. Opinions are stated or interpretations or reasons for an event can be explored. The interview is a little conversation with a purpose. Neuman and Roskos (1993, p. 258) suggest this mini-outline:

A greeting of some kind—"Hello, June."

Expression of interest—"I have some new markers. Would you like to try them?"

Taking turns at speaking—As June draws, she says, "That's my mom's friend's sister." The teacher asks, "What is she doing?" June replies, "She's going in there . . . shopping. She's meeting her friend and buy something." The teacher asks, "What is she buying?" June says, "Milk . . . and cereal . . . egg . . . and orange!" She smiles broadly. "I see she is carrying something." "Her bag," and pointing to the other

Figure 6–2 Children's dictations and drawings give insight into their thinking.

hand, "She puts money in there. She's going to bring a flower for her kid."

Some pausing—"No" she says sadly. (pause) "But I get to go the preception!" (pause) "I'm done. I'm going to play now."

Leave-taking, or way to end the conversation—"I enjoyed our little conversation. I'd like to put your drawing and your story about it in our class storybook. May I? I can make a copy of the drawing so you can take the original home." June nods and runs off.

Efficient questioning techniques and skills make the most of the interviewing method. There is a hierarchy of questions (Bryen & Gallaher, 1983) that yield progressively more information while requiring more complex levels of comprehension.

Yes/no questions—"Do you want a drink?"
What (object)—"What's this?"
What (action)—"What are you doing?"
Where (location)—"Where's the dolly?"
What (attributes)—"What color is this?"
Who (persons)—"Who is picking you up today?"
Whose (possession)— "Whose boots are these?"
Which (selection)—"Which cookie cutter do you want?"
When (time)—"When are you going to paint today?"
How (manner)—"How did you make those dots?"
Why (cause-effect)—"Why did that paper rip?" (p. 103)

Each type of question requires more thought; understanding of the *Wh*-questions, and longer, more revealing answers. A **closed question** is one for which the asker already knows the answer and is testing the receiver. All but the last two of the preceding list are closed questions. They may give information about a child's specific knowledge but not about thinking processes or creativity. An **open question** such as, "What's another way . . . " or "Can you tell me how . . . ?" gives more insight and are more natural conversation models.

Asking children open-ended questions (those for which the person asking does not know the precise answer) is a technique to help the child think, imagine, and solve problems.

EXERCISE: Here are some typical questions. Put a checkmark by the open-ended questions.

❑ Observing—"What do you notice here?"
❑ Recall—"What did you see at the zoo?"

❑ Differences—"How are they different?"
❑ Similarities—"How are these the same?"
❑ Ordering—"Can you order these colors from lightest to darkest?"
❑ Grouping—"Which of these go together?"
❑ Labeling—"What is the name of that group?"
❑ Classifying—"Which cubes here are red?"
❑ Concept Testing—"This cube is blue but does it belong?"
❑ Causes—"Why do you think that happened?"
❑ Effects—"What happens if . . . ?"
❑ Feelings—"How do you think she feels?"
❑ Generalizing—"What usually happens to water in the freezer?"
❑ Questioning—"What could you ask her?"
❑ Anticipating—"What do you think will happen?"
❑ Making choices—"Which one would you like?"

(Adapted from Sigel's Questioning Model in Pelligrini [1991])

All but naming, labeling, classifying, and concept testing are open-ended questions.

Selecting an interview type depends on what the adult wants to know about the child, the cognitive level, and the emotional state of the child.

The style of the questioner is also a factor in interviewing. Some people are more comfortable engaging in a conversation that is spontaneous and flows from the exchange between child and adult. Others may prefer a more structured format for uniformity and comparison as well as comfort with the method. Questions for discussion or interviews with preschool children will be provided for the interview assignments, but the observer or recorder is free to record more natural conversations if that is more comfortable.

What Can You Tell About a Child from Listening?

EXERCISE: In the following categories, list on a separate sheet of paper what you might learn about a child by listening to speech and language as well as content.

Family:
Culture:
Physical development:
Health:
Age or stage of development:
Socioeconomic level:
Cognitive development:
Self-concept:

Needs:
Temperament:
Activity level:
Humor:
Television viewing habits:
Imagination:
Problem-solving abilities:
Social development:

In each category, there are the obvious bits of knowledge that can be acquired by listening or asking the child questions.

Family—manners, attitudes, besides finding out inside information like a new baby is on the way

Culture—customs, holiday celebrations, common activities

Physical development—abilities like riding a bike with no training wheels, interests such as dancing or karate, missing teeth, muscles or structure of the mouth and jaw

Health—nasal congestion, "I threw up before I came to school," "My arm hurts."

Age or stage of development—grammatical construction, "Me do it."

Socioeconomic level—"We're flying to Disney World," or "We slept in the car last night."

Cognitive development—"If I want more cookie I can just break this one up and have lots," "Eight, nine, ten, eleventeen, twelveteen."

Self-concept—"Nobody likes me."

Needs—"Help me, I can't do it."

Temperament—"I CAN'T DO IT!"

Activity level—"I'm gonna swing on a swing then I'm gonna ride a bike, then I'm gonna dig in the sand, then I'm gonna . . . "

Humor—"Where does a sheep get a haircut? In the baabaa shop."

Television viewing habits—"I'm gonna be a Power Ranger."

Imagination—"I have this refrigerator and it follows me wherever I go so I can have a cold drink whenever I want it."

Problem-solving abilities—"I tried it this way but it didn't work so I tried this and it worked!"

Social development—"If you don't give me a turn I won't invite you to my birthday party."

Listen to children talk, sometimes prompted by a few open-ended questions like:

"Do you want to tell me about . . . ?"
"How'd you do that?"
"Then what happened?"
"What do you think will happen next?"
"Hmmmmm"

Confidentiality Issue

Just a reminder to teachers that the child is the client. In that special relationship, what a child tells a teacher is privileged information, just like a doctor or a lawyer. It is important not to use this information for a general topic of conversation, only to help the child. In a later chapter, the child's disclosures of possible abuse are discussed.

Advantages of Conversations and Interviews

They can

- yield multitudes of information both in content and in language production from natural situations.
- be analyzed later.
- show progress of speech and language over time.
- raise child's self-esteem as the focus of a one-on-one conversation, with a closely attentive listener.

Disadvantages of Interviews

They are

- time-intensive when focusing on one child.
- intimidating so the child may be reluctant to speak under certain circumstances.
- intrusive and may appear to probe into confidential areas.

Conducting a conversation or interview gives you the opportunity to gather much information about the child that can be used for assessment. Its effectiveness depends on your own conversational skills; you must listen actively and formulate questions based on the child's lead. A language sample can be gathered effectively in this way through a written record of the child's exact spoken words, taken in the context of the child's activity, usually in conversations with you or other children. A dated series of language samples over time can demonstrate the child's growth and progress (Leonard, 1997).

Using Technology

In the context of this book, **record** is a word used for writing down information. Recording conversations and interviews has a more traditional meaning referring to electronic recording such as audio tape recording. This is an effective method for preserving the conversation for later transcription into words and for a more careful analysis of the child's speech and language. It depends, however, on the comfort zone of

148   CHAPTER 6

both the adult and the child. Tape recording can be intimidating and intrusive. If it is, it modifies the results. Frequent use of the tape recorder for children to record themselves and each other reduces the intimidation and familiarizes them with the tape recorder.

A tape for each child with a collection of recordings made throughout the year is an appropriate addition to the portfolio. Most children enjoy taping and listening to themselves. The teacher also makes written summaries or notes of the tape recordings. This method is recommended for the beginning interviewer so that concentration is focused on the conversation rather than note taking.

Video recording a child's conversations yields even more information than an audio recording because you also see facial and body expressions. Any kind of overt preservation of a child's behavior, writing, audio, or video recording, has the possibility of altering the behavior so care must be taken to obtain a natural sample so that it is objective and authentic.

How to Find the Time

The teacher talks with children throughout the day—carrying out the routines and instructions necessary to achieve the goal of getting through the day. However, the amount of time left for one-on-one or even meaningful group conversations seems to be ever smaller. We know, of course, how important verbal exchanges are to knowing each child, learning what they know, and meeting their emotional, social, and cognitive needs. The teacher can look at every aspect of the day and see opportunities for individual conversations. Arrival time offers an opportunity to have a brief conversation with each child, getting feedback on what has happened since they were last together, how the child is feeling, what the teacher has in store for the group that day. A Class List Log near the entryway can help quickly capture important points. While children are working and playing is an ideal time for the teacher to circulate and comment on the play and extend the conversation. Anecdotal notes, even abbreviated to be expanded upon later, only take a few moments. Class meetings can be an opportune time to have wonderful conversations. The tape recorder or a second person writing notes can preserve these important times that provide developmental information.

Pitfalls to Avoid

Children may be uncomfortable with interviews. If holding individual formal interviews with each child, it is important to emphasize the special conversations will be held with *each* child and *everyone* will have a turn. If a child appears anxious during the interview and is reluctant to speak, the interviewer should stop and observe the child in a more natural setting.

A busy classroom may interfere with the interview, but isolation in another room is not recommended. Find a quiet spot, as free from distractions as possible, within the classroom.

The teacher has an ethical responsibility not to probe into personal family matters and practices. Any information revealed by the child of a personal nature should not be recorded unless it is a child abuse disclosure. (See Chapter 12 for a full discussion of this subject.) Of course, all personal conversations with children are confidential, not to be shared with others without the child's permission. This is a very sensitive area.

What to Do with It

The Structured Interview questions and answers are filed in the child's portfolio. Anecdotal notes or jottings from conversations or Informal Interviews are also filed in the portfolio. Significant parts can be highlighted with a marker to draw attention. The

---

R E V I E W

Conversations or Interviews: Recording a child's verbal interactions either in writing or in audio recording.

Types of Information to Record Using Conversations or Interviews:

Informal conversations that are planned or spontaneous.

Interviews that are structured for a specific purpose

child's viewpoint on school adjustment

child's self-responsibility views

child's self-evaluation of physical skills

child's self-evaluation of friendships and social interactions

child's self-evaluation of emotional difficulties

to listen carefully to child's speech and language

to assess child's attention span for conversations

to assess child's cognitive development:

physical knowledge

logico-mathematical knowledge

social knowledge

to assess child's literacy development

to discuss a child's creative work or play

information yielded can be noted in respective categories on the overview sheet, such as cognitive, social, self-identity, or emotional.

Tape recordings are also filed in the portfolio. A sheet is attached to the tape, listing the dates and subject (and counter number, if possible) of each recording. Full transcriptions are not necessary unless there is some reason to amplify documentation of a developmental area, or provide the raw data, exact wording, for a referral.

The tape recorded conversations or interviews make excellent resources for listening closely to a child's speech and language. The next section on speech and language development gives guidelines for listening and evaluating, both from live and tape recorded conversations.

LISTENING TO LANGUAGE AND SPEECH

"Listen before you speak" is not just wise advice but actually the progression of language development. Listening is also described as **receptive language.**

Receptive and Expressive Language

An important principle of language development is that the receptive language always is greater than the **expressive language** (Figure 6–3). The one-year-old is told "Go give grandma a kiss." The infant crawls, or walks, to grandma and gives her a kiss. He cannot say anything close to, "I want to kiss my grandma," but from his actions that is interpreted. He can understand the words of the request, act on them, but not say or express the words himself. When people are learning a second language, they always can understand far more than they are able to actually say themselves. This principle is also displayed when a person has a thought or idea but has difficulty explaining it to someone else. They say, "I know what I mean, but I just can't explain it." Receptive language, understanding verbal communication, is always greater than the ability to express thoughts verbally.

This has some direct implications for anyone around young children. The phrase, "Little pitchers have big ears" comes from this principle. Although children are physically small, unsophisticated, and unable to speak themselves, they are "taking in" what they hear. It will eventually be expressed. Not only is this a warning for adults to monitor their conversations in the presence of young children, but it is a reminder that this is a fertile learning time. All that is said, read, and sung is received. It emphasizes the

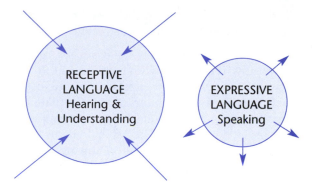

Figure 6–3 Receptive language is always greater than expressive language.

importance of adults talking to babies who cannot yet communicate back. The foundations for vocabulary and language not yet present are laid in these early months and years.

Language Acquisition

Exactly how language is acquired has been the focus of much study and controversy. As infants say their first words—*ma, da, see, bye, hi, no*—they get positive reinforcement to repeat those meaningful sounds when the adults around them smile and repeat the word back to the infant. Behaviorists and social learning theorists, such as Skinner (1957) and Bandura (1977), say this imitation and positive response is how language develops. Children who are deprived of hearing language can end up permanently incapable of learning and using language. Noam Chomsky's (1965) work broadened the view of how language is acquired with studies that indicated that children from all cultures develop language skills in the same sequence at close to the same time, supporting a biological approach to language. His idea of a Language Acquisition Device (LAD) is present in all humans, but not animals. Proof of this are the choices in grammar that children make automatically. No one teaches a child to say "goed." It comes from the internalization of language. The process converts to a past tense using an untaught rule. It also causes the switch from "goed" to "went" a little later. Interactionist theorists, such as Bruner (1983), agree that there are behavioral and biological aspects but emphasize the role of environment where adults support language learning and use. Developmentalists like Chomsky (1968) believe that intelligence precedes language acquisition, as illustrated by the parallel development of cognition and language, whereas Vygotsky (1962) disagrees and believes children are speaking internally to solve difficult problems.

Three key findings from the new brain research relate to language development in the following ways:

- Biology (nature) blueprints the brain for language but positive interactions with nurturing adults (nurture) is also necessary for effective communication.
- Early experiences and interactions stimulate brain circuitry and affect spoken and written language.
- The brain development is dependent on experiences at optimal times for acquiring different kinds of knowledge and skills.

By early experiences, positive interactions, and communication with others, a child learns language, the key to lifelong learning (Willis, 1998). Hart and Risley (1995) found some astounding results in a study that measured the language experiences of children of welfare, working-class, and professional people in the first four years of life. Children between one and four years old in the welfare homes heard 13 million words, children in working-class families heard 26 million words, and in professional homes children heard 45 million words (198). There were also proportional differences in vocabulary used in naming and recalling people, places, and objects; words used to ask or demand; and responsiveness to the child during interactions. The differences that Hart and Risley found at three years of age were strongly linked to school performance at age nine. They concluded that a part-day preschool program at four years of age for children in language-deficient homes could not make up the difference. A conclusion from this study is that language intervention needs to be a priority of every infant/toddler out-of-home program, as well as the focus of family education. The study also concludes that preschool may be too late to make an appreciable difference in a child's language development.

The adult role in language acquisition cannot be denied. When children are provided an environment where people are talking to them, they talk sooner. When adults respond to babies' early sounds, those sounds occur more frequently. Reinforcement, encouragement, expectation, and rewards for language stimulate development. Probably, it is a combination of all of these factors working together. The important principle for parents and teachers of young children is the recognition and response to each child's attempts to communicate.

Speech Development

EXERCISE: **Read the following sentence out loud:**

"Eres el/la heredero de una herencia. Ve inmediatemente a Madrid y pregunta por el alcalde. El te va a indicar lo que debes hacer."

You have just spoken Spanish. You have the speech. You have the sounds, but you do not have the language unless you know the meaning. Have you communicated in Spanish? Only if the hearer or receiver knows the language. (The sentence means: "You are the heir of a fortune. Go at once to Madrid and ask for the mayor. He will direct you.") It would be important to be able to receive that message!

As explained in Chapter 1, the words *growth* and *development* often are used interchangeably. However, they have different meanings. The words *speech* and *language* are so often used together that most people think they are the same also (Figure 6–4). Not so! **Speech** is the sound produced to make the words. **Language** is the term for words and phrases that convey meaning. There can be speech without language (just making random sounds). There can be no audible language without speech. Nonverbal communication is body language or gestures, the way of conveying messages without speaking.

The smallest units making the sounds of the words are the **phonemes,** the sounds of speech. These are phonemes /u/, /o/, /a/, /m/, /p/, /b/, /t/, /n/, /k/, /ng/, /y/, /g/, /f/, /v/, /sh/, /zh/, /l/, /rth/, /ch/. These are in the order in which they appear developmentally. Along with vowels to link them, words are formed. These are called **morphemes,** small units of sound that have meaning. It is interesting that /m/ is one of the first sounds an infant can make, and in most languages of the world, the word for the person who bore them begins with the /m/ sound: *mother, mama, mamone* (Ouseg, 1962).

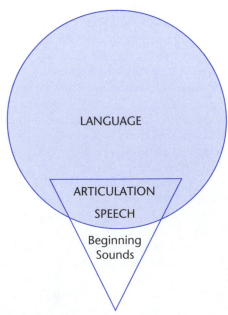

Figure 6–4 Speech as a part of language development

The infant begins to make sounds at birth, crying, not purposefully but by reflex, just like reflex actions in other developmental areas. Within the first month, the crying becomes more differentiated so the caregiver can begin to tell the difference between the hungry cry and the painful cry. During that first month, preverbal infants can even differentiate between the sounds of /ba/ and /pa/ (deVillers & deVillers, 1979).

During the second month, more purposeful and pleasant sounds emerge: cooing and squealing. Those can be written down because the sounds are phonemes that are recognizable as vowels. As the infant gains muscular control of the lips and tongue, the consonants appear in babbling and, later, imitation of adult talking. "Ba ba, ma ma, da da, pa pa," understandable approximations of longer words, are usually frequent by the end of the first year.

Infants can make and hear all the sounds found in every language. The click sound in Southern African languages, or the blowing through his lips like a cross between a /p/ and an /f/ in the Japanese language, are made but later lost by English-speaking children. These sounds are heard in babbles of all babies around the world but disappear or are added by one year, depending on the language they are learning. Kuhl (1993) calls infants "citizens of the world" at this stage. This accounts for the difficulty adult learners have with certain sounds of the second language they are learning. The ability to make those sounds has disappeared from their repertoire. It also makes the case for exposing infants and toddlers to other languages to help preserve those sounds.

The precise articulation or production of phonemes, the sounds of language, is a long developmental period (see Figure 6–5). Some of the more difficult combinations of sounds may not be present until six or seven years old.

EXERCISE: Listen to the tape you made in the exercise again, listening closely and looking at the following articulation chart. This outlines the usual progression and expectation of acquiring certain sounds. Did the children you listened to produce these sounds clearly?

p, w, h, m, n (usually by three years)
b, k, g, d, y (usually by four years)
f, ng, t, r, l (usually by six years)
ch, sh, j, s, z, v, th, zh, br, tr (clear by seven to eight years)

By the time children are four years old, they have usually developed the vocabulary, language structure, and grammatical rules needed to communicate about their world. Because young children are learners, their speech and language will be imperfect. They still may have **articulation** (sound) errors, which will continue to develop into the seventh year, especially those combinations like *wh* (whether), *rth*, *ch*, *sz*. Those imperfections can be categorized but are not necessarily cause for alarm. Some of the common mispronunciations in the preschool years are

substitutions—"wabbit" for "rabbit"
omissions—"tar" for "star"
distortions—"caaa" for "car"
additions—"pisghetti" for "spaghetti"
lisps—"thith" for "this"

Speech and language screening in the preschool years is recommended and especially indicated if the child is very difficult to understand. The role of the early childhood educator is one of facilitator, interpreter, and responder rather than remediator. Content and meaning are the most important aspects when talking with young children.

Stuttering. **Dysfluent,** repetitive speech, or stuttering, "I, I, I, I want it," occurs frequently in the four- and five-year-old. It is for most children a temporary, often short-lived, disorder that disappears without formal intervention. Stuttering persists and requires assistance in only a minority of cases (Yairi, 1999). The adult listener should listen patiently without telling the child, "Now, just slow down," or "Don't talk so fast," or "Your ideas just get ahead of your tongue." Statements like these draw the child's attention to the stuttering and add to the stress. Avoid placing the child in the spotlight to speak or feeling the pressure of the whole group waiting. If this does not pass in a few weeks, further investigation may be needed to look for stressors or other factors. A private conversation with the family should begin the investigation, along with notes on when the stuttering began and the child's reaction to it.

The Development of Language

From the first birthday, vocabulary grows (because it can be measured in numbers) at a fantastic rate (Figure 6–6). Listen again to the taped conversations: Count the number of different words each child said. Did it increase with age? Look at the vocabulary explosion (Figure 6–7).

EXERCISE: Here is a mathematical problem for you. Using Figure 6–7 on page 154, what is the percentage rate of vocabulary growth between one year (use 15 words) and six years?

LEVEL	AGE RANGE	ASSOCIATED SKILLS
Prespeech	Birth to 10 months	Development of sound (perception and production) Development of gestures Concomitant changes in nonlinguistic development
		Rapid development of sound perception; infant a few weeks old can distinguish phonological contrasts in human speech; speech production rooted in infant's crying and vegetative noises; play with speech sounds including reciprocal speech sounds with others begins after three months; between 6 to 10 months consonant and consonant-vowel imitations are evident in babbling
First Words: Emergence of naming	10 to 13 months	Single-word comprehension Single-word production Individual differences in single-word use Gestures that function as words
		Attention can be directed with object names ("see the dog," "Amy, dog"); by 13 monhts receptive vocabulary from 17 to 97 words; as speech production increases, gestures decrease
Word combinations	18 to 24 months	Transition between production of single words with complex meanings to multiword phrases Nature of word combinations and individual differences Parallel developments in other developmental domains
		Use of word combinations initiate shift into sentence use; size of spoken vocabulary undergoing rapid acceleration and expansion of types of words, especially verbs; parallel development includes gestural imitation, classification of objects, and multigesture strings in play indicating the need for accompanying cognitive development to allow language development
Grammaticization	20 to 30 months (fundamentals of grammar) 36 months (competent speaker)	Acquisition of rules of morphology and syntax Speed of morphemic acquisition Nature and sequence of grammatical development Uniqueness of language development for this age Application of rules Mastery of irregular patterns and rules Requires a baseline of cognitive and language development

Figure 6–5 Four Levels of Language Development (From Benner, S. M. [2003]. *Assessment of Children with Special Needs.* Clifton Park, NY: Thomson Delmar Learning.)

Beginning Communication.

EXERCISE: "Mama" is one of the first words a baby says. How many meanings can be interpreted by the way you say it?

The beginning talker starts with one word. It quickly is joined by others, all names for people or objects. They are spoken with various inflections and sometimes accompanied by gestures, such as pointing or arm movements that convey a more sophisticated message than labeling. Single words between 12 and 18 months become requests or questions. These one-word utterances that have meaning are holographic phrases, which are soon followed by short two-word sentences called telegraphic phrases. Examples of the telegraphic phrases are "Doggie gone," and "Look baby." When telegraphic phrases occur, the child has acquired language. She is expressing herself using the sounds of speech.

EXERCISE: Listen to the children on the tape. Did any of them use just one word to convey a whole thought?

Language is developing, changing from simple to complex in a predictable pattern but at individual rates. The child is developing a sense of syntax, the

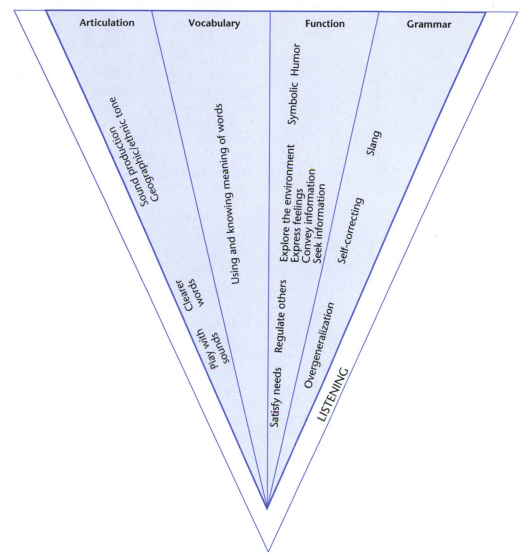

Figure 6–6 Speech and Language Development

order of words in a sentence that make it understandable to others: "Mama go," "Baby ba ba." His language is the combination of heredity, social interactions, and emotional environment. Cognitive or learning ability and physical development all combine to make this happen. The interdependence and simultaneous development of many areas are vividly illustrated in language development.

EXERCISE: **Describe how speech or language might be affected by:**

Hearing:
Muscle development:
Geography:
Abuse:

Siblings:
Heredity:
Ethnicity:

EXERCISE: **From the children you listened to, could you gather any of the preceding information?**

It takes many years for the grammatical construction to move from one-word holographic sentences to the telegraphic but meaningful few-word sentences to complex sentences with prepositional phrases and correct tenses and plurals. Children seem to have an inner sense of picking up plurals and past tense from hearing adults speak. At first they say "mouses," instead of "mice," because they have heard "houses" meaning more than one house. They will say, "I *goed*

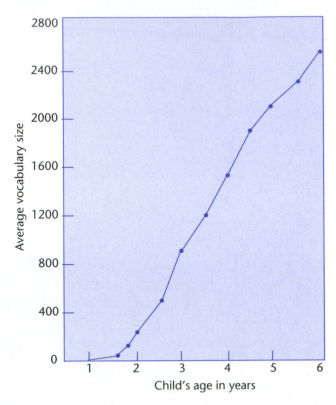

Figure 6–7 The Vocabulary Explosion! (Courtesy of Machado, J. M. 2003. *Early Childhood Experiences in Language Arts* (7th ed.). Clifton Park, NY: Thomson Delmar Learning, p. 80. Reprinted with permission of author.)

to the store," though they have never heard anyone say that. They have heard others say, "I *washed* the dishes." This application of simple grammatical rules to all plurals and past tense words is **overgeneralization.** Children internalize the grammatical rule and apply it to all words in that category. Over time, this self-corrects, usually by five years of age.

The development of grammatical construction (Bryen & Gallaher, 1983) follows this progression:

Uses correct word order (by two-and-one-half)
Uses pronouns (by two- and-one-half)
Gives name (by three)
Uses plurals and some prepositions (by three)
Tells day's schedule in sequence (by four)
Can tell an imaginative story about a picture (by four)
Speaks in adultlike sentences (by four)

EXERCISE: How complex were the sentences in the tape recording of conversations? Were there any examples of overgeneralization?

Language and Literacy Connection. The critical role that early education plays in language and liter-

acy development was emphasized in the National Academy of Sciences report *Preventing Reading Difficulties in Young Children* (Snow, Burns, & Griffin, 1998). In seeking solutions to readying children for school success, researcher David Dickinson points out that language is a literacy activity that provides the vocabulary, structure, and meaning verbally that will be found later in the printed word. In the Home-School Study, Dickinson and Tabos (2001) learned much about the linkage between language and literacy. The income level, vocabulary, the opportunity to hear books read and learn the concept of words and books, and child care quality all have correlations to later school success. This has implications for teachers of young children. Families and child care staff can maximize language use throughout the day.

To encourage children's language development

- At snack and meals, sit with children and have family-style mealtime conversations.
- Encourage discussions about nonimmediate events, remembering details from the past.
- Encourage children to use new vocabulary words learned during class lessons.

When reading to the group

- Identify important words and concepts.
- Encourage children to talk about aspects of the story.
- Respond to children's questions.
- Link books to themes and other activities.
- Avoid long stretches of talk and stay on the subject.

During free play

- Children need opportunities to talk with each other.
- Minimize interruptions—teacher involvement in dramatic play tends to disrupt and disengage the players.
- Engage individual children in conversations using a variety of words, especially novel words. (Dickinson & Tabos, 2001, 252–254)

Functions of Language. Children develop in the more complex use of language. Their first single words convey recognition and description, "Ma ma," "Ba ba." Very quickly they learn that their language can be used to influence others. Those same words can now call others to communicate a need. "Ma ma," "Ba ba." As they gain vocabulary and willfulness, the communication takes the form of commands like "Go," "No bath."

With mobility and experience in a wider environment, their language expands not only in vocabulary but in using it to describe what they see, "My ball." They convey information, "Ball all gone," as they watch the ball going down the toilet. They seek information in the second year with incessant, "Where Daddy go?" "Where doggie go?" and in the third and fourth years with the constant, "Why?" questions. They begin to express feelings, "So sad," after a scolding, the "So sorry," that softens a grandma's heart. By four and five years old, cognitive development is moving toward the symbolic stage when reading and writing develop. The symbolic stage appears in language too, "I have an idea." Humor emerges in double meanings of words and puns. By five, the concept of rhyming appears.

Social and Nonverbal Language. Acredolo and Goodwyn (2000) point out that nonverbal gestures as signs or signals come before words. A baby with arms outstretched is making an understandable but silent plea. Asking a one- to two-year-old, "Where's your nose?" elicits a knowledgeable response months before the child can say the word *nose*. By observing gestures and also listening for words, the caregiver can learn about the child's needs, what he knows, and even what he is thinking.

Very young children without hearing impairments can learn to communicate using sign language even before they can speak. In her fascinating study, Daniels (2001) tells of infants learning to convey important messages such as *more, yes, no, come* months before they could say the words. She also studied the effects of hearing children learning sign language, showing positive results on later reading scores.

Children show social and cognitive skills in their language as well. Think about each of the children on your tape as they talked with you.

Did they demonstrate a "turn-taking" kind of conversation where they knew they were to speak then you would have a turn, or was it more of a monologue?

Did they make eye contact?

What was the facial expression as they spoke?

What gestures did they use, if any?

What could you tell from the tone of voice that just writing down the words would not convey?

EXERCISE: Practice your ability to place bits of language in chronological order of their normal development. Number the following from the earliest to the latest in the progression of development:

❑ "Want milk"
❑ "Waader"
❑ "When I grow up, I'm gonna be a ballerina."
❑ "No"

He Shared His Expertise

Jason was a very quiet four-year-old when he started preschool. Several weeks went by while he just watched other children, without interacting or speaking in the classroom. Some children just need more time to adjust to a situation. We spoke to him about the day, what he was doing, greeted him at the door without pressuring him to speak or commenting on his silence. In private talks with his mother, she said that was his way of coping with new situations. She assured us he was very verbal at home. This continued for weeks and into months with his mother assuring us this was his little game. He did begin to play with objects in the classroom, first the sand and blocks. He eventually began to interact with other children but still without speaking. We still tried not to draw attention to it but spoke to him as we did all the other children in conversation as they played.

One day in February, when dinosaurs were the project theme, he brought in a book from home. At the door he held it open to me and said, "This is a stegosaurus." I was shocked and the children even commented saying, "He talked!" I said, "Jason, that's the first thing you've ever said to me. I wonder why you chose today to talk." He said matter-of-factly, "I wanted to share my expertise about dinosaurs with you." (Exact words, I swear.) From that day on, he talked occasionally with peers and teachers as he played. I often marvel at the strength of will he had all those weeks. His willpower held us all hostage to his little game.

❑ "mum mum mum mum mum"
❑ "I goed to the store."
❑ "Wha's dat?"
❑ "Eeeeeeeeeeeeeeeeeeee"

The sequence is vowels, consonants and vowels, approximations of words, telegraphic speech, questions, refusals (this can come anytime after item number 2), imperfect grammar, and adultlike but self-centered.

Answers are: 6, 3, 8, 5, 2, 7, 4, 1.

Facilitating Language. Children learn language through interaction with adults. Adults initiate and respond in such a way that demonstrates listening, understanding, expanding, and modeling. Kratcoski and Katz (1998) suggest these strategies:

Expansion—respond, expanding holographic and telegraphic sentences
C: "Doggie eat." T: "Yes, the doggie is eating."

Extensions—response and addition of new information
C: "Doggie eat." T: "Yes, the doggie is eating. Doggie is hungry."

Repetition—repeats phrase
C: "Doggie eat." T: "Eat, doggie. Eat, doggie."

Parallel talk—describes child's action
C: "Doggie eat." T: Yes, doggie is eating. You feed the doggie her food."

Self-talk—describes own action
C: "Doggie eat." T: "Yes, doggie is eating. I gave the doggie her food."

Vertical structuring—uses questions to facilitate longer sentences
C: "Doggie eat." T: "Yes, the doggie is eating. Does she want a drink?"

Fill-ins—conversation structured for child to provide word to complete the statement
T: "Doggie wants a drink. Let's get her some _____." C: "Water!"

Play "conversational ball" where the conversation goes back and forth between the two parties. The child is a learner so may drop the ball. The adult always catches or picks it up and tosses it back (Figure 6–8).

Language Role Models. Adults are language role models for children (Figure 6–9).

EXERCISE: Set up a tape recorder in the classroom or wear a small portable one in your pocket. Tape a 30- to 60-minute sample of yourself "for your ears only." Analyze it for your common language habits, and see if any changes need to be made in the language role model you are presenting to children.

Teachers of young children fall into some habits that are not helpful to children. Some are reviewed here to alert the reader to consider the impact on the child.

The Tester. Many teachers of young children know the way to find out what children know is to ask questions. Unfortunately, they translate this into a series of test questions: "What color is the coat you

Figure 6–8 The adult should always return the conversational ball.

are wearing today?" "Is it sunny or rainy?" "How many colors in your picture?" "What month is it?" The child might answer sarcastically, "You're supposed to be the teacher and you don't know so you're asking a little kid?" As language role models and empathetic humans, adults should speak to children in the same manner they speak to peers. An adult would not ask a bystander "What color is your shirt?" or a friend "How many bracelets are you wearing today?" Questions asked of children should be motivated by natural interest and desire to explore the child's thinking, rather than checking if the child knows.

The tester: What color is this?
What day is it?
The universal <u>we</u>, Have we had our nap?
Third person helper: Let Ms. Teacher help you with your shoelaces
"Use your words"
"How would you like it?"
"Hey, you guys, gimme dat"

Figure 6–9 Poor examples of language role models

The Helper. Adults fall into the trap of speaking of themselves by name in sentences spoken to young children, like the much criticized "we" of the health profession. Often teachers say, "Let Mrs. M. help you with your boots," or "Do you want Miss Barbara to push you on the swing?" If a child said of herself, "Mary can do it" it would be considered an irregular language pattern, not using pronouns. As language models, teachers can and should use pronouns when speaking of themselves in sentences. A neighbor would think it odd if a person spoke of themselves when saying, "Mrs. Smith (the speaker) heard your dog barking all night."

"Use Your Words." The underlying reason for this phrase is to encourage children to verbalize their feelings. Unfortunately, these words do not help the child do that. Neither does its accompanying, "Tell him you don't like it when he . . . " It tells the child what she should do but does not give assistance in how to do it. If she knew how to use her words to tell him, she would have said it already. A more appropriate and helpful phrase might be, "Tell him, 'I don't like it when you . . . '" It reminds the child that words are preferred to hurtful actions. The child is given the exact words to say. She also does not have to make the shift from "you" to "I" when using the sentence. Imagine a car stopped at the red light, and the driver behind it sounds his horn. The first driver leans out and says sweetly, "Use your words."

How Would You Like It if She Did That to You?" One of the major characteristics of the egocentric, preoperational child is the inability to see a situation from another's perspective, the inability to put oneself on the receiving end of the action or word. This phrase then becomes meaningless and useless to the child under five or six. A more understandable phrase might be, "Remember when you got sand in your eyes from someone flipping the shovel? That's what you just did to Lois. It hurt your eyes and now her eyes are hurting in the same way. Can you find another way to use the shovel?"

Incorrect Grammar, Slang, and Lazy Articulation. The disagreement of noun and verb plurals is a common grammatical habit. Saying, "We was" rather than "We were" gives children a poor example of grammar. Calling all the children "Kids," or "Guys" rather than by their names is disrespectful. Dropping the /g/ at the end of those *-ing* words is a habit adopted by language learners. By listening to a tape of themselves, teachers can become aware of those habits and try to correct 'em (them). Teachers with an awareness of the potential for misunderstanding or imitation become better language role models for young children.

HELPING ALL CHILDREN WITH LANGUAGE DEVELOPMENT

Society is increasingly more culturally and linguistically diverse as well as aware of differing abilities. It is advisable for teachers to be bilingual, whether in a second cultural language or sign language.

Accepting Other Languages and Dialects

Schools and caregivers must be ready to receive a child speaking languages other than English (Figure 6–10). The following statistics may be surprising but they underscore the reality of the United States—it is becoming more and more multicultural and teachers need to prepare for non-English speakers in

Figure 6–10 Teachers must be ready to receive families of diverse cultures.

classrooms. This increasing diversity has important ramifications for our teaching.

- Spanish is the predominant native language of 79% of the English as a second language learners in the United States. (Kindler, 2002)
- Between the 1997–1998 school year and the 2000–2001 school year PreK–Grade 12 English as a second language students in the United States increased by 15.3%. (Padolsky, 2002)
- The states with the highest growth in English as a second language are surprising: Georgia 210%, South Carolina 127%, Indiana 88%, North Carolina 84%, Wisconsin 75%, Arkansas 57%, Minnesota 64%, Missouri 58%. (Padolsky, 2002)
- The states with the highest number of English as a second language students enrolled were California, Texas, Florida, New York, Illinois, and Arizona. (Padolsky, 2002)

Bilingualism is a great advantage for teachers. There are so many different languages spoken in many classrooms, however, it would be impossible to have teachers fluent in all of them. Therefore, it calls for a sensitivity to the child's needs who does not speak the language of the classroom or the teacher. It may be the child speaks a nonstandard dialect such as Black English **Ebonics** (Hendrick, 1992) in which the hearer recognizes the words and phrases but not the meaning. Many group settings include children who speak English as a second language with another as their first or come into the group knowing no English at all. Many schools have labeled these children Limited English Proficient (LEP), seeing their lack of English as a deficit rather than recognizing their proficiency in the language they have already learned. In the past, assessments given in English indicated major delays and mistakenly prescribed remediation for many of these children.

More tolerant approaches have been developed to help the child become bilingual, not pushing to be monolingual, nor attempting to extinguish the first language. The approach is described as additive, supporting the native language, while adding a second. This can be accomplished by

1. making a commitment to use their language(s) throughout the classroom.
2. labeling classroom items in English and in another language.
3. learning phases, songs, or greeting words in other languages.
4. having classroom charts written in two languages.
5. including books in other languages.
6. learning the numbers in a different language.
7. inviting family members or other persons to teach a simple poem or song to the class.

A basic early childhood principle is the acceptance of each child. It provides an environment, experiences, and support to help the child progress to the next level. Children learning a second language will progress through the same language development stages as an infant and toddler, beginning with single important words, then to telegraphic stages. They proceed through them with the same stage predictability of any other child learning language. The same techniques of teaching and observation are used regardless of the language the child speaks. See more about assessment and culture in this chapter's Topics in Observation.

Children with Differing Abilities in Regular Classrooms

Children with differing abilities of speech, language, or hearing may be placed in regular classrooms. Other children become their role models and communication skills become more functional in the responsive environment. The same strategies that are recommended for effective therapy carried on in the classroom are applicable to any early childhood teacher. Cook, Tessier, and Klein (2000) make the suggestions to

- listen attentively.
- not ask quiz-like questions—"What color is your shoe?"
- talk about the here and now.
- speak in a calm, normal tone of voice.
- expand sentence length as the child's understanding expands. (p. 311)

Sign language, or manual communication, and speech reading (commonly called lip reading) are debated between experts and families of the hearing impaired. The family makes the decision about their child. The early childhood program responds to that decision just as it would to any other family decisions, with sensitivity, and willingness to adapt to meet the needs of the child.

HELPING PROFESSIONALS FOR SPEECH AND LANGUAGE CONCERNS

Speech and language disorders are often diagnosed first in early childhood programs. As children develop, families expect their verbal skills to be

TOPICS
IN
OBSERVATION

Diversity

EXERCISE: In a crowded place—at the supermarket, at the fair, on a bus—just take a look around. Do you see any two people who are alike? Look at noses. Just noses. Are any exactly the same shape or size? People-watching is a fascinating pastime.

Every person is different and yet the same. All have two ears and a nose that are parts of the whole. Because all people are members of the same species, there are expectations of how the parts work and how they change over time. Genetics, age, environment, or trauma cause the variations in the basic mold of a human.

Generalities help to make sense of the whole. Averages have been calculated based on large numbers of people but even then some will not fit within the range of average. Assessments and professional practice are based on averages that may not be a valid measurement. How can a teacher measure vocabulary when the teacher does not speak the same language? How can a teacher write down how long the child can stand on one leg when the child is in a wheelchair? How can a teacher comment on the child's separation and adjustment to the classroom when the child has been in eight foster homes in three years? The dilemma is real!

Diversity is a fact of life, but thinking and attitudes sometimes are so narrow that the truth is overlooked. Adults are supposed to be past the egocentric stage, so they should understand statements such as, "How would you like it if

no one learned how to pronounce your name?"
there never were any pictures of people who looked like you around in your classroom?"
the food never had familiar flavors and spices?"
no one would hold your hand in a circle?"
the teacher planned activities that were always too difficult for you to do?"
you had to have money for school tomorrow for a field trip and your family didn't have it?"
letters always went home addressed to parents and you didn't have two parents (or any)?"
everyone else was thin and you were fat?"

Different notes in a song, colors in a rainbow, or flowers in a field are valued. Why not individual differences? They are often rebuffed, ignored, and rejected, causing disharmony and hurt feelings. While working with children, observing and evaluating their development, comparisons to norms must be done very cautiously. The environment should represent and reflect everyone's individuality, and an attitude of acceptance of all must prevail. Here are some practical ways of accomplishing this.

Individual Differences. While norms give a range of expected growth and development, there will always be some children at both ends of the range that demand attention and decision-making about that difference. No child will be at the same developmental level as another. Even within each child, the level of development may be different in different areas. The child may be more advanced in language, less advanced in large muscle development, in the mid-range of emotional development, and off the map in cognitive development. Those differences deserve to be observed, evaluated, and acted upon if needed, but not seen as unusual or strange.

(continued)

TOPICS IN OBSERVATION

Diversity (continued)

Special Needs. Some children have not developed within the normal range of expected levels. A strengths model looks at the abilities of the child as decision points for the placement. The role of the program is to keep the areas of special need from interfering with other normally developing skills. This opposes the deficit model focusing on the need. Instead, the child should be placed where the child can function to capacity where able, and assisted in areas of lesser ability. Authentic assessment, for every child, then looks at the individual areas of development to note the highest level of achievement rather than what the child cannot yet do.

Cultural/Ethnic Diversity. Caution is advised when broadly accepting any standard of evaluation or professional practice. It might be in conflict with the values or style differences in culture or ethnicity. Developmental and behavioral norms and professional practice are based on the majority culture and may be diametrically opposed to those of a minority culture. Familiarity and sensitivity to the cultural and ethnic differences of the population of the classroom is the only way to meet each child's needs. For example, the separation and independence and move toward autonomy (Chapter 1) may not fit the interdependence highly valued in Middle Eastern families.

Toilet training (Chapter 2) is a topic with great cultural variation and should be approached with the family's preferences in mind. Communication differs in some cultures using more body language and implicit cues. Other cultures respond more to precise, direct language. Cultural differences must be considered when talking to families about their child. Family decision-makers vary between cultures, as do expectations for girls and boys. Acting honestly with a heightened awareness of the differences will help the child. By displaying a willingness to learn and a desire not to offend, families and teachers will build a partnership for the child.

What's in a Name? Throughout this book you will notice children's names, when used as examples, are from a variety of nationalities. A deliberate effort sought out the most popular names in many different cultures from a baby name book. It is extremely important to learn the correct pronunciation of the first and last names of all the families in the class, not giving them American nicknames unless the family especially requests it. It is a learning experience for the teacher and the other children to learn to pronounce ethnic names and can be a point of teaching tolerance, understanding, and cultural awareness. It must begin with the teacher's attitude.

emerging but often are not aware, or choose to ignore, what may be a problem in this area. It is not life-threatening; it often is compensated by the parent and other children in the family; and it can be cute and entertaining.

A speech and language screening is routinely administered to preschool children to detect possible difficulties. Informal interviews may act as that screening.

When to Seek Help in Speech and Language

The family is consulted if the child is nearing three years old without much language. Documented observations over a time showing little progress when compared to a chart of norms can help explain the concern. The teacher presents options for referrals to professionals who will conduct screening or full evaluations. That referral should begin with medical personnel or the pediatrician. Chronic ear infections often go unnoticed and can cause hearing loss that may affect language development. There are many other possible causes. Early detection for diagnosis and possible intervention is recommended. This dialogue takes place with empathy for the family's feelings and also a knowledge of community resources. If potential problems are indicated, a full evaluation usually is recommended either by the child's pediatrician or the program team. Teachers and early childhood programs should have referral lists from which the family can choose an agency or professional to perform this evaluation. Some of the helping professionals that may be involved are:

audiologist—conducts screenings and evaluations and diagnoses hearing problems; assesses hearing aids and teaches clients to conserve hearing and to use residual hearing

speech and language pathologist—conducts screenings, evaluation, diagnosis, and treatment of children with communication disorders

otolaryngologist—physician who specializes in diagnosis and treatment of ear, nose, and throat disorders; sometimes known as ENT (ear, nose, and throat) physician

American Sign Language interpreters—translate spoken language into sign language and vice versa for people with hearing impairments.

OTHER METHODS

Other Methods to Record Speech and Language Development:

Class List Log—a screening device for specific aspects of speech such as clarity, or language such as "talks freely with peers."

Anecdotal/Running Records—when exact quotes are included (as they should be) a sample of the child's speech and language is obtained.

Checklists/Rating Scales—formal evaluation instruments can evaluate progress in development.

KEY TERMS

action research	morphemes
articulation	open question
closed question	overgeneralization
diagnostic interview	phonemes
diversity	receptive language
dysfluent	record
Ebonics	speech
expressive language	structured interview
holographic	syntax
informal conversations	telegraphic
language	

WEEK 6: PLAN A

LISTENING TO SPEECH AND LANGUAGE FOR GROUP A

Students

With the help of the teacher, select two children to interview or have a conversation with.

Practitioners

Select each child in Group A to have a little conversation with each day this week. If it is allowed, tape record the Informal Conversations or Structured Interviews (see the following suggestions) as well as make written notes (literacy role model) as you speak with each child.

Informal Conversation

If you wish, record a conversation you have with the child about the child's play, an event, or an explana- tion of a piece of art or construction. Afterward, ana- lyze the conversation for what it reveals about the child's knowledge, emotional state, social development, and about the child's speech and language using the following checklist.

Structured Interview (sample questions)

Two- and three-year-olds:

"What's your name?"
"How old are you?"
"Go get the book." (receptive)
Say, "I want the ball."
"What's this?"
"What's this sound?" (Ring a bell without child seeing it.)
Show a mirror. "Who is that?" "What's his/her name?"

Four- and five-year-olds:

"What's your name? Last name?"
"Look around the room and tell me what you see."
"What makes you happy (sad or mad)?"
"What do you like to do best at school?"
"Can you tell me about a dream you've had?"
"Do you know any jokes?"

What to Do with It

Filing. Copy the Speech and Language Checklist found in Appendix D for each child.

Analyze the interview for what it reveals about the child's knowledge, emotional state, social development, and the child's speech and language development. Enter a summary, recorder, and date on the Portfolio Overview Sheet, like the example in Figure 6–11.

Sharing with Child and Family. Share with the family and the child, if appropriate, something of interest that came from the interview. For example, "Mrs. Santiago, I was talking with Manuel and he told me about the trip you have planned to visit his grandparents. He is very excited about it. When he gets back we'll be sure to invite him to tell the class about it if he would like to," or "When we had that little talk the other day, Sarah, it really was interesting the way you described your painting. I liked listening to the words you used about the shapes and colors. Any time you want to listen to the tape, let me know."

If a significant lag appears, discuss it with your supervisor to confirm it; then discuss it with the family. Have a list of resources available for the family to locate agencies for a speech and language evaluation.

Is any follow-up needed from the Speech and Language Checklist? Make a note of it, and seek answers or take action.

SPEECH/LANGUAGE			
Documentation	Location	Recorder	Date
AR	Portfolio	BAN	10/11
tape	"	BAN	1/6
video tape	"	MS	2/15
RR	"	BAN	6/19

Figure 6–11 Portfolio Overview Example

Actions.

Read a Book.

Grossman, B. (1996). *My Little Sister Ate One Hare.* New York: Crown.

Meddaugh, S. (1992). *Martha Speaks.* New York: Houghton Mifflin.

Small, D. (1992). *Ruby Mae Has Something to Say.* New York: Crown.

Rattigan, J. (1994). *Truman's Aunt Farm.* New York: Houghton Mifflin.

Young, D. (1995). *Purple Hair, I Don't Care.* Brooklyn: Kane Miller Books.

In the Environment.

• An environment that has new additions every day sparks conversations. The wonder over something from nature, a photograph from a classroom event, a special visitor, food in a new form, an interesting picture on the wall, all can spark conversations that will expand vocabulary, practice conversational turn-taking, initiate questions and responses.

• The psychological environment of "no risk" is necessary for language development. Children need lots of time for speaking with each other and the adults, with freedom to select the topic, be treated with respect, and be encouraged to express opinions or ideas feelings without fear of ridicule from adults or other children.

In the Curriculum.

• Planned times of conversation such as a Class Meeting might be added to the day's routine. The length of time and format should be carefully considered so that long wait times or conversation monopolies are eliminated. Some use a "Talking stick," a stick that is passed so that only the holder may speak. The traditional "Show and Tell" is not conversation, not a simulation of any conversational technique used in everyday life. Its use should be seriously reconsidered. (See Chapter 13 for a more complete discussion of this topic.)

• A real game of "Conversational Ball" can be used as a visual example of how to carry on a conversation. Using a wound-up ball of yarn, or a very soft ball, the adult and child can toss the ball back and forth as they carry on a conversation with appropriate responses. This can demonstrate the responsibility of both to talk and listen.

• The art of description can be practiced and modeled by adults. Describing a child's action, product, or behavior in specific, nonevaluative terms shows that the adult is observant, relates events in sequence, illustrates cause and effect, and gives the child individualized attention. This can be practiced from the very littlest ones to mature players. Everyone wants to be noticed.

In the Newsletter.
- Explain the stages of speech and language development. A short article regarding stuttering as a transitional phase in most children will allay family fears.

- New words learned at school or the word of the month like *discovering, comparing,* or *patterns* can help families reinforce concepts at home.
- Tips can be shared on conversations with children such as expanding or extending a child's comments, and describing the child's actions.
- Cute anecdotes can be sprinkled to bring humor and give insight into children's thinking.
- Be sure your newsletter is translated for those families whose language of the home is not English.

WEEK 6: PLAN B

CLASS LIST LOG OF SPEECH AND LANGUAGE FOR ALL

Use one of the Class List Log forms found in Appendix D, listing children by first names, alphabetically. Jot notes about each child concerning clarity of speech (understandable?), use of language for communication, irregularities, or concerns.

Note an observation on each child's Portfolio Overview Sheet.

What to Do with It

This is a screening for your own use to listen closely to every child's speech and language development this week. In the next month, you will be individually interviewing and audio taping each child to listen more closely. Discuss any concerns with the other staff or your supervisor, then the family.

Note an observation on each child's Portfolio Overview Sheet.

File the Class List Log in the class file.

WEEK 6: PLAN C

REFLECTIVE JOURNAL

Respond to the following in your Reflective Journal, kept in a private file at home.

I like to talk with children about . . .

I feel much more apprehensive when talking about . . .

I think it is because . . .

My language habit I need to work on most is . . .

My thoughts about diversity are . . .

REFERENCES

Acredolo, L. P., & Goodwyn, S. W. (2000). *Baby minds: Brain-building games your baby will love to play.* New York: Bantam Books.

Almy, M., & Genishi, C. (1979). *Ways of studying children.* New York: Teacher's College Press.

Bandura, A. (1977). *Social learning theory.* Englewood Cliffs, NJ: Prentice Hall.

Benner, S. M. (2003). *Assessment of children with special needs.* Clifton Park, NY: Thomson Delmar Learning.

Bruner, J. S. (1983). *Child's talk: Learning to use language.* New York: Norton.

Bryen, D. N., & Gallaher, D. (1983). Assessment of language and communication. In K. D. Paget & B. A. Bracken (Eds.), *The psychoeducational assessment of the Preschool Child.* New York: Grune & Stratton.

Chomsky, N. (1965). *Aspects of the theory of syntax.* Cambridge, MA: MIT Press.

Chomsky, N. (1968). *Language and mind.* New York: Harcourt, Brace and World.

Cook, R. E., Tessier, A., & Klein, M. D. (2000). *Adapting early childhood curricula for children in inclusive settings.* New York: Merrill. (An imprint of Macmillan Publishing Company.)

Daniels, M. (2001). *Dancing with words: Signing for hearing children's literacy.* Westport, CT: Bergin & Garvey.

Dickinson, D. K., & Tabos, P. O. (Eds.). (2001). *Beginning literacy with language: Young children learning at home and school.* Baltimore, MD: Brookes.

Evans, R. I. (1973). *Jean Piaget: The man and his ideas.* New York: E. P. Dutton.

Harste, J., Woodward, V., & Burke, C. (1984). *Language stories & literacy lessons.* Portsmouth, NH: Heinemann.

Hart, B., & Risley, T. R. (1995). *Meaningful differences in the everyday experiences of young American children.* Baltimore, MD: Brookes.

Hendrick, J. (1992). *The whole child.* New York: Merrill. (An imprint of Macmillan Publishing Co.)

Kindler, A. (2002). *Survey of the states' limited English proficient students and available educational programs and services, 2000–2001.* Washington, DC: National Clearinghouse for English Language Acquisition and Language Instruction Educational Programs.

Kratcoski, A. M., & Katz, K. B. (1998). *Conversing with young language learners in the classroom. Young Children,* 53 (3), 30–33.

Kuhl, P. K. (1993). Developmental speech perception: Implications for models of language impairment. *Annals of the New York Academy of Sciences, 682,* 248–263.

Leonard, A. M. (1997). *I spy something: A practical guide to classroom observations of young children.* Little Rock, AR: Southern Early Childhood Association.

Lewin, K. (1948). *Resolving social conflicts, selected papers on group dynamics (1935–1946).* New York: Harper.

Machado, J. M. (2003). *Early childhood experiences in language arts* (7th ed.). Clifton Park, NY: Thomson Delmar Learning.

Moxley, R. A., Kenny, K. A., & Hunt, M. K. (1990). Improving the instruction of young children with self-recording and discussion. In *Early Childhood Research Quarterly, 5,* 233–249.

Neuman, S. B., & Roskos, K. A. (1993). *Language and literacy learning in the early years.* Fort Worth, TX: Harcourt, Brace Jovanovich.

Ouseg, H. L. (Ed.). (1962). *International dictionary in twenty-one languages.* New York: Philosophical Library.

Padolsky, D. (2002). *How many school-aged English language learners (ELLs) are there in the U.S.* National Clearinghouse for English Language Acquisition. http://www.ncela.gw.edu/askncela/01leps.htm. Accessed March 16, 2003.

Pelligrini, A. D. (1991). *Applied child study: A developmental approach.* Hillsdale, NJ: Lawrence Erlbaum Associates.

Skinner, B. F. (1957). *Verbal behavior.* New York: Appleton-Century-Crofts.

Snow, C., Burns, M. S., & Griffin, P. (Eds.). (1998). *Preventing reading difficulties in young children.* Washington, DC: National Academy Press.

Vygotsky, L. S. (1962). *Thought and language.* New York: John Wiley.

Willis, C. (1998). Language development: A key to lifelong learning. *Child Care Information Exchange 121,* May/June 1998, 63–65.

Wortham, S. C. (2001). *Assessment in early childhood education,* 3rd ed. Upper Saddle River, NJ: Merrill Prentice Hall.

Yairi, E., & Ambrose, N.G. (1999). Early child stuttering persistency and recovery rates. *Journal of Speech, Language and Hearing Research,* 22 (5), 1097.

RESOURCES

Derman-Sparks, L. (1988). *Anti-bias curriculum: Tools for empowering young children.* Washington, DC: National Association for the Education of Young Children.

Hildebrand, V., Phenice, L. A., Gray, M. M., & Hines, R. P. (1996). *Knowing and serving diverse families.* Englewood Cliffs, NJ: Prentice Hall.

King, E. W., Chipman, M., & Cruz-Janzen, M. (1994). *Educating young children in a diverse society.* Boston: Allyn and Bacon.

Lynch, E. W., & Hanson, M. J. (1998). *Developing cross-cultural competence,* 2nd ed. Baltimore, MD: Brookes Publishing Co.

For additional information on early education curriculum, visit our Web site at http://www.earlychilded.delmar.com

Using Time Samples to Look at Attention Span

USING TIME SAMPLES

EXERCISE: How much time did you spend in the last week sewing? reading? golfing? shopping?

When is your attention span the longest?

Think about the choices you make. When there is a choice of activities, it is governed by some assumptions:

- You are more likely to do what you *like* to do rather than what you *have* to do.
- You do what you have the opportunity to do. Your sewing machine may be broken. You have no new novel to read. You have no money for golfing or shopping. You would if you could.
- If your first choice, your favorite pastime, is not available, you may choose a related activity. Your sewing machine is broken so maybe you do some hand sewing. You have no new book to read so you reread an old one. Instead of golfing or shopping, you read about it in magazines or the newspaper.
- If you have finished all the sewing projects, read all the books, played that course, or shopped that mall already, you may be bored with those choices.
- If you have a new pattern you want to try, a best-seller waiting, a new golf course or mall just opened, you cannot wait to try it and will avoid all other choices, people, or tasks.
- You are more likely to do it if you feel you will be successful or challenged, but not frustrated. You know you can sew a dress so perhaps you decide to try a jacket. You will work on it until you get to

a difficult part. Depending on your personality, you may work at it, rip it out, and start over, or abandon the project. If you are a slow, deliberate reader then probably reading is not a favorite pastime. If you feel awkward at physical things, then golfing may not be your forté. A person planning to lose weight before the next season might be frustrated with shopping and leave the store after trying on only one bathing suit.

- You may choose your activity because your friends are doing it too. They call and say, "Let's go golfing or shopping." You had not planned to, but you want to be with them so you join them.
- While you are at a task of your choosing, time passes quickly. You look up at the clock and cannot believe you have spent four hours working on that garment, reading that book, playing that golf game, or shopping at that mall. The total absorption in the activity also resents intrusions and attempts to draw you away. The phone rings, you let the answering machine get it. It is time for lunch, so you grab a sandwich and eat it while you are reading. You hurry home from the golf course or shopping and pick up a pizza for dinner. If someone comes and tells you it is time to stop doing that and to come do something else, it makes you angry. You may ignore the first call, the second, and the third.

Factors Influencing Children's Attention Span

What does **attention span** have to do with observing young children? When they have their choice, where, what, and with whom do they choose to spend their time? By observing children's choices of activities, a spectrum of information is gathered. The same principles lead children's activity choices.

The child's choices reveal interests. Avoidance or cursory completion of assigned or chosen tasks may suggest lack of competence. Bessie just loves painting at the easel so she rushes to get there first, puts on her smock, and gets ready. Miss Jones says, "Bessie, before you start painting I want you to come and paint this hand plaque for your mother." Bessie reluctantly goes to the table, quickly paints the plaque, and returns to the easel where she paints for the next fifteen minutes. Miss Jones wonders to herself, and maybe even writes on her Class List Log, "Short attention span, painted part of plaque and left." Was Bessie interested in painting and does she have a long or short attention span? What made the difference?

The child may select related activities when their first choice is not available. William headed straight for the water table after he hung up his jacket. It was

closed. He moved to the climber, but it was taken down, replaced by a writing center. He went into the bathroom, ran water in the sink, wadded up paper towels, and blew them around in the water. Someone had to use the bathroom so he came out. He climbed up on the shelf and jumped off, three times, before the teacher came over and tried to get him to come to the new writing center. He refused. She wondered, "Why is he doing these things today?" Children will find a way to do what they want and need to do. William found water play soothing and climbing helped him work off extra energy. Those were two activities his body, temperament, and development needed but were denied by the environment so he manufactured them himself.

Novel, new activities attract children's interest (Figure 7–1). The next day when William came to the classroom, he saw that there was a computer in the writing center. He ran right over and started touching the keys. Marvella showed him how to turn it on and asked him if he wanted to use the dinosaur program to write a story with her. "Sure." Miss Jones wondered, "I couldn't get William over here yesterday. I wonder what made the difference?"

Children will choose and give attention to activities where they find success. Bessie may have rejected the teacher's painting project, preferring her own. Maybe she never painted a plaque before and

Figure 7–1 New activities attract attention.

was afraid to try. She had trouble controlling the small brushes the teacher provided but she knew how to use the big brushes and many colors at the easel. Easel painting she knew would be successful. William was not lured by the teacher's invitation to the writing center. He had tried to write his name when his mother made him practice, and he could not do it to please her. If he went to the writing center he probably would have to write, "No way! Stay away! I'll just stick with water play and climbing and jumping. I know I'm good at those."

Children are sometimes influenced by their friends' choices of activities. Bessie looked over at the art table. "Oh, my friends are all at the art table with shells and twigs and leaves and stones and bottles of glue. They're calling me over. I've never used glue before. My mom says it's too messy." She joins them and watches for a few minutes. "Now I know how to do it," and works as long as they are there. When they leave she may decide to finish her collage or leave it and follow them to the next activity they choose. She may choose an activity because that is where the adult is. She likes to be near Mr. Jim. If he had invited her to do the plaque she would have stayed there longer.

Children involved in an activity may be reluctant to bring it to a close. Timmy's block building is growing taller and wider. He gets more blocks and makes a road up to the building's door. He gets out the little animals and builds a pen for them. Then he gets a tub of cars and drives it up the road to deliver new animals. The teacher says, "Time for everyone to come to circle time." Timmy keeps building. She says, "Timmy, put the blocks away and come to circle time. You have played there a whole hour." There are too many blocks and animals and cars to put away and the building does not yet have a roof or a barn for the animals. It is not finished and he realizes he did not even have time to play in the water table yet and he always plays in the water table before circle time. He has been in the block area the whole free choice time.

Measuring Attention Span with Time Samples

One of the characteristics commonly used to describe young children is "short attention span." Families will often report that children who cannot sit still one minute at the dinner table will sit for two hours watching a video and never move. (Is it any wonder that families do not fully cooperate with "Television Turn-Off Day?") From the preceding adult and children's examples, there are many variables that determine the length of attention span. By watching

children as they choose and participate in the activities, a wide spectrum of development and behavior can be assessed and evaluated.

The **Time Sample** is an efficient recording method that tracks children's choices, their playmates, and the time they spend in one area. It is a method suitable for children three years old and older in group settings. It may be a mixed age group or homogeneous age group. Obviously, if it is recording the children's choices, it is only used in a program and at a time when children have choices. That assumption is based on developmentally appropriate practice for young children birth through eight years old (Bredekamp & Copple, 1997).

Infants—Observing the infant's cues, the adult is able to judge when the baby would like to be held, carried to a new place, or shifted to a new position. (p. 72)

Toddlers—Adults adapt schedules and activities to meet individual children's needs within the group setting. (p. 84)

Three- through five-year olds—Teachers allocate extended periods of time (at least one hour at a time) for children to engage in play and projects. (p. 126)

Six- through eight-year olds—A variety of work places and spaces is provided and used flexibly. (p. 165)

Here is an example of a Time Sample (Figure 7–2). A segment of the free choice time is selected. One-half hour works well, begun after the children have all arrived and are actively engaged. The learning centers or choices are listed down the left margin. Five-minute intervals are filled in across the top from when the recording is begun. The recorder looks at each area and writes down the names of the children who are in that area at that moment. After a quick glance, a circle can be drawn around the names of the children who are playing cooperatively. That does not refer to the absence of arguments but to the social stage of working together for a common goal, as described in Chapter 4. The recorder notes also if an adult is in that area, then looks on to the next area to be observed. The areas are all scanned, and names of players are written down. A category at the bottom designates the names of children not in any area at the time, perhaps in transition, perhaps wandering around not involved in play.

When the next five-minute period begins, the process is repeated. If the recorder knows a child remained in the area for the last five minutes, a straight line is drawn, saving a few seconds. If the child left and returned, the name is rewritten. Children do move quickly. Every five minutes the process is repeated.

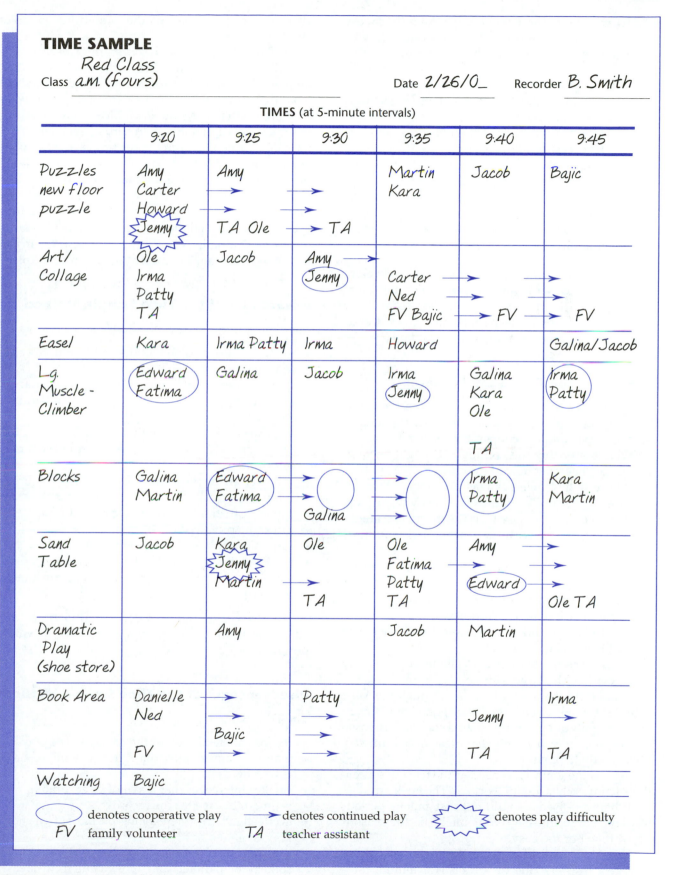

Figure 7–2 Time Sample Example

EXERCISE: From the Time Sample example, choose one child and follow the child for a one-half-hour segment. Draw some conclusions about:

- the child's interests.
- where the child feels competent (probably is most developed).
- where the child may not feel competent (may be the least developed area).
- the stage of play.
- the length of attention span.
- if the child is teacher-dependent or avoids the adults.
- what questions it still leaves in your mind about this child.

Of course, a total evaluation of a child's development is not drawn from one recording, any more than it should be drawn from one test score. Time samples should be done periodically to see trends and to amplify other documentation methods.

Analysis of the Time Sample Example

Who do you think is the oldest child in the class? Probably Edward. He appears to have the longest attention span and is a cooperative player.

Who is probably the youngest? It might be Bajic, or possibly he is just new to the class.

Whose family member was probably the volunteer (see FV for family volunteer)? The FV was probably related to Bajic, or else he is the most dependent.

Who likes to be with the teacher assistant (TA)? Ole.

What are the most popular areas of the classroom? Large motor and sand.

What is the least popular area? Dramatic play. What might be a remedy? Add new props.

What strategy did the TA use? The TA went to where the most children were.

Where was the teacher (T)? The teacher possibly was recording the Time Sample.

What child is missing halfway through the Time Sample? Danielle. She might have gone home sick or gone to a pull-out program such as speech. It is possible she was in transit between areas or just missed. Mistakes do happen.

Who is the child who needed the teacher's attention? Jenny. What finally worked? The book area.

What well-used area did not sustain long periods of play? Large muscle. What might be the reason? Too difficult or too easy.

How long would you expect four-year-olds to stay at a task? A rule of thumb is a minute for a

year of age *unless* one of the preceding variables affects it.

A Time Sample is a closed method because the recorder writes down where children are at that moment (raw data) but does not include details of what they are doing, how they are doing it, or what they are saying. The symbols indicate inferences the observer makes as notes are recorded such as: circles for cooperative play, arrows for uninterrupted play, and a jagged circle for aggressive play. A Time Sample is a very revealing method of gathering and recording information that can be interpreted for many purposes. It even reveals where the adults spend their time and the most and least used areas of the room. Evaluation of children, adults, and curriculum choices all can be made from the Time Sample.

Advantages of the Time Sample Method

The Time Sample is helpful because it

- gathers information on all the children in the class at one time.
- gives quantitative (numerical) information about attention span. (Cindy spent _____ minutes at the easel.)
- indicates child's play and interest preferences.
- gives clues as to children's strongest areas, inferred by choices.
- gives clues about child's less developed areas, inferred by avoidance.
- can indicate the stage of play the child is in.
- can show preferred playmates.
- can track adult positions in the room.
- shows which areas of the classroom are most used.
- shows which areas of the classroom are underutilized.

The recorder can develop abbreviations and adapt the form and method to meet the individual program.

Disadvantages of the Time Sample Method

The Time Sample

- records no details about the nature of the play.
- may not capture children moving while recorder is writing.
- rmakes inferences that may not be accurate.
- is time-intensive for the recorder.
- is effective only where a long period of free choice play is offered.
- is not as effective for toddlers because most play is solitary or parallel, and movement from area to

area is more frequent due to the children's shorter attention spans.
- must be done periodically, or it is too judgmental.

Pitfalls to Avoid

Time Samples should be repeated every few weeks so that too much credence is not placed on one isolated Time Sample (as in the exercise interpreting this Time Sample).

The Time Sample is very time-consuming but is a method that a family member or a volunteer, a non-participant observer, could be assigned.

Children must have free choice of activity areas for the Time Sample to be effective. If there is a teacher-led activity during that free choice time, it can be indicated.

Using Technology

A timer is a useful tool to remind the recorder to scan the room again and note where each child is working. Hand-held computers with timers can be used as well. The Time Sample form can be loaded on a computer using the Documents to Go® program and can then be used to electronically record the names of the children. Later, when the completed form is downloaded, summary results of each child's activities can be stored in an electronic portfolio for each child.

R E V I E W

Time Sample: Documentation of the duration of a child's chosen activity. Can be compiled on an individual child or an entire class by noting each child's location in the room at regular intervals of time.

Types of Information to Record Using Time Samples:

Location of child at regular intervals. It can yield information on

Interests

Areas of strength

Patterns of behavior

Areas that may not be developed by noting activities the child never selects

Playmates

Social play stage

Child's selection or avoidance of adults in the classroom

Length of time a child stays in one area

How to Find the Time

The Time Sample can be time-consuming but on a day when free play or free choice time is going smoothly, the teacher, assistant, or volunteer is only briefly occupied and can perform other tasks between the recording periods. By carefully planning self-directed projects and curriculum, adult intervention is minimized, leaving time for this kind of record-keeping.

What to Do with It

Once a Time Sample is completed, it is stored in the teacher's Class File. Since it has information on all of the children present on that day it is not copied for individual children's portfolios. Information can be summarized on each child and placed in that child's portfolio.

Example: From the Time Sample on pg 169

Amy—At the beginning of the day Amy moved around the room frequently, stopping at puzzles and dramatic play. She painted and worked at the Sand Table for longer periods of time. Her play was solitary. 2/26/03

Edward and a friend moved together from the climber to an involved block-building project that occupied them for more than ten minutes. They then moved to the Sand Table where they played cooperatively. 2/26/03

These summaries give information on play choices, movements, and level of social play. Subsequent Time Samples will be used for comparison to see if the child is in a consistent pattern of play or is moving among the choices in the classroom. These comparisons can be used to measure progress in development as well as to make individual plans for a child who may need some encouragement to extend or experience other choices offered.

LOOKING AT COGNITIVE DEVELOPMENT

EXERCISE: Try the exercise in Figure 7–3 to determine your learning style.

One of the fundamental requirements for learning is a focused attention span. People with brain dysfunctions that prevent them from focusing and filtering all the stimuli that comes into the brain at once have difficulty learning. Cognitive development begins with attention span and is the topic of this chapter and continues into the next.

HOW DO YOU LEARN?

For each item below, check the response that most closely describes your typical behavior.

1. In class or a meeting I…
   - ☐ A. Take lots of notes, often with lots of doodles
   - ☐ B. Sit near the front so I can hear and participate in discussions
   - ☐ C. Tend to get restless quickly, have the urge to move around

2. I get the most from presentations where the leader…
   - ☐ A. Uses lots of audio-visual aids and handouts
   - ☐ B. Is a good speaker
   - ☐ C. Involves participants in exercises and hands-on experiences

3. I get the most from a reading assignment by…
   - ☐ A. Reading it quietly to myself
   - ☐ B. Having it read to me
   - ☐ C. Reading it aloud while pacing about

4. When I need to make a big decision, I prefer to…
   - ☐ A. Analyze my options on paper
   - ☐ B. Sit in a comfortable place and listen to music
   - ☐ C. Do something active like jogging, walking, or working with my hands

5. When learning something new, I learn best when…
   - ☐ A. Reading and writing about it
   - ☐ B. Hearing it explained and talking about it with someone
   - ☐ C. Trying it out in a real-life situation

6. Prior to making a major purchase, I evaluate my choices by…
   - ☐ A. Reading about them
   - ☐ B. Talking to friends to get their advice
   - ☐ C. Trying them out

7. When learning how to use a new piece of equipment, I
   - ☐ A. Read all the directions before trying it out
   - ☐ B. Like to have someone tell me how to get started
   - ☐ C. Like to see if I can figure it out myself

8. When I get angry, I…
   - ☐ A. Clam up and keep it to myself
   - ☐ B. Quickly let others know I am angry
   - ☐ C. Clench my fists, pound the table, storm off

9. In my spare time I prefer to…
   - ☐ A. Watch TV, go to the movies, attend a play, or read
   - ☐ B. Listen to the radio, play tapes, or attend a concert
   - ☐ C. Engage in physical activity

Total your answers. If most of your answers are A's this indicates that you are primarily a visual learner; if most are B's, an auditory learner; and if most are C's, a kinesthetic learner.

Figure 7–3 How Do You Learn? (October, 1988, p. 11. Reprinted with permission from *Child Care Information Exchange*, PO Box 2890, Redmond, WA 98073, 1-800-221-2864.)

Learning is not just a matter of memorizing information. It is highly complex and individually different. Some people learn best by hearing, reading, and memorizing, whereas others learn best by touching, moving, and interacting either with materials or people (Figure 7–3). The art of teaching does not begin with knowing the pupil, but with knowing oneself. Recognizing that others learn in ways different from ourselves profoundly affects understanding and teaching. Teaching then becomes the orchestration of experiences for all modalities or ways of learning. The traditional method of "recite, memorize, and test" has been unsuccessful for many people. The development of cognition, thinking processes, is observable and an area for teachers to consider in environment and schedule planning as well as daily lesson planning.

The development of cognition entwines all other areas already discussed—attachment and separation, physical development, language, and social and emotional development. In the next few chapters, it will be the focus of a closer look. Observers need knowledge and clues to examine closely the changes that take place in children's mental processes. Whether the process is called knowledge, imagination, creativity, reasoning, problem solving, classification, logic, symbolizing, or logico-mathematical reasoning, it all is relevant to cognitive development. The chapter and section divisions are for ease of categorization and description, not separate from one another as the divisions infer.

Piaget and Cognitive Development

No discussion of cognition can be complete without a review of the work of Jean Piaget (1896–1980) and his interpreters (Flavell, 1987; Furth, 1969; Ginsburg & Opper, 1969). He described the kinds of knowledge and the stages of children's cognitive development.

Jean Piaget was a Swiss scientist, psychologist, and epistemologist (a person who studies the methods and grounds of knowledge). His early work studied the adaptation of mollusks (related to the clam) to different types of water; he was trained in exacting observation skills. He had to look closely to see changes in a mollusk. His life changed dramatically, as most do, when he became a parent. He then transferred those observation skills to a more fascinating subject, his own children, looking and theorizing the source and meaning of each movement and new skill. Out of those close observations and sixty years of study (talk about long attention span!) came the foundation for most of what is known about infant and young child maturation cognitive processes.

Kinds of Knowledge. Piaget categorized not only the stages of cognitive development but the types of knowledge developed (Figure 7–4).

Social Conventional Knowledge. **Social conventional knowledge** is described as "the rules of the tribe." It is the type of knowledge that parents teach by instruction and example. These are the accepted social and cultural norms for dress, behavior in different settings, greetings, and ways of addressing others. Some might call this category manners or customs. Language development is another major cognitive category in conventional knowledge. The interactions with other people affect language directly, but certain cognitive processing must be possible before language can appear.

Physical Knowledge. **Physical knowledge** is the accumulation of facts about how the world works. As the child rolls, scoots, crawls, stands, cruises, and climbs, she is inspecting her environment (Figure 7–5). She finds that pushing a ball makes it roll, but pushing

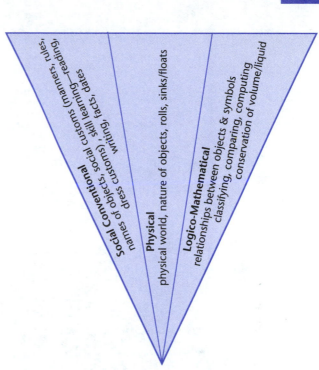

Figure 7–4 Kinds of Knowledge. (Adapted from Peterson, R., & Felton-Collins, V. 1986. *The Piaget Handbook for Teachers and Parents*. New York: Teachers College Press.)

a block does not have the same effect. She soon adapts her hand movements and expectations of results when she pushes round objects and grasps square ones. During the sensorimotor stage, the child is gathering data about the properties of all that is around her by manipulating it and watching the results.

Logico-Mathematical Knowledge. **Logico-mathematical knowledge** is the primary area usually associated with cognitive development, the processing of information to draw conclusions, either verbal or mathematical. Seeking relationships is the main task of this type of processing. It is all about the observation of similarities, differences, and commonalities. Variables are manipulated and the results measured. These abstract concepts are clarified when we watch as a child plays with blocks:

- Similarities and **matching**—He places the same size blocks on top of each other.
- Commonalities and **classification**—He places all the blocks together and all the toy animals together.
- **Cause and effect**—He tries to stand the toy horse on the small block too small for all four feet. Then he tries to stand it up on the large block, which succeeds.
- Measuring and **seriation**—He places the animals in a line according to size.

Figure 7–5 Physical knowledge is acquired through experiences with real objects.

small muscles (Figure 7–6). Vision in a newborn is at the legally blind level (Flavell, 1987) because of the inability to focus or fixate. However, the newborn is able to distinguish between high and dark contrast about seven to eight inches away, figure-ground, shape, and contours. That is just what is needed to look at a human face at close distance. Visual acuity increases rapidly, and by six months it is at the adult level. Hearing is at a near-adult level at birth. Some research suggests an infant can discriminate the mother's voice from others, if it was in "motherese," an up-and-down quality that adults naturally use with babies. The infant has been found able to discriminate between "pa" and "ba" sounds at an early age as well. Touch is well developed, especially the sensors for receptive touch that have caused an interest in baby massage. Those perceptions, along with taste and smell, are present at birth, though at rudimentary levels. Their rapid development necessitates families and caregivers to provide a sensory-rich environment and experiences for even the youngest infant. In this way, they have a healthy start on the road to cognitive development.

Piaget described intricate substages in which information processing takes circular pathways. Each new piece of information goes through this chain, trying to make a match. Piaget called this con-

- **Rote counting**—He orally counts, perhaps inaccurately, or out of order, "1, 2, 3, 6, 8."
- **One-to-one correspondence**—He points to each animal as he accurately counts, "1, 2, 3, 4."
- Object permanence—He knows that if one of the animals falls off the table, out of his sight, it still exists. If he looks for it, he can find it.
- **Conservation**—He knows if he sawed one of the two blocks in half, the two halves would weigh the same as the whole block.

These three areas of cognitive development—social conventional knowledge, physical knowledge, and logico-mathematical knowledge—change in a predictable pattern from simple to complex, over a period of time, at individual rates. They have implications for curriculum planning and assessment.

Piaget's Stages of Cognitive Development

Infancy—Sensorimotor Stage (Birth to 24 Months). Piaget's label of the **Sensorimotor Stage,** birth through 24 months old, gives clues of how the infant is processing information through the senses and acting on information with developing large and

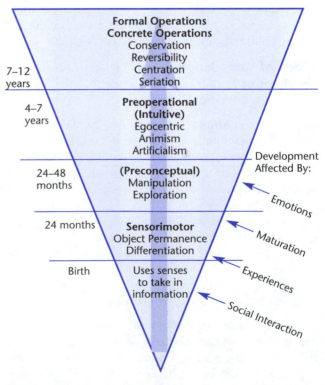

Figure 7–6 Piaget's Stages of Cognitive Development

Figure 7–7 Association

Figure 7–8 Disequilibrium

Figure 7–9 Assimilation

Beginning Geometry

A group of parents and toddlers were gathered to share stories, frustrations, and advice. A less-than-two-year-old toddled over to a swinging door with an automatic closer. When he leaned against it, it opened a little way, then closed with a hissing sound. He seriously looked at the door and tried it again. Push, close, hiss. Push, close, hiss. All this time he was looking up at the top of the door jamb. Mom came running over, "Come away from there." She was probably concerned about pinched fingers and what would happen if he pushed too hard and went on through the doorway. I was fascinated that he was not tempted to do that. He was mesmerized by the action and reaction of the door.

As we took his point of view and looked up as he was, we saw the ceiling produced a bright changing triangle as the door closed. He formed a mental image (schema) of triangles and their changing shapes that day that will be the foundation of later geometry equations. Someday he will measure the degrees of the angles in a triangle. I like to think about the connection between that task and the day he pushed the door open and watched it close.

structing knowledge. This basic principle is the foundation for professional practice. The child is involved actively in exploration and experimentation to form his own knowledge. Knowledge is not the transfer of abstract information but the formation of associations based on information from the senses.

To help you become familiar with this theory, Figures 7–7, 7–8, and 7–9 illustrate your own cognitive processes as you read this passage. If you already know and understand Piaget's concept of association, as you read this and look at Figure 7–7, your brain is processing, comparing this new information with what you already knew (old information) and you make an association. This is an "aha, I know that" moment.

If it is new information for you, for example, if you realize that this use of the word **association** is different from your previous understanding of the definition, you are in **disequilibrium** (mental confu-

sion or imbalance) until you make a match (Figure 7–8). Once you take in the information and form a bridge or relationship to what you already know, it is **assimilation.** You have added another building block, or schema, to existing information or deepened your understanding.

When the new information is associated, assimilated, and added to the old information, you have achieved **accommodation.** You have somewhat changed the structure of what you previously knew and formed new ideas or blocks of knowledge. That is the process of assimilation. Now all of that becomes old information to begin the process all over again the next time a new piece of information is received. You will try to associate it, assimilate it, go into disequilibrium, and then accommodate it (Figure 7–9).

Here is an example: An infant suckles her mother's breast and receives milk. She builds an association between sucking and milk. As she is rolling around in her crib a few months later, the blanket brushes her lips. The reflex motion causes her to suck. "Ugh! I'm not getting milk!" She could not make a match between the previous milk she received and this new substance. She has tried to associate the substance to what she already knew, but it was lint instead of milk. She was in disequilibrium. She spit the blanket out and has now another action or reaction to sucking. She can continue or she can spit it out. She can now assimilate, or make a judgment, and decide on a new course of action, accommodation. She may decide that it is a second-best alternative and continue to chew on it when the nipple is not available.

This process occurs thousands of times a day in nanoseconds (one billionth of a second) without any awareness or conscious decision of the thinker.

The cognitive tasks of the Sensorimotor Stage are self-differentiation and object permanence. Around six months of age, the infant forms the concept that he is a separate entity from the crib, from the car seat, but most of all from the humans around him. This has implications when adults leave the room and the infant wants them back. Remember the discussion on separation in the first chapter?

Very closely allied is the knowledge that items and people still exist even when out of sight. If they drop a spoon over the side of the high chair tray, they will look for it. When their caregiver leaves the room, they may whine or cry until he comes back. By the end of the second year, infants have both mental representations that are leading them into the development of language and on into the Preoperational Stage.

The Preoperational Stage (Two to Seven Years). The **Preoperational Stage** consists of the Preconceptual Period (two to four years old) and the Intuitive Period (four to seven years old).

According to Piaget (Peterson & Felton-Collins, 1986) there are four factors that guide development from one substage to the next.

1. emotions that create feelings and motivate learning
2. maturation of physical growth, including the nervous system
3. experiences (own learning and self-discovery)
4. social interaction and influence of parents, teachers, and peers (p. 4)

Having an understanding of these factors assists the early childhood educator to assess and plan for an environment and curriculum that meets the cognitive needs of this stage.

In the Preconceptual Period, the child is an active participant in learning, intentionally acting on the environment and finding how things work. Problems are attacked mostly by trial and error and manipulation of materials. Instead of just using a spoon to feed herself, she will use it to feed her dolly. This moves her from the function performed on herself, to acting on another. She may even move to the symbolic or dramatic use of the play when she uses the spoon as a microphone like she saw the singer use on television last night. Throughout this substage, the major task is classification, making connections by physically and mentally placing items in pairs and groups. The vocabulary is rapidly building and grammar is expanding. Now sentences convey messages and control the environment and other people.

In the Intuitive Period, as described by Piaget, for the early childhood years four to seven years old, the reasons the child gives for phenomena are based on appearances or intuition rather than understanding. There are many mental processes the child cannot do until the next stage, the Concrete Operational Stage. Flavell (1987) and others have looked at this stage in a more positive light, finding that children in this stage have built large knowledge structures. Although they are present, the child may not yet represent them either in language or art. The receptive processes are greater than the expressive. The child understands much more than he can convey either in words, drawings, or writing.

Some classic terminology and experiments demonstrate what a Preoperational child will attain in the next stage:

egocentrism—The child believes that everyone thinks and feels as he does. (A small screen separates the child and a toy from the examiner who asks, "Can I see the toy?" If the child can see it, she will answer, "Yes," even if a screen blocks the examiner's view.)

conservation—The child does not understand the variables that can make quantity look different although the volume is unchanged. (There are two glasses of water with the same level of liquid.) The examiner asks, "Are they the same?" Then liquid is poured from one glass into a tall, thin beaker. The examiner asks, "Are they the same now?" The Preoperational child, without the understanding of the properties of volume, will say, "No. This one has more." The child will answer by appearance.

reversibility—The child is not yet able to mentally reverse an operation. (The examiner asks, "What will happen if I pour this back? Then will it be the same?")

centration—The Preoperational child is only able to focus on one attribute at a time. (If the child is sorting by color but the blocks also have different shapes, he will have difficulty centering [concentrating] on sorting by color, ignoring the shape.)

seriation—The Preoperational child is not able to place items in a series according to a rule such as height or weight. (They can probably pick out largest and smallest but have difficulty with those in between.)

The Preoperational child makes cognitive errors based on appearance, not reasoning, such as:

animism—The child believes that all objects have properties of being alive. ("My book will be lonely if I leave it home.")

artificialism—The child believes that natural phenomena are man-caused. ("Daddy, make it stop raining so we can go on our picnic.")

Concrete Operational Stage (Seven to Eleven Years). All the processes that the Preoperational child is developing come to bloom in the **Concrete Operational Stage.** Children now can use logical and rational thinking to understand and explain the properties of volume and number, classifying, seriating, centering, and reversing. It does not occur as they celebrate their seventh birthday; it happens in small, incremental steps when major neurological changes take place. Around seven years old, the ways of thinking have changed. The child is now ready physically, socially, emotionally, and cognitively to apply the experiences of the past seven years to the serious business of learning.

The tasks of sorting and classifying, recognizing similarities and differences, is *the* recurring curriculum theme. This is not to be interpreted that ways of learning change from those experiential, hands-on explorations. Piaget's theory is complex and full of terminology but it has practical application for methods, materials, environment, and curriculum in any early childhood program. The environment and curriculum allow each child to construct knowledge by exploration, manipulation, and sensory experiences the adults provide. The role of the adult is still to prepare the environment, facilitate the exploration, support and scaffold approximations of development, and record the progress. If the first roles are fulfilled, there will be progress to record.

Attention

"Attention is the focusing of the individual's perceptual processes upon a specific aspect of the environment. Learning cannot take place unless the individual is able to focus attention." (Cook, Tessier, & Klein, 2000, p. 342). To focus attention the child must concentrate on the object or task at hand while also ignoring other, insignificant stimuli. This is a skill that is being refined from birth and is critical to school performance, social interaction, and even survival. It is one of the three basic processes utilized in information processing, attention, perception, and memory.

Jensen (1998) in *Teaching with the Brain in Mind* gives understandable insight into the workings of the brain. He discusses the purpose of attention for survival and to extend pleasurable states. It provides sensory information on which to base decisions about our next actions. The pathways of attention consist of alarm, orientation, identification, and decision. A child may see the flicker of fire, but without prior experiences on which to base a decision, the attention and decision to seek it out may prove very dangerous. On the other hand, when a child is absorbed in play and the teacher flicks the lights, the decision point is whether to continue the pleasure of play or give attention now to the teacher's agenda. Is it any wonder that children get hurt or in trouble?

The visual system provides 80% of the information needed for this process to take place. The brain has to process or sort out irrelevant data and amplify the relevant data. Chemical changes take place during this process, assisting in heightened attention during times of stress and threat. Attention also flows in cycles from high to low throughout the day and night with periods of inattention of great importance for processing time. When teachers see children gazing out the window or standing and watching, a common response is, "Pay attention." If teachers heeded Jensen's explanation of the processing time, those inactive moments would be seen in a new light. Everyone has experienced profound thoughts that come long after a discussion or experience. The brain just needed that time to process the information and make sense and meaning.

Memory

During the Sensorimotor and Preoperational stages, the child interacts with real objects and builds memory of the properties of these objects and how they react. This assimilation and accommodation is stored in the memory. John Flavell, whose whole career has been devoted to studying cognitive development, reinforces the importance of providing young children with experiences that will increase their knowledge of the world in which they live. He says, "What the hand knows has an enormous effect on what the head learns and remembers" (Flavell, 1987, p. 213). Memory is the construction material of cognitive development.

Those who compare memory to an information processing system say there are three components of the hardware: sensory memory that receives input from the environment, working memory that is the site of ongoing cognitive activity, and long-term memory, a permanent storehouse of knowledge that is present but sometimes hard to access. As children get older they acquire more efficient strategies to solve problems, are able to inhibit distractions, and some cognitive processes become virtually automatic, aiding in faster processing of information. Kail (2001) sees these as smoother transitions between the cognitive stages than Piaget's steps.

EXERCISE: Respond to the following statements about yourself:

I have a (bad/good) memory.
It helps me to remember if I . . .

There are many different aspects of memory. Recognition is the most basic. Piaget's term for it was *association*. It is that matching to a past piece of information. Studies of infants and young children show this basic ability is very high early in life. A 1993 article in *Life* magazine entitled, "Babies Are SMARTER Than You Think," reviewed amazing research experiments. Six-week-old infants remembered lab experiments up to two years later when the same retrieval cues were given (Bernstein & Hollister, 1993). A fascinating study of 360 infants and toddlers less than three years old found that long-term memory does exist, especially when accompanied by verbal reminders and tangible related items (Bauer, Wenner, Dropik, & Wewerka, 2000). This adds evidence to the importance of verbal repetition and presenting children with connected sensory experiences to assist memory. Sensory experiences are usually messy ones that caregivers or families are reluctant to allow. However, they are more than fun and mess, they are important to brain development. The sensory substance infants younger than one year are most often familiar with is their food. Cultural values about playing with food come into conflict with the educational value of sensory experiences. This dilemma must be resolved with sensitivity and an acceptable

solution. Other sensory experiences for infants include massage, bathing, rocking, patting—all done most naturally without thought to their cognitive development implications.

Visual recognition has very high rates of memory. "Ah, yes, I've met you before but I don't remember your name." Recall, the next phase after recognition, is more difficult, placing the name with the face recognized. The strategy used to help in that recall or retrieval of information is mnemonics. Figure 7–10 illustrates six keys that might be used to "unlock" memory:

1. Wait time—One of the most natural keys, used by all ages, involves waiting for a period of time and letting the mind work.
2. Rehearsal—Repeating, either aloud or silently, is a technique that experimenters have taught young children to use (Kail, 1990). However, it is not long-lasting nor does it become spontaneous.
3. Categories or word associations—Older children and adults use this technique to put words into categories to aid in retrieval.
4. Sensory cues—Kail (1990) found that young children use visual and sensory retrieval cues. This reinforces the emphasis on an active, real approach for teaching young children, using multisensory experiences. For example, reading a story about an apple, accompanied by eating one, will help children remember the story about the apple.

Figure 7–10 Keys to Unlock Memory

5. Chunking—Memory is aided by breaking strings of information down into smaller parts, such as Social Security numbers, telephone numbers, or song lyrics. (For example, two, forty-eight, eleven, seventy-nine, seventy-six, or 1-800-FORKIDS.) Teachers who use rebus charts to teach children song lyrics use visual cues and teach small portions of the song at a time.
6. Writing—Writing words down helps implant them in the memory and aids in recall. That is the major reason for *written* observations.

The awareness of the need to remember begins in the Preoperational period. Preschoolers were found to be inaccurate predictors of what they could remember, and ill-equipped to develop or act on strategies. By the time they were seven, however, they could group material into similarities or categories to help them remember. They used common aids like making lists or placing items to remember by their coat (Kail, 1990).

The strategies that different people use to learn and remember have been explored from a number of theories. Multiple intelligences and learning styles are ones that have caught the interest of researchers. Educators also see the profound differences between children, bringing that recognition to the next step, which is adopting an individualized curriculum and expectations based on each child's learning style and strength.

Brain Development. The research on brain development came to the forefront in the late 1990s with the use of new brain imaging technologies linked with growing concern of the status of children in America. The outcome was a heightened awareness in media, and on policymakers and families, of what many teachers and caregivers of the very young knew all along, that these are critical times for learning and growing. The studies prove it is the interplay of "nature" and "nurture" that is necessary for maximum development, that early care has a long-lasting impact on ability to develop, learn, and relate to others. Timing is crucial, and negative experiences have serious and sustained effects. Early intervention is effective (Shore, 1997). The research emphasizes the importance of holistic experiences to learning. Caine and Caine (1991) say, "Brain research establishes and confirms that multiple complex and concrete experiences are essential for meaningful learning and teaching." It is all about making connections between what has been experienced in the past and how this new experience is alike and different from that. Less is known about positive early experiences at critical times than is known about exposure to negative influences like poor nutrition, and drug and alcohol use by the mother that can cause lasting neurological effects (Shonkoff & Phillips, 2000).

Multiple Intelligences and Hemisphericity

Howard Gardner (1983) has looked beyond learning styles and identified seven types of intelligence he calls Frames of Mind. He criticizes schools that only measure and value some while ignoring others. He has identified **multiple intelligences** as

1. *Linguistic intelligence*—remembering what one hears and reads
2. *Logical-mathematical intelligence*—figuring things out logically using reasoning and problem solving
3. *Spatial intelligence*—recreating what one sees, imagines, visualizes, or creates
4. *Bodily-kinesthetic intelligence*—using one's body to learn, interact, and express oneself
5. *Musical intelligence*—innate musical talent
6. *Interpersonal intelligence*—understanding, cooperative, and communicative with others
7. *Intrapersonal intelligence*—comfortable with self, works best alone, and pursues one's own interests

In a later book, *Intelligence Reframed* (1999), Gardner goes beyond these, presenting the idea that there may be any number of other intelligences such as naturalist, moral, and spiritual. Attempts have been made to assess individuals for various intelligences but Gardner resists this "assessment mentality" because tests tend to be biased toward some intelligences and thus would not be a true measure. He has worked instead to "observe children at play (or at work) systematically and to arrive at a quantitative description of their intelligences" (p. 138). This work is called Project Spectrum.

EXERCISE: Think of people you know who fit into each of the multiple intelligences. Where are your strengths or gifts?

By observing and recognizing each child's cognitive style, the teacher can better understand and individualize the curriculum. An environment providing for all modalities sounds very much like a developmentally appropriate early childhood classroom, one that provides

- language-based, print-rich materials
- real objects to explore, manipulate, and experiment with
- art and construction materials to create without models

- music, rhythm, and songs for transitions
- large muscle equipment and opportunities for creative movement
- cooperative activities and a social atmosphere
- alone spaces and individual activities

Another related theory is **brain hemisphericity.** The two hemispheres, or sides, of the brain deal with information and behavioral functions in different ways.

Left—analytical, logical, sequential, orderly, verbal, computational, linear, concrete

Right—intuitive, spontaneous, random, casual and informal, holistic, uses body language, sensory, visual, metaphoric (Springer & Deutsch, 1998)

The study of the brain continues as neurological testing techniques advance. Scientists are still sorting out the contributions of nature and nurture to the functioning of the brain and studying the effects when injury or illness affects one hemisphere.

Many researchers feel traditional educational teaching and testing methods ignore sensory, visual, and intuition functions of the brain. The labeling of right-brained learners as learning disabled is an injustice that lateralization and learning styles theorists seek to eliminate (Armstrong, 1987).

Families can be encouraged to use multiple intelligence strategies as well in game playing and home activities with their children, suggests Reiff (1996):

Linguistic Learners—Scrabble™, Hangman, Yahtzee™

Logical-Mathematical learners—UNO™, checkers, chess

Spatial Learners—Pictionary™ , cards

Musical Learners—Name That Tune™, sing-alongs

Bodily-Kinesthetic Learners—charades, Simon says, hide and seek

Interpersonal Learners—Group meetings for problem solving

Intrapersonal Learners—Keeping a diary or journal

Naturalist Learners—collecting and sorting articles from nature

HELPING ALL CHILDREN WITH ATTENTION SPAN

Cognitive development, with respect to memory and attention span, is affected by physical, emotional, and cultural influences.

IT HAPPENED TO ME

Pay Attention

One of my first-semester college students who worked in an out-of-school program related a story in class one day about a boy with autism in her group. She said she had to speak to the father when he picked up his son. She told the father that the boy was causing a problem because he wouldn't pay attention and follow the rules. She told the father that he should work with his son about that.

What do you think that revealed about the young woman? Did she lack knowledge of a disorder that she knew affected a child in her charge? Did her ignorance lead her to lay a burden on a parent beyond the one he already had? What strategies do you think she had been using to get the boy to pay attention? What would you have said to her if you were the instructor?

Mental Processing Difficulties

Different causes such as birth defects, maternal drug use, and poor nutrition may result in difficulties in the basic cognitive processes.

Attention Deficit. Attention is defined as the ability to focus on a specific aspect of the environment and ignore the other stimuli. Some children with extremely short attention spans, difficulty concentrating, and high distractibility have been diagnosed with **Attention Deficit** Hyperactivity Disorder (**ADHD**) or Attention Deficit Disorders (**ADD**) without hyperactivity. Children with these disorders have been mislabeled sometimes as emotionally disturbed, mentally retarded, or autistic. It is the nature of young children to be impulsive and easily distracted, especially when the classroom does not provide outlets for their energy or appropriate curriculum. This makes the disorder difficult to diagnose. Is it the environment, the curriculum, or the child? Diagnosis begins with gathering information of physical, mental, and social-emotional development from families, medical professionals, and teachers. Federal laws, such as the Individuals with Disabilities Education Act (IDEA) and Section 504 of the Rehabilitation Act of 1973 provide coverage for children with ADD (Council, 1992).

Attention Span and Autism

Autism is a "pervasive developmental disorder" (Kauffman, 1997) because it affects all areas of functioning, such as communication, social, physical, and cognitive development. It occurs in 1 in 400 children, 4:1 boys, has a neurological basis, perhaps with familial links (Mauk, Reber, & Batshaw, 1997; Pericak-Vance, 2003; Powers, 2000). There is some evidence that it appears in clusters (Bertrand et al., 2001; Yeargin-Allsopp et al., 2003). While there is no objective measure for diagnosing autism, its effect on the attention span can be an important clue. In contrast to many other cognitive disabilities, such as ADD or ADHD, its onset can be recognized before the age of three. Autism is a spectrum disorder ranging from high-functioning Asperger syndrome to classic autism to mixed autism associated with other conditions such as mental retardation.

Between year one and year two and certainly by year three, there is a noticeable attention span difference in a child with autism. The child may give little attention to other people, peers or family. Instead the child can be preoccupied with an object or a routine to the exclusion of all other interactions and stimuli. The child's behavior can be extreme in response to altered routines or the denial of the obsessive object. Children with autism have been known to attach to vacuum cleaners, ceiling fans, and spinning toys to the exclusion of social interaction, failing even to make eye contact. They can attend to their chosen item to such a degree that all other outside happenings are completely ignored. Many children with autism who have a less severe attachment to specific objects still have difficulty focusing attention on the relevant stimuli in a task. For example, the child with autism who is listening to a story may be so fascinated by the pattern in the rug on which he is sitting that he never gets the context of the story. Language may be affected by echolalia (repeating a question over and over) but ignoring the answer, giving attention only to the question, never noticing or listening to the response.

Asperger syndrome is on the high-functioning end of the autistic spectrum. This is classified with autism because it too is a pervasive developmental disorder. It involves the physical domain in balance and coordination. The child may be sensory sensitive, have irrational fears, and be easily obsessed about things that might happen in their world that would not be stressful to typical children. This can put children with Asperger syndrome in a terrible state of anxiety. It especially involves their social development because of the inability to understand social cues, their own emotions, or the emotions of others. However, in Asperger syndrome expressive language development is often very advanced, and the child may display a large vocabulary and savant knowledge about an obscure subject.

You as the observer may recognize symptoms of autism spectrum disorder that otherwise may be explained as stubbornness, distractibility, precociousness, or shyness. It is not your role to diagnose but to observe, take specific, accurate information, and share the results with the person who needs to know. Remember, students, it is not for you to approach a family member with any of your suspicions. That must be very carefully done by the teacher or special-services personnel. (This was written with the consultation of Liz Smithmeyer and Michael Logalo.)

The Time Samples of the group will give a quantitative recording of the attention behavior. It also will compare the child in question to his peers. (The word *his* is selected purposefully here because more boys than girls are diagnosed with ADHD.)

Running Records focusing on the child will also aid helping professionals in the diagnosis. Even though a child has a short attention span, high distractibility, high activity, and impulsivity, he may not have ADHD.

It is important for the family or program staff not to impose a label or a diagnosis, leaving that to the professionals. There are brain functioning tests and a breakthrough link to identify the specific gene, recently discovered at the University of Chicago. (*Advance*, 1995, p. 2). Most children with this disorder respond favorably to a stimulant that paradoxically increases attention and decreases impulsivity and activity, along with child and family counseling. There is a national information support group: Children with Attention Deficit Disorders (CH.A.D.D.), (305) 587–3700.

Perception. Perception is the ability to interpret the objects and events stimulating the senses. For children with a limited ability in hearing, sight, taste, smell, or touch, the intake of information limits their cognitive processing. The other modalities may compensate for the limited ones but only as much as the cognitive capacity is able to accommodate. Young children especially depend on sight to cue all kinds of behavior with less attention to verbal language. They carefully watch and imitate rather than listen and do.

Perception depends on the ability to discriminate between appearances, sounds, and textures. With impairments of the receptors or the cognitive structures to process the information, these sensory cues go unrecognized and ignored. The teacher of children with such impaired sensory abilities makes adaptations for the other senses to receive a similar message, such as tapping a rhythm that cannot be heard or associating textures with the words *cool*, *warm*, *rough*, and *soft*.

Memory is the third basic cognitive process, received through attention and perception. It is stored in the central nervous system in the various categories of short-term, long-term, visual, rote, recognition, and recall. Children with nervous system difficulties, such as muscular dystrophy or multiple sclerosis, as well as limited cognitive ability, may experience memory difficulties.

As with all cognitive, physical, or emotional disorders, families, teachers, and Committees on the Handicapped seek to place the child in the least restricted environment, that in which the child can maximize the abilities that are present and make modifications and allowances for the areas of lower functioning.

Cultural Differences in Memory and Attention Span

Research on various cultures has had mixed results. People from a culture with little or no formal school-ing or technological tools to aid problem solving, such as alphabets, calculators, or computers, seem to be more concrete thinkers (Dasen, 1977; Luria, 1976). The assessment of cognitive development must consider the cultural context. When memory tasks used for assessment are unrelated to the child's world they do poorly (Rogoff, 1990), but when tests were culturally relevant few differences in memory are found (Mandler, Scribner, Cole, & DeForest, 1980). This is consistent with the principles of fair testing: The test should be culturally relevant to be a valid measurement of ability.

HELPING PROFESSIONALS FOR ATTENTION CONCERNS

If a difficulty with memory, attention span, or cognitive processing is observed, those concerns are addressed by the teaching team, program supervisor, and then brought to the attention of the family of the child with tact and sensitivity. They are nebulous and often extremely difficult to diagnose and even more difficult to treat and strategize. People who may be able to help are described here.

pediatrician—physician specifically trained to treat children

psychologist or psychiatrist—professionals trained in areas of emotional disorders

neurologist—physician specifically trained in sensory or motor responses due to nervous system impairments

special educators—specialists with knowledge or normal and atypical children's development and appropriate education strategies

OTHER METHODS

Other Methods to Record Attention Span:

Anecdotal/Running Records—In recording an incident or sample of behavior, attention span may be observed and noted.

Checklist/Rating Scales—Criteria may be included where an inference about attention span is noted.

Frequency Count—An individual child could be the focus of a Frequency Count, noting every time the child changes activity by choice, inferring a long or short attention span depending on the number of changes over a certain period.

Conversations or Interviews—When talking with a child, the child's ability to sustain the conversation or to wander and not be able to concentrate could give indications of attention span.

Work Samples—The child's work may show a short or long attention span—one swipe with a paint brush, one block placed on end, compared to page-covered paintings or intricate block buildings.

Media—Photographs showing the child concentrating, audio tapes of involved conversations, or video tapes following the child from choice to choice can document attention span.

KEY TERMS

accommodation	disequilibrium
ADD	egocentrism
ADHD	logico-mathematical
animism	knowledge
artificialism	matching
assimilation	multiple intelligences
association	one-to-one
attention deficit	correspondence
attention span	physical knowledge
autism	Preoperational Stage
brain hemisphericity	reversibility
cause and effect	rote counting
centration	Sensorimotor Stage
classification	seriation
Concrete Operational	social conventional
Stage	knowledge
conservation	Time Sample

WEEK 7: PLAN A

TIME SAMPLE OF ATTENTION SPAN FOR ALL
Students

In one of your visits, complete a Time Sample during free choice time, following the suggestions below.

Practitioners

Select a day this week during a normal free play time. Prepare a Time Sample form by copying the Time Sample Form from Appendix D and adapt it to reflect areas in your classroom. List the learning center areas down the left margin. Begin by noting the time in the top column and proceed to write down each child's name as you scan each learning area. If you have time, circle those children's names who are playing cooperatively, a jagged circle around any who are aggressive. Note where the adults are and if any child is just standing and watching. Five minutes from the beginning time, scan the areas once again. If the child has not left the area, draw an arrow to the next time block and move on. Every five minutes, repeat the scanning and recording.

What to Do with It

Filing. Later that day, draw conclusions and write notes on each child's Portfolio Overview Sheet about

MEMORY AND ATTENTION SPAN

Documentation	Location	Recorder	Date
TS	Class file	MS	10/18
TS	"		1/5
TS	"		3/1
TS	"		6/26

Figure 7–11 Portfolio Overview Example

the child's attention span, play preferences, or social interactions as recorded on the Time Sample (Figure 7–11).

File the Time Sample in the class file. If this Time Sample showed an unusual pattern or you have an explanation for why a certain thing happened, write that down as well. Your incidental observations are important too. For example, note if you observe that there were a lot of children around the water table today because it is new. If you notice a learning center is avoided by all children, you may want to consider the reasons for it and work to make it more interesting or change it to some other emphasis.

Sharing with Child and Family. This kind of observation recording in its entirety cannot be shared with the family because it shows information about all the children in the class. Conclusions drawn from the Time Sample as directed in **What to Do with It** are the types of information that can be shared. Students, of course, do not give information about the child to the family. See **It Happened to Me: Pay Attention.**

Discuss your observations with the family or the child, if appropriate. For example: "Mrs. Johnson, while I was observing in class today I noticed that Shawnalee spent twelve minutes at the easel painting. That was a lot of concentration for a three-year-old." or "Anthony, I noticed today you never played at the new water table. Did you want a turn? There were times when you weren't busy other places. It'll be out again tomorrow so you'll have another chance if you want to play there."

Actions.

Read a Book.
> Carlson, N.L. (1996). *Sit Still!* New York: Viking.
> Seuss, Dr. (1975). *Oh, the Things You Can Think.* New York: Random House.
> Hutchins, P. (1987). *Don't Forget the Bacon.* New York: Greenwillow.

In the Environment.
Evaluate the environment for intrusions on concentration

- Is the Block Area out of the flow of traffic?
- Is the Reading Area in a quiet area of the classroom, somewhat secluded and cozy?

- Are noisy areas such as Large Muscle—climber, jumper, ball toss—buffered from the rest of the room?
- Does the schedule have a long, uninterrupted period of free-choice time?
- Are children not interrupted from play choices to participate in teacher-led activities?
- Is there sufficient warning and transition out of free-choice time so that projects can be brought to a close?

In the Curriculum.
- Provide a way that projects can be long-term, saved from one day to the next to encourage long involvement.
- Allow for differences in attention span by providing alternative activities for those who cannot sit still for a group time that seems to be appropriate for most of the group.
- Provide open-ended activities and equipment so that children can use the materials at their individual cognitive levels.
- Plan activities that build on one another and revisit previous ones to form associations, patterns, and assimilation knowledge.

In the Newsletter.
- Tactfully suggest limits to television viewing as a way to increase cognitive and creative learning.
- Encourage families to play games with children—card games, concentration, old-fashioned guessing games.
- Feature an article about different kinds of intelligence to help families understand the uniqueness of their child's abilities and strengths.

WEEK 7: PLAN B

CONVERSATIONS WITH GROUP B FOR SPEECH AND LANGUAGE

Continue with conversations begun last week, selecting children from Group B to converse with each day this week. If possible, tape record the conversation as well as make written notes as you speak with each child. Do an informal conversation or structured interview as described in Week 6, Plan A.

What to Do with It

Filing. Analyze each conversation for what it reveals about the child's knowledge, emotional state,

social development, and the child's speech and language. (Use the Speech and Language Checklist found in Appendix D.)

Enter the summary. Note your name and the date on the Portfolio Overview Sheet. If a significant lag appears, discuss it with your supervisor to confirm it. Then approach the family. Have a list of sites where a speech and language evaluation may be obtained to give to the family.

WEEK 7: PLAN C

REFLECTIVE JOURNAL

Respond to the following in your Reflective Journal, kept in a private file at home.

I think I am a _____ learner because . . .

When I look at children's learning, I'm interested especially in . . .

I found doing the time sample . . .

It really showed me . . .

I wonder if . . .

REFERENCES

Advance for Speech Pathologists, (5), 16. Researchers Identify Specific Gene for ADHD. April 24, 1995.

Armstrong, T. (1987). *In their own way.* New York: G. P. Putnam's Sons.

Bauer, P. J., Wenner, J. A., Dropik, P. L., & Wewerka, S. S. (2000). Parameters of remembering and forgetting in the transition from infancy to early childhood. *Monograph of the Society for Research in Child Development, 65* (4).

Bernstein, S., & Hollister, A. (1993). Babies are SMARTER than you think. *Life,* July, 1993, 46–60.

Bertrand, J., Mars, A., Boyle, C., Bove, F., Yeargin-Allsopp, M., & Decoufle, P. (2001). Prevalence of autism in a United States population: the Brick Township, New Jersey, investigation. *Pediatrics, 108* (5). http://www.pediatrics.org. Accessed April 1, 2003.

Bredekamp, S., & Copple, C. (Eds.) (1997). *Developmentally appropriate practice in early childhood programs, revised edition.* Washington, DC: National Association for the Education of Young Children.

Caine, R. N., & Caine, G. (1991). *Making connections: Teaching and the human brain.* p. 5. Alexandria, VA: Association for Supervision and Curriculum.

Cook, R. E., Tessier, A., & Klein, M. D. (2000). *Adapting early childhood curricula for children in inclusive settings,* 5th ed. Upper Saddle River, NJ: Merrill Prentice Hall.

Council for Exceptional Children. (1992). *Providing an appropriate education to children with attention deficit disorder.* ERIC Digest ED352747–92.

Dasen, P. R. (Ed.) (1977). Piagetian psychology: Cross-cultural contributions. New York: Gardner.

Flavell, J. H. (1987). *Cognitive development,* 2nd ed. Englewood Cliffs, NJ: Prentice Hall.

Furth, H. G. (1969). *Piaget and knowledge.* Englewood Cliffs, NJ: Prentice Hall.

Gardner, H. (1983). *Frames of mind: Theory of multiple intelligences.* New York: Basic Books.

Gardner, H. (1999). *Intelligence reframed: Multiple intelligences for the 21st century.* New York: Basic Books.

Ginsburg, H., & Opper, S. (1969). *Piaget's theory of intellectual development.* Englewood Cliffs, NJ: Prentice Hall.

Jensen, E. (1998). *Teaching with the brain in mind.* Alexandria, VA: Association for Supervision and Curriculum.

Kail, R. (1990). *The development of memory in children,* 2nd ed. New York: W. H. Freeman & Co.

Kail, R. V. (2001). *Children and their development,* 2nd ed. Upper Saddle River, NJ: Prentice Hall.

Kauffman, J. M. (1997). *Characteristics of emotional and behavioral disorder of children and youth,* 6th ed.) Upper Saddle River, NJ: Merrill.

Luria, A. R. (1976). *Cognitive development: Its cultural and social foundations.* Cambridge, MA: Harvard University Press.

Mandler, J. M., Scribner, S., Cole, M., & DeForest, M. (1980). Cross-cultural invariance in story recall. *Child Development, 51,* 19–26.

Mauk, J. E., Reber, M., & Batshaw, M. L. (1997). Autism and other pervasive developmental disorders. In M. L. Batshaw (Ed.) *Children with disabilities,* 4th ed. Baltimore, MD: Brookes.

Pericak-Vance, M. A. (2003). Discovering the genetics of autism. *USA Today Magazine,* Vol. 131, January 2003, p. 56.

Peterson, R., & Felton-Collins, V. (1986). *The Piaget handbook for teachers and parents; Children in the age of discovery, preschool-third grade.* New York: Teachers College Press.

Powers, M. D. (2000). What is autism? In M. D. Powers (Ed.), *Children with autism: A parents' guide,* 2nd ed. Bethesda, MD: Woodbine House.

Reiff, J. C. (1996). Bridging home and school through multiple intelligences. *Childhood Education, 72* (3) 164–166.

Rogoff, B. (1990). *Apprenticeship in thinking: Cognitive development in social context.* New York: Oxford University Press.

Shore, R. (1997). *Rethinking the brain.* New York: Families and Work Institute.

Shonkoff, J. P., & Phillips, D. A. (2000). *From neurons to neighborhoods: The science of early childhood development.* Washington, DC: National Academy Press.

Springer, S. P., & Deutsch, G. (1998). *Left brain, right brain: Perspectives from cognitive neuroscience,* 5th ed. New York: W. H. Freeman and Company.

Yeargin-Allsopp, M., Rice, C., Karapurkar, T., Doernberg, N., Boyle, C., & Murphy, C. (2003). Prevalence of autism in a US metropolitan area. *Journal of American Medical Association, 289* (1), 87–89.

RESOURCES

Autism Society of America. http://www.autism-society.org.

Cherry, C., Godwin, D., & Staples, J. (1989). *Is the left brain always right: A guide to whole child development.* Belmont, CA: Fearon Teacher Aids.

Kamii, C., & Kamii, M. (1990). Why achievement testing should stop in C. Kamii, (Ed.) *Achievement Testing in the Early Grades: The Games Grown-ups Play.* Washington, DC: National Association for the Education of Young Children.

Jensen, E. (1998). *Teaching with the brain in mind.* Alexandria, VA: Association for Supervision and Curriculum.

Peterson, R., & Felton-Collins, V. (1987). *The Piaget handbook for teachers and parents: Children in the age of discovery, preschool–third grade.* New York: Teachers College Press.

For additional information on early education curriculum, visit our Web site at http://www.earlychilded.delmar.com

Using Standardized Tests to Look at Cognitive Development

USING TESTS

Every family wants to know how their child is doing. Some want to know how their child is doing compared to the rest of the children in the class. Teachers want to know if the children in their class are learning what they have been teaching. Some people (such as school administrators or policymakers) want to know if the children in a class/school/state/nation are learning what they should be learning at a particular age. Politicians want to know if tax dollars are being used efficiently to produce the desired outcomes.

Since the first edition of this textbook was written in 1995, there has been an increase in the use of formal assessments and **standardized tests.** These are being used to make "high-stakes" decisions about children. They have been used to determine "readiness" and "placement" in various levels of kindergarten. Some say they have been used to unfairly penalize children who are poor, of a racial or ethnic minority, whose first language is not English, or who are divergent and creative thinkers (FairTest, 1990; Perrone, 1991). They are being used to determine teachers' and school's effectiveness, with much riding on the results. Often instruction time is focused toward test-taking techniques and content of the test rather than allowing children to construct knowledge in a way that is relevant to them. This chapter is not designed to teach "how to" use standardized tests but to familiarize the reader with their uses and misuses (Figure 8–1).

A World of Tests

We live in a world of tests. Our driving skills are tested before we can obtain a driver's license. Doctors

Figure 8–1 Testing has become the accepted measure of teacher and curriculum accountability but portfolios show what a child knows and can do.

are tested before they can perform surgery or dispense medications. Teachers in most states must take a test before they can be licensed to teach. Manicurists or beauticians must pass a test before they can perform their skills on a person's nails or hair. Tests are administered for specific purposes.

- to gain information on which to act—such as medical tests
- to certify a certain level of competence in order to issue a license
- to assess knowledge and skills learned in a particular environment

There have always been tests in school to assess knowledge, either developed by the teacher (directly connected to what the teacher taught), or developed for the broader purpose of measuring students against students in other classes, across the state, or against a sample of similar students. In the twenty-first century there are movements to test children at younger and younger ages using tests that are developed to compare results on nationwide standards. It is important for the early childhood teacher to understand the use of tests in measuring children's development. It is even more important for teachers to become knowledgeable about when and where tests are appropriate and to advocate on behalf of children when tests are not appropriate.

The Standards Movement

Before one can test, it has to be determined what is being measured. Many states and organizations have set standards for results, outcomes, or expectations—even for preschoolers. The rationale is that nationally recognized standards are set by experts in the discipline and divided into appropriate concepts for age or grade levels. Educators then align curriculum and lesson objectives with the standards. Evaluation and assessment, both in the classroom and nationwide, are based on the standards.

Some organizations or content-monitoring associations that delineate standards for specific content areas are

Art: *National Visual Arts Standards*—National Art Education Association [http://www.naea-reston.org]

English: *Standards for the English Language Arts*—National Council of Teachers of English and International Reading Association [http://www.ncte.org]

English as a Second Language: *ESL Standards for Pre-K–12 Students*—Teachers of English to Speakers of Other Languages [http://www.tesol.org]

Head Start: *Head Start Child Outcomes Framework*—Department of Health and Human Services [http://www.headstartinfo.org]

Health Education: *National Health Education Standards*—American Association for Health Education [http://www.aahperd.org]

High/Scope®:*Key Experiences*—High/Scope [http://www.highscope.org]

Mathematics: *Principles and Standards for School Mathematics*—National Council of Teachers of Mathematics [http://www.nctm.org]

Music: *Benchmarks in Action: Standards-Based Assessment in Music*—The National Association for Music Education [http://www.menc.org]

Science: *Benchmarks for Science Literacy*—American Association for the Advancement of Science [http://www.project2061.org]

Social Studies: *Expectations of Excellence*—National Council for the Social Studies [http://www.ncss.org]

Technology: *National Educational Technology Standards*—International Society for Technology in Education [http://www.cnets.iste.org]

There are also standards for early childhood teacher education preparation programs.

NAEYC Professional Preparation Standards at Associate Degree, Initial Licensure and Advance Degrees—National Association for the Education of Young Children [http://www.naeyc.org/profdev/prep]

Program Standards—National Council for Accreditation of Teacher Education [http://www.ncate.org]

National Board Certification Standards—National Board for Professional Teaching Standards [http://www.nbpts.org]

Child Development Associate Competencies— Council for Professional Recognition [http://www.cdacouncil.org]

Difficulty in Assessing Young Children

Regarding the standardized testing movement from a cautionary perspective, the National Association for the Education of Young Children (NAEYC) and the National Association of Early Childhood Specialists in State Departments of Education (NAECS/SDE) have developed a position statement. It recognizes that learning standards can be valuable in young children's educational experiences but only "if early learning standards (1) emphasize significant, developmentally appropriate content and outcomes; (2) are developed and reviewed through informed, inclusive processes; (3) use implementation and assessment strategies that are ethical and appropriate for young children; and (4) are accompanied by strong supports for early childhood programs, professionals and families" (NAEYC & NAECS/SDE 2002).

Preliterate (birth to age 8) children cannot be assessed by writing answers on a sheet of paper. The purpose of this book is to provide other methods of gathering information about each child's development in order to assess and plan. The change in children's physical, social, linguistic, cognitive, creative, and emotional development is rapid. Because they do not understand the goals of formal testing ("Do your best," "Do it by yourself without help," or "Keep at it until it's finished"), results of pencil-and-paper tests are not accurate assessments. Naturalistic measures such as the ones presented in this text are more accurate methods for describing each child's development but do not make it easy to compare children across classrooms, schools, states, or the nation. There are several reasons put forth for making such comparisons.

- identification of children who need more help in school to succeed
- holding teachers and administrators accountable to carry out the responsibility of helping children to learn
- determining the best practices so they can be applied by others to get better results
- conserving or investing public funding wisely in efficient methods

Those are logical reasons for using formal assessment and there may be times when formal measuring instruments need to be used. This section is designed to be a guide.

Formal Assessment Measures

Fairness is a quality that most people would hold in high esteem. Fairness in assessing children may have even greater appeal.

EXERCISE:

- **This bag of potato chips holds 11.2 ounces and is priced at $1.89. Another bag of potato chips holds 8 ounces and is priced at $1.69. Which is a fairer price?**
- **You take a class and the final exam has 100 questions and 10 essays. Your friend takes the same class taught by another teacher and the final is a take-home exam. In evaluating which of you learned more, is one testing approach fairer than the other?**
- **You have been waiting in line to order food. A clerk opens a new line, another customer walks up, and is waited on before you. "It's not fair!"**

Trying to determine what is fair necessitates a standard measure. To calculate the best value, you need to convert the price to cost per ounce, a standard comparison. To assess how much you each learned from the class, a common exam would be given. To serve customers in the order in which they came to the counter, the store would need a number system or clerks should be instructed to call out, "I'll help the next person in line." Standard measures ensure fairness. The difficulty comes in assessing fairly what one child knows against what another child knows and using a test given on any specific day. To what do we attribute a high or low score? Was it the teacher? Was it the child on that particular day? Was it the family? Fair assessment is always difficult.

Standardized Tests

The word "standardized" means to apply the same measure in the same way to determine an individual result compared to an expected response. Teachers apply standards frequently. The teacher of infants says, "Where's your nose?" to each of her charges 6–12 months of age. She notes that the younger infants cannot respond to her question but the older ones point to their nose with pride. She knows at what age children can understand the question, have the physical control to move their arm and point, and the cognitive processing to discriminate between the words "nose" and other body parts. If the oldest of all of the children cannot perform the function, it may raise questions about the child's development. The teacher of toddlers might ask the same question in a more complex way, gently touching the child's nose and asking, "What's this?" Now the child seeks the answer from a vocabulary bank and comes up with the word, "Nose!" The teacher of preschoolers might present a child with a drawing without a nose and ask, "What's missing?" The teacher of kindergartners might ask his pupils to write the word for the part of the body that helps us smell cookies baking. The teacher of first graders might ask her students to write the word "nose" and create other words using the same letters.

These assessments are standardized. The teacher is finding out what each child knows about noses at a developmental level expected for that age. Each child is demonstrating knowledge in a way that is measured against expected capabilities. The teacher would also expect to see changes in each child's performance over time. If any of the children had a problem with hearing, understanding, speaking, or writing it would be revealed. The checklists discussed in Chapter 3 are standardized based on common expectations for a child of a certain age, based on maturation. All children of that age are measured by the same scale because human development has been studied and determined to be fairly "standard."

A standardized test is constructed by a content specialist, and is designed to measure specific aspects of development or behavior. It is usually administered to a group, by a specific set of procedures and must be completed in a limited time. It has a **quantitative scoring** system. The results are scored against the **norm,** the group on whom the test was researched, identified by age, gender, race, geographic region, and socioeconomic status. The norm group's average scores then become the scores against which later test-takers are compared. There are three types of standardized tests.

Standardized achievement tests measure what children know or can do at a particular age or grade. These outcomes are determined from a cross section of the population and scored in comparison to that population. The more the children are like that group, the closer the scores will be to the average. *Standardized aptitude tests* measure aptitudes or capacity to learn, such as the Scholastic Aptitude Test (SAT), which looks for the results to *predict* later per-

formance levels. Intelligence tests measuring IQ fall into this category. *Standardized screening and diagnostic tests* are used to identify a potential learning problem or developmental delay. They are based on broad abilities that most children will possess, revealing only those children who may need further evaluation (McAfee & Leong, 2002; Pelligrini & Bjorklund, 1998).

Standardized Testing as an Assessment Method. Before any standardized test is given, some questions should be answered.

1. What is the purpose of the test? The test should have a clear benefit to the child or the program.
2. What is the design of the test? Is it **valid?** In testing terms valid refers to whether the test measures what it's supposed to measure. If a test's purpose was to measure the ability to multiply but only asked addition questions it would not be valid. What is the **reliability** of the test? Would the same score be obtained on subsequent tests of the same nature? Because it is difficult to obtain valid and reliable data, especially on cognitive abilities of children under six, only trained professionals with a specific need to know should administer that type of test. Standardized tests must fit the developmental level of the child, be administered individually (not in a group) for children under six, be short in duration, and be given in the child's natural setting (home or school), preferably by a person known to the child.
3. How will the results be used? No single test should be the basis for an important decision regarding the child's placement or diagnosis. Other methods of data collection must be considered, such as input from the family, observational data from the school, and direct information from the child.

Appropriate Uses of Early Childhood Assessments. The National Educational Goals Panel (Shepard, Kagan, & Wurtz, 1998) was formed to "improve methods of assessing the readiness of children for school that would lead to alternatives to currently used early childhood assessments" (Figure 8–2).

Purpose 1. Assessing to promote children's learning and development. The classroom teacher, along with the family, know the child best. Seeing a child day after day, alongside other children the same age, viewed through a lens suffused with the knowledge of child development, an accurate assessment of the child's learning and development can be made without a purchased, standardized test. Observations such as

FAMILY
Observing as child develops with standards determined by cultural traditions as well as accumulated knowledge. Intervention when development does not meet the standard by seeking advice/assistance from professionals.

HEALTH PROFESSIONALS
Formalized health assessments throughout prenatal and childhood through routine health care. Suspected developmental delays or disabilities referred for full evaluation.

EDUCATORS
Informal and formal measures, including observation used to assess learning and to plan curriculum.
SPECIAL EDUCATORS
Individualized educational program based on formal assessment of disability.

POLICYMAKERS
Assessments of aggregates, not individual preschool children to evaluate programs and gather data on trends, living, and social conditions.

BEFORE AGE 8, 3rd grade

Standardized achievement measures
Accountability of students, teachers or schools
High stakes decisions about individual children

Figure 8–2 Appropriate Assessments of Children. (Adapted from Shepard, L., Kagan, S. L., & Wurtz, E. (1998). *Principles and Recommendations for Early Childhood Assessments.* Washington, DC: National Education Goals.)

those supported by this book can provide an **authentic assessment** of what the child knows and can do (McTighe & Ferrara, 1998; Meisels, Bickel, Nicholson, Xue, & Atkins-Burnett, 2001). These are "low-stakes" assessments because significant intervention is *not* taking place based on these assessments. They are used as benchmarks for development and for curriculum planning purposes.

Purpose 2. Assessing to identify children for health and special services. Federal legislation, Individuals with Disabilities Education Act (IDEA) passed in 1975, mandated early **screening** for the identification of children with disabilities. Later amendments required family involvement, and earlier screenings of infants and toddlers. Screening involves testing large numbers of individuals in a short amount of time to find those who need to be further evaluated. Developmental screenings "should be brief, norm-referenced, inexpensive, standardized in administration, objectively scored, broadly focused across all areas of development, reliable, and valid" (Meisels & Wasik, 1990, p. 613). IDEA provided the definition of developmental delay, supported by performance on a standardized assessment instrument and specific observations in developmental domains. After a full evaluation, indicated by the screenings, the law mandates school districts to provide appropriate services. Some screening instruments commonly used are: Hawaii Early Learning Profile (HELP) (VORT Corporation, 1995; Ages and Stages (Bricker, Squires, & Mount, 1995). Some full evaluation instruments commonly used are: Bayley Scales of Infant Development II (Bayley, 1993), and Brigance Diagnostic Inventory of Early Development—Revised (Brigance, 1991). These are known as **high-stakes tests** because they may be used to make classification and intervention plans. Precautions should be taken to rely on multiple sources for information and the family and a range of professionals must reach consensus on an intervention plan.

Purpose 3. *Assessing to monitor trends and evaluate programs and services.* The Goals Panel recommends that preschool programs and services should be assessed on a state or national level focusing only on the conditions of learning, such as the percentage of low-income children who attend quality preschool programs. After age five, early childhood education trends in early learning should be assessed not on individual children's scores but on a matrix or sampling of a nonintrusive standardized test (Shepard, Kagan, & Wurtz, 1998). Individual program assessments are important for quality assurance for the program itself and as an indicator of quality for consumers, families, and funders. See Chapter 13 for a full discussion of program assessment.

Purpose 4. *Assessing academic achievement to hold individual students, teachers, and schools accountable.* This too is called high-stakes testing because these test scores are used to make decisions about the retention of individual students, teachers' tenure, and schools' allocation of funding. The Goals Panel (Shepard, Kagan, & Wrutz, 1998) state, "There should be no high-stakes accountability testing of individual children before the end of third grade" (p. 21). They recommend instructionally relevant assessments should be a part of the educational program in kindergarten through second grade. Teachers should keep records of individual student achievement prior to third grade.

No Child Left Behind. This bill was enacted in 2002 for the purpose of educational reform through stronger accountability results, increased flexibility and local control, expanded options for families and an emphasis on teaching methods that have been proven to work [http://www.nclb.gov]. States are responsible for math, reading, and science learning standards in all grades and tests to measure the progress of each child—and schools—toward those standards. School accountability will be especially measured by progress in test results of students who are economically disadvantaged, from racial or ethnic minorities, have disabilities, or have limited English. These tests are high-stakes tests of the accountability of school districts to make adequate progress toward the standards.

The Case Against Standardized Tests. There are many strong voices against standardized testing for young children birth through second grade. Wesson (2001) points out the misuse of tests such as the widely used SAT. He states that it was devised to predict freshman-year success for "New England-based, college preparatory, male-only schools" and that its widespread use is not a predictor of success for those not in those categories. Wesson believes that test scores closely correlated to socioeconomic characteristics. Kohn is another vocal opponent of standardized tests as an extension of his work on rewards and punishments. He states that the problems with testing young children are

- Standardized testing sets the unrealistic expectation that everyone at the same age acquires the same set of capabilities.
- Standardized assessments cannot produce an accurate picture of what a child can do.
- The stress on young children to perform on the tests interferes with accurate results. (Kohn, 2001)

He encourages teachers to take an organized stand against testing through advocacy with families and administration.

"Accountability shovedown" is the term Hatch (2002) uses to describe the standards movement, stating it is "so pervasive across educational settings today [it] is threatening children in early childhood in the same ways as the curriculum shovedown movement did in the 1980s" (p. 457). He sees child observation changing from a strategy for shaping curriculum to a device for monitoring student progress. His ten reasons for his concern are: pressure on children, pressure on teachers, narrowing of experiences, accountability as punishment, teacher deprofessionalization, performance over learning, individual

Measuring Cognitive Development—Why Not Test?

EXERCISE: Imagine that you took a test and found out you failed. Jot down how each of the possible reasons that follows might have been the cause of your failure:

The room
The person giving the test
The subject matter of the test
The importance of the test to you
The new format of the test
The way the test was scored
Your health
You are physically challenged.
You are in big trouble that has nothing to do with the test.
Your native language is Russian. The test is in English.
Your friend left you here in this strange building to take the test, but you do not know how you will find her later.

These same influences affect the outcomes of a young child taking a test, only more so because they are not able to understand, rationalize, or adjust. This section is a policy statement to defend and uphold authentic assessment methods over standardized or achievement tests. There are three major issues in testing young children: the test itself, the child, and the use of the test.

A standardized test is an evaluation instrument written for a definite purpose and application. When it indeed does measure what it proposes to measure, it is described as valid. Early forms of the test are tried out on a segment of the population that will be taking the test eventually. This early test group is the norm group against which the rest of the scores are measured. If the norm group is significantly different from the subjects taking the test then the scores will be inaccurate. For example, suppose the norm group in the tryout of a new test is ten children. There are eight boys and two girls, ranging in age from five to eight years old, living in south Florida, all attending the same school. Two children are black, three are Puerto Rican, and one has been sexually abused. Their scores on the test will set the standard against which children in Idaho, Connecticut, and Minnesota will be measured. This is an extreme example to demonstrate the point, but unfortunately is not far from reality. It is difficult to select a norm group that represents all the variables in exact proportions to the subjects taking the test. Standardized tests have a high risk of being discriminatory because of the scoring against the norm group. The results may be skewed by factors such as geographic region, urban, suburban or rural, different socialization experiences due to culture, economic situation, family dynamics, and native language.

The second major concern of using standardized tests on young children is the nature of the child. Because young children are just that—young—taking tests may be a new experience for them. The way that children confront new experiences varies from child to child. Some just observe, watch, and wait, paralyzed by the novelty. Others will manipulate it and play with it, not recognizing the purpose. They may not understand or follow directions but explore and adapt it to their own style. If the child takes another form of the same test again in a short time, the score may be drastically different. Now they have experience, or have thought of other ways to try it out.

(continued)

Measuring Cognitive Development—Why Not Test? (continued)

The expectation of standardized tests is that the same subject taking the same type of test in a reasonable period will obtain a similar score. This is test reliability. Many standardized tests for young children are not reliable. They are easily influenced by the new place. The examiner may be a stranger to them. They are separated from their family and may not know how to take a test. They lack the ability to screen out noises, hunger, or fear that may divert their attention.

The original intelligence test developed in France by Binet was for a noble purpose, to provide adequate education for children who were mentally retarded. Many tests administered to children today are for a similar purpose, to identify handicapping conditions for which early intervention would be provided.

Many federal and state laws mandate such testing. P. L. 94–142 (1975) provides a free and appropriate public education for children with disabilities between the ages of 3 and 21. P. L. 99–457 (1986) includes infants and toddlers and their families in comprehensive early intervention services. To implement these mandates, it was necessary to identify children who needed services. This was accomplished through a screening, an initial step in identifying those children who had a high probability of developmental delay. Once a screening indicates there might be a delay or problem, a full evaluation or follow-up provides the diagnosis. The diagnosis will determine the type of intervention needed to provide services for the child in the least-restrictive environment. These laws have been effective in helping many children and families receive the services they need.

The problem arises when the screenings and tests developed for one purpose are used for other, possibly less helpful ones. Meisels (1987) has criticized the Gesell Preschool Readiness Test as an invalid predictor of success in kindergarten. Many schools use this as a developmental screening tool. Based on its results, a recommendation may be made to delay school entrance or a year in a transitional grade between kindergarten and first grade. Meisels contends this is a misuse of a test that lacks reliability and validity. Tests are misused when they are the sole factor in decisions to place a child in special education, or label them as an individual with a handicapping condition. NAEYC's *Developmentally Appropriate Practice in Early Childhood Programs, Revised Edition* (1997) emphasizes the role of observation: "Decisions that have a major impact on children, such as enrollment or placement, are never made on the basis of a single developmental assessment or screening device but are based on multiple sources of relevant information, particularly observations by teachers and parents" (p. 21).

The NAEYC position and constructivist writings, such as Kamii & Kamii (1990) in *Achievement Testing in the Early Grades: The Games Grown-ups Play*, enumerate the abuses of testing:

- Results of standardized tests might be inappropriately used as readiness screening tests for placement decisions.
- Standardized testing increases the academic emphasis of the curriculum, which should be localized, not centralized.
- Achievement tests frequently do not reflect current theory or research about how children learn.
- Many schools "teach to the test" to raise school scores.
- Standardized tests cannot predict how well students will do in the future.

Measuring Cognitive Development—Why Not Test?

- Below third grade, development is uneven and still emergent.
- Racial, cultural, and social biases are evident.
- Numerical results are not useful in curriculum planning for individual students.

How can the effectiveness of teachers and schools be measured if children are not tested? How can a teacher know if the child is learning? How could school boards and voters know their education tax dollars were well-spent but still be sensitive to the population it was examining?

Authentic assessment assumes that children in a supportive setting will initiate and direct their own learning, constructing knowledge at their own rate physically, emotionally, socially, and intellectually. It also assumes that learning proceeds from concrete to abstract. Children learn by interacting with the enriched environment that recognizes and values different intelligences and is facilitated by an adult who has specialized training and skills. Teaching is individualized and in small groups. Individual learning needs are acknowledged based on objective evaluation of each child's strengths, moving the child forward in the continuum of learning through relevant curriculum. Assessment is rooted in principles of child growth and development and involves a collaboration of child, teacher, family, and other professionals as needed (Puckett & Black, 2000).

The form of that assessment is in question. Teachers ask, "How can a test manufactured in New Jersey measure what the children have learned about magnets in my class in Nevada? How can the test maker in New Jersey even know if my class in Nevada has worked with magnets?" The test can only measure it if the teachers know what is on the test and make sure that it is taught in the classroom. In this way, it is the test determining the curriculum, instead of measuring achievement. Methods of authentic assessment, then, must be locally based to measure progress of a distinct group of children. This is done by "keeping track" (Kamii & Kamii, pp. 120, 121) of their work on three levels.

1. Descriptive data about each child that can be analyzed by the teacher as well as outside evaluators
2. Summaries and interpretations of that data by the teacher to evaluate the effectiveness of teaching methods and the individual progress of the child
3. Quantitative information that gives statistical analysis of the whole group, against which individual children may be compared to adjust the curriculum

These principles of performance assessment are consistent with the knowledge of child growth and development, and developmentally appropriate practice. Assessment by observation and recording using multiple techniques is repeated in a systematic way. The portfolio documents the child's progress and is shared with the parents and the child. That describes what can be achieved by *Week by Week* assessment planning.

devaluation, sameness versus diversity, questionable benefits, and corporate mentality. He challenges teachers with this statement, "Our accountability comes from an ethical commitment to do what is right for every child, not from measuring productivity according to an arbitrary set of narrowly defined outcomes."

Stress indicators such as wiggling, chewing on pencils, twisting hair, playing with clothes, complaining of feeling tired and crying were observed in kindergarteners during standardized tests (Fleege, Charlesworth, Burts, & Hart, 1996). These behaviors had not been present in observations done weeks before the California Achievement Test was administered to groups of ten children. In addition to the stress, other behaviors such as copying, refusing to continue, calling out answers, and asking for reassurance of correct answers indicated that children did not understand nor could they comply with test-taking rules. Increased stress and inaccurate results due to the developmental level of children are two of the main arguments against group-administered standardized tests for young children. In a large survey, Paris, Lawton, Turner, and Roth (1991) found that similar behaviors are exhibited by adolescents taking standardized tests. They "are likely to cheat, become nervous, have difficulty concentrating, to guess, to look for answers without reading the passage."

Neuman and Roskos (2000) state

Many of our young children are evaluated, screened, and labeled each year using standardized measures that describe what children do against prescribed developmental markers or average norms. Particularly during these early years, standardized paper-and-pencil measures are not effective in measuring what children know and do not know. Because children's knowledge and skills are in constant motion, these tests tend not to be reliable or valid measures of what children can do in typical situations. (p. 24)

What's a Teacher to Do?

Because tests are becoming a fact of life for early educators, here is some advice for teachers, caregivers, and families with young children (Benner, 2003; Greenspan & Meisels, 1994; Kohn, 2001; Puckett & Black, 2000; Shepard, 1994).

1. No testing of young children should occur unless it can be shown to lead to beneficial results.
2. Know child development ages, stages, and milestones, understanding the range of individual rates and styles for those stages. This will give you a basis against which to measure each child's progress. A red flag should go up when a child does not appear to be progressing in development. Then an evaluation with a standardized instrument may be necessary.
3. If a formal assessment is used, the content, form, validity and standards for interpretation should match the purpose of the assessment.
4. If a diagnostic test is called for to determine the cause or extent of a developmental lag, the following considerations should be made:

- the test should be administered by a qualified professional with carefully selected tests (preferably more than one)
- the child should not be forced to separate from the parents causing undue stress, which could negatively affect the results of the test
- tests that consist of isolated tasks resulting in a score do not give a complete picture of how the child uses those skills in the context of everyday interactions, so the assessment should consist of a wider range of criteria
- the tests should not carry more weight for decisions about the child than testimony from families and teachers and direct observations of the child in familiar environments

5. The test's purpose should be to improve performance, not just monitor it for measuring the effectiveness of a program, teacher, or school.
6. The test should be individually administered. Young children are still developing the skill of following directions so a group-administered test is not appropriate.
7. Formal tests should be skill-based rather than verbal or written, allowing the child as much time as needed to complete the tasks and feel supported by the person administering the test.
8. Do no more preparation than necessary. Time spent in preparation for tests is time not spent on subjects children want to know about. Families and teachers prepping children on items to be tested may also skew test results.

The National Association for the Education of Young Children (1990) has developed a set of guidelines regarding appropriate curriculum content and assessment in programs serving children ages three through eight. In Chapter 14 these guidelines are applied to the *Week by Week* observation and recording plan.

Advantages

Standardized tests, used appropriately, may be

- fair, objective assessments of a child's capabilities.
- recognized tests and scores used by intervention professionals.
- used with other forms of information about the child, to contribute to an overall picture of the child.

Disadvantages

Standardized tests, are used inappropriately when

- children feel pressure during testing.
- norms may not match the child's cultural and socioeconomic circumstances.

R E V I E W

Standardized Tests: A test in which the administration, scoring, and interpretation procedures are prescribed in the test manual and must be strictly followed. A standardized test is usually norm-referenced.

Types of Information Gathered by Standardized Tests:

Literacy level
> Vocabulary
> Comprehension
> Communication of ideas

Mathematics concepts and computation

Science Concepts

Analytical thinking

- young children's performance assessment is affected by the child's lack of experience with testing protocol.
- they are used to make decisions about the child based on a false reading.
- test results punish economically disadvantaged children and children whose first language is not English.

Pitfalls to Avoid

Advice for the use of standardized tests:

- Do not allow testing that places children under stress.
- Be sure the test is administered by a trained professional.
- Advocate for multiple sources of information about the child be used in any decision about placement, readiness, or intervention.

LOOKING AT COGNITIVE DEVELOPMENT: MATH AND SCIENCE

EXERCISE: How do you feel when you read these words?

Mathematics
Physics
Geometry
Hypothesis

In looking further at **cognitive** development, observing and assessing intellectual development, it is important to consider not just the knowledge of the subject matter but the other dimensions of development. Lillian Katz (1988), a great thinking stimulator of the early childhood field, reminds educators that learning is not just knowledge as an accumulation of facts, skills, or the ability to function in a certain way. Knowledge also involves **dispositions,** habits of the mind. Those are the ways that each individual responds to experiences. Some people have the disposition to quit after a defeat or embarrassment. The same situation may cause someone else with a different disposition to try harder, while another casts blame or another reflects and seeks advice.

The dispositions, feelings, or emotional responses to the fields of mathematics and science affect many early childhood educators. Perhaps it is the non-academic track through which some have entered the field. Perhaps it is the manifestation of learning style theory that people with strong logical thinking skills become engineers, while those with interpersonal learning styles and skills become educators. Or it may be the sex role socialization that girls unconsciously absorb from school as the "hidden curriculum," and from media, family, and peers. Whatever the cause, the math and science aversion has kept many early childhood classrooms from having interesting and challenging math and science learning areas. Consequently, the foundations have not been adequately laid on which children can build knowledge.

Rivkin (1992), an early childhood educator, addresses the emotions of science and urges a joy in the beauty of nature and a childlike curiosity and quest to make sense of things. She urges teachers to examine sexist messages that science is a man's field and questions the perpetuation of that idea. Conezio and French (2002) suggest ten benefits of science being at the center of an integrated curriculum.

1. Science responds to children's need to learn about the world around them.
2. Children's everyday experience is the foundation for science.
3. Open-ended science activities involve children from a wide range of developmental levels.
4. Hands-on science activities let *teachers observe and respond to children's individual strengths and needs*.
5. The scientific approach of trial and error welcomes error and interprets it as valuable information, not as failure.
6. Science strongly supports language and literacy.
7. Science helps children who are English language learners to participate in the classroom and learn English.

8. The problem-solving skills of science easily generalize to social situations.
9. Science demonstrations help children become comfortable in large-group conversations.
10. Science connects easily to other areas, including center-based play, math, artistic expression and social studies. (p. 16)

The science process skills (Lind, 2000) sound very much like authentic assessment of a child's development.

observing—concentrated watching and making field notes

comparing—looking at the changes that have taken place by rereading previous field notes

classifying—categorizing the observed behavior into developmental domains (such as an Anecdotal Recording from dramatic play) may give indicators of social, physical, cognitive, creative, language, literacy, and emotional development

measuring—noting specific, quantifiable changes such as minutes of attention span or letters of the alphabet the child can recognize

communicating—informing the child and the family of the progress the child has made

inferring—using experience to make judgments about those inner characteristics like self-esteem, coping skills, temperament

predicting—anticipating what milestones will be approaching and planning curriculum to help achieve them

If teachers have feelings of inadequacy and avoidance of math and science, there will be little to observe. The teacher must become conscious of these emotions. The concepts that follow can be used to heighten awareness of what children are doing as they manipulate their environment. They are actively engaging in math and science, even though it may not be on the daily curriculum plan. This will serve also as a curriculum guide of the concepts that can be incorporated into the early childhood program, enriching children's experiences in math and science. Reflective thinking and concept-building encourage the teacher's explorations.

Observing Developing Mathematical Concepts

EXERCISE: Which of the following children are learning math?

❑ a) The class is looking at the teacher holding the calendar and counting up to today's date, the 23rd.

❑ b) Two children are setting the table for lunch.

❑ c) Two children are shoving each other at the door to go outside.

❑ d) A child is eating orange sections.

❑ e) Two children are playing with clay.

❑ f) Three children and the teacher are making instant pudding.

❑ g) A child is painting at the easel.

❑ h) The group is sitting on a rug singing, "This Old Man."

❑ i) Four children are picking up the blocks and placing them on the shelves.

❑ j) A child in the housekeeping area is squeezed into a doll high chair.

❑ k) A child is passing out birthday party invitations and has one left over.

❑ l) A child is lining up all the shoes in the dress-up corner.

If you checked all of the items except the first one, you are correct.

a) **Rote.** Counting the calendar with nothing to touch or manipulate has little relevance to the child's life. (Why should the child care if it is the 23rd or the 89th?) This is not how children learn mathematical concepts. More effective ways of using the calendar to support children's concepts of time are with shared experiences (Van Scoy & Fairchild, 1993). Calendars record an event that has happened, like a birthday, with an artifact from that event. Children could record individual experiences, much the same as Show and Tell, but drawn, dictated, or written on a calendar by the child. The calendar can be used to plan for anticipated events, how many days until the picnic, and what must be done each day in preparation for it. In this way, calendars are relevant and perform concrete purposes rather than the recital of numbers and words that have little meaning.

It is through direct interaction with real objects that children construct meaning and make those associations that lead to cognitive development (Figure 8–3). Kamii (1982) has studied Piagetian principles and applied them to mathematics in the early years. She says, "It is good for children to learn to count and to read and write numerals, but a more important objective is for the child to construct the mental structure of number" (p. 25). She advocates teaching number through indirect ways in the environment. "Indirect teaching can vary from encouraging the child

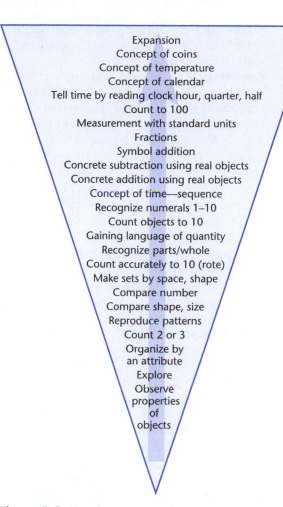

Expansion
Concept of coins
Concept of temperature
Concept of calendar
Tell time by reading clock hour, quarter, half
Count to 100
Measurement with standard units
Fractions
Symbol addition
Concrete subtraction using real objects
Concrete addition using real objects
Concept of time—sequence
Recognize numerals 1–10
Count objects to 10
Gaining language of quantity
Recognize parts/whole
Count accurately to 10 (rote)
Make sets by space, shape
Compare number
Compare shape, size
Reproduce patterns
Count 2 or 3
Organize by an attribute
Explore
Observe properties of objects

Figure 8–3 Developing Math Concepts

to put all kinds of things into all kinds of relationships, to ask him to get just enough plates for everybody at his table" (p. 27). While they are working, the observer records and assesses the child's mathematical and physical knowledge. The activities that follow illustrate children learning math concepts in indirect ways from the environment.

b) **One-to-one Correspondence.** When children are setting the table, placing one cup or one napkin at each place, they are demonstrating the concept of oneness, the most basic concept of number. This is practiced and can be observed in any number of ways. A child puts on a boot and knows she has two feet so there must be another boot somewhere. She does not try to put the second boot on the same foot. Materials in the classroom with pieces that fit, match, or can be counted if the child is at that level all add to

the acquisition of one-to-one correspondence.

c) **Ordinal Numbers.** The idea of **ordinal numbers** (first/second) is learned quickly by children in group settings or in families with siblings. The two-year-old wants his "first." The boys at the door want to be the "first" out. Not that it makes any difference once they get out but it is the competitive drive for first and the disappointment of "last." Would they then tussle to be the "first" in or the "last" in? That would be an indication of their understanding of the terminology of ordinal numbers. In the classroom, the familiarity with the schedule becomes rigidly defined in the lives of two-year-olds. Song time *must* come before the story, and then outside time. If the teacher decides that it looks like rain so today they must go outside "first," many will protest. Having older preschoolers decide which activity to do first, or who will have a first turn, and why, is an excellent way to observe children's understanding of ordinal numbers.

d) **Whole/Part Terminology.** As children interact with the environment, the role of the adult is to observe and provide descriptions for their actions like, "You've eaten half your orange." By inquiring, the adult can encourage further exploration, "How many sections were in the orange?" "Did each section have a seed or only some of them?" This type of description can go on incidentally throughout the day. It shows children individual attention by describing ordinary actions. It adds to their vocabulary, raises self-esteem, and promotes thinking.

e) **Conservation.** Clay manipulated into balls and snakes and scrutinized for more and less is an excellent math medium (Figure 8–4). The conservation of volume is the Piagetian concept that the Preoperational child (two to six years old) has not yet attained. The child uses intuition or appearances by centering attention on one attribute and judging volume by that. Two children have equal size balls. One breaks the ball into several little ones and declares, "I have more." The other one shouts, "Not fair." There have been efforts to teach conservation with limited results but the viewpoint now is that it should develop naturally and *not* be taught. However, clay and the water experiments with tall containers and a short squatty one

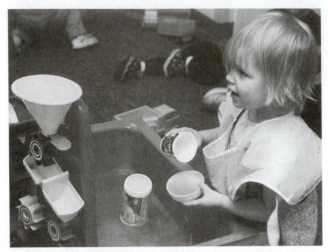

Figure 8–4 The amount never changes even if the shape of the container does—that's Piaget's conservation.

are excellent ways to question children's reasoning to test this hypothesis.

f) **Measurement.** Cooking is an excellent way to apply mathematical principles of measurement, sequence, cause, and effect. In following a recipe, quantities are specified, then measured by different-sized cups and spoons. Johnson and Plemons, in *Cup Cooking* (1993), suggest using multiple measuring utensils, such as three individual teaspoon measuring spoons rather than filling the teaspoon measurer three times. In this way, the child sees the quantity "three" physically present before adding them to the recipe. Recipes are practices in sequencing. The observation of before and after cooking or baking demonstrates cause and effect of heat and prompts description of attributes like hard and soft, liquid and solid.

g) **Geometry of Shape.** The recognition of circle, square, and triangle begins in infancy when the baby reaches out for a ball or a box or a sharp triangular shape. The infant uses all the senses; touching, chewing, seeing, and hearing. Someone says "Ball," "Box." The words are stored and each experience associates with the prior one. "Is this shape like that one? Yes? Then it must be a ball too." The baby is handed an orange. She says "Ball." She is overgeneralizing in calling all round objects balls. As she absorbs more information, those shapes will be differentiated from one another. They will take on more and more meaning by their various differences. They eventually will be the symbols that are

represented in drawing and later writing. Attention to the details and differences are really training for writing skills.

h) **Geometry of Pattern.** Pattern can be the visual image of the regular bars of the crib and the figures printed in a row on the sheets. The repetition of sounds in language and singing also form a pattern. Patterns are expressed in lines painted on the paper at the easel, and the rhythmic clapping of name syllables as they go to wash for lunch. Materials to form patterns are supplied with a card to guide the sequence of shapes, colors, or beads. They begin with two element patterns and gradually increase in complexity. Scientific observation skills are built as the child notices similarities and differences. The teacher watches and notes how the child uses blocks, buttons, and sound to make patterns.

i) **Classifying.** Sorting is such an important skill to cognitive development that it is taken for granted or overlooked as a cognitive activity. The toddler fills and dumps, then puts some in this bucket and some in that one. Finally, by some criteria, he purposefully sorts and selects which ones will go into each bucket. He is on the road to classification skills, which are the basis for scientific discovery. In the block area, the shelves are labeled with the shape of the block that belongs there. All the manipulatives have boxes or trays with picture and word labels. Replacing them is more than keeping the room tidy; it is a cognitive exercise. In the dramatic play area, tools are outlined above the woodworking bench for their replacement. In the art area, supplies are on labeled shelves. Spontaneous classifying occurs at snack time by eating the round pretzels before the straight ones, or separating the peas from the carrots. These all are building cognitive schema against which future associations will be made. Children will sort in ways that are not always predictable. This ability to sort as well as the "wrong" way can be observed, noted, and questioned to investigate the child's thinking.

j) **Visual Spatial Skills.** The estimate of how much space an object will fill sometimes is overcome by strong desire. Fitting into small spaces is a challenge to young children who are still learning the fine art of spatial awareness. They are prone to put fingers into tiny holes, heads through spaces, and bodies into containers. Withdrawing from those spaces sometimes is difficult. This spatial awareness is seen on the playground when a child playing "Duck, Duck, Goose" has difficulty finding the spot to join the circle. It can be observed when a child is doing a puzzle, trying to pound the piece in by force rather than turn it to get it to fit. The sand player fills the container, yet continues to shovel and shovel and shovel. The container overflows with each scoop. Still the child does not indicate a recognition that the space is full and can hold no more. Then comes the day when he lines the containers up and fills each one to the top. Ah ha! A new phase of cognitive development appears.

k) **Problem Solving.** It is James's turn to pass out napkins. Maxine had counted them out because she knows how many children are in the class. "Why do you have one left?" This question invites the child to apply the math skills of how many he started with, how many are in the class, how many children are absent, and then the observation and memory task of deciding who did not receive one. Offering opportunities for problem solving, which uses mathematics, can show children the usefulness of their newfound knowledge. "There are eight crackers left and four children at the table. How can we decide who can have more? How many can they have?" At the computer there are two chairs and the rule is two workers, but three people want to use it. Problem solving does not have to have a mathematical solution to be helpful in cognitive development. It is also the logical process of mentally creating the situation, the dilemma, generating possible solutions, and deciding on one by some criteria. Problem-solving strategies are universal.

l) **Seriation.** Placing objects in order according to some rule, such as size, texture, or color, helps the child to look for similarities but also to distinguish differences. The vocabulary of seriation begins with comparisons (big/little, short/long, heavy/light, empty/full) and expands to middle points and closer variations. This shows the ability to center attention on the one critical variable by which the items are being placed in a series. It is a complex skill that can be observed in its progression. Stories like "Goldilocks and the Three Bears" can lead to concrete activities for manipulating props from the hand to the mind. Con-

cepts of small, medium, and large; first and last; and in and out are introduced. Observing what strategies the child uses to come to conclusions about an item's placement also gives clues about the child's thinking processes.

Mathematics and literacy can be combined by incorporating books into the curriculum that have a mathematical theme. Schiro's (1997) example of Pat Hutchins, *A Doorbell Rang* (1986), gives an example how this book's story line about more and more visitors to share the tea cookies developed into a twelve-day project. It went beyond the obvious exercise in practical division into a critical analysis of the text and illustrations, a dramatization of the book, and a rewrite to incorporate the clarifications suggested by the class. Schiro suggests other titles that can be used in this way: *Alexander, Who Used to Be Rich Last Sunday* (Viorst, 1978), *The Philharmonic Gets Dressed* (Kuskin, 1982), *The King's Chessboard* (Birch, 1988), *Inch by Inch* (Lionni, 1960), and *Caps for Sale* (Slobodkina, 1940/1987). Some of the standards for grades Pre-K–2 from the National Council of Teachers of Mathematics (2000) include:

- *number and operations*—accuracy in counting, number words and numerals, beginning addition and subtraction, strategies for whole-number computations
- *algebra*—sort, classify, and order objects by size, number, and other properties: sequencing; patterns; representations of symbolic notations; symbols for qualitative and quantitative change
- *geometry*—recognize, name, draw, and compare two- and three-dimensional shapes; represent shapes from different perspectives; recognize geometric shapes in the environment
- *measurement*—attributes of length, volume, weight, area, and time; compare objects by these attributes; select appropriate unit and tool for measuring attributes; compare estimates
- *data analysis and probability*—sort and classify objects in sets, represent data using pictures and graphs, discuss experiences as likely or unlikely
- *problem solving*—recognize, analyze, and strategize how to solve problems that occur in experiences that can be solved through mathematical knowledge
- *reasoning and proof*—use pattern recognition and classifying skills to justify answers
- *communication*—use oral and pictorial language to convey mathematical thinking, listen to others, and evaluate ideas
- *connections*—use experiences to make linkages between one mathematical concept and another and between mathematics and real life

- *representation*—represent understanding through oral and written language, gestures, drawing, and symbols

Observing Developing Scientific Concepts

EXERCISE: Check the following science activities that would be appropriate for young children.

- ☐ a) Caves
- ☐ b) Bird's-eye view
- ☐ c) Dolphins
- ☐ d) Making a sandwich
- ☐ e) Let's grow a pumpkin
- ☐ f) The Earth—under, over, on
- ☐ g) Dirty hands
- ☐ h) The food chain
- ☐ i) Shadows
- ☐ j) When will it snow?

Learning activities are appropriate if they are relevant or real to the group of children and the concept can be tested through investigation. These curriculum ideas may be good ones depending on the context of the children in the group, their age, and their interests. Each of them may be the spark for a project for exploration using the project approach (Katz & Chard, 2000).

Common interests and experiences are the key to curriculum that is meaningful and a springboard for the project approach. If a project comes from the teacher rather than the children, there is a risk that it will become a teacher-telling or teacher-directed experience. "The central feature of a project, as we use the term, is that the children, in discussion and consultation with their teacher, take initiative, make decisions, and take major responsibility for what is accomplished" (Helm & Katz, 2001, p. 12).

a) Learning about caves would be relevant for children in several states, such as Kentucky, West Virginia, and states in other mountainous regions.

b) All children have knowledge of birds but thinking about what a bird sees involves moving beyond the egocentric view of the world to see it from above the Earth. This would stimulate not only a study of birds but of positional vocabulary, and a growing understanding of the Earth as an orb.

c) While children are fascinated with benign animals such as dolphins, unless they live in an area where they can experience them, either in the ocean or in an aquarium, it is a stretch for dolphins to develop into a project where children

are constructing knowledge from real, firsthand experiences.

d) Most children have the experience of at least eating a sandwich, but not necessarily making one. It is a familiar food but the sequence of making a sandwich and the choices available are rich with curriculum possibilities.

e) Growing things from seed, especially large rambling plants like pumpkins, can meet many learning objectives. However, climate, season, and indoor/outdoor environmental factors must be taken into consideration.

f) Children have had contact with the Earth but to explore by digging into it, studying things above it and things on it, pose interesting questions that can be explored any number of ways. This will bring in language, science, and imagination.

g) What child hasn't experienced dirty hands? This idea brings with it all kinds of reasons for and possibilities to explore what can be done about dirty hands. Dirty hands can act as a springboard for a health and hygiene lesson and more. Microbes, different cleaners, sensory experiences that get hands "dirty" all would be relevant learning themes.

h) Eating and eliminating are daily activities with which children have an intimate knowledge. Following the cycle for themselves and then thinking about food sources and the whole life cycle chain can be expanded in many different ways.

i) Light and dark, sun and shadows, day and night, are all concepts that touch every child. Using these as springboards for a project can bring about rich learning.

j) Obviously this is not a topic for temperate and warm climates but for those who await the first snowflake. Children can predict when it will occur and projects can be derived from observation of the first snowflake and measurement of accumulation.

The same cognitive processes the child uses for math are also used for science (Figure 8–5). Scientific discovery and mathematic awareness come from exploring the physical properties of objects through all the senses and identifying the similarities and differences between objects and events. Meaning is attached to the symbols of the environment, such as day and night, summer and winter. The ability to focus on selected pieces of information while ignoring the irrelevant is developed. Vocabulary is expanded to express the concepts of knowledge in various subject areas (Kostelnik, Soderman, & Whiren, 1993). These processes have been pointed out as necessary for literacy as well, such as perceptual skills, matching, discrimination, sequencing, describing, and classifying. Science, math, and literacy are all connected to cognitive development. The world of science for the young child contains all of these elements. Their learning is enriched by reading and listening to stories about the natural world, discussing, and hypothesizing. They wonder about how the guinea pig had babies in the night and what happened to the snowman. Small muscles are used in carefully picking up a worm, and large ones are used when they run with paper streamers in the wind. They listen and count the heartbeats of Stephanie's unborn sibling with a stethoscope on her mother's abdomen. Let's get ourselves, then children, excited about science!

What are the building blocks of science in the early years? They are the same ones used in chemistry laboratories in real life. The problem-solving skills in science (Charlesworth & Lind, 2003) are explored every day by young children, constructing their own knowledge.

EXERCISE: Look at the skills and tasks in the chart in **Figure 8–6.** Think of activities to provide these kinds of experiences from the child's interests and familiar world.

Science for Young Children. Appropriate science content that would have meaning to the young child is suggested in Charlesworth and Lind's useful guide *Math and Science for Young Children* (2003) (Figure 8–7).

Life Science. Life science is the study of plants, animals, and ecology. Appropriate to every early childhood classroom are growing, living things. Plants on

Figure 8–5 Developing Science Concepts

IT HAPPENED TO ME

Tornados

I was observing a student teacher leading a "science" activity. She had joined two soda bottles at the neck and gave each child in the circle a turn at tipping them over. They watched the vortex of swirling water as it drained from the upper bottle to the lower one. Some waited patiently, others impatiently, as they waited for a turn to make a "tornado." When it finally completed the circle, she asked the question, "And what did we learn about today?" Many were blank and silent but one dare-to-risk child said "Tomatoes!" There was surprise on the student teacher's face with a where'd-he-get-that? look.

Afterward we talked about a child's need to manipulate, a child's inability to wait, and the importance of relevancy. We discussed why the child said "Tomatoes." She had no idea other than it sounded like tornados. For children living in Kansas who had seen funnel clouds and knew the word *tornado*, this lesson might have been more effective. Four-year-olds in New York could make no connection between a tornado and the water in the bottle. Should she not have done it? Possibly. Perhaps with other kinds of preparations about wind, funnels, pipes, it would have had meaning. This activity did little to promote cognitive development, or any other kind.

---

a windowsill, guinea pigs in a cage, fish in a tank, or a recycling bin next to the garbage can are all informal ways of incorporating life science into the curriculum. These can become more formalized with specific activities to observe, identify, describe, classify, and so on.

Health Science. The most relevant lesson to all is health science—the human body, its workings, and healthy practices. This is a vital area for foundation building, illness prevention, and promotion of life-long wellness. Everyday practices, such as hand-washing, are probably the most important health lessons that early childhood programs teach. Children are curious about their bodies, the appearance, and function internally and externally. Measuring, weighing, and charting hair color, eye color, or

SKILL	TASK	ACTIVITIES
OBSERVING	Discriminating alike, different	Observe any two objects for likenesses and differences: clothing, shoes, pinecones, crackers.
IDENTIFYING	Recognizing, naming	Vocabulary games with pictures. "What's this?"
DESCRIBING	Isolating characteristics Using appropriate terms Building vocabulary	Describing objects by shape, color, origin, function, texture, smell, taste, and sound. "How many shape words do we know?" Color words, things that grow, picky things, etc.
CLASSIFYING	Comparing/Contrasting Arranging/Matching Categorizing	Grouping objects together by a rule. Selecting an object that does not belong in the group using a rule.
DESIGNING INVESTIGATIONS	Asking questions Looking for relationships Following procedures	Playing games like "Hot/Cold" and "Twenty Questions." Manipulating objects to find out more about them, like cutting open a coconut. Cooking.
COLLECTING DATA	Taking notes Measuring	Charting the growth of a plant, or the weight and height of each child in the class.
INTERPRETING	Theories of cause and effect Organizing facts	Brainstorming, wondering. "Why does the plant on the windowsill grow faster than the one in the cubbie? Does the plant grow faster in water or soil?"
COMMUNICATING RESULTS	Summarizing Sequencing Describing	Charting, drawing, writing the sequence of events, such as planting a bean seed to picking the bean
FORMULATING CONCLUSIONS	Evaluating Generalizing Analyzing critically Applying to other situations	Theorizing: "If plants grow best in the sunlight, do people need sunlight to grow?"

Figure 8–6 Process Skills in Science

number of teeth are relevant math and science activities for young children. Having a class baby is a very beneficial activity. At the beginning of the year the class "adopts" a mom having a baby in a month or two. She visits the class and they ask questions and learn about the baby growing inside her. After its birth (which is a class celebration!), the mother visits the class regularly for the children to observe, measure, and investigate the baby's growth. By the end of the school year, the baby is sitting up, crawling,

getting teeth, and becoming social. The children have learned many concepts in math, science, social studies, language, and physical development.

Physical Science. Physical science is the study of force, motion, energy, and machines. Children themselves are force, motion, and energy in one machine. Their fascination with carrying each other around, moving objects, and what makes things run can be capitalized in the classroom. Heavy objects to be moved

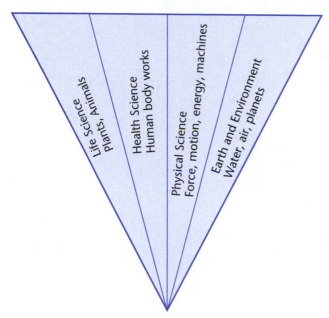

Figure 8–7 Young Children's Science Curriculum

can be moved easily (once they all get moving in the same direction) by a group of 8 or 10 preschoolers. Even the teacher sitting on a table can be carried from place to place. Magnets have always been a part of the classroom without deep explanation of poles of attraction. Manipulation, exploration, and observation can be augmented with charting what the magnet will pick up or attach to and what it will not. Blocks, a staple area of the classroom, can be augmented with ramps, cardboard tubes, and a facilitator who asks what-if questions to expose children to principles of gravity and give experiences in making predictions. "From which tube will the ball come out first if we start them both at the same time—the long one or the short one? Does it make any difference if it is a big ball or a small ball? Does it make a difference if we tip the short tube up higher? Why?" These concepts cannot be fully understood at this age. Most adults use electricity and television without understanding the principles behind them. The exploration of the effects of the forces of air, water, and machines are suitable activities for the early childhood classroom to explore and pose questions. The physical science area is important as these children grow up in the technological age where these skills affect their daily life.

Earth and Environmental Science. All children are in daily contact with weather, water, air, dirt, rocks, sun, moon, and stars. Charting and measuring temperature and rainfall are concrete activities that can be carried on in an early childhood classroom. Exper-

iments with water are carried on naturally as they stick their finger in the faucet to see what happens, or as they plunge a container into the water table and hold it up high to watch the water spill out. The magic of air's invisibility yet power can spark some interesting investigations for young children, laying foundations for the study of aerodynamics or hot air ballooning. Collecting rocks has been done naturally since the child was a toddler, picking up gravel stones from the driveway. Size, color, weight, geography, and effects of the environment all can be concepts to explore in this area. The sky and its lights have fascinated children and poets. Exploring these from all kinds of curriculum areas begins with familiar stories, such as "Good Night, Moon," and singing "Twinkle, Twinkle, Little Star."

Will children understand all the math and science concepts? Probably not. Most adults do not understand how turning a switch will light a lamp, but it is used. Giving children experiences that provide exploration expands their knowledge and logical thinking processes, and poses greater questions that will continue to be explored as they grow older.

Math and science curriculum topics begin with ideas from children's interest, current events, and the natural world around them. Projects and curriculum themes can be webbed or integrated into all of the curriculum areas. These are opportunities to make associations, broaden the experiences, and meet the needs of different learning styles. Here is an example of a curriculum web exploring topics relating to dirt (Figure 8–8).

EXERCISE: Select one of the topics mentioned in this chapter and make a web to explore possible activities in each of the learning centers of your classroom or curriculum areas. Use the blank curriculum web in Figure 8–9.

Mathematics and science are interwoven into daily life so math and science concepts are interwoven into the curriculum in much the same way. They are not discrete subjects but useful ways to make connections and meaning. Every individual is affected. Everyone uses mathematics and science in their daily lives.

Assessing Other Developmental Areas While Observing Math and Science Activities

As children interact with math and science experiences in the classroom in integrated curriculum, developmental areas other than cognitive develop-

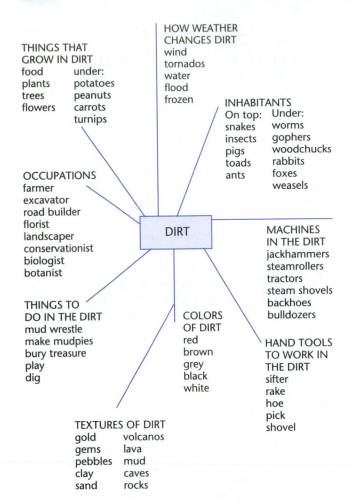

Figure 8–8 Science Curriculum Theme Web

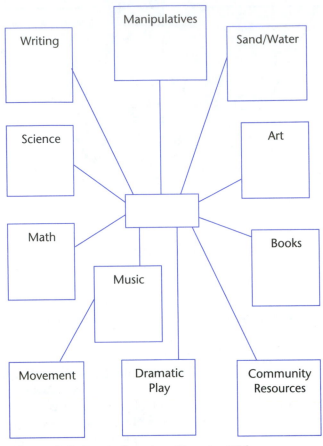

Figure 8–9 Curriculum Area Planning Web

ment can be observed simultaneously. The interdependence of development both contributes to and is an outcome of math and science activities.

Self-Care Skills. The autonomy of doing things for oneself comes as children feel more competent in their environment. When children can count how many napkins they need to set the table for the group, or a child sees her name on the chart as the floor sweeper around the table where marigolds were being planted today, the skills interact.

Large Muscle Development. The coordination of the body is observed as the child is running under the parachute to experience the wind or as she follows the game rules to take six steps backward. Both counting to six and walking backward are observed.

Small Muscle Development. The child places one shell in each compartment of the egg carton in one-to-one correspondence. He gently picks up the baby chick that has just been hatched. Observation of

small muscle skills and math and science come together (Figure 8–10).

Literacy. Many teachers have explored the use of manipulatives and journals to learn mathematics, and the scientific procedures of problem solving worked for preschool and primary age children. The combination of new skills integrates and maximizes the learning (Jones & Courtney, 2002; Whiten & Whiten, 2003).

Other Areas of Development. Visual perception and knowledge of size comparison vocabulary can be noted when the child picks up the bowling ball and calls it the "heaviest."

Language can be assessed by listening as the child speaks about solving the dilemma of three friends who want to sit by her at lunch. There are only two chairs left. Where will the third child sit? The logical resolution considering number of chairs as well as social interactions are observed while listening for clear speech and complexity of sentence structure.

Sharing Play Doh, dividing cookies, and taking turns on two bicycles are opportunities to observe

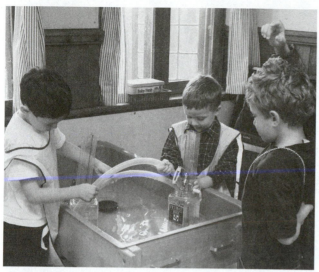

Figure 8–10 Other areas of development may be assessed during math and science activities.

both mathematical concepts and social development. Cooperation in working together to move a heavy object displays not only scientific principles but an understanding of community.

As children discover math and science concepts in a free environment without fear of "wrong" answers, they do not have to memorize or parrot back "right" answers in reply to closed questions. They can take risks to experiment. That is the basis for all inquiry: the elimination of wrong answers until the right one is arrived at through understanding. Children in the classroom environment dedicated to developmental learning can build and demonstrate that kind of self-concept.

Toads

I was observing in a first-grade classroom where the teacher told the children to turn to page 45 in their workbook. She asked, "What is that animal?" One of the children said, "Frog." "No, it's not a frog. It's a toad, /t/, /t/, /t/. The letter of the day is *T* so this has to be a toad. Now copy the word *toad* at the bottom of the page and you can color it in."

It looked like a frog to me. What is the difference? More important, what a learning opportunity was missed for the children and me to learn the difference. Instead, a negative message was sent to the one who answered the question. Do any of those children now know about toads because they wrote the letter or colored it? What if the class had gone out and gathered toads from the window well, watched them squirm down into the dirt, felt them wiggle, and measured their jumps? What if they compared them to a frog someone had captured in a pond and to tadpoles (another *T* word to add to their vocabulary)? Then they could have written, drawn, and dictated a story about a toad and a frog. The teacher would have really met her objective to familiarize them with toads and the letter *T* in a way that they would be more likely to remember. Authentic assessment is a real, not contrived, measurement of a real, not contrived curriculum.

HELPING ALL CHILDREN WITH COGNITIVE DEVELOPMENT

Cognitive development is different for each person, affected by learning styles, strong areas of intelligence, physical, and experiential factors. Early childhood teachers are faced with the challenge of meeting the learning needs of each child. There are some special populations whose cognitive development presents even more challenges.

Minority and Poverty Effects on School Achievement

Equality of educational opportunity has been the theme of Head Start for over thirty years. The Chil-

dren's Defense Fund monitors poverty's effect on school achievement and has found that "each year spent in poverty by a child increases by two percentage points the chances that he or she will fall behind in school and reduces by two percentage points the likelihood that the child will finish high school by age 19" (1995, p. 92). Minority children have higher rates of illiteracy and lower reading levels.

One in four children in America live in poverty and poverty is a strong predictor of poor school achievement, risk for learning disabilities, and need for special education services (Duncan & Brooks-Gunn,

TOPICS IN OBSERVATION

"Real" Curriculum

Educational advertisements fill teachers' mailboxes, promising easy, fun, ready-to-do activities for every curriculum area, especially math and science. They come with attractive containers, dividers for organization, and free sample plans. Most of these and many idea books for math and science curriculum are adaptations of the workbook format. Directions are given such as, "Draw a line to the one that is the same." "Count the red balloons and select the numeral." "Circle the bead that completes the pattern." The purpose of these activities is to teach and assess cognitive concepts. Visual discrimination and classification, counting and reading numbers, and patterning are appropriate learning objectives for activity plans. Using paper-and-pencil tasks, or even teacher-made paper games is not showing the teacher's knowledge of child development.

We know the attributes of the young, developing child. By knowing child development principles and observing and assessing the individual child's physical, social, emotional, and cognitive development, we can develop curriculum and teaching practices (Figure 8–11). It is not necessary nor effective to use workbook pages or folder activities to teach or test concepts. Just watch the child, and help the child do real stuff.

BECAUSE WE KNOW . . .	WE DO
Children learn through their senses.	We provide real, three-dimensional objects for them to manipulate.
Children are making associations with previous knowledge.	We provide materials that are familiar.
Children need time to organize their thoughts.	We provide long periods of uninterrupted time for them to explore.
Children cannot share.	We provide duplicates of popular materials.
Children cannot wait.	We do not require them to all do the same thing at the same time.
Children have different attention spans.	We provide a flexible schedule so children can move at their own pace.
Children are egocentric, only seeing things from their own point of view.	We do not force them to internalize someone else's point of view.
Children learn what they want to know.	We listen to them and provide ways for them to learn it.
Children learn from making mistakes.	We allow the mistakes to happen.
Children are frustrated easily.	We provide an environment and materials that are accessible and easy to manage themselves.
Children learn from accomplishing hard tasks.	We let them try without rushing in with solutions.
Children construct their own knowledge.	We provide a way for them to "teach" themselves.

Figure 8–11 Because We Know, We Do

1997; Hart and Risley, 1995). There are many factors contributing to these depressing statistics. It is even more distressing to know that teaching and assessment methods exacerbated rather than helped minority children and children in poverty to learn. The well-known Rosenthal effect (Rosenthal & Jacobson, 1968) may affect these populations. Teachers' expectations, using IQ scores or labels to categorize people, may contribute to the inequities. Jonathan Kozol's *Savage Inequalities: Children in America's Schools* (1991) captured in several vignettes the differences in schools for the haves and the have nots. Teachers who gave their all to their students under extremely harsh conditions were portrayed along with teachers who did much harm. The book is a call to self-reflection about attitudes and actions by everyone who works with children.

Children Who Are Cognitively Impaired

A whole group of cognitive impairments is categorized as mental retardation, subaverage intellectual function, and adaptive behavior (Figure 8–12). There are many causes, some of which are genetic disorders such as Down syndrome, prenatal influences (maternal illness, drug abuse, fetal alcohol syndrome [FAS]), birth complications such as anoxia (oxygen deprivation during the birth process), postnatal causes, such as illnesses with high fevers, head injury, lead poisoning, and environmental causes such as parental abuse and neglect. The identification and labeling of mild cognitive impairments is difficult in young children because of inaccurate diagnostic methods such as IQ tests and wide cultural definitions of "normal" intelligence. Some symptoms or clues are

- extremely short attention span
- language delays of more than one year
- social and emotional difficulties

Children with undiagnosed cognitive impairments often are detected first by preschool teachers. Approaching families with suspicions or concerns is a very sensitive task, done with concrete data, surrounded with care, understanding, and tact. The teacher may refer the family first to the pediatrician or a clinic specializing in full developmental evaluations.

After diagnosis, a placement decision is made for the child in the least restricted environment. It may be the child can function in a regular classroom. Cook, Tessier, and Klein (2000, p. 358) give these recommendations for children who need extra time and spaced practice.

1. Provide concrete, multisensory tasks.
2. Find the child's most efficient mode of learning.

Figure 8–12 Cognitive development can be affected by many factors, but inclusive programs accept and adapt.

3. Monitor pacing; provide shorter work periods with less information.
4. Provide repetition.
5. Plan for modeling and imitation.
6. Task analyze; use short, simple steps in sequence.
7. Give explicit directions.

Inclusion

Public Law (P.L.) 94–142 specifies that every child must be given access to an *appropriate* education in the *least restrictive environment*. This law and supplementary laws have led to the **inclusion** of children with disabilities into the regular classroom. Children with physical disabilities fare the best in inclusion classrooms. Learning disabilities and cognitive disorders require the teacher to implement an individualized program. With a philosophy that every child is unique, individualizing the curriculum for each child is the goal. There are social benefits as well as social risks to inclusion. Children are forming ideas about *we* and *they* with very basic social skills, so inclusion with peers who may react negatively because they are still learning social skills may bring rejection to the included child. The role of the teacher is expanded here to address social issues and turn inclusion into experiences of greater understanding and caring. Effectiveness in inclusion education depends on the training and support of all people working with the children: teacher, aide, volunteers, and support staff such as bus drivers and lunchroom personnel.

The family of a child with learning disabilities gives this insight and three specific strategies for inclusion but they are really advice for working with all children (Anderson and Weinhouse, 1997, p. 30–31).

1. Never limit your expectations or predetermine the final outcome.
2. Explore all interests and abilities for hidden potential.
3. Include these children in regular education classes and activities whenever possible.

For specific strategies for working with a child with exceptional health, hearing, learning, visual impairments, communication, or physical needs, see *Inclusive Early Childhood Education* (Richey & Wheeler, 2000) and *The Exceptional Child* (Allen, 2005).

Children Who Are Talented and Gifted

This beyond-the-range-of-normal category, **talented and gifted,** is one of the most neglected in working with children with exceptional needs. While high cognitive abilities characterized by advanced linguistic, reasoning ability, curiosity, and superior memory are the most obvious indicators of cognitive giftedness, other areas also are considered in this category. Children with advanced social skills, physical prowess, and musical ability also are included. The same hindrances to early identification of mental impairments also apply to giftedness. Developmental assessments can indicate advanced attainment of milestones and document behavior that alerts teachers and parents of the child's exceptional abilities. The teacher then individualizes the curriculum to provide enrichment opportunities to support the child's area of strength as well as the areas of normal development.

HELPING PROFESSIONALS FOR COGNITIVE CONCERNS

Families with a child with exceptional cognitive development at either end of the range of normal can first seek help from the following medical personnel:

pediatrician—physician specializing in the health and development of children
neurologist—physician specializing in the nervous system and in brain functioning

Within the educational system, specially trained professionals help the classroom teacher and the family meet the needs of the child whether cognitively impaired or gifted.

itinerant teacher—visits classroom or home regularly to see that appropriate methods, materials, and services are provided
resource teacher—assesses placement and provides instructional time outside of the regular classroom

OTHER METHODS

Other Methods to Record Cognitive Development:
Anecdotal/Running Records
Checklists/Rating Scales
Discussions/Interviews
Work Samples
Media such as audio/video and still photography

KEY TERMS

authentic assessment	quantitative scoring
cognitive	reliability
dispositions	screening
high-stakes tests	standardized tests
inclusion	talented and gifted
norm	valid
ordinal numbers	

WEEK 8: PLAN A

Standardized Test

Obtain a copy of one of the standardized tests mentioned in this chapter or one that is used in your program or local school district. Carefully read the manual for the following information:

- purpose of the test
- kind of test—screening, diagnostic, special abilities
- norm group—size of group, ages, geographic location, racial and gender makeup
- reliability
- validity
- method of administration
- method of scoring

Draw conclusions about its appropriateness for the group of children with whom you are working. Under what circumstances, if any, would you suggest using this test?

Share this information with classmates and discuss the issue of standardized tests in early childhood, their use and misuse.

Practitioners

If you are in a program where standardized tests are *not* given, it is important to inform yourself about the standardized tests the children you work with will be taking in the next grades. Be an advocate for their ethical use and inform families of the tests' use, misuse, and their rights to information about the tests, the scoring, and the outcomes for their child, the teacher, and the school.

If you are in a program where standardized tests *are* given, then it is your responsibility to learn all you can about the tests and work as an advocate for their ethical use. Prepare the children in your class to take the tests. Two excellent resources, one by Calkins (1998) and another by Taylor (1998), are listed in the resource section at the end of this chapter.

WEEK 8: PLAN B

MATH AND SCIENCE ASSESSMENT FOR ALL

Students

Complete the Math and Science Checklist in Appendix D for one or two children and use it as an observing guide during children's regular activities.

Practitioners

Copy the Math and Science Checklist in Appendix D for each child, or use the cognitive portion of the developmental checklist used by your program. During this week, observe and mark as many of the criterion as you can from natural activities.

What to Do with It

Filing. Note the assessment on the Portfolio Overview Sheet with the date completed and your name (Figure 8–13). File the checklist in each child's portfolio.

Sharing with the Child and Family. Share your observations with the family or the child, if appropri-

ate. For example: "Mrs. DeRienzo, when I was observing Gino counting today I noticed that besides being able to say the numbers to ten, he can count up to five objects. The counting comes first, then the understanding of number," or "Carmine, here on this paper I'm writing all the numbers and colors and shapes you know. After the holiday, I'll take this paper out again and see how much more you've learned."

COGNITIVE DEVELOPMENT			
Documentation	Location	Recorder	Date
Cag	Portfolio		10/20
CK	"		1/10
CK	"		4/11
CK	"		6/27

Figure 8–13 Portfolio Overview Example

Actions.

Read a Book.
Mathematics:

Bang, M. (1983). *Ten, Nine, Eight.* New York: Greenwillow.

Carle, E. (1994). *The Very Hungry Caterpillar.* New York: Putnam.

Henkes, K. (1995). *The Biggest Bow.* New York: Greenwillow.

Hoban, T. (1992). *Look up, Look down.* New York: Greenwillow.

Science:

Carle, E. (1990). *Pancakes, Pancakes!* New York: Scholastic.

Cowcher, H. (1991). *Tigress.* New York: Garrar.

Ehlert, L. (1990). *Feathers for Lunch.* San Diego, CA: Harcourt Brace and Company.

James, S. (1991). *Dear Mr. Blueberry.* New York: McElderry.

Johnson, S. (1982). *Inside an Egg.* Minneapolis, MN: Lerner Publications.

Livingston, M. (1992). *Light and Shadow.* New York: Holiday House.

Kuhn, D. (1990). *More than Just a Vegetable Garden.* New York: Silver Press.

In the Environment.
- Be sure there are tubs of manipulatives to line up in a row, sort, and count. (These can be purchased for that purpose or be found items of collections such as shells, thread spools, pinecones, macaroni shapes. Use your imagination and change the items periodically.)
- Provide materials and games of varying difficulty to count out spaces, sort, and count.

- Establish a living, changing science discovery area with found items, planned science concept exploration, and accompanying books.
- Add and change equipment regularly in a science/math area such as inclines, balance scale, tops, magnifying glasses, pinwheels, live animals and insects, gears and simple machines, kaleidoscopes.
- Provide materials and experiences for children to test their ideas and challenge their mistakes.

In the Curriculum.
- Incorporate the principles of scientific discovery in the curriculum. Projects that arise can use this approach as a pattern of exploration.
- Help children to see mathematics and science as a part of their everyday world, not an isolated subject. Explore the most common objects for similarities and differences.
- Incorporate graphing and related math games to the curriculum theme.
- Make thematic connections to math and science with seasons, construction, bakery, farm, birth, and even death.

In the Newsletter.
- Review the developmental stages of children's mathematical and science knowledge and skills.
- Write an article to give families ideas about incorporating mathematics and science in everyday household chores, experiences, and discussions.
- Convey some collected anecdotes of children's theories about the how or why of their world. These theories can be documented in panels showing the exploration of the theory.

WEEK 8: PLAN C

CONVERSATIONS WITH GROUP C FOR SPEECH AND LANGUAGE

Continue with the Conversations begun in Week 6, selecting children from Group C to converse with each day this week. If possible, tape record the conversation as well as make written notes as you speak with each child. Do an informal conversation or structured interview as described in Week 6, Plan A.

What to Do with It

Analyze each interview for what it reveals about the child's knowledge, emotional state, social development, and the child's speech and language. (Use the Speech and Language Checklist found in Appendix D.)

Enter the summary. Note your name and the date on the Portfolio Overview Sheet. If a significant lag appears, discuss it with your supervisor to confirm it. Then discuss it with the family. Have available a list of sites where a speech and language evaluation may be obtained to give to the family.

WEEK 8: PLAN D

REFLECTIVE JOURNAL

Respond to the following in your Reflective Journal, kept in a private file at home.

Reading about the emotions and the subjects of math and science made me think that . . .

I wish I knew more about . . .

I remember math and science in school as . . .

I think I'll try . . .

REFERENCES

Allen, K. E., & Cowdery, G. (2005). *The exceptional child*, 5th ed. Clifton Park, NY: Thomson Delmar Learning.

Anderson, M., & Weinhouse, D. (1997). Learning disabilities—Twice blessed. *Young Children, 52* (4), 29–31.

Bayley, N. (1993) *Bayley scales of infant development*, 2nd ed. San Antonio TX: The Psychological Corp.

Benner, S. (2003). *Assessment of young children with special needs*. Clifton Park, NY: Thomson Delmar Learning.

Bricker, D., Squires, J., & Mounts, L. (1995). *Ages and Stages Questionnaires: A parent-completed, child monitoring system*. Baltimore, MD: Brookes.

Brigance, A. H. (1991). *BRIGANC® diagnostic inventory of early development, revised*. Billerica, MA: Curriculum Associates, Inc.

Anderson, M., & Weinhouse, D. (1997). Learning disabilities—Twice blessed. *Young Children, 52* (4), 29–31.

Charlesworth, R., & Lind, K. (2003). *Math and science for young children* (4th ed.). Clifton Park, NY: Thomson Delmar Learning..

Children's Defense Fund. (1995*). The state of America's children yearbook, 1995*. Washington, DC: Author.

Conezio, K., & French, L. (2002). Science in the preschool classroom: Capitalizing on children's fascination with everyday world to foster language and literacy development. *Young Children, 57* (5) 12–18.

Cook, R. E., Tessier, A., & Klein, M. D. (2000). *Adapting early childhood curricula for children with special needs*, 5th ed. New York: Merrill. (An imprint of Macmillan Publishing Company.)

Duncan, G., & Brooks-Gunn, J. (1997). *Consequences of growing up poor*. New York: Russell Sage.

FairTest. (1990). *What's wrong with standardized tests? Factsheet*. Cambridge, MA: National Center for Fair and Open Testing.

Fleege, P. O., Charlesworth, R., Burts, D. C., & Hart, C. H. (1996). Stress begins in kindergarten: A look at behavior during standardized testing. *Journal of Research in Childhood Education, 7* (10), 20–26.

Greenspan, S. I., & Meisels, S. (1994). Toward a new vision for the developmental assessment of infants and young children. *Zero to Three, 14*, 1–8.

Hart, B., & Risley, T. R. (1995). *Meaningful differences in the everyday experience of young American children*. Baltimore, MD: Brookes.

Hatch, J. A. (2002). Accountability shovedown: Resisting the standards movement in early childhood education. *Phi Delta Kappan, 83* (6), 457–463.

Helm, J. H., & Katz, L. (2001). *Young investigators: The project approach in the early years*. New York: Teachers College Press.

Jones, J., & Courtney, R. (2002). Documenting early science learning. *Young Children, 57* (5), 34–40.

Johnson, B., & Plemons, B. (1993). *Cup cooking: Individual child-portion picture recipes*. Ithaca, NY: Early Educators Press.

Kamii, C. (1982). *Number in preschool and kindergarten: Educational implications of Piaget's theory*. Washington, DC: National Association for the Education of Young Children.

Kamii, C., & Kamii, M. (1990). Why achievement testing should stop. In C. Kamii, (Ed.) *Achievement Testing in the Early Grades: The games grown-ups play*. Washington,

DC: National Association for the Education of Young Children.

Katz, L. G. (1988). *Early childhood education: What research tells us*. Bloomington, IN: Phi Delta Kappa.

Katz, L. G., & Chard, S. C. (2000) *Engaging children's minds: The project approach, 2nd ed.* Stamford, CT: Ablex Publishing Corp.

Kohn, A. (2001). Fighting the Tests: Turning frustration into action. *Young Children, 56* (2), 19–24.

Kostelnik, M., Soderman, A., & Whiren, A. (1993). *Developmentally appropriate programs in early childhood education*. New York: Merrill. (An imprint of Macmillan Publishing Company.)

Kozol, J. (1991). *Savage inequalities: Children in America's schools*. New York: Harper Perennial.

Lind, K. K. (2000). *Exploring science in early childhood education*. Clifton Park: Thomson Delmar Learning.

McAfee, O., & Leong, K, J. (2002). *Assessing and guiding young children's development and learning*, 3rd ed. Boston: Allyn and Bacon.

McTighe, J., & Ferrara, S. (1998). *Assessing learning in the classroom*. Washington, DC: National Education Association.

Meisels, S. (1987). Uses and abuses of developmental screening and school readiness testing. *Young Children, 42* (2), 4.

Meisels, S. J., Bickel, D. D., Nicholson, J., Xue, Y., & Atkins-Burnett, S. (2001). Trusting teachers judgments: A validity study of a curriculum-embedded performance assessment in kindergarten-Grade 3. *American Educational Research Journal, 38* (1) p. 73.

Meisels, S. J., & Wasik, B. A. (1990). Who should be served? Identifying children in need of early intervention. In S. J. Meisels and J. P. Shonkoff, eds. *Handbook of early childhood intervention*. Cambridge: Cambridge University Press.

National Association for the Education of Young Children. (1990). *Guidelines for appropriate curriculum content and assessment in programs serving children ages 3 through 8. A position statement*. Washington, DC: Author.

National Association for the Education of Young Children. (1997). *Developmentally Appropriate Practice in Early Childhood Programs, Revised Edition*. Washington, DC: NAEYC.

National Association for the Education of Young Children and National Association of Early Childhood Specialists in State Departments of Education. (2002). *Early learning standards: Creating the conditions for success. Executive summary*. http://www.naeyc.org/resources/position_statements/creating_conditions.asp. Accessed April 18, 2003.

National Council of Teachers of Mathematics (NCTM). (2000). *Principles and standards for school mathematics*. Reston, VA: Author.

Neuman, S. B., & Roskos, K. A. (2000). How can we enable all children to achieve? *Early Childhood Today, 15* (2), 21–4.

Paris, S. C., Lawton, T. A., Turner, J. C., & Roth, J. L. (1991) A developmental perspective on standardized achievement testing. *Educational Researcher, 20* (5) 12–20.

Pellegrini, A. D., & Bjorklund, D. F. (1998). *Applied child study: A developmental approach*. Mahwah, NJ: Lawrence Erlbaum Associates.

Perrone, V. (1991). *On standardized testing: A position paper of the Association for Childhood Education International*.

Wheaton, MD: Association for Childhood Education International

Puckett, M. B., & Black, J. K. (2000). *Authentic assessment of the young child: Celebrating development and learning.* Upper Saddle River, NJ: Merrill Prentice Hall.

Richey, D. D., & Wheeler, J. J. (2000*). Inclusive early childhood education.* Clifton Park, NY: Thomson Delmar Learning.

Rivkin, M. (1992). Science is a way of life. *Young Children, 47* (4), May 1992.

Rosenthal, R., & Jacobson, L. (1968). *Pygmalion in the classroom: Teacher expectation and pupils intellectual development.* New York: Holt, Rinehart, and Winston.

Schiro, M. (1997). *Integrating children's literature and mathematics in the classroom.* New York: Teachers College Press.

Shepard, L. A. (1994). The challenges of assessing young children appropriately. *Phi Delta Kappan, 76* (3), 206–213.

Shepard, L., Kagan, S. L., & Wurtz, E. (Eds.). (1998). *Principles and recommendations for early childhood assessments.* Washington, DC: National Education Goals Panel, U.S. Department of Education.

VanScoy, I. J., & Fairchild, S. H. (1993). It's about time! Helping preschool and primary children understand time concepts. *Young Children, 48* (2), 21–24.

VORT Corporation. (1995). *HELP for preschoolers: Assessment and curriculum guide.* Palo Alto, CA: Author.

Wesson, K. A. (2001). The "Volvo" effect: Questioning standardized tests. *Young Children, 56* (2), 16–18

Whitin, P., & Whitin, D. J. (2003). Developing mathematical understanding along the yellow brick road. *Young Children, 58* (1), 36–40.

RESOURCES

Calkins, L., Mongtomery, K., & Santman, D. (1998). *A teacher's guide to standardized reading tests: Knowledge is power.* Portsmouth, NH: Heinemann.

Chandler, P. A. (1994). *A place for me: Including children with special needs in early care and education settings.* Washington, DC: National Association for the Education of Young Children.

Charlesworth, R., & Lind, K. (2003). *Math and science for young children* (4th ed.). Clifton Park, NY: Thomson Delmar Learning.

Eliot, L. (1999). *What's going on in there?: How the brain and mind develop in the first five years of life.* New York: Bantam Books.

Holt, B. (1977). *Science with young children, Revised.* Washington, DC: National Association for the Education of Young Children.

Kamii, C. (1982). *Number in preschool and kindergarten: Educational implications of Piaget's theory.* Washington, DC: National Association for the Education of Young Children.

Katz, L. G. (2001). *A developmental approach to assessment of young children.* ERIC EDD00036.

Peterson, R., & Felton-Collins, V. (1986). *The Piaget handbook for teachers and parents: Children in the age of discovery, preschool-third grade.* New York: Teachers College Press.

Taylor, K., & Walton, S. (1998). *Children at the center: A workshop approach to standardized test preparation, K–8.* Portsmouth, NH: Heinemann.

For additional information on early education curriculum, visit our Web site at http://www.earlychilded.delmar.com

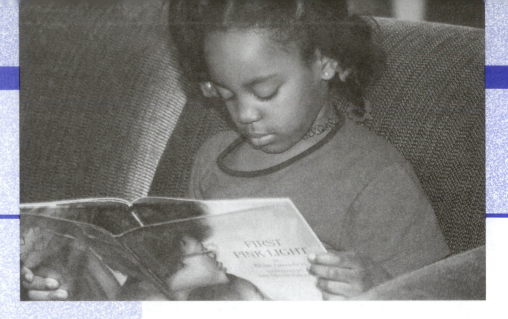

Using Rating Scales to Look at Literacy

USING THE RATING SCALE

EXERCISE: How hungry are you?
   Starved?   A little hungry?   Fully satisfied?
How is the temperature?
   Too cold?   Just right?   Too hot?
How well do you sing?
   Off key? Comfortably with a group?   Soloist?

A **Rating Scale** lists specific descriptions of criteria in a horizontal line from least to most, early developing to later developing, simple to complex, with several choices in between (Figure 9–1).

This Rating Scale contains seven sequential milestones or **quality points** in learning to read. A checklist such as Figure 9–2 contains the same information but in a vertical formation calling for a yes or no response from the recorder. The Rating Scale visually portrays the stages of development of a skill and can even include notations at the in-between stages.

Once the rater becomes familiar with the instrument and the child or setting, a rating is chosen that most closely describes what has been observed. It could be used by the teacher, a family member, a volunteer, or an outside observer. When more than one rater uses the same instrument on the same child, the validity increases, reducing rater bias. This is called **interrater reliability.** The scores are compared and, depending on the number of raters, the highest and lowest scores are cast out and the remaining scores are averaged. This technique is used in research and in Olympic sporting events.

Rating scales, like checklists, are self-made or purchased, and are used to measure certain criteria. The criteria can be a child's development or a setting

Figure 9–1 Literacy Rating Scale

or program's adherence to certain aspects of quality. When a measurement is made against criteria, it is an affirmation of what has been attained and an indicator of what to plan for next. In a child's development this type of measurement indicates progress or reveals lags that may be cause for concern. This tool, like the checklist, gives the teacher that zone of proximal development (Berk & Winsler, 1995), the not-yet-attained skill that the teacher can scaffold and help along with support. For example, a child who can print the first letter of his name is encouraged to do so at every opportunity with the teacher finishing it. Eventually, the child will write more of the letters himself. When a setting or program rating scale is used, it is an effective self-study tool to measure adherence to guidelines and indicate areas to be addressed for improvement.

Because the rater is looking for signs of the specific criteria, a rating scale is a highly **selective method.** Other observations are irrelevant and not recorded while looking for the specific criteria. A Rating Scale is considered a closed method since no raw data or details are recorded. Exact details of the rater's observation leading to the selection of a rating are not recorded.

A Literacy Rating Scale has been developed to assess the interest, skill, and knowledge of young children's reading and writing. Figure 9–3 is an example of a completed Rating Scale. Each criterion is rated from observation and dated at its highest level of attainment. When the quality point or milestone is not

observed, individualized curriculum or activities are planned for that child to encourage this area of development. It may be that the environment is not conducive for this child's learning style to spawn interest in reading or writing, or the materials are not accessible or meaningful. The tool is a way to accomplish the end result, to stimulate and encourage literacy development and record the progress. See Appendix D for a blank reproducible Literacy Rating Scale.

Rating Scale Examples

The quality points take several forms, depending on the design of the rating scale. The scale in Figure 9–1 describes the criteria from which the rater selects the most accurate choice based on observation and the rater's knowledge of the child.

Rating scales, such as *The Work Sampling System* (Meisel, Dichtelmiller, Jablon, Dorfman, & Marsden, 2001), use quality points of "Seldom, Usually, Always," or "Not Yet, In Process, Proficient." A Rating Scale that uses a similar style is the center evaluation of the *National Association for the Education of Young Children Accreditation Self Study* (NAECP, 1998). It uses rating scales with "Unmet, Partially Met, or Fully Met" (Figure 9–4 on page 220). It is a closed method because it does not record exactly what has been observed to meet the criterion.

Rating Scales can translate the written criteria into a number rating that can be added with others to obtain a quantitative score. *The Environmental Rating Scale (ECERS-R)* by Harms, Clifford, and Cryer (1998) has seven subscales: Space and Furnishings, Personal Care Routines, Language-Reasoning, Activities, Interaction, Program Structure, and Parents and Staff. These are broken down into 43 separate rating scales. Each is arranged on a 7-point scale from Inadequate (1) to Excellent (7). Each specific criteria in the Books and Pictures, Section 15, requires an affirmative decision to attain that score (Figure 9–5 on page 221). The quantitative scores are then graphed on the Summary Sheet (Figure 9–6 on page 222), to report areas of strength and areas that need attention. While the ECERS-R does have a small space for rater's notes

---

Checklist Example

- ❏ Recognizes logos and signs
- ❏ Recognizes name
- ❏ Recognizes some alphabet letters
- ❏ Demonstrates purpose of a book
- ❏ Can tell the story from pictures after hearing it once
- ❏ Catches the reader if words are changed
- ❏ Can read some words out of context

Figure 9–2 Checklist Example

LITERACY RATING SCALE

Child's Name __Jeremiah Jones__

INTEREST IN BOOKS

No interest, avoids	Only if adult-initiated	Brings books to adult to read	Looks at books as self-initiated activity
9/10	10/17		

LISTENING TO BOOKS

Wiggly, no attention	Intermittent attention	Listens in one-on-one situation	Listens as part of a group, tuning out distractions
9/21 10/6	11/17 can't last thru whole story		

INVOLVEMENT WITH BOOKS BEING READ

Little or no response	Emotional response, laugh, frown	Comments, asks questions	Joins in during reading
11/11			

HANDLING BOOKS

No voluntary touching	Rough handling	Exploratory manipulation	Books as favorite toys
	9/30	10/29 Stacking up in piles by _color_!	

CONCEPT OF BOOK FORMAT

No idea of front/back, up/down	Holds book right side up but skips pages	Demonstrated front/back concept	Looks at pages left to right
0	0	10/29	2/7 He sat & looked at every page of dinosaur book

CONCEPT OF STORY BOOK   _didn't realize he was listening even though he wasn't sitting_

Labels pictures	Retells story in sequence from pictures	Accurately repeats some story lines	Points to print while accurately re-telling from pictures
11/21	1/16		

PRINT IN THE ENVIRONMENT   _no obs. in this area_

Notices signs, labels	Asks, "What's that say?"	Reads signs, labels out of context	"Writes" signs to label constructions
0 0	0	0	0

BEGINNING READING   _a start. "J"_

Recognizes own name	Recognizes letters in name in other words	Reads simple words	Sounds out letters in unfamiliar words
11/15 0	3/17		

CONTINUED

Figure 9–3 Literacy Rating Scale Example

LITERACY RATING SCALE (continued)

MANIPULATION OF WRITING TOOLS

Fist hold	High hold on pencil	Adult grip, little control	Adult grip, good control
9/30	11/6	4/17 *Work on this!*	

COMMUNICATION THROUGH WRITING

no interest

Communicates ideas through drawing	Will dictate on request	Initiates dictation	Draws and writes words
2/16 0	4/20 0 0		

BEGINNING WRITING

Scribbles, no reference to writing	Named scribbles "Says my name"	Single letters, random	Writes name

WRITING IN PLAY

No reference to writing	Asks for signs, words to be written	Asks for adult to spell words	Sounds out words and writes on own

Figure 9–3 Literacy Rating Scale Example (Continued)

that could amplify the rating, it is still a closed method since the outside reader does not have enough data on which to draw her own conclusions, unlike the Anecdotal or Running Record.

Advantages

The Rating Scale is

- fast and convenient. (The rater reads, decides, circles, or checks.)
- efficient for measuring a large number of criteria quickly.
- informative of what "should be" expected.
- useful for tracking progress or warning of developmental lags.
- an assessment measurement against the ideal and used as a plan for improvement (accreditation).
- revisited to see progress over time.

Disadvantages

The Rating Scale is not

- backed up with raw data.
- objective. (Judgments are made as observation is taking place with little time for considering the

criteria and no place for explanation of circumstances.)
- free of rater bias, with no way for the reader to know that.
- useful as a method to record spontaneous actions or conversations.
- sensitive to a wide range of individual differences.

Pitfalls to Avoid

The Rating Scale recorder should

- make sure the Rating Scale criteria matches the goals and objectives of the program and developmental range of the children.
- have more than one person use the same rating scale and compare ratings for interrater reliability to limit observer bias.
- become familiar with rating scale criteria before using it and be sure that each criterion is observable rather than judgmental: Scribbles/Forms alphabet letters/Writes cursive *not* Still scribbling/Poor spelling/Good writing.
- be sure the quality points describe behaviors rather than attitudes: Leaves when story reading begins/Stays, plays with toys during story reading/Sits,

REVIEW

Rating Scale: Criteria is arranged according to developmental stages or range of quality with the recorder making a judgment based on observation.

Types of Information to Record Using a Rating Scale (depends on focus of Rating Scale):

child development stages

environment appropriateness

teacher performance

watching pages displayed during story reading *not* Not interested /Some interest/ Very interested.

Using Technology

Rating Scales that have numerical scoring lend themselves to electronic storage and computation of the results. Personal computers and hand-held computers can store the form in an electronic file and the observer can enter the numerical rating. Using computer programs that perform computation and graphic reporting, the scores can be saved in individual children's electronic files and also used as aggregate data on the whole group.

How to Find the Time

Completing Rating Scales on individual children's development does take concentrated observation and recording to obtain objective results. Much of observation this can be done during free play time or it requires a person who is not fully responsible for classroom management. Program Rating Scales such as the ECERS can be done as a self-assessment by the teaching team or by an objective evaluator. See Chapter 13 for more discussion of program assessment.

Criterion	Rating			Comments
B-7d Encourage language and literacy development	Not met ☐1	Partially met ☐2	Fully met ☐3	

For example,

Infants/toddlers

Engage in many one-to-one, face-to-face interactions with infants.
Look at simple books and pictures.
Talk in a pleasant, calm voice, using simple language and frequent eye contact while being responsive to the infant's cues.
Verbally label objects and events within the infant's experience.
Respond to sounds infant makes, occasionally imitating infant's vocalization.
Describe children's and adult's actions and the events that occur in the child's environment.
Respond to toddlers' attempts at language in supportive ways, such as expanding their utterances and answering their questions, engaging in meaningful conversation about everyday experiences.

Preschoolers

Read books and poems, tell stories about experiences, talk about pictures, write down experience stories children dictate.
Provide time for conversation, ask child questions that require more than a one-word answer.
Answer children's questions.
Add more information to what a child says.
Label things in room, use written words with pictures and spoken language, provide a print-rich environment.
Use flannel board, puppets, songs, finger plays, rhyming games.
Encourage children's emerging interest in writing (scribbling, drawing, copying, and using invented spelling).

Kindergartners

Actively work to increase children's vocabulary every day.
Read books and poems, tell stories about experiences, talk about pictures, write down experience stories children dictate.
Help children develop book-handling skills and familiarity with the conventions of print (such as story/chapter titles, punctuation, and capital letters).
Help children develop the full range of strategies for reading, for instance, using letter-sound relationships, pictures and their understanding of the text to figure out unknown words.
Provide many opportunities every day for children to write for reasons that make sense to them (such as making lists, labeling their work, and writing notes to their parents).
Give children frequent practice and help in composing, editing, and revising stories and their written products.
Observe and make plans to ensure each child's continual progress in oral language, reading, and writing.

School-agers

Provide opportunities to read books.
Write and produce plays, publish newspapers, write stories.
Share experiences with friends or adults.
Use audio-visual equipment such as tape recorders.
Make own filmstrips, recordings.

Figure 9–4 NAEYC Accreditation Self-Study Criteria (Permission to reprint granted by National Academy of Early Childhood Programs, 1998, *Accreditation Criteria & Procedures.* Washington, DC: National Association for the Education of Young Children.)

Inadequate 1	2	Minimal 3	4	Good 5	6	Excellent 7

LANGUAGE-REASONING

15. Books and pictures

1.1 Very few books accessible.

1.2 Staff rarely read books to children (Ex. no daily story time, little individual reading to children).

3.1 Some books accessible for children (Ex. during free play children have enough books to avoid conflict).

3.2 At least one staff-initiated receptive language activity time daily (Ex. reading books to children,* storytelling, using flannel board stories)

5.1 A wide selection of books† are accessible for a substantial portion of the day.

5.2 Some additional‡ language materials used daily.

5.3 Books organized in a reading center.

5.4 Books. language materials, and activities are appropriate** for children in group.

5.5 Staff reads books to children informally (Ex. during free time, at naptime, as an extension of an activity).

7.1 Books and language material are rotated to maintain interest.

7.2 Some books relate to current classroom activities or themes (Ex. books borrowed from library on seasonal theme).

Notes for Clarification

* Reading may be done in small groups or in larger groups depending on the ability of the children to attend to the story.

† A wide selection of books may include: variety of topics; fantasy and factual information; stories about people, animals, and science; books that reflect different cultures and abilities.

‡ Examples of additional language materials are posters and pictures, flannel board stories, picture card games, and recorded stories and songs.

**Examples of appropriate materials and activities include simpler books read with younger children; large print materials for child with visual impairment; books in children's primary language(s); rhyming games for older children.

Questions

(7.1) Are there any other books used with the children? How is this handled?

(7.2) How do you choose books?

Figure 9–5 Language-Reasoning Rating Scale, ECERS-R (Reprinted by permission of the publishers from Harms, T., Clifford, R.M. and Cryer, D., Early Childhood Environment Rating Scale (ECERS), Revised Edition, (New York: Teachers College Press, ©1998 by Thelma Harms, Richard M. Clifford and Debby Cryer. All rights reserved.), pp. 33, 35 (Section 15) and 59.)

LANGUAGE-REASONING		
15. Books and pictures 1 2 3 4 5 6 7		**Notes**

Y N   Y N   Y N   Y N
1.1 ☐ ☐   3.1 ☐ ☐   5.1 ☐ ☐   7.1 ☐ ☐
1.2 ☐ ☐   3.2 ☐ ☐   5.2 ☐ ☐   7.2 ☐ ☐
                              5.3 ☐ ☐
                              5.4 ☐ ☐
                              5.5 ☐ ☐

Figure 9–6 ECERS-R Score Sheet for Language-Reasoning (Reprinted by permission of the publishers from Harms, T., Clifford, R.M., and Cryer, D., Early Childhood Environment Rating Scale (ECERS), Revised Edition, (New York: Teachers College Press, ©1998 by Thelma Harms, Richard M. Clifford, and Debby Cryer. All rights reserved.), pp. 33, 35 (Section 15) and 59.)

LOOKING AT LITERACY

EXERCISE: What did you read today? What did you write today?

Reading and writing are so natural that they are done automatically. When reading the preceding exercise, thoughts might have gone to formally picking up a book or writing a letter. Do not forget about:

The numbers on the clock
The name of the toothpaste you used this morning
The on/off light switch
Signing a check
Jotting down a phone number
Reading and writing this exercise

"Learning to read and write is critical to a child's success in school and later in life. One of the best predictors of whether a child will function competently in school and go on to contribute actively in our increasingly literate society is the level to which the child progresses in reading and writing" (Neuman, Copple, & Bredekamp, 1999). This is the opening statement of a joint position statement of the International Reading Association (IRA) and the National Association for the Education of Young Children. But how do children learn to read and write? What can families and teachers provide to ensure not just that these vital skills are mastered but that a joy of reading is kindled for a lifetime? It seems to come effortlessly for some, but with great difficulty for others. For most people, though, once it is learned it is there forever, and *very* useful. Becoming literate is like the childhood game of "Mother, May I." It comes in baby steps, tiny little forward motions, then giant steps, leaps that propel it forward. Literacy is not an isolated skill from other development, for it involves motor skills, visual perception, hearing, small muscle development, cognitive development, social interac-

tions, and emotional control. It is simultaneously developing along with language.

Receptive language skills are greater and earlier than expressive skills (Figure 9–7). This is true in literacy as well. Hearing and understanding words precedes speaking them. Reading words usually occurs before writing them. Reading and comprehension ability will always be greater than the ability to write as an expressive form (though some writing seems to be done without thinking).

Holdaway's classic, *The Foundations of Literacy* (1979), chronicled the history of schools' reading instruction by reviewing the alphabetic versus phonetic, versus whole-word approaches. Then came the whole-word versus sentence, then book approaches versus language experiences, and many variations of each. The basal readers were stories consisting of the most common English words, most of them boring. Writing and reading were taught as separate subjects. Holdaway (1979) and many others since have emphasized that children learn to read and write like they

Figure 9–7 The environment is full of literacy.

learn to speak, in a natural progression of meaningful experiences. It all begins with receiving information about print. The whole language movement of the eighties brought back the integrated method with the decoding process still in debate. The debate between the whole language approach or emphasis on phonemic awareness goes on (Carbo, 1996; Ponnuru, 1999). Some imposing evidence offered by Jeynes and Littell (2000) indicates that for low socioeconomic status (SES) children who are not surrounded by a print-rich environment and families who value reading, phonics instruction with a basal reader is more effective.

Literacy Development

The formal instruction of reading and writing was thought to begin in the first grade. As the field of **emergent literacy** expands, it is believed that literacy begins much earlier (Figure 9–8). Children come to school knowing much about reading and writing already.

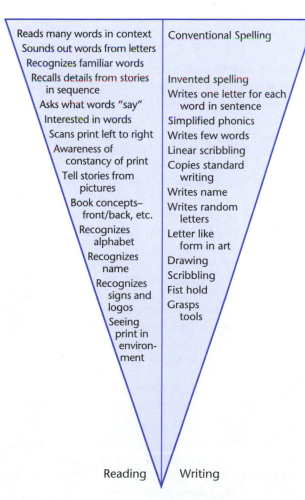

Figure 9–8 Reading and Writing Development

IT HAPPENED TO ME

Permanent Name Writing

A mother came to school one morning and said, "I'm really glad you've been working with name writing and journal writing but last night Jason wrote his name on the side of the car with permanent marker!" Oops, no guarantees.

Print-Rich Environment

EXERCISE: **Look around you right now. List all the reading and writing materials in view.**

Probably your list is very long. It may contain: labels on the television set, phone books, recipe cards, magazines and every other form of print, pens, pencils, markers, paper, computers, and brand labels on manufactured items.

Becoming a reader and writer begins by immersion in a world of print. Young children's environments are filled with the alphabet on everything from blocks, sheets, and cereal boxes. Colorful logos like McDonald's and Sesame Street are recognized long before the actual individual letters and their sounds are known. This is **contextualized literacy,** words and phrases that can be read because they are defined by their context, shape, color, and position. Besides an environment full of print, children look to role models. They see parents reading the newspaper, the advertising on television, or directions on how to put together the tricycle. They often imitate those actions by picking up papers and babbling or pretending to read. Almost every child has picked up a pencil, pen, lipstick, or permanent marker and made some scribbles in a place not meant for writing.

The American Reading Challenge. Despite billions of dollars spent on reading materials, curriculum, studies of various approaches, vast research and national initiatives, the fact remains that a large number of children in America never learn to read well. This has huge implications because of the connection between poverty and illiteracy. Jim Trelease's (2001) findings about the implications of literacy, based on his research, are that

1. The more you read, the more you know.
2. The more you know, the smarter you grow.
3. The smarter you are, the longer you stay in school.

4. The longer you stay in school, the more diplomas you earn and the longer you are employed; thus, the more money you earn in a lifetime.
5. The more diplomas you earn, the higher your children's grades will be in school.
6. The more diplomas you earn, the longer you live. (p. xxv)

The connection between language and literacy was discussed in Chapter 6, illustrated so powerfully with the research of Hart and Risley (1995) who studied the gap between the number of words and kind of language used in high- and low-income homes. That gap correlated to the gap in school performance at age nine. It is not early reading skills that matter, but rather the relationships and connections with the spoken word, including vocabulary, open-ended questions, positive feedback, explanations, descriptions, and running dialogue throughout the day that is true early literacy (New, 2001). The implications of this research are clear; it is too late to begin literacy development in preschool programs. Literacy development begins at birth so the foundation must be laid by the family and the infant and toddler educators.

Babies and Books. An important step toward becoming literate is the shared experience of reading a book with bright pictures and simple words about the child's world.

Look at Figure 9–9.

How does this picture make you feel?
What do you think the adult is feeling?
What do you think the child is feeling?

Young babies are at the Sensorimotor Stage, so their books have to be touchable. The small, cardboard books, ones with texture, cloth, or plastic, ones they can pull on and chew, provide those first experiences. Because infants' language development is at a simple stage, one-word books with repeating sounds soon become their favorites. Even if the reading material is the *New York Times,* building blocks of literacy are being cemented together. The bodies are close. There is a difference in the reading voice from the speaking voice. Awareness is growing that those little marks on the page mean something.

As the child moves into the second year, the memory is lengthening. The child is becoming familiar with books and pointing, laughing, and saying words of identification, like "Choo choo," and "Wha's dat?" They become participants by pretending to read. Words and familiar phrases from favorite books are added to their vocabulary. They ask for their favorites to be read over, and over, and over. When the adult changes a word in a familiar book, the child notices and protests. This shows that they know print and speech are related. By the end of the third year, the child can accurately tell the story from the pictures in familiar books. They will begin to move eyes and fingers along the row of print while saying the words. This is an indication of the child's awareness that those lines and circles are a code to be deciphered (Figure 9–10).

Reading and Preschoolers. Most children learn to listen and speak effortlessly without direct instruction. Traditionally, reading and writing have been taught in formal education. In separate, isolated exercises, the vision and mind for reading and small muscles were trained with "readiness" worksheets or activities. The term *emergent literacy* is a broader term, differing from isolated skills, coming out of the whole-language movement (Clay, 1975). It fits very well into the paradigm of developmentally appropriate practice, child-centered, developmentally based, using curriculum of themes and projects.

Preschoolers who have had early home literacy experiences that included family involvement in reading and writing, and receptive language (hearing many words, complex sentences, descriptions and explanations) have high test scores, directly related to levels of vocabulary, listening comprehension skills, and reading skills in grade 3 (Senechal & LeFevre, 2002).

The common characteristics of these children have most to do with their home environment. They

- were read to on a regular basis.
- had a wide variety of print available in the home, such as books, magazines, and newspapers.
- had paper and pencil available to scribble and draw and copy objects and letters.

Figure 9–9 Even very young children enjoy reading.

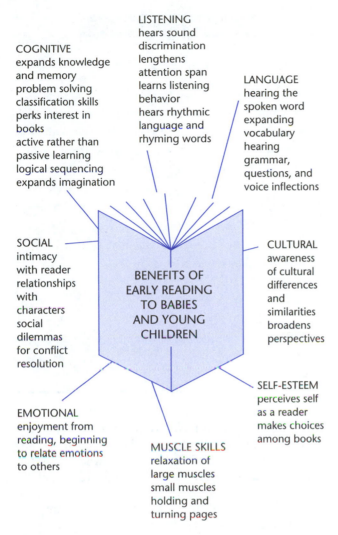

COGNITIVE
expands knowledge
and memory
problem solving
classification skills
perks interest in
books
active rather than
passive learning
logical sequencing
expands imagination

LISTENING
hears sound
discrimination
lengthens
attention span
learns listening
behavior
hears rhythmic
language and
rhyming words

LANGUAGE
hearing the
spoken word
expanding
vocabulary
hearing
grammar,
questions, and
voice inflections

SOCIAL
intimacy
with reader
relationships
with
characters
social
dilemmas
for conflict
resolution

BENEFITS OF
EARLY READING
TO BABIES
AND YOUNG
CHILDREN

CULTURAL
awareness
of cultural
differences
and
similarities
broadens
perspectives

EMOTIONAL
enjoyment from
reading, beginning
to relate emotions
to others

MUSCLE SKILLS
relaxation of
large muscles
small muscles
holding and
turning pages

SELF-ESTEEM
perceives self
as a reader
makes choices
among books

Figure 9–10 Benefits of Early Reading to Babies and Young Children

- had people in the home who stimulated their interest by supporting reading and writing as a worthwhile activity. (Trelease, 2001)

This is not an endorsement for the "superbaby syndrome." Early reading to babies and young children brings many benefits (Figure 9–10). Forced acceleration of reading training has been shown to have no positive effect on school performance by the third grade. While those two concepts seem in opposition, the difference is in the approach. Young children (as early as two years old) have been taught to read and do mathematics through drill and practice. David Elkind, noted child psychologist, has sent out the warning against the "superkid" practices in his book *Miseducation: Preschoolers at Risk* (1987). These techniques are based on behaviorist philosophies rather than on the developmentalists such as Piaget

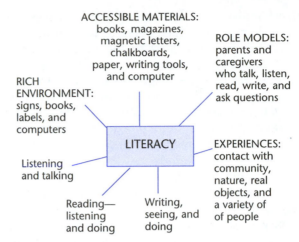

ACCESSIBLE MATERIALS:
books, magazines,
magnetic letters,
chalkboards,
paper, writing tools,
and computer

ROLE MODELS:
parents and
caregivers
who talk, listen,
read, write, and
ask questions

RICH
ENVIRONMENT:
signs, books,
labels, and
computers

LITERACY

EXPERIENCES:
contact with
community,
nature, real
objects, and
a variety of
of people

Listening
and talking

Reading—
listening
and doing

Writing,
seeing, and
doing

Figure 9–11 Interacting with Literacy

and Erikson, on which most early childhood principles and practices are founded.

So how can young children interact with literacy? (See Figure 9–11.)

Literacy begins with communication, verbally and nonverbally. Even the unborn child hears the muffled mother's voice and the rhythm of her heartbeat. Early in the child's life, long before the child can speak to convey thoughts or express feelings, music and visual arts and crafts can be the symbols of thought. The Carnegie Foundation report *Ready to Learn* (Boyer, 1991) reported that only about one-third of America's parents regularly engage in music or arts with their children.

Between two and three years of age children begin to notice and "read" print all around them: McDonald's signs, stop signs, a print advertisement for their favorite cereal box television show. This environmental print can be the springboard to literacy when it is recognized and followed up with books and activities that build on that knowledge.

EXERCISE: Write the alphabet down the side of a piece of paper. Now, begin to think of all the environmental print using the beginning letter. This idea came from *Chicken Starts with CH!* (Xu & Rutledge, 2003). This will get you started:

A—Advertisement
B—Bumper stickers
C—Coins
D—D

Children who have been read to begin to recognize the letter names and the sounds of the letters. They know which side is up in a book and the concept of front to back. In the third year, many recognize familiar logos and signs, their own name, and some short words. They begin to take an interest in the words in books and in the environment, and ask what specific words say. They understand the purpose of a book and begin to turn pages from front to back and scan the pictures from left to right pages. The story sequence of beginning, middle, and end is recognized and can be retold from the pictures. An awareness of rhyming words appears and an association of letters and sounds.

Four- and five-year-old children recognize books as sources of information and entertainment and recognize the difference between story books and pictionary or dictionary format. They can fill in story lines from rebus picture books and sometimes read simple stories word by word. They can retell the story from memory. The story is reconstructed from the pictures. Predictions are made about what might happen next or why a certain event happened, relating the cause and effect concept. Many words are recognized by sight and they are sounding out other words by alphabet letters. This **phonemic awareness** of the sounds of speech in syllables and the relationship of alphabet letters to sounds is a critical stage in the process of learning to read. Children are beginning to notice the space between words and the punctuation marks at the end of the sentence and change their inflection depending on the mark. They act out story characters in their play. Their conversations relate to situations and dilemmas the characters faced and how they solved them. They take an interest in creating and illustrating their own books, either in pretend writing, phonetic spelling, or dictation. Some of them have become readers, either by families' direct instruction, or by natural association of letters and sounds.

IT HAPPENED TO ME

Office

Walking down the hall, a child in my preschool class asked, "Where's the ice?"

"What do you mean? Where's the ice?" I asked incredulously.

He pointed to a door with the sign OFFICE. "It says, 'off ice.' I wonder where the ice is?"

He had learned one aspect of print, the decoding of letters into meaningful words, but had not yet mastered the importance of spacing.

IT HAPPENED TO ME

B L D Z R

This was demonstrated to me by a group of five-year-old boys who dominated a class I had. As we approached the holiday season, they were interested in making their gift wish lists. Having just been inspired by Schickedanz's book (1999), instead of dictating their lists to me, I urged them to write or draw their own. To my amazement they worked hard at it for many minutes (which was amazing in itself). Even more amazing was that I could really read what they wrote:

B L D Z R (bulldozer)

G N (gun)

2 W E L R (two-wheeler)

They were struggling to communicate meaning, and they had done so!

Children enjoy and learn different things from different types of books. They should be exposed to many types. Machado (2003) lists the types, the learning possibilities, and why children like them (Figure 9–12).

Owocki (1999) suggests teachers consider providing literacy materials to explore that fill the functions of written language.

Environmental Print—in the world around us: street signs, instructions, advertising, reference books

Occupational Print—used in the workplace: health records and appointment books, menus, order pads, and money

Informational Print—storing and retrieving information: calendars, clocks, recipes, telephone books

Recreational Print—used for leisure activities: storybooks, poetry books, travel books (p. 58)

Young Children Write

Young children's writing emerges along with language and reading, as well as art. The myth that oral language must be mastered before written language can develop is attacked by Schickedanz. Her book *Much More Than the ABCs: The Early Stages of Reading and Writing* (1999) is a helpful resource for the early childhood educator and families. The first step

Types	Features Teachers Like	Features Children Like
Story books (picture books) • Family and home • Folktales and fables • Fanciful stories • Fairy tales • Animal stories • Others	Shared moments Children enthusiastic and attentive Making characters' voices Introducing human truths and imaginative adventures Sharing favorites Easy for child to identify with small creatures	Imagination and fantasy Identification with characters' humanness Wish and need fulfillment Adventure, Excitement, Action, Self-realization, Visual variety, Word pleasure
Nonfiction books (informational)	Expanding individual and group interests Developing "reading-to-know" attitudes Finding out together	Facts, discovery of information and ideas Understanding of reality and how things work and function Answers to "why" and "how" New words and new meanings
Wordless books	Promote child speech, creativity, and imagination	Supplying their own words to tell story Discovery of meanings Color, action, and visual variety
Interaction books (books that have active child participation built-in)	Keeping children involved and attentive Builds listening for directions skills	Movement and group feeling Individual creativity and expression Appeal to senses Manipulative features
Concept books (books with central concepts or themes that include specific and reinforcing examples)	Promotes categorization Presents opportunities to know about and develop concepts Many examples	Adds to knowledge Visually presents abstractions
Predictable books (books with repetitions and reinforcement)	Permits successful guessing Builds child's confidence Promotes ideas that books make sense	Opportunity to read along Repetitiveness Builds feelings of competence
Reference books (picture dictionaries, encyclopedias, special subject books)	Opportunity to look up questions with the child Individualized learning	Getting answers Being with teacher Finding a resource that answers their questions
Alphabet and word books (word books have name of object printed near or on top of object)	Supplies letters and word models Paired words and objects Useful for child with avid interest in alphabet letters and words	Discovery of meanings and names of alphabet letters and words
Novelty books (pop-ups, fold-outs, stamp and pasting books, activity books, puzzle books, scratch and sniff books, hidden objects in illustrations, talking books)	Adds sense-exploring variety Stimulates creativity Comes in many different sizes and shapes Motor involvement for child	Exploring, touching, moving, feeling, smelling, licking, painting, drawing, coloring, cutting, gluing, acting upon, listening to a mechanical voice, and getting instant feedback
Paperback books and magazines (Golden Books, *Humpty Dumpty Magazine*)	Inexpensive Wide variety Many classics available	Children can save own money and choose for themselves
Teacher- and child-made books	Reinforces class learnings Builds understanding of authorship Allows creative expression Records individual, group projects, field trips, parties Promotes child expression of concerns and ideas Builds child's self-esteem	Child sees own name in print Shares ideas with others Self-rewarding
Therapeutic books (books helping children cope with and understand things such as divorce, death, jealousy)	Presents life realistically Offers positive solutions and insights Presents diverse family groups Deals with life's hard-to-deal-with subjects	Helps children discuss real feelings
Seasonal and holiday books	Accompanies child interest May help child understand underlying reasons for celebration	Builds pleasant expectations Adds detail
Books and audiovisual combinations (read-alongs)	Adds variety Offers group and individual experiencing opportunities Stimulates interest in books	Projects large illustrations Can be enjoyed individually
Toddler books (durable pages)	Resists wear and tear	Ease in page-turning
Multicultural and cross-cultural books	Increases positive attitudes concerning diversity and similarity Emphasizes the realities in our society	Meeting a variety of people

Figure 9–12 Types of Books for Young Children (Reprinted by permission. Machado, J. M. (2003). *Early Childhood Experiences in Language Arts*, 7th ed. Clifton Park, NY: Thomson Delmar Learning, pp. 271, 272.)

in writing begins with the small muscle control of the writing tool, pencil, marker, or crayon. This is influenced greatly by the environment that makes these accessible. The adult is a role model for writing lists to remember. Labels are written on items to signify possession. Writing is demonstrated by the adult who says, "This is how you write your name."

Writing is more than mastery of the tools, or symbols of reading. In fact, researchers have found that many children actually write before they read, driven by the urge to communicate although they are limited in the knowledge of writing conventions. Wells calls this Writing to Read with this powerful statement: "When one has something important to say, and other people are interested in hearing it, it is then that language and thinking most fully interpenetrate in the struggle to make meaning that captures what one has observed and understood and communicate it to others" (p. 107).

Greenburg (1998) proposed twelve principles involved in learning to read, write, and spell well.

- language and literacy environments
- wide variety of experiences
- adult literacy role models
- enjoy books together with an adult
- alerted to sounds of words
- interested in recognizing letters and sounds
- encouraged to communicate in print
- learn that print is language written down
- recognition of name and many other words by sight
- decode other's writing
- principles of spelling and punctuation
- read aloud fluently

Stages of Writing. Writing develops in predictable stages. They are:

Scribbling. The child makes marks as soon as she can hold a writing tool. She begins by stabbing at the paper, the dragging action making lines. She progresses to unclosed circular motions, then to closed circles, vertical and horizontal lines, and eventually boxlike or square shapes. This phase is the preparation

Figure 9–13 Linear scribbles approximate writing.

for both drawing and writing. Many children extend scribbling into wavy lines they call writing after observing adults writing cursive (Figure 9–13).

Drawing. Written communication in the form of pictures has its historical roots in the Egyptian pictorials inside the pyramids. Children (and societies) without writing convey meaningful messages by drawing. Young children are hindered by their lack of small muscle coordination and the ability to represent on paper the ideas they have in their head (Figure 9–14). They have a mental image of a horse but what they draw may not be recognizable as a horse to the viewer. Again, the receptive is greater than the expressive.

Children can express their thoughts by using drawing. This expressive language, known metaphorically as the "100 languages of children" (Reggio Children, 1996), has captivated the world through the work of the children of Reggio Emilia, Italy. Carolyn Pope Edwards, who has studied the Reggio approach in detail, calls the various media, such as photography, clay, or drama, "literacies," extending the child's visual expression beyond writing (Edwards & Willis, 2000).

Making Letters. Between the ages of three and four, children come to realize there is a difference between drawing and writing although it may not be evident to the viewer (Figure 9–15). The first letter they write is usually the first letter of their name. As their knowledge of the sounds and shapes of more letters expands, they will begin to write sentences. The first

letter of each word is sounded out and written down, expecting the reader to be able to decipher the message. It is an approximation that is bringing them closer to the symbols that combine to make words in a sentence. They will often ask for words to be written so they can copy them. They try their hand at **invented spelling,** as the boys did on their gift list, by sounding it out and writing the letter sounds that they hear (see "It Happened to Me: BLDZR").

Organizing Print. Writing is more than knowledge of letters and their sounds; it is the proper sequence, organization on the page, and spaces between that form written language. Random letters will appear in children's paintings and art work whether they have meaning or are just practicing the style.

Name writing can be encouraged with daily sign-in as Green (1998) suggests. Through this early literacy experience, name writing was a transition routine into the classroom that formalized the children's presence, developed their fine muscle control, and documented their writing progress.

Dictation. While a child draws, an adult talking with the child may elicit the thinking that is not revealed in the drawing because of the child's lack of physical ability and representational skills. As the child relates meaning, the adult may ask if the child

Figure 9–14 Children's drawings often are the expression of inner thoughts and words before writing has developed.

Figure 9–15 Drawing and writing are beginning to separate from one another.

wants the story written in words that others can read. If so, in the act of dictation the child is seeing oral language translated into written language. It may even help the child add detail to the drawing by thinking about it more concretely in order to express the meaning to another person. This is an example of scaffolding (Fields & DeGayner, 2000; Oken-Wright, 1998).

Backward Letters. Preschoolers in their experimentation with letters, and perhaps due to their still-developing visual perception, often reverse letters to their family's alarm. Sulzby, who has studied children's writing for over fifteen years, says it is common for preschoolers to write backward and switch from backward to forward (Sulzby, 1993) (Figure 9–16).

Writing to Read. Many Kindergarten classes are encouraging children to write their thoughts and tell about experiences using invented spelling and illustration preceding formal reading instruction. Children demonstrate a level of phonemic awareness by sounding out the words and writing down the sounds they hear. Look at Figure 9–17 and you can almost hear my grandson carefully writing the letters that he hears to convey the meaning of the story about teeth. You can see he has learned about full sentences with subject and verb and the use of a period at the end of each sentence. The teacher has interpreted his words and written the conventional spelling beneath. The illustration of his family all brushing their teeth completes his story. It is a precious artifact of his pathway to literacy.

Incorporate Writing into Play. By ages five and six, children realize that writing serves the function of conveying information. They will make signs to designate territory or "Do not disturb," print their name on their artwork so they can take it home, and use writing to tell stories or write letters. In the dramatic play area, writing materials are provided as they would appear in context. In housekeeping, put a note pad by the phone, include grocery advertisements, list paper, and a pencil nearby. A shoe store would include sales slip books. A restaurant would need menus with pictures and words, server pads, and checkbooks. A grocery store would need flyers, open and closed signs, help-wanted signs, and worker sign-in sheets.

Journal Writing. Many early childhood classrooms have begun daily journal writing for children to make an entry about the day. It may begin as pictures but move to include or become exclusively print. If the child dictates, or the teachers read and interpret the pictures and print, it is a form of personal communication, but also provides a way of ongoing assessment (Williams & Davis, 1994). The *Living Classroom: Writing, Reading and Beyond* (Armington, 1997) gives wonderful examples of children's early writing for expression, full of invented spelling and enchanting children's drawings as representations of thought. Journals allow children to control the topics about which they write, use their abilities at any level without risk, and to communicate original thoughts (Block, 2001).

Literacy and Technology

EXERCISE: How computer literate are you?

Now two-thirds of American homes have computers and many schools and early childhood programs have them as well (U.S. Census Bureau, 2001). Young children have a great interest in using them to imitate adults (Figure 9–18). With the myriad of software available, they are actively involved in the manipulation of symbols, pictures, and letters. The explosion of software for young children has addressed this market but not without controversy. In this age of technology, all advances must be carefully considered for their appropriateness and value to the development of the child.

Computers can serve the same purposes as any other learning area. They can be explored by manipulation, a vehicle of social interaction with peers, and provide a time of interaction with an adult. These all add to the child's general development as well as literacy competency. With the computer, children produce their own pictures, text, and even their own books. Holdaway (1979) prophetically stated, "The difficulty of handwriting and spelling tend to delay

---

IT HAPPENED TO ME

Make Love

Another writing incident is an anecdote I will always remember. A dear, sweet little four-year-old girl came over to me in class one day and said, "Mrs. Nilsen, I know how to make love. Want me to show you?" Gulp! "Sure." She got a sheet of paper and proudly wrote L U V. We rejoiced together!

DEAR. MRS. NILSEN

I MISS. YOU. VERY MUCH
THANK YOU FOR. THE MARKER

LOVE   MEGAN

Figure 9–16 Early writing ignores many rules but is precious for its effort and meaning.

any genuine desire to produce written language for a purpose" (p. 36). The computer removes that obstacle with software that accepts phonetic spelling, spell checks as words are written, and provides picture and word combinations.

The integration of computers into the learning environment is their most effective use. This does not mean a computer lab down the hall where children spend a period of time. True integration of a computer in the classroom uses it as a tool to explore. The computer can enhance language, mathematics, and science and also social interactions (Davis & Shade, 1994).

The teacher's role in using technology as an early learning experience is not different than any other experience. First is to set the environment by safely

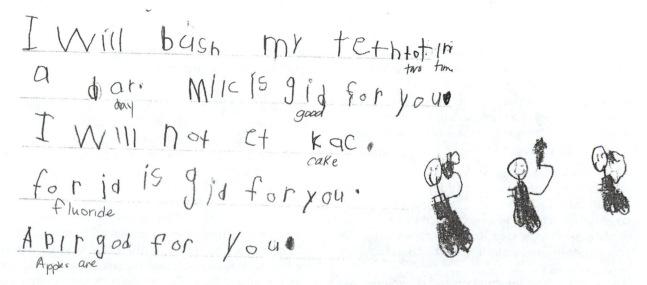

Figure 9–17 This child's early writing testifies to extensive knowledge of good dental hygiene.

Figure 9–18 All writing tools begin with manipulation, mastery, then meaning.

setting up the computer in a place that is inviting and with software that supports class themes. The adult models safe and appropriate use, turn-taking, and works with the children then guides them to explore on their own. Facilitating problem solving by pairing children will encourage peer assistance, and observing children as they use the computer will inform the teacher about the child's communication, collaboration, and problem-solving skills (Haugen, 1998).

Children with learning disabilities and different learning styles have been found to use the computer as a way of finding success in learning. Assistive technology devices were included in the Education of the Handicapped Act Amendments of 1986 (P. L. 99-457) and the Individuals with Disabilities Act (IDEA: P. L. 101-476). Computers promise new ways for the disabled to access not only learning and knowledge but focused behaviors. Behrmann and Lahm (1994) also emphasize the use of computers as a play form in special education that allows children choice, independence, and a mode of expression.

Beaty (2000) says the teacher observes the child move from manipulation level to mastery to meaning and suggests the Computer Area can reveal development in the following areas:

social—turn-taking and sharing
physical—eye–hand coordination, visual discrimination
large motor activities—exercise activities
cognitive—shapes, sizes, colors, opposites, matching, classifying, counting, measuring, sequencing, memory skills
language—giving information and directions, asking and answering questions, discussing operations with a partner, making exclamations

creative—drawing, problem solving, music
emotional—autonomy

An issue of concern is the inequity of access. In a U.S. Census Bureau survey (2000), 94% of high-income homes had computer access compared to 34% of low-income homes and Blacks and Hispanics had half as much access at home as whites. The same survey showed that access to computers at school is closer than was reported in 1995, with 84% for whites and 71% for Blacks and Hispanics. Girls have been found to use the computers less than boys, widening the gap in perceived abilities in the math and science areas. These are valid concerns observant teachers need to keep in mind. Technology offers opportunities beyond imagination but many teachers are still "techno-phobic." Fears of the "teaching machine" are discounted by Davis and Shade (1994): "Potentially powerful and stimulating, the computer is only an inert object that can never be a substitute for the personal touch of the classroom teacher."

There is still the caution about the amount of time a young child spends at a computer and the type of programs the child is using (Kelly, 2000). The Alliance for Childhood, a group of educators and professionals concerned about America's children, made this statement in the executive summary of their publication *Fool's Gold: A Critical Look at Computers in Childhood* (2001): "Those who place their faith in technology to solve the problems of education should look more deeply into the needs of children. The renewal of education requires personal attention to students from good teachers and active parents, strongly supported by communities." (p. 4).

Ways to Document Reading and Writing Progress

Literacy involvement can be observed across all learning areas. A multitude of methods, then, are used to observe the various forms that literacy takes.

Class List Logs can survey the group for a reading and writing interest, behavior, skill, or participation. Taped on the wall in the book area, it is used to record each time a child selects a book as a choice activity, acting as a Frequency Count. A Class List Log could be used to record a child's listening behavior during story reading time. Time Samples indicate how long a child chooses to spend in the book area or writing center. Interviews or asking questions about a story can document the child's understanding of what was read. Anecdotal and Running Records might contain information about the child's use of literacy in structured and unstructured situations. Photographs and videos capture children's reading and writing graphically while their computer-generated stories provide technological evidence. Tape recordings of a child reading or pretending to read give clues not only of reading ability but speech production.

More formalized assessments like checklists of specific reading and writing skills can be purchased or self-made. Samples of the child's writing, dictation, and bookmaking provide information about the level the child has attained. Reading records, sometimes called Running Records, are notations made on scripts of book texts during oral reading (Chittenden & Courtney, 1989). This system requires the individual, concentrated attention of the teacher.

Whatever method is selected, a systematic gathering of documentation shows the progress of literacy.

HELPING ALL CHILDREN WITH LITERACY

Language, whether spoken or written, occurs in the context of children's lives. Children who are Limited English Proficient (LEP) may or may not be literacy limited. It depends on the culture and the family circumstances. "Children who are learning English as a second language are more likely to become readers and writers of English when they are already familiar with the vocabulary and concepts in their primary language" (Neuman et al., 1999), adding English while maintaining their home language. Literacy materials in the classroom should reflect the home language as well as English. All children should be assessed to find the level of development approached as a strength or level of achievement, then individualized plans should be made to help the child attain the next level. When literacy materials are placed throughout the classroom environment, this individualization for diverse populations is also possible.

Physical Disabilities and Literacy

When physical or mental limitations are present, literacy development may be affected. Visual impairments will slow or prevent the progression of reading and writing. By providing high-contrast documents and writing tools, along with tactile materials such as sandpaper, plastic magnetic, or raised alphabet letters, children with limited vision can be included in the world of literacy. Reading to them is also an important part of their literacy world. Children with hearing impairments may have affected

language development, which also affects literacy. Using visual cues for communication may be even more important. It is a critical component of both receptive and expressive language. With the help of assistive and adaptive technology, computers can help overcome visual, hearing, and physical limitations. Braille keyboards, voice activated and audio output computers open the world of literacy. Working with children with hearing deficits in the area of reading and writing is an important facet of the teacher's role.

Learning Disabilities and Literacy

Literacy, the ability to read and write, is the area in which learning disabilities are the most evident. One of the early labels of reading difficulties was dyslexia, often characterized by writing alphabet letters backwards or confusing similarly shaped letters like *b* and *p* (which all children do when learning to write and continue this confusion to six and seven years old). This is just one symptom of a larger range of difficulties. The term learning disabilities describes people within the range of normal intelligence, without significant behavioral disorders, but with low academic achievement because of the inability to read and write.

The actual causes for learning disabilities are still under study. Neurological causes, a brain dysfunction, is one explanation. Vision and perceptual processing difficulties is another theory that has spurred some to seek vision training as a remedy with mixed results. Psychological and emotional causes have been investigated, but academic difficulties affect a child's psychological and emotional well-being so it has been difficult to determine if this is a cause or an effect. Environmental causes, such as extreme poverty and a lack of cognitive stimulation, have been recognized as connected to learning disabilities; however, there are many middle-class children with learning disabilities, so environmental causes cannot be the total answer either.

A recognized definition, diagnosis, and label were needed to secure services for children with academic underachievement. The Association for Children with Learning Disabilities has defined the term *specific learning disability* as "a chronic condition of presumed neurological origin that selectively interferes with the development, integration, and/or demonstration of verbal or nonverbal activities" (in Hallahan and Kaufman, 1986). Young children with learning disabilities are extremely difficult to diagnose because they are in the prereading stage. The two primary behaviors characteristic of learning disabilities are impulsiveness and indiscrimination (the inability to tune out distractions or concentrate on a task in an orderly fashion), as defined by Samuel Kirk, who coined the term *learning disabled* (as cited in Hallahan & Kaufman, 1986). These two characteristics are common in all young children. When they are prolonged or exaggerated, learning disabilities may be suspected. They are also characteristics of hyperactivity and ADHD.

The role of the early childhood observer is to closely monitor the literacy progress, along with other areas of development and behavior, aware of indications of difficulties and referral agents from whom help may be secured.

Literacy and Children Whose First Language Is Not English

Becoming literate and finding school success, overall well-being, and ability to compete in society is complicated when the child's oral and written language is not English. Children are at even greater risk if they come from a home that is economically disadvantaged (Snow, Burns, & Griffin, 1998). Snow found four key components of the home literacy environment: the value placed on literacy, the press for achievement, the availability and use of reading materials, and parent–child book reading. Children who are language learners in a language other than English come into the early childhood setting with a wide range of literacy exposure. They may have observed adults writing and seen a written form of their own language, such as books, newspapers, and letters. They may have story books printed in that language. Early writing follows the same stages: scribbling, drawing, and forming letters. The writing may appear in another form if the symbols are not alphabetic, with scribbles appearing vertically rather than horizontally for Asian children, for example. They will continue to acquire native language literacy from home and an expanded language and literacy in English from the early childhood setting. Children who have little or no early experiences with print come to school at a disadvantage. Neuman and Roskos (1993) say, "Bilingualism often has a negative effect, leading to low levels of ability in both languages" (p. 80).

For all children, and especially English language learners, picture books are excellent ways to communicate universal messages and have a shared experience not based on spoken language. Looking at picture books enhances vocabulary growth. Literacy success in the second language depends on the same factors as oral language for all children, an environment filled with materials and activities. Individual

IT HAPPENED TO ME

Working to Communicate

One of my college students was in a practicum placement in a program in which there was a child from Vietnam who spoke no English. She struggled to communicate. Finally, on her own initiative, she made a book of common items in the classroom from a mail order catalog. She found a translator to write the words for the items in the child's language, as well as phonetic spelling in English so she could pronounce it. That book went back and forth from home to school, aiding both in communicating. Everyone benefited. She received an A.

interactions enhance both language and literacy. The environment and curriculum include real opportunities to use literacy, such as name lists, drawing and writing materials, story books to look at, and adults reading and pointing to pictures and words. Children will write if they have reason to do so, even if they are not able to speak the language (Urzua, 1987). All children need an accepting social atmosphere of language attempts. Adults who allow and encourage native language speaking and writing demonstrate an overall acceptance of the child and the family. Pictorial and word labels in the classroom will help all children associate the object with the written word. Meaningful opportunities to write give older children with limited English a way to communicate. Young children with limited English proficiency can learn vocabulary, customs, and find enjoyment through books and literacy materials. As mentioned previously, the home may already be literacy-rich with books and writing in the family's language. Families should be encouraged to read to their child in the home language and involve the child in community activities in the first language and in English (Grant & Wong, 2003). Stories recorded on tapes, dictionaries that have familiar items in both languages, and books in the first language of every child are helpful toward literacy development. Literacy materials can be sent home for reinforcement and enjoyment by the whole family.

Cultural differences other than native language also affect the child's literacy development. Cultural differences also have been found in the amount and type of early vocalization with infants and young

TOPICS IN OBSERVATION

Books in the Sandbox

EXERCISE: List the literacy materials (reading or writing) in each of the rooms in your home.

   Kitchen   Living room   Bedroom   Bathroom

Most homes have some kinds of literacy materials in every room. From cookbooks to magazines, every room has literacy materials. Why then does the early childhood classroom restrict books to the book area and writing materials to the writing center or art area? It probably is for the protection of the books or the walls from indiscriminate writers. What it does, however, is artificially restrict literacy to certain areas, unlike real life. If the classroom is to be a microcosm of the world outside, then perhaps these restrictions need to be reconsidered. Use the placement and proliferation of books and writing materials throughout the environment as an assessment tool of the literacy-rich environment and the teacher's own literacy priority.

How about books about the beach or archaeology in or near the sandbox? In the art area, books about colors, even art books with prints of the masters, could stimulate interest in color, form, texture, and art expression. Books about buildings and skyscrapers, and pencils and paper to trace blocks or sketch buildings will add a literacy component to the block area. Books or magazines on the back of the toilet might capture the interest of a child not ordinarily sitting in one place very long.

In the dramatic play area, books or magazines and writing materials can connect literacy to whatever dramatic play theme is set up there. A medical office would have an appointment calendar, magazines in the waiting room, and books of anatomy or stories about the hospital. The car repair shop would have auto repair manuals, car magazines, order forms for repairs, and invoices.

Another artificial classroom literacy behavior is reading to the whole group of children at one time. In the outside world, reading and writing are usually individual activities. Individualized reading is enhanced when books and reading materials are integrated throughout the classroom environment. Then the adult can read to every child connected with the context of their play or suggest writing as a mode of communication that facilitates the play. Reading and writing are then associated with their play theme, and assimilated and accommodated into their knowledge base. It is connected with real objects and real purposes, not just another isolated routine on the daily schedule.

By desegregating literacy from the library or writing centers, children see the practical use of reading and writing. The adult role is to help fill the span between their actual ability to read and write and a higher level, to provide that scaffold, by suggesting researching books for answers to questions, or writing as a way to communicate ideas or preserve details.

Care of the books and writing materials is a valid concern, but some principles can reduce the worries.

- Once the decision is made that literacy materials will be accessible throughout the environment, preparations are made for book pockets or racks near the sandbox, easels, and other play areas. A section of the block shelf can just as easily hold books and literacy materials along with wheeled vehicles and block accessories.
- When materials are useful and important to children, they will treat them carefully.
- Adult role models of caring for books and using writing materials in a constructive way will be attended to by the children.

Think about how the opportunities to observe children's literacy skills will be expanded if the materials are included in every area.

children. Middle-class families and teachers are more verbally responsive and referential, giving names to items and repeating them, such as "Doggie. Doggie." Nonmainstream cultures rely more on body language, teasing, and traditional stories using dialects and non-standard English. Many cultures do not consider literacy an important component of the young child's world but hold it as a rite of passage into the adult world. This cultural difference will pose challenges to the early childhood program in helping these children reach the level of familiarity with not only the spoken language but the written language as well.

HELPING PROFESSIONALS FOR LITERACY CONCERNS

Children who need further help in the area of literacy development, reading, or writing should begin first with a physical examination. Vision, hearing, or neurological problems may interfere with literacy development. Speech and language difficulties could be contributing factors, so evaluations in these areas may be considered. Helping professionals in the area of literacy are:

reading specialists—teachers with specialized training in the teaching of reading, and diagnosis and remediation of reading and writing difficulties

special education teachers—teachers with knowledge of literacy disorders and strategies for overcoming learning disabilities

bilingual teachers or interpreters—people who can translate writing materials and communication in the family's first language

OTHER METHODS

Other Methods to Record Literacy:

Anecdotal/Running Records—Narrative about a child's interaction with reading or writing, wherever it occurs

Checklist—Presence or absence of literacy-related skills

Frequency Count—Elements of literacy to measure skills such as recognition of sight words in a passage, hesitations in oral reading, number of misspellings in a passage or list of words

Time Sample—Attention span during story time, ability to sustain in self-reading, amount of time spent writing a passage in a journal or working on a literacy computer program

Conversations or Interviews—Listening to oral reading, discussions about story themes and characters for understanding, conversations preceding writing in a journal or constructing a story

Work Samples—Writing samples, tape recordings of oral reading

Media—Photographs or videos of the child engaged in reading and writing behaviors

KEY TERMS

contextualized literacy	learning disabilities
dyslexia	phonemic awareness
emergent literacy	quality points
environmental print	Rating Scale
interrater reliability	selective method
invented spelling	

WEEK 9: PLAN A

RATING SCALES IN LITERACY

For Students

Select four children and complete the Literacy Rating Scale found in Appendix D. As an additional or alternative assignment, complete the ECERS Rating Scale on the classroom in which you are working.

Practitioners

Copy the Literacy Rating Scale found in Appendix D, or use the literacy assessment tool chosen by your program. Sometime this week, watch how each child uses books, listens to story books being read, and uses writing. Mark the Rating Scale with the date on each attained level. Return to this later in the year to evaluate progress.

What to Do with It

Filing. Make a summary note on the Portfolio Overview Sheet, and file the Rating Scale in the child's portfolio (Figure 9–19).

LITERACY DEVELOPMENT			
Documentation	Location	Recorder	Date
RS	Portfolio	BAN	11/3
RS	"		1/18
RS	"		4/17
AR	"		4/29

Figure 9–19 Portfolio Overview Example

If lower levels of literacy than expected are observed, make notes in your daily plans to give the child some attention or planned activities in that area.

Sharing with the Child and Family. Share your findings with the family or the child, if appropriate. For example: "Mrs. Chen, while I was noting each child's interaction with books, I saw how Mashiko listened so closely to the story and was able to tell it back word for word. That's the first step in learning to read," or "Today when you were playing in the grocery store I saw how you made that sign that said *Coke*. I didn't know you knew how to write!"

Actions.

Read a Book.

Archambault, J., & Martin, B. Jr. (1989). *Chicka Chicka Boom Boom.* New York: Scholastic.

Fleming, D. (1993). *In the Small, Small Pond.* New York: Henry Holt & Company.

Maritin, B. (1967). *Brown Bear, Brown Bear, What Do You See?* New York: Holt, Rinehart & Winston.

Sendak, M. (1962). *Chicken Soup with Rice.* New York: Harper & Rowe.

Van Allsburg, C. (1987) *The Z Was Zapped.* Boston: Houghton Mifflin.

Winch, J. (1998). *The Little Old Lady Who Loved to Read.* New York: Holiday House.

In the Environment.
- This whole chapter speaks of the print-rich environment. Make special provisions for opportunities for reading and writing in every learning center, including active play, blocks, and sand/water.
- Book Center should be filled with many kinds of books including class photo albums. Books should also be placed in the corresponding areas such as art books or books with interesting illustrations in the Art Area, cookbooks in housekeeping, dramatic story books in Dramatic Play area, books about buildings in the Block Area, and even books about the beach near the Sand/Water Area.
- Writing Center could include all kinds of writing materials including greeting card fronts with sample messages to copy, "Happy Birthday," "Get Well," and "I Love You."

In the Curriculum.
- Provide for writing activities from scribbling with the very youngest to daily journals and book production with other children.
- Author studies focus on several books by the same author. Even young children can see the similarities in writing style, illustrations, and themes.
- Books are launching points for curriculum planning in all areas such as *Stone Soup* for sharing (social development discussions and activities) vegetables for the soup (vocabulary, scientific process from hard to soft, raw to cooked), dramatization of the story for language and memory expansion, and modern-day parallels to fear of differences and how they can be overcome.
- Literacy in dramatic play is fostered by providing related props and materials. For example: Post office dramatic play theme encourages writing as does restaurant with carbon order pads, bank with forms and pretend checkbooks.

In the Newsletter.
The first attempts at reading and writing are wonderful to behold. Photographs of early readers, first attempts at writing with "invented spellings" to decode can be interesting ways to further explain the development of literacy.

WEEK 9: PLAN B

CONVERSATIONS IN SPEECH AND LANGUAGE FOR GROUP D

Continue with the Conversations begun in Week 6, selecting children from Group D to have a conversation with each day this week. If possible, tape record the conversation as well as make written notes as you speak with each child. Have an informal conversation or structured interview as described in Week 6, Plan A.

What to Do with It

Filing. Analyze each conversation for what it reveals about the child's knowledge, emotional state, social development, and speech and language development. (Use the Speech and Language Checklist found in Appendix D.)

Enter the summary. Note your name and the date on the Portfolio Overview Sheet. If a significant lag appears, discuss it with your supervisor to confirm it. Then discuss it with the family. Have a list of sites where a speech and language evaluation may be obtained to give to the family.

WEEK 9: PLAN C

REFLECTIVE JOURNAL

Respond to the following by copying this page, making notations and filing it with your Reflective Journal, kept in a private file at home.

My own literacy rating scale:

I am a reluctant reader, for necessity only	I read the daily newspaper and that's about it	I read on vacation or to kill time	I love to read and always have a book going

I think I developed into that kind of reader because . . .

My favorite type of reading is_____ section of the daily newspaper, magazines such as _____,

religious reading such as _____, novels about _____,

nonfiction about _____

I write for:

necessity	to help me remember	to communicate with distant friends/relatives	to clarify or express my thoughts and feelings

This Reflective Journal . . .

REFERENCES

Alliance for Childhood. (2001). *Fool's Gold: A Critical look at computers in childhood—Executive Summary.* http://www.allianceforchildhood.net/projects/computers/computers_reports_fools_gold. Retrieved March 21, 2003.

Armington, D. (1997). *The living classroom: Writing, reading, and beyond.* Washington, DC: National Association for the Education of Young Children.

Beaty, J. (2000). *Preschool appropriate practices*, 2nd ed. Fort Worth: Harcourt Brace Jovanovich College Publishers.

Behrmann, M. M., & Lahm, E. A. (1994). Computer applications in early childhood special education. In Wright, J. L., & Shade, D. D. (Eds.). *Young children: Active learners in a technological age.* Washington, DC: National Association for the Education of Young Children.

Berk, L. E., & Winsler, A. (1995). *Scaffolding children's learning: Vygotsky and early childhood education.* Washington, DC: National Association for the Education of Young Children.

Block, C. C. (2001). *Teaching the language arts: Expanding thinking through student-centered instruction*, 3rd ed. Boston: Allyn and Bacon.

Boyer, E. L. (1991). *Ready to learn: A mandate for the nation.* Princeton, NJ: Carnegie Foundation for the Advancement of Teaching.

Carbo, M. (1996). Whole language vs. phonics: The great debate. *Principal, 75*, January 1996.

Chittenden, E., & Courtney, R. (1989). Assessment of young children's reading: Documentation as an alternative to testing. In Strickland, D. S., & Morrow, L. (Eds.) *Emerging literacy: Young children learn to read and write.* Newark, DE: International Reading Association.

Clay, M. (1975). *What did I write?* Auckland, New Zealand: Heinemann Educational Books.

Davis, B. C., & Shade, D. D. (1994). Integrate, don't isolate!: Computers in the early childhood curriculum. *ERIC Digest.* Urbana, IL: Clearinghouse on Elementary and Early Childhood Education. EDO-PS-94-17.

Edwards, C. P., & Willis, L. M. (2000). Integrating visual and verbal literacies in the early childhood classroom. *Early Childhood Education Journal, 27* (4), 259–265.

Elkind, D. (1987). *Miseducation: Preschoolers at risk.* New York: Alfred A. Knopf.

Fields, M. V., & DeGayner, B. (2000). Read my story: Increasing literacy of preschool children. *Childhood Education, 76* (3), 130.

Grant, R. A., Wong, S. D. (2003). Barriers to literacy for language-minority learners: An argument for change in the literacy education profession. *Journal of Adolescent & Adult Literacy, 46* (5), 386–394.

Green, C. F. (1998). This is my name. *Childhood Education, 74* (4), 226–231.

Greenburg, P. (1998). Some thoughts about phonics, feelings, Don Quixote, diversity and democracy: Teaching young children to read, write, and spell, Part I. *Young Children, 53* (4), 72–82.

Hallahan, D. P., & Kaufman, J. M. (1986). *Exceptional Children.* Englewood Cliffs, NJ: Prentice Hall.

Harms, T., Clifford, R. M., & Cryer, D. (1998). *Early Childhood Environment Rating Scale—Revised Edition.* New York: Teachers College Press.

Hart, B., & Risley, T. (1995). *Meaningful differences.* Baltimore, MD: Brookes.

Haugen, K. (1998). Using technology to enhance early learning experiences. *Child Care Information Exchange, 123*, Sept/Oct. 1998, 47–50.

Holdaway, D. (1979). *The foundations of literacy.* Sydney, Australia: Ashton Scholastic.

Jeynes, W. H., & Littell, S. W. (2000). A meta-analysis of studies examining the effect of whole language instruction on the literacy of low-SES students. *The Elementary School Journal, 101* (1), 21–34.

Kelly, K. (2000). False promise. *U.S. News & World Report, 129* (12), 48–55.

Machado, J. M. (2003). *Early childhood experiences in language arts* (7th ed.). Clifton Park, NY: Thomson Delmar Learning.

Meisel, S. J., Dichtelmiller, M. L., Jablon, J. R., Dorfman, A. B., & Marsden, D. B. (2001). *The work sampling system*, 4th ed. New York: Pearson Education.

National Academy of Early Childhood Programs (NAECP). (1991). *NAEYC Accreditation criteria and procedures.* Washington, DC: Author.

Neuman, S. B., Copple, C., & Bredekamp, S. (1999). *Learning to read and write: Developmentally appropriate practices for young children.* Washington, DC: National Association for the Education of Young Children.

Neuman, S. B., & Roskos, K. A. (1993). *Language and literacy learning in the early years: An integrated approach.* New York: Harcourt Brace Jovanovich.

New, R. S. (2001). Early literacy and developmentally appropriate practice: Rethinking the paradigm. In S. B. Neuman & K. K. Dickinson (Eds.). *Handbook of Early Literacy Research.* New York: The Guilford Press.

Oken-Wright, P. (1998). Transition to writing: Drawing as a scaffold for emergent writers. *Young Children, March, 1998*, 76–81.

Owocki, G. (1999). *Literacy through play.* Westport, CT: Heinemann.

Ponnuru, R. (1999). Fighting words: Why the reading wars aren't over. *National Review, 51* (17), 34–37.

Reggio Children. (1996). *The hundred languages of children: Narratives of the possible. Exhibit Catalog.* Washington, DC: Author.

Schickedanz, J. (1999). *Much more than the ABCs: The early stages of reading and writing.* Washington, DC: National Association for the Education of Young Children.

Senechal, M. LeFevre, J. (2002). Parental involvement in the development of children's reading skill: A five-year longitudinal study. *Child Development, 73* (2), 445–461.

Snow, C., Burns, M. S., & Griffin, P. (Eds.). (1998). *Preventing reading difficulties in young children.* Washington, DC: National Academy Press.

Sulzby, E. (1993). Encouraging emergent writers. *Scholastic Pre-K Today, 7* (4) 30.

Trelease, J. (2001). *The read-aloud handbook.* New York: Penguin Books.

Urzua, C. (1987). "You stopped too soon": Second language children composing and revising. *TESOL Quarterly, 21* (3), 279–305.

U.S. Census Bureau. (2000). *Home computers and internet use in the United States*: August 2000. http://www.census.gov/prod/2001pubs/p23-207.pdf. Retrieved March 23, 2003.

Wells, G. (1986). *The meaning makers: Children learning language and using language to learn.* Portsmouth, NH: Heinemann.

Williams. R. P., & Davis, J. K. (1994). Lead sprightly into literacy. *Young Children, 49* (4) 37–41.

Xu, S.H., & Rutledge, A. L. (2003). Chicken starts with ch!: Kindergartners learn through environmental print. *Young Children, 58* (2), 44-51.

RESOURCES

Burns, M. S., Griffin, P., & Snow, C. E. (Eds.) (1999). *Starting out right: A guide to promoting children's reading success.* Washington, DC. National Academy Press.

Fisher, B., & Medvic, E. F. (2003). *For reading out loud.* Portsmouth, NH: Heinemann.

Haugland, S. W. (2000). *Computers and young children.* ERIC Digest ED438926.

Machado, J. M. (2003). *Early childhood experiences in language arts* (7th ed.). Albany, NY: Thomson Delmar Learning.

Neuman, S. B., Copple, C., & Bredekamp, S. (1999). *Learning to read and write: Developmentally appropriate practices for young children.* Washington, DC: National Association for the Education of Young Children.

Owocki, G. (1999). *Literacy through play.* Westport, CT: Heinemann.

Roskos, K. A., Christie, J. F., & Richgels, D. J. (2003). The essentials of early literacy instruction. *Young Children, 58* (2), 52–60.

Schickedanz, J. (1999). *Much more than the ABCs: The early stages of reading and writing.* Washington, DC: National Association for the Education of Young Children.

Strickland, D. S., & Morrow, L. (Eds.) (1989). *Emerging literacy: Young children learn to read and write.* Newark, DE: International Reading Association.

Trelease, J. (2001). *The read-aloud handbook.* New York: Penguin Books.

For additional information on early education curriculum, visit our Web site at http://www.earlychilded.delmar.com

Using Work Samples to Look at Creativity

USING WORK SAMPLES TO OBSERVE A CHILD'S DEVELOPMENT

EXERCISE: What can you tell about the child who created the drawing in Figure 10–1?

You could probably tell this child has observed a dog closely. The drawing is accurately proportioned and detailed, so the age of the artist could be estimated, by one who knew the usual progressive stages of children's drawing, to be about six years old. Actually, this drawing was done by an active four-year-old with an avid interest in art. Compared to the stages of creative development, it is advanced for the chronological age of the artist.

Creativity comes from within and reveals the self, whether it is a three-year-old with a crayon drawing on the wall, or a great master with oils and canvas. The child's creative products can be used as effective revelations of developmental progress. Almost every developmental area can be assessed from observing a child manipulate creative **media.**

The old saying, "A picture is worth a thousand words," is true also of children's creative products. Children's work, done in the natural home or classroom setting, provides information that would take paragraphs to convey. Individual children and groups produce work that can serve as raw data for assessment. They can be collected over time, showing changes in development (McAfee & Leong, 2002). **Work samples** is the term for any of the child's products including but not limited to visual arts, all of

Figure 10–1 A drawing can tell a lot about a child.

which reveal many aspects of the child's development (Figure 10–2).

Materials can be contributed to the portfolio from various sources—the family, the teacher, or the child—depending on its purpose. In the *Week by Week* portfolio, information and documents are gathered from all three, with equal access as well. The child's access, of course, depends on the age, but even very young children can understand the portfolio is about them. They often want to see it, just as they love to look at photographs of themselves as babies. By including samples of their work, whether drawing, writing, or photographs, they realize its purpose as a chronicle of their development.

Children should be aware of the portfolio and its purpose as a receptacle for information about them. They are invited to add to the portfolio when they have work they feel is important to them. If the portfolio is a file folder, the child can decorate the four panels of the file folder periodically over the quarters of the school year. This personalizes it, but also makes it an episodic documentation of the child's work. The children can comment on their own work

---

IT HAPPENED TO ME

The Story of the Dog Drawing

The child who made me the drawing in Figure 10–1 was a mischievious boy with freckles and a sense of humor. He gave me the drawing as a surprise gift. It was preceded by a promise that I would display it on my refrigerator door. It has been displayed to a far wider audience as a prime example of a child's creative work going beyond expected stages. The drawing reveals so much about him and his development. His sense of humor is seen in the face of the dog.

Figure 10–2 Development Revealed in Work Samples

as a way of exploring their thinking. The observer listens to the child describe the memory of the work and comments on the progress from the child's viewpoint.

Children are very possessive of their work (as they should be) but usually are generous in allowing copies to be made on a copier. The color is lost but the line and form are preserved. Actually having a notebook for each child to draw in over the course of a year is another way of collecting drawings. It is more structured, drawing at the adult's request, and yields less spontaneous and natural art products. It also limits the types of media that can be used.

Three-dimensional creations such as sculpture, collages, mobiles, woodworking, sewing, and even movement can be preserved with photographs, documented, and added to the portfolio (Figure 10–3). Work can be explained with notes attached to the back. The background of the work, how it came to be done, and any dictation or child's words about the work can be written there. The teacher can make notations concerning the child's development that this work especially illustrates.

Portfolios contain samples of the child's work to document progress and illustrate the child's thinking. Because development is seen in children's graphic art products, they are a concrete way to document development. Children's drawings, paintings, scribbles, and block structure photographs or sketches are collected periodically to add to the portfolio. Genishi (1993) recommends reviewing children's art work portfolios when it is time to write progress reports or hold parent conferences. "When you review, look to see how well each child's portfolio captures his or her story of development . . . For example, include a series of paintings that shows a child's changing use of patterns. Use these stories to inform and enrich your written reports and your conversations with parents" (p. 67).

Other Work Samples for the Portfolio. Figure 10–4 is a list of various types of work samples.

The areas of development and other information the teacher gathers about the child can be observed from a child's creative work. Figure 10–5 is the Work Samples Checklist, which includes areas covered in *Week by Week* and some assessment criteria in the creative realm.

Advantages

Collecting work samples is an effective recording technique because it is done

- in a natural classroom setting, with the child selecting materials and working at her own pace

activity choices	manipulative maps
audio tapes	math games
baking projects	models
block constructions	murals
photos	pantomime
sketches	photographs of work
book illustrations	photography by child
book lists	plans and projects
book making	plays
charts and graphs	posters
child-authored books	projects
clay and Play Doh	puppets
manipulations	puzzles
collages	raps
collections	rebus stories
computer constructions	replicas
crafter's handiwork	rhymes
creative movement	rhythms
demonstrations	role play
dictations	rules
dramatic play scenarios	sculptures
exhibits	signs
flannel board depictions	silly sayings
group projects	skits
humor	sociodramatic songs
illustrations	sticker designs
innovations	story themes
jokes and riddles	typing
jump rope rhymes	video tapes
lists	woodworking

Figure 10–4 Work Samples. (Adapted from *Authentic Assessment of the Young Child*, 2nd ed. by Puckett/Black, © 2000, p. 245. Reprinted by permission of Prentice Hall, Upper Saddle River, NJ.)

Figure 10–3 Work samples can be three-dimensional.

WORK SAMPLES CHECKLIST

Child's Name_____ Dates _____

COMMENTS

Separation
- ❑ Separates from adult to work alone
- ❑ Works independently without requiring adult presence or direction

Self-Care
- ❑ Independently selects materials
- ❑ Makes preparations to work (Example: Puts on a smock)
- ❑ Uses materials independently
- ❑ Cleans up spills, messes
- ❑ Writes name on work
- ❑ Places finished product in proper place
- ❑ Washes and dries hands if necessary
- ❑ Replaces materials to storage place

Physical Development
- ❑ Controls whole body movement during work
- ❑ Controls small muscles to hold tool
- ❑ Controls tool to form desired product
- ❑ Draws, prints, paints, pastes
- ❑ Squeezes glue bottle
- ❑ Picks up collage materials
- ❑ Manipulates clay or Play Doh
- ❑ Cuts with scissors
- ❑ Controls body to stay within the space (on the paper, building on a rug, clay on table)

Social Skills
- ❑ Represents important people in his life in his work
- ❑ Desires and can work near other children
- ❑ Shares materials and supplies
- ❑ Engages in positive commentary on other children's work
- ❑ Works cooperatively on a joint project

Emotional Development
- ❑ Uses work to express emotions of happiness, anger, fear
- ❑ Verbalizes feelings about work
- ❑ Enjoys manipulation and creation
- ❑ Controls emotions of frustration when work meets difficulties
- ❑ Uses the media as a stress release, pounding clay, tearing paper, painting

Speech and Language Development
- ❑ Names scribbles, buildings, creations
- ❑ Talks about work using vocabulary connected with materials and design
- ❑ Uses language to describe process, intent, and satisfaction with product
- ❑ Vocabulary reflects knowledge of subject

CONTINUED

Figure 10–5 Work Samples Checklist Example

WORK SAMPLES CHECKLIST (continued)

COMMENTS

Memory and Attention Span
- ❏ Includes details in work from memories of experiences
- ❏ Focuses attention on project to produce a finished work
- ❏ Tunes out distractions of simultaneous play, talk, and work
- ❏ Gives attention and makes connections between environment and own work

Math and Science Knowledge
- ❏ Includes numerals and quantity in work
- ❏ Shows one-to-one correspondence in work designs
- ❏ Shows perceptual awareness of color, space, form
- ❏ Explores cause and effect and experimentation with variables in media
  (Example: sees differences in paint when water and sand are added)
- ❏ Observes similarities and differences, forming theories, and testing them out by manipulating the medium
- ❏ Working with clay or liquid—displays knowledge of the concept of conservation
  (volume stays the same even though form changes—ball flattened is the same amount)

Literacy
- ❏ Includes literacy in work
- ❏ Recognizes the difference between drawing and writing
- ❏ Uses materials to symbolize ideas
- ❏ Work illustrates or connects with stories
- ❏ Gives attention to art in story books and knows the difference between text and illustrations

Creativity
- ❏ Uses materials in a novel way, displaying flexibility in seeing new possibilities in materials
- ❏ Explores all facets of the medium
- ❏ Draws from experiences to create representations
- ❏ Incorporates creativity into other areas of play, constructing with blocks, drawing and constructing in dramatic play, forming designs in sand and other media
- ❏ Demonstrates creativity in sensory awareness (seeing, hearing, touching, smelling, tasting)

Self-Identity
- ❏ Displays risk-free attitude in work
- ❏ Reveals self in content of work
- ❏ Work shows a sense of identity and individuality
- ❏ Expresses satisfaction in work, confident self-esteem
- ❏ Portrays self, family, world in work
- ❏ Work demonstrates child's sex-role identification
- ❏ Work shows child moving from egocentric view of self to an awareness of self as part of larger society
- ❏ Indicates favorite art medium (singular), media (plural)

Group Time Behaviors
- ❏ Participates in cooperative and collaborative work

Interaction with Adults
- ❏ Involves adults in work as (facilitator, participator, director)

©Nilsen, B. *Week by Week: Documenting the Development of Young Children,* 3rd ed. Clifton Park, NY: Thomson Delmar Learning (2005).

Figure 10–5 Work Samples Checklist Example (Continued)

and direction, illustrating many areas of development.

- over a period of time, showing progress of development.
- as an expression of the child's thoughts and feelings more accurately and powerfully than an observer can describe them.

Disadvantages

Work samples might

- make the child overly conscious of manipulation or practice, not meant to be a statement.
- lead the observer to draw erroneous conclusions from the work.
- reflect the inferences of the selector. (The teacher may only gather scribbling or experimental pieces when actually the child does much more advanced work.)

Pitfalls to Avoid

For work samples to be part of an authentic assessment plan, they should be

- dated. (The changeable date stamp comes in handy here. Children can learn to date their work themselves.)
- gathered periodically by joint decision of the recorder and the child.
- accompanied by commentary or narrative concerning the work.
- kept in a separate folder from the portfolio if they become overwhelmingly large or if children want to submit many pieces.

What to Do with It

Children are possessive of their work, and so they should be. To collect work samples one must either file what the child forgets to take home, make photocopies, or take photographs of the work. There may be a tendency to ask a child to create something for the portfolio but that is not what we are seeking here. The purpose is to collect what is called *literacies*, modes of "recording and preserving experiences, reflecting upon, exploring and extending one's thoughts and feelings, and communicating and sharing ideas with others" (Edwards & Willis, 2000). Work samples are another way of documenting the child's development. They are incorporated into the child's portfolio with other documents as proof of development, testimonies from the child that demonstrate physical, social, cognitive, literacy, emotional,

and creative development. At the conclusion of the school year the samples are given to the family. It may be the policy of the school or program to keep copies.

Using Technology

Keeping piles of drawings can get cumbersome and take up valuable storage space. Using technology to file and access work samples is becoming easier and easier. Scanners can turn one-dimensional samples such as writing, drawing, and painting into an easily stored electronic document. Digital photography can capture two- and three-dimensional works such as collages, sculptures, block building, and other constructions. Using technology to store and access work samples as well as other pieces of documentation about each child, it is easier to utilize the information for program planning and sharing with the family. It also keeps the whole portfolio more secure than if it were in a file folder in a drawer or cabinet.

How to Find the Time

Capturing children's work samples is relatively time efficient when using a digital camera. A picture tells a thousand words and the child's work is spoken in a hundred languages or literacies as mentioned above. Taking photos is less time-consuming than writing descriptions or manipulating developmental checklists. It should not be the only method used, but it is very effective.

Observing Creativity with Other Recording Methods

Observing a child during the creative process and preserving the finished product as documentation provides valuable developmental information. The products are not only the outcomes of the child's development but are affected by it as well. Creativity is affected by development, yet by observing creativity, development can be observed and assessed (Figure 10–6).

Developmental checklists with a section on creative development can be used to gather quickly general observed behaviors for the portfolio. The actual work or replicas of it serve as the documentation or evidence for the decisions made on the Checklist or Rating Scale.

Anecdotal Recordings, detailed narratives of the action and exact words the child uses during and after the creation phase, are like the caption to the

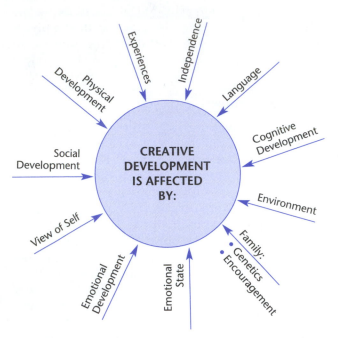

Figure 10–6 Many factors affect creative development.

Work Samples: Observing and collecting a child's product from which to draw conclusions about development, skills, and behaviors.

Types of Information to Record Using Work Samples

- separation
- self-care
- physical development
- social skills
- emotional development
- speech and language development
- memory and attention span
- math and science knowledge
- literacy
- creativity
- self-identity
- group time behaviors
- interaction with adults

illustration. The dictated words or quotations give the background or setting of the work. The action of the work is documented along with the exact quotes of the artist. It can inform the viewer and reader of the special circumstances that affected the child and the work.

Interviews while a child is working on a project are another way of gathering information. They reveal the child's understanding of concepts and increase the observer's understanding of the child's work. The child conveys the process and intent. Then it is not misconstrued by the observer. The child can narrate his thinking during the process. Isenberg and Jalongo (2001, p. 409) suggest questions to ask of the artist:

A Process Interview for the Visual Arts:

1. Why do people (paint, draw, sculpt, weave, etc.) pictures?
2. How do you get ready to make a picture?
3. How do you decide what to make?
4. Do you ever do artwork at home? If yes, how is art at home different from the art you do at school?
5. If you had to explain to a little child how a person makes a picture, what would you tell him or her to do?
6. Show me or tell me about your best art project. Why do you think this is your best work?

LOOKING AT CHILDREN'S CREATIVE DEVELOPMENT

Analyzing children's creative work is a visual demonstration of developmental principles. All children, all over the world, in whatever age they have lived, progress through the same basic stages in art or graphic representation. Historians who have studied pictorials on caves and rocks and alphabetic systems see the same designs that are seen painted by a child in day care in Chicago. Those combinations of circles, squares, straight lines, and curved lines had meaning for those people long ago, just as they do for today's child. Sylvia Fein, in her fascinating book *First Drawings: Genesis of Visual Thinking* (1993), compares artifacts from all over the world with children's first attempts at art. From handprints of the Anasazi Indians on cave walls in New Mexico (Figure 10–7), concentric circles from runic stones in Norway (Figure 10–8), depictions of people from the Caribbean (Figure 10–9), early artists in every age use universal signs.

Children's creative work is recognized as a window into their mind. Before a child symbolizes in writing, and sometimes even verbally, they use

Figure 10–7 Anasazi Indian handprints in New Mexico remind us of fingerpaint handprints that young children make today. (Courtesy of B. Nilsen.)

Figure 10–9 Caribs on the island of St. Kitts in 2500 B.C. drew people in the rocks that resemble preschoolers' early self-portraits. (Courtesy of B. Nilsen.)

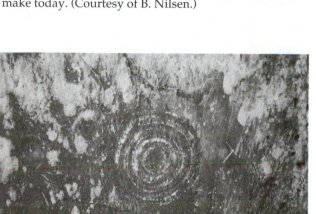

Figure 10–8 Concentric circles every four-year-old makes are similar to these ancient "runic stones" in Norway. (Courtesy of B. Nilsen.)

drawing as an expressive outlet. Many intelligence and psychological tests analyze a child's art to gain insight on the child's thinking and feeling. Careful study and classification of children's drawings have found predictable stages common to children worldwide, with curiously little variation (Kellogg, 1970; Lowenfeld & Brittain, 1987). This reinforces developmental theory that drawing is the representation of inner thought and connected with stages of development. The same factors that affect all other areas of development also affect the creative: genetic, environmental, and cultural. To accurately observe and assess a child's development from creative expression then, knowledge of the stages of creative development is vital.

Stages of Children's Art

Figure 10–10 illustrates the four stages of creative development.

Stage I. Mark-Making Stage (Birth to Two Years). The marks are random, done for pleasure and exploration, involving visual and physical movement. The child uses large muscles and whole-arm movement. Over time, the marks become more organized and are repeated. The tool is held in a tight fist grip, with a rigid wrist.

Stage II. Scribbling Stage (Two to Four Years). Kellogg (1970) analyzed the scribbles of thousands of young children and cataloged them into separate substages. Scribbling becomes more controlled with the development of the small muscles, eye–hand coordination, and cognitive abilities. The child uses a finger grip, with small, more-controlled movements. The marks usually are controlled to the confines of the paper. During this stage, the child is still experimenting with line and practicing muscle control. The child intently works and develops designs in variations of the circle. Once language is developed, the child attaches names to the scribbles. She may have a mental image when she draws but the mind and muscles are not coordinated enough so the drawings are usually not recognizable to others. She might identify drawings, and as the stage progresses they become more representative of her mental image, to the point that the viewer recognizes the object. The

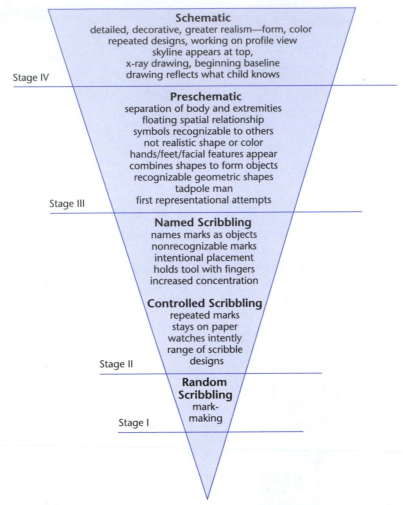

Figure 10–10 The Four Stages of Creative Development (Adapted from Kellogg, 1970; Lowenfeld & Brittain, 1987; Schirrmacher, 2002.)

first representation of humans begins to appear in this stage.

A definite progression of geometric shapes and representations occurs in this order:

1. Circles. As small muscle coordination develops, the circle becomes rounded. Finally, the line connects to close the circle completely.
2. Vertical and horizontal lines. These become more deliberate and crosses and Xs become part of the experimentation with the art medium.
3. Mandalas. A **mandala** (Figure 10–11C) is a combination of a cross inside a circle. The word means *circle* in Sanskrit. In Oriental religion, it is regarded as the symbol of the cosmos. In Jungian psychology, the mandala is representative of the psyche with the collective unconscious (Kellogg, 1970, p. 68). These extended meanings raise the

mandala's significance. All children universally pass through this stage.
4. Suns. The circle with radiating lines (Figure 10–11D) becomes one of the first symbols children draw.
5. Radials. Straight lines radiate from a central point to form a circlelike shape (Figure 10–11E). Radials also occur in the controlled scribbling stage.
6. Tadpole man. During the third and fourth years, children begin to represent humans in a curious symbol that resembles a **tadpole man** (Figure 10–11F). They combine the circles and lines into a head with features. This is understandable when the earliest images are considered. For months, the infant concentrates closely on the human face. The arms and legs are added later just as their awareness of them came later. The circle repre-

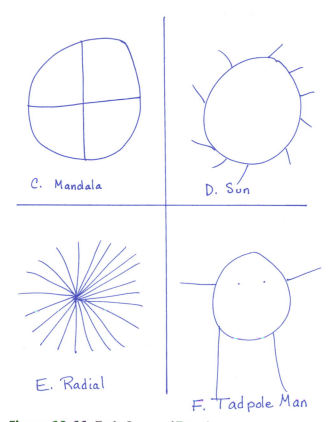

Figure 10–11 Early Stages of Drawing

Older preschoolers are trying to represent their mental images to others and yet much of what they create is still nonrepresentational and without realism to the viewer. They draw what they *know*, not what they *see*. They surely see more than they are able to draw. They experiment with the medium and often play with the tools. No message or intent for representation may be present.

At the beginning of this stage, there is little regard for realism in color, size proportion, or exact details. These aspects continue to be more evident as the stage progresses. By the end of this stage, the child can copy a square by bringing a single line back to the beginning with defined corners.

Details on the human figure increase, with the body becoming more like a snowman. The neck separates the head and body circle, and ovals appear, representing the arms and legs. Hands move from single lines, to more lines, then accurately drawn five digits, and eventually more of a glovelike hand. Anatomical representations appear as the child is striving for realism and gaining knowledge of gender differences.

By the end of this period, the child draws an accurate triangle and often uses a repeated pattern or design of symbols. The child begins to use drawings to express feelings, as well as visual images.

Stage IV. Schematic (Seven to Nine Years). In the schematic stage the child now has a well-developed schema repeated in all drawings to represent humans, homes, trees, clouds, all the relevant, important objects in the child's life. The child's drawing still represents concept rather than perception (what he knows versus what he sees). This is observed in a perspective problem: what to do with the hidden leg of a horse rider or the eyes in a profile view? The child draws these like x-ray vision or with both eyes, signifying he knows there are two legs or eyes. Drawing only one is not acceptable mentally to him. The baseline and skyline appear with a partial sun in the corner. Chimneys on roofs are at right angles to the roof line, making them askew to the baseline. As the child's cognitive development improves, the chimney becomes erect. Attempts at three-dimensional representation are beginning by drawing three sides of a building.

EXERCISE: Based on the developmental stages discussed, number Figures 10–12 through 10–17 one to six, in order of creative development.

Figure 10–12 is an example of a tadpole man with the beginning of some features. The circles and firm, straight lines show small muscle control. The artist is four years, one month old.

sents the whole body as they know it, so a circle with dots for eyes and a line for a mouth is the early person drawing. Arms, then legs, then fingers and toes, and more features appear in an orderly progression. This should remind the student of child development of the principle of cephalocaudal and proximodistal development.

Stage III. Preschematic (Four to Seven Years). Lowenfeld and Brittain (1987, p. 258) call the symbol a child draws for familiar objects a **schema.** The child experiments with drawing through the scribbling and the **preschematic** stages to develop these symbols. They are unique to each child yet similar because they follow the physical and mental developmental stages through which each child moves. Schirrmacher (2002) calls this stage Attempts at Public Representation. These attempts are **nonrepresentational.** It is difficult, if not impossible, for children in this stage to "Think of your favorite . . . and draw it." They are able to think of it but lack the fine muscle skills and cognitive ability to physically represent their thoughts. They are more likely to draw what they can, even a scribble, and say, "This is a butterfly." To the viewer, as well as the artist, it is a blob.

Figure 10–12

Figure 10–13

Figure 10–13 is definitely a scribble but a controlled scribble. The child left a margin around the page and confined marks to a located area. The artist is three years, two months old.

Figure 10–14 has separate, distinct body parts, characters on a baseline, representation of thought by drawing the basketball team and the important parts such as the basket, the basketball, and the scoreboard. Note that the child has numbers on the team uniforms not for counting but for realism. There are many signs this child is moving beyond the preschematic stage. The artist is five years, eleven months old.

Figure 10–15 is very realistic. Of course, this was by the oldest artist in the group. The drawing fills the page with the sky, sun, and clouds overhead and rain coming down. There is a definite baseline on which the person is walking and the cage and "giney pig" are sitting. The artist is attempting a profile—note one eye and no arms drawn—but he just cannot resist the smile, though misplaced. The artist is six years, two months old.

Figure 10–16 was done by the youngest artist at two years, three months. The dots are stabs with the markers and lines run off the paper as the child is attempting to gain control.

Figure 10–17 is the artist's practice, drawing the same form over and over, changing it slightly by the features. Alphabet letters are mixed in with the drawings. The artist is four years, five months.

Your sequence of stages should have been 1—Figure 10–16; 2—Figure 10–13; 3—Figure 10–12; 4—Figure 10–17; 5—Figure 10–14; 6—Figure 10–15. Comparing creative work from different children into developmental stages is not dependable but these are representative of the stages, and their ages happened to correspond. It is not always so. The principles of development prevail. The stages are sequential, but children do not pass through them at the same age. Collecting and comparing the drawings of each child to ones drawn previously is dependable documentation of progress.

Blocks As a Creative Medium

Construction materials are open-ended, used in very different ways by each child. This type of material, like any creative medium, gives the observer knowledge about many developmental areas. Blocks are varied in type but provide this kind of experience. They can be:

Plastic interlocking blocks—Legos or Duplos
Unit blocks—standard units are multiples of each
   other

Figure 10–14

Figure 10–16

Figure 10–17

Figure 10–15

Hollow blocks—standard units of each other but are large; constructed of many pieces nailed and glued together

Cardboard blocks—lightweight, often homemade from milk cartons

Foam blocks—geometric shapes and units; lightweight

Special building sets—Lincoln Logs, Erector sets, Tinkertoys, A-B-C blocks, PVC pipes

Cube blocks—one unit blocks either of wood or plastic, sometimes with locking features

The placement of shaped blocks on shelves, labeled with exact tracings of the block, builds one-to-one correspondence skills. The association of the shapes—square, rectangle, triangle, cylinder—is made not only with the shape but the word, making the literacy connection. Much of what goes on in the block building area is more than construction. It involves dramatic play, social skills, and language practice. The towers with resultant crashes bring excitement and danger themes to the block area. Accompanying props, such as farm and zoo animals, transportation vehicles, and miniature people, expand the play from functional to symbolic. By including textures, such as rug and fabric pieces, small pieces of turflike carpeting, and soft pillows, the area becomes a stress reducer as well (Figure 10–18).

Figure 10–18 Block play areas with accessories, literacy materials, and cross-over play from the dramatic area promote creativity.

Use other media to add details or recreate building

Make labels or write stories about building (with or without adult help)

Build structure large enough to accommodate self and others used in dramatic play

Build elaborate structure with pattern and symmetry

Plan systematically and name what they want to build

Share ideas, cooperate with others on a common building

Buildings with pattern repeated

Buildings related to others'

Using block structures as settings for dramatic play with figures of people, animals, cars

Combinations of enclosures and bridges

Building alongside others

Naming constructions

Building bridges

Enclosures

End to end

Side by side

Stacking

Carrying

Figure 10–19 Block Play Development

There are often physical barriers between the dramatic play area (housekeeping or family area) and the block area. This contributes to gender segregation, which is so common in these areas. By physically removing the barrier and encouraging the crossover of materials, it can help break down the stereotypes of play materials that are already present in preschoolers. Blocks can be taken to the oven to bake as bread. Block structures become homes where dishes and dolls can be added. By carefully planning the environment, the block area becomes another microcosm of development, affording the observer an excellent view of all areas of development.

Stages in Block Play. There are progressive stages in the way children interact with blocks, dependent on cognitive, social, emotional, and physical development (Figure 10–19), adapted from Hirsch, 1996, & Day, 1994).

Stage I. Carrying, Filling, and Dumping (Under Two Years). Children are in the sensorimotor stage, so they are exploring the attributes of blocks by feeling, lifting, and moving them from place to place.

Stage II. Beginning Block Building (Two to Three Years). Children make horizontal rows, laying blocks end to end or stacking. They repeat stacking and knocking down. They are beginning to observe the unstable effect of a small base with large blocks piled on.

Stage III. Bridging (Three Years). Two blocks are placed vertically as pillars with a third block placed

across the top. This takes visual acuity, small muscle coordination, and balance.

Stage IV. Enclosures (Three and Four Years). Four blocks are placed at right angles to enclose a space. This corresponds to the child's ability to draw a square, recognizing the connectedness of the angles and associating inside and outside concepts.

Stage V. Patterns (Four Years). Bridges and enclosures are repeated to form a horizontal or vertical pattern. Symmetry, a sense of balance and equal proportions, is demonstrated.

Stage VI. Naming Structures (Four to Six Years). Names and functions of buildings are assigned to the structures. Additional pieces like cars, animals, and play people add to the play. The play becomes more symbolic.

Stage VII. Reproducing True-life Structures (Five Years and Up). This stage is an expansion of Stage VI by trying to build more realistically and to incorporate dramatic play into the structures by moving play people and animals according to a script.

These block-building stages parallel the drawing stages: manipulation, simple experimentation, patterns, naming, and realistic reproduction.

Dodge, Colker, & Heroman (2002, pp. 244–245) outlined the goals and objectives of block play that serve as key points in observing block play (Figure 10–20).

Other Creative Media

Other materials or media such as clay, woodworking, or collage illustrate the child's development through stages similar to drawing. Small muscles interact with creativity to produce three-dimensional products. These often are not preserved but are materials returned to be manipulated in another way. The stages correspond to drawing (Figure 10–21).

Interaction with a tangible, movable medium is sensory, involving seeing, feeling, and often smelling. It helps the development of logico-mathematical thinking through manipulation. Physical properties of volume, weight, and length are transformed through play.

Creativity and Cognitive Development

Thinking and all the processes that link thinking and learning are integral to creativity. It should not be surprising. There are parallels between the stages of Piaget's cognitive theory (Flavell, 1963), art stages of Kellogg (1970) and Lowenfeld and Brittain (1987), and the social-emotional stages of Erikson (1950). They correspond to stages of development of language, reading, and writing. The ages of these stages are merely guideposts, not firm changepoints (Figure 10–22).

Creativity is dependent on symbolic thought. It is necessary to have existing structures and beliefs in reality against which to measure new data. It is dependent on cognitive ability, past experiences, and the present environment. Observing children's creative efforts can indicate:

1. Long attention span—When the activity captures their interest, they attend longer.
2. Capacity for organization—The organization of their creative work indicates their classification skills.
3. Seeing things in a different perspective—This does not go against the egocentric idea but refers

Social/Emotional Development
- Stands up for rights
- Demonstrates self-direction and independence
- Respects and cares for classroom environment and materials
- Follows classroom rules
- Plays well with others
- Shares and respects the rights of others
- Uses thinking skills to resolve conflicts

Physical Development
- Shows balance while moving
- Controls small muscles in hands
- Coordinates eye–hand movement
- Uses tools for writing and drawing

Cognitive Development
- Approaches problems flexibly
- Explores cause and effect
- Classifies objects
- Compares/measures
- Arranges objects in a series
- Recognizes patterns and can repeat them
- Shows an awareness of position in space
- Uses numbers in counting
- Makes and interprets representations

Language Development
- Expresses self using words and expanded sentences
- Answers questions
- Asks questions
- Actively participates in conversations
- Uses emerging reading skills to make meaning from print
- Understands the purpose of writing

Figure 10–20 Connecting block play with curriculum objectives.

to the child's ability to see things without preconceived notions.

4. Exploring before formal instruction—They have the need to manipulate first, and later organize into more conventional uses of tools and materials.
5. Using silence and time—Every parent knows that a quiet child is one that needs to be investigated, for there probably is some trouble brewing.

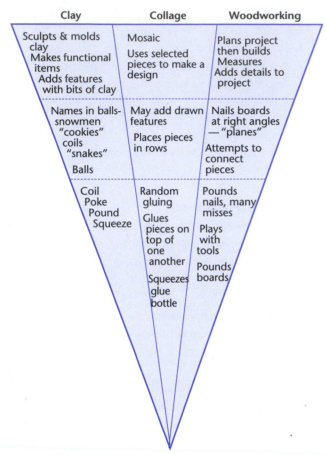

Clay	Collage	Woodworking
Sculpts & molds clay Makes functional items Adds features with bits of clay	Mosaic Uses selected pieces to make a design	Plans project then builds Measures Adds details to project
Names in balls-snowmen "cookies" coils "snakes" Balls	May add drawn features Places pieces in rows	Nails boards at right angles — "planes" Attempts to connect pieces
Coil Poke Pound Squeeze	Random gluing Glues pieces on top of one another Squeezes glue bottle	Pounds nails, many misses Plays with tools Pounds boards

Figure 10–21 Stages of Other Creative Media

Children get into trouble because they try things they do not know are dangerous or forbidden. This is an aspect of creativity like drawing on the sheets with lipstick or painting on the recreation room wall with tar.

6. Taking a "closer look" at things—Creative thinking involves manipulation and being close. It could be apples in a plastic bag at the supermarket or a climb to the top cupboard in the kitchen to investigate.

7. Using fantasy to solve developmental problems—Normal aspects of children's thinking are considered frivolous and even deceitful by adults. Children use creative ideas to explain, defend, and problem solve, such as, "The dog must have ridden my bike to the corner and left it there."

8. Storytelling and song making—Playing with words and music combines mental and creative abilities. Children need opportunities and encouragement to express themselves in the arts.

The child's creativity gives information about her cognitive development. The child does not go to bed one night in one stage and wake up in another. It is a spiral moving slightly upward that keeps returning to previous stages to find reassurance, success, and comfort when new stages become too stressful. Kamii (1982) tells the story of the boy setting the table, who moved from one-to-one correspondence to counting out the tableware. When guests were expected, he was not able to mentally add the number of guests to the number in the family. He had to go back to one-to-one correspondence again.

Disequilibrium sometimes invokes a return to a previous stage or strategy. It is seen in the child who has had a traumatic event in her life return to thumb-sucking, which brought so much comfort in a previous stage. In creative work, there is the return to the manipulation stage with the introduction of each new medium. The child uses sensory exploration of the materials, play without any purpose other than to get in touch with reality without pressure, before going on to actually represent thought.

Giftedness: Creative and Cognitive Development beyond Expected Levels. Many parents believe their child is gifted. The definition traditionally referred to an exceptionally high score on an intelligence test but has been broadened to include exceptional ability in other areas as well. In 1969, P. L. 91–230 contained a model program provision for gifted and talented children. Because of the limitations of standardized tests (see Chapter 8), many children were not identified as gifted because of cultural bias of the tests, resulting in low numbers of minorities in gifted programs. Little federal funding has been allocated for gifted programs but much research has been done in trying to define and identify giftedness. Some have to do with **precocity,** early development in areas such as language, music, or mathematical ability. The Renzulli-Hartman scales (in Torrance, 2000, p. 356) are commonly used for assessing creativity in preschool children.

1. The child has unusually advanced vocabulary for age level.
2. The child possesses a large storehouse of information about a variety of topics.
3. The child has rapid insight into cause-effect relationships.
4. The child is a keen and alert observer; usually "sees more" or "gets more" out of a story, picture, film, sightseeing trip, and so on.
5. The child becomes absorbed and truly involved in certain topics or problems.
6. The child strives toward perfection or excellence and is self-critical.

Piaget's Stages of Cognitive Development	Stages of Art Kellogg; Lowenfeld and Brittain; Schirrmacher	Language Development	Writing/ Reading	Erikson's Psycho-social Stages
Sensorimotor (b–24 months) Moving from reflexes to object permanence	Scribbling and mark-making (b–2 years) Random exploration Nonintentional	Pre/Language (b–2 years) Sounds, telegraphic sentences	Book Handling Skills (b–2 years) Right side up, front/back, turn pages	Basic Trust vs. Mistrust (b–2 years) Consistent experiences
Preoperational 2–7 years Egocentric Representation of objects and events by appearances	Personal Symbol and Design (2–4 years) Controlled scribbling, named scribbling	Beginning Language (2–4 years) Acquiring vocabulary, grammar, social speech	Function of print (2–4 years) Reads symbols in context Read pictures Beginning writing	Autonomy vs. Shame/Doubt (2–4 years) Independence, sensory exploration
	Preschematic (4–7 years) Generalized symbols recognizable to others Nonrepresentational	Language (4–7 years) Symbolic language Humor	Readers and Writers (5–8 years) Decode print Invented spelling Word identity	Initiative vs. Guilt (4–7 years) Constructive activities, own decisions
Concrete Operational (7–11 years) Logical, concrete thinkers. Can conserve, classify, seriate	Schematic/Realism (7–9 years) Representation of what he knows, not necessarily what he sees			Industry vs. Inferiority (7 years to puberty) Sense of duty, academic social competence

Figure 10–22 Stage Comparison of Cognitive and Creative Theorists

7. The child is interested in many "adult" problems such as religion, politics, sex, race, and so on.
8. The child likes to organize and bring structure to things, people, and situations.
9. The child displays a great deal of curiosity about many things and an intense curiosity about something.
10. The child displays a keen sense of humor and sees humor in situations that may not appear humorous to others.

Divergent thinking is the ability to think of a wide range of possibilities. It is associated with giftedness, rather than **convergent thinking,** the ability to arrive at a single answer. Its identification and measurement at an early age is complicated and inaccurate but close observers of children may see signs of giftedness. Assessment of every child's learning level helps meet the child's needs through curriculum planning. This same reason applies to giftedness.

Using Self-Portraits to Know the Child

EXERCISE: Look at the self-portraits by children four to five years old, Figures 10–23 through

10–26. Describe how very different they are in control, detail, and the mood they present.

The child's drawings of humans evolve from the beginning circle with dots for eyes. The child is drawing what is known. The human face, with eyes as predominant feature, represents family and self, drawn by hands still developing control. Arms and legs later protrude from this head and eventually more and more details appear as more "humanoid" drawings in the fourth year. As the child is closer to five, the neck separates the head and body, and limbs begin to take on more substance than just a line. Between five and six, the child usually can outline a drawing of the whole body in one stroke and begin to proportion the height of adults and children more accurately. This is in a predictable sequence (Kellogg, 1970). Three-dimensional work follows a similar sequence. In knowing that sequence, just like in knowing all developmental stage milestones, it helps the observer to recognize change and to anticipate and recognize the next stage when it appears.

The self-portraits in Figures 10–23 through 10–26 were drawn by four-year-old boys. It would be presumptuous to interpret levels of development from

Figure 10–23

Figure 10–24

Figure 10–25

Figure 10–26

Instinct over Knowledge

I had just discussed the responses to children's art with my college class. The next week, a mother with a newborn came to class to demonstrate the reflexes that were still present. She also brought her preschooler with paper and markers to occupy her while we watched her baby brother. As the demonstration drew to a close, I went over to the big sister and looked at her drawing. Out of my mouth came, "What is it?" The whole class gasped then laughed at my embarrassment at doing what I said not to do. It showed how ingrained those old habits are and how easily the instinctive comments slip out from among the learned behaviors. It takes practice and a concentrated effort!

one drawing. However, when the observer periodically collects children's self-portraits, along with the child's commentary about the work, the result is a more valid indication of cognitive and creative development.

Reggio Emilia and Children's Art

A discussion of children's creative development would not be complete without mentioning the child care centers and preschools in Reggio Emilia, Italy. They are the model of community and family collaboration and the integrated project approach to curriculum, but most of all, the incredible creativity of the children. Thousands of visitors from all over the world have been enthralled with the visually sensual learning environment that stimulates children to use a vast array of art materials. The image of the child is one of capability and respect. Teachers consider every aspect of the environment as stimulus for learning, for forming mental images that will be called upon to organize and construct meaning. The environment of beauty and light is breathtaking as one enters spaces of reception that welcome families with antique pieces of furniture and cozy sitting areas. Light streams through every possible opening and is reflected in mirrors, shiny surfaces, and translucent panels.

Observation is the adult's most important role and it is conveyed to the children as well. They are guided to closely observe the smallest seed, insect, or animal, detail of every physical part of the environment. The adult follows the children's interests and supports the graphic representation of what the child sees and explores. Documentation panels or booklets illustrate not just the finished product but the process, looking not at the outcome; their only objective is to make the learning public. This kind of documentation records not just what the child knows or knows how to do, but what the child can do with various kinds of environmental support—the contexts, opportunities, and materials offered to the child (Krechevsky & Stork, 2000). Documenting processes as well as outcomes is research that has its application in evaluation and curriculum decisions. Those who have visited Reggio Emilia have changed forever their ideas about the teacher's role as curriculum planner as well as the capabilities of young children to represent their world. When teachers change their approach, the result is children's creative efforts surpassing long-held developmental expectations (Dighe, Calomiris, & Van Zutphen,1998).

The Hundred Languages of Children (Edwards, Gardini, & Forman, 1998) brings Reggio children's projects to the world both in book and in exhibit form. Reggio advocates point out however that it is not about art but using art and other work samples as products of "children's emotional concerns, social relations, and creative and intellectual pursuits as they occur within the context of collaborative problem solving" (New, 1997). The beauty and richness of the colors, the complete absorption of the children in their work, and the planning of each project piques the curiosity of the viewer.

There is much more to the Reggio approach than simply documenting children's work. The approach begins with the image of the child with legitimate rights, as an active constructor of knowledge through investigation as a social endeavor. The teacher is not the fount of knowledge but a collaborator, colearner, guide, facilitator, and researcher. Curriculum develops from real interests of the children, who decide how to approach learning and then represent what they have learned in a meaningful way (Hewett, 2001). Trust is an important factor in this philosophy, as Linn (2001) points out. First, educators trust children's initiative and intelligence and let them experience things through trial and error, and even be allowed to fail. Parents of Reggio children trust the educators without the necessity of test scores to show that their children are learning. Linn also reminds us that learning is culturally bound and the lesson from Reggio is not to find ways to duplicate it but to "raise awareness about the connection between culture and educational practice in the United States."

After visiting Reggio Emilia, Carol Seefeldt (1995) describes the philosophy of considering creativity a serious work by teachers who

- understand cognitive theories of art.
- motivate children to produce art.
- carefully select teaching strategies. (p. 39)

Assessing Creative Program Goals

When work is not linked to standards and formally assessed, it is seen as less valuable to the educational process and endangered when resources are scarce. It is important for schools and programs to include creativity in goals and to assess creativity systematically as a contribution to cognitive development (Jalongo, 2003). Here are some of those efforts. *Dance, Music, Theater, Visual Arts: What Every Young American Should Know and Be Able To Do In the Arts: National Standards for Arts Education* (Consortium of National Arts Education Associations, 1994), outlines knowledge and skills children must have to fulfill their personal potential, to become productive and competitive workers in a global economy, and to take their place as adult citizens. In the Goals 2000: Educate America Act, the arts are listed as a core academic subject along with English, mathematics, history, science, and foreign language. These are standards for K–12, and are left to individual schools to implement.

Developmentally Appropriate Practice in Early Childhood Programs (Bredekamp & Copple, 1997) recommend "Children have daily opportunities for aesthetic expression and appreciation through art and music. Children experiment and enjoy various forms of dramatic play, music, and dance. A variety of art media such as markers, crayons, paints, and clay are available for creative expression and representation of ideas and feelings" (p. 132).

The *NAEYC Accreditation Criteria and Procedures* (1998) self-study asks programs to rate their opportunities for creative expression and appreciation for the arts.

Koster, in *Growing Artists* (2005), suggests the following for the space designated for art:

- Layout—Art activities should be in an area where the activities of the room are visible and influence the artist.
- Adequate space—Children need space to spread out and work comfortably.
- Traffic patterns—Flexible areas allow more children to explore, both at tables and on the floor.
- Water requirements—Location near the water source or moveable pans of water for prewashing minimizes messes.

- Separate from food areas—Art and cooking activities must be kept separate using separate tables and trays or at least covers for surfaces for one or the other, such as a tablecloth for eating or old shower curtain for art (pp. 106–108).

EXERCISE: Rate your classroom creative environment according to the preceding criteria.

Unmet   Partially Met   Fully met

On a separate sheet of paper, write an action plan to improve aspects of the environment to allow for more creative expression.

HELPING ALL CHILDREN WITH CREATIVITY

Creative work is both expressive and receptive. It requires no spoken language to create or enjoy someone else's creation. Even with limitations of language barriers, physical, cognitive, or psychological impairments, creative arts can be a form of two-way communication.

Cultural Diversity

Art is a universal language. The child may not speak a common language with the rest of the people in the group or share a common culture. Creative work can be a vehicle for becoming absorbed in an activity without pressure to speak or conform. Giving children creative materials with a minimum of direction is appropriate for this population and can be a comforting and successful activity in which to engage these children. It also gives them a way to express feelings and ideas nonverbally.

Ability Diversity

Art plans that are open-ended, designed to explore the medium, can be adapted to meet the needs of special abilities populations. Children with sight or hearing impairments can find great success in manipulating creative materials. Adaptive devices, such as bicycle grips on paintbrush handles, textured finger paint, and Play Doh with scent from powdered, nonsweetened drink mixes, add multisensory aspects to art medium. The manipulation of art materials is also soothing and sustaining for children with attention disorders.

Whatever the cognitive or physical functioning level of the child, open-ended art plans can be implemented and adapted to the child's capability. Frustration and lack of creativity are the outcomes of project-type art (really crafts) that demands a model and closely followed directions. The ability to succeed with these projects is very narrow, leaving most of the group either bored or disappointed.

Creative media are essential parts of every early childhood program. Art involves every developmental area and easily meets the needs of every child, despite their situation. It is a natural place to focus assessment in a nonintrusive way.

HELPING PROFESSIONALS FOR CREATIVE ARTS

Programs or individual teachers who want to enrich the creative environment can enlist the assistance of:

art educators—teachers who specialize in the incorporation of the arts into the curriculum

Individual children may be assisted in resolving emotional conflicts or behavior disorders by specialists who use the arts as therapy, such as:

art therapist—credentialed professional who helps increase self-understanding and emotional release through art media

music therapist—certified professional who uses music in treatment goals for people with handicaps for physical and mental health

OTHER METHODS

Other Methods to Record Creativity:

Anecdotal/Running Records—narratives about a child's approach to work

Checklists/Rating Scales—Work Samples Checklist or the creative portion of a developmental checklist

Conversations and Interviews—recording a child's discussions about work produced

Time Sample—measure the amount of time a child spends on a certain task

Media—use photographs, video or audio taping to document the process or the work produced

KEY TERMS

convergent thinking	preschematic
creativity	schema
divergent thinking	schematic
mandala	scribbling
media/medium	tadpole man
nonrepresentational	work samples
precocity	

TOPICS IN OBSERVATION

Responding to Children's Work

While observing children working, whether it is just enjoyably watching, or observing for a purpose, the adult is often called upon to comment on a child's work. The child may ask, "How is it?" or "Do you like it?" A ready answer is necessary, one that agrees with personal style, program goals, and theoretical philosophy. The following are presented for consideration and practice so that the teacher's repertoire of comments is consistent with beliefs. Different common responses are listed here, along with commentary and suggestions for improvement.

Complimentary

The child may ask or expect a reaction from the adult. A natural response is generalized, polite praise such as "Oh, lovely," "Very nice," "Beautiful." The problem with this approach is that they are empty words with no specific reaction. The child's purpose may not have

(continued)

TOPICS IN OBSERVATION

Responding to Children's Work

(*continued*)

been for it to be "nice" or "lovely." It may be a frightening spider or a bad dream. The adult's comment is a casual remark lacking sincerity. It becomes a denial of the purpose of the artist. It may have been for exploration and practice, not beauty.

Instead: "You worked a really long time at that."

Judgmental

"Great!" "That's wonderful." Again, these are empty words that may not be truthful or reflect what the child is trying to portray. It is valuative from the viewer's opinion. When we consider that young children are egocentric, they only imagine that the viewer will see it just as they do. It is more important for the viewer to determine the child's opinion of the work.

Instead: "What do you like about it?" or "Can you tell me how you did it? What part did you do first?"

Valuing

The adult expresses her personal opinion, "I love it." The goal is to help the child find self-satisfaction as the measuring stick of creative work. An outsider's evaluation is not necessary nor advisable. What the *adult* sees or thinks is not important. How the *child* feels or thinks about it is the important point.

Instead: "What do you like about it?"

Questioning

When the adult asks, "What is it?" or "What's this supposed to be?" a loud message is conveyed, "You were supposed to make something I could recognize. I can't see it so you are not doing it right." The adult should know that young children up to age six and seven are nonrepresentational in their art. They may have a mental image of what they want to draw but their physical abilities for control of the medium and cognitive development concerning perception and reality are still in the formative stages.

Instead: "Would you like to tell me about it?" The child still has the option of saying, "No," rather than answering the command, "Tell me about it."

Probing

When the questioning approach asks the significance of every piece of work, it may be overused and it is probing. From what is known about children's art, much of it is for exploration of the medium. The child is getting the feel of the fingerpaint, or practicing rolling snakes and balls of clay, or watching the glue flow out as the bottle is squeezed.

Instead: Just observe. Watch for indications of what the child is getting from the experience. A simple "Hmmmm" suggests interest, invites the child to comment if she chooses.

Correcting

Of course, early childhood educators should know that children's drawings are unrealistic, so telling a child, "Grass isn't orange. Here's a green crayon for grass" is inappropriate.

Responding to Children's Work

Instead: Allow the child to use materials in any way they wish as long as it is safe for themselves and the environment. Give redirection reminders, such as, "We paint on the paper, not on the wall," or "When you walk around with the brush, you are dripping paint all over. If you want to look at Lizzy's side of the easel, place the brush in the container first."

Psychoanalyzing

Much study has been done on the emotional and psychological meaning of children's creative work. It makes fascinating reading, but it is not for amateurs. Deep psychological significance should not be placed on children's art. It is inappropriate for people without training to make diagnoses about the child's emotional state. Some have said, "She uses black all over the page. She must be depressed." The content of children's creative work and their choice of color is not realistic. The teacher mistakenly commented on the red paint the child used and thought, "He told me this was all the blood from the baby. He must wish his new baby brother was dead. Maybe he's planning to stab him." Forming conclusions about the child's inner mind from one drawing is just as unfair and dangerous as evaluating the whole child from one test.

Instead: Note curious, strange, bizarre creations or comments from the child on a notepad for your own use. If they are repeated or accompanied by behavioral indicators, follow it up. If you are alarmed, talk to your supervisor, then possibly the family, to search for further clarification or evaluation. Sometimes children's art *can be* their way of expressing fears or traumatic incidents that cannot be verbalized.

Modeling

This is an acceptable teaching technique in every other area of early childhood practice *except* art. Modeling in the sense of making a pattern for a child to follow is not good professional practice. Planned art "projects" sometimes present materials for the child to construct the adult's idea of a caterpillar, clown face, or dinosaur. These thwart the whole purpose and theory of children's creative development and its benefits. Many teachers say, "Well, I'm just providing the materials for the clown face, they can do it any way they want." The child knows the adult's expectation but may not have the experience with a clown's face or the desire to make one.

Instead: Provide the child with rich experiences in the world around him. Provide creative materials that the child can use himself and allow the child to create whatever he chooses from those experiences.

Model an accepting attitude to children's explorations.

Model an interest in texture, design, color, and use vocabulary words about them, such as rough, smooth, ridges, pattern, balance, horizontal and vertical, swirls, border, and color names like mauve, lavender, chartreuse. This makes association between the visual image and the word. Young children love big words.

Model processes of using materials by sitting at the clay table and throwing clay to soften it, rolling balls and snakes and pinching pots. This is not direct instruction but scaffolding manipulation techniques that children will adopt when they are ready.

(continued)

TOPICS IN OBSERVATION

Responding to Children's Work

(continued)

Describing

This is the best *Instead* of the preceding approaches. Every area of development that is seen through creative work can be described (not all at once): physical movement, control of the tools, utilization of the space, self-help skills in working on the project, social interactions in the art or in the process, control or expression of emotions, vocabulary to describe the product, writing associated with the creations, math and science concepts, self-identity revealed through the art, and interactions with the group and adults through the process.

"You used a lot of red today." (Making the association between the visual color and the word *red*.)

"You covered the whole page with paint. That took a lot of concentration." (Commenting on space and attention span)

"You made a lot of blue vertical lines and yellow horizontal lines. It made a design that's sometimes called plaid. Look at this. There's the color green where they come together. I don't see any green paint out today. I wonder how that happened?" (Using vocabulary of design, pointing out colors, helping child observe cause and effect and wonder. If he does not understand it this time, he might the next time. The association has been made and the disequilibrium has been pointed out. The child will accommodate this new knowledge into color concepts.)

EXERCISE: Go back to Figures 10–12 through 10–17, which were the drawings in the exercise on the stages of art, and practice your comments to the artist who asks, "How do you like it?"

WEEK 10: PLAN A

CREATIVE WORK SAMPLES

Students

Collect a common work sample from several children of the same age. Note how different they are and reflect on what accounts for the differences. Use the Work Samples Checklist (see Appendix D) to analyze what the samples reveal about development. Collect a common work sample from children ages two through eight and note the differences.

Practitioners

This week collect a sample of creative work from every child. Use the Work Samples Checklist (See Appendix D) or the creative portion of your program's checklist. (You could have them draw on the second panel of the portfolio file folder.)

What to Do with It

Filing. File the Work Samples and Checklist in the child's portfolio. Note the presence of the work on the Portfolio Overview Sheet (Figure 10–27).

Sharing with the Child and Family. Share with the family and child, if appropriate. For example: "Mr. Tower, I made a copy of this drawing Mackenzie did today for her portfolio. She's still in the scribbling stage but she is now staying on the paper. She said this was a bee. I think she was watching the fly we had pestering us in the classroom go round and round. I saw her eyes following it while she was working at the table with crayons. In the next stage we will begin to see more recognizable shapes like a circle. She's just practicing so we provide her with lots of paper, time, and encouragement," or "Caroline, this is the file folder where I keep all the notes I write about you.

CREATIVE – WORK SAMPLES			
Documentation	Location	Recorder	Date
Painting	Portfolio		9/10
AR	Portfolio	MS	10/22
self-portrait	Portfolio		11/7
Drawing	Portfolio		1/23
Designs	Photograph in Portfolio		4/17
Drawing and Dictation	Portfolio		5/30

Figure 10–27 Portfolio Overview Example

Would you like to draw a picture to decorate the cover? You could make a design or draw whatever you wish with the markers on this side, then I'll put it in the drawer with the rest of the papers."

Actions.

Read a Book.

Ackerman, K. (1988). *Song and Dance Man.* New York: Knopf.

dePaola, T. (1989). *The Art Lesson.* New York: Putnam.

Gauch, P. L. (1989). *Dance, Tanya.* New York: Putnam.

McLerrin, A. (1991). *Roxaboxen.* New York: Lothrop, Lee & Shepherd Books.

Winch, J. (1996). *The Old Man Who Loved to Sing.* New York: Scholastic.

Perry, S. (1995). *If . . .* Los Angeles: J. Paul Getty Trust Publications.

In the Environment.

Take a critical look around the room.

- Is natural light available and maximized?
- Are there natural materials to explore, manipulate, and examine closely?

- Is there some wall space that is free from distractions so that light and shadows can be observed?
- Are there beautiful objects on display?
- Are there prints of masterpieces among children's art and panels of projects?
- Does the room produce pleasing sounds of children involved in their work, perhaps with a background of soft classical music, or wind chimes, or soft drums?
- Are the shelves labeled for containers and their placement?
- In the block area, are there wall hangings and pictures that relate to materials, such as vehicles and buildings?

In the Curriculum.

- Bring children's attention to the most obvious to look for the surprises hidden there, such as patterns in the floor or ceiling tiles, where the shadows fall on the floor throughout the day, or the feeling of a slice of bread.
- Use children's interests to learn more about a subject, producing a plan to find out more and document the process. That is a project.
- Introduce new materials and move from simple to complex.
- Block area has thematic connections, such as construction with tools and helmets, or farm animals and buildings and books.

In the Newsletter.

- Point out to readers the technique of looking more closely at objects in the environment. Encourage them to play games and interact with the child in such a way to stimulate curiosity and draw comparisons to previous knowledge.
- Suggest local places to visit where all can enjoy a sensory experience—visual, such as a museum or zoo; auditory, such as a concert or a walk in the forest seeking no sound but those produced in nature.

WEEK 10: PLAN B

ANECDOTAL RECORDING IN CREATIVITY FOR GROUP A

Select all the children from Group A and each day write an Anecdotal Recording about how each child used creative materials. Include all the details and exact quotes written on the left column of the paper. In the right column, comment on each child's development, any special circumstances, and whether this was a usual or an unusual occurrence.

What to Do with It

Filing. Note the recording on the Portfolio Overview Sheet with the date and your name. (See

Figure 10–27.) File the Anecdotal Recording in the child's portfolio.

Sharing with the Child and Family. Share the Anecdotal Recording with the child's family or the child, if appropriate. For example: "Mr. Gonzales, this is Arturo's first painting at school. He's spent a long time watching other children. Today we piled leaves and jumped in them and brought a pile inside and glued them to the bulletin board. He went to the easel and I made notes while he painted. It was fasci-nating! He just used dabbing strokes with all the fall colors until the whole sheet was full. It really shows his interest in those colored leaves made permanent in paint. I took a photograph of it to put into his port-folio. I'm sure he wants to take the painting home when it's dry," or "Mimi, here's your clay ball you wanted to take home. I wrote about how you made it today and how you took the pencil and made all those little holes all over it. You kept saying, 'Let the air out. Let the air out.' 'Yep.'" Sometimes you never know what they were thinking.

WEEK 10: PLAN C

REFLECTIVE JOURNAL

Respond to the following in your Reflective Journal, kept in a private file at home.

When I think about creativity, I . . .

My own background in art has been . . .

It has caused me to . . .

My favorite kind of creative expression is . . .

I (regularly, sometimes, or never) go to art galleries or museums because . . .

REFERENCES

Accreditation Criteria and Procedures (1998). Washington, DC: National Association for the Education of Young Children.

Bredekamp, S., & Copple, C. (Ed.). (1997). *Developmentally appropriate practice in early childhood programs.* Washington, DC: National Association for the Education of Young Children.

Day, B. (1994). *Early childhood education: Developmental/experiential teaching and learning* (4th ed.). New York: Merrill, an imprint of Macmillan College Publishing Company.

Dighe, J., Calomiris, Z., Van Zutphen, C. (1998). Nurturing the language of art in children. *Young Children, 53* (1), 4–9.

Dodge, D. T., Colker, L. J., & Heroman, C. (2002). *The creative curriculum for preschool.* Washington, DC: Teaching Strategies. Washington, DC: Teaching Strategies, Inc.

Edwards, C., Gandini, L., & Forman, G. (Eds.) (1998). *The hundred languages of children: The Reggio Emilia approach: Advanced reflections,* 2nd ed. Greenwich, CT: Ablex Publishing.

Edwards, C. P., & Willis, L. M. (2000). Integrating visual and verbal literacies in the early childhood classroom. *Early Childhood Educational Journal, 27* (4), 259–265.

Erikson, E. H. (1950). *Childhood and society.* New York: Norton.

Fein, S. (1993). *First drawings: Genesis of visual thinking.* Pleasant Hill, CA: Exelrod Press.

Flavell, J. H. (1963). *The Developmental Psychology of Jean Piaget.* New York: Van Nostrand.

Genishi, C. (1993). Art, portfolios, and assessment in *Early Childhood Today, 8* (2), 67.

Hewett, V. M. (2001). Examining the Reggio Emilia approach to early childhood education. *Early Childhood Education Journal, 29* (2), 95–100.

Hirsch, E. S. (1996). *The block book,* 3rd ed. Washington, DC: National Association for the Education of Young Children.

Isenberg, J., & Jalongo, M. (2001). *Creative expression and play in the early childhood curriculum,* 3rd ed. New York: Merrill Prentice Hall.

Kamii, C. (1982). *Number in preschool and kindergarten.* Washington, DC: National Association for the Education of Young Children.

Kellogg, R. (1970). *Analyzing children's art.* Palo Alto, CA: National Press Books.

Koster, J. (2005). *Growing artists: Teaching art to young children* (3rd ed.). Clifton Park, NY: Thomson Delmar Learning.

Krechevsky, M., & Stork, J. (2000). Challenging educational assumptions: Lessons from an Italian-American collaboration. *Cambridge Journal of Education, 30* (1), 57–75.

Linn, M. I. (2001). An American educator reflects on the meaning of the Reggio experience. *Phi Delta Kappan, 83* (4), 332–335.

Lowenfeld, V., & Brittain, W. L. (1987). *Creative and mental growth* (8th ed.). New York: Macmillan Publishing Co., Inc.

McAfee, O., & Leong, D. (2002). *Assessing and guiding young children's development and learning.* Boston: Allyn and Bacon.

New, R. (1997). New steps in teaching "The Reggio way." In Hendricks, J. (Ed.) *First steps toward teaching the Reggio way.* Upper Saddle River, NJ: Prentice Hall.

Puckett, M., & Black, J. (2000). *Authentic assessment of the young child: Celebrating development and learning,* 2nd ed. New York: Merrill Prentice Hall.

Schirrmacher, R. (2002). *Art and creative development for young children.* Clifton Park, NY: Thomson Delmar Learning.

Seefeldt, C. (1995). Art: A serious work. *Young Children, 50* (3), 39.

Torrance, E. P. (2000). Preschool creativity. In B. A. Bracken, (Ed.). *The psychoeducational assessment of preschool children, 3rd Ed.* Boston: Allyn and Bacon.

RESOURCES

Church, E. B., & Miller, K. (1990). *Learning through play: Blocks, a practical guide for teaching young children.* New York: Scholastic, Inc.

Edwards, C., Gandini, L., & Forman, G. (Eds.) (1993). *The hundred languages of children: The Reggio Emilia approach to early childhood education.* Norwood, NJ: Ablex Publishing Corp.

Kellogg, R. (1970). *Analyzing children's art.* Palo Alto, CA: National Press Books.

Koster, J. (2005). *Growing artists: Teaching art to young children* (3rd ed.). Clifton Park, NY: Thomson Delmar Learning.

Lowenfeld, V., & Brittain, W. L. (1987). *Creative and mental growth.* New York: Macmillan Publishing Co., Inc.

For additional information on early education curriculum, visit our Web site at http://www.earlychilded.delmar.com

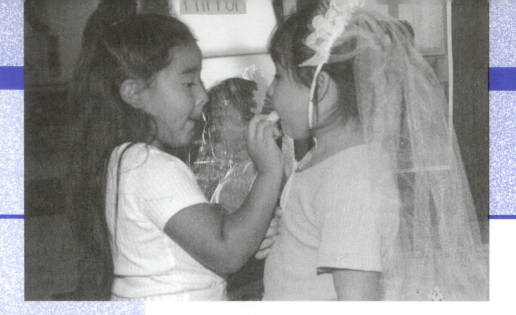

Using Technology to Look at Sociodramatic Play

USING TECHNOLOGY AS DOCUMENTATION

Imagine the end of the day. A mother comes to pick up her child at the child care center. She sits for a few minutes with a cup of coffee and puts on virtual reality glasses. Through them, she views her child in selected video taped segments of the day's activities. The father sitting next to her is doing the same, watching his own child in a virtual reality recording. Each child has been video taped simultaneously, cued to their movements by the "school button" they put on each day as they arrive. The teacher has ended the day's taped segment with a reminder for an e-mail response to the family survey. Other family members have watched portions of the day from home or their workplace through a classroom video connected via the Internet. Parenting workshop choices are reviewed for reception on their television monitors in the next month. They are also reminded to pay the balance of their tuition bill by electronic bank transfer.

Far out? All of this **technology** exists. Can we afford it? Do we agree with it? Do we want it? These are questions many teachers and administrators will be answering soon.

Using technical or electronic medium is not an innovation in classrooms. Tape recorders, cameras, and overhead slide and filmstrip projectors have been used for years. However, electronic and digital technologies have increased the range and quality of products, and ease of equipment use. Lower costs have made electronic media a viable option for documentation in the classroom. Electronic media can capture details that not even the most fluent writer can convey. Tone of voice, nuances of movement, and a visual image all make an incident as alive for the viewer as it was for the original observer. There are considerations of legal and ethical natures that are discussed in the Topics in Observation section of this chapter. A sample release is included in the Plan section.

This recording method section presents the possibilities that are available although many are out of the question for most programs today. In just the right situation, in the future, however, they may be realistic options. A few years ago, who would have dreamed that computers would replace typewriters. Who knows what the future holds? Negroponte opens his book *Being Digital* (1995), saying, "Computing is not about computers any more. It is about living."

Types of Technological Media for Observing and Recording

There are many electronic recording devices. With the arrival of computerization, the options and adaptations are wide. Each has its usefulness along with disadvantages. The early childhood practitioner's knowledge, skills, experience, and creativity may extend far beyond direct interactions with children, into the world of multimedia.

Audio Tape Recording. Recording voices is especially useful for conversations to gather speech and language samples (see Chapter 6). "Transcribing and reviewing these conversations at a later date will provide insights regarding children's learning, thinking, and social skills" (Blagojevic & Garthwait, 2001). Inexpensive tape recorders are available at any electronics supply store. Children's tape recorders make lower-quality recordings but allow the children to record themselves or each other. These can be used as dramatic play props or on project work. Children can record and play back sounds, voices, and music.

Voice-activated **audio recorders** are also available. These can be placed in a selected location where conversations from sociodramatic play, for example, are taking place. The nonintrusive quality is the advantage of this feature, because the teacher does not need to walk over and turn it on. Natural, clear recordings are preserved and may be transcribed and analyzed to assess and evaluate social play level. Problem-solving techniques, learning styles, dramatic play roles, and how the child sustains the role over time can be evaluated.

Parabolic or shotgun microphones (the type sports broadcasts use to catch the coach's instructions and the players' grunts) can be aimed to pick up sound across the room. They can focus on a small, low conversation and screen out all the background noise that is usually going on in an early childhood classroom. They are effective for catching a conversation at the Play Doh table about who has more Play Doh, who made the long snake, or who made all the little balls. Recordings at the sand table might document Caroline's explanation of how she knows which sand is hers and which belongs to Debbie. The self-talk Nicholas uses as he sets the table for snack is captured. His math skills are assessed as he puts out all of the napkins, saying, "Here's one for this chair, one for this chair, one for this chair. Hey, where's the chair for this napkin?"

The advantage of unobtrusiveness is also a disadvantage. Some regard recording without the subject's approval or knowledge as an invasion of privacy. (See Topics in Observation in this chapter.) Another disadvantage is the cost: approximately $200 to $1,000 and up. It also takes some training to become proficient in its operation. This method would be ideal for the classroom with a separate observation booth. Often the sound quality in a teaching lab observation booth is so poor that the value of the audible observation is lost. Remote control of the microphone would help overcome this problem.

Computer microphones with speech-to-text programs can turn children's words into print to add dialogue to their artwork. They can also help children in describing their thinking process or in problem solving. Text-to-speech software can turn children's printed words into audio so they can hear their written stories read back to them.

What to Do with It. Audio tapes of an individual child are kept in the child's portfolio. They can be analyzed for speech and language development. Dictated stories or reading abilities, or informal or structured interviews, can be filed there. These preserve an audible record of the child's thinking revealed through language.

Video. Many children are accustomed to being photographed with a **video recorder** today. Cameras are becoming more affordable, and they are smaller, easier to use, and efficient in almost any kind of light and setting. Zoom capabilities allow recording from a distance. Combined with a parabolic microphone, the video and audio can be remotely controlled from across the room. Mounting a camera on the wall, or in a central location in the room, can record all the events happening in one area. The block area could be recorded on one day and the dramatic play area on another. By mounting the camera and letting it run, children act more natural than if a person is manually pointing the camera at them. If a videographer is used, it is important for the children to become familiar with the process and the person taking pictures. With familiarity, their self-consciousness decreases. A camera could be present, or have a camera person taking blank pictures, days before the actual "shoot" to allow the children to become accustomed to being videotaped. Cameras ranging in price from $900 to $1,500 have point-and-shoot controls, optional date and time, freeze and fast frames, and a bookmark to find the end. The tape can be viewed immediately on a television monitor through the camera. They have a taping capability of thirty minutes to four hours (Holzberg, 1993).

Digital video cameras record images and sounds in digital form on a diskette. The recorded material can be stored on the disk or downloaded to a computer. Most video cameras have a display screen as well, so the event can be viewed on the small screen immediately after it occurs for a playback discussion. Digital photography allows computer editing to zoom in or enlarge portions of the photo. Video printers that can print up to 30 frames per minute, make it possible to capture small changes in action. These can be used for documentation panels of projects, as discussed in Chapter 10 (Trepanier-Street, Hong, & Bauer, 2001).

Lavalieres (electronic signal devices) can be worn that automatically turn the camera to aim at the subject. These are used in distance learning studios by professors who wander around the room. Extremely small cameras, the size of a pencil, can diminish the awareness of being taped. A teacher could wear one behind his ear or in a pocket. Then he can walk around the room or sit "watching" the children play while he is actually video taping. Video taping selected areas could also be done by remote from a control or observation room.

Several companies have combined video and e-mail technologies to provide families a view of their child's day at school. Involved families may want to know more about their child's activities, or concerned families may see this as a protection device. Whatever the motivation, technology is providing the vehicle for electronic observation in the classroom. State-of-the-art child care facilities are outfitted with video cameras in each classroom so that the director has instant access to the day's events and gives some assurance that appropriate actions are taken toward the children there. Recording capability is useful for the teacher to analyze children's or one's own actions for further study.

Hours and hours of tape are unmanageable. There may be segments that are profound, while much of the taping yielded nothing usable for the purpose. Editing the tape can be done by retaping segments from one recorder to another. This is time-consuming and the tape is then second-generation quality. Many public or technical schools have editing machines that may be available to perform this function. The digitizing of video reduces images to mathematical symbols that computers can read. Editing video on a computer with CD-ROM is simple, much the same way paragraphs of text are moved with a computer. They also can be manipulated visually and enhanced, and parts can be erased. Captions and background music can be added to make a very professional production with a minimum of technical training. Nonlinear editing allows changes in sequence of segments or individual images. Large amounts of tape can be stored on one disk, useful when cataloging large amounts of information in the computer's memory for sorting, filing, and rearranging. This sophisticated and expensive equipment may be available through the program's affiliations in the community. Families are frequently resources for technical work.

Something to Think About.

Is Video Taping an Invasion of the Child's Privacy?
By Patricia Amanna, Ed.D.
Director, The Children's Center
at Purchase College, Purchase, NY

I think media and technology can impose an intrusion upon the "private school life" of a child. School is a place where children get the opportunity to see how they fit into the larger world apart from the family. As they develop, they find out about themselves through their interactions with others. Most importantly, they can and should try many different roles in their exploration. In today's world, we often talk about the "rights" of individuals as though we include children in that framework. Many of us would feel horrified and outraged if we were subjected to the invasion of media and technology into our private and professional lives. If our employers decided to video tape us working or look at us doing our jobs using cameras and the Internet, we would be disturbed, to say the least. Yet, we are using video taping in schools without any regard for the individual child, as long as the parents give permission. Moreover, we often fail to set clear guidelines regarding the usage, access, and storage of these video tapes. Even more alarming is our new use of the Internet to peer into the world of the child in the school setting.

This technological ability brings with it questions regarding its use. Those that come to mind are: Do we have a right to unlimited access to a human being? What good does this information really do anyone or society at large? What damage might it cause in relationships between children and "trusted" adults in their lives? How do we make sure that these data are not used against children?

There are many positive applications of media and technology in the schools, but we must be sure we are not teaching children that the technology ability gives us a right to do it. Otherwise the children of today will be the adults of tomorrow who think they have the right to look in on us electronically because they can. Early childhood professionals should apply the basic principals of the NAEYC Ethical Code of Conduct when using media and technology in their classrooms.

What to Do with It. A video tape is a replay of live action. The episode can be viewed repeatedly, hearing and seeing what took place. Segments can be closely examined for relevance to developmental assessment. A commentary can be added for families, or other teachers, or referral agents by voice overlays. The accompanying narrative can point out important details, such as, "Watch the way he is picking up that napkin. Watch the movement of the thumb. Let's go back and slow it down. We can stop it right here."

Other valuable uses of video recorders in the classroom follow:

- historic record—A video tape can be a memento of a special occasion for the whole class. Later viewing of important events, such as the first day, a special visitor, a field trip, or just a normal day, serve as enjoyable memories. Events can take on added importance in the future. Looking at the tape, children can see how much they have grown.
- replay for discussion with the children—A play segment could be taped, shown to the children involved, and discussed, such as, "What happened here? When Audrey did this, see what happened? What could she have done instead?" The tape is then used for problem solving and instruction, more real than any puppet play or discussion with no visual connection.
- video field trip—A teacher was going on a trip so she taped it from the child's viewpoint, as if the child were along with her. She pointed out, "Watch out for that," and "Look over there, see that." It was very effective when accompanied by her artifacts and books. Video can be a teaching tool.
- teacher observation practice—Teachers can watch a selected segment and practice recording methods such as Anecdotal and Running Recordings, Frequency Counts, Checklists, and Rating Scales. Then the teachers can compare ratings (interrater

reliability) to see if they are interpreting the behavior in relatively the same way. This helps them see deficiencies in the system of recording or finding biases that were not realized before. This would make an excellent staff training for improving teachers' professional practice and reviewing child development principles.

- reevaluation and referral—A video recording, authorized with a written release by the family, can be shown to helping professionals for their interpretation or a resource person for an evaluation. It shows the child in a natural setting, capturing usual behavior.
- research—Analyzing video tape can compare small bits of data for research. Ethical principles of voluntary, informed consent are necessary. Family signatures are required after they have been informed of the nature of the research and the techniques to be used. This must be in language they can understand. It is the investigator's responsibility to carefully evaluate the ethical acceptability of the study regarding the "subject at risk" (*American Psychological Association*, 1990, pp. 390–394).
- teacher self-evaluation and reflection—The tape can be used by the teacher to monitor and receive reactions to teaching practices or for personal reflection. The teacher may be unaware of habits revealed on video tapes. The tape may be used to self-evaluate intervention strategies, play involvement, or language usage.

The APA Ethical Principles of Psychologists and Code of Conduct (American Psychological Association, 2002) offers some good advice.

- obtain **informed consent**—this must be given (and understood) by the individual, or family consent must be given for minors
- maintain confidentiality—take reasonable precautions to protect information storage
- obtain prior permission—for voice or image recording, unless they are naturalistic observations in public places and it is not anticipated that the recording will be used in a manner that could cause personal identification or harm

EXERCISE: Record a segment of your classroom if you work with children, or normal routines of your day. Listen and analyze what the recording reveals about yourself.

Photography. Ah, at last something more familiar. Point and shoot. Quality photographs have become much easier to take with automatic focusing, built-in flash, and zoom capabilities. The quality of pictures is *almost* foolproof. Most children are accustomed to being photographed so that photos become a natural documentation of play. That is only true if it is done often throughout the year. This can be expensive but there are ways to reduce the cost. Buying film in bulk makes it the least expensive part of the operation. Developing has become much less expensive with many places offering discounts for nonprofit organizations. Check with the developer for what is known as contact sheets. These are small, postage-sized prints, all on one page. When looking for "just the right shot" this allows many, many pictures to be taken and only the selected ones to be developed.

Digital photography is even less expensive than using and developing film. There are few expenses other than the cost of the camera. Photos can be stored and transferred electronically on disks that are very inexpensive and can hold up to 43,500 still images. The photos can be made into individual or class photo albums or made into slide presentations for a family night. Photos can be printed out on the printer, copied, and distributed. They can be arranged into a desired order, perhaps to show step by step in a project. They can be used to make a book for the children to revive the memory. These images can be incorporated into the curriculum for a sequencing activity. Printing photos on regular paper is much less expensive than making photo prints, and the size of the print can be varied for the purpose, from postage stamp size to poster size. Some digital cameras even have the capability of taking small segments of video as well.

What to Do with It. Many teachers use a photo album in the classroom as a prereading experience, inspiring children to recall details of past events. It helps children get better acquainted with class members. The teacher sends home a school album with a different child each week. In this way, the family can see the other children in the class and some events that have taken place. Conversations about school now have a focus and the family feels more of a connection to the school. A Polaroid educational program, "Presenting Bright Ideas for Child Development" (Herr & Libby, 2004) gives many other activity ideas for using photographs in the classroom.

Hosington (2002) suggests using photographs to support children's science inquiry by helping children revisit and extend their investigations, reflect on building experiences and articulate their strengths, and helping children analyze and synthesize data (pp. 27–29.)

Photographs can be added to the child's portfolio to illustrate comments about areas of development. They add visual information to Anecdotal Records or can be used themselves as the main observation method with notes explaining the photograph. For example, what area of development might the photograph in Figure 11–1 document?

Photographs can be used during the year as vehicles to help the child remember and talk about specific incidents. The visual image is a springboard for a description of the event and the feelings surrounding it. The child's narrative could also be taped or dictated, adding a literacy dimension to the experience.

Photographs of each child taken the first week of school (double prints) can be used in an activity for

IT HAPPENED TO ME

The Gloved Hand

During the days of the taping our hatched chickens were getting bigger so they were allowed some freedom within a circle of children. It made wonderful footage but one got out. Not being an animal person, I had to put on work gloves to pick up the chickens. In one short clip of the tape a black gloved hand appears to scoop up a wandering chicken. Only I know (and now you) the story behind the glove.

Figure 11–1 What do you see in this photograph?

matching or a concentration game. This is a personal and unique way for children to get to know each other. Children can dictate captions for photographs taken in the classroom or during special events, adding them to the class album or making a book of their own. Photographs are self-esteem boosters.

Photographs taken throughout the school year are excellent mementos to give the children at the end of the year. They are a lasting reminder of that school year. Photographs taken of the children could be used in an album, a bulletin board, or placed in the portfolio. At the end of the year, they should be distributed to the children. If the teacher or school is retaining any photographs, a special release form should be signed so the family is aware of that fact and acknowledges consent.

Computers and Scanners. As mentioned before, computers can store vast amounts of documentation data, both text and visual, without taking up closet or file cabinet storage space. Data is easily manipulated into various formats for both individual portfolios and whole group documentation. Hand-held computers can easily capture data on-the-spot with some of the forms and checklists mentioned in earlier chapters programmed into the hand-held computer. Information is later downloaded into the regular computer and stored there, or on a diskette or CD. Scanners can take photographs and drawings and transform them into digital files, easily stored and shared. The child's work can be shared with families via e-mail or computer disk.

Media as Documentation for Other Areas of Development

Audio or video taping or photography can be used to record and document any area of development. Arrivals and separations can give poignant images of hellos and good-byes. Self-care photos can illustrate the accomplishment of milestone tasks, such as dressing for outside or tying a shoe. A video of outside play could be a delightful reminder of the physical, emotional, language, and social actions of the child. It could picture children running down a hill, climbing a slide, or wading in a creek. Social interactions can be preserved with photographs or taped conversations. Emotionally troubled moments are usually best kept private, but there may be circumstances when these might need to be preserved visually or audibly. Language segments on audio or video tape preserve not only the words, but facial and body expressions to make them even more illu-

IT HAPPENED TO ME

Do You Want to Be Pink?

One of the highlights of my days in the classroom was an intergenerational project in which one class of four-year-olds made weekly visits to a nearby nursing home. There are a million stories connected with that but my favorite is about Ethel. She was blind and had David for a little friend. He showed empathy that is supposed to be beyond his Preoperational stage.

One spring day we were making drip dot paintings, so he helped her by placing the paintbrush in her hand and shaking it to make the drips. She got paint on her hand so he asked me for a tissue to wipe it off. As he was wiping, she asked, "What color is it, David?" He answered, "Blue, the color of robin's eggs." (Perceptive, eh?) She sighed, "Oh!" He looked at her and at me and said, "Do you want to be pink?" "I'd love to be pink," she replied. He painted each finger a pastel color and I snapped the most rapturous photograph of her face glowing, with hand outstretched with pastel fingers. The significance of the incident and photograph was even more poignant when I learned later from the activities director that Ethel's love of her life was painting. That photo is precious but, alas, I have no permission to print it, so it will have to glow in your own imagination.

minating. Visual and auditory reminders of past events help expand memory and attention span. They are good teaching tools and document important events. Creative moments, whether art media manipulation or **sociodramatic play,** are meaningfully captured on film or audio tape. Incidents illustrating self-identity, group interactions, or relationships with adults in the classroom are more vividly documented with pictures or audio tape. Any observation can be augmented or recorded using these methods. Further commentary will enhance or add the observer's conclusions to the photograph or tape.

TOPICS IN OBSERVATION

Protecting the Rights of the Child

It is essential to receive the permission of each child's family to permanently record their child using audio, video, or photographic recording methods (Figure 11–2). There are instances when this permission may be denied.

- Some religious groups do not allow photographs.
- The child is under protective services in a protected, confidential placement. An innocent newspaper photograph of an activity that included the child may jeopardize the child's safety.
- There may be personal reasons for which the family may deny permission.

It is important that staff members are aware of the denied photo release. Just as a life-threatening allergy must be made known to all staff, this is important information to be conveyed. The staff should find alternatives to audio taping the child's language sample. If video or still photography is used, either for formal or informal uses, the staff is responsible for making the photographer aware of the prohibition. Sensitivity to the child's feelings is a high priority. The age of the child and reason for prohibition will govern how this exclusion is made. The exclusion from photography or taping should not be obvious to the other children or their family, or even the child, unless it is by the child's request. Techniques of photography could be used to take group casual pictures from the back of the child. All diligence should be given to this serious ethical and legal issue.

Occasionally, photo contests or commercial purposes may arise. If the recordings are used for other than educational or publicity use, the individual child's family should be consulted. A special release form for that purpose must be obtained. It is better to be cautious and guard against any possible recriminations.

Any child who does not want to be taped, video recorded, or photographed has the right to refuse. The program staff has the responsibility to respect the child's wishes, even if the family has given permission. No child should be forced to participate in this kind of an activity. This should be a policy in the program, staff, and family handbook.

AUDIO/VIDEO/PHOTO RELEASE

I give permission for my child to be tape recorded, video recorded, or photographed for educational or publicity purposes while participating in the regular activities of this program.

Date _____

❑ YES   ❑ NO

Signature _____

Figure 11–2 Sample Release

The media portion was written with the help of Katharyn Nannaman.

Advantages

Photographs, video and audio taping are effective observational recording tools because

- they capture visual or real sound images of the episode.
- they are less subject to the recorder's bias or inferences.
- they allow the viewer to form judgments independent from the recorder's.
- they can be analyzed in a number of ways, for different purposes, at different times.
- they are less time-consuming if automatic systems are used.

Disadvantages

Photographs, video or audio taping can be

- expensive.
- complicated and time-consuming.
- intrusive to children and teachers.
- a factor causing unnatural behavior.
- against families' values.

Pitfalls to Avoid

Confidentiality is an issue with media as an observation technique. Children other than the target child may be included in a photo, audio, or video tape recording, thus possibly revealing information about that child's behavior to those who have no need or right to know. This is almost impossible to avoid, especially with video photography. Ethical use of footage is the teacher's responsibility.

Just as equity is important in all other recording methods, it is with media as well. Some children are much more photogenic, do more interesting things, or speak humorously or in an interesting way. When media is used, all children who are allowed to be recorded should be in a fair way, both in number and in content of recording.

View the recordings from the family's eyes. Is it embarrassing? Does it show the child in an uncomfortable situation or looking less competent than peers? Reconsider using that recording.

How to Find the Time

It does take time to learn to use new equipment. Just as a child needs to manipulate a new item, you will need to use it and experiment with it before expecting it to perform perfectly. The more you use the technology the more familiar with it you will become and it will become second nature to use that camera or tape recorder. Once you get to that level, you will see how much time it saves in writing.

REVIEW

Media: Action preserved in photographs, audio, or video tape

Types of Information to Record Using Technology:

any moment or sequence of a child's day, usual or unusual

separation and adjustment

self-care skills

physical development

social development

emotional development

language and speech (audio or video tape)

attention span and interests

cognitive development

literacy

creativity

sociodramatic play

self-esteem

LOOKING AT DRAMATIC PLAY

During dramatic or pretend play, observers see many interesting scenarios unfold. A child puts on a hat, picks up a briefcase, and says, "See ya, honey, I'm goin' to work now." And off she goes. A toddler holds his sweater coiled up in a ball and strokes it saying, "Nice kitty." A four-year-old at the art bench says to himself, "I need a big piece of paper 'cause I'm gonna make a big truck with a trailer. No, I'll use another piece of paper for the trailer and hitch 'em togedder with a piece of tape." Each of these children is displaying imaginative play through his or her thoughts and actions. They are cute to the untrained observer but meaningful to those who know what each incident reveals about the child's development.

While *play* is the word used for not performing any worthwhile function, for young children (and for us all), it has many benefits. Research on dramatic play, solitary imaginative play with or without props, and sociodramatic play, a fantasy episode interacting with other children, has important implications for teachers of young children. Studies have found that children who regularly engage in sociodramatic or imaginative play are more friendly, popular, cooperative, verbal, and creative. They are usually less impulsive and aggressive and more likely to take the perspective of others (Fein & Kinney, 1994). These are logical outcomes of sustained interactions with peers. Other benefits are documented as well. Children between two-and-a-half and five years old who participate in make-believe play are more advanced in general intellectual ability, have better memory, and display higher reasoning ability (Berk, 1994). Bergen's review of pretence (pretend play) literature (2002) found that "representational skills, problem solving abilities and social-linguistic sophistication" were increased by sociodramatic play. These are just the skills necessary for good test performance but most elementary school programs contain few, if any, environments, curriculum, or encouragement of pretend play. Snow, Burns, and Griffin (1998) report the benefits of language development and literacy from play-based instruction with dramatic play scenarios. Nonparticipants, however, had lower school achievement later and exhibited less self-control in social situations and higher rates of delinquency (Singer & Singer, 1990). Machado (2003) lists these benefits of dramatic play. It helps children

- develop conversational skills and the ability to express ideas in words.
- understand the feelings, roles or work of others.
- connect actions with words—actions and words go hand-in-hand in dramatic play.
- develop vocabulary.
- develop creativity—children imagine, act, and make things up as play progresses.
- engage in social interaction with other children.
- cope with life, sometimes through acting out troubling situations, thus giving an outlet for emotion (for example, almost every doll in an early childhood center gets a spanking periodically when children play house).
- assume leadership and group participant roles. (p. 398)

With these benefits, can early childhood programs and elementary schools ignore the importance of providing and encouraging this kind of play?

More fantasy, future plots with strategies
Carries plot into another day
Mostly same-sex playgroups (Boys: Superheroes
Girls: Everyday events)
Plan scenario and carry it out
Danger, excitement-packed themes
Share ideas about roles
"You be . . . and I'll be . . ."
More conversation and gestures in roles
Short sustenance of roles
Assigns and takes roles
Shares play theme
Pretends next to another child
Performs actions on dolls, etc.
Verbal make-believe
Familiar actions on substitute objects
Prop-initiated actions
Plays routines
Imitates

Figure 11–3 Dramatic Play Development

Stages of Dramatic Play

Children play in different ways at different ages and stages (Figure 11–3). Piaget equated that difference in the way they played with the difference in their thinking (Peterson & Felton-Collins, 1986). The changes in imaginative play are easily observed and do correspond with stages of development by several theorists, including Piaget, Erikson, Smilansky, and Vygotsky.

Infancy. The infant and adult are gazing at each other intently. As the adult opens and closes his mouth and slowly sticks out his tongue, the infant imitates the action. Imaginative play has begun. This has been documented to occur in the early days of the infant's life, setting the stage for responding to another human and turn taking. The game of peeka-boo is really the pretend theme of "I'm going away and now I'm back." The repetition of these adult–child interactions is building the foundation for the later plots of sociodramatic play with peers.

Young Toddlers. Between six and eighteen months, the child is exploring the physical world by playing with objects. Close scrutiny of this play illustrates various patterns.

Repetition with Objects. Manipulations are repeated with the objects in every conceivable way. The young toddler takes her bottle and shakes it, throws it, chews on it, sucks on all parts of it, listens to it, and minutely examines it.

Repetition without Objects. The functions she has learned are played out in her imagination without the object. This is the beginning of imaginary play. She puts her fist to her mouth and makes sucking movements and sounds, pretending to suck the bottle.

Substitution. Other objects become stand-ins for the imaginary one. She picks up anything she can handle and puts it to her mouth and pretends, or really, sucks it like a bottle. She is mentally substituting this object for the bottle.

Older Toddlers. Dramatic play occurs just at the time when social rules are being enforced by adults. These rules restrict behavior, such as avoid dangerous situations and do not tear up books or take toys from others. The child then substitutes imaginary situations in which she is in control of the rules and can work them through as she delays immediate gratification. Her parents may be offering her milk from a cup, so she plays the pretend bottle routines as a symbolic way to cope. She now separates thought from action and renounces impulsive action in favor of this situation. She makes the rules.

The child is the center of imaginative play with rituals such as eating and sleeping. The actions become more decentered. Now she is feeding the teddy bear rather than being fed herself. She now can use more language and muscle skills to participate in shared-meaning play with others, but self-control is a problem. Each player must do the acting with the same objects, and none is willing to forego her own desire to possess the toy.

Preschoolers. The three-year-old has an expanded sense of fantasy using semirealistic props for adult roles. Each player has his own role related to the theme but acts independently. The players are trying to represent themselves in roles with which they are familiar. This helps them understand and feel powerful. To be the parent giving the commands, the superhero with super power, or the firefighter as a rescuer, the child takes on the characteristics of another person. They are only able to do this because of expanded vocabulary, experiences with models, and objects that they can mentally transform into props.

Toward the end of the preschool age, the ability to have empathetic thoughts and to want social companionship expands the dramatic play into the sociodramatic stage. Most children are becoming less egocentric and more empathetic. They understand others' points of view and feelings. They are in the Initiative Stage, taking control and leadership of their own play, not dependent on specific props or adult leadership. They are likely to play roles such as family, stereotyped television characters, powerful helpers from the community (firefighter or police), cowboys, pirates, or space creatures. However, now roles are assigned and imaginary experiences are shared through explanations outside the role. Children are frequently heard saying things like, "You be the guy on fire and I'll come with the hose and put the fire out." This often meets with a counterproposal from the victim, "No, *you* be the guy on fire and *I'll* come with the hose." Resolution of the dilemma may indicate language development for negotiation, problem-solving ability, and social status in the group.

Young School-Agers. Sociodramatic play declines in the early school years. The child has a growing contact with reality, feelings of industry, and pride in her motor and intellectual skills. Games with rules are the outlets for these skills and attitudes. Interactions with other children are growing more competitive. Helm and Katz (2001) call this the age of investigations. They are concrete-operational thinkers, ready for group play. Their investigations may be focused on collections of whatever the fad is this week, though Barbie and sports cards have sustained their favor. Games with rules become the play pattern of this age child now that they can accurately keep score, easily take turns, and strategically plan. The sociodramatic play of the earlier stages has prepared the child for these activities.

Using Play Stages to Assess Sociodramatic Play

The social play stages can be used again when assessing and describing dramatic play (see Chapter 4). A variety of methods can record the play, such as Class List Log, Checklist, Anecdotal or Running Record, Rating Scales, or electronically for later analysis.

Onlooker Stage. The child watches the dramatic play of others. The child may lack the entry skills and self-confidence to join the organized play of other children. It may be the child's learning style to watch others before he attempts the play, or it may be the shy personality of the child. The adult can give assistance in play entry techniques if it is warranted.

Solitary Dramatic Play. Any age child may choose to play out individual dramatic or fantasy play alone. The child selects the props for play and may internally or audibly carry on a dialogue. The observer, just as in the Onlooker Stage, can assess the play and decide if intervention is needed to help the child move to social interaction in the play. The scaffolding of an adult as a parallel player may help the child move to the next stage.

Parallel Dramatic Play. Two-, three-, and four-year-olds are social beings and often play out their dramatic roles alongside other children without interactions. The observer, like in the Solitary Stage, assesses the child's social level and choice of parallel play partners. If it is indicated, she can act as an intermediary. Statements such as, "Suzie, you are a Mommy and Joe is a cook. Maybe you could go to his restaurant and order a Kids Meal."

Howe's Peer Play Scale (in Johnson, Christie, & Yawkey, 1987) classifies sociodramatic play in levels.

Level 1—Simple Parallel Play. Children are in close proximity with similar activities, but there is no eye contact or social behavior.

Level 2—Parallel Play with Mutual Regard. Children are involved in similar activities, making eye contact and often imitating each other's play.

Associative Dramatic Play. In the Associative Stage, children are still each playing parallel but share play theme and conversation. This is Howe's:

Level 3—Simple Social Play. Children are talking, smiling, offering objects, and corresponding to associative play. It is the stage of social play in which children are playing near each other, in the same play theme, but not together. They do not share props or final results.

Cooperative Dramatic Play. In the Cooperative Stage, children are working together toward a common goal, contributing parts to the whole. These are Howe's:

Level 4—Complementary/Reciprocal Play with Mutual Awareness. Children offer objects to build a mutual structure, taking turns, but there is no other social exchange. It is a higher level of associative play.

Level 5—Complementary/Reciprocal Social Play. Children engage in social exchanges. They plan and act out make-believe stories.

Smilansky (in Johnson, et al., 1987, p. 160) further defines this level of sociodramatic play as

- Role playing—adopting roles
- Make-believe transformations—symbols stand for objects, actions, and situations
- Social interactions—directly relating to each other in roles
- Verbal communications—(1) statements to organize the play designating the situation, assigning roles, planning story lines, and rebuking players who act in an inappropriate way and (2) pretend communication within the role (p. 158)

By using these finer distinctions in describing dramatic play, the observer can make decisions about the need or desirability of intervening in the play. The adult can help dramatic play by role modeling, making suggestions, asking open-ended questions, or giving direct instruction in carrying out the role. Each of these may help the child extend the play and become a more acceptable play partner.

EXERCISE: Look at photographs of children in the dramatic play area. Using the preceding stages of Howe and Smilansky, determine each child's level or role.

Observing Creative Dramatics

The term *dramatic play* is the spontaneous play in which a child recreates routines they have seen in real life (Figure 11–4). As the child matures, the role is sustained, is accompanied by a monologue or dialogue with another, and then imaginative new play themes are explored. *Sociodramatic play* is the interaction of two or more children in a play theme with each holding separate roles. This often follows family-life routines such as cooking, child care, and male/female interactions.

A third type of creative play is *story play* (Isenberg & Jalongo, 2001) inspired by a book or fingerplay. The classic *Three Little Pigs* or *Goldilocks and the Three Bears* are perfect beginning productions. Block (1997) and Edwards (2001) emphasize the added comprehension of the text and its benefits to learning. This has been very successful in involving children in literature and exercising cognitive thinking to move out of egocentrism. It helps children work out difficult concepts and their reactions (Howell & Corbey-Scullen, 1997). They tell of using creative dramatics as a follow-up to a field trip to the home of Harriet Tubman in trying to understand slavery with very young children and using a play about animals for conflict resolution. A variation of this kind of dramatic play, **story dictation,** has been documented by Vivian Paley (1984, 1988, 1990, 1997) through her accounts of this kind of play in kindergarten class-

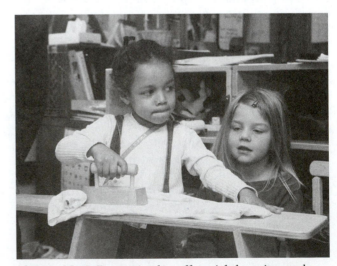

Figure 11–4 Dramatic play offers rich learning and observation opportunities.

rooms. Her work highlights the rich learning outcomes, especially in both cognitive and affective domains. One child, or a group of children, write the story line and act as producers and directors, selecting actors to carry out the story line with the rest of the class as the audience. The teacher is the facilitator, assisting with the production and presentation but the more important role is leading the follow-up conversation about the meaning of the play, the conflicts raised, and possible solutions.

Schoon (1997/98) suggests adding dance and movement to the creative drama to spur children's interest in literature and reading. Schoon (1997/98) recommends books such as:

Color Dance, Jonas, A. (1989)
The Three Billy Goats Gruff: A Norwegian Folktale, Appleby, E. (1984)
Little Blue and Little Yellow, Lionni, L. (1959)
Clap Your Hands, Cauley, L. (1992)
Amazing Grace, Hoffman, M. (1991)
Bringing the Rain to Kapiti Plain, Aardema, V. (1996)

Observing Dramatic Play for Assessing Other Developmental Areas

While children are engaging in dramatic play, they are using other skills and behaviors that can be observed and assessed simultaneously (Figure 11–5).

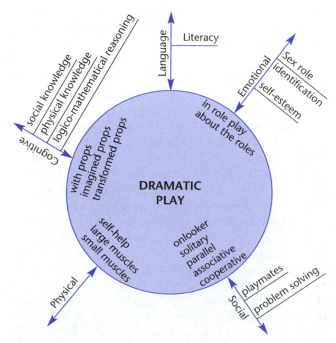

Figure 11–5 Developmental Skills Used and Revealed in Dramatic Play

Cognitive. Sociodramatic play is a progressive step toward abstract thinking. The movement from the real toy to the symbolic leads the preschooler to abstract thinking. This is the link with the Concrete Operations Stage of Piaget. Children who enjoy pretending score higher on imagination and creativity (Berk & Winsler, 1995). During dramatic play, children shift away from self and take the role of another that helps them see situations from a different viewpoint, moving them out of egocentrism. The reversibility of the role, knowing they can leave it any time, helps develop the cognitive structures for understanding the reversibility of operations such as the clay balls and equal amounts of water in different-sized containers (Johnson, et al., 1987). The planning and carrying out of a thematic role through story and fantasy play have been shown to help children's memory for story lines and serve as a foundation for later memory strategies (Kim, 1999).

Language. Sociodramatic play promotes vocabulary growth (Block, 2001; Edwards, 1997), and gives children practice in turn taking and using language to plan as well as carry out roles, sometimes with great expression. This shows the child's ability to move out of egocentrism into the role of another, even using different voices, vocabularies, and gestures for the role. The inner speech, or private speech as Vygotsky (in Kraft & Berk, 1998) calls it, often is audible as children work through a dramatic play episode whether alone or with other children. It reveals the child's inner thoughts. It is as if they were being transmitted directly out of the brain, such as, "Now this is my baby and she has to go to the doctor. Oops, her arm just fell off. I think James did that." Accompanying sound effects and directions to inanimate objects, such as, "Get outta here chair," are often heard in fantasy play.

Literacy. Sociodramatic play is a natural way to integrate literacy into the child's environment, to become a natural and important part of the play theme. The use of literacy materials in areas can be observed, such as sign making in the block area, letter writing, and list making in the dramatic play area. Often children will spontaneously, or the teacher may gently suggest, that a sign or a list could fill a need in the play. It may direct players, like an "Open" or "Closed" sign for a grocery store or labels for buildings with the name of the builder or request to preserve it. Watching the use of literacy materials, including books during play, can give the observer clues about the child's understanding of the usefulness of print.

Social. Dramatic play is encouraged by families who engage in fantasy with their child, provide props, and comment on the play as real. These children tend to be more securely attached and more imaginative. Children's involvement and success with dramatic play depends also on their level of social development (see Chapter 4). When the child is in the Parallel Play Stage, she wants to be near other children playing, but does not have the language, emotional, or cognitive development to engage in interactive play. The adult can recognize the level of social development, help the child find a role that she is capable of, and support her success in that role. Experience in groups greatly affects the child's ability to participate in sociodramatic play. Solving problems in play situations helps children learn the art of negotiation while they divide roles, take turns, and share props. Interacting with an older peer or one more socially experienced will enhance imaginative play. Children seek out familiar same-sex, same-age playmates.

Some children do not participate in sociodramatic play. There are many possible reasons for it and implications for the caregiver. Some children are more object-oriented than people-oriented, which may be their cognitive style (see Chapter 8). They learn through manipulating the physical environment and are convergent rather than divergent thinkers. Children who are withdrawn, nonparticipants in sociodramatic play may later experience peer rejection, social anxiety, loneliness, depression, and negative self-esteem, and even negative school success (Rubin & Coplan, 1998). This emphasizes the importance of facilitating sociodramatic play in the early childhood classroom.

It is well documented that children who are less aggressive are more readily accepted as playmates. The children who introduce wild animal themes and superheroes into dramatic play raise the level of aggressiveness of the play. Research has shown strong relationships between high television viewing and aggressiveness (Johnson, Cohen, Smailes, Kasen, & Brook, 2002: Bushman & Huesmann, 2001; Paik & Comstock, 1994). Effects are also low imagination, more anxiety, and lower reading levels and school performance (Singer & Singer, 1990). These effects can be reduced if adults are mediators of the child's viewing. Talking about the difference between real and fantasy, and the possible results in real life if people did that, can help children gain self-control. Play themes from television are highly aggressive and antisocial, but television can teach prosocial behaviors with careful adult intervention. The National Television Violence Study (2002) says that children below the age of seven are most vulnerable to television violence because of their limited abilities to differentiate between fantasy and reality.

Should superheroes be banned? There is much discussion and disagreement over this topic (see Slaby, et al., 1995; and Carlsson-Paige & Levin, 1990, in Resources). The observer can conduct ethnographic research about the effect of television superheroes on dramatic play through Anecdotal Recordings and Frequency Counts. There is no doubt that children use dramatic play to feel powerful (when they know they are not), feel grown up (when they know they are little), and do dangerous things (when they know they are not allowed). Sociodramatic play can provide a way for a child to behave "beyond his average age, above his daily behavior; in play it is as though he were a head taller than himself" (Sutton-Smith in Berk & Winsler, 1995, p. 68).

Children more frequently play with same-sex playmates, with girls choosing family themes on everyday experiences whereas boys play physically active, superhero roles (Howe, et al., 1993). Studies have been conducted to detect the roots of the differences, biological or cultural. It is the old nature versus nurture question, with the ambiguous answer, "Both." There is no doubt that stereotypical play roles have been reinforced by families, peers, television, storybooks, toy advertising, and even by teachers. This happens overtly in comments like, "You girls might want to play with the new dolls we got for the housekeeping area." It may be covert by not providing dress-up props for boys in the dramatic play area (not the housekeeping area). Observations of dramatic play roles, routines, and partners will give clues about the child's sex role identity. The role of the adult is also to broaden the child's exploration of play things and themes by providing a variety of opportunities.

Emotional. Children's emotions are displayed in dramatic play. Observers of young children have heard and seen the pretend crying of the "baby" or the shrill voice of fear as villains chase the good guys. The obvious enjoyment is seen when children are dressing up to go to the dance. Play therapy has been used extensively in the treatment of children's emotional disorders so the connection between dramatic play as a vehicle for expressing inward emotions is recognized. Important events to the child, such as a new sibling, mommy going to work, moving, or major changes in the family, often are seen played out in the dramatic play themes. Exact conversations and gestures accompany the actions that help the child physically and mentally reenact what is troubling them inside. Recurring themes of going to the doctor, house on fire, spanking the baby all point to the emotional involvement of young children in dramatic play.

Emotional disturbances can be observed in children's dramatic play. Curry and Arnaud (1995, pp. 4–9) present three areas of children's play that may suggest an emotional need for intervention.

1. Thematic content: (a) a preoccupation with a single play theme, unchanging and rigid; (b) highly unusual play themes that may be traumatic events the child has witnessed; (c) play with explicit sexual content; or (d) excessive preoccupation with ordinary objects.
2. Style of play: (a) excessively rigid; (b) play in a style of a younger developmental stage; (c) inability to remove himself from the pretend role; or (d) unusual aggressiveness.
3. Social interactions in play: (a) isolated at a stage in the preschool years when sociodramatic play is at its peak; (b) cannot sustain play because of aggressiveness, disruptiveness, or social ineptness; (c) excessively imitative play; or (d) causes rejections.

Even very young children can have complicated and strange behavior. These can be clues of deeper difficulties or just a unique characteristic. Closer observation of the whole child can help make that determination.

Sociodramatic play, with its rules of varying complexity, calls for self-control of emotions and impulses. This does have the developmental effect of practicing in play what is required in real life. The private speech in fantasy play has a major role in the development of self-control. Children use it to regulate their own activity, such as, "I gotta be careful here. I'll pour carefully so I don't spill it" (Berk & Winsler, 1995).

Physical. The whole body—large and small muscles—is involved in dramatic play. Large muscles are put into action when running away from the robbers and lifting heavy boards to construct a fort. Placing tiny horses in a row on a wobbly block wall or buttoning up opera gloves requires small muscle coordination, attention span, and patience.

An environment enriched with interesting props and possibilities expands dramatic play. When children are engaged in imaginative play, they do adapt their own props from whatever is available. Before that stage however, children first go through the stages of manipulation and exploration. They explored all the physical properties of objects first (Curry, 1992). Toddlers and threes require realistic props to complete their play theme. Children need to physically manage real things in their lives as a significant part of the project approach (Helm, 2003).

Dramatic play incorporates the curriculum areas of art, language, science, math, and social studies. It helps develop interpersonal negotiations, physical coordination, language, and cognitive skills. Children ask their own questions, seek their own answers, and enhance all skill areas with the assistance of the teacher as a support.

Other Techniques for Observing Dramatic Play

Dramatic play can be captured very well through the use of Anecdotal Recording. Some delightful and insightful Anecdotal Recordings of dramatic play comprise the writings of Vivian Gussin Paley. Her book, *Boys and Girls: Superheroes in the Doll Corner* (1984) is a wonderful accompaniment to the discussions of this chapter. (See Resources for others.)

A Class List Log can be used for a quick check on who does and does not participate in fantasy play. This may be expanded into a Frequency Count over the course of a week or so, as children present a dramatic rendition of *The Three Billy Goats Gruff* or some other story. Repeating the Class List Log or Frequency Count will indicate if more children are engaged in sociodramatic play as the year progresses.

Time samples will indicate if play is occurring in the dramatic play area. The observer may want to develop a code for the time sample, perhaps a *D* to designate dramatic play occurring in other areas. Under the climber or outdoors, an exciting

IT HAPPENED TO ME

Fan Fascination

A colleague conferred with me about a child who was preoccupied with fans. He watched the ceiling fan at home for long periods of time, his mother reported. At preschool he searched magazines and catalogs looking for pictures of fans. He carried pictures of them around in his pocket and talked about how things reminded him of fans. He was immature socially but linguistically advanced. Curry and Arnaud's (1995) warning signals reminded me of this child with the fascination and aberration with fans. He was referred to a psychologist and worked with a play therapist. See Chapter 7, "Topics in Observation: Autism."

Thirty Buttons

I watched in amazement as one of the youngest children in the three-year-old class sat for about twenty minutes in the dramatic play area. She had put on a dress with fabric loops for buttonholes all the way down the front. There must have been thirty of them. She sat and buttoned every one. That was patience, long attention span, small muscle coordination, and one-to-one correspondence. A planned activity would never have taught her the lessons she learned that day. It was an observation full of details about her development.

frightening than the cartoons they watch. While taking the time sample, if an event that is interesting or important occurs, the observer could turn the paper over and jot down some notes. Later these could be amplified into a more formal Anecdotal Recording for the class file or child's portfolio.

Developmental Checklists and Rating Scales often have one or more criterion for recording the presence, absence, or level of involvement of the child in dramatic play.

Beaty's (2002) Imagination Checklist includes the following items in a developmental progression:

- pretends an action without taking a role
- assigns roles or takes assigned roles
- takes on characteristics and actions related to role
- needs particular props to do pretend play
- can pretend with imaginary objects
- uses language for creating and sustaining plot
- uses exciting, danger-packed themes
- uses elaborate themes, ideas, details (p. 385)

The Reflective Journal is a place to ponder the meaning of what is seen and heard during fantasy play, to wonder about its roots, and to explore pos-

cops-and-robbers theme may be acted out. In the block area, a city may be constructed in anticipation of an earthquake or a bombing. Children do play out the traumatic events of the news that are even more

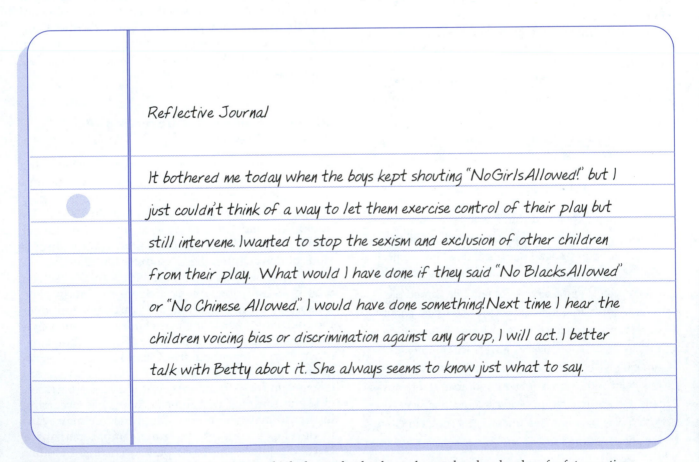

Reflective Journal

It bothered me today when the boys kept shouting "No Girls Allowed!" but I just couldn't think of a way to let them exercise control of their play but still intervene. I wanted to stop the sexism and exclusion of other children from their play. What would I have done if they said "No Blacks Allowed" or "No Chinese Allowed." I would have done something! Next time I hear the children voicing bias or discrimination against any group, I will act. I better talk with Betty about it. She always seems to know just what to say.

Figure 11–6 A Reflective Journal is a place to think about what has been observed and make plans for future actions.

sible actions in the future (Figure 11–6). Thought given to possible scenarios and responses may be considered *before* they occur, to be ready with comfortable, considered answers.

HELPING ALL CHILDREN WITH SOCIODRAMATIC PLAY

It is not surprising that differences exist in the ways children approach dramatic play when they come from diverse backgrounds, cultures, and experiences, as well as varying levels of language, cognitive, and emotional development. Some factors influence the play to such an extent that generalizations can be made that help the teacher reflect on appropriate teaching practices.

Cultural Differences in Dramatic Play

While developmental capacities have individual differences, it is widely held that most are universal. For example, children between one and two all over the world begin to talk. The social and cultural influences on development, attitudes, and dispositions are evident; however, they are even more obvious in dramatic play, especially in the social-emotional realm. Certain cultures do not value fantasy. Those children enter group situations without the desire or skills to interact in this way. Older Mexican-American siblings, however, made expert sociodramatic play partners. In some societies (Russian and East African), fantasy and imaginative play appear to be absent (Johnson, et al., 1987). It is difficult to draw conclusions from limited evidence. The observer should cultivate an awareness so expectations are tempered by the consideration of the many possible factors affecting the development.

Socioeconomic Differences in Dramatic Play

Smilansky and Shefatya's (1990) observations of the play of economically deprived children give insight into the play of these children. It was more object-centered with the object determining the theme rather than the theme suggesting the object. The objects were used in a more rigid way and were possessed with determination. Verbal interactions were more functional for management and announcement of roles. They rarely took on the "voice" of the role they were playing. The language was more authoritative than democratic. They used less humor, more criticism, aggressiveness, and control in dealing with problems.

Differing Abilities and Dramatic Play

Children with physical challenges participate in all kinds of play in the classroom, including dramatic play. The teacher's role supports a higher level of activity by modifications to the environment.

The adult interprets for the hearing impaired, gives sensory experiences to the visually impaired, and mediates for children with serious learning and behavior problems. The teacher looks for ways that the child with disabilities could participate. The child with limited vision or a child who is blind may need explanations about the nature of the play and suggestions of roles or actions she could contribute. Their play is less imaginative and more concrete than sighted children. They are more likely to play alone. The teacher needs to orient the child to choices, offer specific suggestions for symbolic play, and provide props that are sensory-rich (Hughes, 1999).

Children who are hearing impaired will use realistic props to join in the play but may need assistance when the play turns to transformational or representational props. The significance of a rope for a fire hose may not be understood. Children with physical disabilities can use their abilities to join in the play but may need the adult's help. Giving other children ideas about how to involve the child, creating roles for the child, and giving a prop to add to the play are ways that the adult can help (Karnes, 1992.) The application of private speech for children with self-regulatory problems like ADHD is being explored (Berk & Winsler, 1995).

IT HAPPENED TO ME

Empty Eyeglasses

One day in my optometrist's office I offhandedly asked if they ever had any eyeglass frames they could donate to the preschool. They called me in a few weeks with a wonderful collection! These were added to the dramatic play area and at once became favorite props for play. Most of all, they helped all the children relate to a child in the class who wore glasses. It prepared them for that possibility themselves in the future. Sometimes a serendipitous action becomes an important one.

Since play comes naturally to all children and is a central framework for all development, it serves as a context for intervention strategy. Dramatic play facilitates social interaction and communication, seldom is limited by physical disabilities when there are environmental accommodations, and provides a vehicle for success (Cripe & Lee, 1997).

HELPING PROFESSIONALS FOR PLAY CONCERNS

There may be children who exhibit no desire or attention to dramatic play experiences. This does not mean that these children are not creative but this is not an area that interests them. Young children are working out the differences between real and imaginary and become very arbitrary sometimes in only wanting to be involved in the real rather than the pretend, rejecting that as younger behavior. This is usually not a problem, just an observation that one can make from the child's play and interactions with the environment.

On the other hand, there occasionally are some children so caught up in dramatic play and the imaginary world that they lose touch with reality. The causes may be varied, from giftedness in the area of creativity, to escape from a traumatic real-world experience. The observer assesses the range of normal expected behavior, alert to excessive or compulsive behavior that may be a clue of a deeper problem. After observation, documentation, and discussion with the teaching team, the family is consulted for advice and insight. If a referral is made, it may be to one of the psychological professionals such as:

psychologist—professional trained in human behavior

psychiatrist—physician specializing in social or emotional disorders

OTHER METHODS

Other Methods to Record Sociodramatic Play:

Anecdotal/Running Records
Checklist or Rating Scale that has dramatic play criteria
Time Sample—length of time in Dramatic Play area
Work Samples—play written by children, costumes/sets produced

KEY TERMS

audio recorders
digital video cameras
informed consent
sociodramatic play

story dictation
technology
video recorder

WEEK 11: PLAN A

TECHNOLOGY USE IN DRAMATIC PLAY

Students

Get a signed audio/video/photo release from the families of two children. Use some form of technology to record a segment of dramatic play. Analyze the play for its contribution to documenting areas of development.

Practitioners

Get a signed audio/video/photo release from each child's family. File the signed release in each child's program file with family information forms and a copy in each child's portfolio. *If there is no release, or if the family checked no, place a prominent notation on the file and inform all staff.* Use some alternate method for recording dramatic play or blocks.

Use some type of media to record each child's dramatic play. (Use a checklist to be sure you have recorded every child in the class.)

Tape record conversations as children are involved in a dramatic play episode.

What to Do with It

Filing. Transcribe portions of the tape that are significant, noting that the tape is available in the class file. Place individual notes from transcription in each child's portfolio noting its presence on the overview sheet with the date and your name. Make comments in the appropriate developmental area that it documents (Figure 11–7).

Sharing with the Child and Family. Share what you have heard with the family and child if appropriate: "Mrs. Truax, today when I was observing Dionne's block play, the conversation was so interesting I tape recorded it. Would you like to take it home to listen? I wrote down some of the conversation for Dionne's portfolio on imagination."

"Gretchen, today when you were playing with the Play Doh, you were giving the directions to make spaghetti and singing a song about it. Remember when I turned on the tape recorder? Would you like to hear it? Where did you learn that song? Can you tell me about how your mother makes spaghetti? Maybe she'd bring her pasta machine to school some day and you and she could show us all how to do it."

Photographs

Take photographs of each child as they play, even if no dramatic play is observed. If these are groups playing together, take a sequence of shots for the number of children playing there. For example, if three children are building with blocks, take three pictures as the building progresses. It will not only show the sequence but also will give you a picture for each child's portfolio. Or, you can take one picture and have a number of prints made.

What to Do with It

Filing. In each child's portfolio place the photo, the date, and the situation, either on the back or mount the photo on a piece of paper. Make any comments about the child's level of play, conversations heard, interesting points, and questions the play brought up to you.

CREATIVE AND DRAMATIC PLAY			
Documentation	Location	Recorder	Date
Photo Dram Play	Portfolio		11/20
Video	Class tape		12/22
RR - Episode includes doc-tor's office	Portfolio	MS	1/31

Figure 11–7 Portfolio Overview Example

Note the presence of the photo under dramatic play (or relevant area) on the overview sheet, date, and your name.

Sharing with the Child and Family. Share with the family and child, if appropriate. Perhaps have a bulletin board at first with all the photos displayed: "Children at Work." Discuss the situation of the photo and its significance. Tell the family and child it will be in the portfolio and will be given to them at the end of the year.

Video Tape

Take a video of the children as they play. Try to get whole segments of play and as much conversation as you can. Include every child in the class in some way on the tape.

What to Do with It

Filing. Later that day, or as soon as possible, show the tape to the class. They love to see themselves. You could stop after each segment and ask the children involved to explain what they were doing. Invite the other children to ask questions or make suggestions on how the play could have been different. These discussions could be documented as further evidence of sociodramatic play or language practice.

As you view the tape, you can use a Class List Log to check the children's appearance and activity on the tape and file that with the tape as a reference.

You can use the tape to analyze areas of development and make notes in the child's portfolio. Refer to the video tape of (date), or use the counter to indicate the position on the tape.

Sharing with the Child and Family. Show the tape at a family meeting or have it playing as families arrive to pick up the children at the end of the day. File the tape in the class file, and add to it later in the year.

Actions.

Read a Book.
See book list on page 279.

In the Environment.
- Provide an ample supply of dramatic play props for stimulating sociodramatic play.
- Provide housekeeping and work props, interesting clothing with colors, textures, and styles that will appeal to imaginations. One of the best sources are garage sales and family contributions.
- Provide space for many children to be involved in dramatic play.

- Provide a stage made from blocks to feature a short dramatic play episode.

In the Curriculum.

- Use some of the books suggested to try a creative drama based on a favorite. This turns into a project when children catch hold of the idea and want to make costumes, props, and sets. This perhaps can lead to a field trip behind the scenes of a real play or to have the experience of walking onto a real stage; perhaps a local high school would be a willing host.
- Resist the temptation to invite families to view a full-scale production. This may add stress to the children, yourselves, and the families watching. Try to remember, it's the process not the product.
- Make thematic connections in the Dramatic Play area with special materials, such as bakery props: chef's hats, aprons, hot mitts, rolling pins; post office props: mailboxes, canvas tote bags, an assortment of paper, stamps, rubber stamp pads, envelopes; camping props: a child-size tent, pretend binoculars, cameras, picnic baskets, fishing poles, small logs for campfire.

In the Newsletter.

- A narrative article about the benefits of creative dramatics will inform families of the rationale and learning that is going on during this kind of play.
- Some anecdotes from dramatic play or a creative dramatic episode add humorous touches to a newsletter as well as insight into how children think, and perhaps a warning that children are watching and listening, reenacting everything that goes on at home.
- Provide a list of dramatic play props that families could donate. Encourage them to think creatively.

WEEK 11: PLAN B

RUNNING RECORD IN DRAMATIC PLAY/ BLOCKS OR FREE PLAY FOR GROUP B

Each day this week, select children from Group B. Using a Running Record (see Chapter 4), gather a segment of regular play during dramatic play, block play, or free time. On the left column of a sheet of paper, record the child's name, date, your name, and time begun. Follow the child with your recording, telling accurately and descriptively where the child is, what action is taking place, and any conversation in which the child is participating. Just describe without commentary or inferences.

What to Do with It

Filing. Later in the day, in the right-hand column of the Running Record, make any comments, explanations, or evaluations of areas of development. In each child's portfolio, note on the overview sheet the presence of this Record in the area that it most vividly documents, along with the date and your name.

File the recordings in the child's portfolio.

Sharing with the Child and Family. Share the recordings or your observations with the family and the child, if appropriate, such as: "Mr. Williamson, today when I was observing Jared in the block corner he was counting the floors of the building he made. When I was writing down what he was doing he looked over at me and said, 'Did you get that? I counted to ten.' And he had! He is such a character!" or "Taohou, today when I was writing down what you were working on at the puzzle table, I saw you could put together the Lion King puzzle with your eyes closed! How did you know where to put the pieces?"

WEEK 11: PLAN C

REFLECTIVE JOURNAL

Respond to the following in your Reflective Journal, kept in a private file at home.

When I think about using media as an observation technique, I wonder about . . .

It is interesting to watch children in dramatic play. As a child I remember most pretending to be . . .

The role I would like to play is . . .

Because . . .

They call it "private speech" when young children do it. I call it "talking to myself." I notice myself doing it most when . . .

I wonder if it's because . . .

REFERENCES

American Psychological Association. (1990). Ethical principles of psychologists (amended June 2, 1989). *American Psychologist*, 390–395.

American Psychological Association. (2002). *Ethical principles of psychologists and code of conduct.* Washington, DC: Author http://www.apa.org/ethics/code2002.pdf. Retrieved April 7, 2003.

Beaty, J. (2002). *Observing development of the young child* (5th ed.). New York: Merrill, an imprint of Macmillan Publishing Company.

Bergen, D. (2002). The role of pretend play in children's cognitive development. *Early Childhood Research and Practice, 4* (1).

Berk, L. E. (1994). Vygotsky's theory: The importance of make-believe play. *Young Children (50)* (1), 30–39.

Berk, L. E., & Winsler, A. (1995). *Scaffolding children's learning: Vygotsky and early childhood education.* Washington, DC: National Association for the Education of Young Children.

Blagojevic, B., & Gathwait, A. (2001). Observing & recording growth & change: Using technology as an assessment tool. *Scholastic Early Childhood Today, 15* (8), 36–44.

Block, C. C. (2001). *Teaching the language arts: Expanding thinking through student-centered instruction*, 3rd ed. Boston: Allyn and Bacon.

Bushman, B. J., & Huesmann, L. R. (2001). Effects of televised violence on aggression. In D. G. Singer, & J. L. Singer (Eds.). *Handbook of children and the media.* Thousand Oaks, CA: Sage Publications, Inc.

Carlsson-Paige, N., & Levin, D. (1990). *Who's calling the shots? How to respond effectively to children's war play and war toys.* Philadelphia: New Society Publishers.

Consortium of National Arts Education Associations. (1994). *Dance, music, theater, visual arts: What every young American should know and be able to do in the arts: National Standards for arts education.* Reston, VA: Music Educators National Conference.

Cripe, J. W., & Lee, J. M. (1997). Activity-based intervention strategies for serving young children with developmental delays in early childhood programs in Brown, W. H., & Conroy, M. A. *Including and supporting preschool children with developmental delays in early childhood programs.* Little Rock, AR: Southern Early Childhood Association, 49–64.

Curry, N. (1992). Four- and five-year-olds: Intuitive, imaginative players. In V. Dimidjian, (Ed.), *Play's place in public education for young children.* Washington, DC: National Education Association of the United States, pp. 37–48.

Curry, N., & Arnaud, S. (1995). Personality difficulties in preschool children as revealed through play themes and styles. *Young Children, 50* (4), 4–9.

Edwards, L. C. (1997) *The creative arts: A process approach for teachers and children.* Upper Saddle River, NJ: Simon and Schuster.

Fein, G. G., & Kinney, P. (1994). He's a nice alligator: Observations on the effective organization of pretence. In A. Slad, & D. P. Wolf (Eds.). *Children at play: Clinical and developmental approaches to meaning and representation.* New York: Oxford University Press.

Helm, J. H. (2003). Contemporary challenges in early childhood education. In J. H. Helm & S. Beneke (Eds.). *The power of projects: Meeting contemporary challenges in early childhood classrooms.* New York: Teachers College Press.

Helm, J. H., & Katz, L. (2001). *Young investigators: The project approach in the early years.* New York: Teachers College Press.

Herr, J., & Libby, Y. (2004). *Creative resources for the early childhood classroom.* Clifton Park, NY: Thomson Delmar Learning.

Holzberg, C. (1993). Roll 'Em: Camcorders & VCR's for education. *Electronic Learning, 88,* 12.

Hosington, C. (2002). Using photographs to support children's science inquiry. *Young Children, 57* (5), 26–31.

Howe, N., et al. (1993). The ecology of dramatic play centers and children's social and cognitive play. *Early Childhood Research Quarterly, 8,* 235–251.

Howell, J., & Corbey-Scullen, L. (1997). Out of the housekeeping corner and onto the stage—extending dramatic play. *Young Children, 52* (6), 82–88.

Hughes, F. P. (1999). *Children, play, and development.* Boston: Allyn and Bacon.

Isenberg, J., & Jalongo, M. (2001). *Creative expression and play in the early childhood curriculum*, 3rd ed. New York: Merrill, an imprint of Macmillan Publishing Company.

Johnson, M. E., Christie, J. F., & Yawkey, T. D. (1987). *Play and early childhood development.* New York: HarperCollins Publishers.

Johnson, J. G., Cohen, P., Smailes, E. M., Kasen, S., & Brook, J. S. (2002). Television viewing and aggressive behavior during adolescence and adulthood. *Science, 295* (5564), 2468–2471.

Karnes, M. (1992). Dramatic play and children with special needs. *Pre-K Today, 7* (2), 72.

Kim, S. (1999). The effects of storytelling and pretend play on cognitive processes, short-term and long-term narrative recall. *Child Study Journal, 29* (3), 176–191.

Krafft, K. C., & Berk, L. E. (1998). Private speech in two preschools: Significance of open-ended activities and make-believe play for verbal self-regulation. *Early Childhood Research Quarterly, 13* (4), 637–658.

Machado, J. M. (2003). *Early childhood experiences in language arts.* Clifton Park, NY: Thomson Delmar Learning.

National Television Violence Study. (2002). *Executive Summary.* Santa Barbara, CA: Center for Communication and Social Policy.

Negroponte, N. (1995). *Being digital.* New York: Alfred A. Knopf, Inc.

Paik, H. & Comstock, G. (1994). The effects of television violence on antisocial behavior: A meta-analysis. *Communication Research, 21,* 516–546.

Paley, V. G. (1984). *Boys and girls: Superheroes in the doll corner.* Chicago: University of Chicago Press.

Paley, V. G. (1988). *Bad guys don't have birthdays.* Chicago: University of Chicago Press.

Paley, V. G. (1990). *The boy who would be a helicopter.* Cambridge, MA: Harvard University Press.

Paley, V. G. (1997). *The girl with the brown crayon.* Cambridge, MA: Harvard University Press.

Peterson, R., & Felton-Collins, V. (1986). *The Piaget handbook for teachers and parents.* New York: Teachers College Press.

Rubin, K. H., & Coplan, R. K. (1998). Social and nonsocial play in childhood: An individual differences perspective. In O. N. Saracho & B. Spodek (Eds.). *Multiple perspectives on play in early childhood* (pp. 144–170). Albany: State University of New York Press.

Schoon, S. (1997/98). Using dance experience and drama in the classroom. *Childhood Education, 74* (2), 78–82.

Singer, D. G., & Singer, J. L. (1990). *The house of make-believe: Children's play and the developing imagination.* Cambridge, MA: Harvard University Press.

Slaby, R., Roedell, W., Arezzo, D., & Hendrix, K. (1995). *Early violence prevention: Tools for teachers of young children*. Washington, DC: National Association for the Education of Young Children.

Smilansky, S., & Shefatya, L. (1990). *Facilitating play: A medium for promoting cognitive, socio-emotional and academic development in young children*. Gaithersburg, MD: Psychosocial & Educational Publications.

Snow, C. E., Burns, M. S., & Griffin, P. (Eds.). (1998). *Preventing reading difficulties in young children*. Washington, DC: National Academy Press.

Trepanier-Street, M. L, Hong, S. B., & Bauer, J. C. (2001). Using technology in Reggio-inspired long-term projects. *Early Childhood Education Journal, 28* (3), 181–88.

RESOURCES

Carlsson-Paige, N., & Levin, D. (1990). *Who's calling the shots? How to respond effectively to children's war play and war toys*. Philadelphia: New Society Publishers.

Paley, V. G. (1984). *Boys and girls: Superheroes in the doll corner*. Chicago: University of Chicago Press.

Paley, V. G. (1988). *Bad guys don't have birthdays*. Chicago: University of Chicago Press.

Paley, V. G. (1997). *The girl with the brown crayon*. Cambridge, MA: Harvard University Press.

Pugmire-Stoy, M. C. (1992). *Spontaneous play in early childhood*. Clifton Park, NY: Thomson Delmar Learning.

Singer, D. G, & Singer, J. L. (2001). *Make-believe: Games & activities for imaginative play: A book for parents, teachers, and the young children in their lives*. Washington, DC: Magination Press.

Slaby, R., Roedell, W., Arezzo, D., & Hendrix, K. (1995). *Early violence prevention: Tools for teachers of young children*. Washington, DC: National Association for the Education of Young Children.

For additional information on early education curriculum, visit our Web site at http://www.earlychilded.delmar.com

Using Documentation for Child Abuse Suspicions and Looking at Self-Concept

USING DOCUMENTATION FOR CHILD ABUSE SUSPICIONS

Observing children in group settings is not always a pleasant experience. The observer of children has a grave responsibility to fulfill in recognizing and reporting signs of abuse or neglect. This section is

one that everyone wishes would not be necessary but child abuse is a reality. There are people who hurt children physically, psychologically, or use children for sexual purposes.

Neglect is characterized by failure to provide for the child's basic needs, which include physical, medical, educational, and emotional. A form of neglect for infants and young children is organic failure to thrive, caused by physiological problems, or nonorganic, due to nourishment. **Physical abuse** includes any nonaccidental injury caused by the child's caregiver, intentional, or nonintentional. **Sexual abuse** includes a wide range of behavior, including exploitation through prostitution or pornography. **Emotional maltreatment** is psychological or emotional abuse through blaming, belittling, or rejecting a child.

As teachers interact with children, they win the child's trust. They have the opportunity to see and hear what children do and talk about the experiences they have had. They may be the one who prevents neglect or abuse from happening again. People who abuse children need help, and the child needs help and protection. Not reporting suspected abuse allows it to continue.

Physical and Behavioral Indicators of Abuse

Teachers and child care workers must be familiar with the physical and behavioral indicators of abuse. Indicators may give very clear evidence of maltreatment, but they also may have other explanations. Some may result from the personality of the child, a new setting with new adults, poverty, different cultural values, accidents, or illnesses. Judgment must be used, but for the protection of the child it is better to report those suspicions.

Reasonable Cause to Suspect. The suspicion of child abuse or neglect grows from visual observations, verbal disclosures, or an accumulation of circumstances that build to a reasonable cause to suspect. This does not place the reporter in the position of investigator, interrogator, or prosecutor, but just giving an initial alert based on factual observations (Figure 12–1).

The Child's Appearance. For infants and preverbal children, abuse and maltreatment can be observed in the normal routines of being with the child. By the location and formation of bruises, cuts, and inflammations, concerns are raised. Obvious wounds are usually met by a teacher's empathetic comments, such as "Ooo, that bruise looks sore," or interested questions of verbal children such as, "Why are you walking like that? Does something hurt?" The child's response may be a first-hand account of what happened, a **disclosure** statement.

The Child's Description or Disclosure. The child may say, "My daddy twisted my arm," or "Uncle John hurt me in my goo goo." Comments like these always catch teachers by surprise but it is important that facial or verbal expressions not reveal the shock, revulsion, or disapproval of what has happened to this child. An appropriate response is, "Can you tell me what happened?" This expresses concern while gently probing for more details. These disclosures call for immediate action and documentation (Figure 12–2). Besharov (1990) in *Recognizing Child Abuse* stresses that once a mandated reporter has "reasonable cause," probing for all the details is not necessary. In fact, detailed probing may actually place the child in greater jeopardy. The questions should be asked only to answer the question in the reporter's mind: "Do I know enough to *suspect* that this injury or behavior could have been caused by abuse or neglect?" To probe further will inevitably compromise later interviews of the child by child protective authorities. When children must repeat their story to different adults, they may leave out information to protect a loved one. They may recant their story for fear of the consequences, or add untrue details to be more believed. This detailed interviewing is best left to the authorities.

Besharov recommends if the child willingly offers and needs to talk about it, by all means be a ready listener, then accurately document questions and comments by both the child and adult. (See Figure 12–3 on page 294). Conduct the interview in private. Sit next to the child, not across the table or desk. Ask the child to clarify words or terms that you do not understand. Be supportive; the child is likely to be frightened about telling "family secrets." Stress that anything that happened was not the child's fault (p. 269).

Circumstantial Evidence. Suspicious injuries may suggest child abuse or maltreatment. Children's explanations are often protective statements. Behavioral indications by themselves are not sufficient basis for a report, but in combination or continued appearance should be documented and discussed with a supervisor.

Teacher Support. The disclosure, recording, and reporting of child abuse all take an emotional toll on teachers, people who have committed their career to the care and education of children. The first area of support should come from the administration through clear policies, responsive follow-through, and empathy. The local child abuse agency can answer specific questions and clear up any misgivings or doubts about suspected abuse. It may be that the adult will need to spend time with a counselor to sort out feelings of loyalty, betrayal, anger, disappointment, or fear. This is a very sensitive area for all the people involved.

Recording Any Indicators of Maltreatment

The most appropriate method for recording episodes that document suspected abuse or maltreatment is the Anecdotal Record. It is effective for this information because the accounts

- are written shortly after the episode or event occurs, based on notes jotted at the time.
- contain a detailed account, including date and time, people involved in the episode, actions, and exact conversations. This is especially important in situations in which a child reveals to a teacher that someone is hurting him or her. The questions and comments that the adult says must be accurately recorded also. This indicates that the child was not led or influenced in the description of the event.
- contain separate comments by the recorder, such as opinions or questions, from the body of the recording.

Type of Abuse/ Maltreatment	Physical Indicators	Child Behavioral Indicators	Parental Behavioral Indicators
Physical Abuse	* unexplained or inadequately explained bruises, welts, burns, lacerations, abrasions or fractures. * frequent injuries that are "accidental" or "unexplained." * patterned, reflecting shape of article used to inflict injury (e.g., elec. cord, belt buckle). * bilateral (both sides of body) or on several different surfaces. * regularly appearing after absence, weekend, vacation, etc. * in various stages of healing. * human bite marks: <3cm. between canines.	* reports injury by parents. * exhibits behavioral extremes: aggressive, demanding, destructive or shy, withdrawn, compliant, passive. * frequently late or absent from school or comes too early and/or stays late. * wary of adult contacts. * seems frightened of parents. * wears long-sleeved or similar clothing to hide injuries. * afraid to go home or shows little distress at being separated from parents. * seeks affection from any adult.	* seems unconcerned about child. * takes an unusual amount of time to obtain medical care for the child. * offers an inadequate or inappropriate explanation for the child's injury. * gives different explanations for the same injury. * misuses drugs or alcohol. * disciplines the child too harshly considering the child's age or what he/she did wrong. * sees the child as bad or evil. * has history of abuse as a child. * attempts to conceal the child's injury. * takes the child to a different doctor or hospital for each injury.
Neglect	* frequently hungry, inappropriately dressed for the weather, and/or has poor hygiene. * consistently left alone or inadequately supervised for long periods of time or in dangerous circumstances. * often tired or listless. * needs medical/dental care. * has been abandoned. * being exposed to unsafe living conditions.	* frequently late or absent from school or comes too early and/or stays late. * begs or steals food. * constantly falls asleep in school. * exhibits delinquent behavior; uses alcohol or drugs, engages in vandalism or sexual misconduct. * states there is no parent or caretaker. * excessive responsibility for younger siblings.	* misuses alcohol or drugs. * has disorganized, upsetting home life. * is apathetic, feels nothing will change. * is isolated from friends, relatives, neighbors. * has long-term, chronic illness. * cannot be found. * has history of neglect as a child.
Sexual Abuse	* somatic problems (ulcers, migraines, etc.). * has difficulty in walking or sitting. * has torn, stained, or bloody underclothing. * experiences pain or itching in genital area. * has venereal disease (especially in pre-teens). * is pregnant * weight gain/loss. * problems with hygiene.	* poor self-esteem, peer relationships. * is unwilling to participate in physical activities or change clothes for gym. * appears withdrawn, fantasy or infantile behavior, depressed or suicidal. * fear of physical contact. * is engaging in delinquent acts or runs away. * reports sexual assault by parent or caretaker. * change in affect or body language when particular adult is discussed. * sexually acting out/seductive; excessive sexual knowledge. * academic problems, difficulty concentrating.	* role reversal, blurred boundaries. * very protective, jealous, or controlling. * encourages child to engage in prostitution or sexual acts in the presence of caretaker. * misuses alcohol or other drugs. * older siblings leaving home at early age. * history of sexual abuse. * low self-esteem. * socially isolated. * incapacitated mother. * reunited with estranged parent.
Emotional Neglect	* habit disorders (sucking, biting, rocking, etc.) * eating disorders. * physically underdeveloped. * neurotic traits (sleep disorders, speech disorders, inhibition of play). * psychoneurotic reactions (hysteria, obsessions, compulsion, phobias, hypochondria).	* poor self-image. * exhibits behavioral extremes: aggressive, demanding, or compliant, shy, passive. * is overly adaptive, either inappropriately adult or infantile. * exhibits physical, mental or emotional developmental lags. * attempts suicide, self-destructive. * substance abuse. * poor social skills, low frustration tolerance, academic dysfunction.	* poor self-image. * treats children in the family unequally. * doesn't seem to care much about child's problems. * blames or belittles child. * is cold and rejecting. * withholds love. * unrealistic expectations. * substance abuse.

NOTE: Some behavioral indicators may be common to all children at one time. When indicators are noticeable in a sufficient number and strength to characterize a child's overall manner, they may indicate abuse or neglect.

Figure 12–1 Child Abuse and Maltreatment Indicators (Courtesy of New York State Department of Social Services, 1995. *Child Protective Services, Mandated Reporter Manual.* Reprinted with permission.)

As responders it is critical that we be sensitive to issues of poverty and neglect, differing cultural expectations and values, and differing child rearing practices. The outline below should assist you in understanding the minimal standards of care to be expected as well as considerations of poverty, cultural influences, and differing practices.

GUIDELINES/MINIMAL STANDARDS OF CARE

	Expectations	**Considerations**
Supervision	* Young children are not left unattended. * Children are not left in the care of siblings who are too young to provide adequate care. * Children are not left with adult caregivers who are inadequate or unsafe.	* Did the parent/sitter abandon the children? * Are siblings, left to care for younger children, able and responsible? * Are there other child care options available to the parent(s)?
Clothing and Hygiene	* Children are dressed adequately and appropriately for the weather. * Babies and toddlers don't chronically suffer severe diaper rash, or other persistent skin disorders resulting from poor hygiene. * Children are not chronically dirty or unbathed.	* Is too small, clean clothing okay? * Has the child lost his/her winter coat? * Is it "fashionable" from the child's point of view to wear sneakers even in the rain and snow? * Children playing in snow or outside find it difficult to stay dry and clean. * Are they bathed before they go to bed? Are they encouraged to "wash up" for meals?
Medical and Dental Care	* Children who are ill should be receiving proper medical care. * Children should be seen by the dentist and should have proper eye care.	* Are "free" clinics available? * Does the parent know where the clinic is? * Can they afford the appropriate, adequate medical, dental, and eye care?
Education	* Children should attend school on a regular basis. * Older children should not be kept at home to care for younger siblings.	* Are older children needed as interpreters by parents when they go to seek help or services from public and/or private agencies? * Are there ill children/adults home needing care?
Nutrition	* Children should have a sufficient quantity and good quality food. * Children should not continually complain of being hungry. * Severe developmental lags are sometimes indicators of poor nutrition.	* Be aware of poverty factors, as well as cultural factors in terms of what is considered a nutritious meal. * Does parent know how to use food stamps properly? * Does parent know what nutritious meals consist of? * Are children allergic to certain foods?
Adequate Shelter	* Housing should be structurally safe and free of exposed wiring. * There should be adequate heat. * The house should be clean and sanitary.	* Is the landlord/owner of the housing providing proper services?

Figure 12–1   Child Abuse and Maltreatment Indicators (Continued)

Figure 12–2   Hotline reports need to be made immediately.

In addition to the narrative, diagrams and specific descriptions of size and nature of wounds should be made. Explanations or conjecture about their cause should be separate from the diagram.

Some states allow the taking of photographs by mandated reporters, but this should be confirmed in the recorder's state. In most cases, however, photographs taken by those other than the authorities are unnecessary and may be very inappropriate. Photographs by authorized persons are considered to be evidence and can be used as such only under controlled conditions. This is best left to child protection, law enforcement, or medical authorities. Further trauma may be added to the child by photographing the injuries. For many sexually abused children, being photographed may be a part of their history of

When Talking with the Child

DO:

- Make sure the ECE professional is someone the child knows and trusts.
- Conduct the discussion in a place that allows for privacy but is familiar to the child.
- Use only one or two ECE professionals.
- Sit next to the child at his/her level.
- Engage the child in a conversation but do not press the child to talk about the injuries if he/she does not want to.
- Ask the child to clarify words or terms that are not understood.
- Assure the child that he/she has done nothing wrong.

- _____
- _____

DO NOT:

- Suggest answers to the child.
- Probe or press for answers the child does not willingly offer.
- Force the child to remove clothing.
- Display horror, shock, or disapproval of the parent(s), child, or situation.
- Leave the child alone with a stranger.
- Ask "why" questions.

- _____
- _____

When Talking with the Parent(s)

DO:

- Select the person most appropriate to the situation.
- Conduct the discussion in private.
- Tell the parent(s) why the discussion is taking place.
- Be direct, honest, and professional.
- Reassure parent(s) of the program's support to them and to their child.
- Tell the parent(s) if a report was made or will be made.
- Advise the parent(s) of the program's legal and ethical responsibilities to report.

- _____
- _____

DO NOT:

- Try to prove the abuse or neglect; that is not an ECE professional's role.
- Display horror, anger, or disapproval of the parent(s), child, or situation.
- Pry into family matters unrelated to the specific situation.
- Place blame or make judgments about the parent(s) or child.

- _____
- _____

Figure 12–3 Tips for Talking with a Child or Parent (Reprinted from _Caregivers of Young Children: Preventing and Responding to Child Maltreatment_, 1992, p. 24. U. S. Department of Health and Human Services.)

abuse. In any event, photographs, should they be taken, must be turned over to the authorities immediately. _The accurate recording and prompt reporting of suspected child abuse and maltreatment cannot be stressed enough._

Next Steps

Immediate notification of the supervisor is the first step. Short, accurate notes made as soon as possible preserve vital details. The Child Abuse Hotline, required in every state, should be called immediately either by the supervisor or witness, depending on the policies and procedures already in place in the program. The local agency may be called to confer if indeed there is enough suspicion to file a Hotline report. The exception to this is if there is suspicion of sexual abuse or the life of the child is in danger. In that case, the law enforcement agency should be called _immediately_. If for some reason the supervisor does not make the call and the teacher has "reason to suspect" there has been possible abuse, then there is a legal and moral responsibility to make the call.

Legal Process of Reporting. Individual states vary in the definitions of child maltreatment but most include nonaccidental physical abuse, neglect, sexual abuse, and emotional (or mental) maltreatment by a person responsible for the child's welfare.

EXERCISE: According to the laws in your state, reportable child abuse is defined as what?

Every state has laws for reporting child abuse and a reporting number, many of which are 1-800, toll-free telephone calls. School personnel and day-care and child care workers are **mandated reporters** by law in every state. A mandated reporter must report any "reasonable cause to suspect" a child has been maltreated. Not reporting suspected neglect or abuse could result in legal action. Reporters of suspected abuse are not responsible for proving the abuse, just to present the observable facts that led to the suspicions. If the report is **unfounded**—not enough evidence exists to prove it—the reporter is protected from civil action.

EXERCISE: Locate the Hotline or reporting number for child care workers in your state. Find the state and local agency and telephone number to whom you could ask questions. Write them on a separate sheet of paper.

Reporting telephone number
Agency and telephone number

When the Hotline or Law Enforcement Agency Is Called. The reporter will be asked to supply as much of the following information as possible. The lack of complete information *does not* prohibit a report from being made. Requested information includes:

- the name and address of the child and his or her parents or legally responsible guardian
- the child's age, sex, and race
- the nature and extent of the child's injuries, abuse, or maltreatment (including any evidence of prior injuries, abuse, or maltreatment to the child or his or her siblings)
- the child's present location
- the name of the person or persons responsible for causing the injury, abuse, or maltreatment
- family composition; others residing in or at the home in regular intervals
- person making the report, where the person can be reached, and where the information was obtained; names of other relevant school personnel who may provide critical information
- any action taken by the reporting source
- any additional information that may be helpful

Though suspicions of abuse or neglect seem obvious by the very act of calling the Hotline, they must hear the reporter's concerns in those terms: "I believe this child to be abused or neglected because . . ." The report is strengthened if the reporter can

1. detail a pattern (not that a mother was overheard screaming at her child once, but this is how she interacts with her child routinely), *and*
2. state the impact on the child (e.g., behavioral signs, the child is doing poorly in school, and so on).

Needless to say, one would not wait for a pattern of injuries before alerting the authorities. If troublesome behavior by a family member and/or the child, though not reportable, has been observed, that information may be helpful to set a framework for the report to the Hotline. Documentation of these earlier concerns should be recorded in the style of an Anecdotal Recording and kept in a confidential file.

Once the call is made, the written Report of Suspected Child Abuse or Maltreatment should be completed and filed according to the directions in the state (Figure 12–4). A copy is kept in a confidential file, separate from the child's portfolio and separate from the class file, along with any written records referring to these suspicions. For the reporter's own use, a log should be kept of the time of the incident and the witness's exact response (writing anecdotal, reporting to supervisor, action taken). Additions to

the log should be made as each step in the process occurs ("Made out written report, date," "answered questions by . . ."). This should be kept in the reporter's possession.

Do not discuss suspicions with the family or the child. This is the one time when what was observed should not be discussed with family or the child after the initial disclosure. The authorities should be allowed to take further action.

If the family member comes to school and asks who made the report, they should be referred to the supervisor. Families should always be treated respectfully and tactfully. When they know a report has been made, they can be referred to the family handbook where it states the policy of the program and the legal responsibility of mandated reporters. They are offered assistance to seek help and given referrals to agencies and support groups in their area. The family member may be angry and abusive, but the child's safety is of the utmost consideration. Arguing and relating details to the family are inappropriate actions. Supervisors may make a statement such as, "We have observed something that made us suspect the child may be abused and we have a legal obligation to report that suspicion. We have done what we think is best for the child. We stand ready to help in whatever way we can." That is all one needs to say, and all one should say, perhaps even *more* than one should say. It all depends on the circumstances.

DIVERSITY AND CHILD ABUSE

Child-rearing customs and practices are not standard between any two families, but are even more varied because of racial, cultural, economic, and religious differences. Sometimes these come in conflict with

LDSS-2221-A (Rev. 11/97)

REPORT OF SUSPECTED
CHILD ABUSE OR MALTREATMENT

New York State · Office of Children and Family Services

Report Date	Case ID	Call ID
/ /		
Time AM/PM	Local Case #	Local Dist/Agency

SUBJECTS OF REPORT

List all children in household, adults responsible and alleged subjects.

Line # Last Name	First Name	Aliases	Sex (M, F, Unk)	Birthday or Age Mo/ Day/ Yr	Ethnic Code	Relation Code	Role	Lang.
1.								
2.								
3.								
4.								
5.								
6.								
7.								

☐ MORE

List Addresses and Telephone Numbers (Using Line Numbers From Above)	Telephone No.

BASIS OF SUSPICIONS

Alleged suspicions of abuse or maltreatment. Give child(ren)'s line number(s). If all children, write **"ALL"**.

_____ DOA/Fatality

_____ Fractures

_____ Internal Injuries (i.e. Subdural Hematoma)

_____ Lacerations/Bruises/Welts

_____ Burns/Scalding

_____ Excessive Corporal Punishment

_____ Inappropriate Isolation/Restraint(Institutional Abuse Only)

_____ Inappropriate Custodial Conduct(Institutional Abuse Only)

_____ Child's Drug/Alcohol Use

_____ Poisoning/Noxious Substances

_____ Choking/Twisting/Shaking

_____ Lack of Medical Care

_____ Malnutrition/Failure to Thrive

_____ Sexual Abuse

_____ Inadequate Guardianship

_____ Swelling/Dislocation/Sprains

_____ Educational Neglect

_____ Emotional Neglect

_____ Inadequate Food/Clothing/Shelter

_____ Lack of Supervision

_____ Abandonment

_____ Parent's Drug/Alcohol Misuse

_____ Other specify)_____

State reasons for suspicion, including the nature and extent of each child's injuries, abuse or maltreatment, past and present, and any evidence or suspicions of "Parental" behavior contributing to the problem.

(If known, give time/date of alleged incident)
____/____/____ Time_____(AM/PM)

The Mandated Reporter Requests Finding of Investigation   ☐ YES   ☐ NO

CONFIDENTIAL	SOURCES OF REPORT	*CONFIDENTIAL*

NAME	TELEPHONE	NAME	TELEPHONE
ADDRESS		ADDRESS	
AGENCY/INSTITUTION		AGENCY/INSTITUTION	

RELATIONSHIP (✓ = REPORTER, **X** = SOURCE)

☐ Med. Exam/Coroner ☐ Physician ☐ Hosp. Staff ☐ Law Enforcement ☐ Neighbor ☐ Relative ☐ Instit. Staff

☐ Social Services ☐ Public Health ☐ Mental Health ☐ School Staff ☐ Other Specify)_____

For Use By Physicians Only	Medical Diagnosis on Child	Signature of Physician who examined/treated child X	Telephone No.
	Hospitalization Required: ☐ None ☐ Under 1 week ☐ 1-2 weeks ☐ Over 2 weeks		

Actions Taken Or About To Be Taken	☐ Medical Exam ☐ X-Ray ☐ Removal/Keeping ☐ Not. Med Exam/Coroner
	☐ Photographs ☐ Hospitalization ☐ Returning Home ☐ Notified DA

Signature of Person Making This Report	Title	Date Submitted Mo. Day Yr.

Figure 12–4 New York State Child Abuse Report

TOPICS IN OBSERVATION

Dealing with Families Suspected of Child Maltreatment

Figure 12–5 The partnership attitude of teacher and families is never more important than when maltreatment is suspected.

It needs to be said here that discussions with families about their relationship with and treatment of their child is an ongoing dialogue between teachers and families. That basic partnership relationship that has been emphasized throughout this text is never more important than in this section. Whether we feel the family just does not know about good hygiene, appropriate discipline techniques, or are deliberately hurting or neglecting their child to the point of placing them in danger, our position is the same. It is one of advocacy for the child and support and assistance to the family. Look again at the Ecological View of the Child from the Teacher's Viewpoint (Figure I–13). While viewing the child in the cold with no socks or boots, or with a nasty bruise the shape of an adult hand, think again of the surrounding factors. This is not to make excuses but to try to understand the context in which the family lives.

The difference between sympathy, feeling sorry for the child and family, and empathy is doing something about it. In cases where it seems that the child does not have the necessities for health and comfort, such as adequate clothing or food, the teacher's first response is not to report the family to the Hotline but to try to supply the need, if there truly is one. It takes all the tact and caring one can muster to determine if the child does not have a coat or just will not wear one. Then the next step may be some work with the family on parenting skills to help the family take the responsibility for enforcing basic needs (Figure 12–5).

Even in cases in which reports must be made for the health and protection of the child, an attitude of empathy for the family still must prevail. The teacher tries not to see the family as ogres or monsters but people who themselves are so needy or uninformed that these actions are really reactions to their own condition. The reporting then is not "tattling" but an assistance to the family to get the help they all need, as well as protecting the child from harm. This can be communicated again and again to the family but is even more evident by actions that support the family with physical acts of kindness, such as rides to appointments, a home-baked loaf of bread, or a phone call just to see how they are doing.

The teacher is an instrument of change in lives not only of the children in the group but their families. That is an awesome responsibility.

This section was prepared with the help of Jean Rose-Klein, Coordinator of the Broome County Child Abuse Council, Binghamton, NY.

the mainstream practices, and in the case of child abuse, with the legal system. This issue faces people who work with children and families. It is shocking to read child abuse statistics and think about the hurt each statistic represents.

Cultural Differences

Children of families of many cultures are participating in educational experiences. Sensitivity to cultures whose values and customs are different from one's own is an important trait in early childhood professionals. Child-rearing has distinctive differences in various cultures concerning obedience, punishment, dependency, and eye contact. Open discussions about child-rearing will help teachers gain an understanding of other cultures and ethnic groups. The responsibility of the teacher, however, is still to report child abuse and neglect as defined by the state regulations.

Different Abilities

Children with developmental disabilities are also victims of abuse, with some indications that it occurs at higher rates than in the regular population. They are often perceived as an "easy target" with limited defenses or protection. Observation of abuse is even more critical for children with disabilities because they may lack the verbal, physical, or mental skills to protect themselves or disclose what has been happening. The same criteria for signs of abuse are used for children with different abilities, physical, sexual, emotional, or neglect. Any questions that need to be asked should be simple, concrete who, what, when, but *not* why. Drawings, dolls, or a sign interpreter may help the child express the details they want to disclose (Baladerian, 1993). Remember, the observer need not gather all the evidence. All that is needed for a report to try to protect the child is "reason to suspect." Child Protective Services personnel will take the next steps.

What to Do with the Information

Keep your immediate notes, a copy of the report, and a log of the follow-up in a secure place. This is important, but extremely confidential, information. Know the policy of your program or school regarding the storage of this information.

Using Technology

Do not use photographs of the child's body or tape or video recorders of interviews with the child. Leave that to the child protective services. By interrogating the child or gathering this kind of evidence, you may be jeopardizing the veracity of the reporting and investigation process. Remember, you need not *prove* abuse or neglect but you must have reasonable cause for concern. The teacher's role is not to prosecute but to protect.

Pitfalls to Avoid

- Doing nothing when you have strong suspicions.
- Talking about your suspicions to people who do not have a right to know.
- Asking the child too many questions.
- Not writing down all the exact details of the disclosure or your observations.

SELF-CONCEPT AND SELF-ESTEEM

Perhaps no other area of development is more nebulous and difficult to document than self-concept, yet it is at the root of social, academic, and personal success.

Where does the development of self-concept begin? This book began the review of child development with attachment and separation. The circle is complete, coming back to that same important connection to self-concept and self-esteem. Whether it is family and child, family and program, or new concepts and established schemata, relationships and connections are what it is all about. The development of healthy self-esteem is dependent on certain kinds of relationships. This chapter explores the contributing factors to the development of self-esteem, the stages of the development of a sense of self, and how it can be observed in the classroom. Families and teachers are major influences on self-concept, with the goal of helping the child have high self-esteem based on a truthful vision of the self.

Self-concept resides in the cognitive, what one knows about oneself in many different areas. Self-esteem resides in the emotional realm of how one evaluates and feels about oneself. Physical appearance and ability are very important in American culture with millions spent on products, clothing, and exercise machines and clubs to improve that appearance. Sports figures are idols because they can jump, throw, catch, or move with outstanding coordination and skill. People measure themselves against others in appearance and physical ability.

Humans are social beings and crave approval, so interactions with other people profoundly affect how people perceive themselves. Connected to that social dimension is the emotional or affective side where feelings sometimes overrule what one knows to be true. One's ability to function mentally affects not only educational achievements but life's decision-making, possibly affecting economic status, which also has an effect on the perception of self. All of these parts contribute to one's self-perception (Figure 12–6).

Assessing these areas objectively is the self-concept, what one knows about oneself. It is not, however, simply a matter of assessing those areas. Another dimension enters in, the affective domain, the emotions. For example, a person may know their weight is in the range of normal on the charts (self-

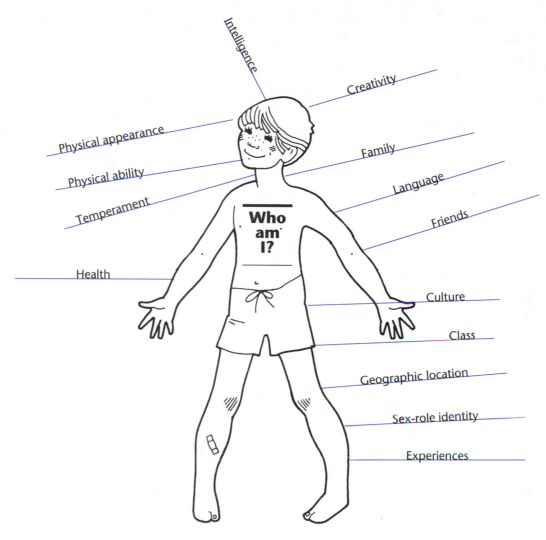

Intelligence

Creativity

Physical appearance

Family

Physical ability

Language

Temperament

Friends

Who am I?

Health

Culture

Class

Geographic location

Sex-role identity

Experiences

Figure 12–6 Who am I? What do others think of me? How do I feel about myself? All may be different.

concept) but feel they are too heavy. They feel fat and not good about themselves (self-esteem). It may not be a true measurement but it is how the person perceives herself. It may be reflected from the appraisal of other people.

EXERCISE: Think about yourself in each of these areas (Figure 12–7). In the left column, write three words or phrases that you *know* about yourself in this category. In the right column, write three words or phrases about how you *feel* about yourself in this area.

Here is the tricky part, the dichotomy as Curry and Johnson (1990) call it, the division or two sides to the issue. They say, "Dichotomous thinking is also evident in the idea that good feelings about the self

are always healthy, whereas bad self-feelings are to be avoided. But good feelings about the self can be self-deceptive and narcissistic (excessive pride)" (p. 4). For example, is it always desirable to have high self-esteem?

- High self-esteem about physical appearance is attained when a person finally diets down to eighty-six pounds?
- High self-esteem in sexual prowess when a man brags he has fathered twelve children by twelve different women?
- High self-esteem in cognitive ability because a person has memorized the phone book?
- High self-esteem in peer acceptance when a high school student gets a twenty on a math quiz because "Dumb is cool"?

Describe what you *know* you are like in these areas.		Describe what you *feel* you are like in these areas.
	COGNITIVE	
	Language	
	History	
	Math	
	Science	
	PHYSICAL	
	Appearance	
	Abilities	
	Sex role	
	SOCIAL	
	Significant others, including family	
	Peers	
	Culture	
	Socioeconomic status	
	EMOTIONAL	
	Temperament	
	Emotional state	

Adapted from Shalveson in Owens (1993); and Lively and Lively (1991)

Figure 12–7 Self-Concept and Self-Esteem Worksheet

- High self-esteem in economic status is proven by lighting a cigarette with a twenty-dollar bill?

Feeling good about oneself is only desirable when abilities are accurately assessed, not based on skewed thinking or misplaced values. For example, is low self-esteem always harmful?

- When low self-esteem about physical appearance prods millions of people into diets and exercise programs?
- When low self-esteem from a social encounter shames one into an apology for saying that unkind, hurtful remark?
- When low self-esteem over educational achievement motivates work on a high school equivalency diploma then on a college degree?
- When low self-esteem over computer phobia prompts a person to enroll in a computer workshop?
- When low self-esteem over cultural ignorance encourages one to attend a concert of multicultural music?

When low self-esteem based on low self-concept, knowing one's shortcomings or inadequacies, brings about action, then low self-esteem "can be constructive and energizing" (Curry & Johnson, 1990, p. 4). Low self-esteem, as a motivator, can raise self-concept and self-esteem.

An interesting study (Kamins & Dweck, 1999) found that praise (and criticism) aimed at the *person* (such as "Good boy," "Bad girl") resulted in more helpless responses and self-blame than praise (and criticism) aimed at the *process* (such as "Great way you picked up your room," or "You haven't picked up your room yet.") It makes sense. Specific actions receiving praise or criticism are not personalized and damaging to self-worth as are criticisms that attribute a value to the whole person.

Well-meaning people giving indiscriminate praise for the purpose of raising self-esteem can actually have the opposite effect. Insincerity, whether expressed to a child or adult, is not believed and tends to be dismissed. When one knows or feels the praise is undeserved, it does not raise self-esteem. If the perception, or self-esteem, is higher than the actual ability, a false pride is present that may prevent future work on this area. This image of self is important to everyone for it directly affects the motivation to change and learn.

EXERCISE: Now look back at those words you wrote in the previous exercise. Where you see low self-esteem, let it be the motivator for a plan. Work to raise the competency, then the self-concept, then the self-esteem: self-improvement plan!

Development of Self-Esteem

Development, the progression from simple to complex over a period of time in sequential stages but at individual times, applies to both self-concept and self-esteem (Figure 12–8).

The First Year. The newborn infant is not aware of separateness from the environment. Actions are merely reflexes to stimuli. There is no recognition of self in the mirror, no recognition of people in his life. Between two and four months, the infant still has no concept of being separate. Now, however, needs are expressed in signals the family comes to understand. Coos and smiles appear as responses back to those people who are cooing and smiling. The child begins to reach toward that image seen in the mirror because it may be something to touch and handle. No, it is just something cold and flat that cannot be put in the mouth to be explored.

By the end of the first year, the knowledge of separateness is attained. The infant now knows he is separate from the people around him and the physical environment. Important people still magically appear and disappear (object permanence). Attempts to keep them present with smiles and sounds work only temporarily. They go away, perhaps never to return. The new mobility of the one-year-old allows the child to go look for those disappearing objects. The knowledge is there that they exist somewhere. If the legs could only support the body, they could be found. The baby reaches for the baby in the mirror. When a toy is seen in the mirror, the baby reaches to

the mirror to grab it. The long journey of individuation has begun, "the process by which the self or personal identity is developed" (Kostelnik, Whiren, Soderman, Stein, & Gregory, 2002, p. 35).

During infancy and toddler ages, the child's self-concept is primarily influenced by the family and those closest to the child. Information is received about being "good," "cute," "lovable," "capable," "smart," and "accepted." This forms the child's ideas about identity and capability.

The Second Year. After walking is mastered, the toddler practices becoming more separate. She now takes journeys away and comes back, farther away, and back again. The toddler is checking each time that a return is possible if necessary. Trust is building that the person will be there when she needs her. Toward the second birthday, if a dot is placed on the child's nose and shown in the mirror, the toddler reaches not to the mirror but to the nose to take it off. Ah, the emergence of self!

Words are multiplying and some important ones that show an increasing sense of self are "me," "mine," "me do it," and "NO." The child displays great pride when attempts to do a task end in success. If efforts fail, the child expresses disappointment. If scolded, the child shows shame. Sometimes a tantrum erupts when the emotions are so strong they cannot be controlled. It may bring embarrassment or a feeling of unworthiness from those the child knows best. Everyone has witnessed or felt helpless when a child throws a tantrum if his wants are not fulfilled. The child is really helpless also, unable to control these strong emotions.

Older Preschoolers. In the preschool years, children talk about being a boy or a girl, how old they are, how big they are, and what toys they have. Toward kindergarten age, they begin to remember the dreams they had last night and they can talk about their thinking. They are beginning to realize their thoughts are part of a private self. No one else can see or know their thoughts unless they are revealed. They used to play with brooms to sweep and trucks to dump, then those brooms became horses and trucks were spaceships. Now they play with their friends in elaborate scenarios in which they leave themselves behind and become other people, talking with other people's words and voices and gestures, doing what grownups do. They constantly read their playmates' faces to look for acceptance. The teacher's words are carefully weighed against what they know they really can do. They are beginning to worry about what others will think of them.

Confronted with many new tasks to try, encouragement and approval of the attempts bring pleasant

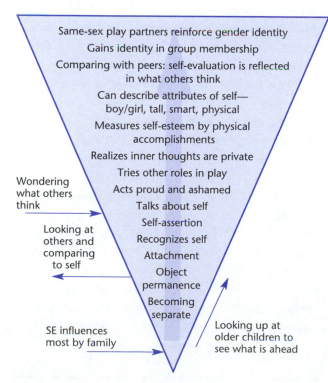

Same-sex play partners reinforce gender identity

Gains identity in group membership

Comparing with peers: self-evaluation is reflected in what others think

Can describe attributes of self— boy/girl, tall, smart, physical

Measures self-esteem by physical accomplishments

Realizes inner thoughts are private

Tries other roles in play

Acts proud and ashamed

Talks about self

Self-assertion

Recognizes self

Attachment

Object permanence

Becoming separate

Wondering what others think

Looking at others and comparing to self

SE influences most by family

Looking up at older children to see what is ahead

Figure 12–8 Self-Concept Development

feelings of competence. This gives motivation to try the next new challenge, expending effort with the confidence of past successes. Success brings more success and even risks at failure. The overall feeling of well-earned, high self-esteem will emerge.

Another child may try as well at all those new things, drawing a circle, tying his shoe, naming his colors. But he is reminded his circle is not round. His shoe does not stay tied. This color is red not green. His attempts at other tasks he is working on may not even be noticed. When he tries again, he feels anxiety because he does not really think he can do it. He could not do it before. Maybe he will not even try or he will try but not very hard, then he will not be disappointed when he cannot do it. He looks to see who is watching but no one is, so he does not even try. Someone comes along and says he did it perfectly and wonderfully but he knows they are wrong. Even when he tries and it works, he believes it was just an accident. He really did not cause it to work. The child's feeling of incompetence is reinforced by powerful adults, such as family members and teachers, that causes a decline in motivation, willingness to try or risk, and results in lowered self-esteem. This is the beginning of the cycle of failure many children experience in school.

The social comparisons of this age are limited to the child's estimation of performance, mainly physical. They have come so far and can now do so many tasks that they could not do in toddlerhood, still a strong memory. They compare themselves to those big seven-year-olds who can ride a two-wheeler. Because of the successes of the past, they have no doubt they will be able to do it. Social comparisons to older, more developed children only bring hope and confidence of coming accomplishments.

School-agers. Feedback from formal schooling will be about peer acceptance, academic and athletic competence, and moral worth, while often removing much of the power (Curry & Johnson, 1990). New abilities may be heightened by new challenges or squashed by criticism and labeling. In this stage of Industry versus Inferiority, as Erikson (1950, 1968) called it, much of the self-esteem is dependent on school success. The child is moving into a new stage of cognitive development, Concrete Operations (Piaget, 1968). She is now in new social settings and more interested in the acceptance of friends than family. Most of the abilities in the physical realm will now be used more competitively in sports and in the writing tasks of school. All of these new opportunities can negatively or positively affect self-concept and self-esteem.

This is the age when comparisons to others and the internalization of what other people think is very important. Constant comparisons and competitiveness bring more reality to self-estimations than in the preschool years. The self-esteem is fragile with inside doubts of abilities and acceptance. Clubs, exclusive friendships, and put-downs of others stem from this quest to feel good about oneself.

Families and Schools That Build Self-Esteem

What makes the difference in children's self-esteem? Basic intellect? Innate ability? The family had more money? The family lived in the ghetto? It is all about acceptance. When efforts and independence are praised, they produce internal rewards (Harter, 1999). This gives the feeling of competence and confidence that motivates greater efforts, more independence, and higher self-esteem. The opposite is also true. Dependence is increased when efforts are criticized. It is accompanied by feelings of incompetency and a lack of control. Anxiety and doubt fail to motivate. Future efforts are then approached tentatively, expecting failure. External rewards and the approval of others,

IT HAPPENED TO ME

Listen to What He Did Now

Every day when Jason's mother would come to school, she had a horror story to relate of Jason's latest episode. He had deliberately poured grape juice on the white rug, painted the basement paneling with tar, and pulled up the neighbor's pumpkin patch. I tried to get her not to talk about these things in front of Jason and all the other families and children, but each day she came with a new story of his escapades. One day as the children arrived I suggested they go check the incubator. "Oh no, you hatched chicks. Don't let Jason go near them. He'll kill them," she exclaimed. Well, you guessed it. Sometime during the free play time, Jason opened the incubator and squeezed a baby chick. Was this Jason's fault? He was just living up to expectations. It is sad that those expectations were not for kind acts, gentle touches, and controlled behavior. I often wonder about what happened to Jason. I wonder what I could have done to try to change his mother's attitude.

which is rarely forthcoming, increases dependency. Competency and self-esteem are lowered.

The socialization of the family toward competency sets the course of the path. Owens (1993) reports that children with high self-esteem had mothers who were content with their role, were calm and poised and accepting of others, and led active personal lives. The mothers gave reasons for behavior control and the fathers took away privileges rather than using punishment. They both used firm follow-through, communicating commitment to the child's welfare, and a willingness to *listen* to the child's ideas.

Children with low self-esteem had families who were coercive, rejecting, and controlling by strict restrictions. They were overprotective or neglectful, either resulting in the child's feeling of incompetence (Owens, 1993, pp. 399–405). The family has a primary influence over the child's self-esteem.

Schools also have a major part to play in the building of a child's self-esteem. Children need to build a sense of competency, to have an environment with experiences that develop real skills in the cognitive, physical, social, and emotional realms. They need to feel they have the power to make things happen. Involvement in decision making, and understanding clear and realistic expectations help children feel powerful. They thrive in a predictable environment where there are plenty of opportunities to make choices. Their opinions and ideas are accepted as worthy and the curriculum capitalizes on their strengths. Teachers give informative praise that gives specific reactions and focuses on what they know and do. Negative labels are avoided. The only labels are on the shelves. Children are seen as individuals. That sounds like the teachers *know* each child and their accomplishments. The teachers have watched closely to determine the level of development of each child and provided an environment where the child could have success. That is a place where a child could go to a portfolio with his name on it and look at a history of his work. He could even add to it or take something out. He knew it was about all the things he could do.

Self-Concept and Acceptance, Power, Morality, and Competence

Curry and Johnson (1990) present four themes, revisited throughout life as each person seeks to define the self (Figure 12–9).

Acceptance. From the attachment of the infant to the desire for friendship, acceptance is the human quest. Young children desire to please adults and

High Self-Esteem
Acceptance
Power
Morality
Competence

Low Self-Esteem
Isolation
Vulnerability
"Bad" Label
Dependent

Figure 12–9 Self-Esteem Factors

other children. They want to feel they are worthy of being heard. From the crawler tugging on dad's pant leg to the tattler telling of other children's misdeeds, self-concept and self-esteem involve acceptance.

Power. The infant is exercising power when he struggles away from the shirt being pulled over his head. The toddler is exercising power when she says, "No." The preschooler exercises power when he chews his bread into a gun shape to escape the "No guns in school rule." The teenager exercises power. Adults exercise power through the vote, purchasing power, in any number of ways. It is all saying, "I can make things happen." That is part of self-concept, the knowledge that one has the ability to influence events rather than passively receive or observe them, resigned to accept their consequences.

Empowerment, Wald (2000) believes, is helping children toward self-awareness, encouraging willingness to take reasonable risks and explore their natural curiosity. To shift from teaching to empowering, she suggests the following:

- design the environment to include child-directed activities
- implement child-initiated curriculum
- recognize individual talents
- encourage peer help
- ask open-ended questions (pp. 14-15)

Morality. Morality is the innate desire to be considered "good" rather than "bad," the recognition between right and wrong by society. Self-esteem is affected by knowing the expectations or the rules and following them. The rules may be social, like manners or certain behavior codes (such as quiet in the movies, or controlled rowdiness at a sports event). They may be legal (such as the speed limit or not stealing) or they may be religious in nature. Self-esteem is increased by following the rules or expectations. Those may even be contrary to the code of the majority of society, like the Code of Thieves, or a cult or terrorist group. No matter what the group's expectations, following them gains acceptance, illustrates self-control, and represents a feeling of competence.

Robert Coles adds his advice to the area of morality in *The Moral Intelligence of Children* (1997) by combining storytelling of children he has interviewed with his thoughts about building character. He explores and wonders about children who are facing insurmountable odds yet have a basic morality or strong character, who are strong and pure, and who are concerned about others above themselves. He does not call it self-esteem and in fact eschews self-absorption and self-satisfaction in favor of self-denial and delayed gratification. He says therein lies the power and moral integrity that families and teachers should seek to impart.

Competence. Satisfaction is the result of accomplishing a task by applying knowledge, skill, and energy and seeing the expected result. This **competence** raises the self-concept and self-esteem because it is the evaluation of the effort and positive feeling from the result. Competence gains acceptance, demonstrates power, and adds to moral worth.

These four aspects are threads that weave through all developmental areas as we observe children's behavior. Their influence affects self-concept and self-esteem.

Sex-Role Identity and Self-Esteem

At the moment of birth, the baby's **gender** is announced and the people around the baby begin to form the **sex-role** or **gender identity** (Figure 12–10). In the first few days of life she receives a name. This distinguishes her sexual identity to the rest of the world. She is held more gently, sometimes covered with a certain color blanket, and congratulations to her parents are sometimes tempered with resignation. She receives gifts that are soft and pastel-colored or toys that inspire nurturing actions instead of construction. She watches her mother to see what women are like and watches her father to see what men are like. Even at two, when she pretends to be grown up, she plays the role of mommy, not daddy. By three she tells people she is a girl, because she has long hair. She knows that someday she will be a woman, though until she is almost six, she may think she can still change her mind. When she looks at toy advertising, she sees that the girls are playing dolls or the boys are building with blocks. When she watches television, she sees that most of the powerful roles are male. When she has boy playmates, they

Figure 12–10 Sex-role identity is affected by society.

say, "You can't do this. You're a girl." Her grandma frowns when she climbs a tree and smiles when she pours the tea. She goes to preschool and the teacher says, "The girls can line up first because they're the quietest."

Children are **socialized,** taught the ways to behave in both overt and covert ways. Sexual identity begins with the physiology, the biological indicators of male or female. The view of one's own sexuality is gender identity, the socialized behaviors by parents, siblings, peers, significant other people, culture, and media, communicated by imitation, direct instruction, and reinforcement. Gender enters the subject of self-concept and self-esteem when it is examined by those four factors that Harter (1999) speaks of as lifelong issues:

- acceptance—Does she feel accepted as a girl, valued for her worth, not just because of her sex, or less because of it?
- power and control—Has she been given autonomy, power over herself in making decisions, allowed to take risks?
- moral virtue—Has she had opportunities to feel useful and "good," not guilty?
- competence—Does she know about all the things she can do well, given opportunities to show her physical strength, logical mind, self-reliant behaviors?

These are much more at issue for girls than boys, so the choice of using "she" in this section was deliberate. Stereotyping female gender behavior, such as dependency and weakness, has prevented girls from feeling powerful and competent, sometimes in very subtle ways. Deaux (as cited in Markus, Cross, & Wurf, 1990) found that girls were socialized to believe that effort brought success, while boys were led to believe it was ability. Thus, when failures came, girls explained it as lack of ability while boys attributed it to lack of effort. The implications of that theory profoundly affect girls' low self-esteem. They will feel, "I just didn't have it" rather than, as the boys would, "I just didn't try hard enough." There is a very great difference.

Perceptions about the body leading to self-esteem can be affected in infancy and toddler stages during diapering. When adults use words like *dirty* or *nasty*, genital areas become associated with negative feelings. Children often engage in masturbation for a variety of reasons, most often because it is pleasurable. If the child perceives adults' reactions as negative, they can have an affect on how the child feels about his body, his sexuality, and total self-esteem. Children will also commonly engage in sex play, just as they play out other adult roles. In a similar way, the breadth of experiences will determine how much reality is incorporated into the play. Children often play out explicit television scenes in the preschool classroom or home playroom. Adult reactions to these simulations will also bring value judgments and affect self-concept and self-esteem about their play and ultimately their sexual identity.

Observing Self-Concept and Self-Esteem

All areas of human development contribute to self-concept and self-esteem. Observable behavior demonstrates what a person knows and can do, and the feeling about that knowledge or ability. Self-esteem has defied researchers' attempts to devise measurement instruments, especially for young children outside of the mainstream (Marshall, 1989). Harter (1990) found two main categories early childhood educators used to define the high self-esteem child:

1. active displays of confidence, curiosity, initiative, and independence
2. adaptive reaction to change or stress

Inferring high or low self-esteem from observing behavior can be highly biased. The indicators of self-esteem adapted from Samuels (1977) parallel the areas of development covered in the preceding chapters of this book.

- unafraid of a new situation
- independent, needs minimal help
- comfortable with physical activities, coordinated
- makes friends easily
- seems to be happy most of the time

- talks freely
- does not rely on others for directions
- experiments with new materials
- creative, imaginative, has own ideas
- participates in classroom activities
- cooperative and largely self-controlled
- trusts people even if they are newly acquainted

The underlying self-concept is observed while the observer has been assessing each child's developmental areas. The Self-Esteem Class List Log (in Appendix D) will be used in Plan A to note these characteristics or behaviors.

Separation. How the child separates from the family member at the beginning of the school year or day depends on the self-concept. The child has the sense of belonging and trust in the adult. He feels so worthy of love and care that he is sure his family member would not think of not returning to reclaim this treasure.

Self-Care. The child who is secure in self-concept will feel capable and competent and want to do things independently. She will want to take care of physical needs and not depend on adults. This is observed in the self-care area of toileting, eating, and dressing. The children whose families have given them instructions, let them try, and rewarded their attempts are more likely to be independent and do things for themselves.

Physical. Physical competence or ability instills pride (Figure 12–11). Climbing to the top of the climber and sliding down, riding the two-wheeler without training wheels, or printing a name can raise a child's self-esteem. The child may have the physical ability but doubts or lacks confidence in the ability. The resulting behavior is avoidance of the activity, need for assistance, or unsteadiness, resulting in a fall. All these behaviors only end in lowering self-esteem. The observer infers self-esteem while watching the physical skills and recording what the child accomplishes. The reactions when attempts are successful or unsuccessful give clues of self-esteem.

Social. Excessive withdrawal from social encounters is a sign the child may not feel worthy to be a friend. There may be other reasons, but self-concept is a strong determining factor in a child's social development. By observing children's interactions, the self-concept can be indicated. Self-esteem can be heightened when classroom activities promote prosocial behaviors.

Emotional. Self-esteem resides in the emotional realm. It is the feeling about the various competencies, the feeling about how capable one is compared

Figure 12–11 I did it!

to other people, the feeling about how acceptable one is as a playmate. This is observable in the demeanor of the child, the facial and verbal expressions that indicate the emotions inside. Children with good feelings about themselves will appear happy, while those who are uncertain of their competencies and worthiness will appear unhappy, sober, or expressionless. The inborn personality or temperament of the child enters here. Care must be taken not to misinterpret a more quiet, introspective person as one with low self-esteem.

Speech and Language. When people are in stressful situations, new encounters where they feel uncertain, it is normal to be more quiet and reserved. They may not risk revealing the self by speaking. As one is more accustomed to a situation, one feels more free to speak and less concerned about the hearer's reactions or judgments. The child who freely talks to teachers, other children, the janitor, the bus driver, or the UPS delivery person is usually displaying a strong self-concept. "I am important enough for you

to listen to what I have to say." Hearing a child constantly say "I can't" will give clues that the child is feeling incompetent and unwilling to risk, indicating low self-esteem.

This is an area in which children who are unsure of their language (especially nonmajority language speakers) are observed and often misjudged as having low self-esteem. Because they cannot or are unsure about their competencies in communication, they do not speak, even after they have learned many words. These children need to find other areas in the classroom in which to feel competent. Language attempts will not be so much of a risk to self-esteem.

Memory and Attention Span. Just as emotions govern self-esteem, cognitive abilities govern self-concept. The child is using the cognitive and memory abilities to observe other children's capabilities. She remembers past attempts and failures. Because so many adult–child conversations rely on closed questions like a constant quiz, "What color is your shirt?" "How many crackers are on your napkin?" "What shape is this puzzle piece?" children form an image very quickly of what they know and do not know in comparison to the adult's expectations. In creating an environment to build cognitive structures and positive self-esteem, opportunities should be presented for divergent thinking, exploring not reciting.

Literacy. School is a place of literacy. Watching the child's contact with the written word, whether it is in signs, books, or attempts at writing, can reveal self-concept. The child who has had the advantage of many opportunities with literacy will feel very comfortable in the literacy classroom. The child who has not will exhibit discomfort there, unable to listen and uninterested in stories. No connections are made between the sign in the block area and the sound. It is difficult for the child to find his name on the helper chart. Behavior observations will inform the watcher. What the child is *not* choosing is as revealing as what is chosen. Those areas and activities the child feels the least competent about will not be chosen.

Creativity. Whether it is wondering about what a magnet will pick up, using a variety of materials to glue a design on a piece of tile, or acting as the pilot on an airplane bound for Disney World, children can be observed exhibiting creativity. There may be a child who is unwilling to try the magnet. A pattern is needed for art projects. Dramatic play is avoided. This gives the observer clues about not just creativity but self-esteem. It takes comfort and confidence in oneself to venture away from the tray of metal pieces the teacher has put out and into the room to test out other materials. It takes boldness to try to glue a nail on end to a collage. It inspires others to announce to the passengers on the pretend plane that she is about to have a baby. Creativity is being observed here as well as self-concept and self-esteem.

Adjustment to a New Setting. Because of that secure attachment with the family, the child has the self-esteem to feel lovable. It makes the child feel capable enough to be comfortable in any setting after a nominal period. The child who learns self-control and follows the routines of the classroom shows confidence. Trust is exhibited that the teacher is a supporter, not an enemy. The child will feel secure enough to want to participate with the group. This gives the observer information, not just about the child's adjustment but about self-concept. Acceptable behavior is assumed and success is expected. This is observable behavior.

Are self-concept and self-esteem observable? Not of themselves, but it appears that by watching the child interact with the environment, peers and adults can make some substantial assumptions about self-concept and self-esteem.

Why Not Ask?

If a person wants the answer to a question, the most logical thing to do is ask someone who is most likely to know. Marshall (1989, p. 46) suggests some questions an observer might ask a child, probably above four years old, that would get first-person information concerning self-esteem:

"What can you tell me about yourself? Why is that important?"
"What can you tell me that is best about you?"
"What are you good at doing?"

This is consistent with the principle of the child as the informant. By asking the child, they verbalize what they may have never thought of before. "What am I good at?" It is a strategy that Bev Bos promotes in her workshops on self-esteem.

HELPING ALL CHILDREN WITH SELF-ESTEEM

It cannot be ignored that different ethnic, racial, and cultural values affect self-esteem. While the toddler's autonomy and the preschooler's independence may be a Western value, other cultures may hold those same accomplishments with contempt for children in their families. Expectations of competence and styles of interpersonal relations vary between cultures. For example, praising a Middle Eastern boy's ability to clear his dishes and wash the table may not raise his self-esteem. The child who refuses to participate in a holiday event may not be antisocial but acting according to a religious tradition. Cultural differences affect behavior. They may be misinterpreted as a self-esteem issue. Conversely, expectations in the classroom may conflict with the positive self-concept and self-esteem of a child of a minority group.

Marshall (2001) cautions that behaviors that are valued and interpreted as indicators of high or low self-concept are strongly culture-based. The Western value placed on independence, individuality, and self-assertion may not be shared by the Eastern, African, and Latino cultures, which value harmonious, interdependent relationships. Marshall makes the following suggestions.

1. Be aware of the ways your own culture influences your expectations of children.
2. Consider the cultural backgrounds of the children in your setting and their community.
3. Learn about the cultures from which the children in your program or school may come.
4. Use your basic knowledge of the culture to talk with each family about its values and practices.
5. Build what you have learned from each family. (p. 22)

Even ethnicity awareness can be identified in a developmental progression. At about three years old, a racial awareness begins and by six years old it is well ingrained (Derman-Sparks & Phillips, 1997). Young children are in the throes of classification tasks. They are sorting by color and shape, looking for similarities and differences, and making matches of everything in their environment. It is only natural for them to look at each other and compare and contrast. They will notice racial cues, mainly color of skin and texture of hair. While they are classifying, they are also labeling objects. Family and societal labels often have values attached, which the child also absorbs. Experiences and attitudes about groups that bear high or low self-esteem are transmitted. The young child absorbs all this as well.

Observation of racial awareness, especially when it is in the form of children's questions or negative comments, should be addressed right away. Derman-Sparks in *Anti-Bias Curriculums* (1989) recommends:

• Do not ignore.
• Do not change the subject.
• Do not answer indirectly.

If you are uncomfortable, identify what gets in the way of your responding directly, matter-of-factly, and simply. (p. 33)

Disabilities and Self-Esteem

When disabilities interfere with a child's functioning while included in a regular classroom, self-concept and self-esteem issues arise (Figure 12–12). Peer relations are especially affected when hearing impairment impedes communication. Visual impairment depends on manual contact and results in less smiling. Physical impairments prevent active participation with other children. Mental retardation may reduce responsiveness or limit play options.

For these children, the self-concept and self-esteem issues are acceptance and the power to be independent and feel competent. Children with disabilities who have difficulty developing peer relationships suffer from loneliness that results in poor self-esteem and increased anxiety and depression. This, in turn, prevents satisfactory friendships and may result in even more serious emotional consequences (Pavri, 2001).

It is the children with normal abilities in an inclusive classroom who become very aware of differences when that social measurement takes place. Observers may see children playing at being visually, hearing, or physically challenged, making up explanations for the disability and exhibiting fear (Kostelnik, et al., 2002). Every child should be recognized for their abilities, rather than the disabilities, labels, or things they cannot do. This attitude or viewpoint will help all gain an understanding of differences not disabilities and give the acceptance that they all want. By recognizing the child's abilities and giving clear explanations of limitations, the other children will be made aware of opportunities to help, but the disabled child must have plenty of opportunity to do for himself what he can. It is that old "Never do for *any* child what he can do for himself"

Figure 12–12 Peer relations are even more important for the self-esteem of an exceptional child.

philosophy. It increases independence, raises competency levels, and ultimately results in positive self-esteem.

These are sensitive, yet vitally important, issues to young children's self-concept and self-esteem. They are challenging.

HELPING PROFESSIONALS FOR CHILD ABUSE AND SELF-ESTEEM CONCERNS

There are many agencies and professionals in most communities to prevent, investigate, advise, protect, and even punish child abuse. Researchers, psychologists, and sociologists are seeking causes and solutions.

Child Protective Services—This is a governmental agency that receives, investigates, and takes action on reports of child abuse or maltreatment. They are a resource for education for mandated reporters, available to answer individual questions and work as advocates for the protection of the child. They protect the confidentiality of all records dealing with the family.

psychologists and psychiatrists—With specialized training in social and emotional disorders, these professionals work with children and families on issues concerning the causes and results of abuse and maltreatment but also issues dealing with self-esteem. Either may interfere with the child's functioning in the social realm. These professionals may serve as educational resources for parenting education for the prevention of child abuse or the development of healthy self-concepts and self-esteem.

OTHER METHODS

Other Methods to Record Self-Esteem:
(Be cautious about making judgments about a child's self-esteem. All that can be observed is the outward behavior, which may be interpreted inaccurately.)

Anecdotal/Running Records
Checklist/Rating Scale
Interviews/Conversations
Work Samples—Be careful about interpreting a child's art
Media

KEY TERMS

acceptance

competence

disclosure

emotional maltreatment

gender

mandated reporters

morality

neglect

physical abuse

power

self-concept

self-esteem

sex-role (gender)

  identity

sexual abuse

socialized

unfounded

WEEK 12: PLAN A

CLASS LIST LOG ON SELF-ESTEEM FOR ALL

Students and Practitioners

Copy the Self-Esteem Class List Log form found in Appendix D. Based on the past 11 weeks of observations, interpret the child's behaviors as they relate to self-concept and self-esteem. Make a note *for yourself*, marking *H* for high or *L* for low under each criteria.

What to Do with It

Filing. Because this is so subjective, *this is for your use only. Keep it in the class file, not in any child's portfolio.* This will be used for individualizing the curriculum and to guide you in your interactions with each child. Relate the ratings to the child's knowledge, skills, and behavior in each area to reflect on the reason for the rating. In areas of high self-esteem, make sure the child has plenty of opportunities to exercise this skill and that the child knows that you know of their success. In areas of lower self-esteem, consider ways you can "scaffold." Your actions can fill in the gap for the child between present ability and next level. The child can then feel successful. Point out the "working on" skills to use the lower self-esteem areas as motivation. For example, the child who is not yet able to write his name: He can write the first letter. "That's a start, good *J*, Jamal, I'll write the rest of your name until you are ready to make the *a, m, a, l*." This shows acceptance of the child at this level of skill. It gives him the power to try or not. He is not labeled "bad" because he cannot write his name yet, but recognizes his competence in making the *J*.

Remember, acceptance, power, morality, and competence are the four components of self-esteem.

Actions.

Read a Book.

    Climo, S. (1991). *King of the Birds.* New York: HarperCollins.

    dePaola, T. (1984). *The Legend of Bluebonnet.* New York: Putnam.

    Fuchshuber, A. (1998). *Two Peas in a Pod.* Brookfield, CT: Millbrook Press.

    Hoffman, M. (1993). *Amazing Grace.* New York: Scholastic.

    Lorbiecki, M. (1998). *Sister Anne's Hands.* New York: Deal.

In the Environment.

- Fill the environment with "Can Do" equipment, activities and equipment that children can accomplish on their own. They are accessible, varied, challenging, yet manageable.
- Arrange the environment to reduce frustration; a rug nap in the Block Area that is a smooth surface for building out of the traffic path, glue bottles that work and ample supplies in the Art area, an adequate number of duplicate toys so that long waits are avoided.

In the Curriculum.

- Activities are planned for successful completion and satisfaction. Those that are too difficult are scaffolded (assisted to the point of success), not taken over by the teacher or abandoned in frustration.
- Interests expressed by the children are used as the basis for projects and curriculum planning.
- Curriculum is planned that builds a sense of community and self-accomplishment.
- Interest is monitored so that activities are changed when interest declines.

In the Newsletter.

- Articles can suggest ways that a sense of acceptance, power, morality, and competence are encouraged.
- Article on the difference between praise and recognition of accomplishment or efforts.

WEEK 12: PLAN B

ANECDOTAL RECORDING TO OBSERVE SELF-IDENTITY FOR GROUP C

Select all the children from Group C and each day write an Anecdotal Recording about how the child displays an aspect of self-identity (how the child sees him/herself) or self-esteem (how the child feels about him/herself). Include all the details and exact quotes written on the left column of the paper. In the right-hand column, make your comments or questions.

| SELF–IDENTITY | | | |
Documentation	Location	Recorder	Date
CL	Class file	Ban	11/27
CL	"		6/12

Figure 12–13 Portfolio Overview Example

What to Do with It

Filing. Note the recording on the Portfolio Overview Sheet with the date and your name (Figure 12–13).

File the Anecdotal Recording in the child's portfolio.

Sharing with the Child and Family. Share the Anecdotal Recording with the child's family or the child, if it is appropriate. For example: "Mrs. Quon, Tia has been working so hard at lacing her new boots and tying a bow. Today she did it! It made her so proud! She hated it when the other children were finished dressing for outside before she was and she had to ask for help. She is a very independent person," or "Alexia, I know you didn't like it when Robert called you a 'bad girl' when that whole pitcher of milk spilled. It hurt your feelings and made you cry. Remember when I told you we have a new cook. She didn't know which pitchers were for our class and not to fill the pitchers so full. It was just too much for you to handle, but not your fault. That is why it spilled, not because you wanted it to. Robert made a mistake and didn't know it was an accident."

WEEK 12: PLAN C

REFLECTIVE JOURNAL

Copy this form, rate your own self-esteem and keep it in a private file at home. Using the similar criteria from the child's self-esteem form, rate your own self-esteem:

❑ I am usually unafraid of new situations.

❑ I am independent, taking pride in doing things for myself.

❑ I am comfortable with physical activities, coordinated, feel all right about my appearance.

❑ I make friends easily.

❑ I feel happy most of the time.

❑ I talk freely in groups.

❑ I show initiative and do not rely on others for directions.

❑ I try new things.

❑ I am creative, imaginative, have ideas of my own.

❑ I participate in social activities.

❑ I am cooperative with coworkers.

❑ I talk comfortably to clerks, cab drivers, and servers.

From the preceding list, I think the thing that helps me most as I deal with children is . . .

I would like to change . . .

Some ways might be . . .

REFERENCES

Baladerian, N. J. (1993). *Abuse of children and youth with disabilities: A prevention and intervention guidebook for parents and other advocates.* Culver City, CA: Disability, Abuse, and Personal Rights Project.

Besharov, D. (1990). *Recognizing child abuse: A guide for the concerned.* New York: The Free Press.

Coles, R. (1997). *The moral intelligence of children.* New York: Random House.

Curry, N., & Johnson, C. (1990). *Beyond self-esteem: Developing a genuine sense of human value.* Washington, DC: National Association for the Education of Young Children.

Derman-Sparks, L. (1989). *Anti-bias curriculum: Tools for empowering young children.* Washington, DC: National Association for the Education of Young Children.

Derman-Sparks, L., & Phillips, C. (1997). *Teaching/learning anti-racism: A developmental approach.* New York: Teachers College Press.

Erikson, E. H. (1950). *Childhood and society.* New York: Norton.

Erikson, E. H. (1968). *Identity: Young and crisis.* New York: Norton.

Harter, S. (1990). Causes, correlates and the functional role of the global self-worth: A life-span perspective. In R. J. Sternberg & J. Kolligan (Eds.), *Competence considered,* 67–97.

Harter, S. (1999). *The construction of the self: A developmental perspective.* New York: Guilford Press.

Kamins, M. L., & Dweck, C. S. (1999). Person versus process praise and criticism: Implications for contingent self-worth and coping. *Developmental Psychology,* 35 (3), 835–847.

Kostelnik, M., Whiren, A., Soderman, A., Stein, L., & Gregory, K. (2002). *Guiding children's social development theory to practice,* 4th ed. Clifton Park, NY: Thomson Delmar Learning.

Lively, V. E., & Lively, E. (1991). *Sexual development of young children.* Clifton Park, NY: Thomson Delmar Learning.

Markus, H., Cross, S., & Wurf, E. (1990). The role of the self-system in competence. In R. J. Sternberg & J. Kolligan (Eds.), *Competence considered,* 205–225.

Marshall, H. (1989). The development of self-concept. *Young Children,* 44 (5) 44–51.

Marshall, H. H. (2001). Cultural influences on the development of self-concept: Updating our thinking. *Young Children,* 56 (6), 19–25.

Owens, K. (1993). *The world of the child.* New York: Merrill, an imprint of Macmillan Publishing Company.

Pavri, S. (2001). Loneliness in children with disabilities: How teachers can help. *Teaching Exceptional Children,* July/August 2001, 52–57.

Piaget, J. (1968). *On the development of memory and identity.* Worcester, MA: Clark University Press.

Samuels, S. C. (1977). *Enhancing self-concept in early childhood: Theory and practice.* New York: Human Science Press.

Wald, G. S. (2000). Moving from "I think I can" to "I know I can." *Young Children,* 55 (4), 14–15.

RESOURCES

Baladerian, N. J. (1990). *Abuse of children and youth with disabilities: A prevention and intervention guidebook for parents and other advocates.* Culver City, CA: Disability, Abuse and Personal Rights Project.

Besharov, D. (1990). *Recognizing child abuse: a guide for the concerned.* New York: The Free Press.

Derman-Sparks, L. (1989). *Anti-bias curriculum: Tools for empowering young children.* Washington, DC: National Association for the Education of Young Children.

King, E., Chipman, M., & Cruz-Jansen, M. (1994). *Educating young children in a diverse society.* Boston: Allyn and Bacon.

Koralek, K. (1992). *Caregivers of young children: Preventing and responding to child maltreatment.* U.S. Department of Health and Human Services, National Center on Child Abuse and Neglect.

Kostelnik, M., Whiren, A., Soderman, A., Stein, L., & Gregory, K. (2002). *Guiding children's social development theory to practice,* 4th ed. Clifton Park, NY: Thomson Delmar Learning.

NAEYC Position Statement on the Prevention of Child Abuse in Early Childhood Programs and the Responsibilities of Early Childhood Professionals to Prevent Child Abuse. (1997). *Young Children,* 52 (3), 42–46.

Saifer, S. (1990). *Practical solutions.* St. Paul, MN: Redleaf Press.

Online Resources

For additional information on early education curriculum, visit our Web site at http://www.earlychilded.delmar.com

Using Program Assessments to Look at Children in Groups

IN THIS CHAPTER

- **Assessing Early Childhood Programs**

- **Topics in Observation: Assessing the Environment—Pointing Back at You**

- **Looking at the Adjustment of the Child to the Program**

- **Helping All Children in Group Settings**

- **Helping Professionals for Program Evaluation and Support**

ASSESSING EARLY CHILDHOOD PROGRAMS

The child is enrolled in an early childhood group setting. It could be in a child care center of many types: for profit, nonprofit, employer supported family day-care home, or a religiously affiliated program. It may be a part-day program called a preschool, nursery, nursery school, play group, or parent cooperative. Head Start programs serve thousands of three- and four-year-olds across the country, and in some places also serve infants and toddlers.

Public and private schools provide educational experiences for children from kindergarten and up. Some schools also have programs for prekindergarten and some for infants and toddlers as well. Many school districts and outside agencies provide programs for children before and after school and on school holidays. There are many programs for children with special needs to receive early intervention in separate settings or included within regular classrooms. Some programs draw specific audiences, such as music, gymnastics, and dance schools.

With the role of the family as the primary educator and socializing agent of children, it becomes increasingly important for all of society to support those roles. When the family is strengthened, society is strengthened. The Family Preservation and Support Services Program Act of 1993 has two major goals: support programs that support families in child-rearing and in providing children with stable and supportive family environments. Children's programs can provide for basic child care for family employment or preparation, provide respite from the stresses of parenting, strengthen child development, and strengthen the family with positive outcomes for all (Brown, 1997).

Whenever young children are in group settings outside their home, the program should be evaluated, by some regulating body or agency, for its safety and appropriateness for children. Each state has its own criteria and process for licensing or regulating the care and education of children in groups.

EXERCISE: **Find out the regulatory agency for the program in which you work or are doing observations.**

> child care—state licensing agency
> school—state agency

Obtain a copy of the regulations and look for the method of program evaluation: yearly review or report, on-site visit, or accreditation.

Program evaluations collect information to make informed judgments and decisions about the program. It could be to

- evaluate the program against a standard.
- assess the program's adherence to its stated mission and philosophy.
- receive feedback from various constituencies such as children, families, program administrators, teachers, funders, community agency personnel.
- assess the program's suitability for an individual child.
- provide measures of accountability. (LaMontagne & Russell, 1998)

Families are the most important evaluators with the greatest risk, their own child. Families have the right and responsibility to freely access the building in which their child is enrolled. They should ask questions and observe that the program meets their expectations and their child's needs. Families should have a voice in evaluating the program, no matter what type it is. There are many family surveys available that can be adapted to ask specific questions about the program. They typically include questions concerning families' satisfaction with the facilities, program, and staff; communication; interactions between the child and staff; comfort with the policies and procedures; and ask for suggestions or recommendations.

Administrators, staff, and families should regularly evaluate all aspects of the program. The *Accreditation Criteria and Procedures of the National Association for the Education of Young Children* (1998) includes criteria from:

- interactions among teachers and children
- curriculum
- relationships among teachers and families
- staff qualifications and professional development
- administration
- staffing

- physical environment
- health and safety
- nutrition and food service
- evaluation

Some sample questions for program evaluation are included in Figure 13–1.

The observation and recording method of this section is not focused on the child but on the program. Several program evaluation tools are presented to familiarize the reader with options available to assess the quality of the early childhood program.

A Setting Observation

EXERCISE: **Let's take a trip to a child care center or school. You can think about one you have visited or make up one in your mind. No children need to be present. You will observe the setting to see what it tells you. Drive into the parking lot.**

What do you see?/What could it mean? (Record your answers on a separate sheet of paper.)

From the parking lot:
Sign for the program:
Playground:
Entranceway:

IT HAPPENED TO ME

Where Is Everyone?

I was attending a meeting at the office of a child care director. I arrived on time and walked through the center without hearing a sound, an eerie feeling. What could that mean?

As I walked down the hall, I smelled, then saw vomit puddles ahead of me. I called out, "Anybody here?" A weak voice from the other end of the hall replied, "In here." It was from the bathroom where two staff people and one child were huddled over sinks. A volatile virus had struck and all other children and staff had been sent home, some sick, and the rest as a precaution. This little person and two staff were the last ones left but were sick as well. What a pitiful sight! I donned gloves and helped them clean up. The meeting had been cancelled since the director had gone home, too sick to think of calling me. Illness can strike quickly and powerfully when people are in group settings.

CHOOSING A TOOL

Evaluation instruments vary with the purpose of the program evaluation. Moreover, a survey of various program evaluations shows that many are designed to be program-specific; that is, the evaluation itself is devised to examine one program only. Individualized assessments are difficult to generalize. However, it appears that most program evaluations assess several, if not all, of the following areas:

The Physical Environment

Are the facilities clean, comfortable, safe?
Are room arrangements orderly and attractive?
Are materials and equipment in good repair and maintained?
Is there a variety of materials, appropriate to age levels?
Are activity areas well defined?
Is cleanup and room restoration a part of the daily schedule?
Are samples of children's work on display?
Is play space adequate, both inside and out?
Is personal space (e.g., cubby) provided for each child?

The Staff

Are there enough teachers for the number of children? How is this determined?
Are the teachers qualified? What criteria are used?
Is the staff evaluated periodically? By whom and how?
Does the school provide/encourage in-service training and continuing education?
Do the teachers encourage the children to be independent and self-sufficient?
Are the teachers genuinely interested in children?
Are teachers aware of individual abilities and limitations?
What guidance and disciplinary techniques are used?
Do teachers observe, record, and write reports on children's progress?
Are teachers skilled in working with individual children, small groups, and large groups?
Does the teaching staff give the children a feeling of stability and belonging?
Do teachers provide curriculum that is age-appropriate and challenging?
How would you describe the teachers' relationships with other adults in the setting? Who does this include, and how?
Can the teaching staff articulate good early education principles and relate them to their teaching?

Family Relationships

How does the classroom include families?
Are family members welcome to observe, discuss policies, make suggestions, help in the class?
Are different needs of families taken into account?
Where and how do families have a voice in the school?
Are family–teacher conferences scheduled?
Does the school attempt to use community resources and social service agencies in meeting families' needs?

The Organization and Administration

Does the school maintain and keep records?
Are there scholarships or subsidies available?
What socioeconomic, cultural, religious groups does the school serve?
What is the funding agency, and what role does it play?
Is there a school board and how is it chosen?
Does the school serve children with special needs or handicaps?
Are the classroom groups homo- or heterogeneous?
What hours is the school open?
What age range is served?
Are there both full- and part-day options?
Is after-school care available?
Does the school conduct research or train teachers?
What is the teacher–child ratio?

The Overall Program

Does the school have a written, stated education philosophy?
Are there developmental goals for the children's physical, social, intellectual, and emotional growth?
Are the children evaluated periodically?
Is the program capable of being individualized to fit the needs of all the children?
Does the program include time for a variety of free, spontaneous activities?
Is the curriculum varied to include music, art, science, nature, math, language, social studies, motor skills, etc.?
Are there ample opportunities to learn through a variety of media and types of equipment and materials?
Is there ample outdoor activity?
Is there a daily provision for routines: eating, sleeping, toileting, play?
Is the major emphasis in activities on concrete experiences?
Are the materials and equipment capable of stimulating and sustaining interest?
Are field trips offered?
Do children have a chance to be alone? In small groups? In large groups?

Tools for program evaluation are woven together to give a more comprehensive look at the total program.

Figure 13–1 Program Evaluation Questions

Inside a classroom:
Children's spaces:
Learning materials:
Displays:
Adult spaces:

Reactions to a Setting Observation. Without ever observing a program in action, much information is gathered, impressions formed, and judgments made. A program's purpose and practices are observed readily and interpreted from the environment. It is healthy to inspect one's own environment with a visitor's eye. It is also an exercise in professionalism to visit other programs. These bits of information are taken in by the senses and associated with information already stored. Reflection on possible meanings infer the values, philosophies, economic sponsorship, and even the housekeeping habits of the teacher. Some decisions for action can result.

"Oh, I can't wait to get back to my classroom and use that idea."
"I could really tell they emphasize . . ."
"I wonder what they did with that? I'll have to ask."
"I wonder how they provide for . . . ?"
"If that were my room, I would . . ."
"I certainly don't agree with . . . but they must have a different philosophy."
"I will not comment on . . . but I can talk about . . ."

Always as a professional courtesy, "I'll write a note and tell them how much I appreciated the visit and that I particularly liked . . ." Remember the evaluation principles: Look for the accomplishments not the deficits; specific praise raises self-esteem.

Program Assessments

EXERCISE: What do these things tell you?

checkbook balance
bathroom scale
speedometer
wristwatch
windsock
mirror
bookmark
diploma
roadmap
report card

Yes, you guessed it. You are so clever. These are all measurements or visual indicators of important facts. Money, weight, speed, time, wind direction, hair check, last chapter read, course completed, roads

travelled, evaluation—constant vigilance is part of life.

In *Week by Week*, many areas of child development have been examined for indicators of progress and possible delays. Programs need evaluation as well, for indicators of progress and warning signs of poor quality situations. Program evaluation can be informal, such as a staff discussion at the end of the year to recap the successes, the difficulties, and forecasts based on the past. Aspects of program quality can be measured with some of the same methods used to observe children's development (Figure 13–2).

An important measuring stick of a program's effectiveness is the growth and development of the children enrolled. Attendance figures give indicators of the health and safety procedures of the program. Young children in close surroundings do not share toys but they do share germs. Staff must give constant consideration to infection control. Children require nourishment to grow. If they are nourished develop-

Child Observation Method	Program Observation
Developmental Checklists	Checklists: Safety Appropriate programming
Anecdotal Records	Teacher's stories
Frequency Counts	Teacher behaviors Use of slang Negative discipline
Time Samples	Assess learning center use Measure effect of adult presence in learning area
Interviews	Family/child surveys Family/teacher conferences
Work Samples	Examples of teacher projects Bulletin boards Newsletters
Observation	Outside reviewers Licensing agents Accreditation validators

Figure 13–2 Observation Techniques for Program Evaluations

mentally, they will show progress. Portfolios measuring children's progress are one indication of an effective program. Another indicator is children's active involvement with the learning environment. Peeks into classrooms should show children busy working on a variety of activities with the adults facilitating the learning. The rooms should be filled with children's voices, talking, and laughing, with a minimum of adult voices. Children can be surveyed to hear what they have to say about the school, the program, and the learning activities. Even very young children can tell what they like about their school or child care center and what they do not. Adults should listen.

Total Program Evaluations

There are many evaluation instruments available, some determined by the type of the program, others elected for use. All have evaluation as their basic premise, the assessment or measurement of aspects of the program, comparison with an accepted standard of quality, and action implemented to bring the program into compliance or increased effectiveness. An informal program evaluation is one that is a self-study, designed to guide program personnel to assess, evaluate, and raise quality. Bentzen and Frost (2003) have developed a guide that also incorporates child observation and recording methods.

Accreditation is a program evaluation completed on-site by an outside body, usually a professional organization, for the purpose of recognizing programs that meet a pre-established criteria. The accreditation process usually begins with an extensive self-study that leads to improvements in the program before the validation visit. Fees are charged for accreditation and usually some kind of periodic reports are required to report the maintenance of the level of quality. Families can use accreditation as a measuring tool when selecting a program. See Figure 13–3 for a comparison chart of some of the systems.

Program Performance Standards. Head Start programs have national **performance standards** by which they are measured. The standards state that the programs must be "developmentally and linguistically appropriate, recognizing that children have individual rates of development as well as individual interests, temperaments, languages, cultural backgrounds and learning styles . . . . support each child's individual pattern of development and learning; provide for the development of cognitive skills by encouraging each child to organize his or her experiences, to understand concepts, and to develop age appropriate literacy, numeracy, reasoning, problem

solving and decision-making skills which form a foundation for school readiness and later school success." (U.S. Department of Health and Human Services, 2000).

Head Start—PRISM. Head Start programs are evaluated using the PRISM (Program Review Instrument for Systems Monitoring) developed by the U.S. Department of Health and Human Services (2004). This evaluation tool measures programs against the Head Start Program Performance Standards adopted in 1998. They include standards for: Early Childhood Development and Health Services, Family and Community Partnerships, Program Design and Management, Implementation and Enforcement.

High/Scope—PQA. High/Scope has developed a program evaluation tool for all early childhood settings, especially those implementing the High/Scope Curriculum, the *High/Scope Program Quality Assessment, second edition* (2002). It has expanded sections for evaluating: Learning Environment, Daily Routine, Adult–Child Interaction, Curriculum Planning and Assessment, Family Involvement and Family Services, Staff Qualifications and Staff Development, and Program Management. Potential uses of the PQA include staff training, program assessment and monitoring, observation and feedback, research and evaluation, and information and dissemination.

NAEYC Center Accreditation. The National Association for the Education of Young Children has an accreditation system for early childhood programs, the *Accreditation Criteria and Procedures of the National Academy of Early Childhood Programs, Revised Edition* (1998), which is the Academy's plan to improve the quality of care and education for young children in settings. Programs are eligible that serve a minimum of ten children from birth through age five in part- or full-day group programs. They have been in operation at least one year and meet the state's **license requirements** by the state or are exempt. The criteria measures interactions between staff and children and staff and families. It also looks at the administration of the program, curriculum, physical environment, health safety, and nutrition. Staff needs are assessed by criterion for staff qualifications and development, staffing patterns, and program evaluation. It does this through a three-step process of self-study in which program personnel and families conduct a self-study, indicating their rating of unmet, partially met, or fully met. This self-study is designed to indicate areas that need improvements; an improvement plan is implemented and ratings are changed. Every classroom staff person, the administrators, and

Crosswalk of Early Childhood Program Standards

	NAEYC Program Accreditation	Head Start Program Standards	National Health & Safety Standards	High/Scope PQA	Environmental Rating Scales (Harms, et al.)
Child Development and Education	A. Interactions among Teachers and Children B. Curriculum	1304.21 Education & Early Childhood Development	2. Program: Activities for Healthy Development 7. IDA Eligible Children	Adult/Child Interaction Curriculum Planning & Assessment Daily Routine	Language-Reasoning Activities Interaction
Child Health and Safety	H. Health and Safety	1304.22 Child Health and Safety	3. Health Promotion & Protection 6. Infectious Diseases	Learning Environment	Personal Care Routines
Nutrition	I. Nutrition and Food Service	1304.23 Child Nutrition	4. Nutrition & Food Service		Personal Care Routines
Mental Health		1304.24 Child Mental Health			Interaction
Family Involvement	C. Relationships among Teachers and Families	1304.4 Family Partnership		Family Involvement & Family Services	Families & Staff
Partnerships		1304.41 Community Partnership	9. Licensing & Community Action		
Management Systems	E. Administration J. Evaluation	1304.51 Management Systems and Procedures	8. Administration	Program Management	Program Structure
Staff Management	D. Staff Qualifications and Development F. Staffing	1304.52 Human Resources Management	1. Staffing	Staff Qualifications & Staff Development	Families & Staff
Facilities and Equipment	G. Physical Environment	1304.53 Facilities, Materials, and Equipment	5. Facilities, Supplies		Space & Furnishings

Note: Letters and numbers refer to the sections in the respective standards as they correlate to the topics in the left-hand column.

Figure 13–3 Program Evaluation Comparison

families have components of the entire criteria to assess. Once the self-study and improvements are complete, the administrator submits the program description to the Academy and applies for a validation visit. The Academy assigns a validator to observe in the classrooms and spot check the documentation of the administrator's report to validate or confirm that the ratings are accurate. That validation report is submitted to a three-person commission for the accreditation decision. Programs are not required to demonstrate 100% compliance. The accreditation is valid for three years, then the self-study and validation are repeated.

NECPA Program Accreditation. *National Early Childhood Program Accreditation (NECPA)* calls for the owner or director to assemble demographic information and lead a self-paced, self-study evaluation. Surveys are completed by staff and families along with classroom observations. Improvements are made to the program based on the evaluations, and the program participates in an on-site verification visit by an assigned validator. The scored indicators and program profile are presented to the NECPA's National Accreditation Council for the accreditation decision. The accreditation is valid for three years. The accreditation system is entering the technological age with a new automated system, Automated Accreditation Indicator Systems (AAIS™).

Family Child Care Accreditation. The National Association for Family Child Care also has an accreditation system for family child care workers: the *National Association for Family Child Care Accreditation (NAFCC)*. These are caregivers who provide licensed or regulated care for other people's children in the provider's home for more than eighteen months. It requires a provider self-evaluation with the assessment profile for family child care, family questionnaires, a family observation, and validator observation. This also is valid for three years.

Special Focus Instruments

There are some formal program assessment tools that can be used to evaluate one aspect of a program. This can be accomplished as a self-study, by the administration, or by a consultant. The advantage of a self-study is the staff considers quality criterion items, standards set by an outside source. These are less threatening and not taken as criticism or a pet peeve but as objective benchmarks against which to compare and consider their appropriateness for this particular situation.

When evaluations are done by the director or administrator, it gives them first-hand information about the program, recognizing the strengths of the program. It also may indicate areas that need attention, from which they can implement change. Often the staff has been aware of the situation and desiring change but were not in a position to make the change themselves. Now that can happen. This type of evaluation can stress the staff and alienate them from administrators if the staff feels they are under scrutiny. Evaluation is only helpful if it focuses on strengths and plans build on those strengths not the deficits. They can be addressed in a cooperative way with group decision making more effectively than from edict or top-down proclamations.

Outside consultants may be enlisted to perform the assessment. This objective outside person can observe, evaluate, and make recommendations without the fear of recriminations from administrators or alienation from the staff. Issues that staff or administrators have been aware of can surface from an outside consultant and can be addressed easier than from within. Whatever the source of evaluation, the outcome should be to discover and proclaim the strengths of the program, and to recommend changes or next steps that are reasonable, attainable, and measurable. This is the same principle that is used in the child's developmental evaluation.

Here are a few program evaluations that may be used and a short description of each evaluation's use.

Early Childhood Environment Rating Scale — Revised (ECERS-R). The ECERS-R (Harms, Clifford, & Cryer, 1998) is a comprehensive Rating Scale to assess personal care routines, furnishings and displays, language reasoning experiences, fine and gross motor activities, creative activities, social development activities, and adult needs. Each is rated on a scale of 1 to 7 with quality points of 1, 3, 5, 7 described in detail. The Rating Scale format gives clear criteria and a goal if a score of less than 7 is determined. The *Infant/Toddler Environment Rating Scale, Revised Edition* (Harms, Cryer, & Clifford, 2002) follows the same format but is specific to younger age groups. Neither one of these rating scales specifically looks at curriculum. The *Family Day Care Rating Scale* (Harms Clifford, 1989) and the *School-Age Care Environment Rating Scale* (Harms, Jacobs, & White, 1995) are two additional Rating Scales measuring environments for special settings.

National Health and Safety Performance Standards (2002). The American Academy of Pediatrics, Public Health Association, and National Resource Center for Health and Safety in Child Care have developed an extensive set of performance standards that include educational, as well as health and safety guidelines. The standards are based on 13 guiding principles that include program policies and procedures.

Staff Performance. There are many instruments created to measure staff performance. *Measuring Performance: The Early Childhood Educator in Practice* (Elliott, 2002) is a comprehensive guide that can be used for both program performance and spot checks on teacher demonstrated cognitive, creative, affective, language/literacy, social, and physical behaviors. It also contains separate checklists for measuring child development, diversity, and safety forms for developing staff and program action plans.

Anti-Bias Curriculum. Derman-Sparks (1989) lists questions to be answered from video taped classroom

Assessing the Environment— Pointing Back at You

When I tattled, my mother always said, "When you point your finger at someone else, three fingers are pointing back at yourself." That axiom has applications in observing children's development or lack of it. When we are careful observers, the attention is focused on the child, pointing at characteristics, skills, and behaviors. We tend to lay the source of the problem with the child. "Why is the child like that?" "Why can't she . . . ?" "What's the matter with that child?"

The finger pointing up can be interpreted as "That's just the way those people are." Substantial elements of a child's development are genetically programmed. The adults in the child's life act as the observers of how that script is played out. However, the three fingers pointing backward are a reminder of the important role the adult plays (Figure 13–4). Rather than blaming the child or the genetic program, some reflection may help. The influence of the adults in the child's life cannot be overlooked.

Figure 13–4 When you point a finger at someone else, three fingers are pointing back at you.

observations. Peers examine interactions between teachers and children that may subtly teach gender, racial, or disability biases. The whole book *Anti-Bias Curriculum: Tools for Empowering Young Children* (1989), is a self-evaluative, consciousness-raising experience for the reader.

Playground Safety. Evaluation is more than assessment. It is making a change because of the assessment. Programs periodically should perform safety checks inside and outside using checklists such as the one in Chapter 3. Deteriorating equipment, overlooked hazards, and bad habits can be detected in these checklist formats for the protection of children's health and safety.

Environment and Development

Repeatedly, the influence of the environment, in particular the early childhood setting, has been emphasized as a powerful force in each area of development. The role of the teacher is to provide, modify, enrich, support, supervise, and adapt that environment for each child. It begins with a knowl-

edge of the child's physical development. How large are they? What do they need to be kept safe? What kind of equipment is needed for the routines and activities of the child while in this environment? That decision is based on the purpose and philosophies of the program. If it is a library story hour then one kind of equipment and materials is appropriate, whereas a gymnastics program may select different criteria.

The cognitive environment in a developmentally based program will provide materials prompting children to ask questions. Answers are sought by following the child's level of thinking. Engaging or participating in the actual manipulation of real objects replaces one-dimensional worksheets, watching an adult, or a video explanation of a principle. The adults in the environment support the exploration by asking open-ended questions, such as, "How do you think that happened?" or "Is there another way . . . ?" "What would happen if . . . ?"

The emotional environment of the early childhood setting provides for realistic expectations. Because young children are spillers, mops, paper towels, brooms, and dust pans are handy for clean up. Group experiences can be noisy and stressful for some children. A quiet, alone space is provided to watch the action or withdraw to rest and reduce the adrenaline flow. Because children are learners, approximations for a task are recognized and efforts are rewarded before full accomplishments are attained. Children are made to feel competent by being trusted with responsibility that matches their ability.

The social atmosphere of the environment is monitored constantly to promote cooperation rather than competition, sociability rather than sarcasm, and friendship rather than isolation. Small groups are encouraged to work and play together by the physical arrangement of the furnishings into small areas. Planned and spontaneous activities bring children physically close to one another. This helps them understand the rights and space needs of each person and the principle of cooperation. Whenever observing the child, give attention to the environment and note its possible influence on the child. If it is in a negative way, changes need to be made. That is the response of a responsible adult.

Suggestions at the end of this chapter give the opportunity to assess the environment. The second assignment helps to assess the suitability to the needs of the child by observing the child's interactions with the group. A program may have a wonderful facility, the nicest equipment, materials, and supplies, but for some reason the child is not comfortable or learning there.

Advantages of Formal Program Assessment

By using internal and external evaluation methods, programs measure and maintain the quality necessary for the safety, health, growth, and development of the children they serve. Other advantages include:

- it ensures that the professionalism of the staff is monitored
- objective criteria is used to measure this program against others of the same type
- staff, administrators, and consultants have an objective instrument with which to measure
- evaluation has program improvement as its goal, not revocation of licensing or censure

Disadvantages of Formal Program Assessment

The disadvantages of formal program assessment are

- there is usually a cost involved
- they are time-consuming

- occasionally, when the instrument does not fit the program, erroneous messages are given, which are not really helpful
- follow-up is necessary so that the assessment is like seeing a smudge on your face and not washing it off
- circumstances, such as economic or leadership, pose barriers to the implementation of evaluation findings

Pitfalls to Avoid

When considering a program evaluation, the disadvantages may be overcome by

- careful consideration of a good match of instrument to program ensures that the results will be helpful.
- planning for the added cost not only of the evaluation process but the implementation helps it not be an exercise in futility.
- using knowledgeable, objective evaluators—they are key components to the success of the evaluation.

Using Technology

Any of the rating systems for program assessments mentioned in this chapter can be tabulated electronically. Using Excel, each of the classroom ratings can be entered and the data can be reported in text or a variety of charts. If you store and use electronic databases for program assessments, strong and weak areas are easily recognized, a quality improvement plan can be made and implemented, and the ratings revisited to see indicators of improvement. Selecting a program assessment instrument that fits the programs goals and objectives can be a very useful tool for use in long-range planning, reporting to administrators and decision-making, bodies and for justification for grants.

How to Find the Time

The director or administrator has many day-to-day responsibilities, but quality assurance should be at the top of the list. Make a plan for program assessment and do more than go through the motions. This should be one of the most important tasks each year (and it *should* be yearly).

Self-assessments are valuable planning tools but to ensure the validity of that evaluation, an outside evaluator is usually used. This should be someone who is familiar with the world of early childhood education but is not a colleague, client, or board member. Those individuals may have a conflict of interest and the evaluation would not be credible for some of the purposes listed above. Some evaluation systems provide the evaluator, such as the NAEYC and the NAFDA Program Evaluations. Evaluation from an outside evaluator not only takes time but involves financial cost, so that is also a consideration. It is a worthwhile endeavor, however.

What to Do with It?

Program assessments should not be done just to fill a notebook and place on a shelf. The time, effort, and cost involved should bring more benefit than simply completing a necessary task. The report itself should be a dynamic document, used for program improvement so its components are the baseline for an ongoing program improvement plan. The report results should be communicated to those who have a need to know and those who should know. A report to families about the findings can include favorable ratings, "Our program received excellent ratings in . . . ." as well as not-so-favorable ratings, "Our program is less effective in . . . and this is how we are working to improve it." This is not only ethical but can help enlist family support in making those improvements, especially those that directly affect them—like record keeping or safety.

Program assessments, especially when they result in an accreditation or certification, should be communicated to the community at large. Press releases, press conferences, letters to government officials, notices to board members and local community agencies all bring positive recognition to the program. Program assessments should be used for affirmation, improvement, and recognition.

(Figure 13–5). Many of the characteristics that have been discussed already as indicators of development are also indicators of appropriateness of a program for a child. These are reviewed along with the impact of group size, adult/child ratio, and program structure on the child's adjustment to the program.

LOOKING AT THE ADJUSTMENT OF THE CHILD TO THE PROGRAM

This section is not about measuring a child's development directly but about observing the child's **adjustment** and how the child is benefiting from the program. It ultimately does affect development. Children's relationships throughout the day, both with adults and peers, have great impact on the child's adjustment to the program. The responsibility lies with programs to give careful attention to transitions, mealtimes, small and large group activities, and peer relations (Gable, 2002). Every quality program may not be a good place for every child. Families and program staff evaluate if the child's needs are being met

Figure 13–5 Does the program fit the child?

Child–adult ratios are one of the most basic indicators of adequate care. When there are too many children or the group is too large, a child's adjustment and even well-being are jeopardized. The National Health and Safety Performance Standards (2002) recommends:

Age	Child/Staff	Maximum Group Size
Birth–12 mos	3:1	6
13–30 mos	4:1	8
31–35 mos	5:1	10
Three-year-olds	7:1	14
Four-year-olds	8:1	16
Five-year-olds	8:1	16
6–8-year-olds	10:1	20
9–12-year-olds	12:1	24

Compare these recommendations to the state-by-state comparison in Figure 13–6.

Children may not, or possibly cannot, say, "I just love going to this program." There are behavioral signs that the child is emotionally, physically, socially, and cognitively comfortable there. Or the opposite may occur. The child may protest attending strongly or may indicate a lack of comfort through regressive behaviors of bed-wetting, thumb-sucking, or other earlier stage behaviors. This is not to put the decision of program choice into the child's domain, but to give families and teachers an indication that the child is not totally comfortable and further investigation is needed.

Sometimes a program may not meet the needs of children. There may be a discontinuity between the child's home situation and the philosophy of the school. A child from a very structured home that stresses adult permission and obedience may have difficulty adjusting to a program that promotes independence and allows choices. A child from a small family with little contact with other children may find the large group setting a hard adjustment. The high energy of a colorful, noisy, busy center may be too much for a highly distractable child. Consideration should be given to the families' values, the program's goals, and the child's personality and experience.

Families and staff watch for signs of that adjustment to judge if the program is meeting the needs of the child. The use of the portfolio to document the child's participation can give specific information on areas of development. Periodically, it is necessary to step back and view the whole child. Looking at the child's adjustment to the program does that. These indicators are for toddlers through early school age. Some require an advanced level, especially in language, but behavior can be interpreted even beyond language.

Behavioral Indicators of Comfort

The child gives behavioral indications of the suitability of the program for developmental needs. Some criterion may be answered with a "No" because the child is going through separation anxiety or another emotional upset. It is important for families and staff to give attention to a child's discomfort. It is a form of communication. The program is appropriate when the child

- begins the day at the program without a fuss.
- knows the schedule for the day and can anticipate what is coming next.
- feels an affinity to the school and says things like, "My school," "My cubby," "My teacher."
- has opportunities to play actively inside and outside every day.
- talks freely at school (at maximum of language level).
- is able to make choices from sufficient equipment and materials.
- is not exhibiting stress, such as crying or regressive behaviors.
- has enough time to work at choice activities.
- is warned of impending change in activities and is given opportunity to finish and clean up.
- moves from one activity to the next comfortably.
- does not have to wait before the next activity can begin.
- does not have to receive step-by-step directions for activities but can explore materials independently.
- is not forced to continue in an activity.
- is able to watch or choose not to participate in an activity.
- displays pride in the work brought home.
- can relate what occurred at school when prompted specifically. (Children need a reminder to trigger memory association.)
- talks about playing with other children in the group.
- knows the teachers' names.
- interacts with the teacher on a one-to-one basis several times during the day.
- goes to the adult for assistance and comfort.
- sleeps, eats, and toilets at school without difficulty.

Families and staff should work together to determine if the child is in the right placement where the

Maximum Number of Children Allowed per Caretaker and Maximum Group Size in Child Care Centers, Selected Ages, 2000

	Children per Caretaker			Group Size		
	9 months	27 months	4 Years	9 Months	27 Months	4 years
Alabama	6:1	8:1	20:1	6	8	20
Alaska	5:1	6:1	10:1	NR	NR	NR
Arizona	5:1/11:2	8:1	15:1	NR	NR	NR
Arkansas	6:1	12:1	15:1	NR	NR	NR
California	4:1	6:1	12:1	NR	12	NR
Colorado	5:1	7:1	12:1	10	14	24
Connecticut	4:1	4:1	10:1	8	8	20
Delaware	4:1	10:1	15:1	NR	NR	NR
District of Columbia	4:1	4:1	10:1	8	8	20
Florida	4:1	11:1	20:1	NR	NR	NR
Georgia	6:1	10:1	18:1	12	20	36
Hawaii	4:1	8:1	16:1	8	NR	NR
Idaho	6:1	12:1	12:1	NR	NR	NR
Illinois	4:1	8:1	10:1	12	16	20
Indiana	4:1	5:1	12:1	8	15	NR
Iowa	4:1	6:1	12:1	NR	NR	NR
Kansas	3:1	7:1	12:1	9	14	24
Kentucky	5:1	10:1	14:1	10	20	28
Louisiana	6:1	12:1	16:1	12	12	16
Maine	4:1	5:1	10:1	12	15	30
Maryland	3:1	6:1	10:1	6	12	20
Massachusetts	3:1/7:2	4:1/9:2	10:1	7	9	20
Michigan	4:1	4:1	12:1	NR	NR	NR
Minnesota	4:1	7:1	10:1	8	14	20
Mississippi	5:1	12:1	16:1	10	14	20
Missouri	4:1	8:1	10:1	8	16	NR
Montana	4:1	8:1	10:1	NR	NR	NR
Nebraska	4:1	6:1	12:1	NR	NR	NR
Nevada	6:1	10:1	13:1	NR	NR	NR
New Hampshire	4:1	6:1	12:1	12	18	24
New Jersey	4:1	7:1	15:1	20	20	20
New Mexico	6:1	10:1	12:1	NR	NR	NR
New York	4:1	5:1	8:1	8	10	16
North Carolina	5:1	10:1	20:1	10	20	25
North Dakota	4:1	5:1	10:1	8	10	20
Ohio	5:1	7:1	12:1	12	14	28
Oklahoma	4:1	8:1	15:1	8	16	30
Oregon	4:1	4:1	10:1	8	8	20
Pennsylvania	4:1	6:1	6:1	8	12	20
Rhode Island	4:1	6:1	10:1	8	12	20
South Carolina	6:1	10:1	18:1	NR	NR	NR
South Dakota	5:1	5:1	10:1	20	20	20
Tennessee	5:1	8:1	15:1	10	16	20
Texas	4:1/10:2	13:1	20:1	10	26	35
Utah	4:1	7:1	15:1	8	14	30
Vermont	4:1	5:1	10:1	8	10	20
Virginia	4:1	10:1	12:1	NR	NR	NR
Washington	4:1	7:1	10:1	8	14	20
West Virginia	4:1	8:1	12:1	NR	NR	NR
Wisconsin	4:1	6:1	13:1	8	12	24
Wyoming	5:1	8:1	15:1	NR	NR	NR
Maximum Recommended Level	3:1 to 4:1	4:1 to 6:1	8:1 to 10:1	8	12	20

NR—Not regulated.

Maximum Recommended Level: As recommended in the accreditation guidelines developed by the National Association for the Education of Young Children and in the National Health and Safety Performance Standards developed by the American Public Health Association Academy of Pediatrics.

There may be some exceptions to these ratio and group size requirements in some states under certain circumstances. For example, some states have different requirements for small centers, classes with mixed-age groups, or different levels of licensing. See original source for details.

Source: The Center for Career Development in Early Care and Education at Wheelock College, *Child/Staff Ratio and Group Size Requirements* (Boston, MA: 2000).

Figure 13–6 Child Group Size and Ratio By State (Reprinted with permission from *The State of America's Children Yearbook, 2001.* Washington, DC: Children's Defense Fund, 2001, p. 138.)

child is receiving not just physical care but learns and feels acceptance and belonging.

Looking at the Program through the Child's Eyes

At times any one or more of the previously listed indicators may be answered with a "No." That does not mean necessarily there is an adjustment problem. It may mean that the child is moving through a developmental phase, struggling with the change in thinking or feeling. It may mean there are personality differences between the child and a staff member. The child may feel threatened by an aggressive child in the group. There may be changes happening at home that are affecting the child at school. A child exhibiting such behaviors should be closely observed in an attempt to learn the cause. There are many factors that influence the child's adjustment to the program.

The Make-Up of the Peer Group. Different activities depend on a certain number of people to be successful.

EXERCISE: How many people would you like in your group for the following activities?

Cheering your team at a football game:
Sleeping:
Changing a light bulb:
Taking a shower:
Talking on the phone:
Eating:
Riding in a car:
Birthing a child:
Numbering all the books in a library:
Playing a card game:

Some activities are solitary, or at least intimate. The space and action also determine the number of people who can participate in certain activities. The size of the task at hand and the skill required, or the occasion, are also factors in group size. When thinking of young children in group settings, some of these same factors need to be considered.

More than 57% of children younger than five whose mothers were employed are cared for by non-relatives. Twenty-five percent of those children are in center-based care while 23% are in family child care homes (Children's Defense Fund, 2001). Children are grouped together by different criteria in different programs. There are rationales, advantages, and disadvantages to each decision.

Chronological Age Groups. Most center-based child care and public schools group children by chronolog-

ical age. Grouping children by age assumes that children who are in the same age range have similar needs and interests. This is usually the case, especially when curriculum is open-ended so that a range of developmental abilities can all find success. Individual differences, especially of exceptional children (those with disabilities or giftedness), and arbitrary age cutoffs sometimes make decisions about group placement difficult. At fifteen months, a child might be advanced physically, walking steadily. She is interested in the wider environment of the young toddler room. Regulations or policies might prevent her advancement into the next group. The wobbly walker may be arbitrarily "promoted" to the young toddler room at eighteen months. For a slow-to-walk infant, a room of two-year-olds is a fearsome place. Grouping of children by age has different criteria and functions for the child's interactions in the group setting.

Mixed-Age or Multi-Age Groups. Mixed-age groups or heterogeneous grouping most resembles the family group with members of different ages (Figure 13–7). It gives young children the opportunity to observe, imitate, and learn from older ones. It gives older children occasions to practice nurturing skills, reteach learned skills, and feel competent. Most family child care settings have children of mixed-age groups since they usually care for siblings. In Kontos's review of group size, the average family child-care group was from five to eight (1992, p. 60). Some centers have mixed-age groups or vertical grouping with the state regulating the size of the group and the adult–child ratio. Prosocial behaviors, such as help-giving, sharing, and turn taking are elicited in the older children toward the younger ones. Older children can lead younger ones to higher levels of cognitive thinking by assisting in collaborative efforts as "experts." Evangelou (1989) recommends the consideration of the optimum age range and the proportion of older to younger children. The allocation of time to the mixed-age group and the curriculum and teaching strategies are crucial to the success of mixed-age grouping.

The Size of the Group. In a large study comparing children at home and in center-based child care, the size of the group and adult–child ratio mattered a great deal. "Children in classes with more children per caregiver made smaller gains in cognitive development, were less socially skilled with unfamiliar peers, and were less compliant. There are apparently some benefits of being in a class with low adult–child ratio; these children learn to curb their aggressive behavior" (Clark-Stewart, Gruber, & Fitzgerald, 1994, p. 240). Family child care studies also indicate that as the group size increased, the interaction of

Figure 13–7 Mixed-age groups bring benefits to all.

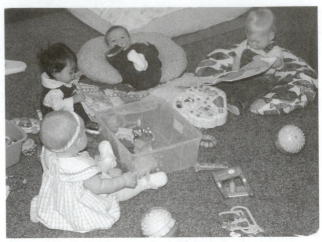

Figure 13–8 Infants need small groups.

adults with children decreased (Kontos, 1992). Even in elementary schools, an experiment in class size including 7,000 children kindergarten through third grade, showed students in classes of 15 raised math and reading standardized scores dramatically (Mosteller, 1995).

The various states have a wide range of children allowed in groups according to age. Figure 13–6 illustrates an interesting comparison from the Children's Defense Fund (2001).

Infants (Birth to 18 Months). It is common sense that the younger the child, the more care they require, so the size of the group should be smaller. Newborn infants need the care and attention from a few of the same people. It is critical that infants receive the required care. The National Institute of Child Health and Human Development (NICHD), in its longitudinal study of children in child care (1996) found that children under two years needed a small group and low staff–infant ratios (Figure 13–8). It also found strong caregiver qualifications predicted positive outcomes. Infants should be cared for in groups no larger than six with two adults, or in a group of three with one adult (National Health and Safety Performance Standards, 2002). The quality and frequency of adult–child interactions are the critical variables in infant care (Cost, Quality, and Outcomes Study Team, 1995). The interaction with adults provides for each infant's individual physical and emotional needs. This includes feeding, diapering, and holding. Infants of younger than eight months interact with the teacher while in close physical proximity to other infants. The space size requirements vary by state regulation, but 35 square feet per child is considered minimum.

Observations of the infant in the group setting would expect to see her looking at other infants, smiling, and touching them. The adult monitors the physical contact, for the infant has no knowledge that her squeezes and hair pullings hurt. She also lacks the self-control to keep from doing it. Other children are part of the world to be manipulated. Once infants become mobile by crawling, creeping, cruising, or walking, they approach other children with simple chase games and peekaboo. They enjoy little finger plays and songs together and a book shared with another child on the lap of the adult. They begin to make vocal exchanges with each other, using vocal signals to invite attention or alert the teacher that they need to be removed from this stressful situation.

The babies' and toddlers' compliance with the adults' requests begin with realistic expectations for children's behavior. Some guidelines for behavior from Jennifer Birckmayer, Cornell University (1995) are

1. Have age-appropriate expectations for children's behavior.
2. Tell children what they can do.
3. Distraction is a good technique to use with very young children.
4. Change the environment instead of the behavior.
5. Offer choices only when you can accept child's decision.
6. Use words and actions to guide behavior.
7. Have a few, simple rules consistently enforced.
8. Recognize children's efforts.
9. Be a friend.
10. Be a good role model.

The teacher watches for developmental milestones that occur almost daily at this age and marks the developmental checklist the program is using. Daily contact sheets are used to document the amount of time and type of activities provided for the infant each day. A copy is kept in the child's file. It is desirable to send a copy home at the end of every day (Figure 13–9).

Toddlers (18 Months to 3 Years). The recommended ratio is five toddlers to one adult and a total group size of ten. This ensures the safety and exchanges with responsive adults needed for this age. Considerations for the toddler in a group setting begin with a safe, healthy environment. The emotional environment provides support, with places to withdraw. The toddler needs consistent teachers and adequate space and materials. He is still developing coordination and has limited social skills. The child is observed as he interacts with the materials, demonstrating his physical development. He can participate in small groups for very short periods of time. This could include songs, finger plays, and short story books. His play with other children is at the functional level, using toys in a repetitive manner but advancing to more make-believe play, simulating grown-up activities. He will pretend to drive a car, bake a cake, sweep the floor, especially when he sees the steering wheel, cake pans, or broom. Interactions with other children will be stormy because of limited language and the inability to take another's viewpoint. He wants the big ball of Play Doh, so he takes it. When the other player protests, there is little self-restraint in the responses.

Toddlers are fast moving, independent, yet needing much adult assistance with self-care skills. Observations include documentation of the child's ability to dress, eat, and the beginning interest in toileting. Socially, the child is taking an interest in other children but with little emotional control or awareness of the feelings of others. This leads to aggressiveness and the possibility for physical harm. The child is rapidly developing language skills but often uses biting as an expression of frustration or aggression.

Toddlers have learned the sequence of the events of the day and depend very heavily on its stability. Arrivals and departures are handled in a routine way that allows for a relaxed, unrushed atmosphere. They need programming that allows them mostly free-play activities from a wide range of choices, including outside play and soft, quiet areas. Sleep and rest time should be adaptable to individual schedules and needs, with some children needing frequent short naps, and others needing long afternoon naps. Eating times are social opportunities with self-care skills, food exploration, and casual conversation included.

Transitions between periods of play, sleeping, eating, and diapering or toileting should be natural and relaxed. Waiting time should be eliminated and children warned that the end of that phase of the day is coming to an end (Psaltis & Stonehouse, 1990). When these elements are included in the program, the child is observed as she follows routines, interacts with adults and children, and maximizes the learning environment (Figure 13–9).

Circle times for toddlers include songs, finger plays, creative movement, and short books or storytelling. Participation should be optional. It can last as long or as short as they are interested. Guidelines for group behavior, including self-discipline, depend on a knowledge of child development to be realistic. The young child is egocentric, not able to put himself in someone else's place. The young child is impulsive without the ability to control emotional urges. Language is not fully developed yet, with vocabulary centered on things rather than ideas and symbolic actions. It is not developed enough to present a rational point of view or to capably negotiate. The young child's experience in life has been limited and memory is still developing, so that does not help in self-control. Adults control the environment by placing matches where the child cannot reach them or by placing furniture where a child cannot use it to climb to forbidden objects in cupboards or on shelves. Adults' directions are clear and specific. They give warning of an impending change in activities. It is the child's desire to please adults yet develop autonomy. The two desires come into conflict. The payoff might be a reward or the absence of punishment. Adults may give direct instruction about expectations of behavior in what is called a "personal message" (Kostelnik, Whiren, Soderman, Stein, & Gregory, 2002):

- rules must be reasonable—within the capability and knowledge necessary to carry out the desired behavior
- rules must be definable—specifying the *exact* behavior that is acceptable
- rules must be positive—telling them what to do rather than "don't . . ." or "stop . . ." (pp. 313–314)

Observing the toddler during play gives information about her concept of right and wrong. She might paint continually on the wall, even after being reminded to paint on paper. It is noted that her inner controls might be missing. She is not understanding the directions. The cause may be emotional in nature, seeking attention, or demonstrating an open defiance to rules.

INFANT DAILY CARE SHEET

Child's Name: _____

Today's Date: _____

PARENT INFORMATION

How did your child sleep last night? _____

Is there medication today? _____

What is your child's feeding schedule? _____

_____

Is there any other information? _____

_____

CAREGIVER INFORMATION
NUTRITION

Bottles:

Snacks:

Lunch:

BATHROOMING

Time	Wet	BM

NAPPING

From _____ to _____

_____ to _____

_____ to _____

Some things we have observed today...

_____ Hand games	_____ Babbled	_____ Rolled
_____ Books	_____ Talked	_____ Crawled
_____ Ball play	_____ Giggled	_____ Stood
_____ Used toys	_____ Cuddled	_____ Danced
_____ Climbed	_____ Cried, but comforted when held	
_____ Outside	_____ Other	

Questions or comments for home:

Signed _____

Figure 13–9 Daily Contact Sheet for Infants and Toddlers (Reprinted with permission from the BC Center, Broome Community College, Binghamton, NY.)

TODDLER DAILY CARE SHEET

Child's Name: _____

Today's Date: _____

PARENT INFORMATION

Is there medication today? _____

Any other concerns? _____

_____

CAREGIVER INFORMATION

NUTRITION:

Breakfast:

Snacks:

A.M.

P.M.

Lunch: None   Some   Most   All

BATHROOMING

Time	Wet	BM

NAPPING

From _____ to _____

Some of the things we did today/special activities...

_____ Books	_____ Markers/Crayons	_____ Legos
_____ Climber	_____ Painted	Special activity of the day was:
_____ Playdough	_____ Outside	_____
_____ Water table	_____ Movement	_____ Puzzles
_____ Housekeeping area	_____ Special games	_____ Music

Questions or comments for home:

Signed _____

Figure 13–9 Daily Contact Sheet for Infants and Toddlers (Continued) (Reprinted with permission from the BC Center, Broome Community College, Binghamton, NY.)

When the child knows clearly what is expected, observing the child adhere to those expectations gives information about memory, cognitive, and emotional development. The child understands and can resist temptation to do what he wants to follow the standard. When adults set firm limits about what behavior is not allowed, children learn to comply, first from outside control, but eventually internalizing the standards. The adults role model and make suggestions about how the child can meet the standards, giving them choices. By providing children with alternative activities, the adult gives a way for the child to focus his own attention and energies in another direction. When the adult indicates what effect the actions have on others, the child is receiving instruction on cause and effect and the consequences of his actions. Giving the child an outside view of how the actions appear to others begins the movement away from egocentrism.

Preschoolers (Three- to Five-Year-Olds). A total group size of 15 to 20 is recommended, with younger children in the lower range. The recommended adult–child ratio is two adults for that size group. Developmentally appropriate practices (Bredekamp & Copple, 1997) recommend that the schedule of the day include long periods of uninterrupted involvement in a variety of areas, commonly called learning centers. These usually are set up for independent use to develop physical, cognitive, creative, and social skills. When integrated curriculum or the project approach is used, there is a thematic connection between learning center areas. Woven throughout the schedule are routines for eating, sleeping or resting, toileting, and outside play. Circle time for the whole group, meetings, plan/do/review groups (High/Scope 2002), and small group gatherings may be included, depending on the curriculum model.

School Age. Children attending public school traditionally have been placed in grades by chronological age. The cut-off dates for school entrance may vary as much as six months. Some are in early summer and others are not until the end of the calendar year. There are many in between. This makes it difficult when children are moving from one school district or state to another. Attempts to place children in classes by developmental age have met with difficulties (Figure 13–10). There are different opinions on the criteria and validity of the instruments. Questions have been raised on screenings.

Children of different ages and at different stages present either a dilemma or opportunity to the school, depending on the philosophy. Some schools have divided each class into smaller groups by abil-

Figure 13–10 Children come in all sizes, ages, and stages—the school's dilemma.

ity. This is to teach lessons closer to the levels of development. Many oppose this early tracking or separating children by abilities. Whole-group instruction is difficult when children are functioning at a wide range of abilities. This is addressed by the exploration of the curriculum and teaching practices calling for "developmentally appropriate" rather than "age appropriate" strategies.

Whole-Group Times. A whole-group time may occur at the beginning of the day as a transition between home and school. It welcomes the group and informs them of the choices of the day. It is sometimes held in the middle of the day, usually right before lunch. Then it serves as a transition to review the work done in the morning and to prepare for lunch and rest time and afternoon activities. At the end of the day, some programs have a whole-group time to summarize the day, recalling the highlights, looking forward to tomorrow, and transitioning to home. Beaty (1996) points out that these whole-group times help children feel a common bond, a sense of community. They can include singing, fingerplays, large motor games and musical games, and creative movement. Hohmann and Weikart (1996) say group times should *not* include rigid routines, competitive games, or teacher-led lessons. They recommend it be held in a spacious location, with a specific plan. The adult should have the materials prepared and draw children in with a transition activity. They begin right away, not waiting until every child is in place. The activity is then turned over to the children. The adult's role is to watch and listen while children are the leaders and to transition the group into the next experience. It is a different vision from the traditional whole-group time.

Unscheduled class meetings may be called to address class announcements, class problems, or mistaken behaviors. Gartrell (2003) refers to Glasser's model (1969) of class meetings that build a sense of togetherness. The general rules are that anyone can talk, take turns, be honest, and be kind. Besides the opening, middle, and closing meetings, unscheduled meetings are called out of necessity for spontaneous discussion. Problem solving by the group is underlined by protection of the dignity of the people involved in the problem. The situation is described using "I" messages; solutions are brainstormed and a course of action is decided by the group. This promotes community responsibility and cooperation.

Questionable Value of Calendar and Show and Tell.

EXERCISE: Imagine you are sitting on the floor. The leader says, "Now let's recite the Dow Jones Averages. What was it yesterday? Which stocks sold the most shares? How much was bid for IBM? How much offered? Now say after me, Alco Standard Corp, Am Home Products, Apple Computer, AT&T, Bell Atlantic, Chase Manhattan. Now you know the top-selling stocks. Don't you?

- Do you *really* know them?
- How would you feel if you couldn't remember?
- What if you heard others around you saying them but you couldn't?

Think about this in relation to children reciting numbers from the calendar and days of the week that have no meaning to them.

There are many programs that include counting the days on the calendar and reciting the days of the week and months of the year. These are abstract principles, not readily understood by young children. This exercise is rote memorization without much value. The time could be better spent on other topics of relevant interest to the children. If counting is the purpose or objective of the group time, there should be concrete objects for the children to count. This is according to child development principles. The association of the numeral is symbolic of the quantity and beyond the level of this developmental stage.

EXERCISE: Now you are sitting on the rug and it is Show and Tell time. Mary brings a full-length mink coat out of her backpack. She puts it on and walks around but you are told not to touch it. You might get it dirty. Then Gabriel brings out a new shotgun his father just gave him. He is so proud of it but the teacher is horrified. "Put that away. We don't allow guns at school." Next, it is Katharine's turn. She has an hour-long video of her trip to the Mall of America. There are things all around you that you want to do but you have to sit there and watch it.

Would you:
- touch Mary's coat anyway?
- feel disappointed and angry that you did not get to talk about your prized gift?
- wiggle, reach for a toy, pinch a neighbor, and not listen to Katharine's trip monologue?

Show and Tell has its champions who claim it raises the self-esteem of children to bring an object from home and talk about it. They point out the value also of speaking before the whole group. Show and Tell usually involves long waiting. The children become disinterested in someone else's object because they are egocentric. The pressure builds to show bigger and better toys. These reasons present contrary evidence of its worth. Many have attempted to resolve the difficulties of Show and Tell with creative alternatives, some of which may be successful. Again, a careful consideration should be given to the objectives of the program. This is because of the knowledge of what young children are like.

They cannot wait and watch without touching.
They learn best by doing.
They have limited capacity to describe an object.
They have sensitivity already to the "haves" and the "have nots."

Teaching practices should be based on what is known about how children learn and develop. Reconsideration of practices sometimes causes resistance and defensiveness in teachers. Calendar and Show and Tell are topics for reflection and reconsideration.

High/Scope Small-Group Time. Without espousing any curriculum model, the small-group time of High/Scope gives effective principles for any program's group time. Small-group time is conducted in an intimate place. It is just the right size for a few children and the adult. The same adult and children hold group time every day in that place, where the adult initiates a learning activity with real materials. The children explore the materials, deciding what to do with them. The adult helps the children carry out their plan if they need assistance. At the end she helps them recall what they did (Hohmann & Weikart, 1995).

Transitions. Even though a daily routine necessitates many changes, most humans are resistant to change.

EXERCISE: **List on a separate sheet of paper all the changes in activities and places you have been today.**

Some people have difficulty getting out of bed, out of pajamas and into clothes, or out of the house and off to work or school. Every change means an adjustment in body position, temperature, sometimes clothing, change in social contacts, and perhaps a change in behavior.

This is difficult for adults but even harder for children. They have no concept of time, minutes, hours, or days. They are stationed in the present. "I am doing this now and I want to continue doing it." They may be forced to change activities. There was not enough time to finish what they were doing. They are led to another activity that they are not so sure they can or want to do. They become stressed. This is the time when children act out, cry, or withdraw.

Transition times need planning with just as much consideration as the activities. Routine signals such as bells, music, gentle whispers, and simple games all give children a clue rather than a command that it is time to make a change. When the schedule of the day is consistent, they quickly come to anticipate and adjust to the changes, especially when they are pleasantly carried out.

When adults consider the child's needs first, plans are made for the program, activities, and interactions to fit those needs. When adults then consider each child as an individual and adapt the plans for that particular child, then the program is truly individually appropriate. If the child is exhibiting adjustment problems, it very likely is the program at fault, not the child.

HELPING ALL CHILDREN IN GROUP SETTINGS

The fit of the program to the needs of the child is vitally important to every child, but for a child with special needs it is critical. *Mainstreaming, integration, inclusion,* and *least restricted environment* are all terms related to the legal-legislative postures as well as child advocates promoting normalizing educational settings for children with special needs. The benefits of regular early childhood settings for children with special needs are many.

- In regular placements, negative views of children with handicaps are reduced because they are not isolated.

- When children of all abilities are grouped together, tolerance and understanding increase.
- Through interactions with typical children, peers become the behavior and skill role models in a demanding environment.
- Early intervention is beneficial for most handicaps.
- Younger children accept others more readily than older children who may have learned to stigmatize those who are different from themselves.

Planning and consideration of many factors ensure a successful placement for children with special needs in regular classrooms. Cook, Tessier, and Klein (2000) suggest some of the same points of consideration discussed earlier in this chapter.

- developmental levels rather than age groupings— By placing children with special needs with younger children, it decreases the developmental differences.
- ratio of integrated children in the group—Some have suggested that when only one or two children with special needs are integrated into a group, they still experience isolation. When more than one and up to one-third of the class is children with special needs, true integration is more likely to be successful. The caveat here is dependent on the nature of the special needs, the training of the teacher, and supplemental classroom assistance available.
- individualized learning experiences—The curriculum for all children should be based on their interests and their strengths. Building on what they can do and modifying the environment and activities so that each child finds success is the principle of developmentally appropriate curriculum for all children.
- partnerships with families—The families of children with special needs must be advocates for their own child. They are involved in more educational decisions about their child than other families and must monitor their child's progress closely. This places the relationship and communication between teacher and families in a priority position.

The placement decisions for children with special needs must be carefully considered so their abilities are maximized and needs are met.

HELPING PROFESSIONALS FOR PROGRAM EVALUATION AND SUPPORT

Help can come from referring to experts or from other people who have had a similar experience.

consultants—The humorous definition of a consultant is someone from more than one hundred miles away. A consultant is a specialist who is enlisted, and paid, for their advice. Programs who want an impartial, outside evaluation often contract with a consultant to provide that service.

support groups—Groups with like concerns often informally or formally band together to discuss, seek answers, commiserate, and give advice to one another. They can become a legislative force for change or a united voice to raise the public's awareness regarding an issue. Many support groups have been formed of families with children who have a specific diagnosed disorder. The program should be aware of these in the local community to make them known to families in the program who may benefit from such an alliance.

OTHER METHODS

Other Methods to Record a Child's Adjustment to Group Settings:

Class List Log
Anecdotal/Running Records
Developmental Checklists
Frequency Counts of social interactions
Conversations and Interviews with the child
Time Samples—measuring activity involvement
Rating Scales

KEY TERMS

accreditation	performance standards
adjustment	program evaluation
license requirements	transitions
mixed-age groups	

WEEK 13: PLAN A

SETTING OBSERVATION

Students

Observe the setting in which you are doing your field experience or practicum, using the Setting Observation Form found in Appendix D.

Practitioners

Use the Setting Observation form in Appendix D. (It can be your own program, but try to look with a visitor's eyes.) You learn so much from visiting other programs.

Make notes of what you observe. After the observation, reflect on the meaning, impressions, inferences, and judgments. Write about how you think the setting reveals the philosophy of the program, the personality and style of the staff, and how the setting may affect the children, families, and people who work there.

What to Do with It

Filing. File the Setting Observation in the class file. Based on the observation, make a plan for improvements to the program. Practitioners, share your plan with other staff. Set a timeline and action plan for implementing improvements.

Sharing with the Child and Family. You may want to share the plan with families and children. For example, in the newsletter, "We've been taking a good look at our classrooms lately and have noticed many pieces of equipment are in need of repair. So we are inviting you to a painting party to help us spruce up and make our learning place more appealing. It won't be all work. Mr. Jones has consented to bring his three-piece band to play for us between 12 and 1 as we eat our lunch, graciously provided by the Wong's Family Restaurant. We hope you can come to help, or even if you just can come for lunch. Please return the reservation form or call the school to let us know how many paint brushes to have available and how many to expect for lunch. Bring the children; we have paint projects for all and the Baby Room will be staffed."

Actions.

Read a Book.
Book selection for this area is for the teacher not the children. There are many excellent resource books for program improvement depending on the area that is being addressed.

Interactions between adults and children:
  Gurewitz, Clemens. (1983). *The sun's not broken, a cloud's just in the way: On child-centered teaching.* Beltsville, MD: Gryphon House.

Curriculum:

Breddekamp, S. & Rosegrant, T. (Eds.). *Reaching potentials: Appropriate curriculum and assessment for young children*, Vol. 1 (1992), Vol. 2 (1995). Washington, DC: NAEYC.

Dodge, D. T. & Colker, L. (2002). *The creative curriculum for preschool*. Washington, DC: Teaching Strategies, Inc.

Relationships among teachers and families:

Hildebrand, V., et al. (1996). *Knowing and serving diverse families*. Englewood Cliffs, NJ: Merrill, an imprint of Prentice Hall.

Staff qualifications and professional development:

Jorde Bloom, P., Sheerer, M., & Britz, J. (1991). *Blue-print for action: Achieving center-based change through staff development*. Beltsville, MD: Gryphon House.

Administration:

Click, P. M. (2004). *Administration of programs for young children, sixth edition*. Clifton Park, NY: Thomson Delmar Learning.

Sciarra, D. J. & Dorsey, A. G. (2003). *Developing and administering a child care center, fifth edition*. Clifton Park, NY: Thomson Delmar Learning.

Staffing:

Carter, M. & Curtis, D. (1994). *Training teachers: a harvest of theory and practice*. St. Paul, MN: Redleaf Press.

Carter, M., & Curtis, D. (1998). *The visionary director: A handbook for dreaming, organizing & improvising in your center*. St. Paul, MN: Redleaf Press.

Health, safety, and nutrition:

Kendrick, A. S., Kaufmann, R., & Messenger, K. P. (Eds.). (1995). *Healthy young children*. Washington, DC: NAEYC.

Environment:

Greenman, J. (1988). *Caring spaces, learning places: Children's environments that work*. Exchange Press.

Anti-bias policies and procedures:

Derman-Sparks, L., Brunson Phillips, C., & Hilliard, A. G. (1997). *Teaching/learning anti-racism: A developmental approach*. New York: Teacher's College Press.

Inclusionary practices:

Allen, K. E. & Cowdery, G. (2005). *The exceptional child: Inclusion in early childhood education, fifth edition*. Clifton Park, NY: Thomson Delmar Learning.

Brown, W. H. & Conroy, M. A. (Eds.). (1997). *Including and supporting preschool children with developmental delays in early childhood programs*. Little Rock, AR: Southern Early Childhood Association.

Catlett, C., Winton, P. J., & Mitchell, A. (2002). *Resource guide: Selected early childhood/early intervention training materials, 11th ed.* Chapel Hill: University of North Carolina, FPG Child Development Institute.

In the Environment.

Based on evaluations, make changes as indicated.

In the Curriculum.

Based on evaluations, make changes as indicated.

In the Newsletter.

- Invite families to participate in regularly scheduled assessments of the program.
- Invite families to feel free to discuss any question they have regarding philosophy or practice with the staff or administration.

WEEK 13: PLAN B

CLASS LIST LOG GROUP PARTICIPATION FOR ALL

Use the Class List Log found in Appendix D and observe the class this week at times when the whole group is together. It may be meeting, circle, planning, lunch, then storytime. Make notes about each child's participation and how each appears to be adjusting to the program. You may also want to make a column for transitions and note the individual behaviors displayed during times of change between activities.

What to Do with It

Filing. Transfer any significant information to the child's Portfolio Overview Sheet. Note each child's level of involvement. If a child appears to be having difficulty, make a plan to do a more detailed observa-

tion (Anecdotal Recording) to look closer for signs of difficulty in adjustment.

File the Class List Log in the class file.

Sharing with the Child and Family. Share the results with the class, families, or a particular child, if appropriate. For example, "Yesterday when I was making notes during Circle Time I saw some people really were interested and some people didn't want to be there. Let's talk about it and see what we can decide," or "I've been observing Latricia for several weeks now and I am concerned that she still does not appear comfortable when presented with the wide range of choices we have in the room. We have decided to narrow it down to two choices for her to get started. Perhaps at home you could give her choices between two shirts, or pants or a dress, or between two acceptable foods. These things will give her more experience and confidence in her own decision-making ability."

WEEK 13: PLAN C

ANECDOTAL RECORDING OF GROUP INTERACTIONS FOR GROUP D

Students

This week select two children to observe. Then follow the instructions below.

Practitioners

Select two children in Group D.

Watch them for any episodes or actions that particularly demonstrate the child's typical interactions with the group. When you see it, jot some notes and amplify into a full Anecdotal Recording, with as many details as possible about action and conversation. In the right-hand column, write your comments, explanations, and questions.

What to Do with It

Filing. In each child's portfolio, note the presence of the Anecdotal Recording on the overview sheet with your name and date (Figure 13–11).

File the recording in each child's portfolio. If there are any follow-up recommendations or questions from the observation, be sure to make a note somewhere to remember to do it.

GROUP INTERACTIONS			
Documentation	Location	Recorder	Date
CL	Class file	MS	12/5
AR	Portfolio	BAN	12/21
CL	Class file	MS	6/9

Figure 13–11 Portfolio Overview Example

Sharing with the Child and Family. Share your findings with family or child if appropriate. For example, "I've been observing some children this week watching for signs of their adjustment or comfort with group activities. Donato fully participates and has an understanding of turn taking, which is unusual for this age. He says you play games a lot at home. That has obviously helped him," or "Patrick, when I was watching you play 'Doggie, Doggie, Where's your Bone?' today, you kept getting angry when no one picked you. Maybe if you pretended to have the bone, like put your hands behind your back, they would think you had it. Maybe you could try that next time and see."

WEEK 13: PLAN D

REFLECTIVE JOURNAL

Respond to the following in your Reflective Journal, kept in a private file at home.

This week when I took the "trip" I noticed . . .

It really bothered me because . . .

I am never going to . . .

I'm worried about . . .

Could it be . . .

I need to remember to . . .

The funniest thing that happened this week was . . .

REFERENCES

American Academy of Pediatrics. (2002). *Caring for our children: National health and safety performance standards.* http://www.nrc.uchsc.edu/COFOC. Retrieved April 20, 2003.

Beaty, J. (1996). *Preschool appropriate practices, 2nd ed.* New York: Harcourt Brace Jovanovich.

Bentzen, W. R., & Frost, M. B. (2003). *Seeing child care: A guide for assessing the effectiveness of child care programs.* Clifton Park, NY: Thomson Delmar Learning.

Birckmayer, J. (1995). *Discipline for babies and toddlers.* Ithaca, NY: Cornell University.

Bredekamp, S., & Copple. C. (Eds.). (1997). *Developmentally appropriate practice in early childhood programs.* Revised edition. Washington, DC: National Association for the Education of Young Children.

Brown, W. (1997). Family-centered practices and inclusive early childhood programs. In Brown, W., & Conroy, M. *Including and supporting preschool children with developmental delays in early childhood programs.* Little Rock, AR: Southern Early Childhood Association.

Children's Defense Fund. (2001). *The state of America's children yearbook, 2001.* Washington, DC: Author.

Clark-Stewart, K., Gruber, C., & Fitzgerald, L. (1994). *Children at home and in day care.* Hillsdale, NJ: Lawrence Erlbaum Associates.

Cook, R. E., Tessier, A., & Klein, M. D. (2000). *Adapting early childhood curricula for children in inclusive settings.* Upper Saddle River, NJ: Merrill Prentice Hall.

Cost, Quality & Outcomes Study Team (1998). *Cost, quality & child outcomes in child care centers.* Denver: Department of Economics, University of Colorado.

Derman-Sparks, L. (1989). *Anti-bias curriculum: Tools for empowering young children.* Washington, DC: National Association for the Education of Young Children.

Elliott, B. (2002). *Measuring performance: The early childhood educator in practice.* Clifton Park, NY: Thomson Delmar Learning.

Evangelou, D. (1989). *Mixed-age groups in early childhood education.* ERIC Digest ED308990 90.

Gable, S. (2002). Teacher–child relationships throughout the day. *Young Children, 57* (4), 42–44.

Gartrell, D. (2003). *A guidance approach for the encouraging classroom, 3rd ed.* Clifton Park, NY: Thomson Delmar Learning.

Glasser, W. (1969). *Schools without failure.* New York: Harper & Row.

Harms, T., Clifford, R. M, & Cryer, D. (1998). *Early childhood environment rating scale (ECERS-R).* Revised Edition. New York: Teachers College Press.

Harms, T., & Clifford, R. M. (1989). *Family day care rating scale (FDCRS).* New York: Teachers College Press.

Harms, T., Cryer, D., & Clifford, R. M. (2002). *Infant/toddler environment rating scale (ITERS), Revised Edition.* New York: Teachers College Press.

Harms, T., Jacobs, E. V., & White, D. R. (1995). *School-age care environment rating scale (SACERS).* New York: Teachers College Press.

High/Scope Press. (2002). *Program quality assessment, 2nd ed.* Ypsilanti, MI: High/Scope Educational Research Foundation.

Hohmann, M., & Weikart, D. (1995). *Educating young children.* Ypsilanti, MI: High/Scope Press.

Kontos, S. (1992). *Family day care: Out of the shadows into the limelight.* Washington, DC: National Association for the Education of Young Children.

Kostelnik, M., Whiren, A., Soderman, A., Stein, L., & Gregory, K. (2002). *Guiding children's social development* (4th ed.). Clifton Park, NY: Thomson Delmar Learning.

LaMontagne, M. J., & Russell, G. W. (1998). Informal and formal assessment. In Johnson, L. J., LaMontagne, M. J., Elgas, P. M., & Bauer, A. M. *Early childhood education: Blending theory, blending practice.* Baltimore, MD: Brookes.

Mosteller, F. (1995). The Tennessee study of class size. In *The future of children.* Cambridge, MA: American Academy of Arts and Sciences.

National Association for the Education of Young Children. (1998). *Accreditation criteria and procedures of the national academy of early childhood programs, Revised edition.* Washington, DC: Author.

National Health and Safety Performance Standards. (2002). http://nrc.uchsc.edu/. Retrieved April 18, 2003.

NICHD Early Child Care Research Network. (1996). Characteristics of infant child care: Factors contributing to positive caregiving. *Early Childhood Research Quarterly, 11* (3), 269–306.

Psaltis, M., & Stonehouse, A. (1990). Toddler centered routines. In A. Stonehouse (Ed.). *Trusting toddlers: Planning for one- to three-year-olds in child care centers.* St. Paul, MN: Toys 'n Things Press.

U.S. Department of Health and Human Services. (2004). *Head Start Program Performance Standards.* Washington, DC: Office of Human Development Services, Administration for Children, Youth, and Families.

RESOURCES

National Association for the Education of Young Children. (1998). *Accreditation criteria and procedures of the national academy of early childhood programs, Revised edition.* Washington, DC: Author.

National Association for Family Child Care Accreditation (1998). NAFCC Accreditation Standards. http://www.nafcc.org/accred/accred.html.

National Early Childhood Program Accreditation (NECPA). http://www.necpa.net.

National Health and Safety Performance Standards. (2002). http://nrc.uchsc.edu/. Retrieved April 18, 2003.

U.S. Department of Health and Human Services. (2004). *Head Start Program Performance Standards.* Washington, DC: Office of Human Development Services, Administration for Children, Youth, and Families.

For additional information on early education curriculum, visit our Web site at http://www.earlychilded.delmar.com

Using the Portfolio to Conference with Families and Looking at the Child's Interactions with Adults

COMMUNICATION BETWEEN HOME AND SCHOOL

Observations have been accumulating in the portfolio. Their effective use in home and school communication is the topic of the final observation feature. "Good information is priceless but if we can't get to it, it's useless," someone said recently concerning the usefulness of becoming computer literate. It could be extended with another phrase, "and if we don't do something with it, it's foolish." That applies to all the information and documentation accumulated about the child. At the end of the year comes the question, "What to Do with It?" The future possession of the portfolio, the class file, and the Reflective Journal conclude this section.

Families are the authorities on their own children. In group settings, children are shared with other people, teachers, who can provide a different perspective on the child. That is an awesome responsibility. Daily contacts with families are the preferable mode of communicating the observations and assessments between home and school. Maximizing these opportunities is discussed. Sometimes written com-

IT HAPPENED TO ME

Families Raising Children

I recently visited an early childhood program during a holiday gathering where families were invited. My eyes were opened to the fact that more than half the adults there were not either of the child's biological "parents." There were grandparents, aunts and uncles, stepparents, foster parents, and other extended family members and some not related but caring friends. I was reminded of Bronfenbrenner's statement about every child needs one person who is crazy about him or her.

The world is constantly changing and so has the configuration of the child's home life. More and more children are living with one parent, or extended family members, or with grandparents as the guardians. Throughout *Week by Week* the involvement of the parent and the program, interacting with the teacher has been stressed. In this third edition, most of the places where "parent" appeared have been changed to "family," which also includes parents. In many cultures, decisions about the child are made by the whole family not just the parent. In an effort to be inclusive, I have been retraining myself to use "family" more often and find that it fits. I am not making a statement that "anyone will do" because I still strongly believe that a child needs a mother and a father to develop, but I recognize that people who fill that role may not necessarily be related by blood.

R E V I E W

Portfolios: A comprehensive collection of teacher observations and children's work to document the child's progress in all developmental areas.

Observation and Recording Methods that May Be Included in the Portfolio:

Class List Log notations (dated)
Developmental Checklists and Rating Scales
Anecdotal and Running Records
Time Sample summaries (dated)
Frequency Count summaries (dated)
transcriptions of Interviews or Conversations
descriptions of Cognitive Task Experiments
Work Samples
media documentation such as photographs, audio or video tape segments
child study
Questionnaires about the child filled out by a family member
Notes inserted by a family member

Portfolios May Include Documentation of:

separation and adjustment to the program
physical development
social development
emotional development
speech and language development
attention span
cognitive development
literacy
creativity
sociodramatic play
self-concept
interaction with adults

munication about the child is the vehicle of transferring information. There are advantages and pitfalls to this mode of exchange. More formal written reports, such as progress reports and child studies, are sometimes warranted, so templates and advice for writing reports about the child are presented. Combining verbal and written reports in a family conference is a unique time of sharing between home and school. More effective family conferences occur with careful preparation and implementation. Guidance will be given for successful family conferences. Occasionally, family conferences of a distinct type are necessary, such as problem solving, questions,

complaints, or an exit interview. Whenever family and staff of a program have a discussion, there is great potential to benefit the child. That is the guiding beacon this section follows.

Children, entrusted to other adults in other settings, must adjust and adapt to other schedules, expectations, and ways of interacting. All have seen the difference in a child's behavior with the parents, then the grandparents. How well they know their allies! In this final section, which looks at child development, this adjustment of the child to other adults is an important one, concluding the child development portion of this book.

A final assessment of the *Week by Week* plan ends this chapter.

USING THE PORTFOLIO TO CONFERENCE WITH FAMILIES

EXERCISE: Using a separate sheet of paper, construct a family diagram for a child you know. Let *M* stand for Mother, *F* for Father. If there are stepparents, grandparents, other adults who are responsible for the child, either legally or in reality, designate them. Let *C* stand for the child. Now draw lines, solid and bold, or dotted or barely visible for the relationship between these adults and the child. For some the diagram is easy; for other children the diagram is complex. Now place a *T* for yourself in pencil that can be erased, for you have a temporary part in that family grouping. You are probably not in the center but closer to the child than you are to the family, yet not in between them. Perhaps you are below them as a support. Draw lines of communication to the family members. It may be by telephone, written communication, now even technology, but whatever form, the goal is to make it a solid, two-way communication to ultimately benefit the child.

Family involvement does not have to be spaghetti suppers, fund-raisers, or discipline classes (though all of those are worthwhile). Involvement, in its truest sense, is the knowledge families have about their child while in the program. Involved families are familiar with the goals of the program, its policies and procedures, and how those relate to their child. They also know what the child's day is like and how the child is functioning in the group setting. Confidence is built that the staff will keep them informed of important facts about their child.

While the family is the most accurate source of information about their child, it has been found that the public at large has some gaps in their knowledge about children in general. In a national study of 3,000 adults, including more than 1,000 parents of young children, it was found that there are vast overexpectations for behavior for babies and young children (Lally, Lerner, & Lurie-Hurvitz, 2001). These include beliefs about the intentionality of behavior by infants and toddlers, "She knows I just sat down to eat and chooses this time to get fussy." It was also found that adults had misinformation about spoiling and disci-

pline, and less understanding of the importance of play. The early childhood professional has the opportunity to educate parents and the public about child development, realistic expectations for behavior, and the effects of the environment (including families, media, health issues) on young children. This can be done through every contact, both formal and informal, not by sermonizing but by constantly pointing out children's actions and what the actions reveals about development. That is exactly what observation, recording, and communicating is all about.

The first step is a well-planned intake process, informing families of the facts they need to know. From the program's personal contacts, families will build trust in the program. Even if they may not understand all the program is about, they can tell these people care about them and their child. This trust is extended in various ways during the year, in daily contacts, written communications, progress reports, and conferences. Whatever the mode, these communications should be positive, descriptive, and personal (Figure 14–1).

DAILY CONTACTS

Personal

The best way for contacts to be personal is if the staff and families know each other. Through home visits, open house, visits to the classroom, phone calls, and notes, the staff establishes rapport with each family. This is not to become friends, though that may happen, but to extend friendliness, courtesy, and partnership in a shared interest—the child. The teacher may have to make the effort again and again. It is like

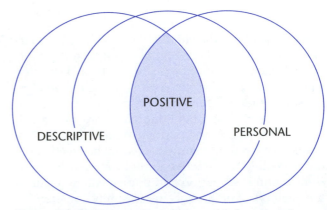

Figure 14–1 Home–school communications must be positive, descriptive, and personal.

the persistent salesperson using different techniques to reach the customer. Many teachers react that it is their job to teach or care for the child, not the family. They cannot adequately and single-handedly do that job without the families' cooperation or at least acknowledgment of the role each plays.

Programs that have daily contact with family members who bring and pick up their children have wonderful opportunities. Each day tidbits of information about the child are casually shared. This gives background and breadth to what the teacher knows about the child to help interpret behavior and help the child develop. Sharing the tidbits of the day with family members at dismissal time gives them insight about the child's day, accomplishments, and attempts. This is an important, crucial part of the teacher's responsibility. The teacher establishes rapport with each family, seeing them day in and day out. Getting to know them and their child should be a priority. Noticing the new hairstyle, or employment badge, or hurried look indicates to the family member they are recognized as human beings. The teacher sees them not just as the client, the tuition check writer, or Amber's daddy. Not all are suited to this task, so the person on the teaching team who is the most adept at personal contacts should be the "doorperson." That person provides a friendly welcoming face and attitude, a receptive ear, and tactful conversation.

Descriptive

It is a luxury to be able to greet families at the end of the day and complete the circle by relating a bit of the child's day. It gives a springboard for later conversations about the day that may need a little nudge. A flood of talk springs forth when families have a little seed to get the child started. The comments at the door also let the family have an idea of not only what the child did but how they are doing. They make comparisons with other children, "Gee, all the children in Heather's class can put on their own boots. Maybe I better work with her to learn how," or "The teacher said Tamiche played for a long time with the Play Doh and she gave me a recipe to make it at home. Maybe that would occupy her while I fix dinner." Family education is occurring in subtle ways.

It is impossible to give daily detailed comments to every family. Using the many communication modes, descriptive little vignettes like those in the assignments should be shared with families often. Just as it is important to observe every child in the group, it is important to share information with every family. It is easy to share those shining moments but for some

children, remembering to turn the water off after they wash their hands is an accomplishment to be shared. It takes tact and practice to describe daily happenings accurately and without sarcasm. With practice it becomes natural. A little tip: The doorperson can keep a Class List Log in a private spot and jot down who received little "gems" at the door. After a few days a spot check will show that some children have not had any good news shared for a while. The teacher can make a conscious effort to observe and share a bit of information.

Positive

All comments shared informally, at the door or in other means, should be *positive* ones. At the end of the day the family member is tired. The child has long forgotten the mistaken behaviors. Other people are present. This is no time to bring out a litany of problems the child had that day. Those conflicts, whether with another child, the staff, or the materials, cannot be solved then so there is no need to talk about them. Staff who tell "bad news" at the end of the day are venting anger. They are displaying their ineptness at guiding the child's behavior. They seem to be expecting the family to take action on something that happened at school. That seems like an unfair request. It could even be interpreted as laying blame on the family for raising such a destructive, aggressive, unruly child. Teachers list "tattletale" at the top of the list of characteristics they do not like in children. Telling families about a child's mistaken behaviors at the end of the day is in the same vein. No, the doorperson should only tell good news (Figure 14–2).

Looking at development is from the positive viewpoint. The baseline is, "What has the child accomplished so far?" Despite the level of development, it has been accomplished and can be shared as good news.

"Derek made it to the bathroom once today."
Rather than: "Derek had three toilet accidents today."
"Cecilia used her blanket for comfort today but did let go of it to go down the slide."
Rather than: "Cecilia whined most of the day and didn't play hardly at all."
"Roshann made an *R* today."
Rather than: "He painted an *R* on the wall."

It may not be possible to relate "good news" stories to every family member at the end of every day, but they should receive frequent, descriptive positive messages. If families pick up their children at the

Figure 14–2 The doorperson only tells good news!

center, *every family* and *every child* should be acknowledged as they leave. It also relieves those anxious moments when suddenly someone says, "I didn't see Serina leave." The doorperson can say, "I was at the door and Mrs. Bigelow was in a hurry so scooted in and out. I saw them leave." A system of signout also safeguards this possibly dangerous time of the day. The personal touch brings closure to the day for the child and reinforces the friendly relationship between the home and program.

High-quality programs make every effort to involve families in a number of ways that fit the families' needs. This emphasizes the partnership, demonstrating the program's recognition of the vital role that families play in the child's life, including their education. Supporting the family's culture is the first step toward this partnership. DiNatale (2002) suggests asking each family to print a welcome sign in their home language for the classroom. Of course, written materials for families should be translated into languages spoken at home, home-language literacy materials in the classroom should be present, and holidays respected.

Ethical Responsibilities to Families

Teachers, caregivers, and the family have a common interest in the child's welfare. The family is the primary teacher and influence on the child. The teacher's role is to collaborate with the family, offering a spe-

cialized knowledge, but always approaching interactions with the family with respect and consideration. The National Association for the Education of Young Children expressed these ideals in the Ethical Code of Conduct (Feeny & Kipnis, 1996):

> To develop relationships of mutual trust with the families we serve.
>
> To acknowledge and build upon strengths and competencies as we support families in their task of nurturing children.
>
> To respect the dignity of each family and its culture, customs, and beliefs.
>
> To respect families' child-rearing values and their right to make decisions for their children.
>
> To interpret each child's progress to parents within the framework of a developmental perspective and to help families understand and appreciate the value of developmentally appropriate early childhood programs.
>
> To help family members improve their understanding of their children and to enhance their skills as parents.
>
> To participate in building support networks for families by providing them with opportunities to interact with program staff and other families.

Written Communication

EXERCISE: Number the following pieces of mail from 1 to 10 in the order you would open them:

_____ card-sized envelope with no return address
_____ credit card preapproval
_____ offer for a free water test
_____ newsletter from an organization
_____ advertisement for a new early childhood magazine
_____ letter from your grandmother
_____ letter from the IRS, stamped "Refund"
_____ telephone bill
_____ letter from the "love of your life"
_____ registered letter from a collection agency

A letter from a friend or someone highly regarded is opened expectantly. Those unsolicited pieces of mail are often not even read. Some mail brings apprehension and anxiety as it is opened, causing feelings of depression, anger, or uncertainty.

Written communications from the early childhood program should be closer to the beginning of the above list than the end. The same points about daily contacts could be made regarding written communications. They should be personal, descriptive, and positive.

Family Handbook. A thorough but reader-friendly Family Handbook is necessary to fully inform families of the philosophy, policies, and procedures the program follows. Educational institutions, from playgroups to universities, have policies, or sets of guidelines under which they operate. The people involved with those institutions need to know what those guidelines are before they can follow them. It is like knowing the rules when playing a game. Early childhood programs should state a clear mission or purpose, policies, and procedures. The people participating in that program need to know the policies of enrollment, services, what they can expect from the program, and what their responsibility is to it. This is usually done in a Family Handbook, a guide with all the necessary information parents need to know. Often families are too busy to read it or the guide book is too involved and intimidating. Efforts to make it user-friendly with indexes, graphics, and concise format have proven to be effective. Orientations where the most important details are presented verbally help the nonreader, the visual learner, and reinforces important elements. Home visits and individual conversations can clarify those points that families need to know most. All of this is done with respect for the families, with an attitude of partnership and consideration for the ultimate benefit of the child.

Newsletters. A periodic newsletter informing families of current news helps with family involvement. Descriptions of past events with short anecdotes from the children give the readers a sense of being there. This should be easy to do from the Anecdotal Recordings. Names of children and volunteers in a newsletter increases its readers' interest. Details families need to know should be bold, concise, not embedded in lines and lines of writing. Short daily or weekly plans in a calendar format will give the families and child a conversation topic. Future events could be anticipated, "It says here that a bunny will visit today. Maybe you want to take a carrot to feed it?" Past events are remembered, "It says here that you had a bee hive and bee keeper visit your class. I didn't know that. Can you tell me about it?"

Positive encouragement for families should be the theme of newsletter writing. It is a tough job. Families are not interested in articles telling them they should be doing more, more, and more.

> "Did you know that we have books to borrow so you don't have to make a trip to the library?"
> *Rather than:* "You should read to your child fifteen minutes every day. If you don't, they won't be good readers."

There are some commercial newsletters that are very well done that can be personalized by additional pages or by using only edited portions of them. The newsletter should be friendly in tone and fun to read, with short, informative articles. The print should be clear and readable with one-half as much white space as there is print. That means that drawings by the children, poems centered in columns, and graphics should comprise one-third of the space. These will catch the reader's eye and illustrate the text. It draws the reader's interest to an article a few paragraphs in length (Figure 14–3).

Happy Notes. In situations in which families and teachers do not have daily contact, happy notes serve the purpose of comments made at the door. They can be written and tucked in a knapsack or handed to a family member with one-line, personal, descriptive, and positive comments about the child that day. Every recording assignment could bring out material from which to draw these comments. Finding the time to do these is a consideration. How about one a day? Does that seem manageable? If so, then use a class list and write one a day, focusing on one positive achievement or skill that child displayed today. See Chapter 1 for an example.

Documentation Panels. These are more than bulletin boards with posted announcements and seasonal decorations. **Documentation panels** articulate to the family the philosophy of the classroom and gives tangible evidence that children are engaged in active learning. Documentation panels can inform the families of the benefits of play and pointing out the learning that is taking place. While the panels are informational, they also should be aesthetically pleasing. The display may contain photographs, children's artwork and dictation, transcripts of the teacher's observations, and curriculum webs, all outlining step-by-step processes around a central theme. They convey much more information than a newsletter and become interactive when the children are the ones explaining the panel, thus enhancing their thinking and language skills.

The documentation panel can communicate information such as

- learning environments
- projects/emergent curriculum
- themes
- special events
- specific curriculum areas
- child development
- skill acquisition (Brown-DuPaul, Keyes, & Segatti, 2001)

CONKLIN PRESCHOOL
MARCH NEWSLETTER

Home is where the heart is, it is as much a state of mind as a physical structure. Children watch construction with fascination, awed by the undertaking of a crew as it creates a structure. At school this month we will be cooperating to build a house, complete with an outside pool! The children will have an opportunity to try some interesting tools. and machines, such as pulleys, hammers and pipes.

This type of hands-on-learning, or play, is a vehicle for the child's mental growth. Play enables children to progress from the sensorimotor intelligence of infancy to pre-operational thought in the preschool years. Play is not only essential to cognitive development but serves important functions in children's physical, emotional, and social development. Come in to PLAY, learn and grow with us at preschool, **we love** to have a mom, dad, grandparent, aunt or uncle on snack day.

FAMILY CONFERENCES

Throughout the school year I have observed your children involved in regular preschool activities. March 15-19 is conference week. There will be no morning classes on the 15th and 16th and no afternoon classes on the 18th and 19th, giving us the opportunity to meet and discuss your child's progress and readiness for school. A sign up sheet for appointments will be posted. If you are unable to make one of these times, we can make alternate arrangements. Call me 775-0511 to schedule an appointment. You are welcome to come early and stay late; we will provide activities and childcare. It is important to be prompt and keep discussions to a maximum of 15 minutes.

TOTE BAGS

On Wednesday, March 17th at 9:00 we will begin to sew tote bags for next year's classes. We need your HELP! We need those who can sew and have sewing machines, those who can iron and pin, and anyone else who can help. Bring sewing machines, pins, white thread, scissors and yourselves. Our goal is to make over 100 bags. The hospitality committee has made arrangements to serve a delicious lunch. Childcare will be provided giving you the opportunity to experience a good old fashion-sewing bee.

CLEANING A ROOM TEACHES ORDER

Did you know that cleaning up a room is a learning activity? It can teach them order and structure. In their room, everything should have a place where it belongs. Toys, for example, each have their place. Teddy Bear goes here, the doll goes there, the ball goes over there. As a child learns about individual objects and the place it goes, they are learning basic lessons about space and how objects are organized in space. Later on in school, this concept will help learn the difference between "b" and "d" and "p" and "q"

Figure 14–3 Newsletter Example (Reprinted with permission. Conklin Preschool, Conklin, NY.)

Technology. Electronic and technical innovations are changing the way people communicate.

E-mail. With e-mail, it is possible to send electronic messages, electronic happy notes, digital photographs, and compressed videos to families who are linked to computer messaging. The day's events or newsletter could be "mailed" to everyone in the class via the computer and a distribution list. Future inventions will modify the way people communicate.

Voice Mail. Families with voice mail (answering machines) can receive short messages of good news from the program. That would be a good welcome home at the end of the day to hear the teacher's voice say, "Mr. and Mrs. Jones, listen to what James learned today. James, want to sing the Snowman song for Mommy and Daddy?" Answering machines at the school could provide reminders for the next day, little parenting tips, or songs by the children. Anyone who wants to call the program in the evening after hours would hear them and leave a message for the teacher "after the beep."

Traveling Journals. Many programs have made traveling journals that go back and forth between school and home. Some are notes written between the family and the teacher. Several programs have a traveling journal in a tote bag with toys or art materials. In one preschool, families were asked to do something with Rags, a cute stuffed puppy, write about it, and send it back to school for the next child. The responses are delightful, showing families' creativity, encouraging the child to draw or write as well. While they have the journal at home, they read the other entries and look at drawing and writing attempts. Here are a few that accompanied a stuffed dog Rags, along with a tape of the songs they would be singing for several weeks. Older children could write their own journal entries for their classmates and their families to read (Figure 14–4). A cassette recorder and a tape on which the teacher has recorded songs sung in school or a short review of projects in progress can inform families of school events. Recordings by each child adding a bit to the tape have also been successful.

Rags' first day at my house was very pleasant. Rags took a nap with my brother Christopher. My brother helped me take care of Rags. Rags went with me to my Daddy's house and spent the night.

Rags also went with me to the babysitter's house. I took Rags in my tent with me. I held Rags and hugged him the whole time he was with me. I had a great time with Rags. I even shared Rags with my brother.

Figure 14–4 Journals from home to school are a part of family communication and involvement. (Reprinted with permission. Conklin Preschool, Conklin, NY.)

Positive, Descriptive, Personal Reports

Why is report card time so dreaded by families, children, and teachers? It is a time of stress. The teacher is placing a value on the child's efforts that may come as a surprise to the families, and sometimes even the child.

EXERCISE: Imagine going to the doctor for a routine physical examination. You feel fine but they run tests and now you are there for the results. What are you feeling?

There is always some apprehension that tests may reveal some unsuspected problem. If that is the case, there are various reactions. First of all, the patient wants to see the file and the test results to verify that there is no mistake. If the doctor will not show the actual test results, suspicions are raised. The diagnosis may be rejected because there were no previous indicators. The doctor must be wrong. The patient may want to wait a while or have the tests repeated to see if there is a change. A second opinion may be sought to decide exactly what the extent of the problem is and how to remedy it. These same apprehensions and reactions are common in family–teacher interactions.

When there is an ongoing exchange of descriptive information from school to home, there are no surprises when progress reports or report cards are issued. When families see the portfolio and know they have access to it, they develop trust that the information about the child is based on credible evidence not just guesses. How often do families say, "She doesn't like my child so she gave him a failing mark." The work in the portfolio documents educational decisions. Even if they never look at the portfolio, when they understand what it is about, they have confidence they can look at it if they want. That knowledge brings trust. The Sunshine Law affords people the right to examine public records. It is only acted upon by a few, but gives everyone confidence to exercise it if the need or desire arises.

The same advice is extended about only positive notes sent home to families. Rather than "telling" on the child, if there is a concern or problem, it is best addressed in person with both parties prepared for the topic. A "bad news note" is like receiving the medical test results in the mail, with no explanation. It leaves a knot of anxiety in the stomach. Most people would rush to the phone to have an explanation. That is exactly what families do. They want to know more, usually calling with feelings of anxiety, anger, and frustration at the bad surprise.

EXERCISE: Read the note in Figure 14–5 the family of a second-grader received. How would it make you feel if you were the family? What elements do you notice?

This is page two of what is at least a four-page note. She went on and on and on. If there were so many concerns, a conference could explain this so much better. Did you notice every comment is negative? Not one positive line! The teacher also is giving a strong order "Please see to it . . ." Would a family treasure this note or would the child feel encouraged to work harder? And what about the form, "Dear Parent"? What if it is not the parent who is responsible for the child? Either the family member would call for an appointment or be so intimidated that no response but anger or resentment would be felt.

EXERCISE: On a separate sheet of paper, write about a report card you remember as a child.

Many people still have report cards on which teachers wrote negative, sarcastic comments and made dire predictions that this person was doomed to fail. Thankfully, most of those people did not believe the teacher and went on to succeed and prove her wrong. Remember, what is written is permanent and could be misinterpreted. The teacher must exercise caution, even in happy notes, that words are not misconstrued or the comments questionable in meaning.

EXERCISE: Rewrite the following comments to be positive, descriptive, and personal.

"She usually shares with other children."
"Grady only will play with other children if he can have his own way."
"Stephanie can't write her name, zip her own coat, or tie her shoes."
"Lynn is always the mother giving orders when playing in the dramatic area."

The word *usually* is one to avoid when writing progress reports. It leaves so many questions about what happens at other times. That is an example of the care and caution in writing progress reports.

Progress Reports. Progress reports are just what the name implies. They are short reviews of development in written format. They give families a glimpse of the child from another's perspective. They should be positive in tone. They are reporting progress. Unless there is some serious trauma, all children make progress over time. It definitely is not at the

PUPIL _Marcy Johnson_   GRADE _2_

Teacher Comment

.She is also behind in the independent reading series in the classroom. She must get caught up in these areas as they are a mandatory part of Reading. She has been allowed to take a few books home to catch up. Please see to it that she works on these. She must learn to use her time wisely!

I am not pleased with Marcy's math grade this term. She must practice.

TEACHER: _Mrs. Marshfield_

Dear Parent:
You may keep this for your records. If you wish to reply to the above comment, then please use the reverse side of this sheet and return it in the envelope. You may call to make an appointment with the teacher.

Figure 14–5 Read this note and see how you would feel as a parent or a family member.

same rate in each developmental area. It most likely is different from any other child. It is still progress (Figure 14–6). (This form also appears in Appendix D.)

A narrative progress report is a more complete report, following very closely the outline of the portfolio. Developmental checklists or charts supply the criteria. A short, descriptive sentence or two in each area is all that is required. An outline and progress at a glance can be included in the portfolio to aid in organizing your thoughts for writing.

It should be headed with the child's name, the date, the writer's full name, and the name of the program (Figure 14–7).

A Positive and Negative Example. Compare the tone and wording of the Progress Reports shown in Figure 14–7.

These reports were written about the same child, telling the same information but giving a whole different tone. The first portrays the child as active and imaginative in the beginning stages of socialization. The second typifies the child as an airhead, not able to do many things that are expected. The second uses language such as one-to-one correspondence and cooperative play stage that is not understood by most families so should be avoided.

Tips for Progress Reports. The following suggestions will aid in writing progress reports.

Short, concise descriptive statements
Positive
Child "can do"
Positive
No technical terms
Positive

Keep a copy in the portfolio and in the class file.

Case Studies. A comprehensive narrative of the child is called a **case study** or **child study.** It can be used as an end-of-the-year report. It can be sent with the family as the child moves to another program or as a report to a referral agency, upon the written request of the family.

A child study follows much the same format as the **progress report** but amplifies the information given in each area and references comments with the documentation. This reference is much in the way an author references information from another source. In this way, the reader can go to that source for further information, possibly as evidence of what the author said or to learn more about the subject. The reader may then draw a different conclusion from that source.

Figure 14–8, on page 350, is a sample child study of the same child in Figure 14–7 at the end of the year.

The reader should feel acquainted with the child by reading the child study and reviewing the

(text continues on page 351)

PROGRESS AT A GLANCE   Child's Name _____

PERIOD 1:   Date_____   Recorder _____

Strengths _____

Areas still developing _____

_____

Educational plan to facilitate development _____

_____

_____

PERIOD 2:   Date_____   Recorder _____

Strengths _____

Areas still developing _____

_____

Educational plan to facilitate development _____

_____

_____

PERIOD 3:   Date_____   Recorder _____

Strengths _____

Areas still developing _____

_____

Educational plan to facilitate development _____

_____

_____

PERIOD 4:   Date_____   Recorder _____

Strengths _____

Areas still developing _____

_____

Educational plan to facilitate development _____

_____

_____

Figure 14–6 Progress at a Glance (form)

XYC CENTER
NICOLE LIND
November 29, year
Age: 4 yrs., 3 mo.
Sandra Richards, Teacher

ADJUSTMENT TO SCHOOL: Nicole had no difficulty from the first day of school. She hangs up her coat and is ready to participate.

SELF-HELP: She can unzip, zip with help. She can pour juice and cut food with ease. She handles the bathroom by herself. She participates in picking up the room.

PHYSICAL DEVELOPMENT: She runs with coordination, balances on one foot. She makes circles and lines with markers and cuts slashes with scissors.

SOCIAL: She plays primarily with two other girls but joins small groups in organized activities.

EMOTIONAL: She smiles a lot and allows herself to be comforted if she is hurt or tired.

SPEECH AND LANGUAGE: She can be understood and speaks freely to adults and other children.

MEMORY AND ATTENTION SPAN: She spends long times in dramatic play and active outdoor play. She knows the words to songs we sing and knows the sequence of the day's activities.

LITERACY: She knows how to look at a book right side up and turn pages. She listens to stories individually read.

MATH AND SCIENCE: She can count out loud to 10. She has a wide knowledge about hamsters, including their birth. She has several at home and has provided little ones for the class.

CREATIVE ARTS: She fills the page with color and notices lines and shapes in her art. She prefers easel painting to table art like collage, watercolors, or clay.

DRAMATIC PLAY: This is the area she chooses most frequently, dressing up, taking on a variety of roles, using her language in an imaginative way.

ADJUSTMENT TO SCHOOL: She seems happy here, comfortably follows the routine, and is making progress mainly in dramatic and physical play.

WORKING ON: Providing her with dramatic play props that require small hand muscle movement. We are beginning small group storybook reading time into the dramatic play area.

XYC CENTER
NICOLE LIND
November 29, year
Age: 4 yrs., 3 mo.
Sandra Richards, Teacher

ADJUSTMENT TO SCHOOL: Nicole is indifferent to parent leaving. Arrives in a whirl.

SELF-HELP: Can't zip her own coat. Serves self more food than she can finish. Licks the spoon. Needs reminding about washing hands after toileting.

PHYSICAL DEVELOPMENT: Runs and climbs. Cannot pedal bicycle yet. Scribbles. Still working on cutting.

SOCIAL: Parallel play stage, not cooperative.

EMOTIONAL: Happy most of the time, sometimes has bouts of silliness.

SPEECH AND LANGUAGE: Talks a lot. Sometimes hard to understand.

MEMORY AND ATTENTION SPAN: Does not participate in whole group activities though she listens to the songs. Reminds teacher what should be happening next.

LITERACY: Not interested in story time yet.

MATH AND SCIENCE: Does not have one-to-one correspondence yet. Often lets hamsters loose in the classroom.

CREATIVE ARTS: Paints whole page one color then paints on lines and circles mixing the paint.

DRAMATIC PLAY: Habitual play area in a fantasy world. Makes up words and imaginary language.

ADJUSTMENT TO SCHOOL: She seems happy here as long as she gets to play in the dramatic area or outside. Those are her favorite things to do. Seems uninterested in learning materials or group times.

WORKING ON: Zipping, cutting, small manipulatives, language.

Figure 14–7 Progress Report Examples: Positive and Negative

XYC CENTER   **NICOLE LIND**   **June 14, year 4 yrs. 9 mo.**

Reporter: Mary McGwinn, 4's Teacher

Nicole is the oldest of three children, all of whom attend the XYC Center. Nicole has been at the XYC Center since September and will be attending kindergarten at Brinker School in the fall. She lives with her family next door to her grandparents with whom she spends much time. She talks about them lovingly. She has many cousins and extended family that make up her social circle. She attends church weekly where she participates in a children's choir. She attends dance lessons on Saturdays and will be dancing in her first recital in a few weeks.

PHYSICAL DEVELOPMENT: She is of average height and weight and in good health as evidenced by her almost perfect attendance record (see attendance record). She was absent for one week with chicken pox and a day occasionally with slight fevers accompanying colds. Her interest in dancing and advanced body coordination skills work together to demonstrate agility and confidence in movement. Her writing and hand muscles for smaller tasks are developing. She can fringe paper with scissors and put together eight-piece puzzles (checklist: physical development). She can write her name in large letters progressing from just the first N to the whole name (samples 10/05/0X, 1/17/0X, 4/4/0X).

SOCIAL DEVELOPMENT: Nicole is comfortable with the staff at XYC seeking help mainly for comfort from falls (which are infrequent) or frustration with small muscle tasks. She has little confidence in her abilities and seeks adults to assist her (anecdotal record 11/1/0X, 3/17/0X). With adults holding the paper or providing her with encouragement, she can perform those tasks she tries. Nicole is called *friend* by many children in the class (photo of Nicole and friends taken 2/2/0X). She plays mostly with girls in the dramatic play area, dressing in the various theme props provided there. She had an especially long play sequence when the area was set up as an animal hospital (class video, running record 3/13/0X). Through this interest in dramatic play she has gained negotiation skills. Compare anecdotal record of 10/6/0X and 2/27/0X. She has moved from playing along side other children along the same theme to interacting and problem solving, assigning, and carrying out intricate play-acting roles, even putting on accents. This is demonstrated on the audio tape.

ADJUSTMENT TO SCHOOL: Nicole has adjusted to the routine of this center since she entered in September. She often goes down the hall "to see how the babies are doing," as she refers to her little sisters. She is welcomed by the teachers and allowed to spend time there, playing with the younger children. She has been observed in a protective, nurturing role captured in some photos (10/1/0X and 12/17/0X). She is comfortable with the routine, using free-play time to be involved in the dramatic play themes. She begins the day with painting since she often arrives before her friends. Her paintings have moved from experimentation with paint (9/29/0X) to more intricate designs (1/6/0X) and on to recognizable forms of people and animals (4/26/0X).

SELF-ACCEPTANCE: She acts independently in caring for her own needs in dressing, eating, and toileting (overview sheet). She independently chooses play areas, companions, and activities (time samples 10/21/0X, 2/03/0X). She exhibits a feeling of competence in physical activities, taking leadership roles (4/7/0X). She has a cheerful temperament. She displays no aggressiveness or antisocial behaviors (frequency counts 10/12/0X, 3/11/0X). She appears to be self-assertive in relations with others. She has a firm sense of self (interviews 11/2/0X, 2/17/0X).

COGNITIVE DEVELOPMENT: Nicole recognizes the letters in her name but not by themselves. She can count to 10 accurately and to 20 if assisted with the "teens." She knows the names of the colors, the names of the geometric shapes, and is beginning to add small numbers mentally (see interview 11/19/0X, 5/2/0X).

She has a wide knowledge of animal life, and a special interest in hamsters. She has raised several litters and provided several classmates with pets along with explicit directions on how to care for them (audio recording 3/22/0X). Her interest and ability in writing is at the beginning stages but her concern for the hamster's care prompted her to write a book. It told her friends how to care for hamsters. She dictated the book then illustrated it (sample, 12/12/0X). This was duplicated and given to each hamster owner. She felt this was a significant work. She talked about it on the tape (12/19/0X).

When listening to Nicole speak on the tape, some irregularities are noticed that are not apparent when talking to her casually (tape 9/29/0X). This was reviewed by her parents and pediatrician and a decision was made

Figure 14–8 Child Study Example

to wait six months for these sounds to develop. Another tape on 04/6/0X showed those sounds were now present. This was reviewed by her parents and the pediatrician and confirmed. No further action was necessary.

CREATIVITY: Nicole's creativity is centered in the dramatic play realm. She can carry out a role imaginatively and encourage others to do so as well, displaying an advanced degree of concentration and social awareness (running record 1/29/0X). Her drawings are more realistic than her daily paintings, almost methodical in nature from one day to the next (samples 10/30/0X, 10/31/0X, 11/1/0X, 11/2/0X). She called it "practicing." She used scissors, collage, and clay in much the same way by experimenting with the same materials day after day then leaving them for months.

Nicole will enter kindergarten with strong social skills, confidence in her physical abilities, and the beginnings of literacy. Her adaptability to the group setting and helping adults should ensure that her school experience is a good one. She talks of school and all the things she will learn there. Once she saw the loft in the kindergarten rooms with extensive dramatic play areas, she was convinced that it was a good place.

I am happy to answer any questions about this review of Nicole's time at XYC Center. She is a joy to know.

Signed _____

Figure 14–8 Child Study Example (Continued)

documentation. It is extensive because there are so many specific details, gathered week by week, on which to draw conclusions. The summaries of the child study are also *positive,* relating what the child can do. The documentation is there for proof of the inferences about the child's progress and development. An extensive child study may not be necessary for every child, especially if the child is remaining in the program, moving from one classroom to another. A series of progress reports may be sufficient.

Template for a Progress Report and Child Study. The mechanics of preparation of the Child Study are much the same as any term paper. (The progress report is shorter with only one or two main points under each topic, without references to documentation although they are present.)

1. Begin by calculating the child's age. The child's age is calculated in years and months at the time the report is written. In the life of a young child, much change takes place in a year so the difference between just three and almost four is very great. This poses a bit of a mathematical problem to report writers.

EXERCISE: Try these for practice:

a) The date is October, 2003. Joseph's birthdate is July, 1991. How old is he? (Simple.)

	2003	10th month
−	1998	− 7th month
	5 years	3 months

b) The date is October, 2003. Martha's birthdate is November, 1999. How old is she? (Trickier.)

	2003	10th month
−	1999	− 11th month

Oops! We have to borrow 12 months from 2003.

	2002	22 months
−	1999	− 11 months
	3 years	11 months

Rule: When the child has not yet had a birthday in that year, you have to borrow 12 months from the current year to calculate the year and month age. Try some:

Janice was born in August, 1999.
Frederick was born in February, 1999.
Natalie was born in October, 1999.

The correct answers will depend on the month and year you are reading and calculating this equation. Now figure your own age in years and months.

2. Next define the topic. Know about whom you are writing and focus on one child at a time.
3. Assemble the raw data, the research, and the reference material. Have the portfolio and notes in either chronological order or organized by developmental area.
4. Prepare an outline. Here it is:

Heading: Child's name, birthdate, name of program, name of reporter.
Family: Birth order, family make-up, contact with extended family, other caregivers, community contacts.

Physical: Appearance, size, build, ways of moving, health, attendance, large and small muscle development.

Social development: With adults—parents, caregivers, other adult helpers, teachers, visitors to the classroom. With children—stage of play, who the child's friends are, how the child interacts with other children, how the child solves problems with other children

Adjustment to school: Separation behavior, areas of interest, participation and avoidance, adjustment to school routines, ability to follow directions, mistaken behaviors requiring guidance

Self-acceptance: Self-care skills, independence, level of self-esteem, emotional development, self-control, aggressiveness.

Cognitive development: What the child knows—numbers, alphabet, shapes, interest in books, language vocabulary, clarity of speech, what the child's attitude toward learning is.

Creativity: Child's use of imagination in art, movement, dramatic play, language.

Closing paragraph, personal best wishes.

Signature of writer, date of report.

5. Write a rough draft from the outline. Think about the child in relation to each of those topics and jot some notes.

6. Refer to sources to document statements. Look through the portfolio and find representative pieces to provide data. Note type of recording and dates.

7. Prepare final document. This is a document that will be preserved maybe for the life of the child. It represents the professionalism of the program and the integrity of the writer. It should be in complete, grammatically correct sentences. Type it, and check for spelling.

8. Proofread. Have a team member who knows the child (for confidentiality, not an outsider), read the document for content, grammar, and tone.

9. Produce the document. Type, or use a word processor, to print the final child study document as perfectly as you can make it. This represents the reputation of the writer and the subject of the study.

10. Copy the document. The family should receive the original either separate or with the portfolio. A copy should be kept in the class file. File the family's written request for a copy to be sent to a referral agent in the class file, along with the program's copy of the document.

These ten steps will become more automatic with experience in writing this type of report. If they are written for the whole class, the task can be divided just as the other observation assignments, with one-fourth of them done each week. The *Week by Week* plan gives you assignments to accomplish this several times a year. It will come easier.

What to Do with the Child Study. Once the child study is printed, two copies are made, one to be kept in the portfolio and one to go in the class file.

The child study belongs to the family. It is best presented to them in a conference (see later section). In this way, each section can be discussed with even more personalized anecdotal remembrances shared with the families. The child study could be mailed if a conference cannot be arranged. The risk is always present that the clarity of the message of writing is more obscure to the reader than the writer. The family may misinterpret the wording of the child study. There should always be an opportunity for reply or challenge.

The child study may be included in the portfolio if it is to be given to the family. With their permission, the child study could be sent to the next program, school, or referral agent such as therapists or medical personnel. In that case, copies of the referenced documentation should be copied.

Family Conferences

The family conference's main purpose should be for a developmental overview of the child. The early childhood program may be the first contact the child and family has had with people outside the family. It is a serious responsibility to be allowed to get so intimately acquainted with their child. This conference is not just the teacher telling the family but an exchange of information, a discussion, a sharing of points of view. The teacher is seeking the advice from the family for the benefit of the child. With this attitude conveyed in word and behavior, the conference has a better chance at success.

Special education and Head Start experiences have proven that family involvement and even guidance in interventions with the child have the best chances for success (Benner, 2003). The strengths-based model (Dunst, Trivette, & Mott, 1994) reminds professionals that families have their own unique strengths and the professional should work not to "fix" the family but to find ways for the family to take responsibility for any behavior changes.

The progress reports and child study can be the reference. These conferences should be held periodically throughout the year or any time at the request of the family. Head Start Program Performance Standards 1304.21(2) (2000) state that parents must be

- invited to become integrally involved in the development of the program's curriculum and approach to child development and education.
- provided opportunities to increase their child's observation skills and to share assessments with staff that will help plan the learning experiences.
- encouraged to participate in staff–parent conferences and home visits to discuss their child's development and education.

Much has been written giving advice about family conferences. Their success is fragile depending on so many variables. Many preparations and precautions should be taken to guarantee an open, informative, positive exchange.

Tips for Family Conferences. Family conferences can be successful exchanges of information, socially satisfying and affirming for family, teacher, and child. Here are some practical suggestions.

1. Be prepared. Have the progress report or child study complete with documentation in an organized system.
2. Make the conference times convenient for the family and provide child care if needed.
3. Prepare the environment by having comfortable chairs, at the same height, next to one another or at right angles with no table between.
4. Make sure the location is private so no one else can hear and there are no interruptions.
5. Begin with social exchange, greetings, small talk.
6. Open the portfolio and let family know what it holds.
7. Make eye contact, lean forward, nod to their comments, listen.
8. Speak in understandable language.
9. Ask questions, ask for questions.
10. Summarize and make plans for further contact.

Conferences with the Child. The portfolio is an excellent tool to discuss with the child. Children above four years old love to look at their work and even nonreaders can understand the concept of all the teacher's notes about them. Looking at work from an earlier stage brings a sense of accomplishment to the child and opens the communication to discuss the meaning of the work and the incidents recorded there. Including the child in the family conference can also be beneficial. Anxiety about what the teacher will say is dissolved. The child hears the teacher review the progress. Of course, this should be a "positive only" conference. This gives the family positive feedback with the child present, hearing what development has occurred this year and indicating the positive effect of their relationship with the

IT HAPPENED TO ME

Excuse Me!

I was holding family conferences midway through the year. They were scheduled every half hour, one after another. Between two conferences I had to leave the room. When I came back, the next parent was looking through all the portfolios I had arranged for the next conferences. I was dumbfounded. What nerve! I got her child's folder and said, "Excuse me! This must be the one you're looking for." My mind raced through what else I could say but I was so angry nothing positive came to mind so I went on with the conference. After all, it was about her child that we came together.

It taught me a lesson that I share with you. Keep all records secure. I did from that day onward.

child. With so many families feeling blame and heavy responsibility, it is an important role of the teacher to give plaudits for a job well done, to the child and the family.

Family Conferences When a Problem Is Suspected. Positive stories are related at the door. Positive statements are printed in the newsletters. Positive progress reports and positive child studies are written. The question arises, "But when do you ever tell them the bad news?" "When do you tell them the truth?" "When do you tell them what the child is *really* like?" When? Only after a certain process has taken place should the teacher talk to the parent about a concern (Figure 14–9).

Documented Observations. If there is a concern for a child in a specific area or areas, it is critically important to gather data. This should be done with the methods that are the least inferential, the most accurate. The Anecdotal Record meets that criteria. If possible, have another member of the teaching team also gather data.

Review Developmental Guidelines. The observers should read some basic information about developmental expectations and have a clear understanding based on research.

Confer with the Team and Your Supervisor. The group should look at the data, review the research,

Regular conferences with family
and referral agents

Observation and documentation

Implementation

Individualized educational plan
evaluation, possible referrals

Discusses concerns
with staff specialists

Meets with family,
explains concerns,
joint problem solving,
decide on action

Discusses concerns with team

Weighs observations against
knowledge base of development

Documents observations

Teacher observes the child

Figure 14–9 Steps in a Problem-Solving Family
Conference

and look again at the child. Theories should be explored, searching for possible causes or influences. Every attempt should be made to eliminate biases, whatever their origin. When it is the consensus of the group that the family should be consulted, the team should decide the approach and who should be involved. Usually the classroom teacher alone is sufficient for the first step in this process. Discussion topics, possible scenarios, and options can be explored. Resources for referral should be researched and prepared for the family beginning with the least alarming, usually beginning with a full physical evaluation.

Approach the Family. In *private,* the teacher conveys concerns and a request for a conference to discuss those concerns. The teacher may ask for the family to be thinking about the areas of concern or give the family some reading material to think about before that meeting.

"We have been noticing and documenting . . . and wondering if you have noticed this at home? When would it be convenient to get together to discuss it?"

"We've been trying different things to help Robert with . . . but we need some suggestions from you. Can we stop by on our way home tomorrow or could you come by here?"

"The next time you take Lucy to the doctor you may want to ask about . . . Would you have time later on this afternoon to give me a call so we could talk about it? I really don't think it's serious but it has been nagging at me and I'd like to see what you think."

Try not to get into a discussion at this time. Set a time when possible. Be prepared to have the meeting within 24 hours, but it is best not to have it immediately. This gives the family time to consider the questions and topic.

The Meeting. The meeting should begin with social pleasantries. It is a meeting of people who have common bonds, but this meeting needs to go on since the topic is serious. The basis for the concerns are presented, referring to documenting evidence. This evidence should be available if needed. Then the family should have the opportunity to respond with their thoughts on the situation or topic. The teacher's role is to *listen.* The teacher must remember the family is the authority on the child.

The Discussion. The meeting is conducted with attempts at clear communication and empathy. Possible solutions can be explored from moderate to drastic. The teacher should be prepared for strong reactions from the family. These may be denial, projection of blame, fear, guilt, mourning or grief, withdrawal, rejection, and finally acceptance (Berger, 1995).

The Decision. The family and teacher come to a decision and to an agreement to carry out the next steps. Referral information should be available if the decision is to seek outside help. The progression is usually to begin with medical personnel to investigate or rule out physical causes. Other agencies may be referred to the family, depending on the nature of the concern.

Follow-Up. The program should make every effort to implement the plan the family has made. It is the responsibility of the program to keep the family informed of the actions taken and the results. If the family is taking an action, they should be asked to keep the program informed.

Documentation. A record of the conference's main points and action planned and the follow-up should be kept in the school's file. It may be warranted to keep it in the confidential file rather than the class file, depending on the nature of the concerns.

Pitfalls to Avoid for a Successful Conference of Any Kind. Gestwicki (2004) lists the following pitfalls:

1. Avoid using technical terminology, such as *motor development* or Piagetian terminology.
2. Avoid the role of "expert." Remember the real experts on the child are the family.
3. Avoid negative evaluations. Avoid using words such as *problem, behind, immature, never/can't,* and *hyperactive.*

4. Avoid unprofessional conversation
   - about other children, families, staff
   - personal topics: marital status, financial, lifestyle
   - taking sides: between family members, between other staff, between this and other programs
5. Avoid giving advice, either requested or unsolicited. Instead, recommend books, or refer to other families.
6. Avoid rushing into solutions. See this as a collaborative effort.

Using Technology

Earlier in the chapter, e-mail and voice mail were mentioned as ways to communicate with families. School Web sites and communication listservs not only send out information and news but act as discussion vehicles. Children's electronic portfolios can be made available to the family by using password-protected areas so that only the family with the password can access the portfolio. Technology advances are occurring faster than many of us can adapt but, rather than become slaves to technology, we can use it to make our job easier and better.

How to Find the Time

It does take time to work with families to keep the lines of communication open. It is essential to value the family as the child's first and foremost teacher and work in partnership with them for the benefit of the child. Then we will find the time, make the time, use the time for this very important part of the job.

What to Do with the Documentation

"What to do with it" has become a common phrase to readers of this book, a point to consider with each piece of written documentation. Now it becomes the question regarding the whole portfolio of each child, the class file and the Reflective Journal (Figure 14–10).

The Portfolio. The program or school implementing a portfolio system should set a policy at that time. The family has the right of access to the portfolio at all times. It remains the property of the school and it is the right of the school to decide when to give it to the family or retain ownership. Any records retained by the school are to be kept confidential, with access only to the family of a child to their own child's file. Child studies are retained as comprehensive overviews and are the property of the program not the

Figure 14–10 What to Do with It

teacher. They can be transferred to other agencies upon the written permission of the family.

The portfolio could be transferred to the:

1. Family. At the close of the year or upon leaving the program, the portfolio may be given to the child and family. For some these become precious mementos. They contain vast amounts of information about the child, along with samples of the child's work.
2. Next teacher within the school. If the child remains in the school or program, it could be passed on and added to by the next teacher. Because of the large volume of material, it may be sorted and reduced in size. The next teacher can refer to the portfolio to come to know the child through it. The teacher may decide not to read the portfolio and form independent viewpoints. That is the teacher's prerogative.
3. Next school. The family may designate the portfolio be sent to the child's next school or program. Upon written authorization, that request is carried out.

4. Referral agent or helping professional. Families may wish to release the portfolio, in writing, to medical or psychological personnel. Observations taken periodically through a multitude of techniques can be very valuable for diagnosis of disorders or disabilities.

What to Do with the Class Files. Again, the school policy is set for the retention of this file. It may be considered the property of the school and retained as a record of that class. It could be used for accountability of the teacher and the program. The class file may be the property of the teacher, kept as a record of the work done that year. The documentation in the class files is of the whole class rather than focused on individual children.

What to Do with the Reflective Journal. This, of course, is the property of the writer. It has been used for personal and professional reflection and represents the thoughts and feelings of the writer. From these thoughts may come insights and deeper understandings of self and the profession. This is what is referred to as action research. This process begins with observation, that kind of "child watching" that comes with the pictures the eyes take and the sounds the ears hear. Those register against what is known about child development. The thinking about what matches and what clashes is the reflective process. This is frequently shared in an informal way.

Action research is a collaborative effort between observers. They get together to discuss the principles, new ideas, questions, and theories. They consider the difference between what is seen and what is known. The environment for this collaboration is of primary importance. It must be among people who trust one another, in an intimate group setting where each is free to speak. Time is provided for an unpressured discussion. It is possible that an article, a book, a video, or a report from one person's workshop could stimulate the discussion. Teachers relate experiences and try to make sense of the dilemma. They may decide to go away and experiment with different approaches and come back to report. The lessons learned from reflection and action research make meaningful reading for others, commonly called teacher's stories, interesting glimpses into the classroom and the teacher's reflections upon the meaning of the occurrences. The Reflective Journals could be used as a basis for action research and teacher's stories. But the journal itself is a private document, for the writer's use alone, and should be protected for privacy.

LOOKING AT THE CHILD'S INTERACTIONS WITH ADULTS

When a child enters a child care program or school, it is the beginning of moving out into the world. The child begins to realize there are differences in people and their views on behavior. As the child gains self-control, adherence to the expectations for behavior is possible. The interactions with adults involve a prosocial model by the adult establishing a secure, trusting relationship with the child. Children have been found to be more socially competent with peers and others when they first feel emotionally secure with their teachers (Howes, Phillips, & Whitelock, 1992). When children are from culturally diverse backgrounds, they experience culture shock and can be overwhelmed with the classroom atmosphere. The teacher is an empathetic mediator with the environment, the language, and peers.

The adults also model behavioral guidance by first establishing a secure attachment, setting the boundaries, communicating realistic expectations, and helping facilitate the child's behavior to meet them. By looking at the child through this lens, the observer gets a glimpse of the child's development in all the other developmental areas.

The role of the teacher is different from that of the family. As a professional, the child is technically the client to be kept at an emotional distance. That definition is foreign to the intensely personal relationship of child and teacher, but the objective detachment must be recognized. The teacher does not love the child as a family member does. Gartrell calls this feeling **unconditional positive regard** (Gartrell, 2003), "full acceptance of the child as a developing human being and member of the group" (p. 65). This is in accord with the positive view of the child's development. Observation assessment methods are used, not to catch children who are failing or to find their "weaknesses." Assessment methods measure individual levels of accomplishments and facilitate the next step in the progressive stage for each child.

How Observation and Recording Aids Child–Adult Interactions

The connection with child–adult interactions should be clear. As observations are made and documented, the adult interacts with the child. The child knows the adult is writing about what he is doing because the teacher tells him. She asks questions about his work and writes about it. Samples of his work are collected for the portfolio the teacher has shown him. He is interviewed, photographed, and audio taped. As a result of observations, the adult knows the child from these interactions. The child knows the teacher's unconditional acceptance. She has not told him he is doing it wrong, but has just observed and written descriptions of what he is doing without judgment. In classrooms where children are treated and moved as a group, where the whole class does art or science or math or story activities, where the teacher's time is spent giving directions rather than interacting, the teacher does not know the individual child. When the curriculum is appropriate with the teacher as the facilitator in the learning, then positive interactions between child and adult occur (Figure 14–11).

The various recording techniques can be used to record the child–adult interactions as well.

- Class List Log—A quick survey of aspects of child–adult interactions can be made, probably from memory. Criterion items could be

  seeks the adult for comfort
  behavior within state guidelines
  guidance needed in situations of . . .
  still gaining self-control in . . .

- Anecdotal or Running Records are ideal for capturing all the factual information of an incident showing the adult and child interacting.
- Frequency Count could measure how many times in a day or week the child needed adult intervention.

- Time Sampling could indicate the presence of the adult and the presence of the child, inferring relationships from contacts with the adult.
- Conversations with the child give information about the nature of the relationship. The child's cooperativeness, comfort with the adult, and willingness to speak indicate a good relationship.
- Work Samples may demonstrate the child's feelings for the adult with love notes and letters, gifts of drawings and work (such as my spotted dog in Chapter 10).
- Checklists and Rating Scales may have criterion regarding adult–child interactions to observe and document. It is the inference of the observer with no details recorded.
- Media, such as photographs and video, may capture the child and adult interactions. It is hoped that if it is to be preserved, they are positive interactions.

The documentation accumulated in the portfolio presents a view of the child from the staffs' eyes, with contributions from the child with work samples. Some ways to use the portfolio to communicate with families and other individuals comprise this last section.

The Teacher's Role in Child Guidance

The adult takes the initiative to get acquainted with the child, recognizing the stages of stranger anxiety, differences in temperaments, and range of experiences the child has had with strangers outside the family. This was discussed in Chapter 1, with strategies for the staff member to begin the relationship with the child and family. It was repeated in discussions on attachment, social and emotional development, and self-concept and self-esteem. The teacher uses different methods in preparing the classroom environment and in interacting with the child.

Preparing the Environment. This has been mentioned many times as the first step in planning curriculum. It is the active involvement of the child with her environment in which she constructs her own learning. The adult's role is to prepare that environment. It is also prepared with thought to help the children control their own behavior. The equipment and materials are organized, accessible, in good condition, varied, and sufficient for the numbers of children in the group. The space is divided into clearly defined areas from which to choose, with enough floor or table space to adequately use the materials. For example, blocks are organized on labeled shelves next to a carpeted surface, free from people walking

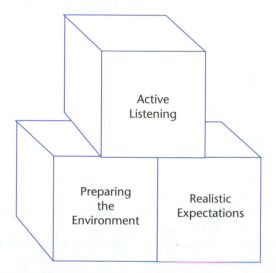

Figure 14–11 Building Blocks of the Teacher's Role in Child Guidance

through. Thus the builders can be comfortable, undisturbed, and not frustrated by constructions being tipped or knocked down. Blocks of time are needed so teachers are not interrupting play for their own purposes.

Realistic Expectations. The observer has a knowledge base of child development against which to measure skills and behavior. When adults expect behaviors that are not appropriate, it is like expecting an infant to walk and punishing him when he does not. Adult's interactions with children must be based on developmental norms and appropriate practice principles so that children are not expected to behave in a way beyond their years or ability. That phrase, "Children can't wait" is so true in many ways. When that principle is understood, then the adult modifies his or her own behavior rather than struggle to make children do what they cannot do. For example, the teacher will not make all the children wait until everyone has washed their hands before they begin to eat.

The realistic expectations are stated in terms that children can understand, from the positive, what they can do rather than not do. When children hear, "Don't run," because of what is known about attention span, selective listening skills, and cognitive structures, young children get the opposite message, "Run." It is the word emphasized, heard last and loudest, without the child's knowledge of the negating feature of the word preceding it.

Active Listening. Another facet of adult–child interactions is listening to the child, listening not only to the words they say but how they are said, and using intuitive ears to really hear the intended meaning. Active listening, a strategy in Gordon's (1975) Parent Effectiveness Training, focuses on what the child is saying, listening actively, and responding to the feelings implied. In the development of emotions, children have strong feelings but lack the vocabulary to express them. They also think that others feel what they feel because they are egocentric. Marian Marion (1999) gives these active listening tips (p. 262).

- Listen carefully.
- Do not interrupt.
- Try to understand what the message means.
- Listen for what the child is feeling.
- Suspend judgment.
- Avoid preaching, giving advice, or trying to persuade the child to feel something else.
- Label the child's feelings as you interpret them.

The adult manages the environment, sets realistic stated expectations, and actively listens. Then the adult and child interactions can focus on more

IT HAPPENED TO ME

The Bare Room

A student teacher warned me of the room's lack of equipment in the setting where she was working. When I visited her, I saw she was not exaggerating. The children were jumping from the top of a play refrigerator, the only piece of equipment in the room besides a table and chairs and a shelf with ditto coloring sheets and crayons. She told me she was having a terrible time "controlling" their behavior, trying to keep them from climbing and jumping off the refrigerator. The story was that each time the children "misbehaved" the lead teacher took away a piece of equipment so they were down to the last piece. Children must play, so they used the refrigerator for the large muscle equipment they were missing. Needless to say, the lead teacher and director were not providing an appropriate environment, nor practicing positive guidance approaches. Behavior problems persist when teachers do not adequately prepare the environment.

important topics, such as where butterflies go when it rains, or how this ball can stay on top of the cone collage base.

Adult Intervention of Problem Behavior

The adult role is first to keep children safe. Sometimes in the execution of that role for one child, interactions with another child strain relationships. A child starts throwing chairs, ripping other children's artwork, or yelling obscenities at another child. In the positive guidance model, children are not punished but guided to help control their own behavior and seek solutions and remedies for problems. Clare Cherry (1983) recommends

- natural consequence: Other children tell her to stop or the adult points out the consequence.
  "When you . . . it hurts, makes them mad, makes them sad."
- logical consequence: Helps the child correct the action or approximates the desired behavior.
  "Place the chair next to the table so that people can use it for sitting," or "Get the tape and try to fix the drawings," or "Call her by her name."

- unrelated consequences: Outcomes by the adult are not related to the act.

  "At recess, you will have to stay inside."

The first two are considered consistent with positive guidance techniques. As a last resort, unrelated consequences are used. This is more like punishment and does not help the child learn to control her own behavior.

Possible Causes of Problem Behavior. The close observer and interpreter of children's behavior looks beyond misbehavior, and considers the consequences, in light of the child's individual situation. Again, it is the empathetic, reflective, professional looking at behavior indicators to seek reasons, causes, contributing factors before blaming the child for deliberately breaking rules. Kostelnik, Whiren, Soderman, Stein, and Gregory (2002) suggests these possible causes for behavior problems.

1. Children are not sure of what the rules are or how to follow them.
2. Children know that certain behaviors are inappropriate, but do not know what to do instead.
3. Children are not capable of following the rule.
4. Children have difficulty controlling impulsive behavior.
5. Children have faulty perceptions about how to gain acceptance.
6. Other significant adults, siblings, or peers advocate certain behaviors that run counter to those advocated by the caregiver or teacher.
7. Children think that the rule is unjustified.
8. Children have learned that unacceptable behaviors are usually ignored and that it makes no difference whether they follow the rule.
9. Children are trying to figure out the real boundaries of a social situation and whether adults will maintain those boundaries consistently. (p. 327)

TOPICS
IN
OBSERVATION

Does the Week by Week Plan Meet NAEYC Guidelines for Assessment?

The National Association for the Education of Young Children (NAEYC) and the National Association of Early Childhood Specialists in State Departments of Education (NAECS/SDE) jointly developed guidelines to evaluate assessment practices. The *Week by Week* system should provide affirmative responses to *all* the questions (NAEYC, 1991, p. 34).

1. Is the assessment procedure based on the goals and objectives of the specific curriculum used in the program?

   The *Week by Week* system guides the teacher to observe each child and plan curriculum to meet the goals and objective. It specifies no particular curriculum and can be adapted to meet the program's uniqueness.

2. Are the results of assessment used to benefit children, i.e., to plan for individual children, improve instruction, identify children's interest and needs, and individualize instruction, rather than label, track, or fail children?

   The purpose of the *Week by Week* system is to provide vehicles for the teacher to *know* the child, to see the child as an individual, and to take action based on that knowledge.

3. Does the assessment procedure address all domains of learning and development—social, emotional, physical, and cognitive—as well as children's feelings and dispositions toward learning?

   The *Week by Week* system not only looks at all areas of development through observation assignments, but includes methods of observation that see the behavior of the child showing the affective approach to learning.

(continued)

Does the Week by Week *Plan Meet NAEYC Guidelines for Assessment?*

(continued)

4. Does assessment provide useful information to teachers to help them do a better job?

    Observations of each child using the *Week by Week* **system help the teacher individualize the curriculum, measure the child's progress, and monitor her own teaching practices.**

5. Does the assessment procedure rely on teachers' regular and periodic observations and recordkeeping of children's everyday activities and performance so that results reflect children's behavior over time?

    Weekly assignments ensure that each child is observed regularly, during activities in the classroom, revisiting each developmental area at least three times during the year to measure progress.

6. Does the assessment procedure occur as part of the ongoing life of the classroom rather than in an artificial, contrived context?

    All observation assignments in the *Week by Week* **system are made while children are interacting with each other, the teacher, and the learning environment.**

7. Is the assessment procedure performance-based, rather than only testing skills in isolation?

    The observer using the *Week by Week* **system observes the child in the normal routine of the classroom environment and activities.**

8. Does the assessment rely on multiple sources of information about children, such as collections of their work, results of teacher interviews and dialogues, as well as observations?

    The *Week by Week* **system collects children's work periodically in a portfolio. These include language samples, writing samples, creative work and electronic reproductions, such as audio or video tape and photography. At least seven different methods of recording are used to control bias and to meet the objectives for the observation. Interviews, both formal and informal, are included in the assignment plan.**

9. Does the assessment procedure reflect individual, cultural, and linguistic diversity? Is it free of cultural, language, and gender biases?

    Natural observation techniques recording raw data or objective criteria are basic to the *Week by Week* **system. The observer's diversity awareness is heightened in the "Helping All Children" sections included in each chapter.**

10. Do children appear comfortable and relaxed during assessment rather than tense or anxious?

    Children are observed and assessed during their regular routine and interactions in the classroom where they are most comfortable. They become aware that observation is the role of the teacher using the *Week by Week* **system.**

11. Does the assessment procedure support parents' confidence in their children and their ability as parents rather than threaten or undermine parents' confidence?

    Families are made aware of the presence and purpose and their accessibility to the portfolio. Since the assessment is an ongoing, regular part of the classroom routine, there is no anxiety to families or children. Their confidence in the *Week by Week* **system is in their ability to look at the portfolio at any time.**

TOPICS IN OBSERVATION

Does the Week by Week *Plan Meet NAEYC Guidelines for Assessment?*

12. Does the assessment examine children's strengths and capabilities rather than just their weaknesses or what they do not know?

   The word *weakness* does not appear in the *Week by Week* system. It is continually emphasized that assessment of development is looking for the measure of accomplishment.

13. Is the teacher the primary assessor and are teachers adequately trained for this role?

   The *Week by Week* system provides the teacher with detailed instructions to adequately use the observation methods. A review of child development principles ensures that each observer, regardless of role—teacher, assistant teacher, family worker, or volunteer—has realistic expectations for behavior and can recognize and classify behavior in appropriate categories.

14. Does the assessment procedure involve collaboration among teachers, children, administrators, and families? Is information from parents used in planning instruction and evaluating children's learning? Are parents informed about assessment information?

   Teachers and all staff people in contact with the child may contribute to the portfolio and the assessment process. In the *Week by Week* system, teachers inform children of the purpose of their observations and invite children's comments on it. Administrators are involved in referrals and concerns about the child. They may read progress reports before they are sent home to be sure they reflect the policies and goals of the program.

   The portfolio begins with the families' information form about the child. This is used by the teachers to know the families' goals for the child and helps to individualize the curriculum.

   Families are invited to read and contribute to the portfolio. They are continually reminded in the *Week by Week* system that the portfolio is a changing collection of documents open for their inspection and comment. Daily contacts concerning the observations are recommended. Regular progress reports are a part of the Week by Week system to keep families informed of their child's progress.

15. Do children have an opportunity to reflect on and evaluate their own learning?

   Throughout the year, using the *Week by Week* system, children are regularly interviewed about their own progress. They have knowledge of the portfolio at their learning level and have opportunities to see and contribute to it.

16. Are children assessed in supportive contexts to determine what they are capable of doing with assistance as well as what they can do independently?

   The observation methods in the *Week by Week* system are implemented during the child's regular activities. The level of independence or need for assistance in performing at this level is noted in many of the observation methods and addressed specifically in some of them.

17. Is there a systematic procedure for collecting assessment data that facilitates its use in planning instruction and communicating with parents?

   That is what the *Week by Week* system is, a collection plan to individualize curriculum and build a portfolio of documentation of development for all.

(continued)

Does the Week by Week Plan Meet NAEYC Guidelines for Assessment?

(continued)

18. Is there a regular procedure for communicating the results of assessment to families in meaningful language, rather than letter or number grades, that reports children's individual progress?

All through the *Week by Week* system, regular communication with families concerning the assessment observations is stressed. A periodic narrative progress report briefly describes the child's accomplishments in each developmental area. These are presented to families in family conferences and become a part of the portfolio. A child study, covering the whole year, is optional as an additional review of the assessment of the child.

It appears that the *Week by Week* system meets the NAEYC and NAECS/SDE guidelines. *Week by Week* assessments of every child's development, using a variety of observation techniques, and professional reflection, have been braided together. Together they make the whole strand stronger—the strand of professional practice.

Through observation and appropriate professional practice, the child in group settings can be assessed for physical and psychological safety. Nonpunitive, positive guidance techniques are used to help the child gain self-control. In this way, the teacher does not give up on any child and has a career of liberation teaching (Ginott in Gartrell, 2003). The teacher sees the child as an individual, recognizing and respecting the cultural differences. Teachers work to help each child be a self-directed, competent, accepted, and moral individual.

HELPING ALL CHILDREN THROUGH HOME AND SCHOOL COMMUNICATIONS

Children from Diverse Backgrounds

Communication is the key component to working in partnership with families. Whether the family speaks a language unknown to the teacher or lives in such a different lifestyle it is almost impossible to comprehend, it is the teacher's responsibility to find some common ground. That common ground is con-

cern for the child and the desire to know and assist the child in development. When that is the motivation, interpreters, adaptions of schedules, overlooking lifestyles without judgments, all can be managed with creativity and conviction.

Children with Special Needs

Families whose children have special needs must be advocates for their child. They want for their child what every other family wants: an opportunity to learn and be treated equally. In the classroom, for some children to receive what they need, some interventions or modifications must be made. It takes an intense amount of understanding between families and teachers to come to satisfactory arrangements that do not overburden the teacher or the program yet provide for the needs of every child in the group. This may mean adding extra adults who specifically help that child. It may mean the teacher modifies the environment and the routines for one particular child while meeting the needs of the rest as well. This can only be accomplished through open communication between the family and teachers, regularly sharing information, frustrations, and problem solving together. It can be done.

IT HAPPENED TO ME

As I Wrote This Book

These are the "truisms" that have come to me in the process of working out this *Week by Week* plan:

Observations cannot be done occasionally because the novelty of being watched changes children's behavior. Children need to see the teacher writing about them every day.

Writing meaningful observations as they are occurring cannot happen in a teacher-directed classroom. The teacher is too busy.

Useful observations cannot be gathered the week before progress reports or family conferences are due.

A fair assessment of the child cannot be gathered with any one recording instrument.

Every child deserves to be observed and recorded individually.

Observing and recording does no good if it does not change the teacher's practices or individualize the approach the teacher uses with each child.

Because some children in the class have reached a certain developmental level does not mean that others should be there too. They have other strengths.

When we look at what the child cannot do, we fail to see all the child can do.

Pointing blame at others—the family, the child, or the program—leaves three fingers pointing back at us. We must reflect on what we could do to make things better for the family, the child, and the program.

Families are the authorities of the child. They lend them to us and we pay them back with interest.

This organized plan comes from a person who is disorganized but enacts plans that get things done.

Teaching is not about transferring knowledge. It is about learning, and the one who learns the most is the teacher.

This book could never have been accomplished had I not set *Week by Week* goals for myself. On a calendar near my computer I plotted chapters, working back from deadlines, so that if I stayed on course I could meet the deadlines. It worked for me. It can work for you!

It is my sincere goal for each one using this plan to know the child. Because we know, we do. In that knowing, we will do what is right for that child.

HELPING PROFESSIONALS FOR HOME AND SCHOOL COMMUNICATIONS

Psychologists and social workers can help as intermediaries between schools, programs, and families. They can assess an individual child's emotional state in relation to the adults in the program, how the program is meeting the child's particular needs, and help the family deal with agencies with its own policies and procedures.

No matter what the circumstances of the family, the teacher's first responsibility is to provide for the needs of the child within the goals and objectives of the program. Working with families in a cooperative partnership helps accomplish those goals.

OTHER METHODS

Other Methods to Record the Child's Interaction with Adults:

Class List Log
Anecdotal/Running Records
Frequency Count
Time Sampling
Conversations/Interviews
Work Samples
Checklists and Rating Scales

KEY TERMS

active listening
case study (child study)
documentation panels
liberation teaching

progress report
teacher's stories
unconditional positive
 regard

WEEK 14: PLAN A

CLASS LIST LOG TO OBSERVE INTERACTION WITH ADULTS FOR ALL

Students

Complete Plan A and Plan C for one child. See your instructor and the supervising teacher for guidelines regarding permission from the family. Submit your Progress Report to your instructor before giving a copy to the family (if they request it). This protects you and the program from erroneous conclusions because of your limited exposure to the child and the program. This is for practice.

Practitioners

Using a Class List Log form, found in Appendix D, jot notes on how each of the children relates to the adults in the classroom. Note behaviors such as cooperation, independence, preferences, reliance, and reaction to new people.

What to Do with It

Filing. On the portfolio overview, note the presence of the observation and transfer a few words to give information about the child (Figure 14–12).

File the Class List Log in the class file.

Sharing with the Child and Family. Share it with the family or the child, if it is appropriate. For example, say privately to a family member, "Today when the firefighters came to school and taught the children 'Stop, Drop, and Roll,' Andrea asked if they were strangers. She was a little afraid of them, I believe. It's a hard one to explain and I know you are trying to protect her safety. It gave me the idea we might want to invite Dr. Greene, the psychologist, to

our Family Night to talk about the topic. Would you like to make the phone call?" or "Ananiy, when I was watching you play outside I saw you ask Mr. Chapin to help Brett get his shoe unstuck from the fence. That was a brave thing you did to go for help and to think of Mr. Chapin, the janitor. I wrote it down so I would remember to talk to you about it. I'll bet Brett was glad."

Actions.

Read a Book.

> Allard, H. (1977). *Miss Nelson Is Missing.* New York: Houghton Mifflin.
> Rosen, M. (1992). *We're Going on a Bear Hunt.* New York: Simon & Schuster.

In the Environment.

- Prepare the environment for family conferences. Be sure the room is neat and clean. Have *all* children's work displayed.
- Have the portfolio available for the families' viewing prior to the conference.
- Provide a comfortable atmosphere with adult-size chairs, refreshments, child care, welcome signs.

In the Curriculum.

- Inform the family that family conferences are times for the teacher and the family to talk about how *well* they have done. Often the family will say they are going to get the report, expecting the worst and instilling dread and anxiety in the child.
- Children can be involved in preparing the environment for the visit by special cleaning (with safe products, of course), project displays, and views in the portfolios themselves, depending on their age. The teacher may talk with the child about the portfolio, letting the child know the progress that has been made.

In the Newsletter.

- Families are informed about the format and topics of the conference.
- Explanations of the portfolio and its contents can give accurate expectations. The positive attitude expressed by the newsletter should put the family at ease and invite them to come prepared for good news.

INTERACTIONS WITH ADULTS

Documentation	Location	Recorder	Date
CL	Class file	Ban	12/12
AR	Portfolio	MS	5/3

Figure 14–12 Portfolio Overview Example

WEEK 14: PLAN B

CHECKLIST ON PHYSICAL DEVELOPMENT FOR ALL

Using the Checklists from Week 3, review each child's large and small muscle development. You may use the same form, just use a different colored pen or write in the new date of this assessment.

What to Do with It

Filing. Note the date of the second observation on the physical development portion of the Portfolio Overview Sheet, and refile the Checklist in the portfolio. If little progress has been observed, take a closer look to see if you can determine a reason. Try to interest the child in more activities that approximate the next criterion on the Checklist. If a serious lag appears, speak to your supervisor and then to the family if it is warranted.

WEEK 14: PLAN C

PROGRESS REPORTS FOR GROUP D

Each day this week, take some time with the portfolios of each child in Group D. Write a progress report following the suggestions in the chapter. Remember: Be positive, descriptive, and personal.

Heading
Family (optional for progress report)
Physical
Social
Adjustment to School
Self-Acceptance
Cognitive
Creativity
Closure

What to Do with It

Have a supervisor check the progress report. Make a copy to place in the portfolio and one in the class file.

Go over the original with the family in a conference if possible. If not, send it home with a note of explanation, such as:

> This year we are instituting a new system of portfolio collections of observations and the children's work. Now that we have been together more than three months, this is a review of your child's development from what we've seen. Please comment or ask questions. We value your information. After all, you know the child best.

NOTE: When you are using the *Week by Week* plan next year you may need to do progress reports earlier than 14 weeks into the school year. Here is a suggestion for earlier assignments:

Week 11: Progress reports for Group A
Week 12: Progress reports for Group B
Week 13: Progress reports for Group C
Week 14: Progress reports for Group D

WEEK 14: PLAN C

REFLECTIVE JOURNAL

Respond to the following in your Reflective Journal, kept in a private file at home.

> *The progress reports make me feel . . .*
>
> *Family conferences wouldn't be dreaded if . . .*
>
> *I think I'd be ready for family conferences when . . .*

The gathering of documentation throughout this book has been a singular work from one source, you. In reality, the responsibility and fun of this should be shared among the teaching team. Reflection on the observations involves much personal thought, which is not shared, but can bring out some revelations that would be valuable as discussion topics. This sounds like a very worthwhile effort to do with the new knowledge you have gained in observation techniques and child development.

Try some of this action research with a few colleagues. Use the skills you have gained in reflection to then write a story of one of the processes. Others can gain from your exploration.

> *Maybe I'll try the action research idea. I'll invite . . .*
>
> *My story would begin with . . .*

REFERENCES

Benner, S. (2003). *Assessment of young children with special needs.* Clifton Park, NY: Thomson Delmar Learning.

Berger, E. (1995). *Parents as partners in education: Families and schools working together.* Englewood Cliffs, NJ: Merrill, an imprint of Prentice Hall.

Brown-DuPaul, J., Keyes, T., & Segatti, L. (2001). Using documentation panels to communicate with families. *Childhood Education, 77* (4), 209–213.

Cherry, C. (1983). *Please don't sit on the kids.* Fearon Teacher Aids, Simon & Schuster.

DiNatale, L. (2002). Developing high-quality family involvement programs in early childhood settings. *Young Children, 57* (5), 90–95.

Dunst, C. J., Trivette, C. M., & Mott, D. W. (1994). Strengths-based family-centered intervention practices. In C. J. Dunst, C. M. Trivette, & A. G. Deal (Eds.). *Supporting and strengthening families: Methods, strategies and practices, Vol I* (115–131). Cambridge, MA: Brookline.

Feeney, S., & Kipnis, L. (1996). *Code of ethical conduct.* Washington, DC: National Association for the Education of Young Children.

Gartrell, D. (2003). *A guidance approach for the encouraging classroom* (3rd ed.). Clifton Park, NY: Thomson Delmar Learning.

Gestwicki, C. (2004). *Home, school, and community relations: A guide to working with parents* (5th ed.). Clifton Park, NY: Thomson Delmar Learning.

Gordon, T. (1975). *P.E.T. Parent Effectiveness Training.* New York: Wyden.

Howes, C., Phillips, D.A., & Whitelock, M. (1992). Thresholds of quality: Implications for social development of children in center-based child care. *Child Development, 63* (2), 449–460.

Kostelnik, M. J., Whiren, A. P., Soderman, A. K., Stein, L. C., & Gregory, K. (2002). *Guiding children's social development* (4th ed.). Clifton Park, NY: Thomson Delmar Learning.

Lally, J. R., Lerner, C., & Lurie-Hurvitz, E. (2001). National survey reveals gaps in the public's and parents' knowledge about early childhood development. *Young Children, 56 (2),* 49–53.

Marion, M. (1999). *Guidance of young children* (5th ed.). Englewood Cliffs, NJ: Merrill, an imprint of Prentice Hall.

National Association for the Education of Young Children and The National Association of Early Childhood Specialists in State Departments of Education (NAEYC and NAECS/SDE). (1991). Guidelines for appropriate curriculum content and assessment in programs serving children ages 3 through 8. *Young Children, 46* (3), 21–38.

U.S. Department of Health and Human Services. (2000). Head Start Program Performance Standards. http://www.acf.hhs.gov.

RESOURCES

Cherry, C. (1983). *Please don't sit on the kids.* Fearon Teacher Aids, Simon & Schuster

Gartrell, D. (2003). *A guidance approach for the encouraging classroom* (3rd ed.). Clifton Park, NY: Thomson Delmar Learning.

Goldberg, P. (1997). *Parent involvement begins at birth.* Boston: Allyn & Bacon.

Marion, M. (2003). *Guidance of young children* (6th ed.). Englewood Cliffs, NJ: Merrill, an imprint of Prentice Hall.

15

Using the Yearly Plan to Observe and Record Children's Development

Students

You have used this book as a guide for observing children throughout a semester but all along you have noticed that this book has a dual purpose. There are extensive directions in the plans at the end of the chapter for practitioners. It is the author's intention that this textbook be used as a reference and guide when you have a classroom of your own. What follows is the *Week by Week* plan for compiling documentation on every child, in every developmental area, every week.

Practitioners

Now you have the tools (the various methods presented in this book). You have the knowledge of how to use the tools (the overview of areas of development). The rest of this book is the building plan for portfolios that contain documentation of all areas of development, revisited at least three times to measure progress.

Appendix A contains the schedule for the *Week by Week* plan. Divide the group into four by alphabetical order, assigning A, B, C, or D. This will give you an arbitrary plan so that certain children are not overlooked in observations while others are frequently observed.

Appendix B contains the plans for weeks 15–40. You may have to adjust for your own program calendar, for vacations or necessary suspensions of recording. But like a diet, even if you slip some, just try to get back into the routine in order to meet your goal: a well-developed portfolio for each child.

Appendix C is a scan of each developmental area and each group to illustrate how the plan works. If you follow the *Week by Week* plan, the portfolios of the children in Group A, B, C, and D will include all of those observations. They are not identical but are numerous enough to give information on which to base decisions about the child.

Appendix D includes the forms you can copy and/or modify for your observations.

Appendix E includes the Reflective Journal pages. You can tear these out, take them home and fill them out week by week to guide your introspection as well as the plans for observing children. Keep these at home, in a private place, and use them to reflect on your own attitudes, practices, and feelings.

REVIEW

Here is your last Review Box, a summary of the methods you have in your toolbox. Use the right tool for the job.

Method	Definition	Useful for Recording:
Class List Log	Alphabetical first name list to record small, specific pieces of information on each child in the class	Single elements of adjustments to routines Single elements of self-care Single elements of physical development Social development stage Clear articulation of speech Single elements of basic concepts in math/science Single elements of literacy Frequency of choices of Learning Centers
Reflective Journal	Personal diary kept separate and private from children's records	Thoughts Expressions of emotions Questions Self-examination
Anecdotal Recording	Detailed incident on one child, including the setting, action/reaction, exact quotes, and result	Separation and adjustment Self-care skills Physical development Social development Emotional development Language and speech Attention span and interests Cognitive development Literacy Creativity Sociodramatic play Child abuse disclosure Self-esteem
Checklists	Listing of related criteria against which skills, knowledge, or behavior is measured indicating yes or no, present or not present. Can indicate milestones attained and areas yet to be developed	Self-care skills Physical development Stages of social development Stages of emotional development Stages of cognitive development Specific criteria such as "knows colors, shapes, recognizes numbers" Stages of literacy Stages of creative development Stages of sociodramatic play Aspects of self-concept
Frequency Count	A recording of predetermined frequently occurring behaviors to quantify their frequency, and later used for comparison after a strategy is implemented	Frequently occuring separation difficulties Frequent requests for assistance Frequent prosocial and antisocial incidents Frequency of language used in certain functions Frequency of choices of activities

CONTINUED

R E V I E W

Method	Definition	Useful for Recording:

Conversations or Interviews	Recording a child's verbal interactions either in writing or in audio recording	Informal conversations
		Interviews to attain:
		    Child's viewpoint on school adjustment
		    Self-responsibility views
		    Self-evaluation of physical skills
		    Self-evaluation of friendships and social interactions
		    Self-evaluation of emotional difficulties
		Evaluate speech /language
		Assess cognitive development
		Assess literacy development
		Discuss creative work or play

Time Sample	Recording children's play area free choices every five minutes for a half hour interval and drawing conclusions about interests, abilities, attention span, preferred playmates, level of social play	Presence of child in area Sustained play in that area Interaction with others in that area Presence of adult
Rating Scale	Criteria is arranged according to developmental stages or range of quality with the recorder making a judgement based on observation	Child development stages Environment appropriateness Teacher performance
Work Samples	Collection of child's products from which to draw conclusions about development, skills, and behaviors	Separation Self-care Physical development Social skills Emotional development Speech & language development Memory and attention span Math and science knowledge Literacy Creativity Self-identity Group time behaviors Interaction with adults
Technology	Action preserved in photos, audio/video tape	Any moment or sequence Separation and adjustment Self-care skills Physical development Social development Emotional development Language and speech Attention span and interests Cognitive development Literacy Creativity Sociodramatic play Self-esteem
Child Abuse Reporting	Precise, descriptive, immediate note taking, State Reporting Form	Indicators of physical abuse Indicators of neglect Indicators of sexual abuse Indicators of emotional abuse

	R E V I E W	
Method	**Definition**	**Useful for Recording:**
Program Assessment	Tool to evaluate program environment, curriculum and administration, staff qualifications and interactions with children, suitability of program for individual child	Interactions among teachers and children Curriculum Relationships among teachers and families Staff qualifications and professional development Administration Staffing Health and safety Environment Nutrition and health service Anti-bias policies and procedures

The purpose is to *know* the child in order to fulfill our responsibility to the global village in helping each one develop into a caring, thinking, reliable human being. This plan is only successful if it helps attain that goal by measuring progress, individualizing the environment or curriculum to assist in development, documenting the child's activities, and sharing with families.

A

Week by Week: An Observation Plan for Portfolio Building (Practitioners)

WEEK	METHOD	AREA	ON WHOM
1	Class List Log Work Samples Reflective Journal	Separation and Adjustment Art	All All Self
2	Anecdotal Recording Class List Log Reflective Journal	Self-Care Self-Care	Group A All Self
3	Checklist Anecdotal Recording Reflective Journal	Physical Development Physical Development	All Group B Self
4	Running Record Class List Log Reflective Journal	Social Development Social Play Stage	Group C All Self
5	Frequency Count Anecdotal Recording Reflective Journal	Emotional Development Emotional Development	All Group D Self
6	Checklist Class List Log Reflective Journal	Speech and Language Speech and Language	Group A All Self

WEEK	METHOD	AREA	ON WHOM
7	Time Sample Checklist Reflective Journal	Attention Span Speech and Language	All Group B Self
8	Checklist Checklist Reflective Journal	Math and Science Speech and Language	All Group C Self
9	Rating Scale Checklist Reflective Journal	Literacy Speech and Language	All Group D Self
10	Work Samples Anecdotal Recording Progress Reports Reflective Journal	Creative Creative Process	All Group A Group A Self
11	Media Running Record Progress Reports* Reflective Journal	Dramatic Play Dramatic Play	All Group B Group B Self
12	Class List Log Anecdotal Recording Progress Reports* Reflective Journal	Self-Esteem Self-Identity	All Group C Group C Self
13	Setting Observation Class List Log Anecdotal Recording Progress Reports* Reflective Journal	Environment Group Participation Group Interactions	Visit All Group D Group D Self
14	Class List Log Checklist Progress Reports Reflective Journal	Interaction with Adults Physical Development	All All Group D Self
15	Class List Log Running Record Reflective Journal	Social Stages of Play Self-Identity	All Group A Self
16	Frequency Count Running Record Reflective Journal	Emotional Development Emotional Development	All Group B Self
17	Checklist Time Sample Reflective Journal	Language Development Attention Span	All All Self
18	Running Record Checklist Reflective Journal	Free Play Cognitive Skills	Group C All Self

*See Week 14, Assignment C

WEEK	METHOD	AREA	ON WHOM
19	Rating Scale Writing Samples Reflective Journal	Literacy	All All Self
20	Work Samples Anecdotal Recording Reflective Journal	Creativity Creative Process	All Group D Self
21	Media Checklist Progress Reports Reflective Journal	Dramatic Play and Blocks Speech and Language	All Group A Group A Self
22	Class List Log Checklist Progress Reports Reflective Journal	Choices in Play Speech and Language	All Group B Group B Self
23	Class List Log Checklist Progress Reports Reflective Journal	Group Time Speech and Language	All Group C Group C Self
24	Time Sample Checklist Progress Reports Reflective Journal	Attention Span Speech and Language	All Group D Group D Self
25	Checklist Anecdotal Recording Reflective Journal	Social Development Creativity	All Group C Self
26	Class List Log Running Record Reflective Journal	Self-Care Free Play	All Group D Self
27	Frequency Count Anecdotal Recording Reflective Journal	Emotional Development Emotional Development	All Group A Self
28	Class List Log Anecdotal Recording Reflective Journal	Adjustment to Routines Literacy	All Group B Self
29	Time Sample Checklist Reflective Journal	Attention Span Cognitive Skills	All All Self
30	Rating Scale Writing Samples Reflective Journal	Literacy	All All Self
31	Work Samples Anecdotal Recording Reflective Journal	Creativity Emotional Development	All Group C Self

WEEK	METHOD	AREA	ON WHOM
32	Class List Log Anecdotal Recording Reflective Journal	Interaction with Adults Self-Identity	All Group D Self
33	Checklist Running Record Reflective Journal	Physical Development Free Play	All Group A Self
34	Checklist Anecdotal Recording Reflective Journal	Social Development Social Development	All Group B Self
35	Frequency Count Checklist Reflective Journal	Emotional Development Speech and Language	All Group C Self
36	Class List Log Checklist Reflective Journal	Group Interaction Speech and Language	All Group D Self
37	Checklist Checklist Progress Reports Reflective Journal	Cognitive Development Speech and Language	All Group A Group A Self
38	Rating Scale Checklist Progress Reports Reflective Journal	Literacy Speech and Language	All Group B Group B Self
39	Class List Log Time Sample Progress Reports Reflective Journal	Self-Identity Attention Span	All All Group C Self
40	Work Samples Progress Reports Reflective Journal	Creativity	All Group D Self

B

Weeks 15 through 40: Plans for the Week

After the completion of Week 14, observation and recording should not stop. This is designed to be an ongoing assessment of each child in the class over a whole year, so each developmental area is revisited and recording methods are used again and again. Weeks 15 through 40 follow with plans for observing all the developmental areas using the methods presented in this book. If the plan is followed, all areas will have several documentations and each child will have group and individual assessments added to his or her portfolio. Progress report plans are included, but may be modified depending on the program

policies and calendar. Of course, all plan topics, methods, and focus children can be modified to meet the policies of the program and the needs of the child. It is important, however, that individual children are not singled out for observations, ignoring the rest of the class. Equality of observation is one of the basic principles of the *Week by Week* plan. See Appendix C for a summary of the developmental areas and child groups.

The forms you will need to complete these plans are printed in Appendix D for you to use as masters to copy.

WEEK 15: PLAN A

CLASS LIST LOG ON SOCIAL STAGES OF PLAY FOR ALL

This week, use a Class List Log form to observe each child's stage of play. You may modify the form by drawing vertical lines to indicate the social play stages: onlooker, solitary, parallel, associative, and cooperative. Observe the children as they interact with each other. Place a check mark in the stage next to their name. If you can, indicate what type of play it is: functional (F), constructive (C), dramatic (D), or games with rules (G).

What to Do with It

Filing. At the end of the week, take the Class List Log and transfer the stage you observed onto the Portfolio Overview Sheet with your name and date of the observation.

File the Class List Log in the class file. If you notice children who have not progressed, plan some cooperative activities and think about modeling some social play strategies to get them started.

Sharing with the Child and Family. Share your observations with the family and the child, if appropriate. For example: "I was watching to see the progress of the children's interactions with each other when I noticed Fatima and how much more social she is now than at the beginning of the school year. She comes in and joins in groups of children who are already playing. That's sometimes hard to do," or "Fatima, I saw how you went right over to the block area when you got here today and joined Manuel and Shawn in building the skyscraper. They liked the way you added the little people on the top floors. How many floors are in the apartment house where you live? Do you ride the elevator or walk up?"

WEEK 15: PLAN B

RUNNING RECORD ON SELF-IDENTITY FOR GROUP A

Each day this week, observe one or more of the children in Group A, selecting a segment of the day when you can write a Running Record of a typical block of time (5 to 10 minutes). Write on the left side of lined notebook paper. Remember to begin with the child's name, the date, and your name. Each day this week, observe and write on each child in Group A.

What to Do with It

Filing. On the right-hand column, note any indicators of the child's knowledge, skills, dispositions, or attitudes, and feelings of empowerment or autonomy that contribute to self-identity.

If further action is needed, make a note of it in the class file and follow through. Perhaps the child needs more encouragement or opportunities to feel successful.

Note the presence of the Running Record with the recorder's name and date on the Portfolio Overview Sheet, and file the Record in each child's portfolio.

Sharing with the Child and Family. Share with family and child, if appropriate. For example: "Mrs. Ramirez, today when I was observing Joseph, I saw him pouring his juice so carefully. When he put the pitcher down, he looked up with a great big smile and said, 'No dejes caev una gota!' ('I didn't spill a drop.') He was so proud of himself and felt the power of doing things for himself."

WEEK 16: PLAN A

FREQUENCY COUNT ON EMOTIONAL DEVELOPMENT FOR GROUPS A AND B, THEN C AND D

Early in the week, select Groups A and B, and later in the week Groups C and D. Observe the children during free choice time for 30 minutes looking for evidence of prosocial or antisocial behaviors. Make a mark each time one of these occurs next to the name of the child in the appropriate column. On another day, repeat the observation with children in Groups C and D.

What to Do with It

Compare this Frequency Count to the one done in Week 5. Do you see differences in the totals for the class? For individual children? Do you think the prosocial curriculum activities for 10 weeks made a difference? If so, write a short summary and send your findings to the authors. They would love to hear it. Share it in your school's newsletter or in a happy gram to the family.

Explore strategies for individual children who may need help in controlling aggression or for the whole group in problem solving or developing prosocial behaviors. Make a plan, implement, and document the results, perhaps with another Frequency Count after implementation. If it did not make a difference, why not? Summarize the project, and file it in the class file.

WEEK 16: PLAN B

RUNNING RECORD ON EMOTIONAL DEVELOPMENT FOR GROUP B

On Monday, watch child 1 in Group B. Select a segment of the day when you can write a Running Record of a typical block of time (5 to 10 minutes). Write on the left side of lined notebook paper. Remember to begin with the child's name, the date, and your name. Each day this week observe and write on each child in Group B. Make notes in the right-hand column of how this sample recording portrays the child's emotional development. If any action is indicated to assist the child or follow up on some other interest or concern, note that also and follow up on it.

What to Do with It

Filing. On the child's Portfolio Overview Sheet, note that the Running Record is present in the portfolio with your name as the recorder and the date.

Sharing with the Child and Family. Share the recording with the family and the child, if appropriate. For example: "Farrah is making progress in leaving at the end of the day. I was observing her yesterday and noticed how that new plan we made worked. I'm glad you suggested having her put all her things in the totebag right after nap. That begins to get her prepared to go home and makes leaving much calmer," or "Marcus, when I was writing about your play today, I noticed that you were angry when Carlo took away the big truck you were on but you just told him you had it first in a big voice and he listened. That's so much better than hitting. Hitting hurts but your words let him know what you wanted."

WEEK 17: PLAN A

CHECKLIST ON LANGUAGE DEVELOPMENT

Review the Speech and Language Checklist in each child's portfolio and note any changes since the checklist in Week 6 and the interviews in Weeks 6, 7, 8, and 9. Use a different color pen to note any changes.

What to Do with It

Filing. Make a note on the Portfolio Overview Sheet with your name and date. Note any changes and place in each child's portfolio.

Sharing with the Child and Family. Share progress with the family or child, if appropriate. For example: "I was observing all the children's language this week and I noticed from my notes that Devon's speech is sounding clearer now. He is pronouncing /l/ and /th/, which he wasn't doing a few months ago. And he's using many more words," or "Shaquinta, where did you hear that great jump rope song you were singing outside? The sounds of the words were such great fun. Would you teach it to me and the class after lunch while we're waiting for the bus? Would you like to add it to your tape in your portfolio?"

WEEK 17: PLAN B

TIME SAMPLE ON ATTENTION SPAN FOR ALL

Select a day this week during free play time without planned interruptions. Prepare the form from Appendix D with learning center areas that are open. Complete the Time Sample.

What to Do with It

Filing. Compare to Time Samples done previously (Week 7). Later in the day, draw conclusions and write notes in the child's portfolio about each child's attention span, play preferences, social interactions, and the changes from the last recording. Note the presence of the recording on the overview chart and file it in the class file. If this Time Sample showed an unusual pattern or you have an explanation for why a certain thing happened, write that down as well. Your incidental observations are important too. For example: "There were a lot of children around the water table today because it is new.")

Discuss observations from the Time Sample with parents or child, if appropriate.

Use the Time Sample to guide curriculum decisions about individual children. For example: "Sara still isn't leaving the art area. I'll try to get her to decorate a bike to ride or encourage her to join her friend Becky in making a sign for the block area." Follow through and make a note of it.

WEEK 18: PLAN A

RUNNING RECORD ON FREE PLAY FOR GROUP C

Select the children in Group C and each day this week write a Running Record of a segment of play, recording as many details as possible about the action, interaction with other children, and exact quotes.

What to Do with It

Filing. On the right-hand column of each recording, make any notes of interpretation, concern, and any explanation for what you saw. Make a note on each child's Portfolio Overview Sheet in the section of development that this observation most illustrates. File in the child's portfolio.

If a question arises from the Running Record, follow it up to help understand it better or plan to include a project in the curriculum to expand this theme.

Sharing with the Child and Family. Share your observation findings with the family or the child, if appropriate. For example: "As I was writing about Laura's play in the dramatic area today, I noticed how she is beginning to use longer sentences and words like *when* and *because*. I didn't think she was doing that a few months ago. When I checked back in the language sample I had in her portfolio, it showed an earlier stage," or "Sammy, when I was watching you play today, I wrote down something you said but I didn't understand it. When you were riding trucks with Peter you told him, 'If you go too fast you'll get popped.' Can you explain what that meant?"

WEEK 18: PLAN B

CHECKLIST ON COGNITIVE SKILLS FOR ALL

Using your program's checklist, review the cognitive criteria and assess each child's level. If your program is not using a developmental checklist, revisit the assessment done in Week 8. Ask the children the same questions and note their level now. If there is little progress, first check the environment and the curriculum. Are math manipulatives and science explorative materials present? Do the teachers facilitate their use, change them frequently, include them in the integrated curriculum tying books, field trips, art, music, and motor activities together with science and math?

What to Do with It

Sharing with the Child and Family. Share your observations with the family and the child, if appropriate. Maybe a happy note would be appropriate.

In October (or when first check was made) your child _____

_____

could _____

_____

and now _____

_____

_____.

Hurray!

WEEK 19: PLAN A

RATING SCALE IN LITERACY FOR ALL

Look again in each child's portfolio at the Rating Scale you did in Week 9. Observe and mark the progress you have seen in each child's reading and writing. Make notes with a different color pen.

What to Do with It

Filing. On the overview sheet, note progress and the date. Refile the Rating Scales. If you noticed no progress in a child's literacy, make a note to yourself to look further at the child's other developmental areas and make some theories and a plan to follow through.

Sharing with the Child and Family. Share your observations with the family or the child, if appropriate. For example: "In the last few months, Hassan has made amazing progress in his awareness of books. He wasn't interested at all when he first entered school and now they've become one of his favorite choice activities. He's really into the small group story time we have every day. Once a book is read, he can take it and tell it back almost word for word. Now I've heard him sounding out words on his own from the letters," or "Dominique, I noticed the story today was too long for you to sit through. Let's look through the books and find a shorter one to read tomorrow, maybe one about that dog Spot since you have a new puppy."

WEEK 19: PLAN B

SAMPLES IN WRITING FOR ALL

This week, try to collect samples of each child's writing. It could be asking them to sign in as they arrive (name writing). Suggest they go to the writing center or art area, and make a book about a topic you have been working on this week. Sitting with them while they do it will give you a close observation of how they approach the task. Write a few notes about it and attach it to the sample.

What to Do with It

Filing. Often children will not want to part with their work, so you may have to make a copy of it on the copier. If a copier is not available, old-fashioned carbon paper is inexpensive and may even be a novel way to get reluctant writers to try it. Be sure to leave it out for later experimentation.

File the sample and your notes attached in the child's portfolio, making a note under literacy that it is there with the date and your name.

Children at three, four, and five years old will exhibit a wide range of written literacy ability. If you notice a much lower level than expected in a child's written language, think about what could be the cause. If there is something that should be addressed, such as possible vision or motor difficulties, discuss it with your supervisor and then the family about a possible follow-up. Provide the family with possible resources in finding out more about it.

Sharing with the Child and Family. Share writing sample observations with the family and the child, if appropriate. For example: "Today when I was gathering some samples of the children's writing Jamal really went to town on his Js. He calls them fish hooks. They do go in every direction but that's normal for this age. He's still experimenting with the shape and will eventually get them turned around most of the time by the time he's five or six," or "Jennifer, you are working so hard at writing your name. It has many letters in it. See here in the middle, you have two that are the same, the ns. Jamal's name also starts with a J but it's shorter and has an l at the end instead of an r like yours."

WEEK 20: PLAN A

CREATIVE WORK SAMPLES FOR ALL

What to Do with It

Filing. This week, collect a sample of creative work from every child. Make comments on the Work Samples Checklist or the creative section of your program's checklist.

Note the presence of the work on the Portfolio Overview Sheet with your name and the date. Note any changes in art stage from Week 10. On a sticky note on the back of the work, write your observations as you watched the child create this work, measurement of the child's developmental progress, and any interesting points to be remembered.

File the sample in the child's portfolio.

Sharing with the Child and Family. Share with the families, "Today Mario made a square for the first time. That's a milestone we've been waiting for. Before they really have those shapes in mind and the ability to draw them, they will be experimenting with them. He's coming right along," or if the child is present, "Anthony spent so long on his painting today he decided he didn't even want a snack, so he just worked right through snack time. Boy, Anthony, you must love painting. You're really an artist."

WEEK 21: PLAN B

ANECDOTAL RECORDING IN THE CREATIVE PROCESS FOR GROUP D

This week, begin with the first child in Group D and write an Anecdotal Recording on each one of them, detailing some aspect of their creativity in art, music, dramatic play, and block building. Include the situation, the details of the action, and exact quotes on the left side of the paper. In the right-hand column give any explanation, judgments, questions you wonder about, or indications of development that the action signifies.

What to Do with It

Filing. Note on the Portfolio Overview Sheet that the Anecdotal Recording is there with the date and your name.

File the photo and the child's dictation in the child's portfolio.

Sharing with the Child and Family. Share your observations with the family, or the child, if appropriate. For example: "Today when I was writing observations of the children's play, I saw that your

Sylvia was involved in a really interesting play episode in our family center. She was obviously the working mother getting ready to go to work but one of the boys argued 'No, you stay home. I go to work.' You have been a role model of a working mother because she came back to him and told him, nose to nose, 'I can be a good mother, go to work and still cook dinner. Now get on the back of this motorcycle.' He did and away they went. Family of the year 2000!" or "Lonnie, when I was watching the block center today, I saw you building a huge tower. You stacked the blocks across then stood one block in each of the four corners and came up with another story. You kept that pattern up until you couldn't reach any farther then you got a chair and carefully stood on it to make a few more stories. I took a picture of it so we can add it to our album. What would you like me to write in the book as the title of your building? 'You can write, "Here's Lonnie's tallest building he ever built."' That's a good description. I'll write it here with my notes so I'll remember. You write your name on this paper and we'll put it next to the building so everyone will know who built it."

WEEK 21: PLAN A

MEDIA DRAMATIC PLAY FREE PLAY FOR ALL

Make sure there are family releases from all families. (Note especially the children's files who have entered the program since Week 11.) *If there is no release, or if the family checked NO, place a prominent notation on the file and inform all staff.* Use some alternate method for recording dramatic play.

On all children this week, use some method of media for recording a segment of play that shows the child's imagination. It may be dramatic play, blocks, sand, manipulatives, or art.

Audio Tape Recording

Perhaps there is a child who loves to sing favorite songs or make up songs. Tape that on their language tape started in Week 9. Perhaps ask a child to tell the tape recorder about the art work as it is being created or the process of making a collage or a Lego construction. A child may want to record a story about the building that is just finished. These make excellent language and imagination samples.

What to Do with It

Filing. Note the presence of the tape recording on the Portfolio Overview Sheet with the date and your name. Make a note from what you have observed in the area of development it most accurately documents.

Sharing with the Child and Family. Share the recording with the family and the child, if appropriate. For example: "When I was talking with Colleen today, she told me about the poem you taught her. It was so beautiful, I had her recite it on the tape that I'm collecting of each child talking. It's in her portfolio. If you want to listen to it sometime I could send it home," or "Marcella, while you were playing with Heather today in the sand I had the tape recorder nearby. It recorded how you were taking turns at using that scoop. That was a friendly thing to do. Would you like to hear it? It's in your portfolio."

Photographs

Take some pictures this week as the children play. Have each child dictate a story or tape record one to tell about what they were doing.

What to Do with It

Filing. Make a bulletin board display of the children's photos and comments for the children to look at. Or place them in a photo album for the book area. Make a note in each child's file of an observation based on the photograph or their comments. Note it on the overview sheet in the corresponding developmental area.

Invite the parents to look at the photo display, especially their child's.

Video Tape

Take a video of children as they play. Try to get whole segments of play and as much conversation as you can. Include every child in the class in some way on the tape.

What to Do with It

Filing. Later that day or soon, show the tape to the class. Show the segment that was recorded earlier. Invite a discussion about what was different then and now. Perhaps make a chart, "Tape 1" and "Tape 2," as they dictate the differences. These discussions could be documented as further evidence of sociodramatic play or language practice.

Sharing with the Child and Family. Share the tape with families at a meeting or have it playing at the entrance as they bring or pick up the children. File it in the class file after you have made any notes to add to each child's file in the area the tape documents. Note its existence on the Portfolio Overview Sheet.

WEEK 21: PLAN B

CONVERSATION OR INTERVIEW AND CHECKLIST FOR GROUP A

Refer to the guidelines and Speech and Language Checklist in Chapter 6.

Select each child in Group A to talk with each day this week. If possible, tape record the interview as well as make written notes (literacy role model) as you speak with each child.

Afterward, analyze the conversation for what it reveals about the child's knowledge, emotional state, social development, and speech and language, using the Speech and Language Checklist.

What to Do with It

Filing. Enter a summary, the recorder's name, and the date on the Portfolio Overview Sheet.

Compare to the Conversations with each child earlier in the year. If a significant lag appears, dis-cuss it with your supervisor to confirm it, then with the family. Have available a list of resources to refer the family to where a speech and language evaluation may be obtained.

Is any follow-up needed?

Sharing with the Child and Family. Share with the family and child something of interest that came from the interview. For example: "I was talking with Jane and noticed how the orthodontics have moved her teeth. Her speech has improved from when she first got them. She has adjusted well, hasn't she?" or "When we made the tape recording of our talk today, I learned how much you knew about iguanas. Maybe someday you could bring one to school. We could play the tape you made and show the storybook that goes with it."

WEEK 21: PLAN C

PROGRESS REPORTS FOR GROUP A

Follow the format from Chapter 14. Each day this week take some time with the portfolios of the children in Group A. Remember: Be positive, descriptive, and personal.

Heading
Family (optional for progress report)
Physical
Social
Adjustment to school
Self-acceptance
Cognitive
Creativity
Closure

What to Do with It

Have a supervisor check the progress reports. Make copies. Place one in the portfolio and one in the class. Go over the original with the family in a conference if possible.

WEEK 22: PLAN A

CLASS LIST LOG ON CHOICES IN BLOCKS AND DRAMATIC PLAY FOR ALL

Use the Class List Log from Appendix D during free play this week, and note the choices that each child makes in the areas of creative and dramatic play.

What to Do with It

Filing. On each child's Portfolio Overview Sheet, note the child's free play choices from the Class List Log and the date observed. File the Class List Log in the class file.

Use this information to individualize curriculum, building on the child's interests by providing additional props, books, and follow-up activities to enrich the play. This also can be used to interest the child in areas not frequently chosen. For example, a child who always plays with blocks but seldom uses small muscles for writing could be encouraged to trace blocks or draw block buildings. A child who always chooses dramatic play could be provided with literacy materials to encourage writing interest.

Sharing with the Child and Family. Share observations with the family and the child, if appropriate. For example: "Today when I was watching Sergi, I saw he spent a long time with the hammer and nails. Tomorrow I'm putting some small mallets out with the clay to see if he can become interested in an area he has not yet tried."

WEEK 22: PLAN B

CONVERSATION OR INTERVIEW AND CHECKLIST FOR GROUP B

Refer to the guidelines and Speech and Language Checklist in Chapter 6.

Select the children in Group B to talk with each day this week. If possible, tape record the interview as well as make written notes (literacy role model) as you speak with each child.

Afterward, analyze the Conversation for what it reveals about the child's knowledge, emotional state, social development, and speech and language, using the Speech and Language Checklist.

What to Do with It

Enter a summary, the recorder's name, and date on the Portfolio Overview Sheet.

Compare to the Conversations with each child earlier in the year. If a significant lag appears, discuss it with your supervisor to confirm it, then with the family. Have available a list of resources to refer the family to where a speech and language evaluation may be obtained. Is any follow-up needed?

WEEK 22: PLAN C

PROGRESS REPORTS FOR GROUP B

Follow the format from Chapter 14. Each day this week take some time with the portfolios of the children in Group B. Remember: Be positive, descriptive, and personal.

Heading
Family (optional for progress report)
Physical
Social
Adjustment to school

Self-acceptance
Cognitive
Creativity
Closure

What to Do with It

Have a supervisor check the progress reports. Make copies. Place one in the portfolio and one in the class file. Go over the original with the family in a family conference if possible.

WEEK 23: PLAN A

CLASS LIST LOG ON GROUP TIME FOR ALL

Some time this week during a time when the group is all engaged in the same activity—eating, outside time, or circle time—use the Class List Log to write a few words about each child's involvement.

What to Do with It

Filing. By this time in the year, children should be displaying signs of comfort and active participation. If you notice a child not participating, look closely at their behavior and draw conclusions. It may be they are new, just learning the language, or are indicating some need. Decide on a follow-up action, such as speaking to other staff about the child.

Write any important information on the Overview Sheet of each child's portfolio, along with the date and your name.

File the Class List Log in the class file.

Sharing with the Child and Family. Share with the family or the child. For example: "Today when I was watching all the children playing the game Loobey Lou, I noticed that Roxanne knows her left from right. That is really unusual for children this age," or "Krissy, today when we were sitting at the lunch table I was making some notes so I wouldn't forget to ask some people some questions. I wanted to ask you about never sitting at Brigette's table. I saw you move your name tag to the other table when you saw Lizette put yours at Brigette's table. Let's talk about Brigette. Does it scare you when she makes those noises because she can't talk yet. Did you know she can only talk when she uses that machine? Later today would you like to see how it works?"

WEEK 23: PLAN B

CONVERSATION OR INTERVIEW AND CHECKLIST FOR GROUP C

Select the children in Group C to talk with each day this week. If possible, tape record an informal Conversation or structured Interview as well as make written notes as you speak with each child. Add this interview to the tape begun in Week 6.

Informal Conversation

If you wish, record a conversation you have with the child about the child's play, an event, or an explanation of a piece of art or construction.

Structured Interview

Two- and three-year-olds:

> What's your name?
> How old are you?
> Go get the book. (receptive)
> Say, "I want the ball."
> What's this?
> What's this sound? (make a toy sound without the child seeing it)

> Show a mirror. Who is that?
> What's his name?

Four- and five-year-olds:

> What's your name? What's your last name?
> Look around the room and tell me what you see.
> What makes you happy? sad? mad?
> What do you like to do best when you aren't at school?
> Can you tell me about a dream you've had?
> Do you remember what we talked about the last time we did this?
> Do you know any jokes?

What to Do with It

Filing. Afterward, analyze the interview or conversation for what it reveals about the child's knowledge, emotional state, social development, and speech and language.

Refer to the Speech and Language Checklist done in Week 6. Make any notations of progress the child has made since then.

On the Overview Sheet, note the addition to the tape and any comments about the child's speech and language or other areas revealed in the conversation.

File the tape in each child's portfolio.

Sharing with the Child and Family. Share the observation with family or the child if appropriate. For example: "I was listening in particular today to Adi speak then I played back the tape I had made many weeks ago. I couldn't believe the difference. His sentences are so much longer and he's using lots of new words. I can tell he just loves having his grandmother here. He talks about her a lot and all the things they do together. He seems so happy," or "April, that was such fun talking with you on the tape recorder. That joke about the chicken crossing the road was one I hadn't heard before. You'll have to tell Bernardo that one. He's really into jokes right now."

WEEK 23: PLAN C

PROGRESS REPORTS FOR GROUP C

Write a progress report on children in Group C. You have spent individual time with them this week in the interview and have a portfolio of past observations as documentation. Follow the format

Heading
Family (optional for progress report)
Physical
Social
Adjustment to school
Self-acceptance
Cognitive
Creativity
Closure

What to Do with It

Filing. Keep a report in the child's portfolio and one in the class file.

Sharing with the Child and Family. Give the report to each child's family individually and privately if possible. Briefly go over the highlights and offer them the opportunity to look through the portfolio some time when they are at school. Ask for them to read it and jot down any questions or comments they may have about it.

WEEK 24: PLAN A

TIME SAMPLE ON ATTENTION SPAN FOR ALL

Select a day this week during free play time without planned interruptions. Prepare the form from Appendix D with learning center areas that are open. Complete the Time Sample.

What to Do with It

Filing. Compare to Time Samples done previously (Week 7 and Week 13). Later in the day, draw conclusions and write notes in the child's portfolio about each child's attention span, play preferences, social interactions, and the changes from the last recording. Note the presence of the recording on the overview chart and file it in the class file.

Sharing with the Child and Family. Share with the child's family how the attention span has lengthened or play choices have changed. Be specific from your notes, showing you are a careful observer and you know their child. Indicate how you plan to use this information to individualize the curriculum. For example: "Edna is staying longer in the story area, taking an interest in looking at books, even when she is the only one there. I think it really helped when we got some books that have flaps to open and wheels to turn. She always has her hands in motion so these books appeal to her," or "Lucienne, I was watching where everyone was playing yesterday and I saw that you stayed for a long time watching the fish. I wonder if you would look through this catalog from the pet store and see what fish we could buy that would cost less than $5. Here's the calculator. Maybe you could get Paulette to help you. She knows how to use it."

WEEK 24: PLAN B

CONVERSATION OR INTERVIEW/CHECKLIST FOR GROUP D

Select the children in Group D to talk with each day this week. If possible, tape record an informal Conversation or structured Interview as well as make written notes as you speak with each child. Add this Interview to the tape begun in Week 7.

What to Do with It

Filing. Afterward, analyze the Interview or Conversation for what it reveals about the child's knowledge, emotional state, social development, and speech and language.

Refer to the Speech and Language Checklist done in Week 6. Make any notations of progress the child has made since then.

File the tape in each child's portfolio.

On the Overview Sheet, note the addition to the tape and any comments about the child's speech and language or other areas revealed in the conversation.

Sharing with the Child and Family. Share the observation with family or the child, if appropriate. For example: "I listened closely to a tape recorded conversation you and Alexia taped at home. I heard the dysfluent speech you were concerned about but it really is common for four-year-olds. Let's talk again in a month and try not to pressure her to talk. Maybe you should mention it to the pediatrician," or "Lorraine, that story you told on the tape recorder about the big dog was really scary. When you see that dog loose from its leash next time, be sure to stay away. Do you want to tell your mom that story or should she listen to the tape? You decide."

WEEK 24: PLAN C

PROGRESS REPORTS FOR GROUP D

Follow the format from Chapter 14. Each day this week take some time with the portfolios of the children in Group D. Remember: Be positive, descriptive, and personal.

Heading
Family (optional for progress report)
Physical
Social
Adjustment to school

Self-acceptance
Cognitive
Creativity
Closure

What to Do with It

Have a supervisor check the progress report. Make a copy to place in the portfolio, and one to place in the class file. Go over the original with the family in a conference if possible.

WEEK 25: PLAN A

CHECKLIST FOR SOCIAL DEVELOPMENT

If your program is using a developmental checklist with a social area, rate each child's social development by that criteria this week or use some of the questions from Chapter 4 from the Social Skills Checklist.

What to Do with It

Filing. Note the presence of the recording on the Portfolio Overview Sheet. Think about the meaning of what you have seen and how it relates to the child's developmental progress.

Make a note if further action is indicated and follow through with some individual curriculum planning.

Sharing with the Child and Family. Share your observations with the family and the child, if appropriate. For example: "This week when I was watching to see how the children's social skills are coming along, I noticed how Henning is now branching out in his friendships. I think he's picking up more English words and that helps," or "Deidre, I saw you waiting your turn when the children were jumping rope and holding Melagro's sweater. That's what friends do."

WEEK 25: PLAN B

ANECDOTAL RECORDING ON CREATIVITY FOR GROUP C

Observe each of the children in Group C this week for an incident that displays an aspect of creativity. Selecting one child a day, record an anecdote with as many details as you can about how the child approached creative media, dramatic play, block building, music, or some other aspect of play. Write a factual account of the incident so the reader has the feel of being there, along with exact quotes of what was said. In the right-hand column, jot down your comments, your interpretation of the incident, and any change in development this incident shows compared to past recordings.

What to Do with It

Filing. Note the presence of the recording on the Overview Sheet with the date and your name.

File the recording in each child's portfolio.

Sharing with the Child and Family. Share the anecdote with the family or the child, if appropriate. For example: "I've been writing incidents as the children play, and today while I was watching Edward I saw a really curious thing. He has been drawing very detailed drawings of houses with doors and windows and trees and swing sets but today when he started to draw a house he started to cry and get very upset. He took a crayon and scribbled all over the page and said 'I hate this house. I hate this house.' I thought maybe he is still holding in the death of his grandpa. He hasn't talked about it at all. Are you seeing any signs of stress like this? Let's make an appointment to talk about it soon. I'd like to discuss what we can do at school to help," or "That sure was an interesting collage you made today with all the buttons piled on top of one another. I was watching you count them and put them all in rows. It looked like you were making stairs with them. Here's my notes where I drew the pattern you were gluing. Does that look like what you were doing? Did I get it right?"

WEEK 26: PLAN A

CLASS LIST LOG ON SELF-CARE FOR ALL

Using the Class List Log from Appendix D, make notes this week about each child's eating, toileting, dressing, personal hygiene, sleeping, and classroom self-care. Review checklist items for the age of the children in your group from Chapter 2, and observe, noting the degree of self-care in each of those areas.

What to Do with It

Filing. Look back in the class file at the Class List Log done in Week 2. On each child's Portfolio Overview Sheet, note the date of the Class List Log and self-care observed and change from that time, along with your name.

File the Class List Log in the class file.

Sharing with the Child and Family. Share your observations with the family and the child, if appropriate. For example: "Over the course of the year, Steven has progressed so far in the ability to care for his own needs in the classroom. This not only shows he is growing more independent but has had a great effect on his self-esteem. He is so proud of all he can now do for himself, like zip, tie, pour, and even help others."

WEEK 26: PLAN B

RUNNING RECORD ON FREE PLAY FOR GROUP D

This week during free play time, select each child from Group D and write a Running Record. Observe and write for 5 to 10 minutes, preserving a specimen of each child's typical behavior. Later in the day, make notes in the right-hand column about the observation, what questions it raises, if this is usual or unusual behavior, and what this incident reveals about the child's development.

What to Do with It

Filing. On the Portfolio Overview Sheet, make a few notes in the developmental area in which the recording is most revealing and the presence of the full recording with your name and date.

File the recording in the child's portfolio.

Sharing with the Child and Family. Share any interesting information with the family or the child, if appropriate. For example: "When I was observing Brenden today, he said the funniest thing . . ." or "You really made me laugh when you told that funny story about your shoe getting stuck in the mud. I wrote it down for your portfolio. If you want me to read it to you sometime I will."

WEEK 27: PLAN A

FREQUENCY COUNT ON EMOTIONAL DEVELOPMENT FOR GROUPS A AND B, THEN GROUPS C AND D

Prepare the Frequency Count form from Appendix D. Early in the week, select children in Groups A and B and observe during free choice time for 30 minutes. Look for evidence of prosocial or antisocial behaviors. Make a mark next to the name of the child in the appropriate column each time one of these occurs. On another day, repeat the observation with children in Groups C and D.

What to Do with It

Filing. Compare your findings with Week 5 and Week 16. What changes do you see? What do you think are the causes? The children are half a year older from the first observation. Can you see that in their emotional control?

Make notes in each child's portfolio and file the Frequency Count form and your answers to the preceding questions in the class file.

For those children still having difficulty with emotional control, make a special plan for them and carry it out, documenting the results.

Sharing with the Child and Family. Share your positive findings and the observation with the family and the child, if appropriate. For example: "I was observing the class today and found that overall there are 50% less aggressive acts than at the start of the year. We've really been working on encouraging prosocial behaviors and it appears to be working."

WEEK 27: PLAN B

ANECDOTAL RECORDING ON EMOTIONAL DEVELOPMENT FOR GROUP A

Select each of the children in Group A. On Monday, observe child 1; Tuesday, child 3; and so on. Observe for incidents that give information about emotional development, such as the child displaying joy, happiness, anger, aggression, and fear. Make notes and by the end of the day write an Anecdotal Record about the incident with as many details as possible on the right-hand column of a sheet of paper. On the left side, comment on the significance of the incident, if it was usual or unusual, and possible contributing factors.

What to Do with It

Filing. In the child's portfolio, jot a few summary words, that the Anecdotal Recording is being included, the date, and your name.

File in each child's portfolio.

If a strategy to help the child cope with emotions is indicated, discuss it with the family or the supervisor to decide on a course of action. Follow through.

Sharing with the Child and Family. Share your observations with the family and the child, if appropriate. For example: "When Tara began school here she cried very easily, with transition times between routines in the day especially upsetting to her. She now knows the routines and is even able to handle the unexpected. I hadn't realized what a change had taken place until I was filing the latest observation in her portfolio and reread some of the previous ones. When you get a chance, stop by and curl up in the parent room and read them. They're better than a Danielle Steele novel," or "Grayson, do you remember how afraid you were whenever we had a fire drill and had to practice how quickly we could leave the building. Now you just stop what you're doing, and help the other children get to the door. How did that change happen?" Grayson replied, "I guess I just growed up."

WEEK 28: PLAN A

CLASS LIST LOG ON ARRIVALS AND DEPARTURES AND ADJUSTMENT TO SCHOOL FOR ALL

Using the Class List Log from Appendix D, make notes about each child's arrivals and departures and adjustments to school this week.

What to Do with It

Filing. Compare your observations to the Class List Logs done on Week 1 and Week 13. Draw conclusions about what the comparison indicates.

Make notes in each child's portfolio from your observation. This would be a good comparison to add to the end-of-the-year report.

File in the class file.

Sharing with the Child and Family. Share your observations with the family or the child, if appropri-ate. For example: "I was observing as the children left the center this week and noticed how much more organized Marco is now. He methodically gathers all his things together and gets them all into his back-pack without any help. He's showing his indepen-dence and anticipating what is coming next. His memory is so much longer and he knows it. He even said, 'I don't forget like I did when I was little,'" or "Brienne, when I was watching all the children arrive on the bus today I noticed you were waiting for Stephanie. It takes her longer because of her crutches. I'm sure it pleased her to have you wait for her so she wouldn't be lonely. She sure moves fast on those computer keys though. I saw how she showed you how to load and start that new program. I guess you two make a good pair."

WEEK 28: PLAN B

ANECDOTAL RECORDING IN LITERACY FOR GROUP B

This week, select the children from Group B to observe, watching for aspects of literacy such as book interest and handling, writing interest and ability, and reading ability (logos, words in context, phonics). Write an Anecdotal Recording on each child that illustrates liter-acy. In the right-hand column, note the meaning, com-ments, and questions you have about this anecdote.

What to Do with It

Filing. Compare these observations with the Litera-cy Rating Scales done in Week 9 and Week 19. Note the child's progress on the Portfolio Overview Sheet, referring to the Anecdotal Recording, the date, and your name. Decide how you can build on what the child can now do to encourage further development. Plan individual curriculum to accomplish this goal.

File the recordings in each child's portfolio.

Sharing with the Child and Family. Share your observations with the family and the child, if appro-priate. For example: "I was watching Lynette as she picked up a book. She looked at it and immediately turned it right side up and began to turn pages from the front to the back, one at a time. That's a milestone for a toddler. I wrote about it for her portfolio," or "Donato, I saw you playing restaurant, pretending to be the waiter. You wrote down people's orders. Could I have their order papers, after they pay their checks, of course? I'd like to include your writing with this writing I did about your play."

WEEK 29: PLAN A

TIME SAMPLE ON ATTENTION SPAN FOR ALL

Select a day this week during a normal free play time without planned interruptions. Prepare the Time Sample form from Appendix D with learning center areas down the left margin. Record where each of the children choose to be and with whom, at five-minute intervals for half an hour.

What to Do with It

Filing. Compare to the Time Sample done previously (Weeks 7, 17, and 24). Later in the day, draw conclusions and write notes in the child's portfolio about each child's attention span, play preferences, social interactions, and the changes from the last recording. Note the recording on the overview chart, and file it in the class file. Write on it any general statements that would help a reader understand what the Time Sample illustrated.

Use the Time Sample to check if a learning center needs to be renewed by the addition of some different materials. If a particular area seems to be the place where a lot of pushing and pulling take place, evaluate if the area has enough materials for the children who are there or if there is something about its arrangement that causes children to infringe on each other's space.

Sharing with the Child and Family. Discuss with the family or the child, if appropriate. For example: "When I was making notes in the portfolio about attention span, I noticed that Huye is playing a lot more with other children as he learns more English words. Here's a new children's book with names of things that might help too," or "When I was watching the class play today I noticed that you really didn't play with anyone else, you just went to places where no other children were playing. This must have been one of those days when you just wanted to be by yourself. Is that the way you were feeling?"

WEEK 29: PLAN B

CHECKLIST ON COGNITIVE SKILLS FOR ALL

Refer to the cognitive portion of your program's developmental checklist. Mark the criteria in this section on each child in the class by observing as they work.

What to Do with It

Filing. File the checklist in each child's portfolio.

Sharing with the Child and Family. Share the progress with the family and the child, if appropri-ate. For example: "Today Anjanette was playing with these tubes and placed them in order according to size perfectly. That shows her mathematical ability," or "Julien, the last time we played this game with the colored bears you had trouble with the color names. This time you knew every one! How'd you remember them this time?"

If you see little or no progress since the last review of the criteria, do a closer observation, making anecdotal notes. Use the child's interests to intro-duce the concepts that are yet to be developed.

WEEK 30: PLAN A

RATING SCALE ON LITERACY FOR ALL

Revisit the Literacy Rating Scale in each child's portfolio. Note the progress and date the observation. Write a short summary on the back of the page about what you've seen over the course of the months and what you think caused the change.

What to Do with It

Filing. Refile the Rating Scale in the portfolio after making a notation on the Overview Sheet, with the date and your name.

Sharing with the Child and Family. Share it with the family and the child, if appropriate. For example: "Well, look at this. I was observing Emilie today and I saw her pick up a new book from the library and pick out many words she knew by sounding them out. At the beginning of the year, she was still learning the alphabet. Isn't it amazing how they learn to read? All those books you borrow every week and read to her have really helped," or "How did you know it was Jamal's turn to water the plants and Jennifer's turn to feed the guinea pig? Here's a list of all the children's names in the class. Can you read them all? I think you can. What a surprise."

WEEK 30: PLAN B

SAMPLES ON WRITING FOR ALL

This week, collect more samples of each child's writing and knowledge of print. You could have them dictate a letter to a sick class member or a thank-you to a recent visitor. From their dictation, you can talk about the writing. If they are to the level of writing themselves, provide interesting paper or tools to encourage their writing, perhaps a pen that writes gold, or print their name with a pencil pressing into a foam meat tray. (Make a copy for the file.) They can then use a paint brayer to make prints of their writing. It will be backwards so warn them and show them how to read it in a mirror. Sitting with them while they work will give you a close observation of how they approach the task. It also is an opportunity for individual time together. Write a few notes about it and attach it to the sample.

What to Do with It

Filing. Compare the writing sample to that done in Week 19. See the progress each one has made and make a note of it on the Portfolio Overview Sheet. File the sample in the child's portfolio.

Sharing with the Child and Family. Share it with the family and the child, if appropriate. For example: "When I was observing and making notes on Matthew's interest in books, I saw that he really pays attention more closely to the story in group time when he sits right up close and often pushes other children and says, 'I can't see.' And when he was writing, he bends right down close to the paper. Have you noticed if he might have trouble seeing other things, like when he's playing with Legos or watching television? A vision check next time you go to the doctor might be a good idea. We also have a pediatric eye specialist who will do a free vision screening for children in our program. Here's her number if you want to follow it up before then," or "K-E-N-D-R-A is one way to write your name in big letters. We call those capitals. Here's another way that also says K-e-n-d-r-a. The capital or big letter is the first letter, then the rest are small letters or lower-case letters. They both spell Kendra and mean you. Do you think that's why you couldn't find your name at the lunch table? How about if we write it in capitals on one side and upper- and lower-case letters on the other so you can always know it's your name."

WEEK 31: PLAN A

WORK SAMPLES ON CREATIVITY FOR ALL

This week, try to collect a sample of each child's creative work. It may be a painting, drawing, collage, clay, or blocks that could be sketched or photographed. It is possible the child may decorate one panel of the portfolio file folder.

What to Do with It

Filing. Compare the work to that done in Week 10 and Week 20. Note the progress from what you know about the stages in children's creative development. File the work samples in the child's portfolio, dated, and with any comments attached to the back of the work with a sticky note.

Sharing with the Child and Family. Share the observations with the family and the child, if appropriate. For example: "Alexis is really advancing in her ability to represent her thoughts in pictures. She worked diligently on a drawing of your house. I would have recognized it driving down the street from her details of the dormers, the bushes, and the letter S on the chimney. She had it all there. That is unusual for a child her age," or "Tom, you made so many little balls from the clay that you used it all up. Are you planning what to do next?"

WEEK 31: PLAN B

ANECDOTAL RECORDING ON EMOTIONAL DEVELOPMENT FOR GROUP C

Select all the children in Group C and watch this week for events or episodes that give information to amplify what you know about the child's emotional development. Make notes and write it down as soon as possible. In the left column, relate the episode in factual terms, describing the participants, the actions, and the exact words spoken. In the right-hand column write your explanations, inferences, and questions raised from what you saw and heard.

What to Do with It

Filing. Note the Anecdotal Recording on each child's Overview Sheet in the developmental area it describes.

File the Anecdotal Recording in the child's portfolio.

Sharing with the Child and Family. Share it with the family and the child, if appropriate. For example: "Today when I was observing April she asked Mrs. Martinez to write down the words to a story. She told this long, involved tale about a boy going on a trip, forgetting his suitcase, losing his ticket, and getting lost in the airport. I hope she wasn't relating your husband's latest business trip. She has quite an imagination but it sounded so real and she appeared quite disturbed about it," or "Robert, you really know a lot about farms. Today when I was watching you build with the farm set we borrowed from the other class, you told all the builders about how the milk goes into a big tank and how the truck comes to pump it out and what they do with the milk at the creamery. Then I remembered, your granddad used to work there. Did he take you there with him so you could watch what happens to the milk in those big steel tanks? You and he were such good buddies. I think playing with this set helps you remember how it was before he died."

WEEK 32: PLAN A

CLASS LIST LOG ON INTERACTION WITH ADULTS FOR ALL

Using the Class List Log from Appendix D, make notes this week about each child's reaction and interactions with adults in the classroom, other teachers, staff, and visitors. Ask another person to watch each child's reaction to you.

What to Do with It

Filing. Transfer your notes to each child's Portfolio Overview Sheet with the date and your name.

File the Class List Log in the class file.

Sharing with the Child and Family. Share your observations with the family or the child, if appropriate. For example: "This week when I was watching Deidre, I saw how she has really made friends with our practicum student Rosa. She loves to touch Rosa's long, braided hair and she looks so closely at Rosa's dark eyes then at her own blue ones in the mirror. They say at two years old children begin to have racial awareness. I believe that's what she is doing. She's really making those observations and taking it all in. Rosa is very understanding and patient with her," or "Luo, today I saw you sitting in Mrs. Wilkins' lap listening to a story. Here's the book *The Foot Book*. You can take it home and read it to your little brother."

WEEK 32: PLAN B

ANECDOTAL RECORDING ON SELF-IDENTITY FOR GROUP D

Select all the children in Group D, and this week observe them as they work in the classroom for signs of how they perceive or feel about themselves. Review Chapter 12 for some of the indicators. Make notes as incidents happen that give you clues about each child's self-identity. Later that day, amplify them with as many details and descriptions as you can, writing them down the left column of a sheet of paper. In the right-hand column, write your judgments, comments, theories, concerns, or questions.

What to Do with It

Filing. On each child's Portfolio Overview Sheet, note the presence of the Anecdotal Record, the date, and your name as recorder. If a child's actions indicate a negative self-identity, make a plan for that child to feel competent and powerful. Implement the plan and revisit the subject with more notes in the portfolio.

File the Anecdotal Recordings in each child's portfolio.

Sharing with the Child and Family. Share positive anecdotes with the family. You may decide the negative ones would not be helpful to be placed in the portfolio. For example: "Mrs. Jamieson, Jerimiah has such a 'can do' attitude. He is never afraid to try a new thing or to say he can't do something. Whatever you did to instill that quality in him has surely benefitted him. He has plenty of friends, is developing in all areas right on track, and seems happy most of the time. Other parents would love to know your secret," or "Marinka, here's a flashlight. You could go over to the block corner and shine it on the buildings like the sun or the moon. I'm sure they will let you be the shiner or will trade a builder's job for the flashlight. Let's see what will happen."

WEEK 33: PLAN A

CHECKLIST ON PHYSICAL DEVELOPMENT FOR ALL

Revisit the Checklist on physical development from Week 3 and Week 14. Using the same form with a different color pen, mark the Checklist.

What to Do with It

Filing. Enter a summary, your name, and the date on the Portfolio Overview Sheet. Note the changes and place in each child's portfolio.

Make note if further action is indicated.

Sharing with the Child and Family. Share accomplishments and progress with the family and the child, if appropriate. For example: "Gretchen can throw and catch a ball, walk the balance beam, and even jump rope. Those are difficult tasks for a three-year-old. Where does she get all that coordination?" or "Christopher, I know you want to climb to the top of the climber and jump off but I can't catch you. When your body tells you it's safe to jump, you will be able to jump without help. For now, climb to step number three and jump from there. That's where you are able to feel safe."

WEEK 33: PLAN B

RUNNING RECORD ON FREE PLAY FOR GROUP A

Select all the children in Group A and each day this week write a Running Record of a segment of play, recording as many details as possible about the action, interaction with other children, and exact quotes.

What to Do with It

Filing. On the right column of each recording, make any notes of interpretation, concern, and any explanation for what you saw. Make a note on each child's Portfolio Overview Sheet in the section of development that this observation most illustrates. File in the child's portfolio.

Record answers to conversations like this at the end of the Running Record to amplify the record.

Sharing with the Child and Family. Share observation findings with the family or the child, if appropriate. For example: "While I was watching Toby at the manipulative area today, I noticed him building a very intricate Lego building. He said he was building the 'monument' and when I asked him about it he told all about your trip to Washington, about staying in the hotel, riding the elevator to the top floor to see the city lights, and going to see the long, black wall with names on it of dead Viet Nam soldiers. He included so many details. What a memory," or "While I was watching you play today and writing about it for your portfolio I could tell you remembered all about the house we built in school back in the fall. I heard you talking into the tape recorder and telling the story from the pictures that we took and you told them all in a row, what happened first, then what happened next. How did you remember all that?"

WEEK 34: PLAN A

CHECKLIST ON SOCIAL DEVELOPMENT FOR ALL

Two months have passed since the last Class List Log on social development. This week, do another, and compare it to the ones done in Weeks 4, 15, and 25. Take one of your Class List Log forms from Appendix D and draw six vertical lines, designating the columns left to right: unoccupied, onlooker, solitary, parallel, associative, and cooperative. This week during free play time, observe the children as they interact. See if the children have progressed from one level to another or are playing at a more sophisticated level.

What to Do with It

Filing. At the end of the day, take the Class List Log and transfer the stage you observed onto the Portfolio Overview Sheet with your name and the date of the observation.

Make a note if further action is indicated.

Sharing with the Child and Family. Share with the family and the child, if appropriate. For example: "Today, Shaun stayed near Sergey all day. A friendship seems to be growing there," or "Kerry, I was making notes today and I saw how you talked with Jessica. I didn't know you knew so many words in sign language."

WEEK 34: PLAN B

ANECDOTAL RECORDING ON SOCIAL DEVELOPMENT FOR GROUP B

Select all the children in Group B. Watch for an episode that tells about this child's social development. Write it as it is happening or jot notes and write the whole episode up by the end of the day while it's fresh in your memory. Record on the left column of lined paper, capturing as many details as possible about where the episode is taking place and who is involved. The selected child is the focus, so be sure to record actions and words carefully to be descriptive. The reader should have the feeling of seeing it through your eyes.

In the right-hand column make your comments, give reasons, indicate if this is usual or unusual behavior, and what you think made the child act in this way. Block out the names of the other children involved unless there is a reason to leave them revealed. This episode may also give a glimpse into the actions of another child. Then you can copy this Anecdotal Recording, blot out this child's name, and file it in the other child's folder with appropriate comments.

What to Do with It

Filing. Note the presence of the Anecdotal Record on the child's Portfolio Overview Sheet under social development.

Make note if further action is indicated.

Sharing with the Child and Family. Share with the family and the child, if appropriate. For example: "He loved playing Uno today and took turns and kept track of other people's turns. Good thinking."

WEEK 35: PLAN A

FREQUENCY COUNT ON EMOTIONAL DEVELOPMENT FOR ALL

Early in the week, observe children in Groups A and B during free choice time for thirty minutes. Look for evidence of prosocial or antisocial behaviors. Make a mark next to the name of the child in the appropriate column each time one of these occurs. On another day, repeat the observation with children in Groups C and D.

What to Do with It

Filing. Compare this Frequency Count to the ones done in Weeks 5, 16, and 27. Do you see differences in the totals for the class? for individual children? Do you think the prosocial curriculum activities for ten weeks made a difference? If so, write a short summary and send your findings to the authors. They would love to hear it. Share it in your school's newsletter or in a happy gram to parents.

If it did not make a difference, why not? Summarize the project and file it in the class file.

WEEK 35: PLAN B

CONVERSATION OR INTERVIEW AND CHECKLIST ON SPEECH AND LANGUAGE FOR GROUP C

Select each of the children in Group C to talk with each day this week. If possible, tape record the conversation as well as make written notes (literacy role model) as you speak with each child.

What to Do with It

Filing. Analyze the Interview or Conversation for what it reveals about the child's knowledge, emotional state, social development, and speech and language, using the Speech and Language Checklist (Week 6, Assignment B). You may use the same sheet, but mark it with a different color pen.

File the tape and notes with the checklist in each child's portfolio.

Sharing with the Child and Family. Share with the family and the child, if appropriate. For example: "Today when I was talking with Mohammed he told me about your vacation to the 'One Thousand Islands.' I'm glad I had the tape recorder on. You can listen to it some time. It is really interesting," or "Oksana, today when we were playing that game with the tape recorder I was so surprised you knew your whole name, address, and phone number. How do you remember all that?"

WEEK 36: PLAN A

CLASS LIST LOG ON GROUP INTERACTION FOR ALL

During group time (small group or whole group, depending on your class's age, your program schedule, and philosophy) do a Class List Log jotting down how each child functions in the group situation.

What to Do with It

Filing. On each child's Overview Sheet under group, make a few notes and reference it to the Class List Log done on (date). File the Class List Log in the class file.

Sharing with the Child and Family. Share with the family or the child, if appropriate, any observation that they might like to hear about the child's group participation. For example: "Today when I was making some notes about each child's functioning in

story time, I noticed Devon was intently listening to the story *When I Was Young in the Mountains*, singing and tapping his feet to the folk musician we had as a guest, and he even danced the Virginia Reel. I believe that is the most involved I've seen him this year. He's come a long way in his attention span and ability to participate in group things. That will help him a lot next year in kindergarten," or "Shequinta, today I was watching you and the other children making hand shadows with Kristy's grandpa. I noticed how well you waited until it was your turn to make your shadow. That was a *long* wait. When you got your turn you did that butterfly he had been showing everyone. The wait must have given you time to watch how to do it so when it was your turn you already knew. Some people learn a lot by watching. I guess you're one of those people. Keep those eyes open and you'll learn a lot."

WEEK 36: PLAN B

CONVERSATION OR INTERVIEW AND CHECKLIST ON SPEECH AND LANGUAGE FOR GROUP D

Select each of the children in Group D to talk with each day this week. If possible, tape record the Conversation as well as make written notes (literacy role model) as you speak with each child.

What to Do with It

Filing. Analyze the Interview or Conversation for what it reveals about the child's knowledge, emo-

tional state, social development, and speech and language, using the Speech and Language Checklist (Week 6, Assignment B). You may use the same sheet, but mark it with a different-colored pen.

Sharing with the Child and Family. Share your observations with the family and the child, if appropriate.

Refile the tape and the Speech and Language Checklist in the child's portfolio. Note any concerns and follow up with a more formal screening or speech and language evaluation if concerns persist.

WEEK 37: PLAN A

CHECKLIST ON COGNITIVE DEVELOPMENT FOR ALL

Using the cognitive portion of the developmental checklist your program uses, assess each child by the criteria listed there. Update the checklist and see the changes since Weeks 18 and 29. As the children play, watch for signs of mathematical concepts, such as counting or one-to-one correspondence; physics, such as recognition of geometric shapes, puzzle problem solving, or changes in the physical environment.

What to Do with It

Filing. File the checklist in the portfolio.

Sharing with the Child and Family. Share the observations of progress with the family in the upcoming progress reports. Give the family specific examples of how the child is exhibiting cognitive development as she interacts with the environment.

WEEK 37: PLAN B

CONVERSATION OR INTERVIEW AND CHECKLIST ON SPEECH AND LANGUAGE FOR GROUP A

Select each of the children in Group A to talk with each day this week. If possible, tape record the Conversation as well as make written notes (literacy role model) as you speak with each child.

What to Do with It

Filing. Analyze the Interview or Conversation for what it reveals about the child's knowledge, emotional state, social development, and speech and languages using the Speech and Language Checklist

(Week 6, Assignment B). You may use the same sheet but mark it with a different-colored pen.

Refile the tape and the checklist in each child's portfolio.

Sharing with the Child and Family. Share your observations with the family and the child, if appropriate. For example: "Audrey has an amazing memory for songs and poems and stories. She just has to hear them once and can say them right back. When you get a chance, take the tape into the family room and spend some time listening to the conversation we had about what happened to the snowman. It's hilarious," or "Manuel, when you are at home you speak Spanish but at school you speak English. Do you know how you keep them separate?"

WEEK 37: PLAN C

PROGRESS REPORTS FOR GROUP A

Review all the documentation in the portfolios of the children in Group A. Note each developmental area and the progress made in 37 weeks in each of the areas. List what the child has accomplished in each area. Remember: Be positive, descriptive, and personal.

Heading
Family (optional for Progress Report)
Physical
Social
Adjustment to school

Self-acceptance
Cognitive
Creativity
Closure

What to Do with It

Have a supervisor check the progress report. Make a copy to place in the portfolio and one to place in the class file. Go over the original with the family in a family conference if possible. Determine what is to be done with the portfolio at the conclusion of the year.

WEEK 38: PLAN A

RATING SCALE ON LITERACY DEVELOPMENT FOR ALL

Use the Rating Scales from Appendix D for literacy development or the literacy section of your program's developmental checklist. Rate each child's interest and abilities to read and write. Make one final entry on the Rating Scale or checklist in a different color.

Refile the Rating Scale in the child's portfolio.

What to Do with It

Filing. Use the Rating Scale as documentation to your comments in progress reports concerning literacy, reading, and writing, at whatever level the child is.

WEEK 38: PLAN B

CONVERSATION OR INTERVIEW AND CHECKLIST ON SPEECH AND LANGUAGE FOR GROUP B

Select each of the children in Group B to talk with each day this week. If possible, tape record the Conversation as well as make written notes (literacy role model) as you speak with each child.

What to Do with It

Analyze the Conversation or Interview for what it reveals about the child's knowledge, emotional state, social development, and speech and language, using the Speech and Language Checklist (Week 6, Assignment B). You may use the same sheet, but mark it with a different-colored pen.

Refile the tape and language checklist in each child's portfolio. Follow up on any concerns that came out of the Conversation or Interview.

Sharing with the Child and Family. Share your observations with the family and the child, if appropriate. For example: "Harriet has been using a lot of baby talk lately. I know this has been a difficult time for her while your mother is sick and you have to spend so much time caring for her. Maybe this is just her way of saying she wants to be cared for like a baby too. Are there any tasks that you could do together or caring things she could do for grandma to be a part of her care? Maybe you could talk to Mrs. Jimenez. She just went through a similar situation," or "Cassidy, I was listening to you and your friends at the snack table when you said Jimmy was the same color as the gingerbread man. You are right, he is just that shade of brown. Can you find some colors in the room that match your skin?"

WEEK 38: PLAN C

PROGRESS REPORTS FOR GROUP B

Review all the documentation in the portfolios of the children in Group B. Note each developmental area and the progress made in 38 weeks in each of the areas. List what the child has accomplished in each area. Remember: Be positive, descriptive, and personal.

Heading
Family (optional for progress report)
Physical
Social
Adjustment to school

Self-acceptance
Cognitive
Creativity
Closure

What to Do with It

Have a supervisor check the progress report. Make a copy to place in the portfolio and one to place in the class file. Go over the original with the family in a family conference if possible. Determine what is to be done with the portfolio at the conclusion of the year.

WEEK 39: PLAN A

CLASS LIST LOG ON SELF-IDENTITY FOR ALL

Using the Class List Log for self-identity from Appendix D, based on how well you know the child, place a rating on each child's self-identity in the areas listed on the Class List Log.

What to Do with It

Filing. Compare this to the Class List Log done in Week 12. Think about each child and what is con-tributing to the child's high or low self-esteem. At this point in the year there is nothing to be done but to use this information and experience to help the next group of children in your class. Self-identity is influenced directly by the feeling of competence, knowledge, power, and acceptance. Vow to do all you can next year to help each child experience those attributes.

File this in the class file. Since it is so subjective, it is not made a part of the child's portfolio.

WEEK 39: PLAN B

TIME SAMPLE ON ATTENTION SPAN FOR ALL

Use the Time Sample form from Appendix D with free choice areas down the left column. For at least one-half hour of free play time, list every five minutes where each child is in the classroom.

What to Do with It

Filing. Compare the Time Sample with those done in Weeks 7, 17, 24, and 29. Draw conclusions about each child's attention span, area of interest, closest playmates, and areas avoided. Use the Time Sample to make summaries and recommendations on the final progress reports.

File in each child's portfolio.

WEEK 39: PLAN C

PROGRESS REPORTS FOR GROUP C

Review all the documentation in the portfolios of the children in Group C. Note each developmental area and the progress made in 39 weeks in each of the areas. List what the child has accomplished in each area. Remember: Be positive, descriptive, and personal.

Heading
Family (optional for progress report)
Physical
Social
Adjustment to school
Self-acceptance
Cognitive
Creativity
Closure

What to Do with It

Have a supervisor check the progress report. Make a copy to place in the portfolio and one to place in the class file. Go over the original with the family in a family conference if possible. Determine what is to be done with the portfolio at the conclusion of the year.

WEEK 40: PLAN A

WORK SAMPLES ON CREATIVITY FOR ALL

This week, try to collect a final sample of work from every child. Make comments on the Work Samples Checklist or the creative portion of your program's checklist.

Note on the Portfolio Overview Sheet that work is present with a few notes, the date, and your name.

What to Do with It

Filing. On the Work Sample Checklist form note the significance of the work and what it demonstrates about the change in the child's development since Week 10.

File in the child's portfolio.

Sharing with the Child and Family. Share the observation with the family or the child, if appropri-

ate. For example: "Here is the drawing Rana did in the fall and here is how she is drawing now. See the details she's now including in her self-portrait: eyelashes, earrings, and pupils in the eyes. We placed a mirror on the drawing table and encouraged the children to look closely at themselves as they drew. It shows not only an advance in physical drawing skills but cognitive skills as well. A scrapbook of her drawings from her first scribbles is a wonderful treasure as she gets older. I'm going to put that suggestion in the newsletter next month if it's okay with you that I give you credit for the idea," or "Uri, look at this. This is the drawing you did on the cover of your portfolio where I keep all my notes. And this is the one you did this week. Look how different they are. You said when you were drawing it that, 'Now I know how to draw.' Why do you think that is? How did you learn it?"

WEEK 40: PLAN B

PROGRESS REPORTS FOR GROUP D

Review all the documentation in the portfolios of the children in Group D. Note each developmental area and the progress made in 40 weeks in each of the areas. List what the child has accomplished in each area. Remember: Be positive, descriptive, and personal.

Heading
Family (optional for progress report)
Physical
Social
Adjustment to school

Self-acceptance
Cognitive
Creativity
Closure

What to Do with It

Have your supervisor check the progress reports. Make a copy to place in the portfolio and one to place in the class file. Go over the original with the family in a family conference if possible. Determine what is to be done with the portfolio at the conclusion of the year.

WEEK 40: PLAN C

FINAL REPORTS

A final report is an excellent way to look back over the year. Reflect on the accomplishments, the difficulties, and their resolutions. Ponder the still unanswered questions and projections for the future. Begin planning for next year now while ideas and resolutions are fresh in your mind. An outline is suggested here to help organize your thoughts.

* When I began the year . . .
* The year's highest accomplishments were . . .
* The children who made the greatest gains were . . .
* The disappointments were . . .
* If I knew then what I know now I would have . . .
* Next year I want to remember to . . .

What to Do with It

When the year comes to a close (that is at different times for everyone), distribute files as program policy dictates.

Portfolios—to families, next teacher, or next program

Class File—to teacher's file, director or administrator, program file

Reflective Journal—teacher's private property to keep or destroy

C

Summary of Plans by Developmental Areas

The *Week by Week* plan is designed to

- use a variety of recording methods.
- revisit developmental areas over the course of a 40-week school year.
- equally focus on individual children who have been arbitrarily assigned to a group A, B, C, or D. (See the note preceding the plans in Chapter 2.)

The pages that follow classify the plans by developmental area and children's groups to demonstrate the equality of the plan.

The abbreviations that are used are:

CL Class List Log
AR Anecdotal Recording
CK Checklist
RR Running Record
FC Frequency Count
I   Conversation or Interview
TS Time Sample
WS Work Sample
M   Media
PR Progress Report

The number following the letters indicates the week of the plan. The square around the recording indicates individual focused observations.

	ARRIVALS AND DEPARTURES ADJUSTMENT	SELF-CARE	PHYSICAL DEVELOPMENT	SOCIAL DEVELOPMENT	EMOTIONAL DEVELOPMENT	SPEECH AND LANGUAGE	MEMORY AND ATTENTION SPAN	COGNITIVE/ MATH AND SCIENCE
	CHAPTER 1	CHAPTER 2	CHAPTER 3	CHAPTER 4	CHAPTER 5	CHAPTER 6	CHAPTER 7	CHAPTER 8
GROUP A	CL1	AR2	CK3	CL4	FC5	1, CK6	TS7	CK8
	CL22	CL2	CK14	CL15	FC16	CL6	TS17	CK18
	CL28	CL26	CK33	CK25	FC27	CK17	TS24	CK29
	RR33			CK34	AR27	1, CK21	TS29	CK37
					FC35	1, CK37	TS39	
GROUP B	CL1	CL2	CK3	CL4	FC5	CL6	TS7	CK8
	CL22	CL26	AR3	CL15	FC16	1, CK7	TS17	CK18
	CL28		CK14	CK25	RR16	CK17	TS24	CK29
			CK33	CK34	FC27	1, CK22	TS29	CK37
				AR34	FC35	1, CK38	TS39	
GROUP C	CL1	CL2	CK3	RR4	FC5	CL6	TS7	CK8
	RR18	CL26	CK14	CL4	FC16	1, CK8	TS17	CK18
	CL22		CK33	CL15	FC27	CK17	TS24	CK29
	CL28			CK25	AR31	1, CK23	TS29	CK37
				CK34	FC35	1, CK35	TS39	
GROUP D	CL1	CL2	CK3	CL4	FC5	CL6	TS7	CK8
	CL22	CL26	CK14	CL15	AR5	1, CK9	TS17	CK18
	RR26		CK33	CK25	FC16	CK17	TS24	CK29
	CL28			CK34	FC27	1, CK24	TS29	CK37
					FC35	1, CK36	TS39	

	LITERACY	CREATIVE ARTS	CREATIVE DR. PLAY BLOCKS	SELF-IDENTITY	GROUP INTERACTIONS	INTERACTIONS WITH ADULTS	PROGRESS REPORTS
	CHAPTER 9	CHAPTER 10	CHAPTER 11	CHAPTER 12	CHAPTER 13	CHAPTER 14	1
GROUP A	RS9 RS19 WS19 RS30 WS30 RS38	WS1 WS10 AR10 WS20 WS31 WS40	M11 M21	CL12 RR15 CL39	CL13 CL23 CL36	CL14 CL32	PR10 PR21 PR37
GROUP B	RS9 RS19 WS19 AR28 RS30 WS30 RS38	WS1 WS10 WS20 WS31 WS40	M11 RR11 M21	CL12 CL39	CL13 CL23 CL36	CL14 CL32	PR11 PR22 PR38
GROUP C	RS9 RS19 WS19 RS30 WS30 RS38	WS1 WS10 WS20 AR25 WS31 WS40	M11 M21	CL12 AR12 CL39	CL13 CL23 CL36	CL14 CL32	PR12 PR23 PR39
GROUP D	RS9 RS19 WS19 RS30 WS30 RS38	WS1 WS10 WS20 AR20 WS31 WS40	M11 M21	CL12 AR32 CL39	CL13 AR13 CL23 CL36	CL14 CL32	PR13 PR14* PR24 PR40

D

Observation Forms

IN THIS APPENDIX

CLASS LIST LOG

Date _____

Observing _____   Recorder _____

_____

_____

_____

_____

_____

_____

_____

_____

_____

_____

_____

_____

_____

_____

_____

_____

_____

CLASS LIST LOG

Date _____

Observing _____   Recorder _____

_____

_____

_____

_____

_____

_____

_____

_____

_____

_____

_____

_____

_____

_____

_____

_____

_____

PORTFOLIO OVERVIEW SHEET

NAME _____ BIRTH DATE _____

SEPARATIONS AND ADJUSTMENT

Documentation	Location	Recorder	Date
_____	_____	_____	_____
_____	_____	_____	_____
_____	_____	_____	_____

PHYSICAL DEVELOPMENT

Documentation	Location	Recorder	Date
_____	_____	_____	_____
_____	_____	_____	_____
_____	_____	_____	_____

EMOTIONAL DEVELOPMENT

Documentation	Location	Recorder	Date
_____	_____	_____	_____
_____	_____	_____	_____
_____	_____	_____	_____

MEMORY AND ATTENTION SPAN

Documentation	Location	Recorder	Date
_____	_____	_____	_____
_____	_____	_____	_____
_____	_____	_____	_____

LITERACY DEVELOPMENT

Documentation	Location	Recorder	Date
_____	_____	_____	_____
_____	_____	_____	_____
_____	_____	_____	_____

CREATIVE—DRAMATIC PLAY

Documentation	Location	Recorder	Date
_____	_____	_____	_____
_____	_____	_____	_____
_____	_____	_____	_____

GROUP INTERACTIONS

Documentation	Location	Recorder	Date
_____	_____	_____	_____
_____	_____	_____	_____
_____	_____	_____	_____

SELF-CARE

Documentation	Location	Recorder	Date
_____	_____	_____	_____
_____	_____	_____	_____
_____	_____	_____	_____

SOCIAL DEVELOPMENT

Documentation	Location	Recorder	Date
_____	_____	_____	_____
_____	_____	_____	_____
_____	_____	_____	_____

SPEECH AND LANGUAGE

Documentation	Location	Recorder	Date
_____	_____	_____	_____
_____	_____	_____	_____
_____	_____	_____	_____

COGNITIVE DEVELOPMENT

Documentation	Location	Recorder	Date
_____	_____	_____	_____
_____	_____	_____	_____
_____	_____	_____	_____

CREATIVITY— ART AND BLOCKS

Documentation	Location	Recorder	Date
_____	_____	_____	_____
_____	_____	_____	_____
_____	_____	_____	_____

SELF-IDENTITY

Documentation	Location	Recorder	Date
_____	_____	_____	_____
_____	_____	_____	_____
_____	_____	_____	_____

INTERACTIONS WITH ADULTS

Documentation	Location	Recorder	Date
_____	_____	_____	_____
_____	_____	_____	_____
_____	_____	_____	_____

OTHER DOCUMENTATION

_____
_____
_____

Center Name _____   Date _____

Target Child's Name _____   Recorder _____

Time _____ Location in Room _____

Anecdotal or Running Record	Comments

PHYSICAL DEVELOPMENT CHECKLIST

(The Frost-Wortham Developmental Checklist)
Gross and Fine Motor

_____ Colored Pen   Date _____
_____ Colored Pen   Date _____
_____ Colored Pen   Date _____

Motor Development: Preschool (Gross Movement)

Level III (approx. age 3)	Introduced	Progress	Mastery
1. Catches a ball with both hands against the chest	❑	❑	❑
2. Rides a tricycle	❑	❑	❑
3. Hops on both feet several times without assistance	❑	❑	❑
4. Throws a ball five feet with accuracy	❑	❑	❑
5. Climbs up a slide and comes down	❑	❑	❑
6. Climbs by alternating feet and holding on to a handrail	❑	❑	❑
7. Stands on one foot and balances briefly	❑	❑	❑
8. Pushes a loaded wheelbarrow	❑	❑	❑
9. Runs freely with little stumbling or falling	❑	❑	❑
10. Builds a tower with nine or ten blocks	❑	❑	❑

Level IV (approx. age 4)	Introduced	Progress	Mastery
1. Balances on one foot	❑	❑	❑
2. Walks a straight line forward and backward	❑	❑	❑
3. Walks a balance beam	❑	❑	❑
4. Climbs steps with alternate feet without support	❑	❑	❑
5. Climbs on a jungle gym	❑	❑	❑
6. Skips haltingly	❑	❑	❑
7. Throws, catches, and bounces a large ball	❑	❑	❑
8. Stacks blocks vertically and horizontally	❑	❑	❑
9. Creates recognizable block structures	❑	❑	❑
10. Rides a tricycle with speed and skill	❑	❑	❑

Level V (approx. age 5)	Introduced	Progress	Mastery
1. Catches and throws a small ball	❑	❑	❑
2. Bounces and catches a small ball	❑	❑	❑
3. Skips on either foot	❑	❑	❑
4. Skips rope	❑	❑	❑
5. Hops on one foot	❑	❑	❑
6. Creates Tinkertoy and block structures	❑	❑	❑
7. Hammers and saws with some skill	❑	❑	❑
8. Walks a balance beam forward and backward	❑	❑	❑
9. Descends stairs by alternating feet			

PHYSICAL DEVELOPMENT CHECKLIST (continued)

Motor Development: Preschool (Fine Movement)

Level III (approx. age 3)	Introduced	Progress	Mastery
1. Places small pegs in pegboards	☐	☐	☐
2. Holds a paintbrush or pencil with the whole hand	☐	☐	☐
3. Eats with a spoon	☐	☐	☐
4. Buttons large buttons on his or her own clothes	☐	☐	☐
5. Puts on coat unassisted	☐	☐	☐
6. Strings bead with ease	☐	☐	☐
7. Hammers a pound toy with accuracy	☐	☐	☐
8. Works a three- or four-piece puzzle	☐	☐	☐

Level IV (approx. age 4)	Introduced	Progress	Mastery
1. Pounds and rolls clay	☐	☐	☐
2. Puts together a five-piece puzzle	☐	☐	☐
3. Forms a pegboard design	☐	☐	☐
4. Cuts with scissors haltingly and pastes	☐	☐	☐
5. Eats with a fork correctly	☐	☐	☐
6. Holds a cup with one hand	☐	☐	☐
7. Puts a coat on a hanger or hook	☐	☐	☐
8. Manipulates large crayons and brushes	☐	☐	☐
9. Buttons and zips zippers haltingly			

Level V (approx. age 5)	Introduced	Progress	Mastery
1. Cuts and pastes creative designs	☐	☐	☐
2. Forms a variety of pegboard designs	☐	☐	☐
3. Buttons buttons, zips zippers, and ties shoes	☐	☐	☐
4. Creates recognizable objects with clay	☐	☐	☐
5. Uses the toilet independently	☐	☐	☐
6. Eats independently with a knife and fork	☐	☐	☐
7. Dresses and undresses independently	☐	☐	☐
8. Holds and manipulates pencils, crayons, and brushes of various sizes	☐	☐	☐
9. Combs and brushes hair	☐	☐	☐
10. Works a twelve-piece puzzle	☐	☐	☐

FREQUENCY COUNT

Date _____ Recorder _____

Make a tally mark in the column next to the child's name each time you observe a behavior which you would classify as prosocial or antisocial.

CHILD'S NAME	PROSOCIAL Helping, sharing, hugging, calling another child by a kind name	ANTISOCIAL Hurting, hoarding, bad-name calling, rejecting another child
TOTALS		

SPEECH AND LANGUAGE CHECKLIST

Child _____ Date _____

Sounds: Underline the ones that you hear. Circle if there is difficulty.

p, w, h, m, n, (usually by 3 years)

b, k, g, d, y (usually by 4 years)

f, ng, t, r, l (usually by 6 years)

ch, sh, j, s, z, v, th, zh, br, tr (clear by 7-8 years)

Language: Underline the ones that are present. Circle if there seems to be difficulty.

Correct word order (by 2½)

Uses pronouns (by 2½)

Gives name (by 3)

Uses plurals, some prepositions (by 3)

Tells day's schedule in sequence (by 4)

Can tell an imaginative story about a picture (by 4)

Speaks in adultlike sentences (by 4)

Note Language Behaviors:

Turn taking—displays understanding of conversational shift

Communication signals

    eye contact

    facial expression

    gestures

    tone of voice

Meaning: What did the conversation tell you about the child? _____

_____

_____

_____

_____

_____

_____

(Adapted from Machado, J. M. [1990] and Breyen & Gallagher [1983]) REPRODUCED WITH THE PERMISSION OF AUTHOR: Nilsen, B. (2005). *Week by Week: Documenting the Development of Young Children*, 3rd ed. Clifton Park, NY: Thomson Delmar Learning.

TIME SAMPLE

Class _____   Date _____   Recorder _____

TIMES (at 5-minute intervals)

LEARNING CENTERS							

MATH AND SCIENCE CHECKLIST

Name _____ Birth Date _____

_____

Dates of Observations

_____ _____ _____   Can sort objects by color

_____ _____ _____   Can name colors: red, blue, yellow, green, orange, purple, white, black, brown

_____ _____ _____   Can name positions: first, middle, last

_____ _____ _____   Can sort objects by size: smallest, medium, largest

_____ _____ _____   Can sort objects by shape: circle, square, triangle, rectangle

_____ _____ _____   Can name shapes: circle, square, triangle, rectangle

_____ _____ _____   Can count by rote to _____ .

_____ _____ _____   Can count _____ objects accurately: 2, 5, 7, 10, more

_____ _____ _____   Can name number before and after: 3, 8, 11

_____ _____ _____   Can mentally subtract (Put out 5 objects. If I took 1, how many
                           would be left?)

_____ _____ _____   Can predict pattern ABABAB (Line up blocks, red, blue, red, blue, red, blue:
                           Which one goes next?)

_____ _____ _____   Can locate: ear, foot, elbow, knee, forehead, wrist

_____ _____ _____   Can name when pointed to: ear, foot, elbow, knee, forehead, wrist

_____ _____ _____   Can repeat two, three, four digits (Say four. "Four." Say two, nine. "Two,
                           nine." Say six, one, eight. "Six, one, eight.")

_____ _____ _____   Where does milk come from? cow, store, carton, other

_____ _____ _____   What's in the sky at night? moon, stars, clouds, other

LITERACY RATING SCALE

Child's Name _____

INTEREST IN BOOKS

No interest, avoids	Only if adult-initiated	Brings books to adult to read	Looks at books as self-initiated activity

LISTENING TO BOOKS

Wiggly, no attention	Intermittent attention	Listens in one-on-one situation	Listens as part of a group, tuning out distractions

INVOLVEMENT WITH BOOKS BEING READ

Little or no response	Emotional response, laugh, frown	Comments, asks questions	Joins in during reading

HANDLING BOOKS

No voluntary touching	Rough handling	Exploratory manipulation	Books as favorite toys

CONCEPT OF BOOK FORMAT

No idea of front/back, up/down	Holds book right side up but skips pages	Demonstrates front/back concept	Looks at pages left to right

CONCEPT OF STORY BOOK

Labels pictures	Retells story in sequence from pictures	Accurately repeats some story lines	Points to print while accurately retelling from pictures

PRINT IN THE ENVIRONMENT

Notices signs, labels	Asks, "What's that say?"	Reads signs, labels out of context	"Writes" signs to label constructions

BEGINNING READING

Recognizes own name	Recognizes letters in name in other words	Reads simple words	Sounds out letters in unfamiliar words

LITERACY RATING SCALE (continued)

MANIPULATION OF WRITING TOOLS

Fist hold	High hold on pencil	Adult grip, little control	Adult grip, good control

COMMUNICATION THROUGH WRITING

Communicates ideas through drawing	Will dictate on request	Initiates dictation	Draws and writes words

BEGINNING WRITING

Scribbles, no reference to writing	Named scribbles "Says my name"	Single letters, random	Writes name

WRITING IN PLAY

No reference to writing	Asks for signs, words to be written	Asks for adult to spell words	Sounds out words and writes on own

WORK SAMPLES CHECKLIST

Child's Name _____   Dates _____

_____

COMMENTS

_____

Separation
❏ Separates from adult to do creative work alone
❏ Works independently without requiring adult presence or direction

Self-Care
❏ Independently selects materials
❏ Makes preparations to work (Example: Puts on a smock)
❏ Uses materials independently
❏ Cleans up spills, messes
❏ Writes name on work
❏ Places finished product in proper place
❏ Washes and dries hands if necessary
❏ Replaces materials to storage place

Physical Development
❏ Controls whole body movement during work
❏ Controls small muscles to hold tool
❏ Controls tool to form desired product
❏ Draws, prints, paints, pastes
❏ Squeezes glue bottle
❏ Picks up collage materials
❏ Manipulates clay or Play Doh
❏ Cuts with scissors
❏ Controls body to stay within the space (on the paper, building on a rug, clay on table)

Social Skills
❏ Represents important people in life and work
❏ Desires and can work near other children
❏ Shares materials and supplies
❏ Engages in positive commentary on other children's work
❏ Works cooperatively on a joint project

Emotional Development
❏ Uses work to express emotions of happiness, anger, fear
❏ Verbalizes feelings about work
❏ Enjoys manipulation and creation
❏ Controls emotions of frustration when work meets difficulties
❏ Uses the media as a stress release, pounding clay, tearing paper, painting

Speech and Language Development
❏ Names scribbles, buildings, creations
❏ Talks about work using vocabulary connected with materials and design
❏ Uses language to describe process, intent, and satisfaction with product
❏ Vocabulary reflects knowledge of subject

WORK SAMPLES CHECKLIST (continued)

COMMENTS

Memory and Attention Span
- ❑ Includes details in work from memories of experiences
- ❑ Focuses attention on project to produce a finished work
- ❑ Tunes out distractions of simultaneous play, talk, and work
- ❑ Gives attention and makes connections between designs, colors, patterns in environment, and own work

Math and Science Knowledge
- ❑ Includes numerals and quantity in work
- ❑ Shows one-to-one correspondence in work designs
- ❑ Shows perceptual awareness of color, space, form
- ❑ Explores cause and effect and experimentation with variables in media
  (Example: Sees differences in paint when water and sand are added)
- ❑ Observes similarities and differences, forming theories and testing them out by manipulating the medium
- ❑ Working with clay or liquid—displays knowledge of the concept of conservation
  (volume stays the same even though form changes—ball flattened is the same amount)

Literacy
- ❑ Includes literacy in work
- ❑ Recognizes the difference between drawing and writing
- ❑ Uses creative materials to symbolize ideas
- ❑ Work illustrates or connects with stories
- ❑ Gives attention to art in story books and knows the difference between text and illustrations

Creativity
- ❑ Uses materials in a novel way, displaying flexibility in seeing new possibilities in materials
- ❑ Explores all facets of the medium
- ❑ Draws from experiences to create representations
- ❑ Incorporates creativity into other areas of play, constructing with blocks, drawing and constructing in
  dramatic play, forming designs in sand and other medium
- ❑ Demonstrates creativity in secondary awareness (seeing, hearing, touching, smelling, tasting)

Self-Identity
- ❑ Displays risk-free attitude in work
- ❑ Reveals self in content of work
- ❑ Work shows a sense of identity and individuality
- ❑ Expresses satisfaction in work, confident self-esteem
- ❑ Portrays self, family, world in work
- ❑ Work demonstrates child's sex-role identification
- ❑ Work shows child moving from egocentric view of self to an awareness of self as part of larger society
- ❑ Indicates favorite art medium (singular), media (plural)

Group Time Behaviors
- ❑ Participates in cooperative and collaborative work

Interaction with Adults
- ❑ Involves adults in work as (facilitator, participator, director)

AUDIO/VIDEO/PHOTO RELEASE

I give permission for my child to be tape recorded, video recorded, or photographed for educational or publicity purposes while participating in the regular activities of this program.

Date _____

❑ YES   ❑ NO

Signature _____

SELF-ESTEEM CLASS LIST LOG

Date _____   Recorder _____

Consider each child's self-esteem in each of the categories. Write an *H* for high or an *L* for low.
For teacher's use only.

Child's Name	Unafraid of a new situation	Independent, needs minimal help	Comfortable with physical activities, coordinated	Makes friends easily	Seems to be happy most of the time	Talks freely	Does not rely on others for directions	Experiments with new materials	Creative, imaginative, has ideas of his own	Participates in classroom group activities	Cooperative and largely controlled	Trusts teacher even though they are strangers

SETTING OBSERVATION

Name of Center _____ Date of Visit _____

Address _____

_____

Phone _____

Type of Program: ☐ Child Care ☐ Nursery School ☐ Kindergarten

Age of children in classroom described below: _____

Number present: _____

1. Describe the building (location, type of building, other uses). _____

_____

_____

_____

2. Describe the entry to the building (signs, decorations, security). _____

_____

_____

_____

3. Classroom
   Draw a floor plan in the space below, indicating room arrangement, furniture, shelves, learning centers, carpeted areas, sink, doorways, windows, and so on. Be as detailed and close to scale as possible.

SETTING OBSERVATION (continued)

4. List and describe other areas used by class (gym, kitchen, bathrooms). _____

    _____

    _____

    _____

5. At the conclusion of visiting this setting, write a paragraph about the "feeling" of this center. What attitudes, values, friendliness, safety, or enrichment did you experience while there? How do you think this environment affects the children, their families, and the staff who work there?

    _____

    _____

    _____

    _____

    _____

    _____

    _____

    _____

6. Complete the following chart on learning centers. Make detailed lists of the following.

Learning Center	Equipment and Furnishings	Materials

PROGRESS AT A GLANCE

Child's Name _____

PERIOD 1: Date _____ Recorder _____

Strengths _____

Areas still developing _____

_____

Educational plan to facilitate development _____

_____

_____

PERIOD 2: Date _____ Recorder _____

Strengths _____

Areas still developing _____

_____

Educational plan to facilitate development _____

_____

_____

PERIOD 3: Date _____ Recorder _____

Strengths _____

Areas still developing _____

_____

Educational plan to facilitate development _____

_____

_____

PERIOD 4: Date _____ Recorder _____

Strengths _____

Areas still developing _____

_____

Educational plan to facilitate development _____

_____

_____

E

Weeks 15 through 40: Reflective Journal

WEEK 15: PLAN C

REFLECTIVE JOURNAL

Respond to the following in your Reflective Journal, kept in a private file at home.

I feel I know more about_____than all the other children.

I think it is because...

I am still puzzled about...

As the children leave for the day, I think...

When I face a loss or a separation, it helps me to...

WEEK 16: PLAN C

REFLECTIVE JOURNAL

Respond to the following in your Reflective Journal, kept in a private file at home.

When children are dependent on me, I feel . . .

The family member I feel the most comfortable with is . . .

I think it's because . . .

The family member I feel the least comfortable with is . . .

I think it's because . . .

Maybe if I . . .

This day would have been better if . . .

The funniest thing I heard a child say this week was . . .

WEEK 17: PLAN C

REFLECTIVE JOURNAL

Respond to the following in your Reflective Journal, kept in a private file at home.

From my observations, I have seen how physical development and self-esteem are connected when...

I think because of that I should...

The benefits to the children would be...

My own life could benefit from...

WEEK 18: PLAN C

REFLECTIVE JOURNAL

Respond to the following in your Reflective Journal, kept in a private file at home.

When I watch children play, I can't help but wonder...

When I talked to families this week I...

I'm looking forward to...

In the ten weeks that have gone by since we last observed cognitive development, the changes that surprised me the most were...

The biggest gains were made by...

I think it is because...

WEEK 19: PLAN C

REFLECTIVE JOURNAL

Respond to the following in your Reflective Journal, kept in a private file at home.

I've been thinking about reading and writing since the last journal entry, and I think...

The most interesting thing I've read recently was...

It made me think about...

When I was gathering the writing samples, I realized...

Because of that, I think I'd better...

WEEK 20: PLAN C

REFLECTIVE JOURNAL

Respond to the following in your Reflective Journal, kept in a private file at home.

Now that I've been watching the children's creations more closely, I see...

I think that has changed my teaching approach so that now I...

I wonder, though, about...

WEEK 21: PLAN C

REFLECTIVE JOURNAL

Respond to the following in your Reflective Journal, kept in a private file at home.

When I listened to children more closely this week, I found...

My work on my own language habit is...

The funniest thing I heard a child say this week was...

The scariest thing I heard a child say this week was...

WEEK 22: PLAN D

REFLECTIVE JOURNAL

Respond to the following in your Reflective Journal, kept in a private file at home.

Is this year half over already?!

Or does it still have... months to go?

What's my attitude?

Why do I feel this way?

Look at the class list and sort the children into two lists using any criteria you want.

List #1   List #2

WEEK 23: PLAN C

REFLECTIVE JOURNAL

Respond to the following in your Reflective Journal, kept in a private file at home.

I'm still thinking about last week when . . .

My body is telling me . . .

Write about an emergency situation you faced and how you reacted.

Draw a doodle that represents how you feel about your job.

WEEK 24: PLAN C

REFLECTIVE JOURNAL

Respond to the following in your Reflective Journal, kept in a private file at home.

I'm really seeing their imagination and creativity developing. I wonder what other things I can do to spark it. Maybe if I . . .

The school year is more than half over (or is it less than half to go?) How do I feel about it?

This media thing is . . .

After all these many weeks I still don't feel like I know . . .

Why don't they . . .

WEEK 25: PLAN C

REFLECTIVE JOURNAL

Respond to the following in your Reflective Journal, kept in a private file at home.

I was surprised to see the Anecdotal Recording show that...

I think I'll try to...

I'm getting to know ... a lot better and that helps because ...

The child who seems to have fewer friends than all the others is ...

I think it's because ...

I'll try to...

WEEK 26: PLAN C

REFLECTIVE JOURNAL

Respond to the following in your Reflective Journal, kept in a private file at home.

I feel like I know...   very well but not...

I wonder if it's because...

I think I need to know more about...

Maybe if I...

It really hurt me when...   said...

I think it's because...

WEEK 27: PLAN D

REFLECTIVE JOURNAL

Respond to the following in your Reflective Journal, kept in a private file at home.

I felt so happy when I saw...

I'm wondering why the curriculum doesn't seem to meet...   needs.

Could it be...

I might try...

It was so funny when...

WEEK 28: PLAN C

REFLECTIVE JOURNAL

Respond to the following in your Reflective Journal, kept in a private file at home.

The ten things that are the most valuable to me are...

Dealing with...   is the most difficult thing I had to
face this week because...

I am achieving...

Next week I will...

WEEK 29: PLAN C

REFLECTIVE JOURNAL

Respond to the following in your Reflective Journal, kept in a private file at home.

As we get closer to the end of the year with only a few weeks left, I really wish I had . . .

I'll be glad that . . .

In thinking more about math and science, I believe . . .

I have the longest attention span when I am . . .

WEEK 30: PLAN C

REFLECTIVE JOURNAL

Respond to the following in your Reflective Journal, kept in a private file at home.

I have the right to...

If I were to compare myself to an animal, I am most like a...
because...

My teaching style has been most influenced by...

If I were going to advise a brand-new teacher, the most helpful piece of
advice would be...

WEEK 31: PLAN C

REFLECTIVE JOURNAL

Respond to the following in your Reflective Journal, kept in a private file at home.

The last time I cried was when...

I would never cry if ...   was around because...

I think crying is...

Thinking about crying helps me to...

Maybe I'll talk with...   about...

WEEK 32: PLAN C

REFLECTIVE JOURNAL

Respond to the following in your Reflective Journal, kept in a private file at home.

My body is telling me. . .

My mind is telling me. . .

My better sense is telling me. . .

I think I'll listen to my. . .   and. . .

WEEK 33: PLAN C

REFLECTIVE JOURNAL

Respond to the following in your Reflective Journal, kept in a private file at home.

When I'm on playground duty, the hardest part is...

My dream playground would look like this. (Draw or sketch if you'd like.)...

The child who seems to have the most difficulty with physical development is...

I think it's because...

Maybe I could...

What smudges appeared on my glass this week? (Look back at the frame of reference.)

WEEK 34: PLAN C

REFLECTIVE JOURNAL

Respond to the following in your Reflective Journal, kept in a private file at home.

I never would have thought that... and... would become friends. I wonder if it's because...

I think... would have friends if he or she didn't...

Next year I'm going to... to help facilitate friendships.

My best friend is...

We are friends because...

I am a good friend to... because...

WEEK 35: PLAN C

REFLECTIVE JOURNAL

Respond to the following in your Reflective Journal, kept in a private file at home.

I just love to hear...

I really need to get started...

The observations this week made me think more about...

WEEK 36: PLAN D

REFLECTIVE JOURNAL

Respond to the following in your Reflective Journal, kept in a private file at home.

The highlight of the week was...

The "low light" this week was...

Here's a drawing of what I do best...

Here's the story...

WEEK 37: PLAN C

REFLECTIVE JOURNAL

Respond to the following in your Reflective Journal, kept in a private file at home.

More than anything I want...

My teaching has changed this week the most in the area of...

I think it is because...

I was really embarrassed when...

This week I thought a lot about...

WEEK 38: PLAN C

REFLECTIVE JOURNAL

Respond to the following in your Reflective Journal, kept in a private file at home.

I think my favorite creative activity this year was...

The reason I liked it so well was...

When I was in school, art...

I now think...

Next year I'd like to try more...

WEEK 39: PLAN C

REFLECTIVE JOURNAL

Respond to the following in your Reflective Journal, kept in a private file at home.

I won't send it, but I'd like to write a letter to _____'s family and tell them...

(If you wish, actually write the letter then tear it up in little pieces.)

I just don't understand why...

Maybe it's because...

or it could be...

I loved my job this week when...

I hated my job this week when...

WEEK 40: PLAN C

REFLECTIVE JOURNAL

Respond to the following in your Reflective Journal, kept in a private file at home.

In this last Reflective Journal entry for these assignments, I would just like to say...

My favorite story from this year is...

I will always remember...   because...

My personal progress report would read...

Draw a map here of the journey you have taken this year, the mountaintops and the valleys. On the back of the paper, make a dotted line for your map of the future, setting your goals to achieve, watching for pitfalls and barriers, building bridges and hurdling high to reach your goals.

Glossary

acceptance—the feeling of being loved and appreciated, contributes to self-esteem (12)

accommodation—takes in new information, balances with previous knowledge, and adjusts response (7)

accreditation—voluntary submission to a standard through a review process, usually consisting of a self-study and verification (13)

action research—informal collection of information about a child or children, nonstandardized (6)

active listening— technique for clarifying the message and the feelings (14)

ADD, ADHD—attention deficit disorders, professionally diagnosed impairments that affect attention span and cause impulsivity and distractibility (7)

adjustment—ability of a child to adapt socially and emotionally (13)

aggression—actions that injure people, things, or emotions (5)

Anecdotal Recording—factual narrative of an incident (2)

animism—preoperational child believes natural world is ruled by willful intent like humans (7)

articulation—the sounds of speech (6)

artificialism—preoperational child believes that humans create and influence nature (7)

assessment—process of observing, recording, and documenting a child's actions, skills, and behaviors (I)

assimilation—information received that adjusts previously related information (7)

association—information received that matches previously related information (7)

associative play—play that is similar, in the same theme but still with each player playing individually (4)

attachment—the emotional bond that infants show to a person (usually the mother) with whom they have had a stable, trusting relationship (1)

attention deficit—inability to focus; medical diagnosis, may or may not be accompanied by hyperactivity (7)

attention span—focus perceptual processes on a specific aspect of the environment (7)

audio recorders—device that makes a taped reproduction of sound (11)

authentic assessment—measurement of knowledge or skill in context, in as realistic a setting as possible (8)

autism—pervasive spectrum disorder with a range of effects on several domains (7)

autonomy—the process of governing oneself (2)

bias—preconceived attitudes that may affect objectivity, either positively or negatively (3)

brain hemisphericity—two hemispheres, or sides, of the brain deal with information and function in different ways (7)

case study (child study)—a comprehensive written overview of the child; it may be documented by written evidence and the child's work (14)

cause and effect—ability to perceive the link between two events with one as a result of the other (7)

centration—focus of attention on one attribute, ignoring other variables (7)

cephalocaudal—sequence of the development of muscle control from head to toe (3)

Checklist—a method of documenting the presence or absence of a skill or behavior in a developmental sequence (3)

Class List Log—method of gathering a specific piece of information on every child in the group (1)

classification—matching or grouping similar data (7)

closed method—the recorder makes a judgment from observation and records it with a check, slash, few words. Raw data is not available for the reader (3)

closed question—one expected answer, like a test (6)

cognitive—knowing, thinking, reasoning, and remembering (8)

competence—the feeling of capability, independence, and autonomy; contributes to self-esteem (12)

Concrete Operational Stage—period of development (seven to eleven years old), using logic and reasoning; mental actions are still related to "concrete" objects (7)

confidentiality—the professional attitude and practice of preserving the privacy of information (I)

conservation—understanding that volume or measurability of objects remains the same if nothing is added or subtracted, but the form is changed (7)

constructive play—manipulating objects, such as blocks, to create a physical product (4)

contextualized literacy—ability to read words when other clues are present, such as cereal names, restaurants, and traffic signs (9)

convergent thinking—the ability to arrive at a single answer, more difficult for young children with still-developing classifying, listening, and attending skills (10)

cooperative play—play where players are in the same theme and working toward a common goal (4)

coping mechanisms—strategies for overcoming uncomfortable circumstances (1)

coping skills—strategies to overcome emotional traumas (5)

core emotions—basic emotions present at birth from which other emotions evolve (5)

creativity—novel thinking or product (10)

criterion-referenced—method that provides a predetermined standard or guideline to look for and measure against. Ex. Checklist, Rating Scales (I)

development—change that takes place in a predictable sequence, from simple to complex, but at a different pace for individual people (2)

diagnostic interview—conversations designed to yield developmental information about a child (6)

diary—journal; a style of recounting past events including feelings these events arouse (1)

digital video cameras—devices that record images electronically (11)

disclosure—a statement that indicates the speaker has been a victim of abuse or maltreatment (12)

disequilibrium—cognitive conflict when new information does not associate or match previous data (7)

displacement—turning angry feelings away from the source of the anger (5)

dispositions—the feelings or responses to a body of knowledge (8)

divergent thinking—ability to think of a wide range of possibilities, associated with creativity and giftedness (10)

diversity—broad range of differences, individual uniqueness (6)

document (verb)—the action of preserving data for later review; documentation (noun)—the product that preserves the data (I)

documentation panels—displays of children's work that show the process of their thinking and planning and the resulting product (14)

dramatic play—symbolic play, pretend (4)

dysfluent—speech disorder in which the speaker repeats a beginning sound or a word (6)

dyslexia— an impairment of the ability to read (9)

Ebonics—nonstandard English spoken by some (6)

ecological view—consideration of all aspects that influence a human being (I)

egocentric—the cognitive stage in which the child is not able to take another's point of view (4)

egocentrism—preoperational child's inability to understand that others do not share his or her perspective (7)

emergent literacy—continuous process of becoming a reader and writer (9)

emotional intelligence—type of intelligence that motivates oneself, persists in frustration, controls impulses, delays gratification, and empathizes with others (5)

emotional maltreatment—psychological damage from blaming, belittling, or rejecting a child (12)

environmental print—the signs and labels that appear on everyday objects in homes, media, and neighborhoods (9)

ethics—the moral principles and practices under which an individual operates (I)

evaluation—comparison of information gathered against a standard or set of criteria (I)

expressive language—messages that are communicated through words and gestures (6)

failure to thrive—developmental delays caused by physical or emotional factors (5)

family—the group of related or nonrelated adults who are legally responsible for a child (I)

file access log—a form in a portfolio that records the name, purpose, and date of each person who views the file (I)

frame of reference—individual point of view influenced by many factors (3)

Frequency Count—recording method to measure how often a specified event occurs (5)

functional play—manipulation of objects with no particular goal other than to examine and practice repetitive motions (4)

games with rules—play where players take turns and act according to a mutually understood standard (4)

gender—general term for the biological differences in the two sexes, male and female (12)

good-bye rituals—established routines to help the child with separation (1)

growth—quantitative change that can be measured in numbers (3)

high-stakes test—on the basis of the tests, decisions are made that affect the child, the teacher, or the school (8)

holographic—one-word sentences that have meaning (6)

inclusion—the practice of including children with special needs into the least restrictive environment (8)

inference—conclusion; judgment; explanation (2)

informal conversations—spontaneous conversations between adult and child that yield information (6)

informed consent—ethical practice of obtaining permission before using a person as the subject of a study or in photos, audio, or video recordings (11)

interrater reliability—two or more raters use the same instrument on the same child to control bias (9)

invented spelling—phonetic spelling with a letter for each sound (9)

invulnerable child—child who escapes from childhood psychological trauma without harm (5)

language—the meaning of the words and gestures that are communicated (6)

large muscle (gross motor)—muscles used in moving the body from one place to another (3)

learning disabilities—an interference with the ability to process written communication (9)

least restrictive environment—legal term referring to the educational placement of exceptional children in regular settings to the maximum extent possible (3)

liberation teaching—theory that the teacher does not give up on any child by seeking to meet the child's needs (14)

license requirements—required standards, usually set by the individual states (13)

logico-mathematical knowledge—understanding principles of the nature of matter by reasoning rather than intuition or appearances (7)

mandala—universal symbol combining circle and intersecting lines (10)

mandated reporters—those individuals who by law must report suspicions of child abuse to specified agencies (12)

matching—recognizing the similarities of an attribute of an object (7)

medium (singular), **media** (plural)—art material(s) (10)

mixed-age groups—also known as heterogeneous, multi-age, vertical, ungraded, nongraded, and family grouping; groups of children not separated by chronological age (13)

morality—characteristic of making choices based on a set of standards set by social group (12)

morphemes—smallest unit of language, words (6)

multiple intelligences—individual ways of processing information (7)

narrative—method that tells a story, includes all the details of an incident. Ex. Anecdotal, Running Record (2)

neglect—the withholding of basic survival needs: food, water, shelter, clothing, medical care; constitutes maltreatment (12)

nonrepresentational—young child's drawing a symbol of mental image; not able to "represent" a recognizable symbol; difficult to draw what they are thinking (10)

norm—standard against which others are measured (8)

object permanence—the cognitive understanding that objects and persons continue to exist even out of sight (4)

objective—detached, impersonal, unprejudiced, data-only recordings (I)

observing—watching children to know more about their development (I)

one-to-one correspondence—ability to count objects accurately by assigning one number to each object (7)

onlooker play—watch others play; may talk or ask questions (4)

open method—recording method that preserves the raw data; only records actions and words so separate conclusions can be drawn (2)

open question—no single, correct answers, creative answers (6)

ordinal numbers—indicating the order or succession, such as first, second, or third (8)

overgeneralization—early stage in grammar construction where child adds "s" to all words for plural and "ed" to all words for past tense (6)

parallel play—play that is near, maybe even doing the same actions or using the same equipment or toys, but not interacting (4)

performance standards—criteria by which individuals or programs are measured (13)

phonemic awareness—child's understanding and conscious awareness that speech is composed of identifiable units, such as spoken words, syllables, and sounds (9)

phonemes—basic unit of sound in spoken language (6)

physical abuse—any nonaccidental physical injury caused by the child's caretaker (12)

physical knowledge—knowledge about the general properties of the physical world: gravity, motion, and nature (7)

portfolio—a systematic collection of documentation about the child's development (I)

power—the ability to control one's actions and destiny, rather than depending on outside agents (12)

precocity—exceptional early development in cognitive or creative ability (10)

Preoperational Stage—stage of cognitive development with distinct characteristics, according to Piaget's theory, ages 4–7 (7)

preschematic—stage in drawing development before the child has attained the motoric and cognitive abilities to draw recognizable symbols (10)

program evaluation—the process of examining all the components of a program to measure effectiveness and quality (13)

progress report—a periodic written overview of short-term goals the child has achieved (14)

proximodistal—development of muscle control from center of body to extremities (3)

quality points—milestones or measurement intervals on a rating scale (9)

quantitative—method that provides a numerical count of individual or group actions. Ex. Frequency Counts, Time Samples (I)

quantitative scoring—an assessment tool that reports results with a numeric score (8)

Rating Scale—measuring a specific behavior, skill, or attribute by choosing from three or more descriptors (9)

receptive language—that which is heard, taken in (6)

record—documentation of an event, may be written, audio or video recorded, photographed (6)

recording—a system or method of writing down what has been observed (I)

referral—a recommendation made for further evaluation by a helping professional (I)

reflection—thoughtful consideration of past events for analysis (1)

Reflective Journal—a private, written record in which to express feelings; not a part of child's record, but property of the writer (1)

reflexes—muscle reactions to stimuli, not controlled by intent (3)

reliability—quality of tests that will produce a similar score by the same individual on the same test (8)

reversibility—concrete operational child understands that any change can be mentally reversed, for example, think of an ice cube as water (7)

rote counting—counting by memory, may be inaccurate or out of sequence (7)

Running Record—detailed account of a segment of time; recording all behaviors and quotes during that time (4)

schema—symbol in art that is repeated over and over representing a real object (10)

schematic—stage in which symbolic representations go through modifications as child develops cognitively (10)

screening—a test given to a broad population to indicate possibilities that are evaluated further (8)

scribbling—experiments with drawing media, can be uncontrolled or controlled (doodling) (10)

selective method—the recording instrument dictates what is to be observed (9)

self-care—ability to eat, toilet, dress, keep clean, and keep safe (2)

self-concept—the qualities one attributes to one's self, self-identity (12)

self-esteem—the valuing of that knowledge based on self and social comparisons (12)

Sensorimotor Stage—stage from birth to age two when the child "takes in" information mainly by sensory means and gains differentiation of self from the environment (7)

separation anxiety—distress when a parent leaves an infant's presence, beginning at eight or nine months and usually disappearing at about twenty-four months (1)

seriation—the ability to order objects by some standard rule, height, weight, shade, or tone (7)

sex-role (or gender) identity—socialized preference of behavior identified with one gender or the other (12)

sexual abuse—sexually explicit conduct with a minor (12)

shyness—hesitance in social situations, self-consciousness (5)

small muscle (fine motor)—muscles that control hands and fingers (3)

social competence—ability to maintain interactions, to have friends (4)

social conventional knowledge—information gathered from influential adults about general rules of conduct acceptable to that group (7)

socialized—behavior learned to adapt to the expectations of the social group (12)

sociodramatic play—fantasy play episode with others involved (11)

solitary play—play that is focused on objects or movements, not involved with others (4)

speech—the sounds produced to make words, phonemes (6)

standardized tests—scores are measured against the norm group that has taken the test (8)

story dictation—children write and produce a story or episode (11)

stranger anxiety—distress when approached by an unfamiliar person, beginning at seven to nine months and ending around one year (1)

stress—physiological reactions to emotional events (5)

structured interview—planned conversations to find out specific information about a child (6)

subjective—influenced by state of mind, point of view, inferential, interpreting the meaning, or cause of an event (1)

syntax—order of words in a sentence that give them meaning; grammar (6)

tadpole man—beginning drawings of humans with lines protruding from circles (10)

talented and gifted—designation for higher than average cognitive, linguistic, social, creative development (8)

teacher's stories—the relating of classroom experiences to child development or professional practice principles; may be related orally or in written form (14)

technology—tools used to perform a task (11)

telegraphic—few-word sentences that have meaning (6)

Time Sample—method of recording where children are by choice at a certain time, measuring attention span and interests (7)

transitions—period between activities, time periods, or programs; may be problematic without planning (13)

unconditional positive regard—feelings a teacher should have for a student (14)

unfounded—child abuse reports that upon investigation lack evidence for criminal or civil charges (12)

unoccupied play—not interested in play, wanders around room (4)

valid—describes quality of a test that measures what it proposes to measure (8)

video recorder—device that makes a taped reproduction of image and sound (11)

work samples—method that preserves the child's work as a documentation of development. Ex. Drawings, writings, constructions, media-preserved work such as audio or video recordings or photographs (I, 10)

zone of proximal development—behavioral levels that can be approximated with assistance (5)

Index